A Historical Phonology of Central Chadic

Of all of the African language families, the Chadic languages belonging to the Afroasiatic macro-family are highly internally diverse due to a long history and various scenarios of language contact. This pioneering study explores the development of the sound systems of the 'Central Chadic' languages, a major branch of the Chadic family. Drawing on and comparing field data from about 60 different Central Chadic languages, H. Ekkehard Wolff unpacks the specific phonological principles that underpin the Chadic languages' diverse phonological evolution, arguing that their diversity results to no little extent from historical processes of 'prosodification' of reconstructable segments of the proto-language. The book offers meticulous historical analyses of some 60 words from Proto-Central Chadic, in up to 60 individual modern languages, including both consonants and vowels. Particular emphasis is on tracing the deep-rooted origin and impact of palatalisation and labialisation prosodies within a phonological system that, on its deepest level, recognises only one vowel phoneme */a/.

H. EKKEHARD WOLFF is Professor and Chair emeritus (African linguistics) at Leipzig University. He has more than 170 publications to his credit (incl. 30 books) on descriptive, typological, comparative, applied linguistics and sociolinguistics of African languages. He is Editor of *The Cambridge Handbook of African Linguistics* (2019) and of *A History of African Linguistics* (2019).

A Historical Phonology of Central Chadic

Prosodies and Lexical Reconstruction

H. Ekkehard Wolff

CAMBRIDGE
UNIVERSITY PRESS

Shaftesbury Road, Cambridge CB2 8EA, United Kingdom

One Liberty Plaza, 20th Floor, New York, NY 10006, USA

477 Williamstown Road, Port Melbourne, VIC 3207, Australia

314–321, 3rd Floor, Plot 3, Splendor Forum, Jasola District Centre, New Delhi – 110025, India

103 Penang Road, #05–06/07, Visioncrest Commercial, Singapore 238467

Cambridge University Press is part of Cambridge University Press & Assessment, a department of the University of Cambridge.

We share the University's mission to contribute to society through the pursuit of education, learning and research at the highest international levels of excellence.

www.cambridge.org
Information on this title: www.cambridge.org/9781009010672

DOI: 10.1017/9781009024310

© H. Ekkehard Wolff 2022

This publication is in copyright. Subject to statutory exception and to the provisions of relevant collective licensing agreements, no reproduction of any part may take place without the written permission of Cambridge University Press & Assessment.

First published 2022
First paperback edition 2025

A catalogue record for this publication is available from the British Library

Library of Congress Cataloging-in-Publication data
Names: Wolff, Ekkehard, author.
Title: A historical phonology of Central Chadic : prosodies and lexical reconstruction / H. Ekkehard Wolff.
Description: Cambridge, UK ; New York : Cambridge University Press, 2021. | Includes bibliographical references and index.
Identifiers: LCCN 2021028425 (print) | LCCN 2021028426 (ebook) | ISBN 9781316519547 (hardback) | ISBN 9781009010672 (paperback) | ISBN 9781009024310 (epub)
Subjects: LCSH: Chadic language–Phonology. | BISAC: LANGUAGE ARTS & DISCIPLINES / Linguistics / Phonetics & Phonology | LANGUAGE ARTS & DISCIPLINES / Linguistics / Phonetics & Phonology
Classification: LCC PL8026.C531 W65 2021 (print) | LCC PL8026.C531 (ebook) | DDC 493/.7–dc23
LC record available at https://lccn.loc.gov/2021028425
LC ebook record available at https://lccn.loc.gov/2021028426

ISBN   978-1-316-51954-7   Hardback
ISBN   978-1-009-01067-2   Paperback

Cambridge University Press & Assessment has no responsibility for the persistence or accuracy of URLs for external or third-party internet websites referred to in this publication and does not guarantee that any content on such websites is, or will remain, accurate or appropriate.

Dedicated to the memory of three excellent fellow Chadicists,
who contributed insights to the study of prosodies in
Chadic languages

Carl F. Hoffmann (1925–2007)
Daniel Barreteau (1950–2007)
Russell G. Schuh (1941–2016)

Contents

List of Figures	*page* xii
List of Tables	xiii
Preface	xv
Acknowledgements	xvii
Glossonyms Used for Central Chadic Languages and Language Variants	xviii
Abbreviations and Symbols	xx

1. Introduction 1
   1.1 Comparative Chadic Linguistics, and Why It Is So Problematic to Reconstruct Lexical Items for Proto-Chadic in General, and for Proto-Central Chadic in Particular 2
   1.2 A Model for the Evolution from Proto-Central Chadic 'Simple Roots' to Phonetic Surface Representations in Central Chadic Languages 17
   1.3 Root Type 20
   1.4 Root Augmentation 20
   1.5 Vowel Pro-/Epenthesis 21
   1.6 Phonological Prosodies 22
   1.7 Morphological Prosodies 23

2. Methodological Preliminaries 27
   2.1 General 27
      2.1.1 The Extra-Linguistic Historical Background 28
      2.1.2 The Exceptional Typology of Central Chadic Languages 30
      2.1.3 The Enigmatic Vocalic Domain 31
         2.1.3.1 The Status of Schwa 32
         2.1.3.2 No True Vowel Contrasts 32
         2.1.3.3 Underspecified 'Weak Radicals': */y/, */w/ 33
         2.1.3.4 Impact of Prosodies 33
      2.1.4 Completeness and Explicitness of Description 34
   2.2 The Comparative Method and Dialectological Approaches 38
   2.3 Internal Reconstruction 41
   2.4 The Database and Conventions of Transcription 46
   2.5 Theoretical Modules Underlying Central Chadic Lexical Reconstruction Work 47
      2.5.1 Epenthesis Theory 48

viii   Contents

2.5.2 Weak Radical Theory	52
2.5.3 Vocalisation Theory	53
2.5.4 Prosody Theory	55
2.5.5 Prosodies as Traces of Diachronically Lost Segments	62
2.6 Confronting Alternative Approaches	65
2.6.1 The Notion of 'Prosody-Type Languages' in Central Chadic	70
2.6.2 The Vocalic Domain in Central Chadic: What to Reconstruct and How Many?	71
2.6.3 The Present Study	74

3. **Proto-Central Chadic Diachronic Phonology and Morphophonology: Inventories and Principles** — 76

- 3.1 General Observations — 76
  - 3.1.1 Templatic Approach: Root-and-Pattern — 76
    - 3.1.1.1 Underlying 'Root Types' — 76
    - 3.1.1.2 Radical Consonant Slots — 77
    - 3.1.1.3 Vocalisation: Vowel Slots and Syllables — 78
    - 3.1.1.4 The Ambiguous Nature of 'Weak Radicals' — 78
    - 3.1.1.5 The Relevance of the Templatic Approach to Historical Reconstruction in Chadic — 79
  - 3.1.2 Diachronically Simple and Augmented Roots — 82
    - 3.1.2.1 Simple Root and Root Types — 86
    - 3.1.2.2 Diachronic Loss of Segments — 88
    - 3.1.2.3 Affixal Root Augmentation and Petrification — 96
    - 3.1.2.4 Reduplicative Augmentation and Petrification — 97
    - 3.1.2.5 Similarity of Inventories of Pre- and Suffixal Augments — 97
  - 3.1.3 Metathesis — 98
  - 3.1.4 Prosodification — 101
- 3.2 Issues in Central Chadic Diachronic Phonology — 103
  - 3.2.1 Inventory: Consonants — 103
  - 3.2.2 The Double Origin of Prosodies — 106
    - 3.2.2.1 Lexical Prosodies: Phonological Palatalisation and Labialisation — 107
    - 3.2.2.2 Grammatical Prosodies: Morphological Palatalisation and Labialisation — 110
  - 3.2.3 Labialisation Prosody — 110
    - 3.2.3.1 Suffixal Augment — 113
    - 3.2.3.2 Prosodising *{-k^w} — 113
    - 3.2.3.3 Non-Prosodising *{-k^w} — 114
    - 3.2.3.4 Is Morphological Labialisation Older Than Phonological Labialisation? — 114
  - 3.2.4 Palatalisation Prosody — 117
    - 3.2.4.1 Suffixal Augment — 119
    - 3.2.4.2 Prosodising *{-y} — 119
    - 3.2.4.3 Non-Prosodising *{-y} — 122
  - 3.2.5 Combined Y- and W-Prosodies — 123
    - 3.2.5.1 Separate Domains for Each Prosody — 124
    - 3.2.5.2 Prosody Fusion in Same Domain (*/a/^{wy} > œ) — 125
- 3.3 Diachronic Sources of Morphological Prosodies — 126
- 3.4 The Origins of Final */a/ and [ə] — 127

	3.4.1	Final */a/	127
	3.4.2	Final Consonant (Ø Vowel)	128
	3.4.3	Final Schwa	128
	3.5	A Note on the Integration of Loan Words into Central Chadic Phonology	129

4. Diachronic Processes in Central Chadic Language Evolution — 133
   4.1 Vowel Epenthesis — 133
   4.2 Prosodic 'Colouring' of Pro- and Epenthetic Schwa — 134
   4.3 Prosodic Effects on */a/ — 134
   4.4 Syllabification of Underlying *y and *w — 135
       4.4.1 Weak Radicals *y and *w in Medial Position — 135
       4.4.2 *y and *w in Suffixal Augments in Final Position — 136
   4.5 Intersegmental Fusion of Features Affecting Radical Consonants — 140
   4.6 Accounting for Differences between Very Closely Related Languages — 141
       4.6.1 Underlying Root Type — 141
       4.6.2 Root Augmentation, Consonantal Sound Changes, and Prosodies — 142
   4.7 From PCC to Modern Central Chadic Languages: Phonemicisation of Allophones — 142
   4.8 On the Emergence of Long Vowels in Modern Central Chadic Languages — 147
       4.8.1 The Emergence of Long [ii] — 148
       4.8.2 The Emergence of Long [uu] — 149
   4.9 Summary of Diachronic Processes from PCC to Modern Central Chadic Languages — 150

5. Central Chadic Languages and the Neogrammarian Hypothesis — 158
   5.1 Individual Language Histories: Evidence from Lamang and Hdi — 161
   5.2 Scrutinising the Notion of 'Regular Sound Correspondence' in the Vocalic Domain — 176

6. Full Lexical Reconstructions — 187
   6.1 Alternative Option for Not Reconstructing ^{x}/ə/ — 187
   6.2 Alternative Option for Not Reconstructing ^{x}/i/ — 191
   6.3 Alternative Reconstructions of the Proto-Central Chadic Lexicon — 192
       6.3.1 Reconstructions Licensing [i] in Phonetic Surface Representation — 193
           6.3.1.1 [i] in Final Position — 194
           6.3.1.2 [i] in Medial Position — 195
           6.3.1.3 [i] in Initial Position — 198
       6.3.2 Reconstructions Licensing [u] in Phonetic Surface Representation — 198
           6.3.2.1 [u] in Final Position — 198
           6.3.2.2 [u] in Medial Position — 200
           6.3.2.3 [u] in Initial Position — 200
       6.3.3 Reconstructions Licensing Mid Vowels [e] and [o] in Both Medial and Final Positions in Phonetic Surface Representation — 201
       6.3.4 Reconstructions Licensing Final Schwa in Phonetic Surface Representation — 201
       6.3.5 Reconstructions Involving */a/ as Medial Vowel — 203
       6.3.6 Regarding Glottal Stop and Glottalisation — 211
           6.3.6.1 Emergence of Glottal Stops in Surface Representations — 212
           6.3.6.2 ['w] (and [p']?) Reflecting PCC */C^w/ — 213
           6.3.6.3 */ʔ/ as an Unidentified Root Augment? — 214

x   Contents

6.3.6.4 Another Look at the Root for 'Water'	214
6.3.6.5 Are there Traces of 'Glottalisation Prosody'?	215
6.4 PCC Lexical Reconstructions: Data and Details	218
arm	221
ashes	224
beard	227
beer	230
belly	231
bite, to	235
blow, to	237
boil, to	239
bone	242
bow	248
brain	253
butterfly	255
camel	258
cook, to	268
cow	271
crocodile	275
cry, to	276
die, to	281
dog	287
donkey$_1$	291
donkey$_2$	295
donkey$_3$	296
dream	299
earth	305
eight	308
elephant	310
extinguish, to	311
faeces	314
five	316
fly	319
foot	327
give birth, to	329
grandfather	336
grasshopper	339
hair	343
hare	345
hedgehog	349
hide, to	351
horn$_1$	353
horn$_2$	357
horse	358
laugh, to	363
lion	368
market	371
moon	377
navel	381
night	385

quiver	391
ram	393
razor$_1$	396
razor$_2$	398
root	400
six	406
spit, to	406
suck, to	411
sun	418
thorn	424
three	428
two	434
wash, to	435
water	439
whistle, to	446
white	450
work	453

APPENDIX: Alphabetical List of Glosses with Alternative Reconstructions and Prosodies	458
References	461
Index: Languages and Lexical Items	466

List of Figures

1.1	Vocoids and contoids	*page* 14
1.2	Abstract model of the evolution of Central Chadic lexical items	19
2.1	Phoneme split affecting the so-called weak radicals */y/ and */w/	32
2.2	Lamang–Hdi: look-alikes or cognates?	42
2.3	Lamang–Hdi: cognation	43
3.1	Diachronic root type dynamics	87

List of Tables

1.1	'nose' and 'ear' in so-called Wandala-Lamang (1)	*page* 8
1.2	'nose' and 'ear' in so-called Wandala-Lamang (2)	9
2.1	Underlying vs. surface representations in the vocalic domain	34
2.2	Representation format of lexical reconstructions	36
2.3	Prenasalisation as prosody?	63
2.4	From segments to prosodies	64
2.5	Alternative reconstructions of diachronic 'root'	69
2.6	Conflated representations and dissolution of root types	69
2.7	Choice of root types	69
3.1	Inventories of pre- and suffixal root augments	98
3.2	Diachronic desegmentalisation and prosodification	102
3.3	Re-segmentalisation and labialisation transfer	102
3.4	Re-segmentalisation and glottalisation transfer	103
3.5	Consonant inventory (1)	104
3.6	Consonant inventory (2)	104
3.7	Different paths of loans into Central Chadic for 'camel'	131
4.1	The vocalic domain of Proto-Central Chadic	144
4.2	Synchronic vowel qualities in Central Chadic languages	145
4.3	The vocalic space in Central Chadic languages: tongue height and position	145
4.4	The vocalic space in Central Chadic languages: diachronic vocoids	146
4.5	The vocalic space in Central Chadic languages: prosodies	147
4.6	Phonetic 'colouring' of epenthetic schwa in Central Chadic languages	147
4.7	Matching of PCC reconstructions with modern forms	152
5.1	Frequency of rule applications	175
5.2	'nose' and 'ear' in so-called Wandala-Lamang (3)	178
5.3	Reconstructing 'nose' in so-called Wandala-Lamang	180

5.4 Consonantal sound changes in so-called Wandala-Lamang (1)   180
5.5 Reconstructing 'ear' in so-called Wandala-Lamang   182
5.6 Consonantal sound changes in so-called Wandala-Lamang (2)   183
6.1 Neutralisation of structural contrasts   189

Preface

Historical-comparative linguistic research in the Afroasiatic language phylum suffers from deficits regarding robust comparative studies in the branches and sub-branches of its African member families, which constitute the vast majority of its currently known 382 member languages. One of the most under-researched language families within Afroasiatic is Chadic, whose almost 200 named languages constitute the largest language family within the phylum. Among the Chadic languages, the Central Chadic (aka 'Biu-Mandara') branch with its about 80 languages again constitutes the majority. Central Chadic languages are notorious for their internal diversification not least due to an assumed immense time-depth, which eminent experts like the late Russell G. Schuh have occasionally compared to Indo-European rather than to any of the latter's constitutive families, like Germanic, Romance etc.

The current volume provides an in-depth study of the historical phonology of Central Chadic, unravelling the structural principles and diachronic developments that link the highly diverse phonetic surface representations in modern Central Chadic languages, as they are spoken in North-Eastern Nigeria, Northern Cameroon and Western Chad, i.e. roughly along the southern shorelines of the former Mega-Chad Lake, to Proto-Central Chadic (PCC) lexical reconstructions. The study rests on an online database (Gravina 2014b) comprising published and unpublished data on 250 lexical items from 60 (plus 6 language varieties) of the then known 78 named languages of this branch (Lewis 2009). The book offers meticulous historical analyses of some 60 selected lexical items, which could be considered controversial in terms of both synchronically underlying and historically reconstructed phonological units that make up the vocalic domain. It covers diachronic processes starting from an archaic *root-and-pattern* structure in PCC to the modern Central Chadic languages, and it distinguishes strictly between the regimes of *phonological* ('lexical') and *morphological* ('grammatical') *prosodies*, which extensively influence the surface forms of lexical items in the present-day languages. Particular emphasis is placed on tracing the deep-rooted origin and impact of *palatalisation* and *labialisation prosodies* within a phonological system that, on its deepest level of analysis, recognises only one vowel phoneme */a/.

The study refines the classic *comparative method* and *internal reconstruction* approaches to cope with the needs of Central Chadic language typology, and it does so in combination with a bottom-up *dialectological* perspective. It remains informed by received typological wisdom from Afroasiatic linguistics regarding root-and-pattern and *weak radical* structures, applying it to a branch of Chadic that had long been considered innovative rather than archaic, because of the almost complete loss of a few diagnostic typological features of the common proto-language (like grammatical gender, broken plurals, etc.), yet ignoring aspects of phonology and morphophonology (like root-and-pattern and weak radicals) that reflect early or even pre-Chadic retentions rather than branch-internal innovations. The book provides new insights into historical (Central) Chadic phonology, in particular with regard to constitutive phonological units in the vocalic domain and their diachronic evolution. By identifying the ultimate segmental sources of palatalisation and labialisation prosodies, it unearths their deep-seated historical origins and describes their continuing effects on synchronic representations that tend to veil etymological relationships between lexical items in modern Central Chadic languages far beyond recognisability.

Acknowledgements

The author gratefully acknowledges valuable comments on a pre-final draft of the book by Paul Newman, with whom the author shares half a century of rewarding professional and personal relationship.

The author further acknowledges welcome input by two anonymous reviewers regarding the overall structure of the final version of the book.

Glossonyms Used for Central Chadic Languages and Language Variants

GROUP	language
BATA	Bachama
	Bata
	Gude
	Jimi
	Sharwa
	Tsuvan
DABA	Buwal
	Mbudum
	Gavar
	Mazagway Hidi
	Daba
MAFA	Mafa
	Cuvok
	Mefele
TERA	Tera
	Nyimatli
	Ga'anda
	Hwana
SUKUR	Sukur
HURZA	Mbuko
	Vame
	Ndreme
MARGI	Bura
	Margi
	Margi-South
	Kilba
MANDARA	Matal
	Podoko
	Mandara
	Malgwa
	Glavda
	Dghweɗe
	Guduf
	Gwara

MOFU	Ouldeme
	Muyang
	Mada
	Moloko
	Zulgo
	Gemzek
	Merey
	Dugwor
	Mofu North
	Mofu-Gudur
MAROUA	Giziga
	Giziga-Muturwa
	Giziga-Marva
	Mbazla
LAMANG	Lamang
	Hdi
	Mabas
HIGI	Kamwe-Nkafa
	Kamwe-Futu
	Kirya
	Psikye
	Bana
KOTOKO-ISLAND	Buduma
KOTOKO-NORTH	Afade
	Mpade
	Malgbe
	Maltam
KOTOKO-CENTRAL	Lagwan
	Mser
KOTOKO-SOUTH	Zina
	Mazera
MUSGUM	Vulum
	Mulwi
	Mbara
	Muskum
GIDAR	Gidar

Abbreviations and Symbols

Ø	deletion of diachronic or synchronically underlying segment; non-representation of category
*__	reconstructed/hypothetical root or segment
x__	invalid reconstruction
/.../	phonemic representation
[...]	phonetic representation; distinctive feature
[±syll]	ambivalent/underspecified for feature 'syllabic'
>	input to output; change to
<	output from input; derived/stemming from
/__#	in (word-) final position
+	juncture between REDuplicated units; re-segmentalisation/phoneme split, e.g. /C^w/ > /C+w/
√	root shape incl. vocalisation slots (blanks, or filled by /a/)
√...(C)a	final lexical root vowel */a/
√...C(a)C...	optional medial slot for */a/
ə	epenthetic vowel schwa
+W	labialisation prosody (operating on the particular lexical item)
+Y	palatalisation prosody (operating on the particular lexical item)
$\_^y$, $\_^w$	indication of prosody (source/affected domain to the left)
aka	also known as
a^y	/a/ affected by Y-prosody: usually yielding [e]
a^w	/a/ affected by W-prosody: usually yielding [o]
$ə^y$	epenthetic vowel affected by Y-prosody: usually yielding [ɨ] or [i]
$ə^w$	epenthetic vowel affected by W-prosody: usually yielding [ʉ] or [u]
C^y	palatalised consonant (by origin, or as affected by Y-prosody)

C^w	labialised consonant (by origin, or as affected by W-prosody)
$^mb, ^nd, ^ŋg, \ldots$	prenasalised obstruents
C	consonant (slot)
CV.CV.CV.	syllable structure
CC	Central Chadic
fn.	footnote
FV	final vowel */a/ (optional, following suffixal root-augmental element)
incl.	including
IPA	International Phonetic Alphabet
PC	Proto-Chadic
PCC	Proto-Central Chadic
PLH	Proto-Lamang-Hdi
RED	reduplicative root augment
SIL	SIL International (formerly Summer Institute of Linguistics)
V	vowel (slot)
vs.	versus, as opposed to

1 Introduction

For a long time in the more than 130 years of history of African linguistics as an academic discipline (Wolff 2019a), Chadic languages in general, and Central Chadic languages in particular, have been underrepresented with regard to detailed monographic descriptions, full-fledged dictionaries, and robust comparative work. If at all and largely to the exception of Hausa, a West Chadic language of wide distribution as lingua franca across large parts of West and Central Africa, Chadic languages were considered minority languages and had only been known from short wordlists and sketchy grammatical notes. Some of these, however, date back to the early nineteenth century, including, for instance, Central Chadic Afade (Seetzen 1810; Sölken 1957) and Wandala/Mandara (cf. Wolff & Naumann 2004).[1]

The first published modern and readable full reference grammars based on extensive and solid linguistic fieldwork for Central Chadic (aka 'Biu-Mandara') languages were Hoffmann (1963) for Margi, truly a pioneer effort, and – twenty years later – Wolff (1983a) for Lamang. One should, however, also mention Roxana Ma Newman's (1971) PhD dissertation on Ga'anda and James Hoskison's (1983) MA thesis on Gude. Unfortunately, Paul Newman's published early PhD dissertation on Tera (1970) was so overloaded with 'generative-transformational' formalism in the spirit of the time that it never qualified as a reference work on the language to be much cited. For these five Central Chadic languages that could boast of major and more recent, i.e. post-1960 descriptive works, however, published full dictionaries were not available until quite recently; all we had was rather limited access to wordlists and small vocabularies. The first late-coming dictionaries to fill that gap were Wolff (2015, Vol. 2) for Lamang, which was based on fieldwork periods between 1968 and 1982, and Frajzyngier et al. (2015) for Hdi, which rests on fieldwork done by both the late Paul Eguchi (1971) in the late 1960s and Zygmunt Frajzyngier after 1991. For the posthumous publication of Hoffmann's vocabulary notes on Margi stemming from his fieldwork in the

---

[1] For a comprehensive bibliography of Chadic and Hausa linguistics, see Newman (2018).

1950s, see Peust (2019). Despite slowly growing numbers of descriptive grammars of Central Chadic languages, dictionary production remains on a deplorably low scale (cf. Newman 2018, 2019: 15). Consequently, serious comparative work on Chadic, including Central Chadic, was hampered by lack of sufficient quantitative and reliable qualitative data in terms of both lexicon and robust language descriptions – until far into the 1980s. For a short history of Chadic linguistics and current state-of-the-art account, see Wolff (in press).

Apart from the generally poor documentation and description of Chadic and in particular Central Chadic languages, the nature of the available data reflected enormous diversity, which tended to make comparative research appear not to be easily feasible, not so much with regard to consonants, but in particular with regard to vowels. To illustrate the point, and thereby anticipating the problems of analysis and description that the present study is about, one could take just three almost randomly selected common words (see 6.4 for all details). For instance, and looking at four Central Chadic languages only, the widely shared word for 'ashes' is represented by highly diverse segmental surface forms, which among themselves display six different vowel qualities in the first two syllables, namely *i*, *œ*, *ə*, *a*, *e*, *o*: *fitœdiye* (Bachama), *bəta* (Dugwor), *bite* (Zulgo), *aftʃo* (Giziga-Marva). As regards the consonants that make up the first two syllables, there is much less diversity: $C_1 = f/b$, $C_2 = t/tʃ$; only Bachama shows more consonantal material ($C_3 = d$, plus ending *-iye*). In the word for 'beard' in just another three languages, one may wonder how, apart from the differences regarding vowels, the forms as such could form 'regular sound correspondences' in terms of cognation and reconstructable proto-language source forms under the so-called Neogrammarian Hypothesis (see Chapter 5): $ag^w oy$ (Matal), *mume* (Podoko), *ɣuɓe* (Kamwe-Futu). Indeed, applying the classic Neogrammarian *comparative method* would appear to come to its limits, if its application were at all feasible to include vowels and consonants, in the light of data such as for 'bone', e.g. *ɬa* (Glavda), *ɠəɬ* (Tera), *ila* (Gude), *uule* (Bachama), *ateɬ* (Giziga-Marva), *'a'aɬ* (Mbazla), *'yithlə* (Kamwe-Futu), *dyahu* (Margi), *ahay* (Buduma), *enʃi* (Mpade), *asis'e* (Mazera), *ɬeŋɬeŋ* (Gidar). That such forms can and must be considered to be cognates, and how they can be reconstructed systematically, i.e. based on regularities, from a common diachronic source system referred to as Proto-Central Chadic (PCC), will be shown in the body of the present book.

1.1 Comparative Chadic Linguistics, and Why It Is So Problematic to Reconstruct Lexical Items for Proto-Chadic in General, and for Proto-Central Chadic in Particular

A first and courageous if somewhat premature attempt to tackle Chadic comparativism, by indicating consonants only and using hyphens to mark the assumed position of vowels, was presented by Paul Newman and Roxana Ma [Newman] (1966) under the fresh impact of Joseph H. Greenberg's seminal classification of *The Languages of Africa* (1963). Greenberg had provided a unified classification of the formerly separated 'Chadohamitic' and 'Chadic' languages under the unifying term 'Chad languages', and added a number of languages in the Republic of Chad and in the Jos Plateau area of Nigeria, which had earlier been ignored from a classificatory point of view. He included the 'Chad languages' in the language phylum that he now called Afroasiatic (formerly known as Hamito-Semitic). The earlier separation of 'Chadohamitic' vs. 'Chadic' languages was based on classifications by Johannes Lukas, such as that of 1936, which had largely been based on typological considerations. These had also found their way into the major pre-Greenbergian reference work, *The Languages of West Africa. Handbook of African Languages Part II*, ed. by D. Westermann and M. A. Bryan (1952) in those sections for which J. Lukas was informally reported to have been partly responsible. The Newman and Ma (1966) pioneer study was followed by a small but illuminating and much more robust comparative-method based study by P. Newman (1977a), which contained at least an attempt, necessarily very tentative at the time, to include vowels in the reconstructions. This again was followed shortly after by a parallel and independent study on reconstructions of again consonantal roots only, compiled by Jungraithmayr and Shimizu (1981). So, by the early 1980s, the ball had slowly begun to roll towards comparative studies involving – or even with a focus on – Central Chadic languages, yet with but a handful of expert linguists becoming involved. The major challenge appeared to remain the provision of additional and reliable descriptive and lexicographic data from more of the almost 200 hitherto largely undocumented languages of the Chadic family with its currently widely accepted four branches (West Chadic, Central Chadic, East Chadic, Masa; cf. Newman 2013), among them about 80 Central Chadic languages, being the family's largest branch in terms of numbers of individual languages. Consequently, Afroasiatic comparativism continued to suffer from the underrepresentation of Chadic data and the lack of robust generalisations, notably since Chadic is the largest family within Afroasiatic, covering more than half of all known Afroasiatic languages.[2]

In the light of slowly increasing new data and the publication of more individual language descriptions, linguists continued to be stunned by the enormous divergence, both typological and genealogical, within Chadic as a whole, and also within the branches, sub-branches and even down to the group level of available Chadic sub-classifications. For as long as it was not feasible

---

[2] According to the latest edition of the Ethnologue (Eberhard et al. 2021), among the 382 recognised Afroasiatic languages, 196 belong to the Chadic language family, among them 79 of the 'Biu-Mandara' branch, i.e. Central Chadic.

to apply the classic comparative method satisfactorily to Chadic languages including both consonants and vowels, and thereby to provide the likewise classic dendrograms of genealogical language classification based on series of regular sound correspondences and shared innovations, even Chadic sub-classifications had to remain somewhat doubtful.[3] Experts in the field appeared to agree on at least one of several potential explanations, namely that there was considerable time-depth involved in this language family, not to speak of the even older heritage from Afroasiatic, to which Chadic doubtlessly belonged (Newman 1980).

P. Newman's pioneering small but illuminating comparative study contained an 'extremely tentative' (Newman 1977a: 12) attempt to include vowels in the reconstructions of Proto-Chadic (henceforth also PC) lexical items. For Chadic as a whole, Newman very cautiously talked about the likelihood that 'PC can be reconstructed as having had **at most** four phonemic vowels *i ə u a*, and possibly only two, *ə* and *a*' (Newman, 1977a: 9).

Their occurrence in surface representations of words in the modern languages, however, would be dependent on the position in the word (initial, medial, final) as well as on whether they occurred in open syllables, etc. More specifically, he stated that '[f]our vowels (*a, ə, i, u*) are used in the reconstructions, although ... the contrastive status of the latter three is open to doubt' (Newman, 1977a: 20) – which brings us back to the assumption of maximally two, if not even fewer, vowel phonemes in the proto-language (see further below).[4] At that time, Newman (1977a: 12) had considered 'a balanced **i, *a, *u* system ... a remote possibility'.[5] Almost 30 years later, Newman (2006)

---

[3] For most recent sub-classifications of Chadic, see Newman (2013) and, with a focus on Central Chadic ('Biu-Mandara'), Gravina (2007, 2011, 2014a: xxi–xxii).

[4] Note that, interestingly and until this day, the choice between such four-vowel (a, ə, i, u) and two-vowel (a, ə) systems corresponds to later popular ideas of the general situation in Central Chadic, and after the situation in Proto-Chadic had been reviewed, see Newman (2006) and below.

[5] A short comparative survey regarding vowel systems in other families of Afroasiatic may be in order here. 1. Berber. Kossmann (2012: 28) mentions vowel systems between three (Tashelhiyt: *i, a, u*) and seven (Ayer Tuareg) vowels. 2. Egyptian. Loprieno and Müller (2012: 116–117) follow Diakonoff (1965) in the assumption of three basic vowel qualities *i, a, u* (long and short) for Earlier Egyptian, which would diachronically undergo a number of historical changes, giving rise in Sahidic Coptic, for instance, to subsystems of two unstressed vowels (e /ə/, a /a/) and seven (long and short) stressed vowels. 3. Semitic. Gragg and Hobermann (2012: 160–163) accept as 'Common Semitic' a similar system of three vowel qualities *i, a, u* (short and long), which undergo historical developments resulting in, for instance, disallowing short vowels in open syllables with subsequent merger to schwa, or a simple /a/ : /ə/ distinction, while historically long vowels remain somewhat more stable. For Afroasiatic southern fringe languages, which are spoken in close neighbourhood to other African languages, a different picture emerges. 4. Cushitic. Mous (2012: 353) assumes as typical five long and five short vowels: *i, e, a, o, u*. 5. Omotic. Amha (2012: 436) also accepts five basic vowels, plus phonemic length. Repeatedly, the quoted authors mention the additional emergence of central schwa, being more or less predictable as to where it occurs.

reviewed achievements in comparative Chadic linguistics and modified his views on the PC vowel system. He now favoured the hypothesis

that PC had 3 vowels (/i, u, a/), although there may have been only a two-way contrast (i/u vs. a) in word-initial position ...

In word-medial position the three vowels could all occur both long and short. There was no length contrast in word-initial position, where the vowels were short. Nor in word-final position, where the vowels were also short except for /a/ which may have been long in CV words, e.g., *saa* 'drink', *ɬaa* 'cow'. The four-vowel system typical of Biu-Mandara, namely /i, u, ə, a/ without length, could easily have arisen from an original 3-vowel system with length by means of a diachronic scenario such as the following: **i* and **u* merged to /ə/, **ii* and **uu* lost vowel length and changed to /i/ and /u/, and **aa* and **a* merged to /a/. (Newman 2006: 193)

Note that in the present study, the focus is exclusively on Central Chadic (= 'Biu-Mandara') languages. The issue of how our PCC reconstructions relate back to hypotheses about PC like those proposed by Newman is not addressed, nor are assumptions about other proto-languages within Afroasiatic allowed to interfere with our focus on PCC. In any case, this opens challenging questions for future comparative research across both Chadic and Afroasiatic.[6]

---

[6] There are two scenarios to be tentatively advanced as plausible, which each still deserve investigation.
   A. Our reconstructions of PCC mirror an Early Chadic if not pre-Chadic situation, which would qualify Central Chadic as diachronically and typologically 'archaic' with regard to *vocalogenesis* (this hypothesis is discussed at some length in Wolff 2017) emerging from a hypothetical proto-system of 'vocoids' */ʕ/, */y/ and */w/, all of them underspecified for the feature [±syllabic]. In syllable-nucleus positions, these vocoids gave rise to [+syll] vowels, which would correspond to Newman's */a, i, u/ and assumptions quoted for Berber, Egyptian and Semitic in the footnote above (disregarding the issue of length at this point). The task then would be to explain the emergence of modern Chadic phonological systems with much richer inventories of phonemic vowels across all branches, mainly by 'phonemicisation' of allophones and/or epenthetic schwa, and/or by contact with non-Chadic languages of presumably Niger-Congo and Nilo-Saharan stock.
   B. The reconstructed situation in PCC represents a largely areal innovation possibly at the time of separation of PCC from the rest of Chadic. The innovation would have been the almost complete breakdown of the PC three-vowel-system (plus length) with losses and extensive merging of vowels (and 'semi-vowels') as suggested by Newman (2006): Short **i* and **u* would have been either lost or merged to *ə* (i.e. schwa, of uncertain phonological status in the emerging synchronic systems) or, together with **ii* and **uu*, in certain positions merged with syllabic **y* and **w*. **aa* and **a* would have merged to */a/ and represent the diachronically most stable vocalic phoneme, which either contrasted only with its absence (resulting in a one-vowel-system, as in Central Chadic Moloko), or with a phonemicised /ə/ (resulting in a two-vowel-system, as more widely spread in Central Chadic languages).
   Lines of further research, therefore, might want to focus on questions relating to the diachronic evolution of 'vowel length' in PC (if not in other branches of Proto-Afroasiatic as well), i.e. whether (i) it was phonemic from the beginning, involving all 'vowels' (if the proto-language possessed a system of 'true' vowel contrasts), or whether (ii) it emerged during later stages, possibly to the exception of and in addition to a very early */a/ : */aa/ contrast, or whether (iii) it more generally came about, as could be assumed for many Central Chadic languages (see 4.8, but notice the groundbreaking contribution by Heide Mirt (1969) on Mandara), by a combination

Another important early attempt towards tentative reconstructions of *Chadic Lexical Roots* was that of Jungraithmayr and Shimizu (1981), who, however, and much like Newman and Ma (1966) before, disregarded vowels almost completely and focused on the consonantal ('radical') skeletons of 'roots' in the narrow sense of Semitic scholarship.[7] Their work stands out with regard to, for the first time, directing our attention to 'affixes' to roots that would need to be taken into account for complete reconstructions of PC lexical items. They describe the research situation at their time as follows:

> To a given reconstructed root ... there are three components: radicals, vowels, and affixes (Footnote: Reconstruction of tone has not yet been attempted). Among these, only radicals can be presented as a truly reconstructable element. The reconstructability of vowels is at least doubtful, if not *entirely impracticable* ... Regarding affixes, much work remains to be done, although some affixes must be postulated and have in fact been proposed. (Jungraithmayr & Shimizu 1981: 24 – emphasis mine)

Their 'three-component' approach to reconstructions is recognised in the present study as a valid starting point.

Mention must also be made of Olga Stolbova's series of contributions towards comparative Chadic etymologies within the wider framework of comparative Afroasiatic (or, in Russian terminology, Afrasian) lexical reconstructions. In her *Chadic Etymological Dictionary* she writes

> Reconstruction of proto-Chadic vowels is considered as the most difficult or even an *unsolvable task* ...
> ... In the present text P[roto-]Ch[adic] vowels are mostly rendered by V. In some cases, however, a short vowel (*-a-, -i-, -u-*) of the first syllable can be reconstructed. (Stolbova 2016: 45 – emphasis mine)

Closer to the focus of the present study and also beginning in the early 1980s, are the historical-comparative works with a special focus on the about 80 Central Chadic languages. Published records begin with Wolff et al. (1981), Wolff (1981, 1983b) and Barreteau (1983, 1987). Both the late Daniel Barreteau (1950–2007) and the present author independently followed leads from synchronic Chadic linguistics that had been developed by, for instance, Carl Hoffmann (1965) for Higi, Roger Mohrlang (1971, 1972) for Higi, James Hoskison (1974) for Gude, Ruth Lienhard and Marti Giger (1975) for Daba, and Roxana Ma Newman (1977) for Ga'anda. Barreteau and Wolff, quite independently but later sharing notes on their respective comparative research on the Cameroonian (Barreteau) and the Nigerian (Wolff) side of the international border cutting through the Mandara Mountains, would appear to

---

and fusion of pro-/epenthetic schwa and any of the postulated proto-language's 'vocoids': *ə+*/y/ > [ii], *ə+*/w/ > [uu], and – possibly – also *ə+ʕ > [aa].

[7] The study was expanded in its much later published Vol. 1 (Jungraithmayr & Ibriszimow 1994).

be the first to apply an innovative 'prosody approach' to diachronic research into selected Central Chadic languages or language groups. They did so with the aim of arriving at an increasingly wider perspective on the linguistic history of the Central Chadic branch of the family in general. Hoffmann (1987) later presented an interesting labialisation–prosody-based comparative approach to selected lexical items from a number of languages belonging to the then so-called Bura-Margi group as a follow-up to his Higi studies of 1965.[8]

The new comparative approach pushed by Barreteau and Wolff in the early 1980s rested on two interrelated modules of a theory that particularly well befitted both the synchronic-descriptive features and assumed diachronic processes of comparative relevance regarding the linguistic situation of Central Chadic (sub-branch A) languages. Whether this pertained to only some better-known or rather all Central Chadic languages was still considered an open question at the time. The two modules were the following:

(a) The postulation of highly abstract phonemic representations that could be assumed to underlie the phonetic surface representations of data from modern Chadic languages as they were provided by the transcriptions of descriptive linguists working in the field. Depending on the degree of abstractness, rather limited inventories of phonemic vowels were recognised: only two (*/a/, */ə/), or possibly only one (*/a/), with schwa being accounted for by pro- and epenthesis in all cases of its occurrence.

(b) The identification of the salient impact of 'prosodies' on the phonetic realisations of actually occurring surface forms, which affected both consonants and vowels. *Palatalisation* and *labialisation prosodies* appeared to provide fairly transparent diachronic processes to allow for satisfactory explanations to account for the existence and distribution of up to 17 (short and long) phonetic vowel representations in the transcriptions of synchronic Chadic data (cf. Wolff 2017), by still being able to relate these to just one or two underlying vowel phonemes in Central Chadic.

This combined approach was another major breakthrough in comparative Chadic linguistics. It rested on comparative bottom-up rather than top-down procedures akin to dialectological methodology, i.e. starting from small sets of closely related (and often immediately neighbouring) languages in order to

---

[8] The author recalls that Carl Hoffmann was about to present this or a similar paper as early as the 2nd International Colloquium on the Chadic Language Family in Hamburg 1981, but was not in a position to provide a written version for the proceedings as invited by the editors (Wolff & Meyer-Bahlburg 1983). His 1987 publication originates from a conference presentation in Marburg 1983, which links his contribution to the broader debate on the value of prosodies for comparative studies of Central Chadic languages following the lead of Barreteau's and Wolff's work in the early 1980s.

Table 1.1 *'nose' and 'ear' in so-called Wandala-Lamang (1)*

	'nose'	'ear'
Dghweɗe	x t i r e	ɬ e m e
Glavda	x t ə r a	h^y i m ia
Gvoko	x t o r	ɬ u w o
Guduf	x t e r e	ɬ i m e
Podoko	f t r a	ɬ a m a
Wandala	ə k t a r e	ɬ ə m a
Gwara	ak^{w}c i n	ɬ i m i
Lamang	x ts i n i	ɬ ə m ə ŋ i

better understand language-internal diachronic processes affecting natural language change.

Earlier researchers had fairly soon realised that it was apparently not feasible to fully apply the classic comparative method (as developed by the Leipzig School of the 'Neogrammarian' tradition in the late nineteenth century) to Chadic languages, particularly with regard to handling surface vowels. Severe problems immediately occurred in the course of comparing pairs of languages from even groups of quite closely related languages when facing the task of identifying regular 1:1 sound correspondences. Between surface vowels, such 1:1 correspondences simply did not exist. Any surface vowel in any position of the word could correspond to practically any other available surface vowel in a corresponding position (cf. first steps, and already envisaging increasingly higher levels of abstract phonological representation, in Wolff et al. 1981; Wolff 1981, 1983b). Wolff (1983b: 215) provides illustrative examples from the rather closely related languages of the then so-called Wandala-Lamang group, among them the reflexes of the obviously cognate lexical items for 'nose' and 'ear', which tend to lead the application of the classic comparative method to vowels *ad absurdum* (Table 1.1).[9]

Any vowel, including its absence (Ø), would appear to correspond to almost any vowel or its absence in any closely related language, with distributional restrictions depending on their position in the word (Table 1.2).

---

[9] According to a more recent sub-classification of Central Chadic, Lamang is no longer considered to belong to the same language group as the other languages but to form a separate LAMANG group together with Hdi (and Mabas). The MANDARA group now comprises the languages Mandara/Wandala (Malgwa), Glavda, Dghweɗe, Cineni, Gava, Guduf, Gvoko, Podoko, Matal. Gwara is not a separate language, but rather a 'substratum' to present-day Margi of the MARGI group, linking up with MANDARA group languages.

1.1 Comparative Chadic Linguistics

Table 1.2 *'nose' and 'ear' in so-called Wandala-Lamang (2)*

	'nose'			'ear'		
	initial	medial	final	initial	medial	final
Dghweɗe	—	*i*	*e*	—	*e*	*e*
Glavda	—	*ə*	*a*	—	*i*	*i(a)*
Gvoko	—	*o*	Ø	—	*u*	*o*
Guduf	—	*e*	*e*	—	*i*	*e*
Podoko	—	Ø	*a*	—	*a*	*a*
Wandala	*ə*	*a*	*e*	—	*ə*	*a*
Gwara	*a*	*i*	Ø	—	*i*	*i*
Lamang	—	*i*	*i*	—	*ə*	(X)*i*

Therefore, attempting to match surface vowels in pairs of languages in order to establish series of regular sound correspondences fails across the board. We will come back to this problem and these data in more detail in section 5.2 further below.

The reasons for the stunning lack of regular sound correspondences among surface vowels were not yet fully understood at the time when the concern about reconstructing vowels in (Central) Chadic began, albeit on a low level of sub-classification. What became obvious quite early was that there was no gain in comparing phonetic surface representations of vowels, but that we needed to identify the underlying (and possibly diachronic) phonological units that had given rise to the emergence of the phonetic surface vowels as transcribed by the field linguist or missionary linguist. It was not even clear how many vowel phonemes each of the languages under comparison actually possessed, nor what governed the distribution of vowels and their likely allophones across the words – based on observations that their distribution would appear to be somewhat restricted. Linguists noted quite obvious cases of 'harmonisation' of vowels across the word, but were, at that time, unable to recognise the more general principles behind such observations, i.e. the diachronic principles and processes that would go beyond the rules assumed to operate in the synchronic phonology and morphophonology of individual languages. (See, for example, the attempts by Wolff (1983b, 2015) to handle the phenomena in synchronic perspective under descriptive terms like 'umlaut' and 'vowel harmonisation'.) In the still rather small scientific community interested in African – or specifically Chadic or even Afroasiatic – comparative linguistics, it was not so much the rather small number of postulated underlying phonemic vowels that irritated fellow comparativists, even though many if not most linguists working on African languages – at the time and until this day – are rather hesitant to accept the idea of underlying linguistic systems with only one, if any at all, underlying phonemic vowel (cf. Wolff 2017). With regard to larger-scale comparisons, experts only later realised that what tended to confuse them was a kind of vicious circle. It seemed to be impossible, for Chadic languages, to reconstruct the consonants of the proto-language without a deeper understanding of the situation with regard to vowels, and it became obvious that the reconstruction of vowels depended to no little extent on our assumptions about reconstructable consonants, both in Chadic in general and in Central Chadic in particular. As Barreteau (1987: 189) had realised quite early: '[L'] important étant de considérer les systèmes vocalique et consonantique comme interdépendants'. It was most of all the palatal(ised) and labial(ised) consonants and their effect on vowels in the same word that raised suspicion. To no little extent, the vicious circle also affects the reconstruction of both vowels and palatalised (in particular coronal) and/or labialised (in particular velar) consonants for the proto-language. The late Russell G. Schuh (1941–2016) much later lucidly describes the challenges as he saw them as follows:

[I]t is difficult to use correspondence sets to unequivocally demonstrate the reconstruction of palatalised and labialised velars as phonemes distinct from their 'plain' counterparts. However, languages in most major groups arguably have at least a series of labialised velars, and many also have a palatalised series. As I will argue here and elsewhere, *what is often interpreted as a distinction in vowels is actually a distinction in consonants that influences the pronunciation of vowels*. (Schuh 2017: 47 – emphasis mine)

Implicit in this statement is the observation that obvious differences in phonetic vowel qualities must not necessarily reflect different underlying vowel phonemes. This links up with the observation that, in some languages at least, conditioned allophones of assumed phonemic vowels 'overlapped', i.e. the same surface vowels could represent – in synchronic terms – different vowel phonemes. It soon became obvious that the various vowel qualities in surface structure could very likely represent the results of phonological processes that historically originated from palatal(ised) and labial(ised) consonants elsewhere in the word. These phonological processes are dealt with here and elsewhere under the term 'prosodies', i.e. we speak of *Y-prosody* to describe larger domains of palatalisation, and we speak of *W-prosody* to describe larger domains of labialisation.[10]

---

[10] The term 'prosody' (aka 'long component') is used to describe a non-segmental functional feature, whose domain is larger than a single phoneme and may extend over a syllable or several syllables, or a word as a whole. In (Central) Chadic languages, we occasionally or regularly observe palatalisation, labialisation, possibly also nasalisation, glottalisation etc. as prosodies, which – stretching over several syllables or the whole word – may affect the articulation and pronunciation of vowels, or consonants, or both at the same time, in a kind of 'colouring' and 'harmonising' manner. To the best of my knowledge, the term '(morphological) Y-prosody'

Therefore and to this day, we suffer from an apparent failure to successfully apply the comparative method in a straightforward way and to arrive at full reconstructions including all surface representations of vowels, i.e. to reach the target of establishing reliable segmentally complete lexical reconstructions. By acquiring the nature of a prosody, formerly present and occasionally later lost segments can no longer be lined up in series of regular sound correspondences (see Chapter 5). Quite obviously in (Central) Chadic languages, surface vowels do not represent underlying vowel phonemes in the same almost 1:1 relationship as may be more usually the case in other and typologically different language families and language phyla, like Indo-European (where, however, we meet with more familiar and somewhat similar *umlaut* phenomena). However, after some 40 years of increasingly sophisticated and abstract phonological research into (Central) Chadic phonology and morphophonology, the tides are beginning to change. The present study aims at exactly the – hitherto considered highly ambitious, if not over-ambitious – target of providing full segmental lexical reconstructions for PCC involving both consonants and vowels, and at describing the diachronic phonological processes that govern the interrelationship between consonants and vowels on the basis of also reconstructing relevant prosodies. For this, we need to introduce the diachronic concept of 'prosodification'. Putting it rather simply: 'prosodification' describes a diachronic process by which phonological segments become desegmentalised completely or partially (also referred to occasionally as 'weakening'), and have one of their phonological features (such as, for instance, labialisation, palatalisation, nasalisation, glottalisation) start 'floating' within given phonological boundaries across morphemes or whole words.

By a very strict application of what we here call the 'prosody-based approach' to lexical reconstruction in PCC, we are now able to suggest alternative lexical reconstructions. These are based on diachronic principles and phonological processes which the author had progressively uncovered in various smaller publications on comparative Central Chadic issues over a period of about 40 years. In the current study, these are now bundled and applied to Central Chadic languages in an all-encompassing way in order to come up with both a coherent history of Central Chadic phonology and solidly based lexical reconstructions. These can now be fruitfully confronted most of all with the valuable lexical reconstruction work achieved by Richard Gravina (2014a). In his pioneer study, Gravina presented an attempt to apply 'the well

---

was introduced into Chadic linguistics by Roxana Ma Newman (1977). Note that, even though the deepest historical origins of the prosodies as we observe them today may have been anchored in near and distant assimilation processes, as *prosodies* they become detached from their original segmental sources in the proto-language and acquire an independent phonological existence, whose effects can no longer be adequately described in terms of simple assimilation processes.

established comparative method' (Gravina, 2014a: 5) based on regular sound correspondences to Central Chadic languages, yet taking into consideration what earlier studies had taught us:

Examining the surface segments is inadequate for establishing regular correspondences and sound changes, particularly for Central Chadic vowels (Wolff 1983[b]). Only by working from underlying segments and prosodies is it possible to understand the historical processes involved. (Gravina 2014a: 6)

Where the classic comparative method failed, therefore, he complemented his efforts with insights from the so-called *prosody theory* (see 2.5.4 below). His study was based on exceptionally rich data from a Central Chadic database containing 250 lexical items from up to 60 languages (Gravina 2014b). This effort must be considered yet another milestone in diachronic Chadic linguistics. Previous to his book-length treatment as PhD dissertation, the gist of his research was presented in a conference paper in 2011 (Gravina 2013). With regard to the vocalic domain, Gravina arrived at reconstructing four salient phonological units for Proto-Central Chadic, namely three vowels (*/a/, */ə/, */i/) and phonemic Y-prosody (i.e. palatalisation).[11]

The motivation behind presenting this study to the linguistics science community is to allow for and stimulate illuminating comparisons across different conceivable theoretical and methodological approaches, but grounded on the same solid language data. Neither of the two approaches, i.e. neither the one presented by Gravina (2014a) nor the one represented in this book, can claim to once and for all solve all problems and answer all questions with regard to full lexical reconstructions for PCC, but we have now come a long way towards that target. Vowels can now be fully integrated into comparative linguistic work on (Central) Chadic, and analytical problems on the way can now be tackled methodologically *lege artis*.

Particularly in the field of Afroasiatic linguistics with its good documentation of certain of its families (in particular Semitic), there is a tendency to come up with sweeping and far-reaching comparisons bridging vast world regions and huge time-depths. Yet they often lack rigid methodology. What is needed is methodologically sound reconstruction on low and intermediate levels of language families and their branches, including Chadic.

Chadic really needs a more extensive, properly-done reconstruction of the proto-language, one that could serve as a point of reference for the next generation of scholars. Independent of or in conjunction with PC reconstruction, Chadic could also

---

[11] Note that, with the exception of language data quoted from the original sources, we have here replaced Gravina's IPA symbol ɨ with ə for schwa, for reasons of long-established practice in Chadic linguistics.

benefit greatly by detailed lexical reconstructions of the four branches of the family approached from within those branches. (Newman 2006: 201)

It remains to be seen, whether at all – and if so, how – our alternative reconstructions have a bearing on reconstructing Proto-Chadic, i.e. beyond the Central branch languages that this study focuses on, and possibly reaching out to reconsidering assumptions and received wisdom even concerning Proto-Afroasiatic. One fundamental question remains still to be answered, as in all historical-linguistic endeavours: whatever the peculiarities of the Central Chadic system are, are we dealing with branch-specific *innovations* or rather with *retentions* from the ancestral Proto-Chadic system (and possibly beyond)? In-depth comparative research into all other branches of Chadic will be needed to arrive at the answer. The pertinent observation, however, namely that *morphological palatalisation* is also reconstructable for other branches within Chadic (see Schuh 2002; Wolff 2019b), could be seen as an indication that we are indeed dealing with rather old features of diachronic Chadic phonology and morphophonology.

The new approach to lexical reconstruction in Central Chadic that is made available here is complementary to previous studies insofar as it differs in at least five basic diachronic assumptions, namely regarding the following.

1. The type of underlying vocalised root (*root type*) within a *root-and-pattern* system. Choice of root type has hitherto been neglected in comparative work other than by the present author since his early works in the 1980s, but proves to be of utmost relevance in creating a coherent systematic picture across all languages.
2. The diachronic phonological relevance of an ultimately underlying class of *vocoids* rather than *vowels* in the narrow sense of the term.[12] Under the label 'vocoids' we group together, for systematic reasons, quite different phonological units that share – partially or completely – in the 'vocalic

---

[12] Without needing and wanting to open any detailed historical or terminological discussion here, it should be remembered that the relationship between syllabic [i, u] and non-syllabic [y, w] has intrigued quite a few seasoned linguists and is reflected in the persistent use of competing terminology, such as *semivowels* and *semiconsonants*, besides *approximants*, *glides*, *vocoids*, and possibly other terms, in opposition to *vowels* and *consonants* (or *contoids* opposed to *vocoids*). For my own historical comparative Chadic research, I have opted for the term 'vocoids', stimulated and encouraged as a young researcher in 1980 by rewarding personal communication with Igor M. Diakonoff (1915–1999) during an academic visit to Saint Petersburg (then Leningrad), Russia, under the umbrella of a twinning agreement between the universities of Hamburg and Leningrad. Attending a presentation of my early research at the then University of Leningrad, Igor Mikhailovich had invited me over to the Russian Academy of Sciences to privately discuss findings from their large-scale comparative Afrasian research project (involving other world-renowned researchers such as Alexander Militarev, Viktor Porkhomovsky, Olga Stolbova) that were similar to and supporting my own small-scale Central Chadic lexical reconstructions.

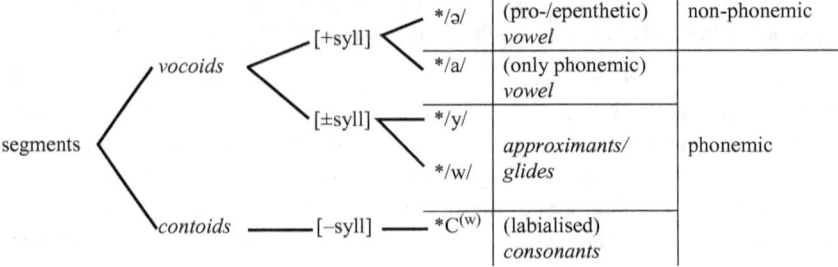

Figure 1.1 Vocoids and contoids

> Note that *y, *w represent 'borderline' phonemic units in terms of syllabicity, i.e. are underspecified in terms of [±syllabic]. In Central Chadic phonological systemics, *vocoids* serve as underlying units for both phonemic [+syllabic] surface vowels (a, i, u) and phonemic [−syllabic] surface consonants (y, w). PCC */a/ stands out among the class of phonemic vocoids by allowing the feature specification [+syllabic] only, meaning that /a/ is the only 'true phonemic vowel' in the vocalic domain of PCC phonology.[13]

space' in PCC phonology and lexical reconstructions as their domain of operation, which is made up of

(a) phonemic vowels (such as reconstructed PCC [+syll] */a/);
(b) non-phonemic vowels (such as reconstructed PCC pro- and epenthetic schwa *ə);
(c) 'weak radicals', i.e. approximants/glides that allow for phonetic surface manifestations in syllable-nucleus positions as vowels (such as reconstructed PCC [±syll] */y/ and */w/, which may surface as [i] and [u]). 'Weak radicals' reflects a notion that refers back to typological heritage as established by Afroasiatic scholarship (particularly in Semitic linguistics).

The notion of 'vocoids' further would allow, if subsequent research should ever or eventually point in that direction, to also relate the reconstructed PCC 'true vowel' */a/ to a historically even deeper-underlying [±syll]

---

[13] This unique status of */a/ as 'only true vowel in the system' only holds under the historically received assumption that – at least currently – *ʕ/ cannot and should not be reconstructed, neither for Proto-Chadic nor for Proto-Central Chadic (3.2.1, but see 6.3.6). Theoretically, however, just like in the cases of */y/ and */w/, a hypothetical vocoid *ʕ/ could also be considered underspecified for the feature [±syll], allowing two complementary allophones: [−syll] /ʔ/ (glottal stop), [+syll] /a/. This would bring us close to prototypical assumptions about the basic Afroasiatic 'vowel system' allowing for three vowel qualities: a, i, u (< *ʕ, *y, *w). Currently and for the purpose of the present study, however, this issue is regarded as open to further research and is of no immediate relevance to our reconstructions of PCC lexical items (but see 6.3.6.4 for our reconstruction of the word for 'water').

phonological unit */ʕ/ (or the like) and create an at least tripartite subsystem of diachronically underlying [±syll] vocoids */ʕ/, */y/ and */w/, which would become 'ancestral', so to speak, to the basic Afroasiatic vowel qualities */a/, */i/ and */u/.
3. The structural/functional relationship between the reconstructed *vocoids* and *contoids* (a term that will not be used any further in this study) in (Central) Chadic, based on specifications regarding the feature [±syllabic]. This relationship is graphically represented in Figure 1.1.
4. The identification of the segmental origin and the nature of *phonological* vs. *morphological prosodies*. Their strict separation serves as a methodological constraint in order to avoid ad hoc (or *deus ex machina*) postulates regarding the diachronic sources of prosodies.
5. The treatment of schwa as either *phonemic* or *pro-/epenthetic* in nature. The – equally valid – choice between the two options should ideally be consistent within the same phonological system.[14] For PCC, the *pro-* and *epenthesis* option is chosen in order to systematically account for the presence of schwa and its prosodically 'coloured' manifestations in the surface structures of modern Central Chadic languages. Note that under our chosen approach, pro- and epenthesis is considered a matter of individual language histories rather than following principles or rules pertaining to the PCC phonological system, which, therefore, is reconstructed without pro- and epenthetic vowels.

These five basic theoretical and methodological assumptions and choices have considerable bearing on the shape of the reconstructed forms, which

---

[14] While two closely related and/or neighbouring languages may differ – in synchronic description – with regard to the phonological status of schwa (as, for instance, in the case of Lamang and Hdi of the LAMANG group, reflecting different theoretical and methodological approaches by the authors of the available monographic descriptions; cf. Wolff 1983a, 2015; Frajzyngier & Shay 2002), the possible option that within the same language schwa may be both, namely phonemic in some instances and epenthetic in others, would prima facie appear to be less probable, but cannot be excluded on a priori grounds. The problem then would be to determine when schwa was phonemic and when it was not. This, however, would rather be a problem of synchronic description and not necessarily one of historical reconstruction. This issue is far from trivial in reconstruction work of PCC since, as is presumably the case, diachronic phonemic */a/ may undergo centralisation and surface synchronically as [ə] in some modern languages in certain positions. This allophone [ə] of */a/ must, of course, be clearly distinguished from inserted epenthetic schwa [ə], a distinction which would be difficult if not impossible to arrive at in purely synchronic analysis. Here, internal reconstruction can and must come in, which would identify positions of underlying */a/ according to root type: wherever surface [ə] occurs in a position held by */a/ in the diachronically underlying root-and-pattern structure, i.e. root type, it can be identified as a centralised allophone of */a/. This, again, provides a strong argument for the pertinence of the notion of root-and-pattern in modern Central Chadic languages.

indeed may look very different in terms of reconstructed 'root material' from reconstructions that have been previously suggested by other authors. On the other hand, it is these assumptions that make the application of Neogrammarian principles and methodology feasible for languages of the (Central) Chadic typological nature.

Our research is based on the generally accepted assumption that all languages that are sub-classified as belonging to the Central Chadic branch of the Chadic language family are genealogically related and share common linguistic ancestry. That ancestry would even go beyond PCC to include Proto-Chadic (PC) and genealogical heritage from Proto-Afroasiatic.

In the present study, we are concerned with tracing the linguistic history of phonetic surface forms of words in modern Central Chadic languages from their diachronically deepest reconstructable common source, i.e. the most abstract 'simple' (and plainly consonantal) root that we would like to associate with the ancestral proto-language, which in our case would be Proto-Central Chadic. In Afroasiatic languages in general, such abstract and plainly consonantal roots, however, tend to associate with vocalisation *patterns* to form 'vocalised roots' (sometimes called 'bases'; cf. Wolff 1977), depending on the available inventory of phonemic vowels of the proto-language. Hence we speak of root-and-pattern structures in Afroasiatic languages, which calls for a templatic analytical approach. For PCC, only */a/ would appear to have been available for forming such vocalisation patterns. The resulting vocalised roots (or 'bases') are referred to in the present study as 'root types'.

As our own and previous research by other expert authors have shown (see sub-section 1.1 above), (Central) Chadic languages pose particular problems for lexical reconstruction. These particular problems are grounded in the peculiar typology of these languages on the one hand, and their linguistic histories on the other. Those histories have been shaped by internal diachronic processes of natural language change, which we will study in much detail further below, as much as by interference from other languages of Chadic and non-Chadic affiliations. Such borrowings would affect individual words and identify them as inter-dialectal and/or inter-language loans. For Central Chadic languages, therefore, we must be aware of three factors in particular that have impacted their linguistic histories:

(a) a presumed considerable time-depth;
(b) influence from inter-dialectal and/or inter-language borrowing;
(c) possibly long periods of relative isolation of speaker communities.

Note that the present habitat of speakers of CC languages is found in areas that are not seldom characterised by difficulties of access from outside. This would include

- the steep and rocky slopes and difficult-to-access plateaus of the Mandara Mountains in Northern Cameroon and along the Cameroon–Nigeria international border,
- the swampy floodplains of the Logone and Shari Rivers in Northern Cameroon and Chad, and
- the partly floating islands in Lake Chad, which is bordered by the modern states of Nigeria, Cameroon, Chad, and Niger.

Such more or less permanent areas of refuge were considered safe havens for potential victims of military raids. More or less successfully, they allowed access to be blocked for troops on horseback in the service of regional empires and marauding slave-raiders in previous centuries.

It would not be surprising to find considerable internal divergences even among close geographic neighbours, which by their surface appearances and neighbourhood are generally presumed to also be close genealogical relatives. On the other hand, close geographic neighbourhood over long periods of time is likely to enhance convergence processes that blur any pre-existing greater genealogical distance. One must be aware, therefore, that areal features reflecting language contact scenarios override straightforward 'natural' intergenerational language change (Cf. a discussion along these lines in terms of grammaticalisation chains pertaining to expressions of 'verbal plurality' in Wolff (2001). Note, further, that the suggested fundamental 'Typology of Central Chadic Phonologies' (Gravina 2014a: 87–221) may also reflect such areal feature distribution.) Such contact scenarios may render more or less naïve applications of the comparative method futile. And indeed, as emerges from our comparative research, words in modern Central Chadic languages tend to have rather complex histories and have undergone remarkable changes in the course of time, which only occasionally are fully paralleled even in the most closely related sister languages within the same language group. However, it is not only time-depth that poses problems for analysis from a diachronic perspective, it is also the complex multi-tiered structure of words. This book is about unravelling these complexities in all possible detail in the following chapters and sections.

1.2 A Model for the Evolution from Proto-Central Chadic 'Simple Roots' to Phonetic Surface Representations in Central Chadic Languages

In order to provide an orientation early in this book to be used as a kind of road map for the evolution of Central Chadic lexical items from reconstructed PCC to modern languages, the following abstract model is presented. It identifies the major ingredients that will be looked at in more detail in the following sections of this book, and that contribute to the diachronic development. It starts off from the most simple (and purely consonantal) root and proceeds via vocalisation pattern (root type) and eventual *root augmentation* by fused and petrified morphological elements, plus tracing the palatalisation and labialisation prosodies stemming originally from segmental material of such simple or augmented roots – even in cases of complete desegmentalisation and prosodification (*/$C^{y~w}/ > Ø^{y~w}$) of the source of such prosodies. The model is based on the application of various methods of historical reconstruction, namely from *internal reconstruction, dialectology*, and the comparative method (see Chapter 2), and it fundamentally follows a bottom-up approach.

For this abstract model (Figure 1.2), we will symbolise any etymological root (for illustration purposes, we will use a triradical root in the model) by either its plain consonantal skeleton √ C C C or by any of its potential vocalised shapes, i.e. root types: √ C C Ca, √ CaC Ca, √ C CaCa, and √ CaCaCa. Note that for historical and typological reasons, only */a/ qualifies as the phonemic vowel to fill the systemic vowel 'slots' in the root, thereby establishing the root type. For PCC reconstructed roots, non-phonemic pro- and epenthetic vowels, as common as they are in modern Central Chadic languages, are not considered. The model also applies mutatis mutandis to biradical and monoradical roots. We further assume that on systemic grounds 'simple' roots carry by default a final lexical */a/, irrespective of root type. This final */a/ may, however, undergo diachronic loss ('deletion' */a/ > Ø) or change in quality ('centralisation' */a/ > [ə]).

In our model, the potential distinction of root types as being either *lexical* or *formative/grammatical* in nature on the level of PCC must remain purely speculative at this point in time. As argued in Wolff (2009), what the author has elsewhere called 'formative a-vocalisation' was used in PCC to create, more likely by insertion of a morphological marker ('infix') *{-a-} rather than by 'vocalisation pattern', so-called pluractional forms of verbs (cf. Newman 1990), as many modern languages still do productively on the synchronic level. In other languages, however, such processes can and must be viewed as non-productive or 'petrified', i.e. as lexicalised by only occurring with certain verbs. We remember that so-called 'internal a' has played an at times highly controversial role in the study of Afroasiatic languages in general, and also in Chadic linguistics (cf., for instance, P. Newman 1977b, 1990; Jungraithmayr 1978; Wolff 1977, 1979, 1982, 1984a, 2009). The controversies pertained to (a) its distribution in nominal and/or verbal grammar, (b) its phonological and/or morphological nature, and (c) its original function(s).

Further below (sub-sections 1.3–1.7), we will illustrate the five steps, not necessarily reflecting a strict chronological order, along such an evolutionary

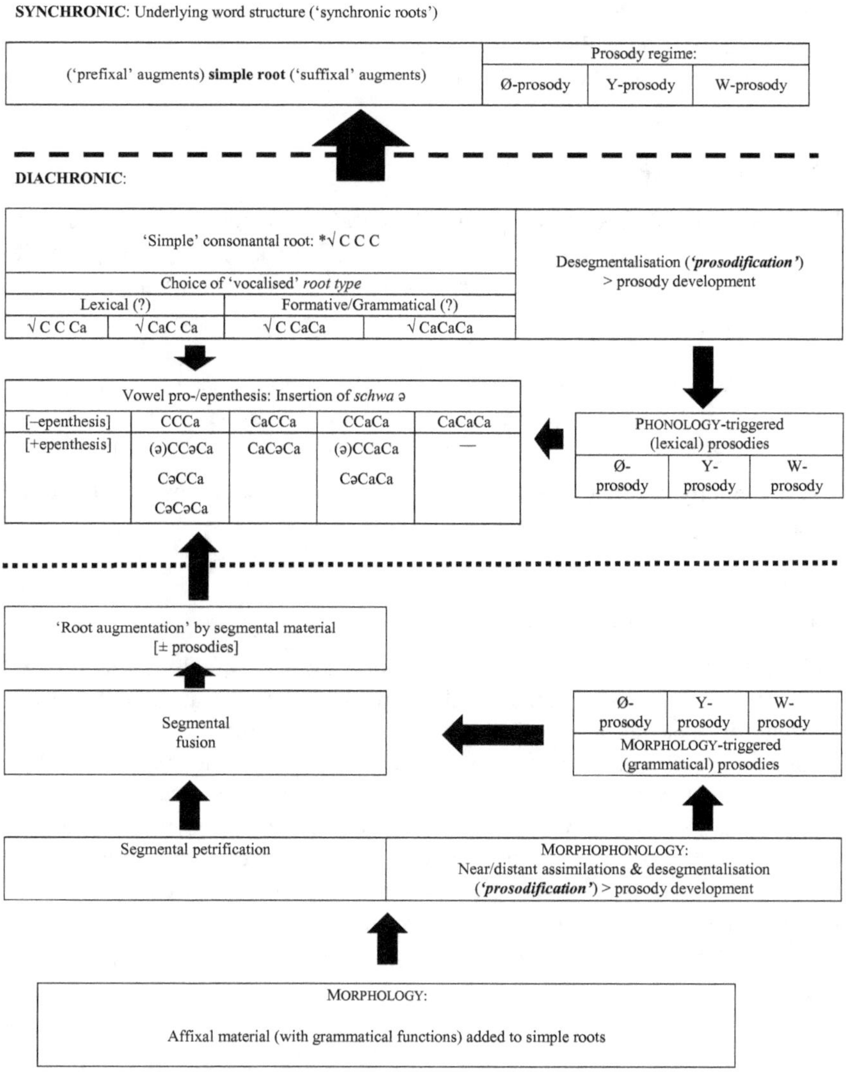

1.2 Evolutionary Model

SYNCHRONIC: Underlying word structure ('synchronic roots')

('prefixal' augments) **simple root** ('suffixal' augments)	Prosody regime:		
	Ø-prosody	Y-prosody	W-prosody

DIACHRONIC:

'Simple' consonantal root: *√ C C C			
Choice of 'vocalised' *root type*			
Lexical (?)		Formative/Grammatical (?)	
√ C C Ca	√ CaC Ca	√ C CaCa	√ CaCaCa

Desegmentalisation (***'prosodification'***)
> prosody development

Vowel pro-/epenthesis: Insertion of *schwa* ə				
[–epenthesis]	CCCa	CaCCa	CCaCa	CaCaCa
[+epenthesis]	(ə)CCəCa	CaCəCa	(ə)CCaCa	—
	CəCCa		CəCaCa	
	CəCəCa			

PHONOLOGY-triggered (lexical) prosodies

Ø-prosody	Y-prosody	W-prosody

'Root augmentation' by segmental material
[± prosodies]

Segmental fusion

Ø-prosody	Y-prosody	W-prosody

MORPHOLOGY-triggered (grammatical) prosodies

Segmental petrification

MORPHOPHONOLOGY:
Near/distant assimilations & desegmentalisation
(***'prosodification'***) > prosody development

MORPHOLOGY:
Affixal material (with grammatical functions) added to simple roots

Figure 1.2 Abstract model of the evolution of Central Chadic lexical items

path from diachronic simple roots to synchronic surface forms by some selected examples from various Central Chadic languages for each step:

1. choice of root type;
2. root augmentation;

3. vowel pro-/epenthesis;
4. emergence of phonological prosodies;
5. emergence of morphological prosodies.

1.3 Root Type

For the simple PCC root ***s(a)w(a)na** 'dream', for instance, three different root types are being made use of across different languages, depending on the occurrence and position(s) of */a/: √ s w na ~ √ s wana ~ √ sawana.[15]

(1) Root type distinctions

MOFU	Zulgo	*suna*	< swna	< *s w na	⎫	
BATA	Cuvok	*suwana*	< səwana	< *s wana	⎬ < ***s(a)w(a)na**
KOTOKO-NORTH	Malgbe	*yawara*		< *sawana	⎭	

The potentially possible root type √ CaC Ca ˣsawna has not been found to be used for this particular lexical item.

1.4 Root Augmentation

Quite a lot of synchronically underlying roots are not 'simple' by nature and origin, but rather must be considered 'augmented'. This means that they carry 'frozen' or 'petrified' accretive segmental material that originally did not belong to the simple root, such as former affixes that belonged to the PCC morphological system. These former affixes must be considered semantically bleached and segmentally frozen or petrified, i.e. they are synchronically no longer productive. Their sporadic and totally unpredictable presence or absence may be a distinguishing feature even among the most closely related modern language pairs and variants within the same languages, like, for instance, *{-k(a)} in the LAMANG group:

---

[15] A note on conventions of representation of data in this study: reconstructed roots, incl. variant root types, will be marked by preceding *; invalid reconstructions by raised ˣ; actual synchronic data as transcribed by (field) linguists and contained in the database will be given in *italics*. Occasionally and somewhat redundantly, the symbol √ will be used to indicate 'root type', and potential positions for vowels by blanks. Forms unmarked by * or by *italics*, often preceded by '<' or '>', illustrate hypothetical intermediate forms, either diachronic or in terms of deep-level phonological representation that would, however, include both phonemic and non-phonemic units (like pro-/epenthetic schwa). On the ultimate level of PCC reconstructions, roots will be given in the shape of conflated formulas, indicating the positions to be filled by */a/ or not, as (a), i.e. using parentheses to indicate choices of presence or absence, e.g. ***s(a)w(a)na** 'dream'.

(2) LAMANG
　　　Lamang　　*fiti*　　　　　　　　　　　　　　'sun'
　　　Hdi　　　*fitik*　　　　　　< *fiti-k(a)　　'sun'
　　　Lamang　*pala ~ palak(a)*　< *pala-k(a)　'rock'
　　　Hdi　　　*pala*　　　　　　　　　　　　　　'stone'

Despite their fairly limited distribution and occurrence, root-augmental elements, i.e. former grammatical markers of sorts, show a vast array of forms and manifestations across Central Chadic. Most frequently they take a suffixal position to the simple root, like in the LAMANG group examples showing *{-k(a)} in (2), but quite often they are also found in prefixal position to the simple root. Some elements are very frequently recurring across the board, independent of individual languages, some are rare and may even be confined to occurrence with only one word in one language in the reconstructed data. For more details see section 3.1.2 below.

Among these frozen or petrified former affixes, besides several other rather frequent candidates, *{-y} is the probably most frequent and is, at the same time, a potential source for palatalisation (Y-prosody). Interestingly, in a number of Chadic languages of both the Central and West Chadic branches of the family, it gave and still gives rise to so-called morphological palatalisation (see Schuh 2002; Wolff 2019b; and further below). Less frequent is the element that we reconstruct as *{-k^w}, which we take to be the source for morphological labialisation (which, to the best of my knowledge, has not yet been described as such in Chadic literature).

1.5 Vowel Pro-/Epenthesis

Again using the simple PCC root *s(a)w(a)na 'dream' for illustration, we note that for the same root, in only one of the available root types are all vowel 'slots' filled by /a/, namely *sawana. The other two root types leave potential vowel slots open, and these are characteristically – but optionally and as part of the history of individual languages or language groups – filled by epenthetic schwa. This option is chosen, for instance, by Cuvok, where epenthetic schwa is inserted between C_1 and C_2 (for the actual surface realisation of schwa as [u] see further below). For clarity, we occasionally indicate syllable structure by the notational convention CV.CV.CV.

(3)　　BATA　　Cuvok　　*su.wa.na*　　< sə.wa.na　　(< *s wana √ C CaCa)

Vowel epenthesis does not operate in Zulgo in this word, since the first option to take precedence over vowel epenthesis in this language is syllabification of an underlying vocoid (approximant/glide), in this case /w/ > [u]:

22   Introduction

(4)   MOFU   Zulgo   *su.na*   (< *s w na √ C C Ca)

Note that, in (3) and (4) above, the apparently identical surface vowel [u] has different origins and histories. In (3), it is the result of prosodic 'colouring' of epenthetic schwa triggered by (or transferred from) the labial component of underlying /w/, while in (4) it is the syllabic manifestation of underlying */w/, which represents C_2 on the level of the diachronic root. Such structural ambiguities of surface vowels present considerable challenges to language comparison. They are, however, characteristic of Central Chadic languages and represent typologically peculiar features of the languages under review.

For Malgbe, none of the above options operates since all vowel slots are already being filled by /a/:

(5)   KOTOKO-NORTH   Malgbe   *ya.wa.ra*   (< *sawana √ CaCaCa)

Epenthetic schwa insertion is a highly frequent phonological process in Central Chadic languages, stimulated by the fact that PCC only had one phonemic vowel */a/, leaving several potential vowel 'slots' open, depending on root type. Occasionally and in particular when a root/word begins with a consonant cluster, vowel prothesis is triggered, i.e. the prothetic insertion of non-phonemic schwa (phonetically 'coloured' under prosodic impact as the case may be) to precede the initial consonant cluster, e.g.[16]

(6)   'beer' PCC simple root **v(a)x^{w}a**
         BATA   Gude   √ C Ca   *n-v x^{w}a   > n-vØ^{w}a   > ənv^{w}a   > ənv^{w}a

(7)   'faeces' PCC simple root **ɣ^w va**
         MANDARA   Mandara,   √ C Ca   *g^w va-y   > g^{w}va-Ø^y > ə^{w}gva^y > ugve
                    Malgwa

1.6   Phonological Prosodies

Pro- and epenthetic vowels in particular, but also */a/ and certain radical consonants of the simple root, may come under the effect of prosodies. In

---

[16] We use raised ^{w} and ^{y} to indicate two different but interrelated observations. As illustrated in the following examples, x^w and g^w symbolise reconstructed underlying segmental sources of (labialisation) prosody, while v^w and ə^w symbolise the target segments affected by the labialisation prosody in surface representations, and a^y the target segment of the palatalisation prosody. In both cases, the raised symbol ^{w} or ^{y} is placed immediately to the right of its segmental origin or target. Note that the segmental source of a prosody may become historically 'lost' (here we would speak of complete desegmentalisation) but still maintain its prosodic effect on a target segment elsewhere in the word (hence we speak of prosodification); this is symbolised by Ø^w or Ø^y.

the case of simple (i.e. non-augmented) roots, palatalisation (Y-prosody) and labialisation (W-prosody) stem from either */y/ or any labial(ised) root consonant */C^w/ including */w/. In our examples of the root 'dream' above, */w/ is present in underlying structure and has a labialisation (= simultaneous lip-rounding) effect (indicated by raised ^{w}) on the preceding epenthetic schwa. Technically and on the surface of things, we could speak of a simple case of '(near) assimilation' in individual cases like this – and possibly individual cases of 'distant assimilation' elsewhere – but given the whole picture of Central Chadic phonology in both diachronic and synchronic perspectives, all this is more appropriately subsumed under the term 'prosody' in the sense of a (morpho)phonological subsystem of its own with special properties that developed varying functional domains of inclusion and exclusion. As surface effect in the present case, the lip-rounding feature of W-prosody (labialisation) on schwa yields a back-round surface vowel ə^w > [u], as is transcribed in the Cuvok data:

(8)   BATA Cuvok   *su.wa.na* < sə^{w}wana < səw^{w}ana (< *s wana √ C CaCa)

Since the source of the prosody is root-internal, we speak of phonological (or 'lexical') labialisation in this instance of W-prosody.

Phonological Y-prosody effects may originate from */y/ as radical consonant of a (simple) PCC root, as in the following example of √ C C(a)Ca *ɗ y(a)ɬa 'bone':

(9)   BATA   Tsuvan   √ C C Ca   *Ø y ɮa   > y^{y}ɮa^y > *iɮe*
        TERA   Ga'anda   √ C C Ca   *a-Ø y la   > a^y-Ø^{y}la   > *ela*

In Tsuvan, after deletion of the initial consonant, root-internal */y/ ends up in syllable-nucleus position, where it is phonetically realised as [i], in a parallel fashion creating a Y-prosody effect on the final lexical vowel */a/ + ^{y} > a^y > [e]. Likewise in Ga'anda, the initial consonant is deleted, but the root is augmented by prefixal *a-. Root-internal */y/ desegmentalises and prosodifies > Ø^y, i.e. thereby creating Y-prosody, which changes preceding prefixal [a] + ^{y} > a^y > [e].

Note that Ø-prosody will not be marked; it is simply the absence of either Y-prosody (marked by ^{y}) or W-prosody (marked by ^{w}) or both (marked by ^{yw}).

1.7   Morphological Prosodies

As already mentioned, reconstructed segmental root augments can also be identified as diachronic sources of prosodies, namely *{-y} and *{-k^w}. They give rise to morphological palatalisation and labialisation, each of which may have different manifestations in modern languages.

Reconstructed root-augmental *{-y} has basically two manifestations in modern Central Chadic languages which, however, may combine. One will be dealt with under *syllabification*, the other is complete or partial desegmentalisation to Y-prosody (*prosodification*). Using again the PCC simple root *s(a)w(a)na 'dream' for illustration: root-augmental *{-y} regularly syllabifies in nucleus position of the final syllable of the word, after deletion of the lexical final vowel */a/, to become phonetically [i]. (By root-internal syllabification, underlying /w/ will yield the surface vowel [u].)

(10) 'dream' (PCC simple root *s(a)w(a)na)
      MARGI   Bura   su.ni < swn-i   < swnØ-y   (< *s w na)
      LAMANG   Lamang   su.ni < swn-i   < swnØ-y   (< *s w na)

Likewise, the suffixal root-augment *{-k^w} can undergo partial desegmentalisation to /w/ plus/minus further prosodification to /w^w/; eventually /w/ may further syllabify > [u], mostly in the final syllable of the word. In some languages, the root-augment *{-k^w}, therefore, can end up as word-final vowel [u]. See the following examples for the simple roots (a) 'ashes' (PCC *p ts(a)ɗa) and (b) 'bone' (PCC *ɗ y(a)ła), both of which are reconstructed with a suffixal augment *{-k^w} among others, in the languages illustrated here:

(11) 'ashes' (PCC simple root *p ts(a)ɗa)
      MAROUA   Mbazla   fu.tʃu   < fə^{w}ts^y-Ø^y-w^w < f ts ØØ-y-k^w (< *p ts ɗa)
      MARGI   Kilba   pə.tsə.du   < pətsəɗ-w   < p ts ɗØ-k^w (< *p ts ɗa)

(12) 'bone' (PCC simple root *ɗ y(a)ła)
      MARGI   Margi   ɗya.hu   < ɗya.x-w   < ɗ yaxØ-k^w (< *ɗ yała)

In Mbazla, */k^w/ weakens to /w/ which, however, retains the coarticulative labialisation feature of */k^w/, here symbolised by /w^w/, which serves as diachronic source for morphological W-prosody, which in turn will affect the epenthetic schwa that is inserted in the first syllable. /w/ then syllabifies, because it finds itself in syllable-nucleus position, to yield word-final [u]. Since the augmented root also contained *{-y}, this desegmentalises and prosodifies completely to Y-prosody (symbolised by Ø^y), which affects the original C_2 of the simple root by palatalising it: */ts + ^{y}/ > ts^y > [tʃ]. (Note also C_1 */p/ > /f/.)

In Kilba, */k^w/ weakens to /w/ with no survival of its original (and potentially prosodising) labialisation feature; the medial epenthetic vowels, therefore, remain unaffected by any prosody. In absolute word-final position, /w/ ends up in syllable-nucleus position and accordingly syllabifies to [u].

Margi behaves like Kilba, in that */k^w/ weakens to /w/ (with no prosodic effects) and ends up as word-final [u]. (Note also C_3 */ł/ > /x/.)

Note that in such cases, final [u] in surface representation does not require the reconstruction of a PCC vowel */u/. This is corroborated from the observation that there is independent evidence of the existence of the suffix *{-k^w} in Central Chadic languages. On the other hand, there is no independent

1.7 Morphological Prosodies

evidence for the existence of a phonemic vowel */u/, because word-medial and word-initial surface representations of [u] also find different diachronic explanations.

As the case may be, root augmentation can also be prefixal, as in the following example, again for 'dream' (PCC simple root *s(a)w(a)na), root type √ C C Ca *s w na:

(13) 'dream' (PCC simple root *s(a)w(a)na)
      MAFA Mafa *nʃu.wi.ne* < n-s^{y}ə^w.wə^y.na^y < n-səw^{w}əna-Ø^y < *n-s w na-y

Mafa shows a prefixal augment *n-, which does not interfere any further with the final shape of the surface form of the verb. Morphological palatalisation stemming from suffixal *{-y} of the augmented root affects all three syllables of the root (to the exception of prefixal n-) by changing /s/ > [ʃ], epenthetic [ə] > [i] in the penultimate syllable, and /a/ > [e] in the ultimate syllable. In addition, there is also phonological labialisation operating in the word, stemming from the medial /w/ of the simple root, namely changing [ə] > [u] in the antepenultimate syllable.

We have seen syllabification to result in surface vowels in, for instance, word-final position, as in the examples for *{-y} and *{-k^w} above. Both *{-y} and *{-k^w} may in addition undergo complete desegmentalisation (prosodification) and become 'floating' prosodies (aka 'long components'), which may affect any number of (usually preceding) segments in the word, be they consonants or vowels. Also, different prosodies may co-occur on the same word. A minimal and frequent effect of morphological prosodies stemming from *{-y} and *{-k^w} is to palatalise lexical final /a/ > [e] and labialise lexical final /a/ > [o]; e.g.

(14) 'dream' (PCC simple root *s(a)w(a)na)
      KOTOKO-CENTRAL Lagwan[17] *swa.ne* < swa.na^y-Ø^y < *s wana-y

(15) 'ashes' (PCC simple root *p ts(a)ɗa)
      MAROUA Giziga-Marva *af.tʃo* < af.ts^{y}a^w < a-ftsa-Ø^y-Ø^w < *a-f tsa-y-k^w

(16) 'butterfly' (PCC simple root *p(a)ra)
      GIDAR Gidar *mo.to.po.lo.po.lo* < ma^{w}ta^{w}pa^{w}la^{w}pa^{w}la^w-Ø^w
      < *ma-ta-pala-pala-k^w

Desegmentalisation and prosodification of, for instance, *{-k^w} may be complete, i.e. */k^w/ > Ø^w, but it may also be only partial, i.e. */k^w/ > w^w.

---

[17] In Chadic literature, this language is better known under the name 'Logone'. In order to avoid using different name variants for the same languages, the present study sticks to the nomenclature used in Gravina's (2014b) database for easier cross-reference.

For complete desegmentalisation, see the following example, in which the labialisation feature reassociates with another consonant in the root:

(17) 'beer' (PCC simple root *v(a)x^{w}a)
      BATA Gude ənv^{w}a < nv^{w}a < n-vØ^{w}a < *n-vx^{w}a

In Gude, the labialisation feature stemming from the final root consonant */x^w/ becomes divorced from */x/, which subsequently desegmentalises completely and only leaves W-prosody behind (symbolised by Ø^w), i.e. undergoes complete prosodification. The labialisation feature then associates not with an adjacent vowel, but with the initial root consonant: /v + ^{w}/ > [v^w]. The initial consonant cluster /nv^w/ triggers prothetic insertion of schwa.

Further, any labialised velar */C^w/ may become divorced from its labialisation feature */C^w/ > /C+w/ ~ /C+^{w}/ (here we speak of 're-segmentalisation'), which in turn may undergo *metathesis* or target and associate with a vowel or consonant immediately preceding or elsewhere in the word, e.g.

(18) 'butterfly' (PCC simple root *p(a)ra)
      HURZA Mbuko ma.pə.rok < mapəra^{w}k < ma.prawk < ma-pra-kw < *ma-pra-k^w

In Mbuko, the labialisation feature stemming from *{-k^w} associates with the immediately preceding vowel /a/ > [o], while delabialised /k/ survives segmentally. We may assume intermediate metathesis */k+w/ > /w+k/.

In some cases, both manifestations of the same prosody combine. For instance, a word may end in syllabified */y/ > [i] (< *{-y}) and still have a palatalising prosodic effect on other segments in the word (indicated by raised ^{y} as in -i^y), like /s/ > ʃ and [ə] > [i] in Kilba, as again for the root 'dream' (disregarding for the time being the somewhat irritating glottal stop preceding 'w):

(19) 'dream' (PCC simple root *s(a)w(a)na)
      MARGI Kilba ʃi.'u.ni < s^{y}ə^y.'w.n-i^y < sə'wnØ-y^y < s 'w na-y (< *s w na)

2 Methodological Preliminaries

2.1 General

Chadic, being the largest language family within the Afroasiatic phylum, is doubtlessly of great age. Its remarkable internal divergence would partly be explained by the time-depth, partly by long histories and differing scenarios of language contact. The languages in question are distributed at the southern fringe of the Sahara desert in the Sahel zone west, south and east of Lake Chad, whence the family received its name. Historiography and historical anthropological and ethnographic research for this area is still poor, so there is only little knowledge about historical events leading to large- or small-scale migrations in the past that would suggest reliable contact scenarios that could enlighten current scholarship on relevant extra-linguistic data that would be helpful for historical linguistic work (see 2.1.1). It is for further research to establish whence populations ancestral to peoples speaking present-day (Central) Chadic languages arrived at and settled along, the southern shores of the former Mega-Chad, possibly during or following the Holocene Wet Phase (Neolithic Subpluvial) and the beginning of the youngest desertification period of the Sahara desert several thousand years ago.

Chadic, and in particular Central Chadic, languages would appear to display somewhat exceptional phonological and morphophonological features in terms of typology regarding diachronic prosodification of underlying segments and a particular phonological organisation of the 'vocalic space' (see 4.7). This entails a possibly unique evolution of their synchronic vowel systems (elsewhere referred to as 'vocalogenesis'; see Wolff 2017), which may have come about by continuous phonemicisation of both underlying phonemic 'vocoids' and their allophones as well as of originally non-phonemic (pro- and epenthetic) vowels, towards phonetic representations as surface 'vowels' in modern languages. These diachronic processes were historically based on a submerged and synchronically largely hidden genetic heritage from Afroasiatic in terms of an underlying *root-and-pattern* structure (see 2.1.2 and 2.1.3).

With regard to historical linguistic analysis and description, the present study is guided, first of all, by two sets of very basic general methodological concepts. The first set encompasses attempts at descriptive adequacy and economy of description. This entails the search for maximal generalisations, which are based on a minimal number of distinct phonological or grammatical units and – ideally – avoiding as much as possible any 'exceptions' to general principles and rules. The second set targets completeness and explicitness of description; this will be taken up in some more detail in sub-section 2.1.4.

2.1.1 The Extra-Linguistic Historical Background

In serious literature on the subject, there are hardly ever concrete figures in terms of millennia available to go by, but it is received wisdom among experts that Chadic as a language family is very likely of great age. By implication, the age of Afroasiatic as a language phylum would be even greater, for which individual researchers have proposed an age of between 12,000 and 16,000 years, which would reach back well into the period of the Holocene Wet Phase of the so-called 'green Sahara'. Accordingly, the enormous time-depth of Chadic and its branches, including Central Chadic, can be held accountable for the considerable linguistic diversification between branches, sub-branches, language groups and even close clusters of no-longer-mutually-intelligible former dialects of the same languages. In addition and as a corollary of such time-depth, various and different language-contact scenarios can be assumed to have played an important role.

We have little if any robust insight into population movements in the history of the area where Chadic languages are spoken today. As a matter of fact, we are still practically blind to contact scenarios between speakers of different Chadic languages, or speakers of Chadic languages and non-Chadic languages, in any period in the past. Apart from the westward extension in historic times of the Kanem Empire from the eastern shore of Lake Chad into Borno along the northern periphery of both Central and West-Chadic language territories since the beginning of the thirteenth century at the latest, the most unlikely scenario is that of large-scale migration of whole populations (*Völkerwanderung*). Rather, local histories in much more recent times, as told by elders in the villages – as far as their own and collective memory goes – suggest fairly frequent small-scale migrations by individuals or very small groups of refugees (be it from ecological disaster or continuous threats of slave-raiding, for instance), which accounted for the trickling in of non-natives to the area, who then settled and procreated and formed new lineages and descent groups.[1] In the absence of any normative socio-cultural agencies in

---

[1] Scenarios like this were reported to me by elders during my fieldwork among Lamang speakers in the Gwoza area in north-eastern Nigeria (cf. Wolff 2006b; for the original accounts, see Wolff 1994), however, not reaching very far into the past, i.e. covering lifespans of seven to eleven

2.1 General

charge of preserving 'language purity', this would have meant tolerance of non-perfect acquisition of the language of the host group in the new settlement and would have allowed for establishing substratum influence from the original home language of the migrants. Theoretically, this could have resulted in the emergence of neighbouring language variants that were marked by multiple cases of *abrupt* rather than persistent *gradual* language change.

Another scenario, reaching well into present times, would relate to exogamous practices of local speaker communities, by which inter-language marriages were being arranged on a more or less regular albeit restricted basis between settlements across language boundaries. Again, this would bring individuals from other language communities into new environments, particularly young women and mothers when culture-specific post-nuptial residence rules required them to live with their husband's family. They often might be poor speakers of their husband's language and would still have to pass it on to their children in the present habitat, yet with 'contaminations' to be expected from the mother's own home language. Such scenarios would again explain the recurrent observation that a fair number of lexical items do not conform to expected patterns of so-called regular series of sound correspondences

---

generations. What might be safe to assume is that prior to the sustained advent of European colonialism, there was a dramatic spillover into the Lake Chad area from the *Mahdist War* (1881–99) in Sudan that was linked to extensive slave-raiding in the territories where Central Chadic language speakers lived. This followed centuries of repeated raids by forces of the Kanem-Borno Empire, i.e. events that might have forced individuals and small groups of people to flee from their home villages towards purported safe havens in the mountains and/or river swamps that were difficult to access by the cavalry of the slave-raiders.

In retrospect, these territories might have been originally characterised by fairly stable patterns of geographic separation of communities speaking the same language or varieties thereof, with only occasional instances of individual bi- and multilingualism with certain members of society. (By personal observation during fieldwork in the Gwoza Hills and Mandara Mountains in the late 1960s and early 1970s, the author witnessed still fierce enmity entailing encounters leading to bloodshed between members of different speaker communities, who settled almost in sight of each other on neighbouring mountain plateaus and/or adjacent plains. Until well into the 1940s, for instance, in the Gwoza area of North-Eastern Nigeria, there were practically no local markets in existence where people of different ethnic and linguistic background would meet on a regular basis.) The somewhat rare multilingualism would have encompassed, in addition to one's mother tongue or first language, one or two neighbouring local languages and most likely a language of wider distribution, i.e. a lingua franca linked to a regional hegemonic polity (like, for instance, Hausa spreading from the so-called *Hausa States*, Kanuri as associated with the *Kanem-Borno Empire*, Fulfulde as linked to the *Sokoto Caliphate* and its extension into *Adamawa*, etc.) and, possibly but not very probable for Central Chadic-A languages, spoken local varieties of Arabic. (Note again that during the author's fieldwork in the late 1960s and early 1970s, in the market town of Gwoza, then a so-called Native Authority Headquarter and seat of the Emir of Gwoza, there were only a handful of formally educated adults (all males), who would have some command of Hausa, the major lingua franca in the area, possibly some of Fulfulde, and practically no Kanuri – not to speak of English, the official language of post-independence Nigeria. Fifty years later, Hausa and Fulfulde are now the major lingua francas spoken, plus English.)

between pairs of languages, which would be the basis for successful application of the classic *comparative method*. Obviously, many words from other Chadic languages have entered neighbouring Chadic languages as loans, replacing original cognates from shared linguistic ancestry. Here, we would speak of processes akin to inter-dialectal borrowing.

Therefore, stable bilingualism involving neighbouring Chadic mother-tongue languages with speakers having close to native-speaker proficiency in both languages might have been quite rare, beyond the scenarios of exogamous relationships between neighbouring groups of people speaking different Chadic (or other) languages, possibly resulting in cases of more or less pronounced semilingualism. Such scenarios would explain a remarkable absence of closely knit nets of widespread and highly regular sound correspondences between languages, even between (sub-)branches or language groups, which would make them close to exceptionless (as assumed by the *Neogrammarians* of the Leipzig School and protagonists of the *comparative method* in Indo-European comparativism in the late nineteenth century). Such scenarios of localised small-scale language contact might have fostered a fair amount of rather 'sporadic' and not widely 'established regular' sound changes and correspondences between pairs or groups of languages. (Cf. the comparative observations provided by Gravina (2014b) which accompany his reconstructions. For immediate consultation of his observations, they are consistently quoted in the introductory part of our own reconstructions in section 6.4.) In such scenarios, the well-established classic comparative method comes to its limits, in particular when it is applied to genealogically more distant languages within the family. Therefore, it may be more illuminating for understanding the linguistic history of the languages under research to look at language change among most closely related languages and varieties of the 'same' languages, i.e. use bottom-up approaches known from dialectology. It is one of the striking finds in the database that for some languages there are multiple entries, sometimes but not always going back to fieldnotes of different linguists, which illustrate two or three different forms for the same lexical item, reflecting different formation processes, even differences in the application of quite different diachronic processes of so-called natural language change. This points towards instances of 'broken transmissions' (Thomason & Kaufman 1988) of inherited vocabulary through contact-induced changes or borrowings from closely related languages ('inter-dialectal borrowing').

2.1.2   The Exceptional Typology of Central Chadic Languages

Central Chadic languages tend to be typologically somewhat exceptional insofar as they would appear to defy the strict application of Neogrammarian procedures in terms of establishing series of 1:1 regular sound correspondences, not so much with regard to consonants, but definitely with regard to surface vowels. These languages represent a particular language type that pushes the application of the classic Neogrammarian Hypothesis, just like the classic comparative method, to its limits, as has been shown by the previous research referred to further above. The details of this particular language type with regard to the historical origin and diachronic development of the 'vocalic domain' from Proto-Central Chadic (PCC) to the modern languages will be unravelled and illustrated in the body of this book.

In the linguistic history of these languages, certain diachronic segments have turned, partially or completely, into prosodies. Referred to here as *prosodification*, these historical processes dissolve the neat distinction among autonomous units that make up the segmental structure of morphemes and words, such as unequivocally defined vowels and consonants. This means that originally integral features of segments (like palatalisation and labialisation) may become disassociated from the original segment carrying them and become autonomous 'floating' elements (i.e. 'prosodies'). We are thus forced to deal with the somewhat unusual language-internal sound changes that will be discussed in this book under labels such as 'desegmentalisation' (partial or complete) and 'prosodification'. Together with the kind of floating nature of the resulting prosodies, in particular palatalisation and labialisation, plus the surprisingly frequent occurrences of notoriously irregular metathesis involving adjacent consonants in 'roots', Central Chadic languages challenge our received Neogrammarian notions regarding the regularity of diachronic change and series of regular sound correspondences, particularly in the vocalic domain. Therefore and accordingly, we have to refine the methodological apparatus of traditional Neogrammarian comparativism and adapt it to the needs of this particular language type and linguistic history.

2.1.3 The Enigmatic Vocalic Domain

Central to this study is the diachronic analysis and description of the vocalic domain in PCC. In our chosen prosody-based approach to Central Chadic lexical reconstructions, we attempt to adhere to the basic methodological concepts of descriptive adequacy and economy of description, and also follow the Neogrammarian approach as far as possible. However, we need to recognise the particular typological nature of Central Chadic languages in terms of the essential role that prosodies play in their linguistic history, and do all this in confrontation with the groundbreaking work provided by Richard Gravina (2014a). As indicated above, applying a different approach is not so necessary for the consonantal domain, rather it is the vocalic domain that poses particular analytical challenges. This leads us to refine the comparative method in order

32   Methodological Preliminaries

to sensitise it to the specificities of Central Chadic data and adjust the methodological apparatus accordingly. The peculiarities to be addressed and taken care of relate to (a) the nature and phonological status of schwa, (b) the absence of true (phonemic) vowel contrasts, (c) the ambivalent nature of so-called weak radicals, and (d) the essential impact of prosodies.

2.1.3.1 The Status of Schwa
In line with the principle of economy of description, our decision to treat schwa, at variance with Gravina (2014a), as essentially *pro- and epenthetic* in nature, is based on the observation that in most cases where schwa occurs, it is predictable by the phonological environment, in particular by the given underlying root type (3.1.1.1). Therefore, it need not be postulated as a separate phoneme. Generally, it would appear to be simpler, i.e. more economic, to predict its occurrence on a general principle rather than describing the language-specific rules for its deletion after it had been reconstructed by default in a position within a regular CV.CV.CV sequence – only to be immediately deleted again, which would be the alternative approach.

2.1.3.2 No True Vowel Contrasts
Based on the analysis of schwa as pro- or epenthetic wherever it applies our long-time comparative research has led us to profitably work with the assumption of just one underlying diachronic vowel phoneme */a/, which contrasts only with its absence, but with no other vowel phoneme. This makes PCC a proto-language with no true vowel system, as we usually predict to exist in probably most human languages. This is, at the same time, the simpler, i.e. more economic, option compared to postulating at least two distinct vowel phonemes, namely */a/ and */ə/, as has been assumed by various authors in the past, not to speak of postulating three distinct vowel phonemes */a/, */ə/ and */i/ (plus distinctive Y-prosody) as in Gravina (2014a) or, as Newman (2006: 193) suggests as likely for Central Chadic, a four-vowel system with *a, *ə, *i and *u.

Reconstructed */a/, however, not being part of a more usual 'vowel system' and together with the [±syllabic] underspecified approximants */y/ and */w/, forms a class of here so-called *vocoids* (see Figure 1.1 further above). Vocoids share the feature that, in syllable-nucleus position, they all surface as phonetic vowels, namely [a, i, u] – thereby creating, on the level of phonetic surface

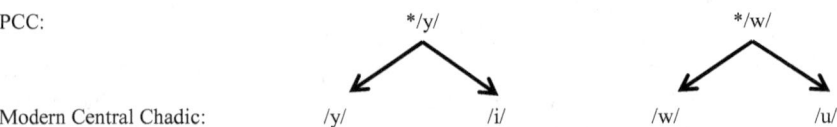

Figure 2.1 Phoneme split affecting the so-called weak radicals */y/ and */w/

representations, a system of phonetic vowels at variance with the underlying phonemic structure, on which level we would be dealing with */a/, */y/, */w/.

2.1.3.3 Underspecified 'Weak Radicals': */y/, */w/

With the deep diachronic level of PCC being in focus (and not necessarily applying to the level of synchronic descriptions of modern Central Chadic languages), we consider the adoption of the well-established notion of *weak radicals* from Semitic and Afroasiatic scholarship to contribute to our purpose. By weak radical we refer to the underspecified [±syllabic] nature of approximants/glides (also traditionally known as 'semivowels' and 'semiconsonants'), according to which they can function as both consonantal and vocalic segments depending on their position in the syllable. Hence we treat them, together with */a/, as forming a particular phonological class of vocoids. For Central Chadic reconstructions, therefore, *y and ^{x}i on the one hand, and *w and ^{x}u on the other, will not be treated as four different PCC phonemes, but only two, with each having two principal allophones in complementary distribution: vocalic/[+syllabic] (i, u) in syllable-nucleus position, and consonantal/[−syllabic] (y, w) in syllable-onset and syllable-coda positions. Such assumptions about PCC phonology do not, of course, necessarily predict the same situations in the phonologies of modern Central Chadic languages, where /i/ and /u/ may appear as phonemic vowels of their own standing in the synchronic systems, in addition to /y/ and /w/.[2] Rather, our assumptions for PCC phonology would allow for diachronic 'phoneme splits' as depicted in Figure 2.1, which are part of a more general historical scenario of *vocalogenesis* in (Central) Chadic languages (cf. Wolff 2017).

2.1.3.4 Impact of Prosodies

Central to our comparative approach to Central Chadic languages is the notion and impact of prosodies, first of all palatalisation (Y-prosody) and labialisation (W-prosody), which massively influence the phonetic realisation of words. Most of all this affects the actually occurring surface vowels, namely both */a/ and pro-/epenthetic schwa, changing their phonetic realisations to [e~ɛ, o~ɔ] and [i~ɨ, u~ʉ] respectively most of the time. This means that what might look like an apparently characteristic four-vowel-system in Central Chadic of *a, i, u,* and *ə* (cf. Newman 2006) in surface representations, in diachronic terms reflects an underlying phonemic system of */a/, */y/, */w/ plus epenthetic schwa, whereby transcriptions of high vowels *i* and *u* could either represent */y/ and */w/, or prosodically 'coloured' manifestations of epenthetic schwa

---

[2] Note, however, that even in synchronic phonological systems of CC languages, [i] and [y] as well as [u] and [w] may function as allophones in the same complementary distribution, i.e. reflecting systemic retentions from PCC typology.

34   Methodological Preliminaries

Table 2.1 *Underlying vs. surface representations in the vocalic domain*

| | Segments [+syll] | | | |
	*/a/	schwa	*/y/	*/w/
Ø-prosody	a	ə~ɐ~a	i	u
Y-prosody	e~ɛ~æ	i~ɪ~i		
W-prosody	o~ɔ	ʉ~ʊ~u		
Y+W-prosodies	œ	ʏ		

under Y- or W-prosody respectively. (Note that a lot depends on the transcription conventions used by the field or missionary linguist; see Table 2.1.)

The prosody-based approach on which this study is based has another advantage in terms of economy of description. With the assumption of (i) just two prosodies, namely palatalisation and labialisation, plus (ii) one underlying diachronic vowel */a/, and (iii) the notion of pro- and epenthetic vowel insertion – and (iv) by taking into account synchronic vowel length which, however, plays no role in our PCC reconstructions – we are able to predict and describe the emergence of up to 17 phonetic surface vowels in present-day Chadic languages, which, however, do not enter into any systematic 1:1 sound correspondences among themselves between even the most closely related languages, as already noted in previous research (Wolff 1981, 1983b, and again 2017). It is this prosody-based approach which, in the end, allows for a successful application of the comparative method to Central Chadic languages, namely by (i) identifying the original phonological segmental units to be reconstructed for the Proto-Central Chadic lexicon, and (ii) diachronically tracing the 'prosodies' back to the segments from which they originate, irrespective of whether these sources are still segmentally present in the modern CC languages or not.

2.1.4 Completeness and Explicitness of Description

As regards methodologically desired completeness and explicitness of description, whatever language data we use in this study is analysed completely; none is omitted or passed over just because it may pose difficulties for analysis and reconstruction, or could be considered somewhat doubtful and/or based on a somewhat obscure source.[3] All phonological processes that are assumed to

---

[3] This would apply, for instance, to some 'Nyimatli' (TERA) forms (Nyimatli being the autonym for Tera, according to P. Newman p.c. 2020) from a source that is not identified in Gravina (2014a), but is continuously quoted in the database (Gravina 2014b).

2.1 General

have applied to the reconstructed roots are traced and are graphically represented in one way or the other in the multi-tiered reconstructions, for which comments will also be provided in telegraphic style. Rare exceptions and problems of analysis will be identified in accompanying notes or by footnote. Thus, in principle, all diachronic processes that are likely to have occurred in the history of the individual languages are presented in an explicit format and can be evaluated by the reader. A summary of relevant diachronic phonological processes or 'rules' is supplied in section 4.9. In particular and inspired by dialectological research (see 2.2), all data selected and reanalysed from the database make all and even the tiniest formal differences between languages and language varieties transparent in a unified fashion of presentation, which tend to be passed over in more sweeping and top-down linguistic accounts of comparative issues. For instance, variant forms from the same named language, Matal (MANDARA group), like the following for 'fly' (noun) will be meticulously listed and commented upon along the following lines (but in a slightly different format, see below):

(20)   MANDARA   Matal   √ C CaCa
                          z wayØ   > zway   Note: No comment[4]

                          √ C CaCa
                          zəwayØ   > zəway   Note: Vowel epenthesis

                          √ C CaCa
                          zəw^{w}ayØ
                          > zə^{w}way   > zuway   Note: Vowel epenthesis;
                                                   W-prosody affecting
                                                   epenthetic vowel

For such purposes, I have adopted the following two basic formats of representation and illustration of data and examples in this study.

I. The actual reconstructions (Table 2.2; cf. sub-section 6.4)
The top line of reference identifies, in the following order of columns, gloss, language GROUP (always in capitals), the individual language of that group from which the data are taken, followed by prefixal augments to the root (if any), the diachronic simple root type (indicated by the symbol √) and the actual root, suffixal augments to the root (if any), final vowel (FV, if present), identification of active prosodies (if any).

In this format, the usually five lines in the columns pertaining to the (simple or augmented) root follow the order of

---

[4] Deletion of segments, symbolised by Ø, will not be commented on in accompanying notes, because it is self-evident. Instead of explicitly stating 'no comment', the potential space for 'notes' will simply be left empty.

Table 2.2 *Representation format of lexical reconstructions*

Gloss	GROUP	Language	Prefixal augment	Simple root	Suffixal augment	FV	Prosody
cry, to	MANDARA	Matal		√ C Ca			
			ma-	*t wØ	-a	-y	
			ma-	təw	-a	y	
				mətəway			
				(Note) Vowel epenthesis			
		Glavda		√ C Ca			+W
				*t wØ	-k	a	
				təw^w	-k	a	
				tə^{w}w	-g	a	
				tu:ga			
				(Note) Vowel epenthesis; prosodification of /w/; prosody affecting epenthetic vowel; syllabification of /w/; tə^{w}w > tuw > tu:			

1. The most abstract representation of simple root type, e.g. √ C Ca, plus indication of prosody operating (+Y, +W), single or both.
2. The specific simple root (preceded by *) as internally reconstructed for the individual language, reflecting the PCC reconstruction in terms of phonemic consonants (correspondences) and vowels (i.e. */a/) and deletions (indicated by Ø) of diachronic segments of the PCC reconstructed root; plus all (petrified) prefixal and suffixal augments including FV (Final Vowel) /a/ for the individual language.
3. Indications of vowel pro- and epenthesis and the impact of prosodies, either phonological or morphological in origin, indicated by raised ^{y} and ^{w} for both source and target domains (to the left of raised ^{y} and/or ^{w}) of the respective prosody.[5]

---

[5] The raised symbols ^{w} and ^{y}, always transcribed following the segment of origin and/or its domain of impact, indicate two phonologically distinct but phonetically closely related phenomena:

1. They indicate labialised and palatalised consonants $C^w \sim C^y$, such as k^w or ts^y (= tʃ), irrespective of their phonemic status, i.e. either representing consonantal phonemes, or symbolising phonetic changes under the impact of prosodies.
2. They indicate segments under the regime of the corresponding prosody including vowels. That is, vowels, whether phonemic or epenthetic, under prosody impact are given as follows (in combination with /a/ and mainly in final position, prosody effects may be represented in the available transcriptions of data as either monophthongs or diphthongs):

2.1 General

    Occasionally for complex example types, such as including instances of metathesis, epenthetic schwa insertion and prosodies are given in an extra line for the purpose of increased transparency.
4. The phonetic surface realisation (always in *italics*) as transcribed by the field researcher or dictionary compiler and as contained in the database, yet without diacritics.
5. (Notes.) Highlighted diachronic processes involved (telegraphic style), largely disregarding diachronic changes affecting consonants.

II. Discussing diachronic phonology and processes

In the body of the study, data will be used for illustration of inventories, principles and processes. Here and for ease of reading, we use an abbreviated format, which is also closer to the usual conventions of handling examples in linguistic descriptions. Again, language GROUP and individual source language will always be identified, followed by the internally reconstructed diachronic underlying root (simple or augmented, augments being separated from the root and from each other by '-', deletions from the original PCC root are indicated by Ø), which is always preceded by an asterisk (*). In the next column(s) to the right and again introduced by '>', there is the synchronic underlying root including epenthesis of schwa and indications of prosody domains (left of the raised prosody symbol ^{y} or ^{w}) and further deletions of segments. The rightmost column, again introduced by '>', gives the transcription of the data from the database (always in *italics*). E.g.

(21)   'ashes' PCC *(a-) **p ts(a)ɗa** (-y, -k^w, -n; FV)
       MAROUA   Giziga-Marva   *a-f ts Øa-y-k^w > aftsa-Ø^y-Ø^w > afts^{y}a^w > *aftʃo*

Occasionally, the order of data presentation will be reversed, e.g. for Kamwe-Futu (HIGI group) *ʒiwi* < √ C C Ca *z k^w ya 'fly' (noun) from PCC simple root ***dz(a)k^w(a)ɗa**, we may give

(22)   GROUP   language   surface form   < underlying forms   < *root

       HIGI   Kamwe-Futu   *ʒiwi*   < z^{y}ə^{y}wi^y < zəwy^{y}Ø   < *z k^w ya

If considered necessary for analytical transparency, underlying root types may also be made explicit, e.g.

                    'schwa'   /a/
Y-prosody: ə^y > ɨ ~ i   a^y > ay ~ ey ~ e
W-prosody: ə^w > ʉ ~ u   a^w > aw (~ ow) ~ o

Note that in the database, transcriptions of surface vowels, particularly those under the effect of prosodies, tend to be inconsistent and often depend on the individual conventions used by the transcribing (field/missionary) linguist rather than reflecting different contrastive units in the language under description. Therefore, we will maintain the individual transcriptions as contained in the database (Gravina 2014b), but allow for (internal) reconstruction purposes to interpret them in the way described above.

(23) 'dream' PCC *(n-, ...) s(a)w(a)na (-a, -y, -k, -n; FV)
MAFA Mafa √ C C Ca *n-s w na-y > n-səw^{w}əna-Ø^y > n-s^{y}ə^{w}wə^{y}na^y
                                                          > *nfuwine*
      Cuvok √ C CaCa *s wana > səw^{w}ana > sə^{w}wana
                                              > *suwana*

2.2 The Comparative Method and Dialectological Approaches

The classic comparative method is based on word-by-word and sound-by-sound comparisons between pairs of languages. It rests on an initial assumption of genetic/genealogical relationship between the languages compared, and is at the same time used as proof of such relationship. By applying the comparative method, we arrive at hypotheses about properties of the common ancestor languages (so-called proto-languages). Characteristic results of the comparative method are the establishment of so-called regular sound correspondences (in original Neogrammarian terminology: *sound laws*) between pairs of languages, and of reconstructed forms of ancestral proto-languages (either the ultimate proto-language for the whole language family, or that for branches, sub-branches and groups reflecting intermediate stages of the linguistic history of present-day languages or groups of languages). As has been amply shown for Central Chadic languages in the available literature reflecting previous research, the comparative method comes to its limits here for three major reasons:

- the particular nature of the phonological systems and the diachronic processes behind them in the languages' histories;
- the absence of written documentation from previous centuries for practically all the languages (except Hausa) that would allow recognition of visible historical changes in phonology, grammar and lexicon;
- the considerable time-depth involved and absence of knowledge about migration processes and contact scenarios of the populations involved.

Therefore, like with most African language data, rather than using 'vertical' historical techniques and etymology, Chadic historical linguistics requires 'horizontal' techniques akin to dialectological methods, in what has also been termed *multilateral comparison*. Important to note is that in order to arrive finally at representations that can be submitted to the comparative method with some success at a later stage, data have to be *pre-processed* in terms of identifying their underlying, i.e. more abstract, phonological representation. For this, one can make use of the method of *internal reconstruction* (2.3).

Second, an areal perspective needs to be introduced in order to detect traces of language contact regarding individual lexical items that may have been

2.2 Comparative Method & Dialectological Approaches

borrowed inter-dialectally, i.e. between very closely related languages, or across robust language boundaries, if not between languages originating from different families or phyla. Characteristically, such cases conflict with the more or less established regular sound correspondences between languages and thus may throw doubt on the applicability of the comparative method. In order to zoom in on the linguistic history of individual word forms, the methods adopted from dialectology come in handy. Ideally and in keeping with techniques known from dialectological research, one would want to draw maps of isoglosses for individual words or properties of words in a given geographic area. (It is worth noting that Gravina (2014a) makes ample use of maps in his study, all in all 60, including 26 maps of 'isoglosses', without, however, explicitly reflecting on dialectological methods and techniques.) Often and justifiably, individual word histories ('etymologies') have to replace the more encompassing regular sound changes and correspondences that we would expect under strict application of the Neogrammarian Hypothesis.

Third, with the availability of data from fairly closely related languages on the group level of Central Chadic language classification, including data from different varieties of what are considered the same (named) languages, we can draw almost microscopic pictures of minimal phonological differences between languages and among their dialects, which help in understanding the type and nature of processes that – over time – have led to considerable linguistic diversification between languages within the same language groups, and across Central Chadic. Remarkably, as Gravina's and our study show, even closely related language groups or dialect clusters may display a fair variety of forms and diachronic processes that have affected them.

See, for example, the word for 'to cry' from five fairly closely related languages of the MANDARA group. They display the following surface representations: *mataway – tawa – $k^y ua$ – $k^y uwa$ – tu:ga*, which we all consider to ultimately derive from a PCC simple root **ts(a)wa**, which occasionally also shows petrified prefixal and suffixal augment material (see 6.4).

1. All five languages show PCC *ts > t for the initial root consonant; two of them show a peculiar effect of Y-prosody on this consonant: *ts > t; $t + ^y > t^y > k^y$.
2. Three of the five languages retain the lexical final vowel /a/, one (Matal) deletes lexical final /a/ before suffixal augment *-a-y, one other (Glavda) deletes final /a/ after syllabification of the preceding weak radical consonant.
3. Only one (Podoko) of the five languages makes use of the root type √ CaCa, all others use √ C Ca.

4. Only one (Matal) of the five languages uses prefix {ma-} and multiple suffixal augment *-a-y (together presumably representing a citation form for verbs), all others don't.
5. Only one (Glavda) of the five languages makes use of multiple suffixal augment *{-k} + FV.
6. Three of the five languages use suffixal augment *{-y}, two (Podoko, Glavda) don't.
7. Out of the three languages that use suffixal augment *{-y}, only two (Mandara, Malgwa) show presence of accompanying Y-prosody with palatalisation of the initial consonant of the root, the third one (Matal) doesn't.
8. Out of the four languages that use the root shape √ C Ca, two (Mandara, Malgwa) syllabify the second root consonant */w/ > [u], the others (Matal, Glavda) use epenthetic vowel insertion (ᵊ) to separate the two root consonants.[6]

(24)   'cry, to' PCC *(ma-) **ts(a)wa** (-a, -y, -k; FV)

GROUP	language	root type	root	intermediate	surface
MANDARA	Matal	√ C Ca	*ma-t wØ-a-y	matᵊway	*matəway*
	Podoko	√ CaCa	*tawa	tawa	*tawa*
	Mandara	√ C Ca	*t wa-y	tʸwa-Øʸ	*kʸua*
	Malgwa	√ C Ca	*t wa-y	tʸᵊwa-Øʸ	*kʸuwa*
	Glavda	√ C Ca	*t wØ-ka	tᵊwka	*tu:ga*

Similar diverse reflexes within closely related language groups of common underlying roots can be illustrated with the following examples involving the word for 'faeces': MARGI group *kivi – tʃivi – ibi*, and again from the MANDARA group *ugve – guva – gəve*. With the exception of Glavda (MANDARA), five languages show reflexes of morphological palatalisation stemming from root-augmental *{-y}. Bura has two forms that differ in the degree of palatalisation of the initial consonant (/k + ʸ/ > k⁽ʸ⁾ ~ tʃ). Kilba deletes C_1, and C_2 undergoes consonant change /v/ > b. In addition to the MARGI group languages, Dghweɗe has lost the labialisation feature of its initial consonant (*/gʷ/ > /g/) prior to its potential prosodification, so it remains the only MANDARA group language without reflex of phonological labialisation, which in the other languages of the group 'colour' prothetic (Mandara, Malgwa) and epenthetic (Glavda) schwa to surface as [u] in the first syllable.

---

[6] For reasons of increased transparency, pro- and epenthetic schwa will be indicated, only in the following examples, by raised ᵊ in intermediate representations. Elsewhere in this book, this convention will not be used, since the use of the graphic symbol ə is by itself indication of the epenthetic nature of this vowel, unless it can be identified as allophone of */a/.

(25) 'faeces' PCC *(ŋ-) ɣʷ va (-a, -y, -n)

GROUP	language	root type	root		intermediate		surface
MARGI	Bura	√ C Ca	*k vØ-y	kᵊv-iʸ		> kᵊʸv-i	kivi
			*k vØ-y	kᵊv-iʸ		> kʸᵊʸv-i	tʃivi
	Kilba	√ C Ca	*Ø bØ-y	ᵊb-iʸ		> ᵊʸb-i	ibi
MANDARA	Mandara, Malgwa	√ C Ca	*gʷ va-y	ᵊgʷva-Øʸ		> ᵊʷgvaʸ	ugve
	Glavda	√ C Ca	*gʷ va	gʷᵊva		> gᵊʷva	guva
	Dghweɗe	√ C Ca	*g va-y	gᵊva-Øʸ		> gᵊvaʸ	gəve

2.3 Internal Reconstruction

While the comparative method is used to establish features of the ancestor language of two or more related modern languages, i.e. of languages belonging to the same language family, the method of internal reconstruction uses complexities, if not apparent irregularities, in a single language to make inferences about an earlier stage of that language. Internal reconstruction, therefore, is based on evidence from one language alone.[7] However, knowing what went on diachronically in closely related other languages can serve as an eye-opener.

Even before beginning diachronic analysis, i.e. already for synchronic analysis and description, the at times rather complex phonological nature of Central Chadic languages can only be understood by reference to rather abstract levels of representation. For this, one can make use of the method of internal reconstruction, which allows one to identify for each word an underlying structure on a high level of phonological abstraction, which at the same time is likely to more or less accidentally mirror (stages in) the diachronic history of the word form. In many cases, if not always, the forms arrived at by internal reconstruction bring us closer to the reconstructable form of the word in the individual ancestral language, if not that of the language group into which the particular language is classified. And only by knowing the history of the word form behind its surface phonetic representation can we then proceed to comparisons with other languages, because we have almost automatically identified the phonological entities that can and must be compared (cf. illustrations for the words for 'nose' and 'ear' in selected CC languages, in sub-section 5.2 further below).

With the following example, we can illustrate the method and results of internal reconstruction by looking – in a parallel fashion – at two very closely

---

[7] For a valuable independent parallel appraisal of the method of internal reconstruction with illustrative application to a Chadic language, namely West Chadic Hausa, see Newman (2014).

related languages, namely Lamang and Hdi of the LAMANG group (for a detailed comparative study of the two languages, see Wolff 2015 Vol.1: Chapters 3 and 4). As a matter of fact, both languages are, on the one hand, structurally so similar that they would merit being considered varieties of just one and the same language separated by a high and steep mountain slope and an international border (between Nigeria and Cameroon); on the other hand, however, they are dissimilar enough in terms of surface structures that they are no longer mutually intelligible 'dialects' of the same language and should, for practical reasons, be considered distinct languages. Still, their linguistic nearness allows us to apply the method of internal reconstruction to both at the same time and show how applying the method to one language helps to gain insight into the other in mutual enlightenment.

Linguistic intuition would tell us that the somewhat similar words for 'wound' (noun), i.e. Lamang *wulki* and Hdi *luku*, could be cognates and display dialectal variants of the same word. Such intuition rests on the superficial impression that the two words might be historically the same, because of (a) their shared meaning, and (b) a similarity in terms of segments that make up the words, namely because they both contain the consonants /l/ and /k/ (in that order) and they share one identical vowel, namely [u]. But exactly how can we prove their etymological identity? On second sight, they are disturbingly dissimilar in that one language has [i] where the other one has another [u], and Lamang has a /w/ where Hdi obviously has nothing. And the sequential order of /l/ and [u] is not the same in both languages. How do we tie the loose ends together based on sound linguistic methodology? The surface forms only allow us to identify three 1:1 sound correspondences between segments, but three others would not even have a counterpart in the other language. Even the sequence of the corresponding segments would appear to be only an incomplete match, since correspondence lines cross (see Figure 2.2).

Figure 2.2 Lamang–Hdi: look-alikes or cognates?

2.3 Internal Reconstruction

With this not very successful first attempt to match segments in this pair of languages, one might consider the comparison abortive, declare one's intuition about cognation to be false, and speak of 'look-alikes' that are only partially similar in sound, while they accidentally share the same meaning. Still, such negative evaluation of the data would appear to be counter-intuitive vis-à-vis the overall picture of remarkable structural and lexical similarities between the two languages.

This is where internal reconstruction comes in and shows us, that and why we are indeed dealing with true cognates. Rather than comparing the surface structures *wulki* and *luku*, we need to look at the underlying structures for each word and re-try our comparison based on these. For doing this, however, we need a fair amount of insight into the languages, to understand their phonological 'mechanics', so to speak, and to use intuition supported by experience from comparative work with related other languages of the same language family. In a kind of sloppy way of saying, it needs a seasoned comparativist to take over from where the linguistic rookie fails. Based on thorough insight into the individual languages of the group and by knowing what diachronic phonological processes are likely to have operated in the history of these words, we can apply the method of internal reconstruction and will arrive at the following underlying structures and the hypothetical (so-called reconstructed) common root. In this process, we identify underlying triradical simple roots in both languages that involve a weak radical /w/ as well as an instance of metathesis of radical consonants involving this /w/, so that we recognise a complete match of five segments. Two of the five reconstructed segments, however, are no longer present in the synchronic forms of the individual words, one in each of the two languages. Thus, we arrive at internally reconstructing five segmental units, which together even in their sequence create a perfect match between the two languages, yet on a fairly abstract level of underlying structure (Figure 2.3).

In order to arrive at the surface forms of the words in the modern languages, we can now tell the whole story in a step-by-step account, starting off from the reconstructed common root of the word in proto-LAMANG. (For additional examples illustrating divergent language evolution in the most closely related Lamang and Hdi, see sub-section 5.1 further below.)

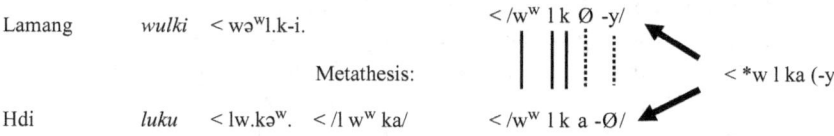

Lamang   *wulki*   < wəʷl.k-i.

                            Metathesis:

Hdi   *luku*   < lw.kəʷ.   < /l wʷ ka/

Figure 2.3 Lamang–Hdi: cognation

1. The hypothetical reconstructed simple root is triradical and of the root type √ C C Ca, i.e. ***w l ka**. This root is the starting point for then slightly different diachronic developments in the two languages.
2. In both languages and in a parallel way, the weak radical /w/ becomes partially desegmentalised by becoming the source of phonological W-prosody (indicated by w^w), which will have effects on, for instance, epenthetic and centralised vowels (see steps 6 and 7).
3. One language (Lamang) takes on a diachronic suffixal root augment, namely *{-y}, the other (Hdi) doesn't. Here, Lamang *{-y} corresponds to Hdi Ø.
4. While in Lamang the lexical final vowel /a/ is deleted in front of the suffixal root-augment *{-y}, it is retained in Hdi where no such element is added. Here, Hdi /a/ corresponds to Lamang Ø.
5. In Hdi only, the root consonants /w/ and /l/ undergo metathesis, i.e. the original sequence of segments /w l ka/ is changed to /l w ka/. (Note that in the Central Chadic languages in general, metathesis involving */w/ is quite frequent.)
6. In both languages, the intermediate structures undergo syllable formation. Hdi chooses the option to syllabify /w/ in syllable-nucleus position, i.e. it creates a first syllable /lw./ > [lu.]. Lamang chooses another option, namely vowel epenthesis, i.e. it inserts schwa between the first two consonants to create a first syllable [wəl.]. For second syllables, Hdi retains the lexical final vowel of the root, but – as many Central Chadic languages do – centralises it to its allophone [ə], thereby creating an intermediate second syllable of the shape [kə.]. Lamang, on the other hand, syllabifies root-augmental *{-y} in syllable-nucleus position to yield a second syllable [ki.].
7. Subsequently W-prosody, originating from partial desegmentalisation of the weak radical /w/ > $/w^w/$, affects the epenthetic schwa in the first syllable in Lamang, yielding a syllable [wə^{w}l.] > [wul.]. It likewise affects the centralised allophone schwa in the final syllable in Hdi, yielding a syllable [kə^w.] > [ku.]. In both cases, the resulting surface vowel from labialised schwa is [u].

Finally, the modern phonetic surface representations *wulki* and *luku* have been arrived at by the application of a series of Central Chadic diachronic phonological rules of natural language change, operating on the internally reconstructed proto-LAMANG simple root ***w l ka**.

Note that the resulting surface structures give a totally misleading picture of what could be the underlying root type in both languages: Lamang *wulki* looks like a √ CVCCV structure, while Hdi *luku* looks like a √ CVCV structure – yet both derive from a common underlying root type √ C C Ca. This is a common and often confusing phenomenon in Central Chadic, so that in this book we occasionally make it a point to explicitly identify the underlying root type for individual examples in order to provide additional diachronic transparency.

Hence, internal reconstruction is essential for both synchronic analysis and historical explanation of diachronic processes for each word in a given language – particularly so for Central Chadic languages. They are notorious for phonetic surface realisations of vowels and their distribution within the word, which together tend to blur the picture and veil the identity of the phonemic units and epenthetic vowels that were originally, i.e. diachronically, involved.

There is, however, a methodological caveat in order here. Language-centred internal reconstruction may occasionally lead to ad hoc decisions by the linguist as to which of two explanatory hypotheses to follow and to give precedence over the other. For instance, when in a given word there is obviously a prosody operating, the question arises whether to attribute this prosody to an original lexical/phonological or grammatical/morphological origin. When on first sight there may be no apparent phonological source of the prosody from within the simple root of the word, the linguist may be led to postulate – in an ad hoc fashion – a 'lost' morphological source for the prosody, and subsequently 'reconstruct' the presence of, for instance, the palatalising suffixal root-augment *{-y}, which would reflect a distinct morpheme in PCC grammar. For illustration of this point, let us look, for example, at the word for 'fly' (noun) in languages of the HIGI group. There is obviously Y-prosody operating in the languages from which the following examples are taken. By looking at the data and the surface forms of the words, a first step would be to reconstruct an apparently biradical root of the underlying root types √ C Ca and √ CaCa, i.e. ^{x}z k^{w}a ~ ^{x}zak^{w}a or the like. Further, one would – in a kind of ad hoc fashion – reconstruct *{-y}, which then presumably deleted the preceding final */a/ of the simple root, then desegmentalised and only 'survived' in the shape of Y-prosody, which affected the initial root consonant (by changing */z/ > ʒ) as much as the vowels, by changing phonemic */a/ > [e] and epenthetic [ə] > [i]:

(26) HIGI Kamwe-Futu ʒiwi   < z^{y}ə^{y}w-i   < zəwØ-y^y < ^{x}z k^{w}a-y
           Bana   ʒiɓ(i) < z^{y}ə^{y}ɓ-i   < zəɓØ-y^y < ^{x}z k^{w}a-y
           Kirya   ʒew   < z^{y}a^{y}w-Ø   < zawØ-y^y < ^{x}zak^{w}a-y

Such diachronic development of the synchronic forms would be quite plausible in the light of the overall behaviour of Y-prosody with roots of this type and shape. However, taking the wider picture into account by also involving languages from other groups for comparative purposes, if not already other languages from the same group (if data were available), a different scenario emerges, which helps to identify the palatalisation prosody in these examples as NOT being of morphological nature, but to have a lexical phonological source. (The comparative scenario, therefore, dismisses the reconstruction of Y-prosody stemming from morphological *{-y} as unjustified and ad hoc.) First of all, we need to recognise that the root behind the word for 'fly' is triradical **dz(a)kʷ(a)ɗa**, with at least two root types involved, namely √ C C Ca and √ CaC Ca. The final root consonant */ɗ/, however, tends to weaken to [y] and even get lost, leaving behind a trace in the shape of Y-prosody. Therefore, it is a weak radical /y/ (being a reflex of the original C₃ of the PCC simple root: */ɗ/ > /y/) that is the source for the palatalisation across the word. Thus, we are more likely dealing with phonological palatalisation rather than with *morphological* palatalisation.[8] Hence, we arrive at an alternative path to diachronically derive the modern forms in the HIGI languages from their Proto-HIGI and ultimately PCC origins:

(27) HIGI   Kamwe-Futu   ʒiwi   < zʸəʸwi   < zəwyʸØ   < *z kʷ ya
              Bana   ʒiɓ(i)   < zʸəʸɓi   < zəɓyʸØ   < *z kʷ ya
              Kirya   ʒew   < zʸaʸwØ   < zawyʸØ   < *zakʷ ya

In all three languages and under this analysis, the palatalisation effect stems from an underlying final root consonant /y/ (< */ɗ/) rather than from the ad hoc postulated highly frequent suffixal root-augment *{-y}. In Kamwe-Futu and Bana, the final weak radical /y/ has syllabified to [i] in syllable-nucleus position and has prosodified to further change epenthetic schwa in the first syllable to [i] and initial /z/ > [ʒ], while in Kirya it has been completely desegmentalised and only survived as Y-prosody, which changed the medial /a/ > [e] and initial /z/ > [ʒ]. The different diachronic developments in Kamwe-Futu and Bana on the one side, and Kirya on the other, are explained by the previous choice of root types: Kamwe-Futu and Bana have opted historically for √ C C Ca (*z kʷ ya), while Kirya has opted for √ CaC Ca (*zakʷ ya). For Proto-HIGI, therefore, we would have to allow for at least two root-type options and indicate this by a conflated reconstruction: **z(a)kʷ ya**.

Examples like the above show that and how a multi-method approach in comparative Chadic linguistics as chosen for the present study implies corrective elements to mono-method approaches.

2.4   The Database and Conventions of Transcription

This book rests exclusively on the remarkably rich database made available online by Richard Gravina (2014b), which includes his reconstructions and

---

[8] Such observations and interpretations, if historically correct, open up insights into the relative chronology of language change. Assuming *phonological* Y-prosody, the */ɗ/ > y change could be assumed to have preceded the emergence of Y-prosody, while the assumption of *morphological* Y-prosody (stemming from a hypothetical suffix *{-y}) could link the */ɗ/ > y change itself to the assumed existence of the suffix *{-y}, i.e. attribute the consonantal sound change to an effect of pre-existing Y-prosody.

surface-form representations from a wide variety of languages and which he identifies as follows:

> The present study includes data from 60 of the 78 Central Chadic languages listed in Lewis (2009), together with data from six varieties treated as dialects in Lewis (2009), which amounts to 66 varieties used in this study. (Gravina 2014b: 11)

The database includes both data that were already published at the time of Gravina's compilation, and unpublished data from hard-to-come-by SIL surveys and fieldnotes of fellow linguists that he was able to solicit for his PhD project. After finishing his PhD project at Leiden University in 2014, the database was made available online. Only on rare occasions when corresponding data were missing, have I added data from Lamang and Hdi of the LAMANG group from more recent sources, namely Wolff (2015, Vol.2) and Frajzyngier et al. (2015).

Note that in Gravina's database, 'the data is as presented by the original author, except that word forms have been normalised into IPA'. This was a justifiable decision to make, but for the present study we will use the established conventions in Chadic linguistics, some of which are at variance with IPA, for practical and convenience reasons:

1. We will render the frequent non-low central vowel schwa by ə (Gravina uses /ɨ/, which phonetically may probably be more adequate for most modern Central Chadic languages) for simple reasons of long-established practice and usage and in order to avoid graphic confusion between Gravina's /ɨ/ and phonetic surface realisations of the vowels [i] and [ɨ] – unless, however, the individual transcription in the fieldnotes contains [ɨ] (or [ʉ], for that matter).
2. Further, IPA j is in this study rendered by the more common *Africa Alphabet* symbol y also for the simple reason of long-established practice and usage; this also allows us to use the same symbol for both segmental y and Y-prosody, the latter graphically symbolised by raised ^{y}.[9]
3. In our own PCC reconstructions involving velar fricatives, we will replace Gravina's *h and *h^w more appropriately with *x and *x^w, even though individual language sources may also represent these by h and h^w.

2.5 Theoretical Modules Underlying Central Chadic Lexical Reconstruction Work

One of the most challenging tasks for the reconstruction of Proto- (Central) Chadic phonology and lexicon is the identification of and processes pertaining

---

[9] Note that on very rare occasions of combined Y- and W-prosodies, ʏ (not to be confused with y) will be used in its IPA value as front-rounded vowel; in these rare cases, we may mark this somewhat redundantly by the expression 'IPA ʏ' or 'ʏ (IPA)'.

to, non-consonantal segmental phonological units, whether we call them vowels, vocoids, weak radicals, or the like, and how this may link up with issues concerning the phonological status of schwa. This leads to the fundamental question in diachronic (Central) Chadic linguistics whether – in the light of a plethora of phonetic surface vowels that may occur in any individual language – all of them can really be historically derived from just one or two vowels in the proto-language, namely */a/ and possibly schwa (of uncertain phonological status). As outlined further above, the assumption of such minimal inventories of 'true' vowels has been debated in the relevant literature for quite some time. Based on many years of dealing with low-level reconstructions within Central Chadic since the mid 1970s, and profiting from professional exchanges with other experts in (Central) Chadic linguistics and Afroasiatic languages as a whole for half a century, the present author has meanwhile developed a promising unified approach to comparative (Central) Chadic that is in keeping with generally accepted typological assumptions about Afroasiatic as a whole and Chadic languages in particular. It rests on four theoretical modules, which will be sketched out shortly in the following sub-sections. These modules are referred to as (1) *epenthesis theory*, (2) *weak radical theory*, (3) *vocalisation theory*, and (4) *prosody theory*. As a bundle and under these labels, they were presented in Wolff (2004), but had been developed earlier for the low-level comparison of the languages of the then so-called Wandala-Lamang Group within Central Chadic in Wolff (1983b) and – somewhat almost in passing – have been applied to Vulum (MUSGUM group) in Wolff (1984b).

2.5.1   Epenthesis Theory

As repeatedly pointed out, one of the difficult questions in analysing Central Chadic vowel systems concerns the phonological status of schwa.[10] Some authors consider schwa a full vowel phoneme in a given language, other authors, as we do here for PCC, claim that schwa and all its conditioned

---

[10] In this study and also elsewhere, I use the term 'epenthesis (theory)' as conveniently shortened from 'pro- and epenthesis (theory)'. In Central Chadic languages, from both diachronic and synchronic perspectives, we find frequent insertions of schwa (ə) either *within* or *preceding* a root/word, in the latter case usually but not always preceding initial consonant clusters. Instances of both *epenthesis* and *prothesis* will be conveniently subsumed here under 'epenthesis (theory)'. Note that occurrence of schwa at the end of a reconstructed root will not be subsumed, nor is it discussed in this study, since we assume all PCC simple roots by default to end in */a/, and we treat augmented roots as optionally carrying a final vowel */a/ (FV) or simply as ending in a consonant. These final vowels may, however, undergo centralisation to yield underlying or surface [ə]. So-called *epithesis* or *paragoge*, therefore, is not considered to be an issue in our PCC reconstructions, since all word-final occurrences of schwa will be automatically assumed to represent centralised representations of word-final /a/.

2.5 Theoretical Modules in CC Lexical Reconstruction

variants are fully predictable *epenthetic* vowels.[11] As such, they merit no status in the phonemic reconstruction of roots of the proto-language, which are made up solely of phonemic consonants and the only PCC vowel phoneme */a/. However, in order to move from reconstructed phonemic structures to phonetic surface representations in the individual present-day languages, we need to take the very frequently occurring epenthetic vowels into account. It is with their help that underlying forms are transformed according to the requirements of syllable structure and are thus made 'pronounceable' as acceptable words in the language. It is, therefore, imperative for comparative Central Chadic linguistics to, first of all, scrutinise surface vowels with regard to their underlying phonological nature as either 'true' vowel or diphthong (*/a, ay, aw/ > [a, e, ɛ, o, ɔ]), syllabified representations of underlying weak radicals (*/y/ > [i], */w/ > [u]), or pro-/epenthetic schwa ([ə, ɨ, ɪ, ʉ, ʊ], the latter occasionally also transcribed as [i, u] in fieldnotes or for practical orthographies).

Pro- and epenthetic vowels, however, tend to be somewhat unstable in terms of distribution and phonetic realisations. They tend to be perceptually shorter than other surface vowels to the extent of not being heard and transcribed at all, and may not be allowed to occur phonetically 'long', for instance, under stress. Quite characteristically, transcriptions by individual linguists may try to capture intermediate degrees of vocalisation by using conventions of the type CəC ~ C°C ~ CC symbolising anaptyxis or open phonetic transition between consonants. As pro-/epenthetic vowels, they are sensitive to the phonotactic requirements of the individual language. Their phonetic realisations may be different (e.g. [ɨ, ɪ, ʉ, ʊ]) from or identical to (e.g. [a, ə, i, u]) those of surface vowels with underlying phonemic status (i.e. */a/, */y/, */w/). Pro-/epenthetic vowels are easily affected by assimilatory pressure from the phonological environment. In Central Chadic languages, they most of all come under the influence of so-called prosodies, i.e. 'long-component' effects of palatalisation and labialisation (see below for *prosody theory*). Despite being non-phonemic in nature, epenthetic vowels – which we refer to as schwa, and which on abstract levels of analysis we render graphically by ə – contribute as much to the shape of a word as do occurrences of phonemic */a/ (see below for

---

[11] The issue can be neatly illustrated by comparing the full descriptions of two very closely related CC languages, namely Lamang and Hdi from the LAMANG group, which are considered separate languages within a linguistic continuum just beyond being mutually intelligible dialects. For both we have extensive descriptive monographs (Wolff, 1983a, 2015; Frajzyngier & Shay, 2002). While Wolff describes Lamang under the provision that schwa is epenthetic in nature and totally predictable wherever it occurs, Frajzyngier and Shay treat /ə/ as a phoneme in Hdi. Both approaches allow plausible descriptions of synchronic linguistic structures. The question, therefore, is often not one of 'right' or 'wrong', but of theoretical orientation and methodological preference on the part of the describing linguist.

vocalisation theory), other vocoids, i.e. */y/ and */w/ (see below for *weak radical theory*), and consonants.

See the following examples from groups of closely related languages for the manifold surface representations of epenthetic schwa, namely giving rise to [ə], [ɨ], [i], and [u], depending on the effects of prosodies and the transcription conventions used in the original data. Note that underlying phonemic /a/ has entirely different reflexes in some of the languages, namely [e] in final position in Bata, Bachama, Hwana and Dghweɗe, and [œ] in medial position in Bachama, again under the effect of prosodies.

(28)   'ashes' PCC *(a-) **p ts(a)ɗa** (-y, -k^w, -n; FV)

BATA	Bata	√ C C Ca	*f t Øa-y	> fəta-Ø^y	
				> fə^{y}ta^y	> *fite*
	Bachama	√ C CaCa	*f tadØ-y-k^{w}a	> ftaɗ-y^y-Ø^{w}a	
				> fə^{y}ta^{yw}ɗə^{y}ya^y	> *fitœɗiye*
TERA	Tera	√ C C Ca	*p dz tØ-y	> pədzət-Ø^y	
				> pədz^{y}ə^{y}t	> *pədʒit*
	Nyimatli[12]	√ C C Ca	*p z tØ-y	> pəzət-Ø^y	
				> pəz^{y}ə^{y}t	> *pəʒit*
	Hwana	√ C C Ca	*f s Øa-y	> fəsa-Ø^y	
				> fə^{y}s^{y}a^y	> *fiʃe*
MANDARA	Dghweɗe	√ C C Ca	*f ts t'a-y-k^w	> ftsət'a-Ø^y-Ø^w	
				> ftsə^{w}t'a^y	> *ftsut'e*
MAROUA	Giziga-Muturwa, Mbazla	√ C C Ca	*f ts ØØ-y-k^w	> fəts-Ø^y-w^w	
				> fə^{w}ts^{y}w	> *futʃu*

A note on transcriptions of schwa (ə) as i and u

As was pointed out elsewhere (cf. also Gravina 2014a), Central Chadic language data transcriptions are not always consistent with regard to representing the central non-low vowel schwa, independent of whether it is considered to be phonemic or epenthetic by individual linguists for individual language

---

[12] According to P. Newman (p.c. 2020), Nyimatli is the autonym for Tera and is not a different language in the TERA group. The source for this is somewhat doubtful, given as 'Harley' (a compiler of several wordlists of different Central Chadic languages) in Gravina's database, but otherwise remaining unidentified in Gravina's (2014a) 'Bibliography' with regard to providing a Nyimatli/Tera wordlist. In order to stick as closely as possible to the database, and in view of certain differences of transcription between 'Tera' (wordlist by Newman) and 'Nyimatli' (wordlist by Harley), both sources, wherever providing slightly different word forms, remain quoted separately in the present book. P. Newman (p.c. 2020) also identified the convention u (used by Harley for Nyimatli) as representing schwa in local missionary practice; therefore, in the present study and at variance with the database, the symbol ə will be used instead of u̱.

2.5 Theoretical Modules in CC Lexical Reconstruction

descriptions. The most widely used convention is ə, while some researchers use the convention ɨ, which 'is the most common realisation of the vowel in different languages' (Gravina 2014a: 351) as a slightly fronted central-high ([−round]) rather than central-mid vowel. In his reconstruction work, Gravina consistently uses /ɨ/ rather than /ə/ to symbolise the non-low central vowel schwa. Our present study, however, will consistently follow established usage and represent schwa by ə. It should be noted that whenever we are quoting language data from the database, we will follow the original conventions of individual researchers as indicated in the database, i.e. we will maintain a distinction between, for instance, [ə], [ɨ] and [ʉ] as found in the transcriptions. More specifically, and despite the risk of over-interpreting the conventions, we will treat [ə] and [ɨ] as [−Y] and [+Y] variants of epenthetic vowels, i.e. we will make the effect of Y-prosody responsible for the [ɨ] variant.[13] See, for example, alternative treatments in the following examples from the KOTOKO group languages.

(29)   'blow, to'   PCC *(ma-) v ɓa (-a, -y, -ɗ, -kʷ, -n)

   (a) In the following interpretation of a set of available transcriptions, the notation ɨ is taken to indicate Y-prosody effect on the root, therefore we postulate morphological palatalisation stemming from *{-y}:

(29a)   KOTOKO-NORTH   Mpade   √ C Ca   +Y
                                  *f lØ   -y
                                  fəʸl   -Øʸ
                                  fɨl

         KOTOKO-CENTRAL Lagwan   √ C Ca   +Y,+W
                                  *v lØ   -y -kʷ -n
                                  vəʸl   -Øʸ-wʷ-əʷn
                                  vɨlwun

                         Mser   √ C Ca   +Y
                                  *v lØ   -y
                                  vəʸl   -Øʸ
                                  vɨl

   (b) If we were to replace ɨ as conventional graphic representation with ə for the same examples and not paying attention to the potentially and possibly implied [+high] value of the phonetic symbol [ɨ], we would arrive at not recognising the presence of morphological Y-prosody (if it was really there!):

---

[13] Admittedly, this may constitute a case of over-differentiation. If the reader pleases, s/he may undo the indication of Y-prosody in such examples in which the symbol [ɨ] is the only trace of the prosody, i.e. in the absence of other Y-prosody effects; see our discussion of alternative options below.

(29b)　　KOTOKO-NORTH　　　Mpade　　√ C Ca
　　　　　　　　　　　　　　　　　　*f lØ
　　　　　　　　　　　　　　　　　　fəl

　　　　　KOTOKO-CENTRAL　　Lagwan　√ C Ca　　　　　　　　+W
　　　　　　　　　　　　　　　　　　*v lØ　　-k^w -n
　　　　　　　　　　　　　　　　　　vəl　　　-w^w-ə^{w}n
　　　　　　　　　　　　　　　　　　vəlwun

　　　　　　　　　　　　　　　Mser　　√ C Ca
　　　　　　　　　　　　　　　　　　*v lØ
　　　　　　　　　　　　　　　　　　vəl

2.5.2 Weak Radical Theory

The *weak radical theory* is inspired by centuries of Semitic and Afroasiatic scholarship. By 'radical' (short for 'radical consonant'; cf. Latin *radix* for 'root') we refer to a consonant that is part of the simple root, which in the narrow reading of Afroasiatic and Semitic linguistics comprises only the consonantal skeleton of such root. The *weak radical theory* is based on the characteristic typological observation that the [+syllabic] high vowels [i] and [u] are in complementary distribution with their [−syllabic] counterparts, namely the approximants/glides when they are used as consonants [y] and [w], i.e. [i] and [u] only occur in syllable-nucleus position, [y] and [w] elsewhere. When occurring in syllable-nucleus position, the vocoids */y/ and */w/ become [+syllabic] and function like ordinary vowels, namely [i] and [u]. When occurring in non-nucleus positions of the syllable, i.e. onset or coda positions, the same vocoids function like ordinary consonants, i.e. they become [−syllabic]. Further in Afroasiatic scholarship, it can be shown that */y ~ i/ and */w ~ u/ can each be treated as being the same phonological units with complementary distribution of allophones, and that in systemic terms they can or must be counted as radical consonants, even if considered somewhat 'weak'. Thus, and in terminological agreement with Afroasiatic scholarship, we say that /y/ and /w/ function as *weak radicals* ([±syllabic]) also in Chadic, hence the name for this second theoretical module of Chadic diachronic linguistics. Not to observe the systemic relationship between *y ~ [i] and *w ~ [u] would dramatically blur the picture and produce misrepresentations of diachronic phonological processes, which consequently would lead to lexical reconstructions that could be considered to be 'historically wrong'.

Our Central Chadic reconstructions contain many examples in which such weak radicals surface as vowels in phonetic transcription. In the following example, which is just one out of many, both medial */w/ and final */y/ find themselves in syllable-nucleus positions within the same word, and thus surface as [u] and [i] respectively (note that syllable boundaries are indicated by '.' and RED stands for reduplicative root augment).

2.5 Theoretical Modules in CC Lexical Reconstruction   53

(30)   'dream' PCC *(ma-, ma-RED-, RED-, n-) **s(a)w(a)na** (-a, -y, -k, -n; FV)
         MARGI   Bura   *s w na-y   > sw.nØ-y.   > *su.ni*.

Comparative evidence, sometimes even internally reconstructed evidence from the same language, clearly shows the underlying vocoid */w/ (if not, in this case, ultimately */x^w/, see Podoko) functioning as a consonant rather than an underlying 'true' vowel ^{x}/u/; see for the same root 'dream':

(31)   MANDARA   Podoko   *s x^{w}ana   > sə.x^{w}a.na.   > *səh^{w}ana*
         LAMANG   Lamang   *s waŋa   > sə.wa.ŋa.   > *suwaŋa*
         HIGI   Kirya   *s w ØØ-y-k^w > s^{y}ə^y.w-Ø^y-w. > *ʃiwu*
         KOTOKO-   Lagwan   *s wana-y   > swa.na^y-Ø^y.   > *swane*
         CENTRAL

See also the examples from two closely related languages of the MUSGUM group below, which each follow a different strategy with regard to the feature [±syllabic] in the derivation of intermediate and final phonetic surface forms.

(32)   'cook, to' PCC *(k-, ma-, RED-) **da** (-a, -y, -k, k^w; FV)
         MUSGUM   Mulwi   *da-y   > dØ-y   > d-i   > *di*
                    Mbara   *ta-y   > tØ-y^y > tə^{y}y   > *tii*

While Mulwi, after deleting the lexical final /a/ of the monoradical root *da, allows the underlying suffixal root-augment *{-y} to syllabify to become the vowel [i] in word-final and syllable-nucleus position *dØ-y > *di*, Mbara treats */y/ as a consonant thereby creating an intermediate CVC sequence *tay, from which */a/ is then deleted, yielding an intermediate CC structure *tØy. Vowel epenthesis then shifts /y/ into syllable-coda position *tay > tØy > təy, which – under the regime of Y-prosody originating from the final *{-y} – phonetically changes *tə^{y}y > *tii* to yield a long surface vowel [ii]. In the end, reconstructed *{-y} ends up as surface vowel [i] in both languages. However, only an intermediate structure where /y/ is treated as a consonant is able to explain the difference in vowel length between the two languages: *di* vs. *tii*.

2.5.3   Vocalisation Theory

Starting from the assumption that the proto-language (PCC) only has one true, i.e. phonemic, vowel, namely */a/, it is extremely helpful to group lexical morphemes in Chadic according to 'vocalisation patterns' with regard to the distribution of */a/. Such vocalisation patterns are part of an old overall root-and-pattern structure in Chadic which, explained again by typological heritage, is characteristic for Afroasiatic languages as a whole. The root in its simplest form and in the narrow sense of the term, consists of the consonantal skeleton alone, disregarding any vowels. In Afroasiatic language typology, it is such roots that carry the basic meaning of the lexeme. Vocalic 'patterns' are then added to create vocalised roots; these patterns are made up of the available phonemic vowels. For PCC vocalised roots (in this study referred to as root types; see 3.1.1.1), only */a/ is available. By restricting the notion of 'pattern' to the occurrences of phonemic */a/, so-called epenthetic vowels (see *epenthesis theory* above) automatically do not count for such patterns. It is this fundamental distinction that renders the application of comparative linguistic methods feasible with Central Chadic languages, as first tentatively sketched out in Wolff (1983b).

For Proto-Central Chadic, therefore, vocalised roots are made up of only consonants and occurrences of */a/ in particular slots in the chain of segments, i.e. √ C C Ca, √ CaC Ca, √ C CaCa, √ CaCaCa, for instance. Not all potential slots for vowels between consonants of a root need to be filled by */a/; they may remain empty, even all of them, as is the case with the √ C C Ca root type (disregarding */a/ in final position for a moment, but see below). These slots are then often, but not always, filled by epenthetic vowels (see *epenthesis theory* above).

Therefore, two basic vocalisation patterns can be reconstructed as underlying and can be considered relevant for all historical reconstruction work in (Central) Chadic:

- *Ø-vocalisation*, when the root morpheme contains no phonemic vowel in non-final positions, i.e. the root is considered 'vowelless' (disregarding the word-final vowel for systemic reasons, since all roots are assumed to end in */a/ by default). This does not exclude the presence of one or more epenthetic vowels occurring between the consonants of the root. Such Ø-vocalised roots are symbolised by the root types √ C C Ca, √ C Ca.
- *A-vocalisation*, when at least one non-final syllable nucleus in the phonemic representation of the morpheme is filled by */a/. The a-vocalisation pattern is a priori assumed to be lexical in nature in PCC, i.e. it does not necessarily carry any overt morphological information.

    A-vocalisation may, however, be 'formative' and indeed carry overt morphological information, as is the case in individual present-day languages, such as found in pluralisation in both verbal and nominal morphology. One of the basic challenges for comparative Chadic phonology and morphology is to tell 'lexical' a-vocalisation from 'grammatical' a-vocalisation. Apparent synchronic grammatical a-vocalisation (also known as 'internal a' formations in Afroasiatic and Chadic scholarship) can be explained historically by different diachronic processes, which have nothing to do with each other: (i) by infixation of *{-a-} (as in cases of pluractional verb formations), (ii) by diagnostic changes of vowel patterns (as in cases of *internal* or *broken plural* formations of nominals), (iii) by *distant assimilation/umlaut* of medial vowels from suffixes carrying /a/, if not (iv) by what some authors would consider to be instances of *ablaut/apophony* whereby they may at times confuse grammatically conditioned changes (*infixation* and true *ablaut*) and phonologically conditioned changes (*assimilation, umlaut*). (For details of so-called 'internal a' formations in Chadic, see Newman 1990, 2006; and in particular Wolff 2009.)

A-vocalised roots can be symbolised by the root types √ CaCaCa, √ CaC Ca, √ C CaCa, and √ CaCa.

Characteristically, two features contribute to a relevant typology of roots: (a) number of radical consonants within the root, i.e. we distinguish mainly triradical, biradical and monoradical roots, and (b) vocalisation pattern in terms of how many and where in medial position of the root */a/ fills one or more slots (a-vocalisation), or none (Ø-vocalisation).

Somewhat outside the vocalisation pattern is the vowel in the absolute final position, at least in terms of our proposed PCC reconstructions. It would appear that all simple roots, whether reconstructable for PCC or obviously borrowed from neighbouring non-Chadic languages (here so-called 'pseudo-PCC' roots), must end in a lexical final vowel */a/ in diachronically underlying structures for systemic reasons. This 'lexical' final */a/ may, however, undergo deletion (*/a/ > Ø) or centralisation (*/a/ > [ə]) as the case may be on the level of individual language histories. We will, therefore, reconstruct PCC lexical items always with a lexical final */a/. This is also true for so-called Ø-vocalised roots, i.e. those in which final */a/ is the only occurrence of */a/ in the root. Therefore and for analytical clarity, we usually distinguish between 'medial' or 'non-final' and 'final' positions of */a/ in the vocalised root.

2.5.4   Prosody Theory

The *prosody theory* (short for the more precise *prosody-in-Central-Chadic theory*) allows us to describe and explain in a unified manner some highly irritating observations that characterise a fair number of Central Chadic languages:

- A multitude of phonetic surface vowels (see Wolff (2017) for a list of Chadic languages with vowel inventories, short and long, adding up to 17 vowels per language) can be reduced, in Central Chadic, to maximally two synchronically underlying phonemic vowels (often represented by the pair */ə/ : */a/), and in some languages to only one: */a/, or even none.
- Several vowels within a word stem tend to share most if not all phonological features – researchers speak of vowel 'harmonisation' (Wolff), even 'vowel harmony' (Gravina).

- 'Harmonisation' in terms of labialisation and/or palatalisation tends to affect not only vowels but also has effects on consonants, quite often on both at the same time.

All this together can best be ascribed to the effect of *prosodies*. Prosodies (also known in general linguistics as 'long components') may stretch over individual segments, segments belonging to the same syllable, across several syllables or across the phonological word – as the language-specific or word-specific case may be. In a way, prosodies may be described as phonological features that have the potential to 'float', in more or less regular or at times erratic ways, within words and phonological boundaries. The notion of 'prosody' allows for a unified description of all related phenomena of potentially 'long' phonological features (such as, for instance, palatalisation, labialisation, nasalisation, voicing, glottalisation, and possibly others), involving consonants or vowels or both in the same language. For instance and most conspicuously so in CC languages, phonetic mid vowels emerge from underlying /a/ under the effect of palatalisation (giving phonetic [e]) and labialisation (giving phonetic [o]), sometimes via intermediate diphthongs /ay/ and /aw/, whose sources may be actually or formerly present segments anywhere in the word. Under the effect of prosodies, epenthetic central vowels also receive their conditioned 'colouring', i.e. slight or complete fronting under palatalisation prosody ([ə] > [ɨ] or [i]), and slight or complete back-rounding under labialisation prosody ([ə] > [ʉ] or [u]). Likewise, 'plain' consonants may receive coarticulation features like palatalisation ($C > C^y$), labialisation ($C > C^w$), nasalisation ($C > {}^N C$), glottalisation ($C > C^?$) etc. under respective prosody effects, triggered by actually or formerly present segments anywhere in the word. Obviously, as we now have come to realise, such prosodies are essential typological features of Chadic languages and are presumably of great age in the family; they would appear to be particularly virulent, but not exclusively, in the Central Chadic branch of the family. For phonological and lexical reconstruction work in Central Chadic, therefore, it is essential to identify prosodies and their impact on segmental units and keep them analytically distinct from any 'plain' (in this study sometimes referred to as 'Ø-prosody') counterparts.

The term *prosody* as conveniently used in Chadic synchronic as much as diachronic linguistics serves as a morphophonological construct on a deep level, which – in historical perspective – has origins in the historical segmental structure of roots and words. Its ultimate diachronic sources may have been near and distant *assimilation* and *umlaut* phenomena stretching over potentially several segments and syllables, starting off from certain segments in the segmental chain of the word in the proto-language. These diachronic segments are reconstructable by methods of internal reconstruction and/or by comparative analysis between genealogically related languages. The source segments of prosodies may either be synchronically still present in the segmental chain of the word, or they may have been desegmentalised in the course of time, either completely (i.e. being segmentally reduced to zero and said to be simply 'lost' without trace; this will be symbolised by Ø) or partially (i.e. by losing their segmental properties but leaving behind traces of their former existence in terms of prosodies; this will be symbolised, for instance, by Ø^w and Ø^y). In the latter case, 'lost' segments can thus be conveniently reconstituted in the reconstructions from the presence of prosodies on the basis of internal reconstruction and/or the application of the comparative method.

Prosodies as we find them widely across Central Chadic languages tend to 'harmonise' the phonetic appearance of words, with regard to both synchronic vowels and consonants. In Central Chadic languages, they originate historically from segments that are reconstructable on the root level, but later may have been lost in the course of diachronic developments of the word in individual languages. They may leave traces of their former existence in the shape of prosodies, from which they can be 'reconstructed'. The source segments may either belong to the root in the narrow sense, i.e. what we call the simple root, or to an augmented root – depending on what serves as the reference structure that underlies the synchronic shape of the word. As a rule, W-prosody (labialisation) results from diachronic labial(ised) consonants (*/w/, */C^w/), and Y-prosody from segmental */y/. Both form part of either roots or the inventories of suffixal augments to roots; their segmental part is often lost and only leaves the prosody behind as a trace of its former presence. Hence we speak of 'desegmentalisation' and 'prosodification' of, for instance, *{-y} > ^{y}, and *{-k^w} > ^{w}. In some cases, however, the segmental part is still present, along with the simultaneous effects of the corresponding prosody. In such cases, we speak of partial desegmentalisation, e.g. *y > y^y ~ i^y and *k^w > w^w (~ u^w). The segmental survival of such sources of prosodies in some modern languages provides the comparative justification for reconstructing such sources even where they have become fully desegmentalised in other modern languages and must be considered completely 'lost'. (Such occasional survival prevents us from a *deus ex machina* automatism, by which we would invent any such sources ad hoc as we go along.) Prosodies in Central Chadic, therefore, may have reflexes in the shape of surface vowels, e.g. [i] and [u], or [ɨ] and [ʉ], or as C^y or C^w – depending on the individual language or the individual linguist and her/his transcription conventions. Note that very closely related languages within established language groups, including dialectal varieties of the same (named) languages, may differ with regard to the presence and/or manifestation of prosodies (see 4.6).

In terms of notational conventions, any localised source or effect of a prosody will be indicated by a raised symbol: ^{y} for palatalisation (Y-prosody),

58   Methodological Preliminaries

and ^{w} for labialisation (W-prosody). Raised ^{y} and ^{w} also indicate coarticulation with series of consonants, i.e. /C^y/ and /C^w/ respectively, which may serve as diachronic sources for the respective prosodies. Cf. the following examples.

In the example from Bata for the simple PCC root ***s(a)w(a)na** 'dream', root-augmental *{-y} syllabifies to surface as [i], while the accompanying Y-prosody palatalises the epenthetic vowel [ə] > [i] and the initial consonant of the root /s+^{y}/ > [ʃ]:

(33)	GROUP	Language	Prefixal augment	Simple root	Suffixal augment	FV	Prosody	Gloss
	BATA	Bata		√ C C Ca				dream
				*s w ra	-y		+Y	
				s Ø rØ	-i^y			
				s^{y}ə^{y}r	-i			
				ʃiri				

In Zina and for the simple PCC root ***ts(a)wa** 'cry, to', the root-augmental *{-y} is retained as approximant/glide in the onset of the second syllable. Radical C$_2$ /w/ creates W-prosody that affects the preceding epenthetic vowel [ə] > [u], while the accompanying Y-prosody stemming from *{-y} palatalises the initial consonant of the root /ts+^{y}/ > [tʃ]:

(34)	KOTOKO-SOUTH	Zina	√ C Ca				cry, to
			*ts w a	-y	a	+Y,+W	
			tsəw^{w}Ø	-y^y	a		
			ts^{y}ə^{w}wØ	-y	a		
			tʃuwya				

Prosodies have different scope and reach. They may affect vowels only or consonants only, be restricted to individual syllables of the word, or affect combinations of syllables, or operate across the whole word.

In the following examples, the prosody affects all vowels in the words whether lexical or epenthetic in nature:

(35)	HURZA	Vame		√ CaCa			butterfly
			RED	*pala	-y	+Y	
			pa^{y}l	pa^{y}la^y	-Ø^y		
				pelpele			
	GIDAR	Gidar		√ CaCa			butterfly
			ma-ta-RED	*pala	-k^w	+W	
			ma^w-ta^w-pa^{w}la^w	pa^{w}la^w	-Ø^w		
				motopolopolo			
	MAROUA	Mbazla		√ C Ca			dog
				*k ra	-y	+Y	
				kə^{y}ra^y	-Ø^y		
				kire			

2.5 Theoretical Modules in CC Lexical Reconstruction   59

In the following example from Mbudum, the prosody affects only epenthetic vowels within the root, but not the vowel of the prefixal augment:

(36)   DABA   Mbudum   √ C Ca   butterfly
                        ma-RED   *p la   -k^w +W
                        mə-pə^{w}l pə^{w}la   -Ø^w
                                    məpulpula

There are also examples with the prosody affecting only epenthetic vowels within prefixal augments, after deletion or centralisation of phonemic */a/ in the prefixal augment:

(37)   MAROUA Giziga-   √ C Ca   butterfly
                Muturwa ma-RED   *p la   -y   +Y
                         mə^y-pla- pla   -Ø^y
                                     miplapla

                Giziga-   √ C Ca   butterfly
                Muturwa ma-RED   *p la   -k^w +W
                         mə^w-pla- pla   -Ø^w
                                     muplapla

It remains, however, an occasional problem to distinguish a prosody effect originating deeper down in language history from rather shallow assimilation processes in phonetic surface representation. In the above cases of *ma-pl-pla > *məpulpula* and *ma-pla-pla > *miplapla* ~ *muplapla*, and if the overall importance of prosodies had not been established for Central Chadic as a whole, at least [u] could be derived from a natural assimilation effect by the labial feature of the preceding /m/ (*ma- > mə- > mu-) and /p/ (*pəl > pul), but still leaving the conditioning factor for [i] open, unless [i] was a default realisation of schwa (*ma- > mə- > mi-?). Questions like these, however, must be answered by thorough synchronic phonological analysis of individual languages in combination with dialectological approaches. But once languages are known (if not typologically notorious) for displaying effects of prosodies, as we can assume for most if not all Central Chadic languages as amply sketched out in this book, historical linguistic work has to take this into account with high analytical priority – even though occasionally 'old' prosodic effects of diachronic concern would be hard to tell from 'recent' plain cases of simple assimilations among adjacent segments of synchronic concern.

There is, however and a priori, no reason why the two different types of processes, i.e. prosodification and assimilation, should not co-occur in the same word in the same language. In the following examples for the verb 'to give birth', we are dealing with both instances of phonological Y-prosody (stemming from root-internal C_3 */y/), and assimilation of C_1 */w/ > [y] under the impact of */y/, which after (double) metathesis becomes adjacent to */w/.

For both Sukur and Bura, the database contains two slightly different surface forms: *yiiha ~ yi*, and *iya ~ yia*.

(38) 'give birth, to' PCC *(ma-) **w(a)x(a)ya** (-k^w, -n, -l; FV)

    SUKUR   Sukur   *w x ya   > w y xa > y^y w xa   > y^{y}yxa   > *yiiha*
                                                                                                     > yə^{y}yxa

Note: Root-internal original C$_3$ *y double-metathesises into C$_1$ position; it partially desegmentalises and prosodifies y > y^y, thereby creating Y-prosody; new C$_1$ /y/ assimilates adjacent C$_2$ /w/ > y; vowel epenthesis inserts ə between C$_1$ and C$_2$; Y-prosody 'colours' ə > i; C$_2$ y now in syllable-nucleus position syllabifies to yield i: yə^{y}y > yiy > *yii*.

                Sukur   *w x ya   > w y xa > y w xa   > yyxa   > *yi*
                                                                                                          > yyØØ

Note: Root-internal original C$_3$ *y double-metathesises into C$_1$ position; new C$_1$ /y/ assimilates adjacent C$_2$ /w/ > y; C$_3$ /x/+/a/ is deleted; y (< /w/) now in syllable-nucleus position syllabifies to yield i.

    MARGI   Bura   *w x ya   > w y xa > y w xa   > yyØa   > *iya*

Note: Root-internal original C$_3$ *y double-metathesises into C$_1$ position; new C$_1$ /y/ assimilates adjacent C$_2$ /w/ > y; C$_3$ */x/ is deleted; new C$_1$ y now in syllable-nucleus position syllabifies to yield i.

                Bura   *w x ya   > w y xa > y w xa   > yyØa   > *yia*

Note: Root-internal original C$_3$ *y double-metathesises into C$_1$ position; new C$_1$ /y/ assimilates adjacent C$_2$ /w/ > y; C$_3$ */x/ is deleted; C$_2$ y (< w) now in syllable-nucleus position syllabifies to yield i.

Note that it would appear to be language specific whether, for instance, Y-prosody affects all vowel types in the word, or only phonemic /a/, or only epenthetic schwa, and whether it would also affect consonants, and in which positions. Therefore, no wider generalisations are being attempted here to identify domains of prosodies on the level of PCC. This would be a matter of individual grammatical descriptions, if not individual words in a given language.

Note also that prosodies in Central Chadic languages tend to work, almost as a rule, from right to left, i.e. their 'colouring' or 'harmonising' impact operates mainly by *anticipation*. There are, however, a few cases in our reconstructions, quite rare if not exceptional, in which prosodies also operate by *spreading* when affecting phonological material, i.e. from left to right.

The present study accepts the methodological primacy of phonology-triggered prosodies over morphology-triggered prosodies (see 3.2.2). Justification for this is that, whenever we need to account for the appearance

2.5 Theoretical Modules in CC Lexical Reconstruction 61

of prosodies, our internal reconstructions (see 2.3) of abstract underlying synchronic as much as diachronic structures may lead us to hypothetically postulate (in historical-linguistic terms: 'reconstruct') morphological markers as part of the root-augmental material (see 3.1.2) that we assume to be sources of palatalisation (*{-y}) or labialisation (*{-k^w}), but which may have been lost in the course of the history of modern Chadic languages. Here we would speak of *morphology*-triggered (or grammatical) prosodies. This, of course, has the characteristics of a *deus ex machina* that we could evoke at any occasion as we go along, as plausible as the assumption of the existence of such suffixal elements is for the diachronic history of Chadic languages in general. On the other hand, certain reconstructed roots already contain potential sources of prosodies, namely */y/ for palatalisation prosody, and all labialised *C^w and */w/ for labialisation prosody. Prosodies originating from these root-internal segments we refer to as sources of *phonology*-triggered (or lexical) prosodies. For methodological reasons of transparency, therefore, we give primacy to phonological prosodies: wherever */y/, */w/ or */C^w/ are contained in the reconstructed simple root, we take these to be the sources of prosodies, when they occur. Only in the absence of the former, or for other good reasons, shall we 'reconstruct' diachronic morphological prosodies, i.e. assume suffixal *{-y} and/or *{-k^w} as synchronically petrified root-augmental material.

Note that by this principle-guided procedure, we may miss out on the potential occurrence of both types of prosodies in the same word. This, however, would have no bearing on 'explaining' surface forms in present-day language that show reflexes of a prosody. Note further that the same prosodies do not accumulate, i.e. there are no traces of 'double' Y- or W-prosody. Note also, however, that different prosodies (i.e. Y+W-prosodies) may combine even on the same segments; such occurrences will be symbolised as X^{wy}.

A note on nasalisation prosody in Central Chadic
The present study focuses on palatalisation and labialisation prosodies, which are the most frequent and salient prosodies for understanding both modern Central Chadic language phonologies and the historical development of the Central Chadic lexicon from the proto-language (PCC). These, however, may not be the only prosodies that play a role, as was pointed out very early for the synchronic description of individual languages, such as, for instance, Higi (Hoffmann 1965; Mohrlang 1971, 1972). Other candidates for prosodies that have been debated in Chadic linguistics are prenasalisation, possibly voicing and, occasionally, informal mention has been made of glottalisation (see 6.3.6). The present study will not discuss these in any detail for the simple reason that

potential reflexes of such prosodies are too few in the selected data to merit separate treatment in this volume, and they would have no meaningful implication for the analysis of surface vowels and their underlying segments that this study focuses on. But we note here, for the sake of completeness, some fairly transparent instances of prenasalisation of (initial or final) root consonants stemming from both prefixal and suffixal nasals. Some suffixal nasals take part in metathesis, prefixal nasals appear not to; they do, however, occasionally surface phonetically as prenasalisation feature accompanying radical consonants. Our somewhat erratic treatment of prenasalisation in this study may, therefore, not reflect the true historical nature of the development. See, nonetheless, the following list of candidates for (pre)nasalisation prosody culled from our reconstructions (Table 2.3); we have adapted the transcriptions for this purpose to a (pre-) nasalisation prosody approach, indicating the source by capital N and the effect by raised $^n \sim ^ŋ$, purposefully disregarding explicit indication of other prosodies that may be operating on the same word. As for glottalisation as a potential candidate for prosody in Central Chadic, see the discussion under 6.3.6. For detailed treatment of these prosodies see Wolff (forthcoming).

2.5.5 *Prosodies as Traces of Diachronically Lost Segments*

One of the strategic principles in our reconstruction of PCC lexical items is the 'recovery' of diachronically lost segments through their traces in the shape of prosodies, i.e. either palatalisation or labialisation. These segments may have belonged to the simple root (see 3.1.2), we then speak of phonological prosodies. Or, the segments may have belonged originally to the PCC grammatical system and later fused with simple roots to form so-called augmented roots (see 3.1.2), hence we speak of their 'petrification' and of morphological prosodies. (The distinction between phonological and morphological prosodies and the recognition of its relevance for Chadic linguistics goes back to Schuh (2002), see also Wolff (2019b) and 3.2.3 below.) Methodologically, we follow a two-step approach.

Step 1: In the presence of prosodies such as palatalisation (Y-prosody) and labialisation (W-prosody), we first look for potential sources of such prosodies among the segments making up the simple root. Given our assumptions about the PCC consonant and vocoid inventory, candidates would be root-internal */y/ (or *[y] as allophone of another radical consonant, e.g. */ɗ/ > [y]) for palatalisation prosody and */w/ and any labialised consonant */C^w/ for labialisation prosody. In cases where we find such root-internal segments, we will treat the prosodies as being phonological (or lexical) in nature and relate them diachronically to these segments. Occasionally, however, these segments have been lost in some individual modern languages, while they are still present in

2.5 Theoretical Modules in CC Lexical Reconstruction   63

Table 2.3 *Prenasalisation as prosody?*

Gloss	PCC simple root	GROUP	language	underlying	surface
beard	*gʷma	GIDAR	Gidar	a-N-ga-Øma-y	$a^n geme$
beer	*v(a)xʷa	BATA	Gude	N-vwa	$ə^n vʷa$
bite, to	*dza	MAFA	Mafa	N-dza-y	$^n dʒe$
		MANDARA	Podoko	N-dza-y-kʷa	$^n dʒewe$
			Dghweɗe	N-dza-xa	$^n dzaxa$
bone	*ɗy(a)ɬa	KOTOKO-NORTH	Afade, Malgbe	a-N-ØyɬØ > a-N-ɬy	$e^n ɬi$
			Mpade	a-N-ØysØ > a-N-sy	$e^n ʃi$
		KOTOKO-CENTRAL	Mser	a-N-ØysØ > a-N-sy	$e^n ʃi$
brain	*r(a)ɬa	MOFU	Ouldeme	a-N-daɬØ-y	$a^n deɬ$
			Muyang	a-N-dɬØ-y	$a^n diɬ$
camel	*k(a)l(a)g(a)m(a)w(a)	LAMANG	Hdi	N-galØbwa-y	$^n galibwa$
five	*xʷt(a)fa	MARGI	Bura	N-wtfØ > Ntfw	$^n tufu$
		HIGI	Nkafa	N-wtsfa-y > Ntswfa-y	$^n tʃufə$
			Kirya	N-Øtsfa-y	$^n tʃifə$
fly (noun)	*dz(a)kʷ(a)ɗa	MANDARA	Podoko	N-dzwayØ	$^n dʒəwe$
			Mandara	N-dzawØa-N	$^n dza^n wa$
			Glavda	N-dzwya	$^n dzuya$
foot	*sa	KOTOKO-NORTH	Afade	a-N-tsØ-y	$e^n tsi$
			Mpade	a-N-sØ-y	$e^n si$
moon	*t(a)ra	DABA	Mbudum	N-tra	$^n təra$
		TERA	Hwana	N-dra-y	$^n dre$
night	*r(a)v(a)ɗa	KOTOKO-CENTRAL	Lagwan, Mser	N-Øvaɗa-y	$^n vaɗe$
spit, to	*t(a)fa	MAFA	Mafa	N-dzfØ-y	$^n dʒif$
		HIGI	Kamwe	N-tfØ-y	$^n tivi$
			Kirya	N-tfa	$^n təfə$
suck, to	*s(a)wɓa	KOTOKO-CENTRAL	Mser	N-s'fa-y	$^n s'afɨ$

others. This is where multilateral comparison will assist internal reconstruction. We can illustrate this below, for instance, with the KOTOKO-NORTH language Mpade regarding the emergence of W-prosody, whose effect is to change underlying final /a/ to surface [o]. Compare our PCC reconstruction (containing two C^w-type consonants in the simple root in C_1 and C_3 positions, namely $*x^w$ and $*k^w$) and the MANDARA group language Matal, in which the likely source still surfaces as C_3 /w/. In Mpade, C_3 is diachronically lost, but its labialisation feature $Ø^w$ is still present and affects the preceding vowel /a/ with the effect of its being phonetically realised as word-final [o]:

(39)

PCC simple root Root type √ CaCaCa	MANDARA Matal	KOTOKO-NORTH Mpade			Gloss
$*x^w ayak^w a$	$*xayawØ > hayaw$	$*xayawØ > xayaØ^w$	$> hayo$		grasshopper
		$*gayawØ > gayaØ^w$	$> gayo$		

Step 2: Only when there is no source to be identified for phonological (lexical) prosodies will we assume morphological prosody to be the source, i.e. we will tentatively 'reconstruct' the hypothetical presence of a former morphological element that we consider to be the source of the prosody. Candidates for such prosodies are $*\{-y\}$ for Y-prosody (palatalisation), and $*\{-k^w\}$ for W-prosody (labialisation). For both we assume partly parallel historical developments, which allow for different phonetic surface representations as listed in Table 2.4.

Such reconstruction will take place independent of whether there is comparative evidence from other languages to the segmental presence of the source

Table 2.4 *From segments to prosodies*

	$*\{-y\}$	$*\{-k^w\}$
Partial desegmentalisation ('weakening', without prosody effect)	—	$>w$
Partial desegmentalisation ('weakening', with prosody effect)	—	$> w^w$
Syllabification (without prosody effect)	$> i$	$> u$
Syllabification (with prosody effect)	$> i^y$	$> u^w$
Complete desegmentalisation and prosodification	$> Ø^y$	$> Ø^w$
Deletion (without prosody effect)	$Ø$	$Ø$

2.6 Confronting Alternative Approaches

in any of the languages for the lexical item under reconstruction. Given, however, the wide coverage of Central Chadic languages in the database (Gravina 2014b), such segmental presence can be quite often found in at least one of the other languages.

2.6 Confronting Alternative Approaches

As a follow-up on previous and critically reviewed research, Gravina's (2014a) study provides highly valuable input to the ongoing discussion with regard to lexical reconstructions in Proto-(Central) Chadic involving consonants and both vowels and prosodies. His groundbreaking study has stimulated the work behind the present book. Without access to Gravina's (2014b) rich database, it would not have been possible to undertake this study.

The work presented here is meant to provide alternative reconstructions to those proposed by Gravina, not in order to falsify his reconstructions, but in order to illustrate the analytical power inherent in different methodological and theoretical approaches. The present study is based on a complex 'multi-module' approach, which rests on different theoretical and typological assumptions, which the present author has found useful and has been following during his comparative research on certain Central Chadic languages over the last 40 years. Not surprisingly, and based on the different theoretical and typological assumptions, some of which tap into the common history of all Afroasiatic languages, the present study yields more or less divergent results from those presented by Gravina and from any previous research by other authors.

Central to the present study is the diachronic analysis and description of the vocalic domain in Proto-Central Chadic. Our study allows us to draw a coherent and transparent picture of Central Chadic diachronic developments from PCC reconstructions to individual modern Central Chadic languages. It allows for comprehensive generalisations on phonological units and processes, and it dissolves the enigmatic relationship between synchronic phonological systems of individual languages that each may display large sets of phonetic surface vowels.[14] These many phonetic surface vowels do not enter 1:1 correspondence sets among each other but relate unequivocally to various sources, namely PCC reconstructed */a/, so-called weak radicals (see 4.4 below), and the principles of vowel pro- and epenthesis (see 4.1 below). Given that the comparative method has its limits when it is applied in a straightforward fashion to the Central Chadic situation, additional theoretical

---

[14] See Wolff (2017: 31–32) for a list of 'vowel inventories in selected Chadic languages' illustrating the wide range of variation across Chadic, with synchronic inventories between 1 (e.g. Central Chadic Moloko) and 17 (e.g. East Chadic Tumak) vowels.

and methodological tools are required and the classic comparative method of the Neogrammarian School needs to be refined. Following this necessity, Gravina (2014a) made additional use of the prosody approach, which meanwhile can be considered well established in Central Chadic linguistics. Put in an over-simplistic way, for Gravina's reconstructions, Y-prosody comes in when the comparative method doesn't really work. Nonetheless, his study yields an interesting and illuminating way forward to the reconstruction of PCC lexical items, but it leaves a number of questions open and provokes some methodological criticism.

Our own approach differs from Gravina's with regard to a number of central assumptions. Like Gravina (who followed earlier insights like, for instance, those put forward by Wolff (1983b)), we do not take the phonetic surface representations as reflected in the transcriptions of the data by field linguists as a starting point, but – by establishing abstract underlying phonological structures and by using the method of internal reconstruction – first of all submit all data to some kind of pre-processing. Unlike Gravina, however, we start by looking at the effects of prosodies first, i.e. by 'undoing' potentially prosody-triggered sound changes. To cut a longish story short: after highly abstract phonological analysis and application of the method of internal reconstruction, we arrive at 'reconstructions' of lexical items involving consonants (among them labialised velars */C^w/, but no palatalised ones ^{x}/C^y/), plus only one reconstructed vowel phoneme */a/, plus instances of syllabification of the weak radicals */y/ and */w/. Also at variance with Gravina's approach, who singles out and 'reconstructs' Y-prosody as a phonological unit for PCC while attributing a different history to the emergence of W-prosody (Gravina 2014a: 293), we treat palatalisation and labialisation prosodies on equal terms and in a parallel fashion. Our approach is based on a strict application of the prosody approach first, i.e. before we look at phonological units to compare across languages under the comparative method. While Gravina accepts schwa as phonemic, we rather allow for principles of pro- and epenthetic schwa insertion to apply for the creation of syllable structures of phonetic surface representations. Not surprisingly, by applying these techniques (that we call the 'strict prosody-based approach') we arrive at alternative reconstructions that occasionally may look quite different from those suggested by Gravina or any previous researchers.

While Gravina (2014a) reconstructs three vowels (*/a/, */ə/, */i/) plus Y-prosody (*/^{y}/) as four distinct phonemic units in the vocalic domain, our alternative reconstructions are based on just one phonemic vowel (*/a/). Further, we do not accept Y-prosody as a phonemic unit, but treat it as a phonological feature and process historically linked to a parallel existing reconstructed segment, namely *y, whose former or current presence allows for Y-prosody to occur and begin to 'float'. Likewise, W-prosody is linked to labial(ised) segments that are postulated on independent grounds. Further, Gravina's reconstructions are based on a rather ad hoc hypothesis that cannot be justified from received knowledge about the typology or genealogy of Chadic/Afroasiatic languages in general, namely that PCC served the regime of a rigid syllable-structure constraint of the shape CV.CV.CV. Our own study is based on the assumption of the relevance of the so-called root-and-pattern structure for PCC as inherited from Afroasiatic linguistic ancestry and for which only the presence or absence of */a/ in inter-consonantal 'slots' counts in establishing vocalisation patterns, i.e. the so-called root types in the present book.

The confrontation of the two hitherto most comprehensive comparative approaches to Central Chadic should provide interesting and challenging questions for future investigations into more general comparative Chadic linguistics, if not – in a still wider sense – into comparative Afroasiatic linguistics.

The major points of confrontation regarding Gravina's (2014a) and the present study can, therefore, be summarised as follows.

1. Treatment of schwa

At variance with Gravina's approach, our decision to treat schwa as principally pro- and epenthetic in nature is based on the observation that in most cases, where it occurs, schwa is predictable by the phonological environment and need not be postulated as a separate phoneme. Generally, it would appear to be the simpler, i.e. the more economical, solution to predict its occurrence on a general principle rather than describing the language-specific rules for its deletion after it had been reconstructed by default in a position within a regular CV.CV.CV sequence, and only to be immediately deleted again. This essentially diachronic perspective does not exclude the validity of analysing schwa as a phonemic vowel in synchronic descriptions of present-day languages.

2. Number of diachronic and/or underlying vowel phonemes

With schwa being identified in diachronic perspective as a pro- and epenthetic vowel, the present study is based on the assumption of just one underlying diachronic vowel phoneme */a/. Again, this is the simpler, i.e. more economical, option compared to postulating at least two distinct vowel phonemes, namely */a/ and */ə/, as has been assumed by various authors in the past, not to speak of postulating three distinct vowel phonemes */a/, */ə/ and */i/ (plus distinctive Y-prosody) as in Gravina (2014a) or, as Newman (2006: 193) suggests as likely for Central Chadic, a four-vowel-system with *a, *ə, *i and *u.

3. Diachronic root-and-pattern structure

At variance with the approach proposed by Gravina (2014a), in this study we do not propose a rigid systemic sequence of consonant and vowel slots on the most abstract synchronic (and diachronic) phonological levels, like /CV.CV.CV/, in which the vowel slots (indicated by V) must be filled by any reconstructed vowel phoneme. Our alternative approach works with the hypothesis of root-and-pattern typology in Central Chadic, which is well motivated by received wisdom and overwhelming evidence from Afroasiatic typology and genealogy (cf., for instance, Frajzyngier & Shay 2012; Meyer & Wolff 2019). Accordingly, we propose as basic the notion of root type, such as, for instance, $\sqrt{C\,C\,Ca}$, $\sqrt{CaC\,Ca}$, $\sqrt{C\,CaCa}$, $\sqrt{CaCaCa}$, etc. Based on the input by root type, the remaining potential slots for schwa-epenthesis become apparent, which, however, may be filled or not by a process referred to as vowel epenthesis (see 2.5.1). Therefore, the most explicit of our alternative reconstructions for PCC as presented in this study will indicate the reconstructed root type, both in terms of numbers of consonants, vowel slots (either filled by /a/ or left empty for potential insertion of epenthetic vowels), and potential left or right augments that may have petrified in individual synchronic languages (see 3.1.2).

4. Simple vs. augmented roots

Most previous approaches were only concerned with what we here call 'simple' roots (see the relevant distinction between 'simple' and 'augmented' roots; 3.1.2), while the present study takes into account the full forms of the words in the database (and thereby includes reconstructed sources of prosodies from beyond the simple root, which nevertheless form part of the transcribed 'word' as a whole). This means that our study works with both simple and augmented roots as equally valid starting points for lexical reconstruction. One of the major analytical decisions to take is to identify what is part of the most simple root shape, and what to consider 'root-augmental' material. Therefore, when confronting our own with Gravina's reconstructions, even the forms of the simple root may differ, as the examples in Table 2.5 show.

5. Conflated representations of roots

Our reconstructions present conflated representations with medial phonemic */a/ given in parentheses, for the reason that individual languages – retrospectively – are free in the choice of root type that they use as underlying structure. In more explicit terms, the reconstructions in Table 2.5 provide choices in terms of root types (Table 2.6).

Not all theoretically possible root types are necessarily made use of in every case, as the data suggest. Therefore, we make the underlying root type transparent

2.6 Confronting Alternative Approaches

Table 2.5 *Alternative reconstructions of diachronic 'root'*

	Gravina (2014b)	Present study
'earth'	*hʷaɗik	*(a-, ya-, RED-) **xʷ(a)yɗa** (-y, -k; FV)
'grasshopper'	*haɗikʷ	*(a-) **xʷ(a)y(a)kʷa** (-ɗ, -ŋ ?)
'thorn'	*haɗik	*(a-, xa-, ma-, va-) **ɗ(a)yka** (-t, -y)
'night'	*viɗ	*(a-, x-, m/n-, sa-, ta-) **r(a)v(a)ɗa** (-a, -y, -k, -kʷ, -n, -ŋ; FV)

Table 2.6 *Conflated representations and dissolution of root types*

		ROOT TYPE			
		√ C C Ca	√ C CaCa	√ CaC Ca	√ CaCaCa
'grasshopper'	*xʷ(a)y(a)kʷa	xʷykʷa	xʷyakʷa	xʷaykʷa	xʷayakʷa
'night'	*r(a)v(a)ɗa	rvɗa	rvaɗa	ravɗa	ravaɗa

Table 2.7 *Choice of root types*

		√ C C Ca	√ C CaCa	√ CaC Ca	√ CaCaCa
'earth'	*xʷ(a)yɗa	*xʷyɗa	—	*xʷayɗa	—
'thorn'	*ɗ(a)yka	*ɗyka	—	*ɗayka	—

throughout much of the present study. For some items selected from the database, for instance, only two root types are reflected in the modern Central Chadic languages where the root occurs (Table 2.7).

6. Consonants

As regards the reconstruction of consonants and related sound changes and correspondences between languages, in this volume we largely follow Gravina (2014a) unless we assume that there is good reason not to do so. With only few and noted exceptions, none of his reconstructions and assumptions concerning consonants are discussed in this study. The exceptions concern the full inventory of PCC consonants (3.2.1), including the phonological status of */f/. In addition, in our own PCC reconstructions we have replaced *h and *hʷ by the more appropriate *fricative* symbols *x and *xʷ. Consonants will be treated in detail in a follow-up publication (Wolff, forthcoming).

7. Application of the comparative method

With regard to the application of the comparative method to arrive at PCC reconstructions of lexicon, there is another methodological difference between the approach chosen by Gravina (2014a) and the present study. Gravina takes the methodologically perfectly justified path via intermediate group-level reconstructions:

> the reconstructions are made based on at least two layers of history. Reconstructions are made for each group within Central Chadic, and then these are used to reconstruct the form for Proto-Central Chadic. In some cases, it is possible also to reconstruct forms for the proto-languages of sub-groups within a group, or of the proto-language of a major group that was ancestral to a number of groups. (Gravina 2014a: 6)

The present study omits the intermediate steps of group-level reconstructions. We derive our alternative PCC forms from a simultaneous comparison of all internally reconstructed underlying forms directly from the individual languages. This procedure is akin to the method of so-called *multilateral* (or 'mass') comparison. We thereby avoid unwanted interference into our reconstructions from a priori existing ideas about language groupings based on some pre-conceptualised sub-classification.

2.6.1 The Notion of 'Prosody-Type Languages' in Central Chadic

One of Gravina's (2014a) creative and challenging insights concerned his 'typology of Central Chadic phonologies' in terms of classifying language groups by *prosody type*. He distinguishes (2014a: 87) the following:

> *Vowel prosody languages:* 'where their primary characteristic is the presence of vowel harmony caused by prosodic features of palatalisation or labialisation'.
> *Consonant prosody languages:* 'These languages are characterised by complex systems of labialised and palatalised consonants.'
> *Mixed prosody languages:* 'where elements of vowel prosody and consonant prosody have combined'.
> *Kotoko languages (or no-prosody type languages):* 'whose phonological system doesn't fit any of the other systems'.

Interestingly yet not surprisingly, the prosody type relates in significant ways to areal/geographic distribution and linguistic subgroupings. This typology of phonological systems has been made basic to Gravina's study by providing a framework through which he approaches the reconstruction of vowels, consonants and prosodies for PCC.

2.6 Confronting Alternative Approaches   71

Our present study does not take this typology as a framework or guideline, but rather considers it an interesting and illuminating case of areal distribution of typological features within Central Chadic. It tends to strengthen our hypothesis that quite a few neighbouring Central Chadic languages have been engaged in inter-dialectal borrowing over long periods of time.

Favouring a more general alternative approach, our concept of prosody is much wider and would not allow such neat typology to be used as a starting point of analysis. Accepting prosodies as essential features in Central Chadic languages and for adequate linguistic analysis and description from both diachronic and synchronic perspectives, we subject all potential prosodic processes to a *unified prosodic analysis*. Once the relevance of prosodies has been established for a particular language, we will note but not accept 'classic' assimilation of adjacent segments or across minimal distance as being something different from prosodic effects, but consider them to be just more localised prosody effects. (With some data, therefore, we may be guilty of under-analysis, if local surface assimilations were to be considered more pertinent than the overall pattern of palatalisation and labialisation prosodies that we have established over all Central Chadic languages under research.)

2.6.2   The Vocalic Domain in Central Chadic: What to Reconstruct and How Many?

Our major departure from Gravina's (2014a) reconstructed PCC phonology concerns the vocalic domain – usually referred to in synchronic language descriptions as 'vowel system' – in Proto-Central Chadic. Gravina justifiably accepts schwa as a phonemic vowel in PCC and reconstructs a total of three vowel phonemes */a/, */i/ and */ə/ (note again that Gravina in his work prefers to represent the non-low central vowel schwa by the symbol */ɨ/) plus Y-prosody as a separate phonemic unit also operating in the vocalic domain and used as such in the PCC reconstructions. In those languages that synchronically have only two underlying vowels, namely /a/ and /ə/, he assumes diachronic merger of */i/ with */ə/, yielding synchronic two-vowel systems. For other languages, he assumes the surface mid-vowel [e] to represent PCC */i/, where the present study reconstructs */a/ to be represented by the surface allophone [e] under the palatalisation prosody effect.

A major difference in the two approaches lies in the adoption of the Vocalisation theory (2.5.3). Gravina does not take into account the systematics of vocalisation patterns that rest on the assumption of an overall root-and-pattern analysis of (Central) Chadic languages. As we will maintain and illustrate throughout this study, we consider it essential to know which diachronic root type we are dealing with, i.e. where – for each single language ancestor – reconstructed */a/ filled which position in the vocalised root, and which other slots remained to be filled or not to be filled by epenthetic schwa. With only one phonemic vowel available in PCC that contrasts only with its own absence rather than with other vowel phonemes, we can no longer speak of PCC having had a 'vowel system' in the usual sense of this notion. Therefore, we prefer to speak of a subsystem of 'vocoids' within the phonological inventory.

Still within the domain of vocalic representations and at variance with Gravina, we have introduced the Weak radical theory (2.5.2) into historical Chadic linguistic reconstructions. This means that the vocoids */y/ and */w/ are considered ambivalent or underspecified as regards the feature [±syllabic]. According to this theoretical approach, which is typologically and genetically justified from general Afroasiatic linguistic typology, [+high] phonetic surface vowels [i] and [u] may in certain cases represent underlying and diachronic */y/ and */w/. This typological feature, likely inherited from Proto-Afroasiatic, does not figure in Gravina's reconstructions. Therefore, we do not reconstruct separate */i/ and */u/ in addition to */y/ and */w/.[15] Note, however, that surface transcriptions of [i] and [u] may also represent variants of epenthetic schwa under prosody effects, depending on the transcription conventions used by individual field linguists.[16] Not keeping surface [i] < */y/ distinct from the 'i-coloured' representation of epenthetic schwa will necessarily lead to some confusion in the reconstruction work. The same will happen when we do not keep surface [u] < */w/ distinct from the 'u-coloured' representation of epenthetic schwa. Reconstructing the underlying root type, however, should tell us exactly what we are dealing with, because the reconstructed root type will automatically identify any diachronic (and often synchronically underlying) */w/ and */y/ (see 6.4).

As has already been pointed out, our approach is also based on the Epenthesis theory module (2.5.1), which does not accept schwa to be a phonemic vowel, neither diachronically in PCC nor synchronically in many present-day Central Chadic languages. This does not mean that in synchronic descriptions of modern Central Chadic languages schwa should never be

---

[15] In this context it may be interesting to note, as P. Newman (p.c. 2020) reminded me, that August Klingenheben (1886–1967), an excellent researcher in African linguistics with a solid background in Semitic linguistics, for his article on *Die Silbenauslautgesetze des Hausa* (1927/28), chose to represent y and w in West Chadic Hausa by using the vowel symbols i and u plus a diacritic, namely as i̯ and u̯. He may have had his reasons. His seminal study later became widely known as 'Klingenheben's Law' (see Newman 2004).

[16] Using 'broad' rather than 'narrow' transcription conventions, and in the case of phonologically non-contrasting [ɨ~i], [ɛ~e], [ɔ~o], [ʉ~u], field linguists may feel inclined to choose the common and simpler typewriter graphic symbols i, e, o, u rather than the more complicated IPA symbols ɨ, ɛ, ɔ, ʉ for their transcriptions, not to speak of practical considerations in terms of orthography creation, which was very much in the interest of missionary linguists in order to provide Bible translations and Christian scripture in the so-called vernaculars.

2.6 Confronting Alternative Approaches 73

considered to be phonemic; in some modern languages this may indeed be the superior approach in order to simplify the phonological descriptions. As we will point out in section 4.7, we assume that the system reconstructed for PCC has undergone considerable changes in the history of individual languages and language groups, including the phonemicisation of vowels which, in the PCC system, were just conditioned allophones or variants of other reconstructed segments. Hence and for the purpose of this study, Gravina's assumptions concerning a vowel-system sub-type with two vowels */a/ and */ə/ is not shared. We assume just one phonemic vowel to operate in PCC, namely */a/ and account for the emergence of other surface vowels by reference to conditioned allophones of */a/ (namely [e~ɛ] and [o~ɔ]), vowel pro- and epenthesis (namely [i~i] and [ʉ~u]) – depending on transcription conventions used – and syllabification of the two other underlying vocoids in the system besides */a/, namely */y/ and */w/ when syllabified to yield [i] and [u] in syllable-nucleus positions. This approach allows us to relate a minimum of eight vowel qualities, namely [a, e, o, ə, i, ʉ, i, u] (plus occasionally even more, like IPA [ɐ, ɪ, ʊ, ɛ, ɔ, œ, æ, ɣ] in narrow phonetic transcriptions) to (a) three underlying vocoids (*a, *y, *w), including just one underlying 'true' phonemic vowel, namely */a/, and (b) the processes of 'colouring' pro- and epenthetic, i.e. non-phonemic schwa.

Gravina reconstructs Y-prosody as a phonological unit on a par with his three reconstructed vowels, so that reconstructions will need to identify Y-prosody as a reconstructable feature indicated by superscript ^{y}, e.g. in Gravina's transcription conventions ***hwitsin** ^{y} 'nose', ***sihwani** ^{y} 'dream' etc. This, one might argue, constitutes a somewhat counter-intuitive system of four phonologically relevant units in the vocalic domain, namely */a/, */i/, */ə/, and */^{y}/, with a suspicious phonetic clustering of these vocalic units in the upper front section of the vocalic space (and opposing the clustering of back-round units that are associated with a whole series of labialised velar consonants).

None of these potentially controversial issues emerge under our present approach, in which Y- and W-prosodies are not reconstructed as phonemic units but as phonological processes, which originate as 'long components' from given segmental phonemes in the proto-language. Underlying */y/ is the source of Y-prosody, and underlying */w/ or any labialised consonant */C^w/ is a potential source for W-prosody (see 2.5.4 for Prosody theory).

Another irritation concerning descriptions of the vocalic domain in Central Chadic lies with quantitative facts. As Gravina (2014a: 354) reports, the three vowels reconstructed by him for PCC have a surprisingly different frequency of occurrence: *ə (= *i in Gravina's transcription) 'is the most common of vowels (64%), followed by *a (27%) and *i (9%)'. This highly disparate distribution of vowels, however, goes well with our alternative assumption, namely that schwa is epenthetic in nature with practically ubiquitous distribution, that */a/ is the most stable yet less common – because the only phonemic – vowel in a system that widely respects inherited root types (see 3.1.1) in terms of vocalisation patterns, and that occurrences of [i] can and must be explained by reference to processes stemming from outside the 'narrow vowel system', namely being either a conditioned allophone of /y/ in syllable-nucleus position, or a conditioned high-front 'i-coloured' variant of epenthetic schwa.

Summing up: our reconstructions confirm the a priori held assumption, which is based on many years of comparative research, that PCC phonology operated without a true 'vowel system' in the sense of an inventory of several contrastive and independently motivated vowel phonemes. Rather, the 'vocalic domain' of the proto-language was inhabited by what we here call phonemic vocoids and epenthetic schwa. The reconstructed phonemic vocoids were */a/, */y/ and */w/, together allowing for [+syllabic] manifestations as [a], [i] and [u]. (This compares well to Newman's (2006) assumptions about Proto-Chadic, but also with certain hypotheses held about Berber, early Egyptian, and Semitic.) */a/ allowed 'colouring' by prosodic impact to yield phonetic [ɛ~e] and [ɔ~o], and occasionally [œ]. Pro- and epenthetic schwa was phonetically realised (and/or transcribed) as [ə, ɨ, ɪ, ʉ, ʊ] but also [i, u] and sometimes [ɐ, a] and IPA [ɣ] (although not in the data selected for this study). All phonetic surface 'colourings' can be related in a regular manner to the effect of two highly frequent prosodies, namely Y-prosody (palatalisation) and W-prosody (labialisation).

2.6.3 The Present Study

In the present study, we are solely concerned with issues related to vowels and prosodies. Suprasegmental features of stress, pitch and tone are not considered for reconstruction largely due to the lack of sufficient data and robust analyses concerning suprasegmental phonology for most of the languages contained in the database. Rare cases of consonant and vowel length are addressed where they occur, because they may actually 'hide' a so-called weak radical or come about as a result of a non-transparent diachronic process. The ultimate purpose of this study is to provide reconstructions that are based on linguistically sound but alternative approaches as compared to Gravina (2014a, 2014b), from which readers and researchers can draw their own conclusions and stimuli for further studies targeting the fascinating and diverse history of the Central Chadic languages.

Summarising our main concerns and goals in this study, we arrive at the following agenda:

1. Provide conclusive reconstructions with regard to the phonological units that underlie the various synchronic vowel systems in Central Chadic languages.

2. Identify the deepest historically reconstructed *root type* in terms of vocalisation pattern, i.e. regarding the occurrence and distribution of */a/ in the most basic *root-and-pattern* representation.
3. Describe the diachronic processes that govern the language-specific effects of *Y-* and *W-prosodies* on both syllabic and non-syllabic segments.
4. Provide structural analyses of simple and augmented roots by identifying morphological augmentation material that has fused with the *simple root* and created *augmented roots* by petrification.
5. Illuminate (based on the method of internal reconstruction) ideally all diachronic processes that have affected the abstract underlying structures, which provide the connecting link between the phonetic surface representations and our reconstructed PCC roots (or 'pseudo'-roots in the case of fully integrated loans from other languages).

We thereby wish to progress beyond what Gravina was able to do in his groundbreaking study, who states that

[a]t this stage, reconstructions are fairly tentative, since very little is known about sound changes affecting vowels that have taken place in the history of Central Chadic. (Gravina 2014a: 333)

The present study aims at providing exactly these, namely the descriptions of 'sound changes affecting vowels that have taken place in the history of Central Chadic' under the proviso, however, that no 1:1 series of regular sound changes for surface vowels – comparable to, for instance, the situation in Indo-European languages – can be established due to the different phonological nature of diachronic sources for synchronic vowels and the regime of prosodies. We maintain, however, that, with the present study available, any synchronic surface vowel in any modern Central Chadic language can be attributed its linguistic history by systematically relating it to PCC lexical reconstructions that rest on what is here called the 'strict prosody-based approach'.

For a comprehensive and detailed historical analysis of the whole set of data, which comprises some 250 lexical items from more than 60 Central Chadic language varieties, and for detailed reconstruction and identification of consonantal sound changes plus recognising two further essential prosodies in Central Chadic languages, namely (pre-)nasalisation and glottalisation, see Wolff (forthcoming).

3 Proto-Central Chadic Diachronic Phonology and Morphophonology
Inventories and Principles

3.1 General Observations

3.1.1 Templatic Approach: Root-and-Pattern

So-called root-and-pattern structure is usually associated most of all with the phonology and morphology of Semitic languages, but it is considered by many typologists as being a salient feature that can be attributed to Afroasiatic as a whole. However, Afroasiatic languages that belong to families outside Semitic like Chadic, for instance, show less pronounced manifestations of this typological feature. In individual languages and for their synchronic description, assumptions about root-and-pattern may even be considered irrelevant. Characteristically, therefore, contemporary descriptive grammars of Central Chadic languages usually do not contain references to root-and-pattern structure. Historical linguistic analysis may nonetheless reveal that at least traces of root-and-pattern structure can be found, and that we may be safe to assume that root-and-pattern has played a role in the choice and distribution of vowels ('pattern') in the root or beyond (i.e. in the whole phonological word) at some time in the linguistic history of a particular language or language group. However, as our previous and current comparative research into CC languages suggests, there was only one 'true' vowel phoneme available to take part in the formation of 'patterns' in PCC, namely */a/. Hence, the approach chosen here rests on the basic assumption that root-and-pattern structures were of relevance in Proto(-Central)-Chadic. Throughout this study, therefore, reference to here so-called root types will play a clarifying role with regard to the underlying structures of words.

3.1.1.1 Underlying 'Root Types'

In addition to the basic assumption of an underlying and diachronically relevant root-and-pattern structure, another fundamental assumption is that of the existence of only one true vowel phoneme for PCC, namely */a/. These two basic assumptions combined, we expect reconstructable PCC lexical items to conform to root-and-pattern structures, which allow the formation of different root types, depending on the number of radical consonants and the distribution of vowel 'slots' that are filled by */a/.

There is reason to assume that the most basic (and so-called 'simple') roots contained, in addition to usually between one and three radical consonants (only rarely more), at least a final vowel /a/, which can be reconstructed as being a formal requirement for PCC roots (also including loans when these are becoming integrated into Central Chadic phonological systems, see 3.5). We refer to this as the 'lexical' final vowel. This lexical final /a/, like all other segments of a root, simple or augmented (see 3.1.2), may undergo diachronic deletion, i.e. /a/ > Ø. When the final /a/ is retained, it synchronically surfaces as /a/ [a] or undergoes centralisation /a/ > [ə] and then could be accidentally confused with epenthetic schwa, with which it indeed shares phonetic 'colouring' by palatalising or labialising environments. (Note that on systematic if a priori grounds, for our PCC reconstructions we exclude epithetic (paragogic) insertion of schwa at the end of roots or words.) Quite often, final /a/ comes under the effect of prosodies, which would account for allophones [e] (under Y-prosody) and [o] (under W-prosody).

Note that for the discussion of 'radical structure' in terms of consonantal roots and vocalisation patterns in the sub-sections of section 3.1, prosodies and their effects, as central as they are to comparative Central Chadic linguistics, will temporarily be left largely aside, in order to focus on diachronic processes affecting the 'plain' segments, i.e. consonants and vowels, themselves. For complete phonological and historical analysis, see the later sub-sections and particularly section 6.4.

3.1.1.2 Radical Consonant Slots

For reasons of analytical clarity, we will refer to the consonantal segments of simple roots (also referred to as 'radical consonants' or simply 'radicals') in terms of their position relative to each other in the root, occasionally using index numbers for further clarity, e.g.

Position in the simple root:	initial	medial	final
	C_1	C_2	C_3

However, these terminological conventions come to their limits when we are dealing with diachronic processes of loss of radical consonants, when, for instance, originally medial consonants become synchronically initial or final by deletion of any other or all other consonants in the root (see 3.1.2.2 below). Or when in monoradical roots the only consonant must be considered to be both initial and final. Such distinctions are not trivial, since phonological rules may apply to consonants in certain positions, so their identification as initial, medial or final may become pertinent.

3.1.1.3 Vocalisation: Vowel Slots and Syllables

It goes with the assumption of underlying root-and-pattern structure that – on a highly abstract level of analysis – there are systemic 'slots' for consonants and vowels. For Central Chadic languages and, therefore, for the purpose of this study, we need to distinguish two types of vocalic 'slots', namely systemic slots for the phonemic vowel /a/ to occur (here we speak of 'a-vocalisation' patterns, see 2.5.3), and potential slots for the occurrence of epenthetic schwa. The root-final slot, however, is systemically reserved for /a/, which may itself undergo centralisation or deletion in individual languages according to language-specific processes.

Like radical consonants (see 3.1.1.2 above), root-internal vowels can and must also be identified by their position in the word in terms of surface syllable structure. Since the most basic notion of 'root' comprises only the consonantal skeleton, even 'simple' (i.e. non-augmented) consonantal roots must undergo some kind of vocalisation in terms of insertions of underlying phonemic /a/ and/or epenthetic schwa in order to produce 'pronounceable' words. This happens in reference to admitted syllable structures. In the processes of word formation, therefore, the formation of syllables in the segmental chain is mandatory, at least with regard to surface (phonetic) representation. We will distinguish, counting from right to left, *ultimate – penultimate – antepenultimate syllables*; occasionally, we will speak also of initial and final syllables and/or, counting from left to right, speak of first, second or third syllables, as may be analytically appropriate.

3.1.1.4 The Ambiguous Nature of 'Weak Radicals'

The vocoids */y/ and */w/ (see 'weak radicals', 2.5.2) most frequently occur in consonantal slots (and are, therefore, counted among the radical consonants in terms of root types), which typically coincide with the onset or coda of a syllable in phonetic surface representation. However, due to their ambivalent nature in terms of underspecification for [±syllabic] as 'semivowels' or 'semiconsonants', they may shift, under the phonological processes targeting the creation of valid syllable structures to ensure phonetic 'pronounceability', into syllable-nucleus position, in which they will become syllabified to yield phonetic surface vowels ([i] and [u]). By the syllabification of weak radicals, the underlying original consonantal structure of the root becomes blurred, if not veiled completely.

See, for instance, the following examples, where the synchronic forms apparently point to an underlying root of the structure $\sqrt{}$ CVCV and, in one language (Merey) involving an augmental prefix (CV-). Internal reconstruction and comparative evidence, however, clearly show that we are dealing with a triradical root structure $\sqrt{}$ C C Ca (plus Ca- prefixal augment in Merey) plus instances of the syllabification of an underlying weak radical */w/ > [u]. (Note further that in the same set of examples, suffixal *{-y} occasionally likewise syllabifies to yield surface [i] in final positions.)

(40) 'dream' *(ma-, ma-RED, RED, n-) s(a)w(a)na (-a, -y, -k, -n; FV)
HURZA	Mbuko	√ C C Ca	*s w na-y	>	sune
MARGI	Bura	√ C C Ca	*s w nØ-y	>	suni
MOFU	Zulgo	√ C C Ca	*s w na	>	suna
	Merey	√ C C Ca	*ma-s w na-y	>	məsune
LAMANG	Hdi	√ C C Ca	*s w nØ-y	>	suni

The same holds true for syllabification of /y/ in both medial and final positions, as illustrated by the following examples. Here, underlying quadriradical root types surface as apparently bi- or monoradical roots due to the syllabification of /y/ in syllable-nucleus positions. Note that /y/ may syllabify and/or prosodify to yield /y^y~i^y/, with a palatalising effect on, for instance, neighbouring epenthetic vowels.

(41) 'hare' PCC *(ma-, na-) x^w(a)d(a)y(a)va (-k^w, -n; FV)
BATA	Jimi	√ C C C Ca	*ØdyvØ-n	> vyd-ən	> vidən	
	Tsuvan	√ C C C Ca	*ØtyvØ-k-n	> vy^{y}tə-kən		
				> vytə^y-kən	> vitikən	
SUKUR	Sukur	√ C C C Ca	*ØlyvØ	> və^{y}lya	> viI^{y}a ~ vilya	
MARGI	Kilba	√ C C C Ca	*ØtypØ	> pyta	> pita	
MANDARA	Podoko	√ C C C Ca	*ØryvØ	> vyra	> vira	
	Glavda	√ C C C Ca	*ØØyvØ	> vəy^y		
				> və^{y}y	> vii	
		√ C C C Ca	*Ødyva	> vəy^{y}da		
				> və^{y}yda	> vi:da	
LAMANG	Lamang	√ C C C Ca	*Ølyva-k^{w}a	> vyla-k^{w}a	> vilak^{w}a	

Note: In all languages metathesis is involved. Syllabification of medial /y/ > i appears to be consistent across the languages. However, some underlying /y/ ends up in syllable-initial position, where – as in Sukur – it surfaces either as such (vil.ya) or as palatalisation feature on the preceding consonant (vi.l^{y}a), but still in syllable-onset position.

3.1.1.5 The Relevance of the Templatic Approach to Historical Reconstruction in Chadic

The essential templatic structure of (Central) Chadic within Afroasiatic accounts for the apparent impossibility of using the *comparative method* for vowels in a straightforward way, as opposed to consonants, where the method works more or less well. As was already noted in the earliest attempts to reconstruct vowels in the then so-called Wandala-Lamang group (Wolff, 1981, 1983b), we need to carefully distinguish what was there called *a-vocalisation* and *Ø-vocalisation*, and we need likewise to know whether we are dealing with reflexes of underlying/diachronic /a/ or schwa (of assumed non-phonemic, i.e. pro- and epenthetic, nature). Comparing any vowel in one language with any vowel in another language, in same positions in the word (initial, medial, final), does not yield any satisfactory results in terms of assumptions of common origin in the proto-language, since any surface vowel in any position can correspond to practically any other surface vowel in the corresponding position across the languages. Also, one would need to know whether one is dealing with the phonemic vowel /a/ or with a reflex of non-phonemic schwa. Not taking these distinctions into account made full lexical reconstructions not feasible in Chadic for a long time. Consequently, some authors did not even attempt to include vowels in their reconstructions (see, for instance, Newman & Ma 1966; Jungraithmayr & Shimizu 1981), or authors had to come up with only 'very tentative' (Newman 1977a) suggestions, or propose 'a short vowel (-a-, -i-, -u-) of the first syllable' for only 'some cases' (Stolbova 2016). Therefore on methodological grounds, what needs to be done first of all is to identify vowel slots in the templatic structure that are filled by /a/, and these can then only be compared with other languages where the same slot is also filled by /a/. This means that we have to identify the underlying root type first. We can only compare language pairs in a 1:1 fashion when we are dealing with the same underlying root types and comparing vowels in the same slots filled by /a/ on the one hand, and epenthetic vowels in other slots, on the other. Depending on root type, we also need to allow for a fair number of /a/:Ø and ə:Ø correspondences. Note that under such premises, /a/:ə correspondences would be legitimate only where we can be sure that [ə] was a centralised allophone of /a/ in the particular position within the root-and-pattern structure.

For comparisons, the effects of prosodies must be identified and undone, i.e. underlying */a/ must be identified behind surface representations like [e] and [o]. The same is true for epenthetic schwa, which must also be identified behind its most common surface representations [ə], [ɨ~i], [ʉ~u]. With regard to underlying structures, such identification of vowels is further complicated by potential effects of local assimilations by immediate consonantal environment, in particular with regard to palatal(ised) and labial(ised) consonants.

Likewise, the 'semivocalic' vocoids /y/ and /w/ obscure the picture. In some surface forms in a certain language, they may occur as vowels [i] and [u] (having undergone syllabification), but have no corresponding vowels in the other language with which it is being compared, because in that language, the same segment may be in non-nucleus position of the syllable and, therefore, appear as a 'semiconsonantal' approximant/glide. Only the templatic approach allows us to identify the justification of a comparative series involving /y/ and

3.1 General Observations

[i] on the one hand, and /w/ and [u] on the other. This can be illustrated from examples like the following.

(a) /w/ : [u]

(42) 'beard' PCC *(a-, m(a)-, RED) **gʷ ma** (-a, -y)

MANDARA	Matal	√ C Ca	*a-gʷ ØØ-a-y		> agʷay
			*a-gʷ ØØ-a-y	> agʷaʷy	> agʷoy
	Podoko	√ C Ca	*m-w ma-y	> mwma-Øʸ	
				> mwmaʸ	> mume
	Mandara	√ C Ca	*w ma		> uma
	Malgwa	√ C Ca	*kʷ ma	> kwʷma	
				> kəʷuma	> kuuma
			*w ma	> əwʷma	
				> əʷuma	> uuma

Note: In the MANDARA group, initial labialised /Cʷ/ as still apparent in Matal /gʷ/ (and hidden in underlying Malgwa /kʷ/) may weaken to /w/ in initial position. This /w/ surfaces as [u] in languages like Podoko (as medial [u] of a left-augmented root), Mandara (as initial [u]) and Malgwa (as medial [u]).

(b) /y/ : [i]

(43) 'grasshopper' PCC *(a-) **xʷ(a)y(a)kʷa** (-ɗ,-ŋ?)

BATA	Gude	√ CaC Ca	*Øay wa	> ayʸəwa	
				> ayəʸwa	> ayiwa
DABA	Buwal	√ CaCaCa	*wayakØ		> wayak
MAFA	Cuvok	√ C CaCa	*Ø yakʷØ		> yakʷ
MANDARA	Mandara	√ C C Ca	*Ø y wa		> iwa
	Malgwa	√ C C Ca	*Ø y wa	> əyʸwa	
				> əʸiwaʸ	> iiwe
MAROUA	Giziga-Muturwa	√ C C Ca	*Ø y kʷØ	> yəkwʷ	
				> yəʷku	> yuku
LAMANG	Hdi	√ C C Ca	*x y 'Ø-y		> hi'i
HIGI	Bana	√ CaC Ca	*xay ØØ		> xay

Note: In Mandara, Malgwa and Hdi, underlying /y/ surfaces as vowel [i] in all positions (initial, medial, final). In the other languages, /y/ occurs in syllable-initial or syllable-final positions, in which it surfaces as /y/.

(c) /a/ : [e ~ o]

(44) 'butterfly' PCC *(kʷa-, ma-, ma-ta-, RED, ...) **p(a)ra** (-y, -kw, -n; FV)

MAROUA	Giziga-Muturwa	√ CaCa	*ma-pala-pala		> mapalapala
HURZA	Vame	√ CaCa	*pal-pala-y		
			> palpala-Øʸ		
			> paʸlpaʸlaʸ		> pelpele
GIDAR	Gidar	√ CaCa	*ma-ta-pala-pala-kʷ		
			> matapalapala-Øʷ		
			> maʷtaʷpaʷlaʷpaʷlaʷ		> motopolopolo

Note: In these three languages from different groups, /a/ surfaces in qualities which depend on the absence or presence of prosodies. Giziga has Ø-prosody, Vame has Y-prosody, and Gidar has W-prosody. All occurrences of /a/ are affected by prosodies in the same way across the word.[1]

The same holds for epenthetic schwa. Wherever it is inserted in a vowel slot, prosodies may impact the phonetic realisation, so various phonetic vowel qualities can still be said to correspond regularly between pairs of languages and thus meet the requirements for the application of the comparative method.

(45) (d) schwa corresponding to [ə], [i], [u] under the regime of prosodies
'horn$_1$' PCC ***d(a)r(a)ma** (-y, -k^w)

MOFU	Merey	√ C CaCa	*d ramØ	> dəram	> *dəram*
MARGI	Bura	√ C C Ca	*t l ^{m}ba-y-k^w		
			Metathesis		
			> t ^{m}b lØ-Øy-Ø^w	> tə^{ym}bə^{w}l	> *ti^{m}bul*
MAROUA	Giziga-Muturwa	√ C C Ca	*d r mØ-k^w		
			> d r m-Ø^w	> də^{w}rə^{w}m	> *durum*

Note: In Merey, epenthetic schwa is under Ø-prosody and surfaces as [ə]. In Bura, apart from metathesis involving C$_2$ and C$_3$ plus change from */m/ > ^{m}b, Y-prosody affects the epenthetic vowel in the first syllable, which surfaces as [i] (while W-prosody affects the epenthetic vowel in the second syllable, which accordingly surfaces as [u]). In Giziga, W-prosody affects the epenthetic vowels in both syllables, which surface as [u].

Summing up: in order to 'pre-process' (Central) Chadic language data on abstract levels of phonological analysis before such data can be used for application of the comparative method, i.e. in order to arrive at full lexical reconstructions involving all relevant segmental phonological units, there are three methodological requisites:

- identification of underlying root types and weak radicals;
- recognition of the distinction between underlying /a/ and epenthetic schwa;
- understanding of the nature and relevance of prosodies.

3.1.2 Diachronically Simple and Augmented Roots

One of the major insights that struck the present author in early publications (1981, 1983b, and elsewhere) and also, for instance, Jungraithmayr and

---

[1] Hence the somewhat unhappy idea by Gravina (2014a) to call this 'vowel harmony', which is a term that usually refers to a typologically different morphophonological construct. I prefer to use the purposefully slightly different term 'vowel harmonisation'.

3.1 General Observations

Shimizu (1981) and Newman (1991), was the observation that synchronic Chadic roots obviously contained petrified root-augmentation material, both to the left and the right of a reconstructable more 'simple' root.[2] That insight is considered central to the present reconstructions insofar as all root-augmental segments including (mainly leftward) reduplication (RED) of parts of the simple root are meticulously identified and explicitly reflected in the reconstructions presented here.

Hitherto, such petrified root-augmental segments have been noted rather in passing than forming part of detailed reconstruction work for PCC (but see Wolff 2004, 2006a for more detailed discussions with a focus on languages of the LAMANG group). Together with occasional diachronic loss of segments of the simple root (see 3.1.2.2), root augmentation by a range of added segments (at times apparently in sort of 'compensation' for lost segments) contributes to the difficulty of identifying what actually the units are to be compared across pairs of languages under the comparative method. For illustration, see the following examples reflecting the root 'work' in some selected Central Chadic languages, whose variant surface forms require considerable insight in order to identify the respective underlying structures, as they might be composed of elements of the 'simple' root and root-augmental material (for detailed analysis, see further below and, in particular, section 6.4):

(46)   'work' PCC *(a-, ka-, ma-) ɬ(a)na (-t, -y, -k, -k^w, -n, -l; FV)

		Simple root	Augmented root	Surface form
MANDARA	Glavda	√ C Ca		
		*ɬ Øa	—	> ɬə
MARGI	Bura	√ C Ca		
		*ɬ rØ	*k-ɬr-y	> kiɬir
BATA	Tsuvan	√ C Ca		
		*ɬ nØ	*ɬn-y-k-n	> ɬinikən
MOFU	Moloko	√ C Ca		
		*ɬ ra	*ɬra-y-la	> ɬərele
BATA	Bata	√ CaCa		
		*lanØ	*lan-t-y-k^{w}a	> lento

Another issue of potential relevance for comparative Chadic relates to the question whether root-internal vowels could have 'derivative' functions other than the well-known derivation of pluractional verb stems (Newman 1990) by so-called 'internal-a' (which, according to Wolff (2009), should be diachronically analysed as a morphological marker by itself, i.e. 'infix', while other authors prefer to refer to the formation as 'ablaut', i.e. a grammatically

---

[2] The issue of root 'growth' as opposed to 'decay' has been lucidly discussed with regard to West Chadic Hausa, the by far best-researched Chadic language, in a paper by Paul Newman (1991).

conditioned change of vocalisation pattern). Since the available database contains two practically identical verb roots with, however, related but different meanings, and which would appear to be derivations from the same underlying simple root, Gravina (2014b) raises the question whether one root should not be considered a 'causative' derivation of the other, the more so since he felt compelled to reconstruct both roots slightly differently (i.e. ***mits** vs ***məts**):

mits v. to extinguish éteindre (8 groups, 14 languages) B rel. to: mɨts.
   The basic meaning of this verb is 'to put out a fire'. This root is very similar to the root for 'to die', the only difference is that *i is reconstructed. It could possibly be a causative form, i.e. 'to cause (a fire) to die'.

In the present study, both roots are reconstructed with practically much the same results, yet with – accidental (?) – slight differences with regard to the suffixal root-augmental inventory, i.e. 'die' may take a suffix root-augment *{-k} in the available data, which does not occur with 'extinguish'. Cf.

(47)   'die, to'   PCC *(k-, ma-) **m(a)ta** (-a, -y, -k, -k^w, -n, -ŋ; FV)

(48)   'extinguish, to' PCC *(k-, m(a)-) **m(a)ta** (-a, -y, -k^w, -n, -ŋ; FV)

When we compare the two verbs in the 11 individual languages where we have reflexes of both verbs, we find that in only two instances are both forms completely identical, namely in Cuvok (BATA group) and Giziga-Muturwa (MAROUA group). In Cuvok, the 'simple' root *mətsa* serves both purposes, while in Giziga-Muturwa the augmented root *mutʃ* for both meanings shows traces of both morphological Y- and W-prosodies resulting from the presence of reconstructed *{-y} and *{-k^w}. In the majority of the other nine languages, however, there are formal differences between the forms of the two verbs relating to choice of root type and choice of combinations of augmental material. In Podoko (MANDARA) and Ouldeme (MOFU), 'die' uses a Ø-vocalised root type √ C Ca, while 'extinguish' uses the a-vocalised root type √ CaCa. In terms of suffixal root-augment chains, the differences are the following:

(49)

		'to die'	'to extinguish'
BATA	Jimi	-n	-y-n
DABA	Mbudum	-y	-y-k^w
	Daba	-y	-y-n
HURZA	Vame	—	-y-k^{w}a
MANDARA	Matal	-a-y	-y-ŋ
	Glavda	-y-ka	-y
MOFU	Ouldeme	—	-y-ŋ
LAMANG	Hdi	—	-a-y

Gravina's hunch that the medial *i reconstructed by him for 'extinguish' (***mits**) as opposed to schwa for 'die' (***məts**) could have something to do with

3.1 General Observations

deriving one from the other (see quote above) is not corroborated by our own reconstructions. Rather, the 'derivative' relationship between the two would appear to hinge – in a still non-transparent manner – on choice of suffixal root augmentation, which reflects distinctions of derivative morphology regarding the respective source forms underlying the difference of meaning. Note that for 'extinguish', all languages listed in (49) show a potential source of morphological palatalisation, namely *{-y}, which could explain the occurrence of medial [i~i] in the simple root – but the same *{-y} occurs widely also with 'die'.

The synchronically non-productive ('frozen', 'petrified') nature of most root-augmental segments becomes apparent when we observe that and how they also become involved in metathesis in addition to consonants of the 'simple' root (see 3.1.3 for examples).

Two limiting statements must, however, be made at this point in time and for the present study:

- Looking at both prefixal and suffixal root-augmental elements, we note a remarkable similarity of inventory. Whether or not we are dealing with historically identical markers remains yet to be ascertained, as much as the question whether this might be an indication of diachronic – at least partial – ambifixal marking in PCC grammar (see 3.1.2.5).
- The (petrified) augmental elements are presumably morphological in nature, to the likely exception of the FV ('final vowel'). However, no attempt is being made here to identify any original grammatical function, apart from relating – in passing – a fair number of them to the Proto-Chadic determiner system as reconstructed by Schuh (1983). (A likely historical relationship between Schuh's reconstructed PC determiners and West Chadic Hausa nominal plural formations has been already discussed in Wolff (1993: 165–177, 1995). See also Schuh (2002) and Wolff (2019b) on rather widespread so-called morphological palatalisation in Chadic.)

As already noted by Gravina (2014b, *passim*), in some languages there appears to be a tendency to use (petrified) prefixal root augmentation in particular to compensate for the loss of segmental root material, such as replacing the initial root consonant or a sequence of initial */Ca/. Occasionally, reduplication (RED) of root material is also prefixed, less commonly suffixed, for likely the same reason.

Note that root-augmental elements may combine, independently of their position relative to the simple root, i.e. both as prefixal and suffixal elements.

As had also been noted by Gravina (2014b, *passim*), especially with verbs, some of the forms offered as (augmented) roots are, in fact, citation forms that carry additional grammatical markers, such as for nominalisation of verbs. Candidates for such are the fairly widespread prefix {ma-} and the ending {-(a)y ~ -(e)y} with verbs in certain languages, which may be synchronically productive rather than diachronically 'petrified'. However, in order not to manipulate the data from the database, all the available forms have been subjected to our reconstruction approach irrespective of their 'productive vitality' in the modern languages.

3.1.2.1 Simple Root and Root Types

In order to arrive at the identification of simple roots, we need to identify in synchronic underlying structures all augmental material in prefixal and suffixal positions that may have petrified in the course of time. PCC lexical reconstructions then reveal one of the following root types for each simple root. Potential slots for epenthetic vowels are indicated by blanks.

Triradical structures:	√ C C Ca, √ C CaCa, √ CaC Ca, √ CaCaCa
Biradical structures:	√ C Ca, √ CaCa
Monoradical structure:	√ Ca

Note that synchronic lexical items for which we can reconstruct the diachronic source in PCC may relate to any of the above root types on a reductive downward or accretive upward cascade of types in terms of number of reconstructable segments, vowel slots filled by /a/, and number of consonants. When a root loses a consonant, this will affect the root type in underlying structure. (This reductive process has occasionally been referred to elsewhere as 'root thinning' or 'decay', see 3.1.2.2). However, if the lost consonant was the source of a prosody, then the prosody may survive as a trace of its former presence and help us to identify, for instance, an underlying apparently biradical root to originally have been a triradical root, which could then be reflected in our PCC reconstruction.

Therefore, assumptions about the synchronically underlying or reconstructable ultimate diachronic root type may be premature, until one has done larger-scale comparative studies for the specific lexical item. In principle, any root type could diachronically correspond to any other, by invoking reductive and accretive processes in the course of the history of individual languages. Not only individual occurrences of consonants and the vowel /a/, but also complete /Ca/-syllables can be affected by deletion and become diachronically 'lost'.

Instantiations of /a/ would, first of all, depend on 'choice' of root type for individual PCC lexical items, whose governing principles are not yet understood. Theoretically, diachronic 'formative a-vocalisation' may have played a role, for instance, when verb pluractionals were formed by so-called 'internal a' (i.e. infix *{-a-} plus/minus consonant replication) and, possibly, noun plurals by *ablaut*-type changes of vocalic pattern. The diachronic 'root type dynamics' can be depicted by the diagram in Figure 3.1.

3.1 General Observations

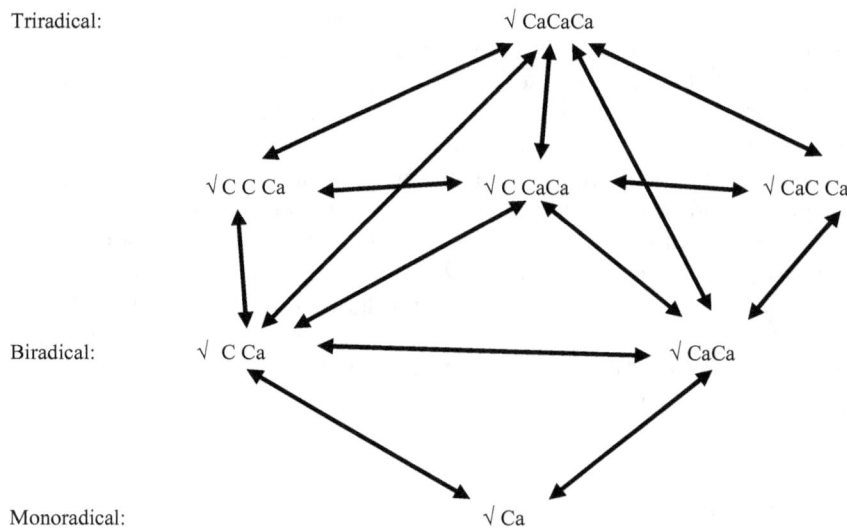

Figure 3.1 Diachronic root type dynamics

As indicated, this does not mean that all PCC roots originally were triradical and that the only direction of diachronic development was reduction, decay or simplification. Some roots were biradical or even monoradical by origin. On the other hand, accretive processes also occurred, leading to expanded vowel patterns and/or compensatory elaboration, often by fusion and petrification of affixal material, after diachronic loss of original root material. Subsequently, synchronically underlying roots may have more segments than the reconstructed original PCC root as much as vice versa. Therefore, for the fully transparent reconstruction of PCC lexical items, it is necessary to always keep the distinction between simple and augmented roots in mind (3.1.2).

Note that, whether by accident or not and despite synchronic occurrence in modern CC languages, the examples selected for this study from the database do not contain, for the proto-language level, obvious instances of (formative) consonant replication, such as are likely to be confused with (formative) consonant gemination, and as known to play a role in the synchronic grammar of many Afroasiatic languages, including Chadic. The selected data do, however, show (mainly leftward) REDuplication of simple-root material, yet without currently allowing any functional semantic value to be attached to it. Also, widely occurring choice of root type, such as contrasting Ø-vocalised with a-vocalised roots on the proto-language level, can currently not be related to any formative purposes, such as, for instance, forming pluractional verb stems or nominal plurals. If it was plausible to assume that this was the case on the level of the proto-language, then the data under review would suggest that, for many languages or language groups, the formative processes were no longer productive, and that 'vocalised' roots (i.e. root types) became lexicalised in the individual language histories – and thereby, retrospectively, allowing what we in this study refer to as 'choice of root type'. On the other hand, productive formative a-vocalisation has rudimentarily survived in many modern CC languages (in particular with plurals for certain kinship terms and domestic animals). In many languages, also infixation of *{-a-} still serves to derive pluractional verb stems from simple underlying roots. The diachronic details of loss and maintenance of such formative principles in Central Chadic still deserve further research.

3.1.2.2 Diachronic Loss of Segments

A recurrent diachronic process in the history of Chadic languages is the – at times massive – loss of segmental root material, occasionally referred to as 'root thinning' (a term presumably coined by H. Jungraithmayr) or root 'decay' (the term used by Newman 1991). Such loss of segments may affect consonants as well as */a/, and even whole Ca-syllables. Simple roots as a rule contain between one and three radical consonants which, in addition to lexical final /a/, may have at least one systemic medial vowel slot filled by /a/, i.e. besides √ C C Ca this would be √ CaC Ca, √ C CaCa or √ CaCa. Simple roots of the shape √ CaCaCa would appear to be somewhat less frequent, but cannot be considered exceptional. Rather, 'exceptional' could be considered roots that contain more than three radicals, even though they do occur.

Any root may undergo deletion of radical consonants and phonemic vowels. Triradical roots would yield reduced roots of the types √ C Ca, √ CaCa, and √ Ca. Likewise, original biradical roots of the shapes √ C Ca and √ CaCa may undergo loss of segments to yield synchronically reduced monoradical roots of the shape √ Ca.

√ C C Ca > √ C Ca > √ Ca   Loss of radical consonants from original triradical to synchronic underlying biradical structure can be illustrated by the following set of examples.

(50)   'hair' PCC *(ma-) **s(a)b(a)ta** (-y, -k^w)
(a) Retention of triradical structure: √ CaC Ca ~ √ C CaCa ~ √ C C Ca
√ CaC Ca
BATA   Bata   *saw ta-y-k^w > sawta-Ø^y-Ø^w > ʃewto
                                             > s^{y}a^{y}wta^w

3.1 General Observations   89

√ C CaCa
MOFU   Moloko   *m-s bata-y-k^w   > sə^mbata-Ø^y-^wk
                                                     > sə^mba^yta^y-^wk   > səmbetewk
√ C C Ca
BATA   Sharwa   *s ɓ^w tØ-y   > səɓ^wət-i^y
                                                     > s^yəɓ^wət-i   > ʃəɓ^wəti
             Tsuvan   *s ɓ^w ta-y   > səɓ^wta-Ø^y
                                                     > sə^wɓta^y   > suɓte
SUKUR   Sukur   *m-s b tØ-y-k^w   > sə^mbət-Ø^y-Ø^w
                                                     > s^yə^{wm}bə^wt   > ʃu^mbut
LAMANG   Hdi   *s w dØ-y   > səwəd-i^y
                                                     > səwə^yd-i   > səwidi
HIGI   Kamwe-   *s m tØ-y   > sənt-i^y
             Nkafa   > s^yə^ynt^y-i > ʃint^yi

(b) Reduction to surface biradical structure: √ C C Ca > √ C Ø Ca
LAMANG   Lamang   *s Ø dØ-y   > səd-i^y
                                                     > sə^yd-i   > sidi
HIGI   Bana   *s Ø tØ-y   > sət-i   > səti
                                                     > st-i^y
                                                     > s^yt-i   > ʃti

With the following examples of original triradical structure, we are able to illustrate three historical developments (a) retention, (b) apparent reduction to surface biradical structure by syllabification of a weak radical, and (c) obvious reduction to surface biradical structure by deletion of a weak radical.

(51)   'dream' *(...) s(a)w(a)na (-a, -y, -k, -n; FV)

         (a) Retention of triradical structure: root types √ C C Ca ~ √ C CaCa ~
             √ CaCaCa
         MAFA   Mafa   √ C C Ca   *n-s w na-y   > n-səw^wəna-Ø^y
                                                           > n-s^yə^wwə^yna^y   > nʃuwine
                     Cuvok   √ C CaCa   *s wana   > səw^wana
                                                           > sə^wwana   > suwana
         MANDARA   Podoko   √ C CaCa   *s x^wana   > səx^wana   > səh^wana
         LAMANG   Lamang   √ C CaCa   *s waŋa   > səw^waŋa
                                                           > sə^wwaŋa   > suwaŋa
         KOTOKO-   Mpade   √ C CaCa   *s wara-y   > swara-Ø^y
         NORTH   > swara^y   > sware
                     Malgbe   √ CaCaCa   *yawara-y   > yawara-Ø^y
                                                           > yawara^y   > yaware
         KOTOKO-   Lagwan   √ C CaCa   *s wana-y   > swana-Ø^y
         CENTRAL   > swana^y   > swane
                     Mser   √ C CaCa   *s wara-y   > swara-Ø^y
                                                           > swara^y   > sware

(b) Reduction to surface biradical structure by syllabification of weak radical */w/ > [u]

HURZA	Mbuko	√ C C Ca	*s w na-y	> swna-Ø^y	
				> swna^y	> sune
MARGI	Bura	√ C C Ca	*s w nØ-y	> swn-i	> suni
MOFU	Zulgo	√ C C Ca	*s w na		> suna
	Merey	√ C C Ca	*ma-s w na-y	> məswna-Ø^y	
				> məswna^y	> məsune
LAMANG	Hdi	√ C C Ca	*s w nØ-y	> swn-i	> suni

(c) Reduction to surface biradical structure by deletion of weak radical */w/

BATA	Bata	√ C C Ca	*s Ø rØ-y	> sər-i^y	
				> s^{y}ə^{y}r-i	> ʃiri
	Gude	√ C C Ca	*s Ø na-y	> sənə-i^y	
				> sənə^y-i	> sənii
	Jimi	√ C C Ca	*s Ø nØ-y-n	> sən-i^y-n	
				> sə^{y}n-i-n	> sinin
	Sharwa	√ C C Ca	*s Ø nə-y'a	> sənə-Ø^y'a	
				> s^{y}ə^{y}nə'a	> ʃinə'ə
DABA	Daba	√ C C Ca	*s Ø nØ-y	> sən-i^y	
				> sə^{y}n-i	> sini
MANDARA	Mandara	√ C CaCa	*s Øana-y	> sana-Ø^y	
				> s^{y}a^{y}na^y	> ʃene
	Malgwa	√ C C Ca	*s Ø na-y	> səna-Ø^y	
				> s^{y}ə^{y}na^y	> ʃine
	Glavda	√ C C Ca	*s Ø nØ-y-ka	> sən-Ø^y-ka	
				> sə^{y}n-ka	> siŋga
MOFU	Dugwor	√ C C Ca	*ma-s Ø na-y	> məsna-Ø^y	
				> məsna^y	> məsne
	Mofu North	√ C C Ca	*ma-s Ø na-y	> ma-səna-Ø^y	
				> ma^y-səna^y	> mesəne
MARUA	Giziga-Marva	√ C C Ca	*ma-s Ø nØ-y	> ma-sən-Ø^y	
				> ma-sə^{y}n	> məsin
HIGI	Kirya	√ C C Ca	*sØnØ-y	> sən-Ø^y	
				> s^{y}ə^{y}n	> ʃin

Some of the most spectacular cases of 'root thinning' from tri- down to monoradical underlying synchronic roots can be found in the following examples. Loss of radical consonants has been compensated in quite a few languages, as it would appear, by adding prefixal augmental materials, including leftward reduplication (marked below by RED+). In the following example of the root for 'bone', only one language of the MANDARA group, namely Glavda, does not compensate and retains the simplest possible √ Ca structure: ɬa, besides also allowing for a reduplicated form.

(52) 'bone' PCC *((')a-, a-n-, a-ta-, ma-, ma-ta-, RED-a-) ɗy(a)ɬa (-a, -y, -k^w, -t, -n)
      MANDARA Matal   √ C C Ca *a-RED+Ø Ø ɬØ > a-ɬa+ɬ > aɬaɬ
                 Podoko √ C C Ca *RED+Ø Ø ɬa > ɬa+ɬa > ɬaɬa

3.1 General Observations

	Mandara	√ C C Ca	*RED+Ø y x^{y}a	> x^{y}a+Ø^{y}x^{y}a	
				> x^{y}a+x^{y}a^y	> h^{y}ah^{y}e
	Malwa	√ C C Ca	*RED+Ø y x^{y}a	> x^{y}a+Ø^{y}x^{y}a	
				> x^{y}a^y+x^{y}a^y	> h^{y}eh^{y}e
	Glavda	√ C C Ca	*Ø Ø ła		> ła
		√ C C Ca	*RED+Ø Ø ła	> ła+ła	> łała
	Dghweɗe	√ C C Ca	*RED+Ø Ø ła-y	> ła+ła-Ø^y	
				> ła+ła^y	> łałe
MOFU	Ouldeme	√ C C Ca	*a-RED+Ø Ø łØ	> a-ła+ł	> ałał
	Muyang	√ C C Ca	*a-Ø Ø ła-t		> ałat
	Mada	√ C C Ca	*a-RED+Ø Ø łØ	> a-ła+ł	> ałał
	Zulgo, Gemzek	√ C C Ca	*a-ta-Ø Ø łØ		> atał
	Merey, Dugwor	√ C C Ca	*ma-ta-Ø Ø łØ		> mətał
	Mofu North	√ C C Ca	*ma-ta-Ø Ø łØ	> m-ta-ł	> ^{n}dał
MAROUA	Giziga-Muturwa	√ C C Ca	*ta-Ø Ø ł(a-y)	> ta-ł(-a-Ø^y)	
				> ta^y-ł(-a^y)	> teł(e)
	Muturwa, Marva	√ C C Ca	*a-ta-Ø Ø łØ-y	> ata-ł-Ø^y	
				> ata^y-ł	> ateł
	Muturwa	√ C C Ca	*a-ta-Ø Ø łØ-y	> ata-ł-Ø^y	
				> a^{y}ta^y-ł	> eteł

In the following example, the very widely spread original triradical root for 'to give birth' displays two weak radicals among its three radical consonants of the consonantal root *w x y, which show a strong tendency to metathesise and/or be deleted. In many modern languages reflecting this triradical PCC root, we find surface monoradical roots. (Note that henceforth, for purposes of condensing illustrations of language-specific historical developments, phonological ('lexical') prosody origins are occasionally already indicated in the quotation of the diachronic roots.)

(53)   'give birth, to' PCC *(ma-) **w(a)x(a)ya** (-a, -y, -k, -k^w, -n, -l; FV)

	MAFA	Mafa	√ C C Ca	*Ø Ø ya		> ya
		Cuvok	√ C CaCa	*Ø xaya		> haya
	TERA	Tera	√ C C Ca	*Ø x Øa		> xa
	SUKUR	Sukur	√ C C Ca	*w x ya		
				> w y xa		
				> y y xa		
				> yy^{y}xa	> yə^{y}ixa	> yiiha
			√ C C Ca	*w x ya		
				> w y xa		
				> y w ØØ	> yy	> yi
	HURZA	Mbuko	√ CaCaCa	*waxayØ		> wahay
		Vame	√ CaC Ca	*wax Ø(a)		> wah(a)
	MARGI	Bura	√ C C Ca	*w x ya		
				> Ø Ø y^{y}a	> ə^{y}ya	> iya

		√ C C Ca	*w x ya		
			> y w Øa		
			> yya		> yia
	Margi, Margi-South Kilba	√ C C Ca	*Ø Ø ya		> ya
MANDARA	Podoko	√ C C Ca	*Ø x Øa		> ha
	Malgwa	√ C C Ca	*Ø Ø ya		> ya
	Glavda	√ C C Ca	*w x ya-ka		
			> w y xa-ka		
			> w y ØØ-ka	> yy-ka	> yiga
		√ C C Ca	RED+Ø Ø ya-na		
			> ya+ya-na		> yayana
	Dghweɗe	√ C C Ca	*w x ya-ka		
			> w y xa-ka		
			> y w xa-ka		
			> yyØØ-ka	> yi^y-ga	
				> yi-ga^y	> yige
MOFU	Ouldeme	√ C C Ca	*w Ø yØ		> wi
	Moloko	√ C C Ca	*w Ø Ø^{y}a	> wa^y	> we
	Zulgo	√ C C Ca	*w Ø Øa		> wa
	Gemzek	√ C C Ca	*ma-w Ø Ø^{y}a	> ma^{y}wa^y	> mewe
		√ C C Ca	*ma-w Ø Øa		> mawa
	Merey	√ C C Ca	*w Ø Øa		> wa
	Dugwor	√ CaC Ca	*ma-waØ yØ		> maway
	Mofu North	√ C C Ca	*ma-Ø Ø y^y-a-y	> ma^{y}ya^{y}y	> meyey
	Mofu-Gudur	√ C C Ca	*Ø Ø yØ		> y-
MAROUA	Giziga-Marva	√ C C Ca	*w x ya		
			> w y xa		
			> ywØØ	> yy	> yi
		√ C C Ca	*Ø Ø y^{y}a	> ya^y	> ye
	Mbazla	√ C C Ca	*w x ya		
			> w y xa		
			> wyØØ	> yy	> yi
		√ C C Ca	*RED+w x ya		
			> RED+w y xa		
			> RED+y w xa		
			> ya+y^{y}w'Ø	> ya^y-yy'	> yɛyi'
LAMANG	Lamang	√ C C Ca	*Ø Ø ya		> ya
	Hdi	√ C C Ca	*RED+Ø Ø yØ		
			> ya+y		> yay
HIGI	Kamwe-Nkafa	√ C C Ca	*Ø Ø yə		> yə
	Kamwe-Futu	√ C C Ca	*Ø Ø y^{y}a-ka	> ya^y-ka	> yekə
		√ C C Ca	*Ø Ø y^{y}a-k-g^{w}a	> ya^y-kəg^{w}a^w	> yekəg^{w}o
	Kirya, Bana	√ C C Ca	*Ø Ø ya		> ya
KOTOKO-ISLAND	Buduma	√ C C Ca	*w^w Ø yØ	> wə^{w}y	> wuy
		√ C C Ca	*w^w Ø ØØ-a-y	> wə^w-ay	> wuəy
KOTOKO-NORTH	Afade, Mpade	√ C C Ca	*w Ø Ø^{y}a	> wa^y	> we
		√ C C Ca	*w Ø Øa-n		> wan

3.1 General Observations   93

	Malgbe	√ C C Ca	*w Ø Øa-k^w-n	> wa-w^wən	
				> wa-wə^wn	> *wawun*
KOTOKO- SOUTH	Zina	√ C C Ca	*w Ø y^ya	> wə^yya	> *wiya*
MUSGUM	Mulwi	√ C C Ca	*w Ø yØ		> *wi*
	Mbara	√ C C Ca	*w Ø y^yØ	> wə^yi	> *wii*
GIDAR	Gidar	√ C C Ca	*RED+w Ø Øa		
			> w+w^wa	> ə^wuwa	> *uuwa*
		√ C C Ca	*RED+w Ø Øa		
			> w+w^wa	> ə^wwa	> *uwa*
		√ C C Ca	*w Ø y^yØ-na	> wə^yina	> *wiina*

√ C Ca > √ Ca   Also, PCC biradical roots may undergo deletion of one of the two radical consonants and end up as synchronic underlying monoradical roots. Occasionally, the lost radical leaves a trace in terms of labialisation or palatalisation or is hidden behind its own syllabification. Such examples have the surface appearance of underlying monoradical roots. For example (note metathesis *w v > v w in Jimi, Sharwa and Sukur and subsequent fusion of the sequence /v+w/ > [v^w] or syllabification of /w/ > [u]):

(54)   'faeces' PCC *(ŋ-) ɣ^w va (-a, -y, -n)

	BATA	Jimi	√ C Ca	*w vØ-y-n	> vw-in	> *v^win*
		Sharwa	√ C Ca	*w vØ-a-y	> vw-ay	> *v^way*
	DABA	Buwal, Gavar, Mbudum	√ C Ca	*ŋ-Øva		> *ŋva*
	SUKUR	Sukur	√ C Ca	*w vØ	> vw	> *vu*

Diachronic Loss of */a/

For PCC simple roots in lexical reconstruction, we structurally distinguish medial */a/ and final */a/. Evidence suggests that all reconstructed simple roots end in */a/ by default. This implies that final */a/ in simple roots is lexical in nature, not grammatical. This lexical final */a/, however, can be subject to deletion or centralisation as a language-specific process. See, for instance, the following examples.

(a) In Bata and Gude, the lexical final */a/ is deleted:

(55)   'cry, to' PCC *(ma-) **ts(a)wa** (-a, -y, -k; FV)
       BATA   Bata, Gude   √ C Ca   *t w^wØ   > tə^ww   > *tuu*

(b) In Sharwa, the lexical final /a/ is centralised:

(56)   BATA   Sharwa   √ C Ca   *t w^wa   > tə^wwə   >   *tuwə*

(57) (c) In Bura and Zulgo, the lexical final vowel is retained:
MARGI   Bura   √ C Ca   *t wʷa   > təʷwa   > *tuwa ~ tua*
MOFU   Zulgo   √ C Ca   *t wʷa   > təʷwa   > *tuwa*

Note that we also postulate /a/ as part of suffixal root-augmental material when it is followed by the very frequent additional augment *{-y} and yielding -*ay* ~ -*ey* in word-final surface representation. This, however, is just a convenience transcription in order to distinguish diphthong-like forms from word-final assumed monophthong palatalisation of root-final /a/, which yields [e]. In this way, we create what may be an over-differentiation between the two realisations of the final syllable surface vowels, namely diphthong [ay] and monophthong [e]. E.g.

(58)   'faeces' PCC *(ŋ-) ɣʷ **va** (-a, -y, -n)
        BATA   Sharwa   √ C Ca   *w v-a-y
                                        Metathesis: vw-ay   > vʷay
        MANDARA   Dghwed̶e   √ C Ca   *g va-y   > gəva-Øʸ
                                                     > gəvaʸ   > gəve

Further, some augmented root forms show what is here termed FV ('Final Vowel', a term adopted from Bantu linguistics), which typically follows other suffixal augment material. This FV behaves phonologically like simple-root final /a/ in terms of potential centralisation. (Deletion of FV is either by default in all other cases or the FV is not there from the beginning; therefore and simply, we do not reconstruct it as default only for it to be deleted again, which, however, would be a legitimate analytical option in order to provide full parallel treatment of root-final /a/, whether with simple or with augmented roots.) See the following reduplicated example that shows both deletion of the lexical final /a/ before [i] (syllabified from *{-y}) and centralisation of the FV. (Note that in the following example from Gude, the leftward REDuplication not only involves segmental material from the simple root *pra, but also encompasses augmental */y/, i.e. *pr-y; in the light of the selected examples from the database for review in this study, this process must be considered to be 'exceptional'.)

(59)   'butterfly' PCC *(…, RED) **p(a)ra** (-y, -kʷ, -n; FV)
        BATA   Gude   √ C Ca + RED   *p rØ-y+p rØ-y-na > pri-prina > pəripərinə

As has already been described above, linguistic ancestors of present-day languages, as a rule, can be associated with particular shapes of the underlying simple roots in terms of presence or absence of medial /a/ for individual lexemes. These root types may vary across languages of the same language groups. In most cases, reconstruction of the root type presents no problem to the analysis. E.g.

3.1 General Observations 95

(60) 'dream' PCC *(...) **s(a)w(a)na** (...)
 MOFU Zulgo √ C C Ca *s w na > *suna*
  Cuvok √ C CaCa *s wʷana > *səʷwana*
    > *suwana*
 KOTOKO- Mpade √ C CaCa *s wara-y > *swara-Øʸ*
 NORTH   > *swaraʸ*
    > *sware*
  Malgbe[3] √ CaCaCa *yawara-y > *yawara-Øʸ*
    > *yawaraʸ*
    > *yaware*

There are rare cases of reduplicated synchronic forms, for which the reduplication (RED) suggests the presence of medial /a/ (which was also reduplicated) in the first syllable of the simple root, which, however, is no longer there in the synchronic phonetic surface form of the word. Here, we assume deletion of root-medial /a/ plus occasional substitutive schwa insertion, as in the following examples:

(61a) 'suck, to' PCC *(ma-, n- RED) **s(a)wɓa** (-a, -y, -n)
 MAFA Mafa √ CaC Ca *sa-sawɓa > sa-sØwʷɓØ
    > saʷ-swɓØ > *sosuɓ*
  Cuvok √ CaC Ca *sa-sawɓa > sa-sØØɓa > *sasɓa*
 MOFU Zulgo √ CaC Ca *sa-sawɓa > sa-sØwɓa > *sasuɓa*
  Mofu √ CaC Ca *ma-sa-sawɓ-a-y > ma-sa-sØØɓ-a-yʸ
  North   > maʸ-saʸ-səɓ-aʸy > *mesəsəɓey*
  Mofu- √ CaC Ca *sa-sawɓa > sa-sØØɓØ
  Gudur   > sa-səɓ > *sasəɓ*

(61b) 'fly' PCC *(a-, xa-, m-, n-, RED) **dz(a)kʷ(a)ɗa** (-y, -n, -ŋ)
 DABA Buwal √ CaCaCa *dza-dzawaɗØ-y > dza-dzØwaɗ-Øy
    > dzʸaʸ-dzʸəwaʸɗ > *dʒedʒəwed*

(61c) 'give birth, to' PCC *(ma-, RED) **w(a)x(a)ya** (a, -y, -k, -kʷ, -n, -l; FV)
 MAROUA Mbazla √ CaC Ca *RED-waxya
    > RED-wayxØ
    > RED-yay'
  ya-yayʸ' > yaʸ-yØy' > *yɛyi'*

Note that for Mbazla, we assume a palatalisation effect triggered by C₂ /y/ that also changes C₁ /w/ > y and is reflected as such also in the REDuplicated syllable. One might wish to argue that this suggests that, after C₂~C₃ metathesis, the palatalisation assimilation chronologically preceded the REDuplicative prefixal augmentation:

---

[3] For Malgbe, this analysis holds because initial /y/ is a reflex of root-initial */s/ in some Kotoko-North languages.

*waxya > wayxØ > way' > yay' > ya-yay$^{y'}$ > ya-yØy$^{y'}$ > ya^y-yØy' > yɛyi'.

In any case, the REDuplicative syllable retains the original medial vowel /a/, which, in its original position, is 'lost' preceding syllabified /y/ > i.

3.1.2.3 Affixal Root Augmentation and Petrification

In terms of the presence or absence (and choice of) root-augmental elements in modern Central Chadic languages, there is little if any consistency even among most closely related languages. Part of the picture is also the observation that certain word-final vowels, in particular [i] and [e], are being offered in parentheses by the transcribing linguist, apparently indicating a not fully predictable presence or absence even in the same language or language variety. (Note: in this study, we take such information very seriously, because such final front vowels are considered to be historically traceable to a reconstructable root-augment *{-y}, which is the source of morphological Y-prosody.) Across languages of the same closely related language groups, there is considerable variation as to the overall presence or absence, but also choice of, for instance, suffixal root-augmental material. See the following examples from some MOFU group languages of a simple root of straightforward √ CaCa root type. (Note that, for instance for Ouldeme, the database does not indicate which of the five different forms represent synchronically productive derivationally extended verb stems that merit polymorphemic analysis, and which of the five must be considered to contain petrified/fused root-augmental material, thereby establishing, in synchronic terms, a monomorphemic underlying structure despite its obvious polymorphemic origin.)

(62) 'wash, to' PCC *(ma-) **b(a)na** (-a,-y,-k^w, -n, (fa-)ŋ, -x, RED; FV)

		√ CaCa	Root augment	
MOFU	Zulgo	*bara	Ø	> bara
	Moloko	*balØ	-a-y	> balay
	Muyang	*barØ	-a-y	> baray
		*bara	RED	> baraba
	Ouldeme	*bara > barə	-ya	> bariya
		*bara	-ya	> bereya
		*bara	-y-ŋ	> bereŋ
		*bara	-xa	> baraha
		*bara	-ka	> baraka

Currently, most questions regarding the original morphological function of the diachronic markers behind the reconstructed root augments must remain open. Serious research into reconstructing PCC morphology has hardly begun.

However, and as has been noted by the current author in several earlier publications, quite a few of the fused elements show a remarkable similarity to the inventory of Proto-Chadic determiners that were reconstructed a long time ago by Schuh (1983): *n, *t, *k, *ɗ, and *i (see inventory in 3.1.2.5).

Some root-augmental material that is reconstructed in this study may, indeed, also have a transparent history from the synchronic study of Central Chadic languages and low-level comparison. Nouns and deictic markers may still show traces of Schuh's reconstructed PC determiners, while verbs in their citation form may come in the shape of synchronically or diachronically identifiable nominalised forms, i.e. verbal nouns.

3.1.2.4 Reduplicative Augmentation and Petrification

Besides quasi-autonomous segmental materials fused and petrified for prefixal and suffixal root augmentation and also with at times compensatory function (see 3.1.2.3), some languages make use of mainly leftward (partial) reduplication (RED) of segmental material from the simple root. Such reduplicative root augmentation is duly identified and explicitly represented in the reconstructions (see 6.4). The RED augment may, in individual languages, combine with other prefixal augmental material. Rarely, it also occurs in suffixal position to the right of the simple root, see MOFU group Muyang *bara-ba* for 'to wash' above, where we assume rare suffixal RED (< *bara-bara?) rather than the occurrence of an otherwise also rare augmental -b(a).

3.1.2.5 Similarity of Inventories of Pre- and Suffixal Augments

Our PCC lexical reconstructions show separate inventories of here so-called prefixal and suffixal root-augmentation material that have become more or less petrified in the diachronic history of the individual languages and can or must be considered, from a synchronic descriptive perspective, to form an integral part of the underlying roots. They are, however, identifiable as additional segmental material by comparison among languages; even the most closely related ones may differ by the presence or absence of such root-augmental elements. From our reconstructions (see 6.4), we receive the inventories shown in Table 3.1 according to position relative to the simple root.

This list raises the question whether the high degree of correspondence between prefixal and suffixal elements could be a reflex of original ambifixal marking in some cases, or whether PCC dialects were free to pre- or postpose such originally grammatical markers in relation to the root. See, for instance, the word for 'night' (PCC simple root **r(a)v(a)ɗa**) in two KOTOKO groups: in Lagwan and Mser, two KOTOKO-CENTRAL languages, the synchronic form is *nvaɗe* (internally reconstructable as *n-Øvaɗa-y), while in Zina (KOTOKO-SOUTH) the cognate modern form is *ləvin* (internally reconstructable as *lv-y-n). The same augmental element *n is present in both groups, yet

Table 3.1 *Inventories of pre- and suffixal root augments*

Prefixal	Suffixal	
RED	RED (rare)	
(')a-	-a (and FV)	
b-	-b	
d-	(corresponding to -l ?)	
ɗa-	-ɗ	
x(a)-	—	
ka-	-k	
kʷa-	-kʷ	
(corresponding to d- ?)	-l	
m(a)-	—	
n(a)-	-n	
ŋ-	-ŋ	
ŋga-	—	(combined *n-/ŋ-ka- ?)
t(a)-	-t	
va-	—	
w-	-w	(different from -kʷ ?)
wr-	—	
ya-	-y	

it takes prefixal position in KOTOKO-CENTRAL languages as opposed to suffixal position in KOTOKO-SOUTH. At present, this question cannot be answered since no research along such lines has as yet been undertaken by the present author, but see Wolff (forthcoming), nor is he aware of any such research having been undertaken by any other author; the study of historical (Central) Chadic grammar has barely begun.

3.1.3 Metathesis

Metathesis of consonants occurs quite frequently in the data. It mostly involves (a) simple-root internal segments, rarely it involves (b) segments within only root-augmental material, and at times it involves (c) both simple-root and root-augmental material combined. We take in particular the latter type of metathesis to be strong evidence that in synchronically underlying structure augmented roots are being treated as unique and single, i.e. (pseudo-) monomorphemic, roots, which historically they most likely are not.

It is worth noting that in the vast majority of cases observed in the data, metathesis takes place among consonants only. However, there are rare instances of apparent metathesis involving a consonant and the vowel /a/, which will be duly discussed whenever a particular example requires this (see 6.3.6).

3.1 General Observations

Metathesis of consonants within simple roots is quite frequent, at times being responsible for slightly different phonological processes affecting closely related languages. While metathesis mostly involves two neighbouring consonants (whether separated by a vowel or not), it may also occur more than once in the same word and, in the end, involve all three root consonants and create a reverse order of consonantal segments in surface representation, as in the following example in which the order $C_1 C_2 C_3$ is reversed to $C_3 C_2 C_1$.

(63)   'suck, to' PCC *(ma-, n-, RED) **s(a)wɓa** (-a,-y,-n)
       MANDARA   Dghweɗe   √ C C Ca
                                              *ts w ɓa   > ɓ w tsa   > *p'utsa*

       Note: We consider this to be the result of multiple metathesis occurring subsequently in the same word: *ts w ɓa > ts ɓ wa > ɓ ts wa > ɓ w tsa.

In the following examples, labial(ised) C_1 metathesises with C_2 and subsequently becomes either desegmentalised, i.e. prosodised to W-prosody, i.e. via labialisation of the original C_2 (BATA and HIGI group languages), or is syllabified and gives rise to final [u] (Sukur).

(64)   'faeces' PCC *(ŋ-) **ɣʷ va** (-a, -y, -n)
       BATA   Jimi   *w vØ-y-n   > vw-yn   > *vʷin*
                    Sharwa   *w vØ-a-y   > vw-ay   > *vʷay*
       HIGI   Kirya   *w vØ-y   > vw-y   > *vʷi*
       SUKUR Sukur   *w vØ   > vw   > *vu*

Occasionally, metathesis involves both simple-root and root-augment consonants, as in the following examples, where root-augmental *-ŋ and root-final /w/ metathesise to yield a sequence /ŋw/ fusing to [ŋʷ]:

(65)   'fly' PCC *(a-, xa-, m-, n-, RED) **dz(a)kʷ(a)ɗa** (-y, -n, -ŋ)
       MANDARA   Mandara   √ CaC Ca
                                          *n-dzaw ya-ŋ   > n-dzawØʸa-ŋ
                                                                                 > n-dzʸawŋa   > ⁿdʒaŋʷa
                         Malgwa   √ C C Ca
                                            *n-dz w ya-ŋ   > n-dzəwØʸa-ŋ
                                                                                 > n-dzʸəwŋa   > ⁿdʒəŋʷa

Notes:
1. There is good reason to assume chronologically intermediate consonant change */ɗ/ > /y/, which would allow phonological palatalisation to emerge and 'survive' even after deletion of the third radical consonant: */ɗ/ > /y/ > yʸ > Øʸ. Alternative explanation: if one were to search for the origin of such */ɗ/ > /y/ change, one could postulate morphological palatalisation from a reconstructed augment *{-y}.

Mandara:
*n-dzawɗa-y-ŋ > n-dzawɗʸa-Øʸ-ŋ > n-dzawØʸa-ŋ > n-dzʸawŋa > ⁿdʒaŋʷa

2. The reconstructed PCC */kʷ/ in C_2 position of the simple root ends up as a labialisation feature of the original root-augmental */ŋ/ in final-consonant position, after */kʷ/ had been partially desegmentalised to [w] before it was shifted to the right to associate with */ŋ/ as a coarticulation feature, which then metathesises with the preceding lexical final vowel /a/ of the simple root).

Malgwa:
*n-dz kʷ yʸa-ŋ > n-dzwØʸaŋ > n-dzʸwaŋ > n-dzʸŋwa > ⁿdʒəŋʷa

There are quite spectacular cases of multiple metathesis to be found (see also triple metathesis in the Dghwedɛ example for 'to suck' in (63) above), i.e. when two instances of metathesis happen within the same word, one feeding into the other. In the following examples, the simple root allows double metathesis when the original order C_1 C_2 C_3 is changed to C_2 C_1 C_3 and further to C_2 C_3 C_1, e.g.

(66)   'five' PCC *(m-, n-) **xʷ t(a)fa** (-y, -k; FV)

			Root type		
BATA	Jimi	√ C CaCa	√ CaC Ca		
		*w tafa	Metathesis	Metathesis	
			tawfa-y	> tafwə-Øʸ	
				> taʸfwə	> tefʷə
MARGI	Bura	√ C C Ca	Metathesis	Metathesis	
		*n-w t fØ	n-twʷf	n-təʷfw	> ntufu
	Kilba	√ C C Ca	Metathesis	Metathesis	
		*w t fØ	> twf	> təfw	> təfu

Note that the Jimi example further necessitates the assumption of a rare shift of root type from √ C CaCa (*wtafa) to √ CaC Ca (tawfa); the Jimi example also shows the effect of Y-prosody stemming from root-augmental *{-y}.

In the following example, it is the final root consonant C_3 */k/ that metathesises with the */y/ of the suffixal root augment before it subsequently allows /k/ to metathesise again with augmental /n/ to undergo prenasalisation to [ⁿg] in the synchronic surface form:

(67)   'root' PCC *(RED) **ɬ(a)r(a)ka** (-a, -y, -kʷ, -n; FV)
       HIGI   Kirya   *ɬ r kØ-y-na > ɬ r yʸ k-na > ɬrØʸnka > ɬəʸrnka > ɬirⁿga

Comparable cases can be illustrated from languages of the HIGI and LAMANG groups, where the ubiquitous root-augmental *{-y} metathesises with the final simple-root consonant or the other root-augment *{-kʷ}, as in the following examples.

(68)   'horn₁' PCC ***d(a)r(a)ma** (-y, -kʷ)
       HIGI   Bana   √ C C Ca
                         *t l ma-y   > t l y ma   > təlimə

3.1 General Observations   101

                    Kamwe-Futu √ C C Ca
                            *t r ma-y-k^w > t r y ma-Ø^w
                                              > tərima^w > tərimo
         LAMANG Lamang, Hdi √ C C Ca
                            *d l ØØ-y-k^w > d l-k^w-y > d k^w l-y > d w l-y   > duli

         Note: For Lamang and Hdi, an alternative and simpler analysis is available according to
         which *{-k^w} is not involved at all, but a root in which C$_3$ is /w/. This alternative
         analysis, however, would rest on a known yet only sporadically occurring m : w
         correspondence, which to assume for this example remains highly speculative:
         *d l mØ-y > d l w-y > d w l-y > duli

3.1.4   Prosodification

Central to our 'prosody-based' approach to historical Central Chadic linguistics is the concept of *prosodification* of reconstructed diachronic segmental phonological units. This diachronic process could be seen as belonging to the more general scenario of 'diachronic loss of segments' (see 3.1.2.2). For Central Chadic languages, it makes sense to distinguish *abrupt* loss (or deletion) from *gradual* loss, i.e. partial desegmentalisation (also occasionally referred to here as 'weakening') and complete desegmentalisation, which both could but may not necessarily include prosodification.

Partial desegmentalisation (aka consonant weakening) would, for instance, change any labialised consonant */C^w/ > /w/ with subsequent neutralisation of the former contrast between them. /w/ can then be syllabified > [u], like */y/ can be syllabified > [i], when occurring in syllable-nucleus positions. /w/ (including /w/ < */C^w/) and /y/ can be partially prosodified, i.e. become sources of labialisation and palatalisation prosodies, without, however, losing their segmental characteristics: /w/ > /w^w/, and /y/ > /y^y/. (This also applies to their syllabic allophones in syllable-nucleus position, i.e. /y^y/ > [i^y], /w^w/ > [u^w].) At the same time, the prosodic characteristics 'float' within the phonological word. Under complete prosodification, however, /w/ and /y/ would lose their segmental characteristics, they 'survive', so to speak, only by 'floating' as suprasegmental prosodies. Eventually, desegmentalisation may become complete to the extent that both the segmental and the suprasegmental properties of the former segments */C^w/, */w/, and */y/ are deleted without any traces left. (See Table 3.2.)

Somewhat related to the above-described process of prosodification is what we here call 're-segmentalisation' of labialised consonants, which leads to cases of 'phoneme split' of the type */C^w/ > /C + w$^{(w)}$/. Basically, this means that the labial feature may become disassociated from the 'plain' consonant and is being treated as a segmental phoneme by itself. As such, and whether we assume intermediate steps of metathesis, however, it may again fuse with

Table 3.2 *Diachronic desegmentalisation and prosodification*

	Diachronic stages of development						
Stage I	Stage II		Stage III		Stage IV		Stage V
Fully segmental	Partial desegmentalisation ('weakening') & neutralisation		Partial prosodification		Complete prosodification		Deletion
	[−syll]	[+syll]	[−syll]	[+syll]			
*/Cʷ/	w	—	wʷ	—	Øʷ		Ø
*/w/		u		uʷ			Ø
*/y/	y	i	yʸ	iʸ	Øʸ		Ø

Table 3.3 *Re-segmentalisation and labialisation transfer*

		Root type	PCC simple root	*Cʷ > C+w⁽ʷ⁾	Metathesis	Prosodification	
BATA	Sharwa Bata	√ CaCa	*ɓaɣʷa	ɓaxwʷØ ɓaØwʷa	ɓawʷx	ɓØʷax ɓaØʷaʷ	ɓʷah ɓoo
MOFU	Jimi Muyang	√ C Ca	*ɓ ɣʷa	ɓ ɣwʷa-n ɓ ØwØ	ɓwʷɣa-n	ɓØʷəɣa-n	ɓʷəɣən ɓu

another consonantal segment, a process, which at the surface creates 'labialisation transfer' from one segment to another. This, then, again can be seen as being part of an overall prosodification tendency in Central Chadic languages. For illustration, see some examples of the word 'hide, to' in languages of the BATA and MOFU groups (Table 3.3); for more details see 6.4.

Mention must be made here of another type of re-segmentalisation, which links up with the hitherto unsolved question of whether 'glottalisation' can or must also be seen as a relevant prosody in Central Chadic languages, albeit with much lower frequency of occurrence compared to palatalisation and labialisation (see 6.3.6). Highly localised and possibly affecting mostly languages of the KOTOKO groups (as far as the data under review suggest), we observe a re-segmentalisation (i.e. phoneme split) affecting */ɓ/ > /ʔ+f/, i.e. the glottal feature becomes delinked from the bilabial 'plain' consonantal element, which in turn surfaces synchronically as /f/, and associates finally with the initial consonant /s/ > [s']. See the PCC simple root *s(a)wɓa 'to suck' in Table 3.4. For details of glottalisation prosody, see Wolff (forthcoming).

Table 3.4 *Re-segmentalisation and glottalisation transfer*

		Root type	Root: *ɓ > ʔ+f	Metathesis	Prosodification	
KOTOKO-NORTH	Afade	√ C C Ca	*swʔfØ	sʔfw	sʔfw^w > sʔə^{w}fw	s'ufu
	Mpade	√ CaC Ca	*sawʔfØ	saʔfw	sʔafw > sʔafw	s'afu
	Malgbe	√ CaC Ca	*saØʔfa-y		sʔafəØ^y > sʔafə^y	s'afɨ
KOTOKO-CENTRAL	Lagwan	√ C C Ca	*swʔfØ-y-n	sʔfw-y-n	sʔəfəw^{w}Ø^{y}ə^{w}n > sʔə^{y}fə^{w}wə^{w}n	s'ifuwun
	Mser	√ CaC Ca	*n-sawʔfa-y		nsʔafəØ^y > nsʔafə^y	ns'afɨ

3.2 Issues in Central Chadic Diachronic Phonology

The present study is essentially a follow-up to Gravina's work as a University of Leiden PhD thesis published under the title *The Phonology of Proto-Central Chadic: The Reconstruction of the Phonology and Lexicon of Proto-Central Chadic, and the Linguistic History of the Central Chadic Languages* (2014a). The thesis has a high scientific value in itself, and at the same time provides a solid and most welcome basis for follow-up studies. Gravina presents arguments for his diachronic interpretation of the rich data representing maximally 66 languages and language variants, which he compiled and later made available in the form of an electronic database (Gravina 2014b). As already indicated further above, our main purpose in this study is to provide alternative solutions to lexical reconstructions in PCC, which are based on an alternative approach based on a number of different assumptions about the history of Central Chadic languages, namely regarding

1. the relevance of observing *root-and-pattern* structures inherited from much earlier stages of linguistic history;
2. the more general role of *prosodies*, in particular palatalisation and labialisation;
3. the assumption of only one reconstructable *phonemic* vowel */a/*, which entails the treatment of schwa as pro- and epenthetic and, therefore, *non-phonemic*;
4. the recognition of [+syllabic] i and u as *conditioned allophones in complementary distribution* (occurring only in syllable-nucleus position) with [±syllabic] */y/* and */w/* (occurring as [−syllabic] approximants elsewhere).

3.2.1 Inventory: Consonants

Gravina (2014a: 231) gives the consonantal system of Proto-Central Chadic as in Table 3.5.

Table 3.5 *Consonant inventory (1)*

	Labial	Alveolar	Laminal	Velar	Labialised velar
Plosive	p	t	ts	k	k^w
	b	d	dz	g	g^w
Implosive	ɓ	ɗ			
Fricative		ɬ	s	h	h^w
	v	ɮ	z	ɣ	$ɣ^w$
Nasal	m	n			
Prenasalised	^{m}b	^{n}d	^{n}dz	(^{n}g)	($^n g^w$)
Liquid		r			
Approximant			j		w

Table 3.6 *Consonant inventory (2)*

	Labial	Alveolar	Laminal	Velar	Labialised velar
Plosive	p	t	ts	k	k^w
	b	d	dz	g	g^w
Implosive	ɓ	ɗ	ʔy		
Fricative	f	ɬ	s	x	x^w
	v	ɮ	z	ɣ	$ɣ^w$
Nasal	m	n		ŋ	($ŋ^w$)
Prenasalised	^{m}b	^{n}d	^{n}dz	(^{n}g)	($^n g^w$)
Liquid		r			
Approximant	w		y		

It is worth observing that there is a series of labialised velars, but the inventory lacks any palatalised consonants. Gravina's table does not necessarily correspond to generally accepted wisdom among Chadicists. Personally, the present author is inclined to follow P. Newman (p.c. 2020), who assumes PCC to allow the reconstruction of

- both /p/ and /f/;
- additional velar /ŋ/;
- and at least a third glottalised consonant in addition to ɓ and ɗ (with as yet uncertain place of articulation, symbolised tentatively as *ʔy in the modified Table 3.6; see also 6.3.6.4).

Further, and at variance with Gravina's largely IPA-based conventions, we will represent the palatal approximant/glide by y (rather than j), as this is a long-established convention for African languages in general, and for Chadic languages in particular. And we will represent voiceless velar fricatives by *x rather than by *h. This would give us the modified Table 3.6 for potentially reconstructable PCC consonants and approximants that we will use for our own reconstructions of PCC lexical items.

It is worth noting that the inventory listed in Table 3.6 for PCC does not correspond to, for instance, the inventory assumed for Proto-Chadic, see Newman (1977a) and specifically Newman (2006: 190–192). In particular, we note the absence of a palatal series (like č, ʤ, š, ɲ) and palatalised velars (like k^y, g^y, x^y, $ɣ^y$). Synchronically, these consonants do occur in modern CC languages, but are easily accounted for by effects of reconstructed Y-prosody.

Note, however, that the reconstructions by P. Newman (1977a) were presented prior to the identification of the eminent role of prosodies in the comparative study of Central Chadic languages, which – in all modesty – could be said to have begun with Wolff (1981, 1983b) and further developed in, for instance, Wolff (2004, 2006a, 2011, 2017), with due respect also to contributions by D. Barreteau (1983, 1987). Consequently for Newman at the time, the reconstruction of palatalised and labialised consonants and a set of four tentatively reconstructed vowels for the proto-language took precedence over presenting complex accounts of the interplay of consonants and vowels and the effects of prosodies on both. Also, Newman's (2006) retrospective state-of-the-art account for comparative Chadic was written long before Gravina's (2014a) and our present study on comparative Central Chadic were in sight.

In past discussions of diachronic Chadic phonology and reconstruction, the option that Y-prosody might be essentially responsible for the occurrence of a palatal(ised) series of consonants in Chadic languages had never been considered, to the best of the author's knowledge. Rather the other way around, Schuh (2017: 47), as quoted in sub-section 1.1 above, had assumed that 'what is often interpreted as a distinction in vowels is actually a distinction in consonants that influences the pronunciation of vowels'.

Based on the insights of our present study of historical Central Chadic phonology, however, a major issue for general Chadic diachronic linguistics to address would be to establish how the now obvious 'prosodising' typological nature of Central Chadic historically matches up with the apparently widely 'non-prosodising' typological nature of Chadic languages in other branches, where such prosodies have not (yet?) been recognised to play a comparable role. While it would appear to be certain that PCC, and PC, for that matter, had a series of labialised (velar) consonants, the ultimate status of a palatal(ised) series outside Central Chadic deserves further research. We remain reminded, however, that morphological palatalisation has been established to also occur outside Central Chadic, namely in the West Chadic branch (cf. Schuh 2002), which we tentatively reconstruct as originating from one or several grammatical markers of the shape *{-y} (see Wolff 2019).

3.2.2 The Double Origin of Prosodies

Prosodies, in particular palatalisation and labialisation prosodies, are essential features of both synchronic and diachronic Central Chadic phonology. The first researcher to point out in a general fashion the salient distinction between phonology-triggered and morphology-triggered prosodies in Chadic languages was Schuh (2002, cf. Wolff 2019). Writing about palatalisation, Schuh's insights can now also be transferred to labialisation; see the following quote from the abstract of his paper.

Morphological palatalisation is a phenomenon whereby palatal articulation (fronting of vowels, adding palatalisation as a secondary articulation to consonants, changing alveolars to alveopalatals) is *a property associated with an entire morpheme, not with individual segments*. Within the Chadic language family, morphological palatalisation is best documented in the Biu-Mandara [i.e. Central Chadic – HEW] branch, but it has been inherited as a feature in the West branch as well. This paper explores palatalisation phenomena in the West Branch that conceivably trace their origin to morphological palatalisation. In Miya, morphological palatalisation operates much as it does in Biu-Mandara languages, *affecting entire morphemes and associating with specific morphological processes*. Duwai exhibits remnants of morphological palatalisation in certain verb alternations. Bole shows alveolar/alveopalatal variations in specific lexical items that have no local phonological explanation. In Hausa, the origin of palatal consonants has long been a source of controversy. The paper argues that local phonological processes of palatalisation cannot account for a large number of the palatals in modern Hausa, a claim that has *implications for the analysis of the system of high vowels*. (Schuh 2002: 97; emphasis mine)

The distinction between phonological ('lexical') and morphological ('grammatical') prosodies is a simple one, but rests on solid internal reconstruction within individual languages and on comparative studies involving languages groups and branches within the Chadic language family. In short:

- We speak of *phonological prosodies* in cases where the source of the prosody can be found among the segments of the simple root (3.1.2), which may contain labial(ised) or palatal(ised) consonants or approximants/glides.
- We speak of *morphological prosodies* in cases where the source of the prosody can be found outside the simple root but within the same word. In synchronic perspective, the source of the prosody would be a productive grammatical morpheme; in diachronic perspective we would be looking for it among the segments of the (usually suffixal) augmental material (3.1.2) to the simple root. It can be assumed that the root-augmental materials originally had morphological function which, however, has often become semantically bleached, with the segmental part becoming fused with the simple root to yield petrified synchronically underlying ('augmented') roots (see 3.1.2.3). Nonetheless, in some languages and under certain conditions, morphological prosodies may even be observed to (still) operate in the synchronic grammars of Chadic languages.

Usually, it is not problematic to identify the nature of a prosody under review. There are, however, a few cases in which the distinction between phonological and morphological prosody is blurred, namely and for instance, when root-internal /y/ and root-augmental *{-y} could be assumed to have co-occurred in the same word. As a rule and on methodological grounds, in conflicting cases we give priority of phonological over morphological prosodies; a complex example in point is discussed in a special note introducing 'fly' in section 6.4.

A rare case of co-occurrence of root-internal /y/ and root-augmental *{-y} in the data under review concerns the word for 'give birth, to' in Mofu North (MOFU), see 6.4. Here, the triradical PCC simple root **w(a)x(a)ya** is reduced to a synchronic monoradical simple root *ya. In the form contained in the database, which most likely is a citation form, the simple root combines with a prefix *ma- and the ending *-ay and yields the present surface representation *meyey*. Clearly, the two occurrences of the mid vowel [e] are reflexes of palatalisation prosody, whose source, however, remains unidentified. We could be dealing with phonological prosody originating from the root-internal C_3 /y/. We could also be dealing with morphological prosody originating from the root-augmental *{-y} as being part of the ending *{-a-y} > [ey]. We could argue that the two surface mid vowels each could have a separate history of origin, one of phonological nature, one of morphological nature. In any case, prosodies share the same phonetic outcomes independent of their origin, and they do not accumulate and establish degrees of palatalisation, so that we cannot distinguish between single or double effects.

3.2.2.1 Lexical Prosodies: Phonological Palatalisation and Labialisation

Proto-Central Chadic can be assumed to have had a series of labialised velars but no palatal(ised) consonants other than the palatal vocoid/approximant */y/ (see 3.2.1). This could be viewed as a branch-specific diachronic development within Chadic, namely a systematic loss of (alveolo-)palatals, when we compare it with the consonantal inventory reconstructed by P. Newman (1977a: 9; see also Newman, 2006: 191) for Proto-Chadic, which contains series of palatal(ised) post-alveolar consonants and mentions the occurrence of palatalised velars (see also 3.2.1 above).

In Central Chadic languages, the sole source of phonological palatalisation (Y-prosody) would be */y/, since Gravina's and our reconstructed PCC roots would not contain any other phonemic palatal(ised) segments. However, while there are many examples for (postulated) morphological palatalisation (see below), those for purely phonological palatalisation are less frequent and not so easy to find. The following examples show phonological palatalisation at work (see also 3.2.5), in which both origin and effect of prosodies are made redundantly explicit by raised ^{y} and ^{w}.

(69) 'bone' PCC *((')a-, a-n-, a-ta-, ma-, ma-ta-, RED-a-) **ɗ y(a)ła** (-a, -y, -k^w, -t, -n)

BATA	Bachama	√ C C Ca	*Ø y la-k^w	Metathesis	
				y k^w la	
				> əy^y w^w la	
				> ə^w Ø^y u^w la^y	> uule
	Tsuvan	√ C C Ca	*Ø y ɮa	> i^y ɮa	
				> iɮa^y	> iʑe
TERA	Tera	√ C C Ca	*ɗ y ɬØ	> ɗ Ø^y əɬ	
				> ɗ^y əɬ	> ɠəɬ
	Ga'anda	√ C C Ca	*(a-)Ø y la⁴	> aØ^y la	
				> a^y la	> ela
MANDARA	Malgwa	√ C C Ca	*RED+Ø y x^y a	> RED+Ø^y x^y a	
				> x^y a^y +x^y a^y	> h^y eh^y e
MAROUA	Giziga-	√ C C Ca	*ta-Ø y ła	> ta-Ø^y ł(a)	
	Muturwa			> ta^y ł(a^y)	> teł(e)
		√ C C Ca	*a-ta-Ø y ɬØ	> ataØ^y ɬ	
				> a^y ta^y ɬ	> eteł
HIGI	Kamwe-	√ C C Ca	*' y ła	> 'y^y əła	
	Nkafa			> 'yə^y łə	> 'yithlə
KOTOKO-	Mazera	√ C C Ca	*a-RED+' y sa	Metathesis	
SOUTH				a-RED-'sya	
				a-RED-s'ya	
				> a-s+s'Ø^y a	
				> asə^y +s'a^y	> asis'e

Note: In some languages, medial */y/ is assumed to be responsible for changing final */a/ > [e] (Bachama, Tsuvan, Malgwa, Giziga, Mazera). In one language, */y/ syllabifies to [i] (Tsuvan) – a process that we do not subsume under Y-prosody. In at least one of the languages, it would be responsible for palatalising and shifting the preceding initial consonant from alveolar to velar position (Tera ɗy > ɠ).⁵

Phonological palatalisation may not be as immediately evident from the PCC reconstructed root as in the example above. In the following example, its source may only come about by consonant change in some language groups, like */ɗ/ > y. See the situation in the MANDARA and MOFU groups for example:

(70) 'fly' (noun) PCC *(a-, xa-, m-, n-, RED) **dz(a)k^w(a)ɗa** (-y, -n, -ŋ)

(a) */ɗ/ > y, without emerging Y-prosody

MANDARA	Matal	√ C CaCa	*z wayØ	> zway ~ zəway ~ zuway
MOFU	Ouldeme	√ C CaCa	*z wayØ	> zuway
	Merey	√ C CaCa	*dz wayØ	> dzuway

---

⁴ For initial [e] in Ga'anda, there are two options for analysis: (a) presence of a prefixal augment *a-, or (b) insertion of a prothetic vowel [a] in front of an initial consonant cluster, both resulting in *ayla > ela. Vowel prothesis is a widespread Central Chadic strategy to create pronounceable syllables for words with initial consonant clusters.

⁵ The emergence of an implosive velar ɠ stemming from the fusion of ɗ+y in Tera would appear to be counter-intuitive, but has parallels in some languages of the MANDARA group (Mandara, Malgwa, Glavda), where palatalised alveolars emerge as palatalised velars, see under 'cry', 'grandfather', 'moon' in section 6.4.

(b) */d/ > y, with Y-prosody effect

MANDARA	Podoko	√ C CaCa	*n-dz wayʸØ	> n-dzʸwaØʸ	> ⁿdʒəwe
	Mandara	√ CaC Ca	*n-dzawØʸa-ŋ	> n-dzʸawa-ŋ	
				> n-dzʸaŋwa	> ⁿdʒaŋʷa
MOFU	Muyang	√ C C Ca	*a-z wʷ yʸØ	> ay-zəʷwiʸ	> ezʉwi
	Moloko	√ C CaCa	*dz wayʸØ	> dzʸway	> dʒəway
	Zulgo	√ C CaCa	*dz wayʸØ	> dzəʸwaØy	> dziwe
	Gemzek	√ C CaCa	*dz wʷayʸØ	> dzəʷwaØʸ	> dzuwe
	Dugwor	√ C CaCa	*dz wʷayʸØ	> dzʸəʷway	> dʒuway

With regard to phonological labialisation, we note that reconstructed PCC roots may contain any of several labial(ised) segments, such as */w/, */kʷ/, */gʷ/, */xʷ/, */ɣʷ/ and /ᵑgʷ/. These serve as sources for phonological labialisation (W-prosody). As noted by Gravina (2014a), phonological labialisation of consonants in Central Chadic tends to preferentially target labial consonants, i.e. we often see a transfer of the labialisation feature from velars to labials, which reminds one of the grave vs. acute features of early distinctive feature theory (as associated with Roman Jakobson and Morris Halle). Of course, vowels (both epenthetic schwa and phonemic */a/) also undergo labialisation under the impact of prosody. The following is an example to show phonological labialisation at work (see also 3.2.4).

(71)   'hide, to' *(ka-) ɓ(a)ɣʷa (-n)

(a) Labialisation feature transfer from velar to labial consonant

BATA	Jimi	√ C Ca	*ɓ ɣʷØ-n	> ɓʷɣ-n	> ɓʷəyən
	Sharwa	√ CaCa	*ɓaxʷØ		> ɓʷah

(b) Labialisation feature transfer from velar consonant to vowels

BATA	Bata	√ CaCa	*ɓaɣʷØ	> ɓaʷw	> ɓoo
DABA	Daba	√ CaCa	*ɓaxʷØ	> ɓaʷx	> ɓoh
HIGI	Bana	√ C Ca	*ɓ ɣʷa	Metathesis	
				ɣʷɓa	
				> ɣəʷɓə	> ɣuɓə

(c) Labialisation feature becoming syllabified after 're-segmentalisation' /Cʷ/ > C+w

MOFU	Muyang	√ C Ca	*ɓ ɣʷØ	> ɓw	> ɓu

(d) No prosody effect emerging from underlying labialised velar

DABA	Buwal, Gavar	√ CaCa	*ɓaxʷØ	> ɓah
	Mbudum	√ CaCa	*ka-ɓaxʷØ	> kəɓah
MANDARA	Podoko	√ C Ca	*ɓxʷa	> ɓəhʷa

Note that in the DABA languages, the underlying final consonant is 'de-labialised', while in Podoko the original labialisation feature is retained *in loco*, without any prosodic effect on the rest of the word.

3.2.2.2 Grammatical Prosodies: Morphological Palatalisation and Labialisation

As pointed out above (3.2.2), in diachronic perspective we would look for sources of morphological palatalisation and labialisation among the segments of the reconstructable root-augment materials (3.1.2), usually to be found in suffixal augment position in relation to the simple root. Candidates among these are *{-y} for Y-prosody and *{-k^w} for W-prosody. Both diachronic root-augmental suffixes may, in absolute word-final position, undergo either straightforward syllabification, like *{-y} > -i when the synchronic root deletes its lexical final /a/ and now ends in [i], or weakening of *{-k^w} > w and further syllabification of w > [u], when the synchronic root ends in [u]. E.g.

(72)   beard   HIGI   Kirya   *g^w ma-y   > ɣ^{w}mØ-y
  > ɣə^{w}m-i   > *yumi*
           bone   MARGI   Margi   *ɗ yaha-k^w > ɗyahØ-w   > *dyahu*

Ideally, we would want to know what the original grammatical function(s) of such markers were in PCC, and derive their postulation for underlying or diachronic structure also from that. Such questions regarding the original function of such diachronic morphemic markers must remain open. However, and as has been noted by the current author in several earlier publications and above, quite a few show similarity to the inventory of Proto-Chadic determiners that were reconstructed by Schuh (1983): *n, *t, *k, *ɗ, and *i.

Some root-augmental material that is reconstructed in this study may, indeed and further, have a transparent history from the synchronic study of Central Chadic languages and low-level comparison. This may be particularly true for morphological markers that accompany the nominalisation of verbs in a fair number of Central Chadic languages, where the data reflect citation forms rather than roots.

3.2.3 Labialisation Prosody

Labialisation prosody is triggered by a labialised consonant (*/C^w/) or /w/ either within the root or as part of (petrified) root-augmentation material, such as *{-k^w}. Labialised consonants may undergo partial desegmentalisation ('weakening') to *w, which then may occasionally further syllabify to [u] when shifted into syllable-nucleus position. In a historical perspective on Central Chadic, therefore, labialisation prosody could have been both phonological and morphological in nature.

However, as far as the author is aware, morphological labialisation prosody has not been described as a synchronic process in present-day Central Chadic languages.[6] Our reconstructions, however, reveal that we have to reconstruct

---

[6] Even though it has not been explicitly described in synchronic grammars under the term 'morphological' labialisation, we may find the phenomenon hidden behind other descriptive

3.2 Issues in CC Diachronic Phonology

sources of W-prosody from the root-augmental materials for the many cases in which there is no source for phonological labialisation detectable within the simple root. We represent this reconstructed diachronic marker as *{-k^w}. Note, however, that a petrified morpheme *{-k^w(a)} can likely be reconstructed for PCC on independent evidence anyway.

Clear cases of phonological W-prosody affecting underlying */a/ can be illustrated with a highly restricted root for 'horn$_2$', which contains a labialised consonant */x^w/, which in the examples in (73) is responsible for the labialisation of */a/ in Mbara (MUSGUM) and Gidar (GIDAR). In KOTOKO-SOUTH group languages, Zina retains the inherited labialised consonant without further changes, but in Mazera */x^w/ re-segmentalises into */x + w/ with subsequent syllabification of /w/ > [u]. Additionally in Mazera, morphological Y-prosody plays a role by affecting the vowel of both the first and final syllable. The PCC simple root is reconstructed as *x^w**ala**.

(73) horn$_2$ KOTOKO-   Zina   *a-x^{w}alØ   > *ah^{w}al*
                SOUTH   Mazera   *ma-x^{w}aØØ-y   > ma-xwa-Ø^y
                                                      > mə^y-xua^y > *mihue*
                MUSGUM   Mbara   *ma-x^{w}aØØ   > ma^{w}xa^w > *moho*
                GIDAR   Gidar   *ma-x^{w}aØØ   > ma^{w}xa^w > *moho*

Looking for other instances of phonological W-prosody, such can be illustrated from the following examples, in which the labial feature is again part of one of the radical consonants. In the languages to be discussed below, the labial(isation) feature becomes somewhat detached from the original consonant and is transferred to another segment, for instance a following vowel, whether epenthetic or */a/ (as seen in Mbara and Gidar above), as the following example shows. In two languages (Mbudum, Hdi) it is completely lost. Occasionally, additional (morphological) Y-prosody plays a role as well.

(74)   'boil, to' PCC *(ma-) **k^w(a)ɗ(a)xa** (-a, -y, -ŋ)

   Note: All cases are listed in which any or none of the two prosodies is operating. Note also that this is a root in which potentially all vocalic slots may be filled by */a/ (full a-vocalisation) and which allows a variety of root types, including Ø-vocalisation in some languages.

   (a) W-prosody affecting epenthetic schwa, or centralised /a/ > [ə], to yield [u]
   DABA   Daba   √ C C Ca   *k^{w}ɗØØ-a-y   > kə^{w}ɗay   > *kuday*
   MAFA   Cuvok   √ C CaCa   *k^{w}ɗaxa   > kə^{w}ɗaxa   > *kudaha*
   TERA   Tera   √ C CaCa   *k^{w}raxØ-y   > kə^{w}rax-i   > *kuraxi*

terms, like 'vowel harmonisation' or 'umlaut'. See, for instance, the description of simple verbal noun formation in Lamang (Wolff 2015, Vol.1: 167), which – from the more general and diachronic perspective of the present study – is a clear case of *morphological labialisation*.

	Nyimatli	√ C CaCa	*kʷɓakxØ	> kəʷɓakh	> kuɓakh
MARGI	Bura	√ C C Ca	*kʷdØa	> kəʷdəʷ	> kudu

Note: An alternative analysis is feasible for these examples that would avoid the assumption of vowel epenthesis. We could assume initial */kʷ/ to become re-segmentalised yielding /k + w/, with subsequent syllabification of /w/ > [u] in the first syllable. This alternative analysis is illustrated by the following examples. - In Bura and under both analyses, W-prosody originating from kʷ or wʷ would be responsible for changing centralised final */a/ > [ə] > [u].

DABA	Daba	√ C C Ca	*kʷdØØ-a-y	> kwday	> kuday
MAFA	Cuvok	√ C CaCa	*kʷdaxa	> kwdaxa	> kudaha
TERA	Tera	√ C CaCa	*kʷraxØ-y	> kwrax-i	> kuraxi
	Nyimatli	√ C CaCa	*kʷɓakxØ	> kwɓakx	> kuɓakh
MARGI	Bura	√ C C Ca	*kʷdØa	> kwʷdəʷ	> kudu

(b) W- prosody affecting /a/ to yield [o]
MOFU Muyang √ CaCaCa *kʷadaxØ-a-y   > kaʷdax-ay   > kodahay
MOFU Dugwor √ CaCaCa *ma-kʷadaxØ-a-yy   > makʷaʷdaʸx-yʸ > məkʷodehey

(c) Y-prosody affecting /a/ to yield [e]
DABA Mbudum √ C CaCa *k daxØ-y   > kdax-Øʸ
                                      > kʸdaʸx   > kydeh
MOFU Gemzek √ CaCaCa *ma-kʷadaxa-y > makʷadaxa-Øʸ
                                      > maʸkʷaʸdaʸxaʸ > mekʷedehe
      Dugwor √ CaCaCa *ma-kʷadaxØ-a-y > makʷadaxayʸ
                                      > makʷaʷdaʸxaʸy > məkʷodehey
      Mofu   √ CaCaCa *ma-kʷadax-a-y > makʷadaxayʸ
      North   > maʸkʷaʸdaʸxaʸy > mekʷedehey

(d) Y-prosody affecting only C₂
BATA Bachama √ CaCaCa *kʷadasa-y > kʷadasa-Øʸ
                                 > kʷadʸasa
                                 > kʷadʸasa

(e) Ø-prosody
HURZA	Mbuko	√ CaCaCa	*kʷadaxØ		> kʷadah
	Vame	√ CaCaCa	*kʷadaxa		> kʷadaha
MANDARA	Podoko	√ CaCaCa	*kʷadaxa		> kʷadaha
	Malgwa	√ CaCaCa	*kʷadØØa		> kʷada
MOFU	Mada	√ CaCaCa	*ma-kʷadaxØ		> makʷadah
	Zulgo	√ CaCaCa	*kʷadaxØ		> kʷadah
LAMANG	Lamang	√ CaCaCa	*kʷadaxØ		> kʷadah
	Hdi	√ C CaCa	*kdax-a-y	> kədaxay	> kədahay

The transfer of the labial(isation) element may also affect other consonants in the root; labials in particular are targeted for such transfer. See the following example for /xʷ/ being prosodified to ʷ and fusing with the preceding labial /v/ in the root in some languages; in other languages it targets the epenthetic vowel schwa to yield surface [u]. In two languages (Gavar, Podoko) it is lost

3.2 Issues in CC Diachronic Phonology   113

completely, while in another (Buwal) it survives as segmental w, not the least due to the fact that Buwal uses a different root type, namely √ CaCa.

(75)   'beer' PCC *(ma-, n-, ⁿga-) **v(a)xʷa** (-y, -n)
        BATA   Bata   √ C Ca   *v wa-y   > vwa-Ø^y
                                                > vway   > vʷe
                Gude   √ C Ca   *n-v wa   > ənvwa   > ənvʷa
                Jimi   √ C Ca   *ⁿga-v Øʷ Ø-n > ⁿgavəʷn   > ⁿgəvun
                Sharwa √ C Ca   *v xʷ Ø   Re-segmentalisation
                                                & metathesis
                                                v w x
                                                > vwəx   > vʷəh
                Tsuvan √ C Ca   *v wa-y   > vwa-Ø^y
                                                > əvway   > əvʷe
        DABA   Buwal   √ CaCa   *ma-vawØ   > mavaw
                Gavar   √ C Ca   *ma-v Øa   > ma-va   > mavə
                Mbudum √ C Ca   *ma-v wØ   > ma-vw   > mavu
                Daba   √ C Ca   *ma-v wØ   > ma-vwʷ
                                                > maʷ-vw   > movu
        MANDARA Podoko √ C Ca   *p xØa-y   > pəxa-Ø^y
                                                > pəʸxaʸ   > pihe

The next examples involve metathesis, like in Sharwa above. The resulting abutting radical consonants /v/ + /w/ (<*/ɣʷ/) yield surface vʷ. Note also syllabification of root-augmental *{-y} > i in Jimi and Kirya.

(76)   'faeces' PCC *(ŋ-) **ɣʷ va** (-a, -y, -n)
        BATA   Jimi   *ɣʷ vØ-y-n   > w v-yn   Metathesis: v w-in   > vʷin
                Sharwa *ɣʷ vØ-a-y   > w v-ay   Metathesis: v w-ay   > vʷay
        HIGI   Kirya   *ɣʷ vØ-y   > w v-y   Metathesis: v w-i   > vʷi

3.2.3.1 Suffixal Augment

The reconstructed – sometimes hypothetical – suffixal root-augment *{-kʷ}, which is occasionally also found as a petrified suffix in synchronic data, is considered to be responsible for morphological labialisation where it occurs. We observe two different manifestations of the resulting phonological effects. Either *{-kʷ} desegmentalises completely, i.e. it prosodifies to survive only in the shape of W-prosody with effects on preceding consonants and/or vowels (here we speak of the 'prosodising' variant), or *{-kʷ} is weakened to /w/, usually in absolute final positions, and syllabifies to [u] and may not have any further prosody effect on the rest of the word (here we speak of the 'non-prosodising' variant). Both processes will be looked at separately below.

3.2.3.2 Prosodising *{-kʷ}

As said, *{-kʷ} may desegmentalise completely and survive only in the shape of W-prosody with effects on preceding consonants and/or vowels. Examples that neatly show the different targeted domains and the difference between epenthetic and phonemic vowels are, for instance, the following. Note the use of different root types in the individual languages to explain the presence or absence of underlying */a/.

(77) 'butterfly' PCC *(..., ma-ta-, RED) **p(a)ra** (-y, -k^w, -n; FV)
      MAROUA Giziga- √ C Ca *ma-RED+pla-k^w > mə-plapla-Ø^w
              Muturwa   > mə^w-plapla   > *muplapla*
      GIDAR   Gidar   √ CaCa *ma-ta-RED+pala-k^w > mata-palapala-Ø^w
                                                                           > ma^{w}ta^{w}pa^{w}la^{w}pa^{w}la^w > *motopolopolo*

> Note that in Giziga-Muturwa *muplapla*, the [u] in the first syllable could also be attributed to very shallow assimilation of centralised /a/ > [ə] > [u] by the labial feature of the initial /m/. The W-prosody analysis is preferred here in the light of the assumed occurrence of *{-k^w} with this lexical item in other languages as well, like in Gidar.

(78) 'hair' PCC *(ma-) **s(a)b(a)ta** (-y, -k^w)
      BATA   Sharwa   √ C C Ca   *s ɓ tØ-y-k^w > sə.ɓə.t-y^y-Ø^y
                                                                                           > s^{y}ə.ɓ^{w}ə.t-i   > *ʃəɓ^{w}əti*
               Tsuvan   √ C C Ca   *s ɓ ta-y-k^w > səɓ.ta-Ø^y-Ø^w
                                                                                          > sə^{w}ɓ.ta^y > *subte*
      SUKUR   Sukur   √ C C Ca   *m-s b tØ-y-k^w > sə.^{m}bət-Ø^y-Ø^w
                                                                                          > s^{y}ə^w.^{m}bə^{w}t   > *ʃu^{m}but*
      MOFU   Moloko   √ C CaCa   *m-s bata-y-k^w > sə.^{m}ba.ta-Ø^y-wk
                                                                                         > sə.^{m}ba^y.ta^{y}wk > *sə^{m}betewk*

> Note that for Sharwa, Tsuvan and Sukur the labialisation feature could also be considered, though less plausibly, as intrinsic in the articulation of C$_2$ /^{m}b$^{(w)}$/~/ɓ$^{(w)}$/. Strong evidence for the presence of *{-k^w}, however, comes from Moloko.

> Note further that in Moloko, W-prosody anticipation is blocked by the obvious primacy of simultaneous Y-prosody. Here, *{-k^w} is re-segmentalised */k+w/ with unique metathesis > /w+k/. This /w/ becomes more ore less syllabified and likely accounts for the surface diphthong [ew] in the final syllable.

3.2.3.3 Non-Prosodising *{-k^w}

In a second scenario of morphological labialisation, we observe partial desegmentalisation ('weakening') of *{-k^w} > w and subsequent syllabification of w > [u] (see also 6.3.2), but without any prosodising effect on preceding syllables:

(79) 'bone' PCC *(...) **ɗ y(a)ɬa** (-a, -y, -k^w, -t, -n)
      MARGI   Margi   *ɗ yaxØ-k^w > ɗya.x-w   > *ɗyahu*

(80) 'dream' PCC *(...) **s(a)w(a)na** (-a, -y, -k^w, -n; a)
      HIGI   Kirya   *s w ØØ-y-k^w > səw-Ø^y-w > s^{y}ə^y.w-w > *ʃiwu* (vb)

3.2.3.4 Is Morphological Labialisation Older Than Phonological Labialisation?

An interesting historical question concerning relative chronology is raised by the following set of examples for 'horn$_1$', which show two different

3.2 Issues in CC Diachronic Phonology

potential sources for labialisation, namely – at least theoretically – both morphological and phonological. Gravina (2014b) mentions the issue as being quite irritating:

> Another difficulty is the presence of labialisation in many of the groups. The change *m to /w/ in the Mandara group is regular, and in the Lamang group is a common sporadic change. However we also have labialisation in the Mafa, Sukur, Maroua and Higi groups that has not come from *m. In the Maroua group this is a common sporadic change, but the present reconstruction does not account for the introduction of labialisation in the other groups.

We would be talking about phonological labialisation if in the languages that underwent a change */m/ > w (regular in the MANDARA group, sporadic in the LAMANG group) this w triggered W-prosody – but it doesn't. And there is so far no evidence that PCC had ^{x}/m^w/ as a consonant phoneme that might have given rise to phonological labialisation in this root. Wherever W-prosody occurs across the language groups, therefore, it must be morphological in nature. We could take this to be an indication that morphological labialisation is older than phonological labialisation, if we assume that the change */m/ > /w/ (and metathesis in the LAMANG group) chronologically preceded the combination with *{-k^w} but as such did not create W-prosody. On the other hand, it remains an interesting observation that in those languages that underwent the */m/ > /w/ change, there would be no sign of the presence of *{-k^w} that might have induced W-prosody nonetheless. Postulating morphological labialisation by *{-k^w}, therefore, would appear to be the most transparent and economic explanation.

(81)   'horn$_1$' PCC **d(a)r(a)ma** (-y, -k^w)
       (a) Forms with Ø-prosody (note differences in root type)

MARGI	Kilba	√ C C Ca	*t l mØ	> tələm	> taləm
MANDARA	Matal	√ C CaCa	*d rawØ		> draw
		√ C CaCa	*d rawØ	> dəraw	> dəraw
	Podoko	√ C CaCa	*d rawa	> dərawa	> dərawa
	Glavda	√ C C Ca	*d r Øa	> dəra	> dəra
		√ C CaCa	*d rawa		> drawa
	Dghweɗe	√ C CaCa	*d rawa	> dərawa	> dərawa
MOFU	Mada	√ C CaCa	*d ramØ		> dram
	Merey	√ C CaCa	*d ramØ	> dəram	> dəram
	Mofu North	√ C CaCa	*t lamØ	> təlam	> talam
		√ CaCaCa	*talamØ		> talam
	Mofu-Gudur	√ C CaCa	*t lamØ	> təlam	> təlam

       (b) Forms with Y-prosody

MAFA	Cuvok	√ C CaCa	*d ramØ-y	> dəram-Ø^y	
				> dəra^{y}m	> dərem

MANDARA	Mandara	√ CaC Ca	*dar ma-y	> darma-Ø^y	
				> da^yrma	> derma
	Malgwa	√ C C Ca	*d r ma-y	> dərəma-Ø^y	
				> dərəma^y	> dərme
MOFU	Muyang	√ C CaCa	*a-d ramØ-y	> adram-Ø^y	
				> a^ydra^ym	> edrem

(c) Forms with W-prosody

MAFA	Mafa	√ CaCaCa	*talamØ-k^w	> talam-Ø^w	
				> ta^wla^wm	> tolom
		√ C CaCa	*d ramØ-k^w	> dəram-Ø^w	
				> də^wra^wm	> durom
	Mefele	√ C C Ca	*d r mØ-k^w	> dərəm-Ø^w	
				> dərə^wm	> dərum
SUKUR	Sukur	√ C CaCa	*taØ mØ-k^w	> tam-Ø^w	
				> t^wam	> twam
MOFU	Dugwor	√ C CaCa	*d ramØ-k^w	> dəram-Ø^w	
				> dəra^wm	> dərom
MAROUA	Giziga-Muturwa	√ C C Ca	*d r mØ-k^w	> dərəm-Ø^w	
				> də^wrə^wm	> durum
		√ C C Ca	*d r mØ-k^w	> drəm-Ø^w	
				> drə^wm	> drum
	Giziga-Marva	√ C CaCa	*d ramØ-k^w	> dəram-Ø^w	
				> də^wra^wm	> durom
	Mbazla	√ C C Ca	*d r mØ-k^w	> dərəm-Ø^w	
				> də^wrə^wm	> durum

(d) Forms with both Y- and W-prosody

MARGI	Bura	√ C C Ca	*t l mba-y-k^w		
			Metathesis		
			t mb lØ-y-k^w	> təmbəl-Øy-Ø^w	
				> tə^ymbə^wl	> ti^mbul

(e) Forms with W-prosody and non-prosodising *{-y}

LAMANG	Lamang	√ C C Ca	*d l ØØ-y-k^w	> d l-y-w	
			Metathesis:	d l-w-y	
			Metathesis:	d w l-y	
				> dul-i	> duli^7

---

[7] Recalling my own fieldwork on Lamang, I seem to remember that I was intrigued by the occasional extra-length of the medial vowel [u], which appeared to be longer than would be expected under the usual penultimate stress. But, since Lamang does not have phonemic but only morphophonemic vowel length, the word is usually simply transcribed as *duli* (cf. Wolff 2015). Until now, I had no explanation for the slightly disturbing issue of relative vowel length. Revisiting the issue in diachronic perspective again for this study, however, it would appear plausible to relate the occasionally heard extra length to the underlying intermediate structure with vowel epenthesis *də^ww.li > du:li* rather than assuming simply syllabification from underlying dw.ly > duli. Possibly, if not likely, Central Chadic languages allow for competing options

3.2 Issues in CC Diachronic Phonology 117

		√ C C Ca	*d l ØØ-y-kʷ	> d l-y-w	
			Metathesis:	d l-w-y	
			Metathesis:	d w l-i	
				> dəʷul-i	> du:li
	Hdi	√ C C Ca	*d l ØØ-y-kʷ	> d l-y-w	
			Metathesis:	d l-w-y	
			Metathesis:	d w l-i	
				> dul-i	> duli
HIGI	Kamwe-Nkafa	√ C C Ca	*t r mØ-y-kʷ		
			Metathesis :	trm-kʷ-y	
				> tərm-Øʷ-i	> tərmʷi
	Kamwe-Futu	√ C C Ca	*t r ma-y-kʷ		
			Metathesis:	tryma-kʷ	
				> təryma-Øʷ	
				> tərimaʷ	> tərimo

3.2.4 Palatalisation Prosody

Palatalisation prosody has attracted the attention of Chadicists, more so than labialisation prosody, mainly because of its obvious synchronic morphological function in a few present-day languages. It has been observed mainly in Central Chadic languages, beginning with a pioneer study on Ga'anda (TERA) by Roxana Ma Newman (1977) and having been lucidly described for Podoko (MANDARA), for instance, in works by Elizabeth Jarvis and Jeanette Swackhamer, but it also has reflexes in other Chadic branches, such as West Chadic (cf. Schuh 2002; Wolff 2019b).

This provides very strong evidence to justify our 'prosody-based' approach to Central Chadic lexical reconstruction as presented in this study. It rests on the assumption that, when we have good evidence for identifiable diachronic morphological sources of Y-prosody that have characteristic effects in present-day languages, we are justified in assuming and internally reconstructing the diachronic presence of such sources, wherever we see such palatalisation effects in present-day languages (and where sources for phonological palatalisation within the simple root are likely to be excluded). This is further supported by the observation that, in the absence of PCC palatal(ised) consonants other than /y/, practically all instances of Y-prosody must originate from palatalising root-augmental material, i.e. *{-y} (of possibly various original functions in PCC (see Wolff 2019b), among which likely the determiner *i as

---

when it comes to creating 'pronounceable' syllables from underlying phonemic structures, see also Bana (HIGI) in (93) below.

reconstructed for PC by Schuh (1983)). As was pointed out further above (3.2.2.1), there are comparatively few clear cases for phonological palatalisation stemming exclusively from */y/ within a simple root. See the following examples for morphological Y-prosody affecting both consonants and epenthetic schwa, and also lexical final /a/ in Hwana:

(82)　　'ashes' PCC *(a-) **p ts(a)ɗa** (-y, -k^w,-n)
　　　　TERA　　Tera　　　*p dz tØ-y　　> pədzət-Ø^y
　　　　　　　　　　　　　　　　　　　　> pədz^{y}ə^{y}t　　> pədʒit
　　　　　　　　Hwana　　*f s Øa-y　　> fəsa-Ø^y
　　　　　　　　　　　　　　　　　　　　> fə^{y}s^{y}a^y　　> fiʃe

In the following examples, only vowels are affected to the exclusion of consonants:

(83)　　'ashes' PCC *(a-) **p ts(a)ɗa** (-y, -k^w,-n)
　　　　MOFU　　Muyang　　*v t-y　　> vət-i^y
　　　　　　　　　　　　　　　　　　　> və^{y}t-i　　> viti
　　　　　　　　Zulgo　　　*b ta-y　　> bəta-Ø^y
　　　　　　　　　　　　　　　　　　　> bə^{y}ta^y　　> bite

(84)　　'blow, to' PCC *(ma-) **v ɮa** (-a, -y, -k^w, -n)
　　　　BATA　　Bata　　　*f lØ-y　　> fəl-Ø^y
　　　　　　　　　　　　　　　　　　　> fə^{y}l　　> fil
　　　　MOFU　　Zulgo　　　*v ɮØ-y　　> vəɮ-Ø^y
　　　　　　　　　　　　　　　　　　　> və^{y}ɮ　　> viɮ

Our reconstructions show that morphological palatalisation plays an enormous role in the derivation of modern language forms. The full gamut of representations of *{-y} in modern Central Chadic languages can be illustrated by the following examples. It is found behind surface endings [i], [e], [uy], [ay], and [ey]. Note that the presence of *{-y} does not necessarily trigger Y-prosody (as it does in Moloko below); the reconstructed morpheme may just be represented segmentally as /y/ (as in the MAROUA languages), or syllabify as [i] (as in Muyang).

(85)　　'cry, to' PCC *(ma-) **ts(a)wa** (-a, -y, -k; FV)
　　　　MOFU　　Muyang　　　　　　*t w^{w}Ø-y　　> tə^{w}w-i　　　> tuwi
　　　　　　　　Moloko　　　　　　*t wa-y　　　> təwa-Ø^y
　　　　　　　　　　　　　　　　　　　　　　　　> təwa^y　　　> təwe
　　　　MAROUA　Giziga-Muturwa　　*t w^{w}Ø-y　　> tə^{w}wə^w-y　> tuwuy
　　　　　　　　Giziga-Marva　　　*t w^{w}Ø-a-y　> tə^{w}w-ay　　 > tuway

These forms can be compared to a variant form in Giziga-Marva, which does not contain any reflex of *{-y}:

(86)　　　　MAROUA　Giziga-Marva　　*t w^{w}a　　> tə^{w}wa　　> tuwa

3.2 Issues in CC Diachronic Phonology

The ending variant [ey] is found, for instance, in the following word:

(87)   'dog' PCC ***k(a)ra** (-a, -y, -k^w; FV)
         MOFU   Mofu North,   *g da-y   > gəda-y^y
                 Mofu-Gudur   > gəda^yy   > gədey

One of the issues still to be resolved is the question of under which conditions, if there are any to be discovered, suffixal *{-y} creates Y-prosody and becomes completely desegmentalised and prosodified to Ø^y, as opposed to cases where it creates Y-prosody and is segmentally retained intact as either /y/ or [i] in synchronic description (see below). The latter cases are here symbolised by -y^y or -i^y.

3.2.4.1 Suffixal Augment

The reconstructed root-augment *{-y} (or its possible synchronic reflex as ending i~y in some modern languages) is very frequent in the data. We observe two different manifestations of the resulting phonological effects. Either *{-y} desegmentalises/prosodifies completely and only leaves traces in the shape of Y-prosody with effects on preceding consonants and/or vowels ('prosodising' variant), or *{-y} syllabifies to [i] (with 'prosodising' and 'non-prosodising' variants), or it becomes part of a final diphthong [ay~ey] (mostly, but not always non-prosodising). Both variant processes will be looked at separately below.

3.2.4.2 Prosodising *{-y}

The prosodising effect of *{-y} on vowels, whether epenthetic ([ə] > [ɨ ~ i]) or phonemic (/a/ > [e]), is illustrated by the following simple set of examples. In word-final position, *{-y} syllabifies to [i] when the preceding lexical /a/ is deleted. When lexical final /a/ is maintained, /a/ + *{-y} diphthongise (yielding intermediate [-ay~ey]) and subsequently may monophthongise to [e].

(88)   'cry' PCC ***ts(a)wa** (-a, -y, -k; FV)
         MARGI   Margi-   *t wØ-y
                     South,   > təw-i^y
                     Kilba   > tə^yw-i   > tiwi
         MANDARA   Matal   *ma-t wØ-a-y   > ma-təw-ay   > matəway
         MOFU   Gemzek   *ma-t wa-y   > ma-təw^wa-Ø^y
                                                     > ma^ytə^wwa^y   > metuwe
         KOTOKO-   Afade   *ts wa-y   > tsəwa-Ø^y
         NORTH   > tsə^ywa^y   > tsɨwe

Note that in Matal there is no prosodising effect, because – as in most but not all cases – the *{-y} remains segmentally present as part of the final diphthong -ay.

A second set of examples illustrates the prosodising effect of *{-y} on consonants (for instance /l/ > l^y; /r/ > ɽ), for instance in languages of the HIGI group:

(89) 'dog' PCC *k(a)ra (-a,-y, -kʷ; FV)
        HIGI   Kamwe-Nkafa   *k la-y   > kəla-Øʸ   > kəlʸa   > kəlyə
                Kamwe-Futu   *k la-y   > kəla-Øʸ   > kəlʸaʸ   > kəlye
                Kirya   *k rØ-y   > kər-yʸ   > kərʸ-i   > kəɽi

Note: In Kamwe-Nkafa only the final consonant is affected by Y-prosody. In Kamwe-Futu both final consonant and final /a/ are affected. In Kirya, *{-y} syllabifies to [i] and also affects the phonetic realisation of final /r/.

It is this latter type that is well attested over much of Central Chadic, i.e. the simultaneous syllabification of *{-y} to [i] in final position plus further Y-prosody effects on other root segments. For example (note that we will exclude all such roots in which phonological palatalisation could play a role, i.e. for which we have been able to identify and reconstruct */y/ in the root):

(90) 'dog' PCC *k(a)ra (-a,-y, -kʷ; FV)
        MAROUA Giziga-Muturwa *k rØ-y   > kər-iʸ
                                            > kəʸr-i   > kiri
        HIGI   Kirya   *k rØ-y   > kər-iʸ
                                            > kərʸ-i   > kəɽi

(91) 'dream' PCC *(...) s(a)w(a)na (-a, -y, -k, -n)
        BATA   Bata   *s Ø rØ-y   > sər-iʸ
                                        > sʸəʸr-i   > ʃiri
        DABA   Daba   *s Ø nØ-y   > sən-iʸ
                                        > səʸn-i   > sini

(92) 'faeces' PCC *(ŋ-) ɣʷ va (-a, -y, -n)
        MARGI   Bura   *k vØ-y   > kəv-iʸ
                                      > kəʸv-i   > kivi
                          *k vØ-y   > kəv-iʸ
                                      > kʸəʸv-i   > tʃivi

(93) 'hair' PCC *(ma-) s(a)b(a)ta (-y, -kʷ)
        BATA   Sharwa   *s ɓ tØ-y-kʷ   > səɓət-iʸ-Øʷ
                                                > sʸəɓʷət-i   > ʃəɓʷəti
        LAMANG Lamang   *s Ø dØ-y   > səd-iʸ
                                                > səʸd-i   > sidi
                Hdi   *s w dØ-y   > səwəd-iʸ
                                                > səwəʸd-i   > səwidi
        HIGI   Kamwe-Nkafa   *s m tØ-y   > sənt-iʸ
                                                > sʸəʸntʸ-i   > ʃintyi
                Bana   *s Ø tØ-y   > sət-i   > səti
                                *s Ø tØ-y   > st-iʸ
                                                > sʸt-i   > ʃti

Note that Bana allows both a prosodised and a non-prosodised form of the same word.

3.2 Issues in CC Diachronic Phonology   121

(94) 'lion' PCC *(a-, RED, wu-) **l(a)vara** (-y)
      SUKUR   Sukur   *l varØ-y   > ləvar-i^y
                                        > lə^{y}var-i   > *livari*
                           *r varØ-y   > rəvar-i^y
                                        > rə^{y}var-i   > *rivari*
      LAMANG   Hdi   *r varØ-y   > rvar-i^y
                                        > rva^{y}r-i   > *rveri*

(95) 'moon' PCC *(n-, ŋ-) **t(a)ra** (-y, -k^w; FV)
      HIGI   Kirya   √ C Ca   *t rØ-y   > tər-i^y
                                                        > tər^y-i   > *tɽi*
      KOTOKO-NORTH   Afade   √ CaCa   *daɗØ-y   > daɗ-i^y
                                                        > da^{y}ɗ-i   > *deɗi*

(96) 'navel' PCC *(ma-) **z(a)b(a)-x^w(a)ɗa** (-y, -n)
      HIGI Kamwe-Nkafa √ C C Ca *m-z bØ^{w}ØØ-y > zə^{m}b^w-i^y
                                                   > z^{y}ə^{m}b^{w}i   > *ʒi^{m}b^{w}i*
            Kamwe-Futu   √ CaC Ca *m-zabØ^{w}ØØ-y > za^{m}b^w-i^y
                                                   > z^{y}a^{ym}b^{w}i > *ʒe^{m}b^w i*

(97) 'night' PCC *(a-, x-, m-/n-, sa-, ta-) **r(a)v(a)ɗa** (-a, -y, -k, -k^w, -n; FV)
      MARGI   Margi   *Ø v dØ-y   > vəɗ-i^y
                                                  > və^{y}ɗ^y-i   > *vi'i*
                 Margi-South   *Ø v dØ-y-k^w > vəɗ-i^y-Ø^w
                                                  > v^{w}ə^{y}ɗ^{y}i > *v^{w}i'i*
      LAMANG   Lamang   *r v dØ-y   > rvəɗ-i^y
                                                  > rvə^{y}ɗi   > *rviɗi*
      HIGI   Kamwe-Futu   *Ø v dØ-y   > vəɗ-i^y
                                                  > və^{y}ɗi   > *viɗi*
                 Psikye   *Ø v dØ-y   > vəɗ-i^y
                                                  > və^{y}ɗi   > *viɗi*

(98) 'root' PCC *(RED) **ɬ(a)r(a)ka** (-a, -y, -k^w, -n; FV)
      BATA   Sharwa   *ɬ r gØ-y   > ɬərəg-i^y
                                                  > ɬ^{y}ər^{y}əgi   > *ɬ'ər^{y}əgi*
      MOFU   Ouldeme   *ɬ l kØ-y   Metathesis:
                                                  ɬ k l-y
                                                  > ɬəkəl-i^y
                                                  > ɬə^{y}kə^{y}li   > *ɬikili*
      MAROUA   Mbazla   *s l kØ-y   > səlk-i^y
                                                  > s^{y}ə^{y}lki   > *filki*

(99) 'spit, to' PCC *(ma-, n-, ŋ-) **t(a)fa** (-a, -y, -k^w, -n, -l ; FV)
      BATA   Gude   *t fØ-y   > təf-i^y
                                                  > tə^{y}f-i   > *tifi*

(100)   'suck, to' PCC *(ma-, n-, RED) **s(a)wɓa** (-a, -y, -n)
        HIGI   Kamwe-Nkafa,   *s Ø ɓØ-y   Metathesis:
               Kamwe-Futu   ɓ s-y
                                           > ɓəs-iʸ
                                           > ɓəʸs-i   > ɓisi

(101)   'sun' PCC *(a-, xa-, d-, RED) **p(a)ta** (-a,-y,-k, -kʷ, -n; FV)
        MARGI   Bura   √ C Ca   *p tsØ-y   > pts-iʸ
                                                      > ptsʸ-i   > ptʃi
                 Margi-South,   √ C Ca   *p tsØ-y   > pəts-iʸ
                 Kilba   > pətsʸ-i   > pətʃi
        LAMANG   Lamang   √ C Ca   *f tØ-y   > fət-iʸ
                                                      > fəʸt-i   > fiti
        HIGI   Kamwe-Nkafa   √ CaCa   *vatsØ-y   > vats-iʸ
                                                      > vaʸtsʸ-i   > vetʃi
                 Kamwe-Futu   √ C Ca   *v tsØ-y   > vəts-Øʸ
                                                      > vəʸtsʸ   > vitʃ
                 Kirya, Psikye   √ C Ca   *v tsØ-y   > vəts-iʸ
                                                      > vətsʸ-i   > vətʃi
                 Bana   √ C Ca   *v tsØ-y   > vts-iʸ
                                                      > vtsʸ-i   > vtʃi

3.2.4.3   Non-Prosodising *{-y}

In a fair number of cases, *{-y} is added to the root without any prosodising effects on the root, other than either creating a final diphthong [ay~ey] by fusing with a preceding /a/, or monophthongising the intermediate diphthong to [e]. Note that in order to keep the two processes – possibly by over-analysis – transparent, different notational conventions are being used in this study:

    Diphthongising: √ C(a)C-a-y   > C(a)Cay ~ C(a)Cey (> C(a)Ce)
    Monophthongising: √ C(a)Ca-y   > C(a)Ce

These conventions leave the historical nature of the preceding /a/ in limbo (as either the lexical /a/ of the simple root or a morphological element of sorts), because there is (yet) no data or robust argument to show that forms of the shape C(a)Ce necessarily reflect monophthongisation of a previous final diphthong C(a)Cay – even though this may be the most plausible explanation. At the risk of being guilty of over-analysis, however, the distinction between final monophthong and diphthong will be maintained. E.g.

(102)   'blow, to' PCC *(ma-) **v ɮa** (-a, -y, -kʷ, -n)

        (a) Diphthong analysis
        MOFU   Dugwor   *ma-v ɮ-a-y   > mavəɮ-a-yʸ   > mavəɮaʸy   > məvəɮey
        LAMANG   Hdi   *v ɮ-a-y-kʷ   > vəł-a-y-Øʷ   > vəʷłay   > vułay

3.2 Issues in CC Diachronic Phonology   123

(b) Monophthong analysis
MOFU   Gemzek   *ma-v ɠa-y   > ma-vəɠa-Ø^y   > ma^yvəɠa^y   > mevəɠe
HURZA   Mbuko   *v ɠa-y   > vəɠa-Ø^y   > vəɠa^y   > vəɠe

In other cases, *{-y} syllabifies to [i] in word-final position and has no further prosodising effect on the root (there may or may not be W-prosody operating on the root). E.g.

(103)   'belly' PCC *(a-) x^w(a)ɗa (-y, -ɗ, -k^w)
        LAMANG   Lamang, Hdi   *x^w ɗØ-y   > x^wəɗ-i
                                                         > xə^wɗ-i   > xudi
        HIGI   Kamwe-Nkafa, Kamwe-Futu   *x^w ØØ-y   > x^w-i   > h^wi

(104)   'cry, to' PCC *(ma-) ts(a)wa (-a, -y, -k; FV)
        MARGI   Margi   *t ØØ-y   > t-i   > ti
        MOFU   Muyang   *t w^wØ-y   > tə^ww-i   > tuwi
        MUSGUM   Mulwi   *t w^wØ-y   > tə^ww-i   > tuwi

(105)   'dog' PCC *k(a)ra (-a,-y, k^w; FV)
        LAMANG   Hdi   *k rØ-y   > kər-i   > kəri
        KOTOKO-ISLAND   Buduma   *k lØ-y(a)   > kəl-i(a)   > kəli(ə)

(106)   'dream' PCC *(...) s w(a)na (-a, -y, -k, -n)
        MARGI   Bura   *s w nØ-y   > swn-i   > suni
        LAMANG   Hdi   *s w nØ-y   > swn-i   > suni

(107)   'faeces' PCC *(ŋ-) ɣ^w va (-a, -y, -n)
        LAMANG   Lamang, Hdi   *ɣ^w vØ-y   > ɣ^wəv-i
                                             > ɣə^wv-i   > ɣuvi
        HIGI   Kirya   *w vØ-y   Metathesis:
                                             v w-y
                                             > vw-i   > v^wi

(108)   'root' PCC *(RED) ɬ(a)r(a)ka (-a, -y, -k^w, -n; FV)
        SUKUR   Sukur   *ɬ Ø ØØ-y   > ɬ-i   > ɬi
        LAMANG   Lamang   *ɬ r kØ-y-n
                           Metathesis: ɬ r k-n-y
                           Metathesis: ɬ r nk-y   > ɬərŋk-i   > sləɲi

3.2.5 Combined Y- and W-Prosodies

It has been noted in synchronic descriptions of Central Chadic languages, that Y- and W-prosodies may jointly occur in the same word. As a rule, they impact different domains in the word. Occasionally, however, they share in the same domain, giving rise to phonetically 'exceptional' surface vowels, such as rounded front vowels (IPA y and œ). We will look at such examples separately in the following sub-sections.

3.2.5.1 Separate Domains for Each Prosody

The database (Gravina 2014b) contains many examples in which both Y- and W-prosodies occur in the same word. As a rule, each domain targets a certain syllable, consonant or vowel to the exclusion of other syllables or segments that are (or are not) targeted by the other prosody. E.g.

(109) 'cry, to' *(ma-) **ts(a)wa** (-a, -y, -k; FV)
MOFU   Gemzek   √ C Ca   *ma-t wa-y   > ma-təw^{w}a-Ø^y
                                       > ma^y-tə^{w}wa^y > metuwe

Note: Vowel epenthesis (penultima) is affected by phonological W-prosody (source */w/); morphological Y-prosody (source *{-y}) affects /a/ in both prefix and final root position.

KOTOKO-   Zina   √ C Ca   *ts wØ-ya   > tsəw^w-y^{y}a
SOUTH   > ts^{y}ə^{w}w-ya   > tʃuwya

Note: Vowel epenthesis (penultima) is affected by phonological W-prosody (source */w/); morphological Y-prosody (source *{-y}) affects initial consonant; /y/ survives segmentally in syllable-onset position due to presence of FV.

(110) 'dream' *(n-, ...) **s(a)w(a)na** (a, -y, -k, -k^w, -n; FV)
MAFA   Mafa   √ C C Ca   *n-s w na-y   > n-səw^{w}əna-Ø^y
                                         > n-s^{y}ə^w.wə^y.na^y > nʃuwine

Note: Vowel epenthesis in antepenultima is affected by phonological W-prosody (source */w/) and in penultima by morphological Y-prosody (source *{-y}); Y-prosody also affects root-initial consonant and lexical final /a/.

(111) 'faeces' *(ŋ-) **ɣ^w va** (-a, -y, -n)
MANDARA   Mandara,   √ C Ca   *g^w va-y   > əg^{w}va-Ø^y
          Malgwa   > ə^{w}gva^y > ugve

Note: Vowel prothesis (conditioned by initial consonant cluster) is affected by phonological W-prosody (source */g^w/); morphological Y-prosody affects final /a/.

(112) 'hair' *(ma-) **s(a)b(a)ta** (-y, -k^w)
BATA   Bata   √ CaC Ca   *saw ta-y   > saw^{w}ta-Ø^y
                                      > s^{y}a^{y}wta^w > ʃewto

Note: Morphological Y-prosody (source *{-y}) affects initial consonant and medial /a/; phonological W-prosody (source */w/) affects final /a/.

3.2 Issues in CC Diachronic Phonology

BATA   Tsuvan   √ C C Ca   *sɓʷta-y   > səɓʷta-Øʸ
                                      > səʷɓtaʸ   > subte

Note: Vowel epenthesis in penultima is affected by phonological W-prosody (source /ɓʷ/); Y-prosody (source *{-y}) affects final /a/.

SUKUR Sukur   √ C C Ca   *s b tØ-y-kʷ   > səᵐbət-Øʸ-Øʷ
                                          > sʸəʷᵐbəʷt   > ʃuᵐbut

Note: Vowel epenthesis in both first and second syllable is affected by morphological W-prosody; morphological Y-prosody affects initial consonant.

(113) 'razor' PCC *p(a)ɗ(a)kʷa (-y, -ɗ)
       MARGI Bura   √ CaC Ca   *par kʷa-y   > parkʷa-Øʸ
                                              > pʸaʸrkəʷ   > pʸerku
       HIGI   Kirya   √ C C Ca   *p r kʷa-y   > pərəkʷa-Øʸ
                                              > pəʸrəʷkəʷ   > piruku

Note: Morphological Y-prosody stemming from desegmentalised *{-y} affects first syllable (in Bura both consonant and vowel, in Kirya only the epenthetic vowel); phonological W-prosody stemming from labialised final consonant affects preceding epenthetic vowel in Kirya and centralised final /a/ in both languages.

3.2.5.2 Prosody Fusion in Same Domain (*/aʷʸ > œ)

In the database there are examples, in which both Y- and W-prosody, both originating from suffixal root-augmental material (*{-y} + *{-kʷ}), share the domain of the penultimate syllable containing the originally medial vowel /a/.

(114) 'ashes' *(a-) p ts(a)ɗa (-y, -kʷ, -n; FV)
       BATA   Bachama   √ C CaCa   *f taɗa-y-kʷa   Metathesis
                                                   f taɗa-kʷ-ya
                                                   > fətaɗa-Øʷ-yʸa
                                                   > fəʸtaʷʸɗəʸyaʸ   > fitœdiye

Note: Metathesis in the root augment *{-y}+*{-kʷ} > -kʷ-y; *{-kʷ} prosodifies completely and only leaves W-prosody behind, *{-y} survives segmentally as initial consonant of the ultimate syllable; W- and Y-prosody combine on medial /a/ > [œ]; Y-prosody affects centralised lexical final /a/ > ə > əʸ > i in penultimate syllable.

(115) 'razor₁' PCC *p(a)ɗ(a)kʷa (-y, -ɗ)
       SUKUR Sukur   √ C CaCa   *p ɗakʷØ-y   > pəɗakʷ-Øʸ
                                                > pəʸɗaʸʷk   > pidoek'

HURZA   Mbuko   √ C CaCa   *pɗak^w∅-y   > pəɗak^w-∅^y
                                        > pəɗa^{yw}k-∅^y   > pəɗæk

Note: *{-y} prosodifies completely and only leaves Y-prosody behind; the labialising component of */k^w/ shifts to the preceding vowel /a/ where it combines with Y-prosody stemming from *{-y}, combined they change /a/ > [æ]. (Note: Emergence of final glottal stop in Sukur remains unaccounted for here.)

3.3 Diachronic Sources of Morphological Prosodies

As has been pointed out above and elsewhere, one of the historical sources of morphological prosodies across Chadic languages can be assumed to be the Proto-Chadic determiner system, as reconstructed and presented by Schuh (1983). As Schuh pointed out (1983: 201), these determiners are of great age and 'can be reconstructed for Proto-Afroasiatic as well'. They have undergone various shifts of function in the course of the history of the languages in which they still occur.

Among the PC determiners established by Schuh, *i as 'marker of definiteness (gender neutral)' very likely corresponds to one of possibly more sources of the suffixal root-augment *{-y} that we take to be the origin of morphological Y-prosody in Central Chadic languages and beyond. This, however, may raise the question why *{-y} (and other 'determiners'?) should occur with apparently verbal roots, unless we assume that the reconstructable augmented roots reflect what originally were nominalised citation forms. On the other hand, root-augmental *{-y} as reconstructed here may have more than only one source in the morphology of the still largely unknown grammar of PCC. Note that Wolff (2019b: 191) tentatively identified four source morphemes for grammatical palatalisation, thereby offering a 'glimpse into hitherto under-researched comparative Chadic grammar'.

Schuh also establishes *k as 'a marker of previous reference (gender neutral)', but does not mention *{-k^w}. In our Central Chadic reconstructions, we find both *{-k} and *{-k^w} as elements that form part of suffixal root-augmental material. Presently, we have no indication whether these were separate or basically the same diachronic segment. *{-k^w} in particular is considered an ultimate source for morphological W-prosody, including the assumption that *{-k^w} could weaken to w and prosodify further to ^w (W-prosody). There is no indication yet as to what the original grammatical function of *{-k^w} might have been, and whether it was distinct from *{-k}. In order not to become guilty of under-differentiation, we keep *{-k} and *{-k^w} distinct in the present study (like we keep *{-k^w} and *{-w} distinct);

3.4 The Origins of Final */a/ and [ə]

this does not preclude any later more focused study that would establish a common proto-language origin.[8]

3.4 The Origins of Final */a/ and [ə]

On an abstract level of theoretical options and given our still limited insights and assumptions about PCC phonology and grammar, for roots or words there would have been three options regarding potential endings:

- final */a/
- final consonant (Ø vowel)
- final [ə].

3.4.1 Final */a/

Given its wide and consistent distribution, we will treat final /a/ as part of the simple root (see 3.1.1), i.e. we postulate final /a/ as 'lexical' in this position by default. Augmented roots would appear to have had the choice of ending either in /a/ (= FV) or in a consonant, i.e. we assume FV to have been an optional ending (but subject to further research, see below). Currently, there is no comparative evidence to suggest that ubiquitous root-final /a/ in PCC is a grammatical morpheme of sorts that would be added to basically consonant-final lexical roots.

However, some present-day Central Chadic languages are known to synchronically neutralise all apparent final vowel contrasts to /a/ in pre-pausal position, such as phrase- or clause-final. Therefore, citation forms could be assumed to require such pre-pausal neutralisation of originally different lexical final vowels of roots, if there ever were any. Whereas this may be a relevant observation for analysis of present-day languages that operate synchronic multi-vowel systems, it would be irrelevant for our reconstructed PCC system, which only recognises one vowel phoneme anyway, namely */a/. Therefore and under this assumption, it is not really surprising to find /a/ in final positions of PCC roots as long as they can be considered vowel-final, since /a/ is the only phonemic vowel in our reconstructed phonological system.

However, and in order to reconcile the various available observations on final vowel behaviour in Central Chadic languages, reconstructing (word-)final /a/ as basic would appear to make a lot of sense, if we tentatively assume that,

---

[8] We cannot, at present, exclude a historical scenario in which *{-k} (as reconstructed by Schuh 1983) was the original PC morpheme and *{-k^w} was a PCC variant. The somewhat rare occurrence of reflexes of *{-k} (and *{-w} for that matter) in Central Chadic languages could then be just variants of non-prosodising *{-k^w}. This question, however, must be left open for further research. At the time of finalising this book, a follow-up study is already under way, in which PCC consonants will also be analysed in more detail (Wolff forthcoming).

for each individual language, one, some or all of the following rules would apply:

- Final /a/ is maintained in pre-pausal environments.
- Final /a/ is deleted in non-pre-pausal environments.
- Final /a/ has a centralised allophone [ə] in language-specific environments.
- Final /a/ is affected by prosodies and changes its quality accordingly.
- Final /a/ is subject to non-prosodic assimilation by its immediate phonological environment and changes its quality accordingly.
- Final /a/ merges with suffixal segments to yield diphthongs or monophthongs of different quality.

Consequently, several vowel qualities and even absence of a vowel in final positions of words could still be accounted for as regular reflections of reconstructed */a/, based on principles and rules, throughout much if not all of Central Chadic.

3.4.2   Final Consonant (Ø Vowel)

In the database, we do find both Ø and schwa in the position of the expected lexical final vowel /a/. Final zero (Ø) is then explained simply as language-specific deletion of final /a/ with so-called simple roots. With augmented roots, the situation is more complicated. Many augmented roots (see 3.1.2) would appear to be consonant-final, while others contain a final */a/, which we here refer to as FV ('Final Vowel'). There is no indication when and where FV is present or absent, and whether absence automatically presupposes the previous presence and hence deletion of the FV. Therefore, our reconstructions will indicate whether or not any language in the database displays the FV. With augmented roots, therefore, we will not reconstruct FV by default, as we do in the case of simple roots. This, however, may give room to another analysis should further comparative research require this.

3.4.3   Final Schwa

Accounting for final schwa allows for at least two plausible explanations. One is that */a/ is allowed to centralise in this position, so that schwa can be considered a conditioned allophone of */a/, and as such it would not be necessarily restricted to final position but could also occur word-medially, i.e. /a/ occasionally centralises in medial position of a word or root. This allophonic variation [a~ə] would be the simplest way of accounting also for final schwa, according to a language-specific rule of the type

>   */a/ > [ə] /X (where X could also be __#)

3.5 Integration of Loan Words into CC Phonology   129

Or, after deletion of /a/ > Ø in final or any other position, the systemic vowel slot, now being empty, is re-filled by epenthetic schwa; in the case of this happening in final position, we would have to speak of *epithetic* schwa. This is the more complex and possibly even counter-intuitive account. In the end, the question is irrelevant, since all schwas, whether in final position or not, behave alike phonologically under the effect of prosodies, independent of their origin as phonemic /a/ or epenthetic schwa.

Whatever account we wish to follow, resulting allophonic schwa in final position undergoes the same 'colouring' by phonological environment, in particular under prosody effects, as all epenthetic schwas would do. This makes it at times difficult to identify surface representations of schwa as either reflexes of underlying /a/ or epenthetic vowel. Summing up: in the framework of our approach to PCC reconstructions, the distinction in final position between */a/ > [ə] on the one hand and insertion of epithetic schwa on the other doesn't really matter, the more so since it does not carry any distinctive functions anyway.

3.5   A Note on the Integration of Loan Words into Central Chadic Phonology

An interesting side-effect of our study involving internal reconstruction is to observe how obvious loans, for instance from or via Nilo-Saharan Kanuri, become integrated into the peculiar history of Central Chadic phonology.

The integration strategy would appear to be that foreign surface forms of loans are reanalysed and phonologically accommodated in terms of root types and potential effects of prosodies, and are then treated as if they were of Central Chadic heritage, i.e. the newly created underlying forms correspond to the constraints of PCC phonological and morphological typology, and no longer to their original phonological nature. Part of the game is that Central Chadic languages allow these loans to be attributed several different root types based on number of radical consonants and vocalisation patterns, a procedure that contradicts assumptions about the unitary nature of borrowed lexical items from outside Chadic or Afroasiatic. This supports the implicit plausible assumption that loans were integrated not into PCC, but during the histories of individual languages or language groups. In a way and when integrating loans, the CC phonological typology uses the same 'pre-processing' procedures (see 2.6 further above) that we have found necessary to introduce for the present study.

The following examples taken from the database are more or less obvious loans from Kanuri or have entered Central Chadic languages via Kanuri, the most influential lingua franca in the area before the more recent dynamic spread of Hausa and Fulfulde set in. It remains remarkable, however, how these loans have been incorporated into the system and allow 'pseudo-reconstruction' as if they were part of the PCC lexicon, which of course they are not. (For the details see 6.4.)

Kanuri *beli* 'razor' is reanalysed as if stemming from PCC **b(a)la* (-y). Individual languages assign it one of the following root types: √ C Ca, √ CaCa, even √ C C Ca (MOFU: Zulgo). In order to accommodate the mid vowel [e] in medial position of the loan, it is reanalysed as underlying /a/ undergoing morphological palatalisation by **{-y}*, which nicely matches the presence of final [i], which is reanalysed as stemming from the syllabified same **{-y}*: ***bal-y** > *beli*. Since underlying root types are options for individual Central Chadic languages, the root type √ CaCa underlying forms with medial [e] can be undone in favour of a parallel root type √ C Ca. Here, epenthetic schwa would be inserted and palatalised under the reanalysed effect of **{-y}*. These strategies allow phonologically fully integrated Central Chadic surface forms like ***bal-y** > ba^{y}l > *bel*, ***bala-y** > ba^{y}la^y > *bele*, both based on the √ CaCa root type, and ***bl-y** > bə^{y}l > *bil*, ***bla-y** > bə^{y}la > *bila*, both based on the √ C Ca root type, and ***byla** > bə^{y}yə^{y}la > *biyila*, based on the √ C C Ca root type, etc.

Kanuri *koro* 'donkey' provides another example of full phonological integration by reanalysis as a triradical root ***k(a)w(a)ra** (-y, -t), which is characteristically assigned three parallel underlying root types: √ C CaCa, √ CaC Ca and √ C C Ca. Positing an underlying vocoid */w/ in C_2 position allows the system to license desegmentalisation/prosodification to ^{w} and thereby to give rise to phonological labialisation prosody, which in turn changes assumed underlying /a/ to surface [o]. Interestingly, some languages retain the hypothetical underlying structure in surface representation, like Giziga-Muturwa (MAROUA) √ CaC Ca *kawra*, while other languages again derive from this in a 'regular' manner the surface form *koro*, which corresponds exactly to the assumed Kanuri original.

In a similar way, Kanuri *kasugu* 'market' (ultimately from Arabic *suq*) is integrated into Central Chadic phonological systems. Again, the assumption of an underlying vocoid /w/ is central here, which turns the tri-consonantal Kanuri original into a somewhat exceptional quadri-radical underlying simple-root structure in Central Chadic: ***k(a)swka**. Characteristically again, up to three root types are associated with this newly integrated simple root: √ C C C Ca, √ CaC C Ca, √ CaCaC Ca. Being adjacent to a velar consonant, /w/ undergoes metathesis in quite a number of languages from *w k > k w, which subsequently allows for labialised velars (k^w) to emerge from the new sequence /k+w/. In accordance with general rules of Central Chadic phonology, we find a wide variety of surface forms from *səku* and *fik^{w}i* to *gosku* and *k^{w}asak^{w}a* and others, which all derive from underlying pseudo-PCC-conform ***k(a)swka**.

Also, Kanuri *fi* 'foot' could possibly be the source for one of the several words for 'foot, leg' in a particular area where Central Chadic languages are spoken. Given its particular surface form, it would be a candidate for reflecting morphological palatalisation in Central Chadic, i.e. carrying a reconstructable suffixal root-augmental marker *{-y}, among others. If this was really a loan from Kanuri, which is not at all certain, it might be a fairly old one, as reflected in its rather divergent representations involving a fair number of petrified root-augmental elements. Etymologically related modern surface forms in Central Chadic range from *hi* via *entsi* to *ms'ɨkɨ*, but also encompassing *tʃu*.

The word for 'camel' is particularly interesting, which we reconstruct as pseudo-PCC root **k(a)l(a)g(a)m(a)wa** with an exceptional five radicals. This is an obvious loan and thus qualifies as a 'pseudo-PCC' root insofar as it has been streamlined into Central Chadic phonology systems to the extent of being apparently 'reconstructable'. This root may have entered CC languages at different times via different donors, like Fulfulde (*ⁿgeelooba*) and Old Kanuri (*kaligimo*). Ultimately, the original source may be Berber **alyəm*. It would also appear that the pseudo-PCC root has undergone some reanalysis in some of the borrowing CC languages. Kanuri is known to make ample use of a nominal prefix *{k(V)-} (often in the form of *ka- or *kə-), so in many modern reflexes of the pseudo-root **k(a)l(a)g(a)m(a)wa** the initial consonant has been deleted based on reanalysis undertaken during the borrowing process (see 6.4). Gravina (2014b) keeps three – as we see it: all cognate – proto-language forms distinct, namely (in his own transcription) **ɓigʷamiʸ**, **ⁿgʲaluba**,

Table 3.7 *Different paths of loans into Central Chadic for 'camel'*

GROUP	Language	Set A	Set B	Set C
BATA	Bata	*lukʷap-to*		
	Jimi	*ligʷam-ən*		
	Sharwa		*ⁿgyaluba*	
	Tsuvan	*ɓəⁿgume*		
TERA	Nyimatli	*ɓimokh*		
	Ga'anda		*ⁿgelupa*	
KOTOKO-ISLAND	Buduma	*loguəme*		
KOTOKO-NORTH	Afade			*girgimu*
	Mpade			*galdʒimu*
	Malgbe	*logomo*		
	Maltam			*girdʒimu*
KOTOKO-CENTRAL	Lagwan			*kurguma*
	Mser			*gurguma*
KOTOKO-SOUTH	Mazera			*kurguma*

and **kaligimo**. At variance with Gravina, however, we propose a common pseudo-PCC root from which all modern forms could be diachronically derived. This does not exclude repeated borrowing from different donor languages in individual CC languages, for which we would appear to have evidence. Such evidence would consist of the apparent differences in sets of forms in languages from within the same language groups – exactly what must have led Gravina to reconstruct three different PCC roots (even though recognising their nature as loans), see Table 3.7 for illustration. Gravina connects set C with Old Kanuri *kaligimo*, and set B with Fulfulde *ngeelooba*, and set A ultimately from Berber *alyəm*. Note that in our own reconstruction, we treat all three sets as being ultimately cognates (see 6.4). Set A stands out by assumed deletion of the characteristic Kanuri nominal prefix *{kV-} and metathesis of *l g m w > *l gw m (Jimi, Tsuvan, Buduma, Malgbe; Bata further changing *m > p /__t,) or *l g m w > *l m w g (Nyimatli). Set B likewise has deleted assumed Kanuri *{kV-} and undergoes different and double metathesis of *l g m w > *g l w m (Sharwa, Ga'anda), with a change of *m > b/p. Set C retains the original Kanuri nominal prefix *{kV-}, with three KOTOKO- CENTRAL and -SOUTH languages metathesising *k l g m w > *k l g w m.

4 Diachronic Processes in Central Chadic Language Evolution

4.1 Vowel Epenthesis

The notion of vowel epenthesis is central to our approach to comparative Chadic linguistics. We have already referred to the notoriously difficult decision for each single Central Chadic language, whether to treat the non-low central vowel schwa (ə) as being phonemic or epenthetic in nature. Clearly, for the synchronic description of Central Chadic languages, any one of the two options may be preferable in the light of other salient features of synchronic language structure (or in the light of the particular theoretical inclination of the linguist providing the description, if not for practical reasons of creating a standardised orthography). For the diachronic study of Central Chadic languages, however, treating schwa as epenthetic throughout has considerable theoretical and methodological advantages. Hence our approach to accept but one true phonemic vowel for PCC, namely */a/. Apart from frequent syllabifications of the other two vocoids besides */a/, namely */y/ and */w/ (also referred to as 'weak radicals'), which yield [+syllabic] allophonic phonetic surface representation as secondary, i.e. non-phonemic vowels [i] and [u], the only other vocalic unit found in these languages will be considered to represent epenthetic (or prothetic, as the case may be) schwa, i.e. a non-phonemic vowel that is highly if not completely predictable in its distribution. The occurrence and distribution of schwa [ə] and its 'coloured' variants [ɨ~i~ʉ~u] across roots and words is highly, if not totally, predictable from the reconstructed shape of the underlying root-and-pattern structure, where systemic vowel slots are being filled by */a/ depending on root type (see 3.1). Slots not filled by */a/ are potential positions for epenthetic schwa to occur. Roots of the shape √ CaCaCa and √ CaCa leave no slot for epenthetic schwa to be inserted, while roots of the shapes √ C CaCa, √ CaC Ca, √ C C Ca and √ C Ca do leave slots that are potentially open for epenthetic schwa to occur. It is, however, not necessary for all slots to be filled by either */a/ or schwa, abutting of consonants in roots (simple and augmented) may be licensed under the constraints of either underlying root type or under the principles underlying surface syllable structure.

Besides rather frequent vowel epenthesis, there are also occasional occurrences of vowel prothesis in the reconstructed data. In a number of languages, initial consonant clusters may require the insertion of a prothetic vowel, which – synchronically – may come in any 'colouring' depending on environment and be transcribed as a, ə, e, o, i, and u.

Note, however, a source of potential confusion between epenthetic schwa and the centralised allophone of */a/, which are both graphically represented by the symbol ə. Epenthetic schwa insertion is a highly frequent phonological process in Central Chadic languages, while low-vowel /a/ centralisation would appear to be less frequent. Both processes are relevant in synchronic as well as diachronic perspectives. We'll return to this issue further below (sub-section 6.3.4).

4.2 Prosodic 'Colouring' of Pro- and Epenthetic Schwa

Characteristically, pro- and epenthetic schwa is frequently subject to phonetic 'colouring' by prosody effects originating from segments in the phonological environment, giving rise to phonetic variants [ɨ] and [ʉ], but also [i] and [u] (often a matter of convention of transcription by individual linguists), under the impact of palatalisation (Y-prosody) and labialisation (W-prosody). For Central Chadic language data, therefore, it is essential to 'read' and identify the likely underlying structure behind the surface transcriptions, since

- *i* can be an allophone ([+syllabic]) of underlying */y/ or an instance of high-front 'colouring' of schwa, which may elsewhere be represented as [ɨ] or [ə];
- *u* can be an allophone ([+syllabic]) of underlying */w/ or an instance of high-back-round 'colouring' of schwa, which may elsewhere be represented as [ʉ] or [ə];
- ə can be the centralised allophone of underlying */a/ or an instance of non-colouring 'neutral' ('Ø-prosody') representation of the epenthetic vowel schwa.

4.3 Prosodic Effects on */a/

Like epenthetic schwa (see above), */a/ too can be subject to impact from the phonological environment, i.e. in particular palatalisation and labialisation prosodies. Typically, these processes give rise to conditioned allophones under Y-prosody and W-prosody, namely [e] (occasionally also transcribed as [ɛ]) and [o] (occasionally also transcribed as [ɔ]), for which we could assume an intermediate stage of diphthongisation and subsequent monophthongisation, i.e. *a^y > ay~ey > [ɛ~e] and *a^w > aw > [ɔ~o]. Characteristically for Central Chadic languages, and often reflected in variant transcriptions of the same words by field linguists, phonetic realisations for certain vowels would appear to be rather unstable at times and, accordingly, may be represented by variant representations by the same authors and/or by individual transcription conventions by different authors. Once allophonic variations of [ɛ~e] and [ɔ~o] have been established as non-contrastive, authors of linguistic descriptions may opt for a unified representation as consistently either [ɛ] and [ɔ], or as [e] and [o]. Likewise, final [ay] and [ey] can mostly be identified as being non-contrastive surface variants and thus their representation may be conventionalised as either *ay* or *ey*. Also and at times, it may be hard to distinguish clearly between diphthongs and monophthongs in cases of transcriptions like *ay, ey, e^y, e*.

Since the segmental sources of the prosodies are sometimes still present in the root-and-pattern structure of the word and may end up in the immediate neighbourhood of */a/, the resulting phonetic representation may be that of a diphthong, i.e. */a/ + */y/ > ay~ai and */a/ + */w/ > aw~au, which often – but not always – monophthongises again, yielding medial vowels, namely [e] and [o] respectively. (Note that in the current study, there is a graphic convention by which we distinguish [e] as both front-mid allophone of /a/ and monophthongisation of an intermediate diphthong *ay~ai from the maintenance of the diphthong in surface representation transcribed as *ay~ey*.)

4.4 Syllabification of Underlying *y and *w

The concept of weak radicals (2.5.2) and their potential for syllabification is central to the internal reconstruction and application of the *comparative method* to Central Chadic languages, i.e. both diachronic and potentially also synchronically underlying */y/ and */w/ can be expected to surface as [i] and [u] in syllable-nucleus positions. This can be illustrated from the neat cases of the augmented root for 'dream' that contains both of these vocoids, i.e. one as weak radical within the root (*/w/), the other as suffixal augment *{-y}. Both diachronic vocoids end up as phonetic vowels [u] and [i] respectively in surface representation in, for instance, Bura and Hdi from different groups within Central Chadic.

(116)   'dream' PCC *(...) s(a)w(a)na (-a, -y, -k, -k^w, -n; FV)
      MARGI   Bura   √ C C Ca   *s w nØ-y   > *suni*
      LAMANG Hdi   √ C C Ca   *s w nØ-y   > *suni*

4.4.1   Weak Radicals *y and *w in Medial Position

As illustrated above, *y and *w may occur word-medially and end up in syllable-nucleus position where they are expected to be realised as vowels [i] and [u].

136   Diachronic Processes in CC Language Evolution

(117)   (a) Syllabification of medial /w/ > [u]
'cry, to' *(ma-) **ts(a)wa** (-a, -y, -k; FV)
BATA   Bata, Gude   √ C Ca   *t wØ   > tw^w > tə^{w}w   > tuu

Note that in Bata and Gude, word-medial C$_2$ /w/ ends up in word-final position after deletion of lexical final /a/.

MANDARA	Glavda	√ C Ca	*t wØ-ka	> tw^w-ka	> tə^{w}w-ka	> tu:ga
	Mandara	√ C Ca	*t wa-y	> twa-Ø^y	> t^{y}wa	> k^{y}ua
KOTOKO-ISLAND	Buduma	√ C Ca	*ts wØ-y	> tsw-y^y	> ts^{y}w-y	> tʃuy

(b) Syllabification of medial /y/ > [i]

(118)   'hare' PCC *(ma-, na-) **x^w(a)d(a)y(a)va** (-k^w, -n ; FV)

BATA	Gude	√ C C C Ca	*Øtypa	> py^{y}ta	> pit^{y}a
	Jimi	√ C C C Ca	*ØdyvØ-n	> vydən	> vidən
	Tsuvan	√ C C C Ca	*ØtyvØ-k-n	> vy^{y}təkən	
				> vitə^{y}kən	> vitikən
SUKUR	Sukur	√ C C C Ca	*Ølyva	> vəØ^{y}la	
				> və^{y}l^{y}a	> vil^{y}a
MARGI	Bura	√ C C C Ca	*ØtypØ	> pty	> pti
	Margi	√ C C C Ca	*Øtypa	> pyta	> pitə
	Margi-South	√ C C C Ca	*ØtypØ-k^w	> pyt-w	> pitu
	Kilba	√ C C C Ca	*Øtypa	> pyta	> pita
MANDARA	Podoko	√ C C C Ca	*Øryva	> vyra	> vira
	Mandara	√ C C C Ca	*na-Øryva	> navy^{y}ra	
				> navira^y	> navire
	Malgwa	√ C C Ca	*na-Øryva	> navy^{y}ra	
				> navə^{y}yra	> naviira
	Glavda	√ C C Ca	*ØØyvØ	> vy^y	
				> və^{y}i	> vii
		√ C C Ca	*Ødyva	> vy^{y}da	
				> və^{y}yda	> vi:da
LAMANG	Lamang	√ C C Ca	*Ølyva-k^{w}a	> vylak^{w}a	> vilak^{w}a
	Hdi	√ C C Ca	*Ølyva-k^w	> vylak^w	> vilak^w
HIGI	Kamwe-Futu	√ C C Ca	*Øryva	> vyra	> vira
	Kirya	√ C C Ca	*Øtypa	> pyta	> pitə

Note the widely occurring metathesis involving C$_2$ and C$_4$.

4.4.2 *y and *w in Suffixal Augments in Final Position

Syllabification of the widespread root-augment *{-y} is quite common, giving rise to a number of synchronic lexical items ending in the surface vowel [i] (after deletion of the preceding root-final /a/). In combination and fusion with

4.4 Syllabification of Underlying *y and *w   137

final /a/ the result is quite often a final surface vowel [e]. Therefore and at variance with Gravina (2014a), we do not reconstruct lexical */i/ in PCC, not even where syllabic [i] occurs in final position in the phonetic surface representation of a word. Note that word-final [i] (< *{-y}) is at times prosodising (symbolised as -i^y) and affects other segments in the word, and at times it is not (symbolised as -i). The principles or rules that govern this divergent behaviour, if there are any, currently remain opaque.

(119) 'butterfly' PCC *(...RED...) **p(a)ra** (-y, -k^w, -n; FV)
      BATA Gude √ RED+C Ca *p rØ-y+p rØ-y-na > pəripərinə > pəripərinə
      HIGI Bana √ RED+C Ca *p l+p lØ-y > pəl-pəl-i > pəlpəli

(120) 'cry, to' PCC *(ma-) **ts(a)wa** (-a, -y, -k; FV)
      MARGI Margi √ C Ca *t ØØ-y > t-i > ti
        Margi-South, Kilba √ C Ca *t wØ-y > təw-i^y
            > tə^{y}w-i > tiwi
      MOFU Muyang √ C Ca *t wØ-y > tw^w-i
            > tə^{w}w-i > tuwi
      MUSGUM Mulwi √ C Ca *t wØ-y > tw^w-i
            > tə^{w}w-i > tuwi

(121) 'dog' PCC ***k(a)ra*** (-a, -y, -k^w; FV)
      LAMANG Hdi √ C Ca *k rØ-y > kər-i > kəri
      HIGI Kirya √ C Ca *k rØ-y > kər-i^y
            > kər^y-i > kəṭi

When the suffixal augment *{-y} prosodically affects lexical final /a/, it will in most cases create an effect of changing /a/ > [e], conceivable as the result of monophthongisation of an intermediate diphthong: */a/ + y^y > a^y~ai > [e]. We take this to be a highly regular and very frequent case in Central Chadic languages, some of which only allow /a/ and [e] (assumed < *a^y < *-a-y) in word-final positions.[1]

---

[1] This development, we would now say, lies behind the analytical problems in Mandara, which led Heide Mirt (1969) to her remarkable pioneer study of postulating only two underlying vowels, namely /a/ and /ə/, for that language. P. Newman (1977a: 12fn.) considers 'Mirt's modest paper ... a major breakthrough in the analysis of Chadic vowel systems.' In Mirt's consistent analysis of the Mandara 2-vowel system, the only final vowels in that language, namely [a] and [e], were assumed to reflect that distinction between /a/ and /ə/. In a focused historical perspective and with the more recent notion of prosodies available, the issue of how to account for only two but different final vowel qualities in Mandara, namely [a] and [e], was taken up again in Wolff and Naumann (2004). In keeping with the insights concerning prosodies in Central Chadic, we analysed final [e] in Mandara as palatalised /a/ under Y-prosody. Accordingly and slightly at variance with Mirt's analysis, we would say that Mandara has two vowels medially, namely /a/ and /ə/, but only one vowel in final position, namely /a/. This leaves room for the

Note that in rather few cases across Central Chadic, this rule of diphthong monophthongisation does not appear to work, so that we find surface forms that end in diphthongs, usually transcribed as words ending in *ay* or *ey*. For the purpose of this study, I have chosen to represent these cases by a differentiating convenience convention, which – as already noted further above – may be guilty of being a case of phonological over-differentiation, yet without any noticeable morphological implications:

(a) monophthong convention

$\quad\quad$ X Ca^y > X Ce $\quad$ Y-prosody effect on final /a/, also conceivable as monophthongisation of an underlying diphthong *ay~ey.

(b) diphthong convention

$\quad\quad$ X C-a-y > X C-ay $\quad$ Non-prosody creating sequence of *{-a} and *{-y} suffixal augments, also emerging as surface structure diphthong *ay~ey.

With regard to the impact of our reconstructed suffixal morphological marker *{-y}, there are considerable differences of interpretation regarding the synchronic data and their reconstructions between Gravina (2014b), who at times would appear to use Y-prosody as a *deus ex machina* in his restricted focus on simple roots, and the present study, which takes both simple and augmented roots into account. See below, for instance, the item 'beard' that Gravina reconstructs with underlying schwa in both syllables plus Y-prosody, assuming a triradical simple root. Our own reconstruction finds no reflex of a final consonant /ɗ/ (and accordingly assumes a biradical simple root), other than ubiquitous traces of *{-y}. See also Gravina's note on consonantal correspondences, which kind of blurs the distinction between prosody effect and 'regular' sound change:

ɣʷimiɗ ʸ n. beard barbe (9 groups, 14 languages) B

The final *ɗ under palatalisation is realised as *j in almost all cases, which is a regular change. This has then been vocalised in Proto-Margi and Proto-Mandara. The palatalisation prosody is retained only in Gidar. *ɣʷ has a wide range of reflexes, as expected.

Given the wide distribution of *{-y} across Central Chadic languages, we reconstruct 'beard' as a candidate for morphological palatalisation in many but not all individual languages. Note, however, that Gravina's reconstruction can also be considered valid when we accept that the source of Y-prosody in this lexical item is not morphological but phonological, i.e. has its origin in a

reanalysis of medial schwa as also epenthetic for this language, which would posit for Mandara an underlying diachronic phonological system with only one vowel phoneme, namely */a/.

4.4 Syllabification of Underlying *y and *w   139

consonant change from radical */ɗ/ (as reconstructed by Gravina as the final consonant of the simple root) > [y]. Both reconstructions would appear to be justified, unless we have reason to prioritise one type of prosody, i.e. morphological or phonological, over the other (see also 3.2.3.4) chronologically. In our own analysis, we reconstruct 'beard' as a biradical root and postulate morphological palatalisation in a number of languages.

(122)   'beard' PCC *(a-, m(a)-, RED) **gʷ ma** (-a, -y)

SUKUR	Sukur	√ C Ca	*ɣ mØ-a-y		> ɣəmay	> yəmay
HURZA	Mbuko	√ C Ca	*ɣ mØ-a-y		> xəmay	> həmay
MARGI	Bura	√ C Ca	*kʷ mØ-y		> kʷəʷm-y	> kumi
MANDARA	Matal	√ C Ca	*a-gʷ ØØ-a-y			> agway
			*a-gʷ ØØ-a-y		> agʷaʷy	> agwoy
	Podoko	√ C Ca	*m-w ma-y		> mwma-Øʸ	
					> mwmaʸ	> mume
	Mandara	√ C Ca	*w ma			> uma
	Malgwa	√ C Ca	*kʷ ma		> kwma	
					> kəʷwma	> kuuma
			*w ma		> əwʷma	
					> əʷwma	> uuma
MOFU	Ouldeme	√ C Ca	*ma-Ø mØ-a-y		> mamay	> mamay
	Gemzek	√ C Ca	*x ma		> xəma	> həma
MAROUA	Giziga-Muturwa	√ C Ca	*RED+*xʷ ma-ŋ		> xʷ+xʷ mØŋ	
					> xʷə-mməŋ	
					> xəʷ-mməʷŋ	> hummuŋ
LAMANG	Lamang	√ C Ca	*ɣ ma			> yma
	Hdi	√ C Ca	*ɣʷ mØ-a-y		> ɣʷəmay	
					> ɣəʷmay	> yumay
HIGI	Kamwe-Futu	√ C Ca	*ɣʷ ɓa-y		> ɣʷəɓa-Øʸ	
					> ɣəʷɓaʸ	> yuɓe
	Kirya	√ C Ca	*ɣʷ mØ-y		> ɣʷəm-i	
					> ɣəʷm-i	> yumi
GIDAR	Gidar	√ C Ca	*aⁿga-Ø ma-y		> aⁿgama-Øʸ	
					> aⁿgaʸmaʸ	> aⁿgeme
					> ayⁿgaʸmaʸ	> eⁿgeme

Syllabification of *w in final root-augment position is somewhat less common, giving rise to a number of synchronic lexical items ending in the surface vowel [u]. Therefore, we do not reconstruct lexical ˣ/u/ in PCC, not even where [u] occurs in final position. (Note that also Gravina (2014a) saw no need to reconstruct ˣ/u/ for PCC.) In all these cases, we assume morphological labialisation to have played a role by allowing root-augmental *{-kʷ} to weaken to w, which would subsequently syllabify in syllable-nucleus position and give rise to final [u].

(123)   'belly' PCC *(a-) **xʷ(a)ɗa** (-y, -ɗ, -kʷ)

Note that in the following example, for which we offer alternative descriptions, the source of labialisation could also be assumed to be phonological, i.e. C_1 */xʷ/ > wʷ rather than morphological, i.e. a postulated suffixal augment {-kʷ}. However, examples from other languages (see immediately below) suggest that {-kʷ} could have played a role here as well.

MAROUA	Mbazla	*(a-)w rØ-k^w	> (a-)wər-w^w	
			> (a-)wə^{w}r-w	> *(a)wuru*
		*(a-)w ra	> (a-)w^{w}rə	
			> (a-)wə^{w}rə^w	> *(a)wuru*

(124) 'bone' PCC *(...) ɗ y(a)ɬa (-a, -y, -k^w, -t, -n)
     MARGI   Margi   *ɗ yaxØ-k^w > ɗyax-w   > *dyahu*

(125) 'root' PCC *(RED) ɬ(a)r(a)ka (-a, -y, -k^w, -; a)
     HIGI   Psikye   *ɬ Ø kØ-k^w > ɬəg-w^w
                                                                             > ɬə^{w}gw   > *ɬugu*

4.5 Intersegmental Fusion of Features Affecting Radical Consonants

Modern Central Chadic languages may or may not have consonant inventories that include labialised velars plus palatalised consonants. All languages would appear to have series of labialised velars, but do not have labialised non-velars. However, the latter do occur in some examples and can be accounted for by some kind of transfer of the labialisation feature ^{w} from an original source among the underlying phonemic labialised velar series */C^w/ or */w/. Occasionally, metathesis involving velar consonants or */w/ can be found to have triggered the process. The same holds true for the emergence of palatalised consonants, where languages do not have palatalised consonants (usually alveolars or post-alveolars, sometimes velars) in their synchronic inventories. In our present study, such transfers of labialisation and/or palatalisation features will be accounted for by the appropriate prosodies, quite often assuming intermediate steps of metathesis.

Note that transcription conventions for Chadic language data are not always clear as to the phonological nature of some graphic combinations, which is also true for nasalisation, i.e.

mb = ^{m}b or m+b	bw = b^w or b+w	ky = k^y or k+y
nd = ^{n}d or n+d	kw = k^w or k+w	ty = t^y or t+y
ŋg = ^{ŋ}g or ŋ+g	sw = s^w or s+w	etc.

See, for example, the following clear cases of feature transfer to create potential surface representations [v^w] and [l^y]. Our diachronic analysis shows that historically we are dealing with segment sequences involving separate root material, namely v+w (< *ɣ^w) and l+y (after metathesis):

(126) 'faeces' PCC *(ŋ-) ɣ^w va (-a, -y, -n)
     BATA   Jimi   *ɣ^{w}vØ-y-n   Metathesis: v w-yn   > *v^{w}in*
                Sharwa   *ɣ^{w}vØ-a-y   Metathesis: v w-ay   > *v^{w}ay*

4.6 Accounting for Differences   141

(127)   'hare' PCC *(ma-, na-) x^w(a)d(a)y(a)va (-k^w, -n ; FV)
        SUKUR   Sukur   *Ø l y va   Metathesis: v l ya   > vəlØ^ya   > vəl^ya
                        *Ø l y va   Metathesis: v l ya   > və^ylØ^ya   > vil^ya

4.6 Accounting for Differences between Very Closely Related Languages

It is one of the challenges for comparative Central Chadic linguistics to account for the stunning differences in the phonetic surface representation of cognate lexical items in even the most closely related languages, if not so-called dialects of the same (named) languages. Our study shows that it is mainly four major factors, which happen to reflect peculiarities of the inherent typology of Central Chadic languages, that create such remarkable differences:

1. choice of root type, involving number of radical consonants and positions of both phonemic */a/ and epenthetic schwa;
2. presence (and choice) or absence of root-augmentation materials;
3. more or less regular *sound changes* involving consonants;
4. presence or absence of *prosodies*, which may be either +Y and/or +W prosodies, or combined.

4.6.1   Underlying Root Type

The following examples from the MANDARA group illustrate the salient impact of choice of root and vowel patterns (root type) for differentiating five variant forms of the same root for the lexeme meaning 'root' between the languages: ɬılıh, ɬalwe, thlalawe, thlali, ɬəla. Three languages maintain a triradical root, two have deleted the final root consonant and surface as biradical roots √ C Ca < √ C C Øa < √ C C Ca. Among the three languages that have chosen to retain a triradical root type, each has opted for a different vocalisation pattern regarding medial /a/: √ C C Ca, √ CaC Ca, √ CaCaCa. Also, the biradical root surface variants differ in this regard: √ C Ca, √ CaCa. Additional differentiation comes from presence (in four languages) versus absence (in one language) of Y-prosody effects, and from differences regarding suffixal root-augment materials: one language has none (Dghweɗe), three languages have *{-y} only (Matal, Mandara, Malgwa), and one language has *{-y} plus FV /a/ (Glavda).

(128)   'root' PCC *(RED) ɬ(a)r(a)ka (-a, -y, -k^w, -; a)
        MANDARA   Matal   √ C C Ca   *ɬ l xØ-y   > ɬələx-Ø^y
                                                   > ɬə^ylə^yx   > ɬılıh
                  Mandara √ CaC Ca   *ɬal wa-y   > ɬalwa-Ø^y
                                                   > ɬalwa^y   > ɬalwe
                  Malgwa   √ CaCaCa   *ɬalawa-y   > ɬalawa-Ø^y
                                                   > ɬalawa^y   > thlalawe

Glavda	√ CaC Ca	*ɬal Øa-ya	> ɬala-yʸa		
			> ɬaləʸya	> ɬaliya	
Dghwed́e	√ C C Ca	*ɬ l Øa	> ɬəla	> ɬəla	

4.6.2 Root Augmentation, Consonantal Sound Changes, and Prosodies

The following examples for 'night' (PCC simple root *$r(a)v(a)ɗa$) from the MARGI group illustrate the salient impact of prosodies for differentiating four variant forms between the languages: *vir(i)*, *vi'i*, *vʷi'i* and *vu'i*. All four languages make use of the same choice of root type. They all delete the first root consonant √ C C Ca > √ Ø C Ca. They all use vowel epenthesis by inserting schwa in the medial vowel slot: √ Ø CəCa. They differ, however, in terms of the prosodies related to suffixal root-augment materials, and with regard to sound changes affecting the final consonant of the simple root.

All four languages undergo changes originating from suffixal *{-y}, which is syllabified and yields final [i] in phonetic surface representation, and which regularly deletes the root-final /a/: √ Ø CəCØ-y > CəC-i. In addition, there is a consonantal change in Margi, Margi-South and Kilba *ɗ > ʔ, which together with the root augment yield the word-ending 'i. (Note that Bura undergoes a different change *ɗ > r.) Suffixal *{-y} > -iʸ becomes the source for Y-prosody, which in Margi, South-Margi and Bura (but not in Kilba) affects the epenthetic vowel of the first syllable and changes ə > [i]. Margi-South and Kilba are the only two languages of this set to also show root-augmental *{-kʷ}, which desegmentalises and prosodifies to yield W-prosody; this W-prosody affects the first-syllable vowel in Kilba by changing epenthetic ə > [u], but affects the initial consonant in Margi-South by transfer of the labialisation feature of *{-kʷ} onto C_1 to yield [vʷ]. See

(129)	MARGI	Margi	√ C C Ca	*Ø v dØ-y	> vəʔ-iʸ	
					> vəʸʔi	> vi'i
		Margi-South	√ C C Ca	*Ø v dØ-y-kʷ	> vəʔ-iʸ-Øʷ	
					> vʷəʸʔi	> vʷi'i
		Kilba	√ C C Ca	*Ø v dØ-y-kʷ	> vəʔ-i-Øʷ	
					> vəʷʔi	> vu'i
		Bura	√ C C Ca	*Ø v dØ-y	> vər-iʸ	
					> vəʸr-i	>vir(i)

4.7 From PCC to Modern Central Chadic Languages: Phonemicisation of Allophones

The linguistic situation in Chadic is intriguing, because we are faced with the contrast – if not apparent contradiction – between

(a) a whole range of up to ten short *phonetic surface vowels* (totalling up to seventeen when counting long vowels), as found in the transcriptions of

4.7 From PCC to Modern Central Chadic Languages

individual languages by individual researchers, of which several are candidates for being considered phonemic in the respective synchronic phonological descriptions;
(b) the fact that a fair number of these surface vowels can often be identified as conditioned variants (allophones) of a much lower number of *synchronically underlying vowel phonemes*, often just two (/a, ə/) or even only one (/a/), depending on the individual language and the level of phonological abstractness chosen by the linguist for descriptive purposes;
(c) the assumption, in *diachronic perspective*, of just one underlying PCC vowel phoneme, namely */a/.

On the one hand, seasoned linguists working in the Central Chadic field may justifiably describe any phonological system as having between only one and six or more phonemic vowels, and dealing phonetically with ten or more vowel qualities when counting in all assimilated allophones and conditioned or free 'phonetically coloured' variants. On the other hand, we are led to assume that PCC had only one 'true' vowel phoneme */a/ (in concert with two other vocoids, namely */y/ and */w/ that would account for syllabic allophones [i] and [u]). We know that the odd Central Chadic language may well be described even synchronically as having only one vowel in underlying abstract phonological terms, as, for instance, Moloko (MOFU, cf. Bow 1999; Gravina 2014a: 90ff.). Wolff and Naumann (2004) have shown that it is feasible also to attribute only one underlying vowel phoneme */a/ to Mandara. And where there are apparently only two vowel phonemes operating in the system, these are /a/ and /ə/. But then we are being told that schwa, possibly most of the time, may be accounted for as epenthetic in nature rather than being truly phonemic, and that, where synchronically it is best described as phonemic, this could be the result of a process of 'phonemicisation' of a former, i.e. from a diachronic perspective, purely epenthetic vowel. Carrying abstract phonological analysis to its extremes, we may end up having to accept that on the ultimate diachronic level, Central Chadic languages were truly vowelless.[2] All this is quite confusing to the non-initiated, who intends to approach modern (Central) Chadic languages from the 'classic' and somewhat Indo-European-centric comparative perspective.

In order to account for the present situation in the almost 80 modern Central Chadic languages, we must obviously assume large-scale diachronic phonemicisation of the proto-languages' allophones and other systemic variants of

---

[2] Reanalysing the diachronic phonology of Lamang (see Wolff 2015 Vol.1: 64–76) and discussing 'vocalogenesis' in (Central) Chadic in more general terms (see Wolff 2017), one could even arrive at an ultimate abstract level of diachronic analysis that would do without any phonemic vowels at all, if we take the theoretical implications seriously when we speak of 'vocoids' rather than 'vowels' on the level of the proto-language. Note that Barreteau (1988) has shown for Mofu-Gudur that it is possible 'to reduce the number of underlying vowels to zero, and to predict the surface vowels just from the consonants, prosodies and tone' (Gravina 2014a: 72).

segments, which can and must be assumed to diachronically underlie the phonetic vowel representations in the synchronic phonological systems of modern Central Chadic languages. Hence the present author has suggested the concept of and has spoken about and has published on 'vocalogenesis' in Chadic on several occasions since the early 1980s. As we can see from the PCC reconstructions in this book and their reflexes in the modern languages, and expectedly so, most present-day surface vowels indeed have their origins in systemic units and their conditioned variants of the PCC system as reconstructed in the present study, namely stemming from

- the only reconstructable 'true' vowel */a/, yielding – in the absence of prosodies – allophones [a] and centralised [ə];
- the syllabification of the other two 'vocoids' */y/ and */w/, yielding allophones [i] and [u];
- conditioned allophones of */a/ under the effect of Y- and/or W-prosody, yielding allophones [ɛ~e, ɔ~o];
- conditioned variants of schwa as a highly predictable pro- and epenthetic vowel (as we postulate in the present study, but which theoretically could also be reconstructed as phonemic */ə/), under either Ø-prosody or under the effect of Y- and/or W-prosody, yielding allophones [ə, ɨ~ɪ, ʉ~ʊ] and also – depending on transcription conventions – [i, u].

The basic units and correspondences are summarised in Table 4.1.

The above inventory would fill a remarkable vowel chart for surface representations, a selection or all of which could indeed represent synchronic inventories of phonetic surface vowels in individual modern Central Chadic languages (Table 4.2).

Behind this chart of phonetic surface vowels lies, in terms of our proposed 'prosody-based' approach to historical Central Chadic phonology, the interaction of three diachronic (and potentially also underlying synchronic) phonological subsystems, which in a parallel fashion share in and organise the 'vocalic space' in Central Chadic languages. These three subsystems involve

Table 4.1 *The vocalic domain of Proto-Central Chadic*

Phonological nature of segments		Syllabic variants under prosodic impact			
non-phonemic (pro-/epenthetic)	phonemic	Ø prosody	+Y prosody	+W prosody	+Y+W prosodies combined
ə		[ə]	[ɨ ~ ɪ ~ i]	[ʉ ~ ʊ ~ u]	IPA [y]
	*/a/	[a]	[ɛ ~ e]	[ɔ ~ o]	[œ]
	*/y/	[i]			
	*/w/	[u]			

4.7 From PCC to Modern Central Chadic Languages

Table 4.2. *Synchronic vowel qualities in Central Chadic languages*

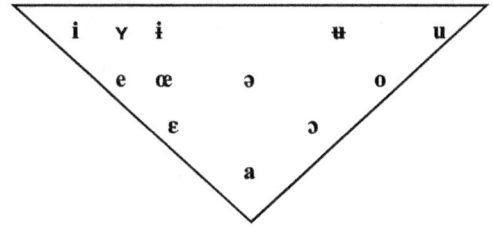

Table 4.3 *The vocalic space in Central Chadic languages: tongue height and position*

	Vocalic space		
	front	**central**	**back**
[−low]	+	(+)	+
[+low]		+	

- articulatory phonetics: tongue height and position
- segmental phonology:
  - diachronic vocoids (phonemic)
  - pro-/epenthetic schwa (non-phonemic)
- suprasegmental phonology: Y- and W-prosodies

The vocalic space could be represented by a basic grid relating to tongue height and positions (Table 4.3).

As for vocalic units to fill this grid, we are dealing with subsystems under the proviso that the '+' marked fields are the domains of phonemic units, here referred to as 'vocoids', whereas the '(+)' marked non-low central field remains the domain of vowel epenthesis (unless schwa should also considered to be phonemic, which would be a legitimate alternative option).

1. Subsystem of PCC vocoids (Table 4.4)

   The vocoids remind us historically and typologically of the weak radicals in other Afroasiatic language families. This subsystem would appear not only to lie at the bottom of diachronic processes but can probably be assumed to also synchronically underlie a fair number of modern Central Chadic languages.

Table 4.4 *The vocalic space in Central Chadic languages: diachronic vocoids*

	Phonologically distinct diachronic VOCOIDS[3]		
	front	central	back
[−low]	*/y ~ i/		*/w ~ u/
[+low]		*/a/	

2. Subsystem of PROSODIES (Table 4.5)

The prosodies systemically emerge from the phonological system behind the vocoids, namely Ø-prosody being affiliated with */a/, Y-prosody being affiliated with */y/, and W-prosody being affiliated with */w/ and */C^w/.

3. Subsystem of VOWEL PRO-/EPENTHESIS (Table 4.6)

Pro- and epenthetic schwa is frequently inserted into diachronically and synchronically underlying structures in order to create acceptable syllable structures in surface phonetic representations.

These are the diachronic and systemic ingredients from which all synchronic modern Central Chadic 'vowel systems' are made. Therefore, we need a multi-tiered approach to understanding Central Chadic comparative linguistics since the units from the different subsystems enter complex relationships among each other between pairs of languages. For this reason, straightforward 1:1 correspondences resulting from 'classic' applications of the comparative method to synchronic surface representations of Central Chadic lexical items

---

[3] It remains a legitimate yet still speculative question, which came up quite early in discussions with fellow linguists on the matter of vocoids in Chadic, why in the reconstructed proto-system, the unique vowel */a/ should not also be treated like the other vocoids, thereby establishing a hypothetical diachronic neat triple vocoid series of the type *ʕ~a, *y~i, *w~u and suggesting that the proto-system reflected a truly vowelless ideal type. Whatever the phonetic features such a hypothetical third vocoid might have had, if it ever existed, it has currently not been found necessary to reconstruct */ʕ/ (or any pharyngeal/glottal approximant) for either PC or PCC. Note, however, that a glottal stop occurs in the phonological and/or phonetic inventory of some modern (Central) Chadic languages reflecting more recent developments, as it would appear (see, in particular, Newman 2006: 192). Therefore and in terms of 'vocalogenesis' (as discussed more recently and in detail in Wolff 2017), the potential relationship between hypothetical and possibly pre-Chadic ˣʕ and */a/ could be considered to remain theoretically open for further comparative research. Note that this issue remains highly speculative and has no bearing on the present study of lexical reconstruction in PCC. If we were to follow the idea any further, however, the issue might eventually link up with the likewise still open question regarding the occasional emergence of long vowels in modern (Central) Chadic languages, in particular long /aa/. By linking the occurrence of synchronic long high vowels to underlying combinations of schwa + */y/ and */w/, i.e. *əy > [ii] and *əw > [uu] (see 4.8 below), this would open a line of investigation towards answering the question of whether synchronic [aa] eventually could be derived from a deeply underlying hypothetical *əʕ, if not simply from *aØa.

Table 4.5 *The vocalic space in Central Chadic languages: prosodies*

	PROSODIES stemming from diachronic and/or synchronically underlying segments		
	front	central	back
[−low]	Palatalisation Y-prosody		Labialisation W-prosody
[+low]		Neutral Ø-prosody	

Table 4.6 *Phonetic 'colouring' of epenthetic schwa in Central Chadic languages*

	Phonetic 'colouring' of PRO-/EPENTHETIC SCHWA		
	front	central	back
[−low]	i ~ ɨ ~ ɪ	ə	ʉ ~ u ~ ʊ
[+low]		(ɐ)	

do not work. They will, however, work between units of sub-domains of different diachronic subsystems.

4.8 On the Emergence of Long Vowels in Modern Central Chadic Languages

The linguistic history of vowel length in (Central) Chadic has also long been considered enigmatic. As quoted in 1.1 further above, P. Newman (2006) suggested that Biu-Mandara (i.e. Central Chadic) lost PC vowel length distinctions in word-medial positions and also with likely *Caa monoradical words, and that PC *ii, *uu and *aa shortened to */i/, */u/ and */a/ respectively, while PC *i and *u merged to */ə/. In this way, PCC would end up having a four-vowel system with no vowel length. However, modern Central Chadic languages do show long vowels in their synchronic phonological systems. Regarding these, however, our internal reconstructions in this study show that and how surface long vowels may emerge in present-day CC languages independently and neither necessarily stem from long vowels that need to be reconstructed for PCC, nor reflect pre-existing long vowels that might be reconstructed for PC. As was already suggested in

Heide Mirt's (1969) early study of Mandara vowels, synchronic long vowels may have their own history from combinations of underlying weak radicals with (epenthetic or phonemic) schwa, thereby creating long high vowels *ə+*/y/ > [ii] and *ə+*/w/ > [uu] in surface structures. Note that in the reconstructions undertaken so far, comparable parallel emergence of vowel length from *ə+*X > [aa] has not been observed. Note also that schwa never actually appears with vowel length in surface manifestations of data from the modern CC languages that have been used for the present study.

4.8.1 The Emergence of Long [ii]

Surface [ii] in modern languages apparently emerges from combinations of epenthetic schwa (under Y-prosody) with syllabified */y/.

(130)   'arm' PCC **dz va** (-y, -k^w, -n ; FV)
        BATA   Gude   *ts ØØ-y-na
                                    > tsə-y^y-na
                                    > ts^{y}ə^y-i-nə   > tʃiinə

(131)   'cook, to' PCC (k-, ma-, RED) **da** (a, -y, -k, k^w; FV)
        MUSGUM   Mbara   *tØ-y   > tə-y^y
                                     > tə^y-i   > tii

(132)   'dream' PCC (ma-, ma-RED, RED, n-) **s(a)w(a)na** (-a, -y, -k, -k^w, -n; FV)
        BATA   Gude   *s Ø na-y   > sənə-i^y
                                        > sənə^y-i   > sənii
        MUSGUM   Mulwi   *x w nØ-y   > xəwn-i^y
                                        > xə^{y}w^{y}n-i
                                        > xə^{y}yn-i   > hiini
        Note that the Mulwi analysis assumes a somewhat rare (but elsewhere indeed more than once observed) assimilatory change from /w/ > y under Y-prosody, including subsequent syllabification of y > i.

(133)   'extinguish, to' PCC (k-, m(a)-) **m(a)ta** (-a, -y, -k^w, -n, -ŋ; FV)
        BATA   Jimi   *m ta-y-n   Metathesis
                                        myta-n
                                        > məy^{y}tə-n
                                        > mə^{y}itə-n   > miitən

(134)   'give birth, to' PCC *(ma-) **w(a)x(a)ya** (-k, -kw, -n, -l; FV)
        SUKUR   Sukur   *RED+x ya   Metathesis
                                        RED+yxa
                                        > yə-y^{y}xa
                                        > yə^y-ixa   > yiiha
        MUSGUM   Mbara   *w Ø yØ   > wəy^y
                                        > wə^{y}i   > wii

4.8 The Emergence of Long Vowels   149

  GIDAR Gidar *wØyØ-na > wəy^y-na
              > wə^{y}i-na > *wiina*

(135) 'grasshopper' PCC *(a-) **x^w(a)y(a)k^{w}a** (...)
  MANDARA Malgwa *Ø y wa > əy^{y}wa
             > ə^{y}ywa^y > *iiwe*

(136) 'hare' PCC (ma-, na-) **x^w(a)d(a)y(a)va** (-k^w, -n; FV))
  MANDARA Malgwa *na-Øryva > navəy^{y}ra
             > navə^{y}ira > *naviira*
       Glavda *ØØyvØ > vəy^y
             > və^{y}i > *vii*
          *Ødyva > vəy^{y}da
             > və^{y}ida > *vi:da*

(137) 'sun' PCC (a-, xa-, d-, RED) **p(a)ta** (-a, -y, -k, -k^w, -n ; FV)
  MUSGUM Vulum, Mulwi *f ta-y-k^w > fəta-i^y-Ø^w
             > fə^{w}tə^y-i > *futii*

(138) 'water' PCC (a(x^w)-) **ʔy(a)ma** (-a, -y, -k^w, -n; FV)
  MANDARA Glavda *y Øa > y^{y}a
            > iə^y > *ii*

(139) 'white' PCC (m(a)-, RED) **k^w(a)ɗ(a)ka** (-y, -l; FV)
  MUSGUM Mulwi, *m-k^w ɗ Metathesis
       Vulum Øa-y m-ɗk^w-y
            > mə-ɗək^{w}a-y^y
            > mə^{w}ɗə^{w}k^{w}ə^{y}i > *muduk^{w}ii*

(140) 'whistle, to' PCC *(ma-, RED) **f(a)y(a)k^{w}a** (-a, -y, -n)
  MANDARA Malgwa *f y k^{w}a > fəy^{y}k^{w}a
            > fə^{y}ik^{w}a > *fiik^{w}a*

4.8.2 The Emergence of Long [uu]

Surface [uu] in modern languages tends to have a more complex linguistic history than [ii] as described above. Like [ii], however, it could emerge from combinations of pro-/epenthetic schwa (albeit under W-prosody) with a syllabified reconstructed PCC vocoid (/w/).

(141) 'cry, to' *(ma-) **ts(a)wa** (-a, -y, -k; FV)
  BATA Bata, Gude *t wØ > təw^w
            > tə^{w}w > *tuu*
  MANDARA Glavda *t wØ-ka > təw^w-ka
            > tə^{w}w-ka > *tu:ga*

(142)   'give birth, to' PCC *(ma-, RED) **w(a)x(a)ya** (-k, -k^w, -n, -l; FV)
        GIDAR   Gidar   *RED+w Ø Øa   > w^w+w^{w}a > ə^{w}u.wa.   > *uuwa*

Occasionally, however, the approximant has previously come about by weakening from PCC */C^w/ > w, either within the root or as part of a suffixal augment. For root-internal origin of w, see

(143)   'beard' PCC *(a-, m(a)-, RED) g^w ma (-a, -y)
        MANDARA   Malgwa   *w ma > əw^{w}ma   > ə^{w}u.ma.   > *uuma*

For root-external origin of w, see the following two examples. In Bachama, root-augmental *{-k^w} metathesises and prosodifies to w^w and affects prothetic schwa; original C$_2$ */y/ prosodifies > Ø^y and changes final /a/ > [e]:

(144)   'bone' PCC *((')a-, a-n-, a-ta-, ma-, ma-ta-, RED-a-) **ɗy(a)la** (-a, -y, -k^w, -t, -n)
        BATA   Bachama   *Ø y la-k^w > Ø^{y}k^{w}la > əw^{w}la^y > ə^{w}ula^y > *uule*

In Lamang, the word for 'horn$_1$' has occasionally been heard during my own fieldwork with longer-than-usual medial [u]. Presumably, root-augmental *{-k^w} weakened to w and subsequently underwent double metathesis to end up in C$_2$ position, where it combines with epenthetic schwa to yield a long(er) medial vowel:

(145)   'horn$_1$' PCC **d(a)r(a)ma** (-y, -k^w)
        LAMANG   Lamang   *d l ØØ-y-k^w > d l-y-w
                                            Metathesis
                                            d l-w-y
                                            Metathesis
                                            d w l-y > də^{w}wl-i   > *du:li*

4.9   Summary of Diachronic Processes from PCC to Modern Central Chadic Languages

In order to arrive at our reconstructions of PCC lexical items, we had to unravel 'reconstructable', i.e. frequent and more or less generalised, phonological processes that we assume would have affected the PCC forms during their historical development towards the synchronic surface representations that we find in the database, i.e. that reflect the situation in modern Central Chadic languages. Basically, we are dealing with 15 phonological processes, which we may group somewhat arbitrarily as belonging to five process types (see below). It is plausible to assume that these processes did or do not apply in a haphazard order but follow either some intrinsic logic or reflect a chronological sequence of application.

As can be expected, not the least in view of the presumed time-depth involved, many if not most reflexes of the reconstructed PCC forms will have

4.9 Diachronic Processes   151

undergone considerable changes which, at times, make the etymological identity of lexical items very hard to recognise – even for the initiated. This, however, is a common experience in historical linguistics.[4] On the other hand and quite accidentally, as also in other language phyla and families, some modern languages will show apparently no effect of diachronic rules of so-called natural language change, i.e. some of their current phonetic representations correspond exactly, or almost exactly, to the form that we have reconstructed for the PCC lexicon. This, by the way, would give us an indication of how some of the reconstructed PCC items might have been phonetically realised – if we were to take PCC to be more than just a fictive system of etymological reference, namely a set of language varieties that were indeed spoken at some time in the past.[5]

See the following selective list of formal matches (by observing the appropriate root type and also counting rather localised reconstructions for only a few language groups) between our reconstructions of simple roots and modern Central Chadic language reflexes (Table 4.7).

Further down, we will give a list of 15 historical phonological processes, which all contribute to diachronic change in individual languages, either in a highly frequent and general or in a sometimes rare if not language-specific manner. Since, in this study, we are not concerned much with consonants nor with natural or contact-induced language change affecting consonants, the likes of the following will have to be acknowledged as equally relevant processes of natural language change (and have been described in more or less detail by Gravina (2014a)) and have occasionally been noted in the body of this book, but will not be listed among the diachronic phonological processes below.

1. Voicing and devoicing
2. Spirantisation
3. Glottalisation (but see 6.3.6)
4. Prenasalisation (but see 2.5.4)
5. Assimilation to abutting other consonants
6. etc.

---

[4] One never fails to impress linguistic laypersons (incl. first-year students of linguistics) by showing that the English word *hundred* can be systematically related etymologically to the Russian word *sto* of the same meaning, by regular sound correspondences, based on earlier forms like *centum* [kentum] and *satem* [ʃatem] coexisting in the history of Indo-European languages.

[5] Note that this is also true of obvious loans into Central Chadic languages, for instance from or via Nilo-Saharan Kanuri, when and after they have been structurally integrated as a PCC pseudo-root into the Central Chadic phonological systematics. Take as an example Kanuri *koro* 'donkey', which has been reanalysed in Giziga-Marva as being of underlying triradical structure and is also realised synchronically as such:

    'donkey$_3$'   *kawra (< *k(a)w(a)ra) *kawra*   Giziga-Marva (MAROUA)

Table 4.7 *Matching of PCC reconstructions with modern forms*

Gloss	PCC reconstruction	Modern form	Language (GROUP)
boil, to	*k^wadaxa	k^wadaha	Vame (HURZA)
bow	*raga	raga	Gude (BATA)
cook, to	*da	da	Buwal (DABA)
cow	*ɬa	ɬa	Mbuko (HURZA)
cry, to	*tawa	tawa	Podoko (MANDARA)
die, to	*mta	mta	Bura (MARGI)
dog	*kra	kra	Gidar (GIDAR)
donkey$_1$	*zaŋ^{w}a	zaŋ^{w}a	Cuvok (MAFA)
eight	*tɣasa	tɣasa	Lamang (LAMANG)
five	*x^{w}tafa	h^{w}tafa	Lamang (LAMANG)
six	*ɬara	ɬaara	Vulum (MUSGUM)
suck, to	*swɓa	suɓa	Giziga-Marva (MAROUA)
sun	*pata	pat	Dugwor (MOFU)

Further, two more restrictions need highlighting here: root augmentation and choice of root type.

We will disregard root augmentation (3.1.2) as a diachronic phonological process, because originally the processes leading to root augmentation were morphological in nature. However, the phonological processes listed below apply to both historically simple and augmented roots.

Neither does choice of underlying root type qualify as a diachronic phonological process, yet it is of high importance in the historical development of modern surface forms of words. Choice of root type is part of the language-internal pre-processing of the reconstructed forms by choosing the vocalisation pattern for the consonantal skeleton of the root, which – in a most general way – follows from the Afroasiatic heritage of root-and-pattern structure in phonology and morphology. This means that each individual language 'chooses' usually one possible root type from various options (but occasionally the same language uses more than one root type for the same lexical item in a parallel fashion), which will function as historical simple root, and on which all diachronic phonological processes will operate (see 3.1.1 further above). It does make a difference whether we are dealing with Ø-vocalised simple roots, which do not contain any */a/ apart from the lexical final vowel, or whether we are dealing with a-vocalised simple roots, where it also matters how many and which inter-consonantal slots are filled by */a/ and which are not. Note that we have not been able to detect traces of productive choice of root type for indication of categorial distinctions in our reconstructions (see also 3.1.2 further above; Wolff 2009). This is unlike in quite a few (but not all)

4.9 Diachronic Processes

modern Central Chadic languages, in which different root types (such as characterised by so-called 'internal a' and/or consonant repetition) may have synchronic relevance for marking pluractional verb stems or forms that specialise in being used for marking categories in the inflectional system of the language, e.g. verbal 'aspect' in a given T(ense-)A(spect-)M(ood) system, or noun pluralisation. However, we have noted that closely related languages of the same groups occasionally make use of different root types for the same reconstructed lemma. For our reconstructions and for each individual language and for each word, therefore, we present conflated structures, which embody the options of root-type choice for PCC.

Any of the following 15 diachronic processes can operate on any of our reconstructed PCC lexical roots, not necessarily only once per root/word. Or they may not operate at all (see the list of 'unchanged' simple roots above). The process typology I–V that structures the list below does not necessarily imply a temporal sequence in terms of relative chronology, but it would appear to do so in many individual cases.

I. Processes *sequentially* or *quantitatively* affecting the segmental structure of the word in either underlying (and likely diachronic) or phonetic surface representation.
   1. **Metathesis** involving consonants and weak radicals (*/y/, */w/); occasionally, a word may undergo two or more subsequent instances of metathesis;
   2. **Re-segmentalisation** (phoneme 'split') of labialised */C^w/ > */C/ + */w/;
   3. **Deletion** of phonemic segments, either consonantal [−syllabic], specified vocalic vocoid [+syllabic] (*/a/), or underspecified [± syllabic] vocoid (*/y/, */w/);[6]
   4. **Vowel pro- and epenthesis**, i.e. insertion of schwa (ə);
   5. **Partial desegmentalisation** (or weakening) of */C^w/ > */w/.
II. Prosodification processes *bridging* the separation between segmental and suprasegmental structures and thereby creating prosodies ('prosodification').
   6. **Prosodification of */C^w/ and */w/ > ^{w}**, i.e. emergence and extension of labialisation (W-) prosody;
   7. **Prosodification of */y/ > ^{y}**, i.e. emergence and extension of palatalisation (Y-) prosody.

---

[6] Quite frequent and more likely 'irregular' apocope of final /a/ is subsumed here, which could also be viewed as a different rule, comparable to 'irregular' metathesis (Rule 1).
  Pro- and epenthetic schwa (ə) – for not being considered phonemic – does not form part of any reconstructed root and, therefore, cannot be deleted. Rather and on very many occasions, schwa is inserted as pro- or epenthetic vowel by a highly frequent diachronic phonological process, as listed next.

III. Syllabification processes *qualitatively* affecting the segmental structure of the word in either underlying (and likely diachronic) or in phonetic surface representation.
    8. **Syllabification of */w/ to [u]** in syllable-nucleus positions;
    9. **Syllabification of */y/ to [i]** in syllable-nucleus positions.

IV. Centralisation processes *blurring* the distinction between phonemic */a/ and non-phonemic schwa.[7]
    10. **Centralisation of simple-root final lexical vowel** */a/ > [ə];
    11. **Centralisation of FV of augmented roots** */a/ > [ə].

V. Prosody extension processes.
    12. **W-Prosody affecting vowels**, whether phonemic */a/, non-phonemic schwa, or both;
    13. **W-Prosody affecting consonants**, independent of position in the segmental chain;
    14. **Y-Prosody affecting vowels**, whether phonemic */a/, non-phonemic schwa, or both;
    15. **Y-Prosody affecting consonants**, independent of position in the segmental chain.

Note that the above list of 15 phonological processes could be considered to be redundantly explicit. In terms of economy of description, one could easily condense it to a list of just nine major processes:

1. Metathesis
2. Re-segmentalisation (phoneme 'split'): $*/C^w/ > */C/ + */w/$
3. Deletion
4. Vowel pro- and epenthesis
5. Partial desegmentalisation (weakening): $*/C^w/ > */w/$
6. Prosodification of palatal(ised) and labial(ised) consonants
7. Syllabification of approximants
8. Centralisation of final */a/ > [ə]
9. Prosody extension (affecting vowels, consonants, or both)

For repetitive summarising purposes, the following examples of simple and augmented roots from selected languages are chosen to illustrate the sequential application of sets of these processes (numbered 1–15) with the same roots.

---

[7] The centralised allophone [ə] of /a/ behaves like non-phonemic schwa under the effects of prosodies in terms of 'colouring'. As indicated before, for our reconstructions we prefer the assumption of 'centralisation' of final */a/ > [ə] over the assumption of schwa epithesis after deletion of */a/.

4.9 Diachronic Processes

The first example is from Ouldeme (MOFU) and shows a Ø-vocalised root type √ C C Ca; the simple root does neither contain any 'weak radical' nor any labialised consonant, but it carries root-augmental *{-y}, which is the source of morphological Y-prosody:

(146)

Simple root	Gloss	Phonological process	Input	Output
PCC:	root	1. Metathesis	*ɬka-y	ɬkla-y
*ɬ(a)r(a)ka		3. Deletion	ɬkla-y	ɬklØ-y
Ouldeme:		4. Vowel epenthesis	ɬklØ-y	ɬəkəl-y
*ɬlka		7. Y-Prosodification	ɬəkəl-y	ɬəkəl-y^y
		9. Y-Syllabification	ɬəkəl-y^y	ɬəkəl-i^y
		14. Y-Prosody on vowels	ɬəkəl-i^y	ɬə^{y}kə^{y}l-i
				> ɬikili

The second example is from Bura (MARGI) and shows an a-vocalised root type √ CaC Ca; the simple root also does not contain any weak radical, but it contains a labialised velar as final root consonant, which is the source of phonological W-prosody, and it again carries root-augmental *{-y}, which is the source of morphological Y-prosody. In this example, therefore, we see both prosodies at work at the same time, but operating on distinct domains within the word.

(147)

Simple root	Gloss	Phonological process	Input	Output
PCC:	razor$_1$	7. Y- Prosodification	*park^{w}a-y	park^{w}a-y^y
*p(a)d(a)k^{w}a		3. Deletion	park^{w}a-y^y	park^{w}a-Ø^y
Bura:		10. Centralisation lexical /a/	park^{w}a-Ø^y	park^{w}ə-^{y}
*park^{w}a		12. W-Prosody on vowels	park^{w}ə-^{y}	parkə^w-^{y}
				> parku-^{y}
		14. Y-Prosody on vowels	parku-^{y}	pa^{y}rku-^{y}
				> perku-^{y}
		15. Y-Prosody on consonants	perku-^{y}	p^{y}erku
				> p^{y}erku

The third example is from two very closely related languages, namely Mandara and Malgwa (MANDARA). It shows a Ø-vocalised root type √ C Ca; the simple root contains an initial labialised consonant, which weakens to w and becomes syllabified to [u], and which gives rise to phonological W-prosody. Interestingly, there are three forms for this word available, i.e. Malgwa *kuuma ~ uuma*, Mandara *uma*, which show different steps of desegmentalisation and deletion in the development from a labialised consonant-initial root to a vowel-initial one:

(a) Malgwa

(148)

Simple root	Gloss	Phonological process	Input	Output
	beard	2. Re-segmentalisation C^w > C+w	*k^{w}ma	kwma

PCC: *gʷ ma	4. Vowel epenthesis	kwma	kəwma
Malgwa:	6. W- Prosodification	kəwma	kəwʷma
*kʷma	8. W-Syllabification	kəwʷma	kəuʷma
	12. W-prosody on vowel	kəuʷma	kəʷuma
			> *kuuma*
	5. Weakening Cʷ > w	*kʷma	wma
	4. Vowel prothesis	wma	əwma
	6. W- Prosodification	əwma	əwʷma
	8. W-Syllabification	əwʷma	əuʷma
	12. W-prosody on vowel	əuʷma	əʷuma
			> *uuma*

(b) Mandara

(149)

Simple root	Gloss	Phonological process	Input	Output
PCC: *gʷ ma	beard	5. Weakening Cʷ > w	*kʷma	wma
Mandara:		8. W-Syllabification	wma	*uma*
*kʷma				

Note: The re-segmentalisation of */kʷ/ > /k+w/ > w in Malgwa, which is not a unique instance in the data, requires vowel epenthesis in one instance and prothesis in the other, and thus explains the occurrence of the long vowel [uu] as opposed to Mandara, which syllabifies weakened /w/ (< */kʷ/) to yield short [u].

The following examples illustrate the less frequent application of processes numbered above 11 and 13. Final vowel (FV) centralisation is even rarer than the low frequency of occurrence of the FV in the first place; remember that the FV occasionally follows suffixal root-augmental material, wherever such is present. Both Gude (BATA) and Bana (HIGI) provide examples, in which the FV appears as centralised allophone [ə] of FV /a/ in the data. Note that in Gude root-augmental *{-y} syllabifies to [i] in final position without, however, creating Y-prosody that would affect other segments within the word. In Bana, the same *{-y} does create Y-prosody that affects other segments within the word. Note further that in Bana rather exceptional rightward reduplication of root material occurs, which is not contained as a 'diachronic rule' in our list of rules above and, therefore, remains unnumbered and is given as 'X. Internal reduplication' below.

(a) Gude

(150)

Simple root	Gloss	Phonological process	Input	Output
PCC:	root	3. Deletion	*ɬrga-y-na	ɬrgØ-y-na
*ɬ(a)r(a)ka		4. Vowel epenthesis	ɬrgØ-y-na	ɬərəg-y-na
Gude:		9. Y-Syllabification	ɬərəg-y-na	ɬərəg-i-na
*ɬrga		11. FV centralisation	ɬərəg-i-na	ɬərəg-i-nə
				> *lhərəginə*

4.9 Diachronic Processes   157

(b) Bana (with language- and word-specific root-internal reduplication)

(151) | Simple root | Gloss | Phonological process | Input | Output |
|---|---|---|---|---|
| PCC: | root | 1. Metathesis | *xlga-y-na | xlyga-na |
| *ɫ(a)r(a)ka | | 1. Metathesis | xlygana | xlynaga |
| Bana: | | 3. Deletion | xlynaga | xlynØga |
| *xlga | | 4. Vowel epenthesis | xlyØnga | xəlynga |
| | | 7. Y-Prosodification | xəlynga | xəly^{y}nga |
| | | X. Internal reduplication | xəly^{y}nga | xəly^y-ly^y-nga |
| | | 9. Y-Syllabification | xəly^y-ly^y-nga | xəli^y-li^y-nga |
| | | 11. FV centralisation | xəli^y-li^y-nga | xəli^y-li^y-ngə |
| | | 14. Y-prosody on vowels | xəli^y-li^y-ngə | xə^{y}li^y-li^y-ngə > xili^y-li^y-ngə |
| | | 15. Y-prosody on consonant | xili^y-li^y-ngə | x^{y}ililiŋə |

For W-prosody affecting (non-velar) consonants, see the following examples from Zulgo (MOFU) and Kirya (HIGI):

(152) | Simple Root | Gloss | Phonological process | INPUT | OUTPUT |
|---|---|---|---|---|
| PCC: | donkey$_1$ | 6. W-Prosodification | *xa-m-zag^{w}a-y | xa-m-zag^{W}a-y |
| *z(a)g^{w}a | | 7. Y-Prosodification | xa-m-zag^{W}a-y | xa-m-zag^{W}a-y^y |
| Zulgo: | | 3. Deletion | xa-m-zag^{W}a-y^y | xa-Ø-za^{ŋ}g^{W}a-Ø^y |
| *zag^{w}a | | 13. W-prosody on consonant | xa-za^{ŋ}g^{W}a-Ø^y | xa-z^{w}a^{ŋ}ga^y |
| | | 14. Y-prosody on vowels | xa-z^{w}a^{ŋ}ga^y | xa^y-z^{w}a^{yŋ}ga^y > hez^{w}eŋe |

Note that W-prosodification is here indicated by raised capital ^{W}. The process of nasalisation transfer (*m-z-g^w > z-^{ŋ}g^w) is left unconsidered at this point. For a detailed account of nasalisation prosody affecting consonants in CC see Wolff (forthcoming).

(153) | Simple root | Gloss | Phonological process | Input | Output |
|---|---|---|---|---|
| PCC: | faeces | 1. Metathesis | *ɣ^{w}va-y | vɣ^{w}a-y |
| *ɣ^w va | | 3. Deletion | vɣ^{w}a-y | vɣ^{w}Ø-y |
| Kirya: | | 5. Weakening C^w > w | vɣ^{w}Ø-y | vw-y |
| *ɣ^{w}va | | 6. W-Prosodification | vw-y | vØ^w-y |
| | | 9. Y-Syllabification | vØ^w-y | vØ^w-i |
| | | 13. W-prosody on consonant | vØ^w-i | v^{w}i |

5 Central Chadic Languages and the Neogrammarian Hypothesis

In Chapters 1 to 4 we have been discussing and illustrating principles and rules of diachronic change in Central Chadic, which will take us to the actual lexical reconstructions that are based on those principles and rules, in Chapter 6. Knowing what at this point we think we now know about Central Chadic linguistic history, it may be worth pausing to summarise and look back on the most salient issues that have impeded progress in (Central) Chadic reconstruction so far. This has to do with the implicit or explicit adherence to the so-called *Neogrammarian Hypothesis* in historical linguistics, which was proposed by a group of linguists in the second half of the nineteenth century at the University of Leipzig, who became mockingly referred to in German as *Junggrammatiker* ('Neogrammarians'). Their innovative major theoretical and methodological concerns were the following:

(a) In describing the history of an individual language, the focus must be on the 'regularity' (ideally, exceptionlessness) of sound changes; apparent exceptions to regular sound changes must be accounted for likewise by regularities that would condition such apparent exceptions (cf., for instance, 'Verner's Law' in Indo-European, 'Klingenheben's Law' in West Chadic Hausa).
(b) Postulation and proof of genealogical relationships between languages must be based on established series of regular sound correspondences (in original Neogrammarian terminology: 'sound laws'), arrived at via word-by-word comparisons between pairs of languages, i.e. by the classic so-called *comparative method*.

Their rigid (and as such from the start and to this day partly controversial) and undoubtedly very successful approach, by which they attempted to place historical linguistics – in the spirit of their time – close to natural sciences as apparently likewise governed by 'laws' of nature, soon and thereafter came under criticism based on studies concerning the impact of lexical and phonological borrowing (including inter-dialectal borrowing), restricted so-called lexical diffusion, grammatical conditioning of sound changes, etc. Issues were and still are whether to accept only gradual changes (as governed by regularities, i.e. what they conceived of as 'sound laws', in intergenerational "linear' transmissions of language) or also allow for abrupt changes stemming from 'broken' transmission of language. (The salient distinction between 'linear' and 'broken' transmission of language goes back to Thomason and Kaufman (1988).) One of the important issues was and still is whether sound changes must be expected to cover the complete lexicon of a language or can be accepted as being interrupted and only spreading incompletely, as dialectological approaches and maps of isoglosses tend to show. Taken to its extremes, however, criticism of the Neogrammarian Hypothesis would end up by only studying individual words in individual languages and their individual linguistic history known as 'etymology', and thereby lose all generalising potential of historical linguistic methodology.

As was pointed out in sub-section 1.1, for as long as it was not feasible to apply the classic comparative method satisfactorily to Chadic languages, including both consonants and vowels, and thereby not being able to provide the likewise classic dendrograms of genealogical language classification based on series of regular sound correspondences and shared innovations, even Chadic sub-classifications had to remain somewhat doubtful – until this day.

Therefore, (Central) Chadic languages are not unique in raising the theoretical and methodological question as to the universal validity of the Neogrammarian Hypothesis according to which all diachronic sound change should be highly 'regular' and, ideally, not allow any exceptions. In the case of our present study, another question is whether and to what extent the original Neogrammarian Hypothesis would also be valid for language groups or families of different typological heritage, like Central Chadic. Here, languages have historically developed a regime of prosodies that, in the vocalic domain, appear to operate with just one diachronic vowel phoneme, namely */a/. A minimal requirement for marrying such 'exceptional' language typology with the Neogrammarian Hypothesis would be that 'regularity' should be found both in the application of only a limited set of general, i.e. non-ad hoc, diachronic rules shared by individual languages, and in the establishment of a reasonable number of series of regular sound correspondences between the phonological units, consonants or other, of related languages, on which the so-called comparative method rests – even if this does not meet the strict requirements of 1:1 correspondences in the narrowest possible sense.

For the present study, we have chosen an established two-step approach in order to arrive at lexical reconstructions and diachronic rules of sound change involving both consonants and vowels. In a first step, we have applied a number of a priori assumptions about Central Chadic, based on analyses and descriptions of their synchronic structures as well as pertaining to their genealogical Afroasiatic heritage, to a theory of Proto-Central Chadic that we have developed in an *inductive* manner. In a second step, these assumptions have then been applied in a *deductive* manner to the available data from individual Central Chadic languages. (This two-step approach is, of course, reminiscent of the successful approach to the reconstruction of Proto-Bantu in early African linguistics, see Gerhardt & Roux (1998).) In doing so we also followed the method of *multilateral comparison* rather than by confronting pairs of languages, as suggested by the classic comparative method, in order to arrive at the proposed reconstructions. The central assumptions used for inductively building our theory of PCC are based on several decades of experience with studying Chadic languages in the context of Afroasiatic and general African linguistics. The salient assumptions pertain, in particular, to accepting as given

- the diachronic relevance of *root-and-pattern* structure;
- a relevant distinction between consonants and *vocoids* rather than 'vowels' (in the narrow sense), with */a/ representing the only true vowel phoneme in the diachronic system of vocoids;
- the diachronic emergence of the essential *prosodies* of palatalisation and labialisation from partial or full desegmentalisation of palatal(ised) and labial(ised) segments ('prosodification'), including the language-specific, if not word-specific, freedom of prosodies to associate with any type or number of surface vowels, or consonants, or both;
- the predictability of surface vowel qualities due to the effects of Y- or W-prosodies
  – on either */a/ (which is anchored in the particular root-and-pattern structure),
  – or on pro- and epenthetic schwa, and from syllabification of underlying vocoids */y/ and */w/;
- the 'irregular', i.e. non-predictable, occurrence of both *metathesis* and *apocope*.

Such a priori assumptions, however, deserve to and can be justified by evidence from their frequent if not 'regular' operation in the diachronic development of individual languages, if not groups of languages, ideally under the label 'regular sound changes' along the lines of the classic Neogrammarian Hypothesis. This justification, however, may not be fully reached in the present study on Central Chadic for several reasons. At the current state and stage of our research, the ideal-type 'regularity' of sound changes according to the Neogrammarian Hypothesis is practically impossible to ascertain, for at least two reasons. One reason is the quantitative limitations of the data that we have been able to analyse and compare.[1] Whatever is to be considered 'regular' would rely not least on quantitative if not statistical underpinning. For this, unfortunately, we do not have enough comparative data at our disposal within the limitations of the present book. The other reason is that this would mean establishing a meaningful 'regularity' of correspondences between segmentally defined 'units' on the one hand, and the almost unbounded phonological nature of 'prosodies', which simply do not behave, so to speak, like bounded segments, on the other, because, by their nature, segments and prosodies do not enter stable sets of 1:1 correspondences. This situation in Central Chadic brings the Neogrammarian Hypothesis to its limits, just like it brings the comparative method to its limits, while not rendering them obsolete (see 5.2 below). We do observe instances of regular sound correspondences not only between consonants among pairs or groups of languages, but also between surface vowels, once we distinguish between correspondences involving */a/ and keep them separate from correspondences involving epenthetic schwa, in both instances by simultaneously observing the conditioning factors of prosody effects. Regularity exists in terms of how to explain occurring sound changes from the phonological environment including prosodies, in a *consistent* and *recurring* way (see 5.2). In addition, regularity exists in terms of access to the rather *restricted pool of diachronic rules* and *choice of rules* that individual languages use, or do not use, for individual words – even if in an apparently ad hoc fashion (see 5.1 below). Consequently, we are faced with the need to kind of 'adapt' or 'refine' the comparative method to the needs imposed by Central Chadic language typology.

5.1 Individual Language Histories: Evidence from Lamang and Hdi

Under the provisions and limitations sketched out above with regard to the Neogrammarian Hypothesis, in this sub-section, for further illustration purposes we look at two closely related languages of the LAMANG group, namely Lamang and Hdi, which the author happens to be particularly familiar with and which are both rather well documented (Wolff 2015 Vols. I & II;

---

[1] Our current study rests on 64 potentially controversial lexical items out of a total of 250 reconstructed items from about 60 languages in Gravina's (2014b) database. Enlarging the present study to encompass all 250 items would have massively gone beyond the limitations and scope of this book, which aims at providing justification for and illustrating the feasibility of, alternative historical-linguistic approaches to the lexical reconstruction of PCC. Readers should feel encouraged and enabled to themselves apply our alternative approach to any number of further lexical items from the database. Our own comprehensive analysis of all 250 items will be contained in Wolff (forthcoming).

Frajzyngier & Shay, 2002; Frajzyngier et al. 2015). We will observe – in a parallel fashion across the selected data from both languages – whether, which and how diachronic principles and rules apply in order to provide evidence for their plausibility and validity in transforming PCC lexical reconstructions into present-day language words. By looking at two rather closely related languages, which even share identical surface forms for a fair number of lexical items, we hope to show how the diachronic rules that we have identified turn individual languages progressively divergent despite their common origin from a shared proto-language for the group (LAMANG group) and the Central Chadic branch as a whole.

We here make use of all reconstructed lexical items (see 6.4) that are shared by both Lamang and Hdi. The tabular representations for the individual lexical items are structured in the following way. The most general and often conflated representation of our PCC reconstruction is given first and is confronted with what we tentatively take to represent Proto-Lamang-Hdi (PLH). However, no systematic reconstruction of PLH is attempted here, the hypothetical reconstruction merely serves the purpose of a generalising illustration. For a detailed treatment of issues of comparative phonology, grammar and lexicon of Lamang and Hdi, see Wolff (2015, Vol. 1: 345–493). Interestingly, in a number of cases we arrive not at a single PLH form from which both languages derive their present-day forms, but are forced to accept variation already at the proto-language level, like choice of different root types, and/or the presence or absence of root-augmental materials. The latter indicate that, in historical perspective, morphologically different forms have been turned into and are used as diachronic 'roots'. In the sequence of the application of rules (which we identify by numbering, cf. section 4.9, and a keyword identification), we keep to the potentially intrinsic ordering, even though such ordering in itself has not yet been proven to be a valid assumption regarding the relative chronology of rule applications. The final line of the table gives the actually occurring present-day forms – in *italics* – as transcribed in the various sources.[2] We also include pseudo-PCC reconstructions, which presumably have entered individual languages separately as loan words from or via Kanuri.

---

[2] Note that, according to source, the following varying transcriptions for consonants may occur:
    voiceless lateral fricative: ɬ, hl, sl
    voiced lateral fricative: ɮ, zl
    voiceless velar fricative: x, h (also labialised: x^w, h^w)
    voiced velar fricative: ɣ, gh (also labialised: $ɣ^w$, gh^w)

5.1 Individual Language Histories

(154)

arm	PCC	*dz va (-y, -kʷ, -n; FV)		
	PLH	*dzva-kʷ		
		Lamang	Hdi	
		—	dzvØ-kʷ	3. deletion of lexical final /a/
		dzva-w	dzv-w	5. partial desegmentalisation *kʷ > w
		dzva-ʷ	—	6. W-prosodification
		—	dzv-u	8. W-syllabification
		dzvaʷ	—	12. W-prosody on vowel
		dzvo	*dzvu*	

(155)

belly	PCC	*(a-) xʷ(a)ɗa (-y, -ɗ, -kʷ)		
	PLH	*xʷɗa-y		
		Lamang	Hdi	
		xʷɗØ-y	xʷɗØ-y	3. deletion of lexical final /a/
		xʷəɗ-y	xʷəɗ-y	4. epenthesis
		xʷəɗ-i	xʷəɗ-i	9. Y-syllabification
		xəʷɗ-i	xəʷɗ-i	12. W-prosody on vowel
		huɗi	*xuɗi*	

(156)

bow	PCC	*(a-, xa-, ma-ᵑga-, ᵑga-, g-nd-, RED-) r(a)ga (-a, -y, -ɗ, -n, -ŋ)		
	PLH	*l(a)ɣa (-y-ɗ)		PLH *r > 1, *g > ɣ Lamang √ CaCa; Hdi √ C Ca
		*laɣa-y		Lamang: *-y
			*l ɣa-y-ɗ	Hdi: *-y-ɗ
		Lamang	Hdi	
		laɣa-Øʸ	lɣa-Øʸ-ɗ	7. Y-prosodification
		laʸɣaʸ	lɣaʸ-ɗ	14. Y-prosody on vowel
		leghe	*lgheɗ*	

(157)

camel		ˣ*kaligimo*	Old KANURI loan, entering languages individually
	Pseudo-PCC	*(n-) k(a)l(a)g(a)m(a)wa (-y, -n, -t, FV)	
	Pseudo-PLH	ˣ(n-) k(a)l(a)g(a)m(a)wa (-y) ˣkaɓgamawa ˣn-galgbwa-y	Lamang √ CaC CaCaCa Hdi √ CaC C C Ca Lamang *l > ɓ Hdi *k > g, *m > b Hdi *n-, *-y
		Lamang	Hdi	
		ØØɓgamawa	—	reanalysis and deletion of pseudo-prefixal material *ka- > ØØ
		— ɓgamawØ	n-galØbwa-y —	3a. deletion C₃ ˣg > Ø 3b. apocope
		—	n-galəbwa-y	4. epenthesis
		ɓgamaØʷ	—	6. W-prosodification
		—	n-galəbwa-Øʸ	7. Y-prosodification
		ɓgʷama	—	13. W-prosody on consonant
		—	n-galəʸbwa	14. Y-prosody on vowel
		ɓgwama	ngalibwa	

(158)

cook, to	PCC	*(k-, ma-, RED) da (-a, -y, -k, kʷ; FV)	
	PLH	*da	
		Lamang	Hdi
		da	da

5.1 Individual Language Histories

(159)

cow	PCC	*(a-, k-, n-, wa-, wr-) **ɬa** (-a, -y, -n; FV)	
	PLH	*ɬa	
		Lamang	Hdi
		sla	hla

(160)

cry, to	PCC	*(ma-) **ts(a)wa** (-a, -y, -k; FV)	
	PLH	*tawa	PLH *ts > t
		Lamang	Hdi	
		—	*tawØ	3. deletion of lexical final /a/
		tawa	taw	

(161)

die, to	PCC	*(k-, ma-) **m(a)ta** (-a, -y, -k, -kʷ, -n, -ŋ; FV)
	PLH	*mta
		Lamang	Hdi
		mta	mta

(162)

dog	PCC	***k(a)ra** (-a, -y, -kʷ; FV)	
	PLH	*kra-y	
		Lamang	Hdi	
		—	krØ-y	3. deletion of lexical final /a/
		kra-Øʸ	—	7. Y-prosodification
		—	kr-i	9. Y-syllabification
		kraʸ	—	14. Y-prosody on vowel
		kre	kri	

(163)

dream	PCC	*(ma-, ma-RED, RED, n-) **s(a)w(a)na** (-a, -y, -k, -n; FV)	
	PLH	*sw(a)na(-y,-k; FV)	Lamang √ C CaCa Hdi √ C C Ca
		*swana (*swana-ka?) *swna-y	Lamang: *-ka (?) Hdi: *-y
		Lamang	Hdi	
		swaŋa³	—	
		—	swnØ-y	3. deletion of lexical final /a/
		—	sun-y	8. W-syllabification
		—	sun-i	9. Y-syllabification
		swaŋa	*suni*	

(164)

earth	PCC	*(a-, ya-, RED-) **xʷ(a)yɗa** (-y, -k; FV)	
	PLH	*xʷayɗa	Hdi *xʷ > x
		*xayɗa-k	Hdi: *-k
		Lamang	Hdi	
		—	xaɗya-k	1. metathesis
		xʷaØɗa —	— xaɗyØ-k	3a. deletion of C₂ *y > Ø 3b. deletion of lexical final /a/
		xʷaɗa	—	6. W-prosodification (xʷ > xʷ)
		—	xaɗi-k	9. Y-syllabification
		xaʷɗaʷ	—	12. W-prosody on vowels
		hoɗo	*xaɗik*	

---

³ The 'sporadic' sound correspondences Lamang /ŋ/ and Hdi /n/ still deserve focused comparative research. In certain cases like the present, root-augmental *{-k} might have played a role in Lamang, which, however, is not reconstructed here with confidence. (Tentative alternative reconstruction for Lamang: *s wana-ka > swanØka > swaŋka > swaŋØa > *swaŋa*).

5.1 Individual Language Histories

(165)

eight	PCC	*(m-) t ɣ(a)sa (-y, -kʷ)	
	PLH	*tɣasa	
		Lamang	Hdi	
		—	*tɣasØ	3. deletion/apocope
		tghasa	*tghas*	

(166)

faeces	PCC	*(ŋ-) ɣʷ va (-a, -y, -n)	
	PLH	*ɣʷva-y	
		Lamang	Hdi	
		ɣʷvØ-y	ɣʷvØ-y	3. deletion/apocope
		ɣʷəv-y	ɣʷəv-y	4. epenthesis
		ɣʷəv-i	ɣʷəv-i	9. Y-syllabification
		ɣəʷv-i	ɣəʷv-i	12. W-prosody on vowel
		ghuvi	*ghuvi*	

(167)

five	PCC	*(m-, n-) xʷ t(a)fa (-y, -k; FV)	
	PLH	*xʷtafa	
		Lamang	Hdi	
		—	xʷtafØ	3. deletion/apocope
		—	xʷətaf	4. epenthesis
		—	xəʷtaf	12. W-prosody on vowel
		hʷtafa	*xutaf*	

(168)

fly	PCC	*(a-, xa-, m-, n-, RED-) **dz(a)kʷ(a)ɗa** (-y, -n, -ŋ)		
	PLH	*zkʷɗa-y		PLH *dz > z
		Lamang	Hdi	
		—	zɗkʷa-y	1. metathesis
		zØɗa-y	—	3a. deletion of C_2 *kʷ > Ø
		zØɗØ-y	zɗkʷØ-y	3b. deletion of lexical final /a/
		zəɗ-y	zəɗəkʷ-y	4. epenthesis
		zəɗ-yʸ	zəɗəkʷ-Øʸ	7. Y-prosodification
		zəɗ-iʸ	—	9. Y-syllabification
		zəʸɗ-i	zəʸɗəʸkʷ	14. Y-prosody on vowels
		zidi	*zidikw*	

(169)

give birth, to	PCC	*(ma-) **w(a)x(a)ya** (-k, -kʷ, -n, -l; FV)		
	PLH	*ya		PLH deletion of C_1 and C_2: *w > Ø; *x > Ø
		Lamang	Hdi	
		ya	ya	

(170)

grandfather	PCC	*(a-, b-, a-d-) **dz(a)dza** (-a, -y, -kʷ, -n; FV)		
	PLH	*dzdza-y		
		Lamang	Hdi	
		dzdzØ-y	dzdzØ-y	3. deletion of lexical final /a/
		dzədz-y	dzədz-y	4. epenthesis
		dzədz-yʸ	dzədz-yʸ	7. Y-prosodification
		dzədz-iʸ	dzədz-iʸ	9. Y-syllabification
		dzəʸdz-i	dzəʸdz-i	14. Y-prosody on vowel
		dzidzi	*dzidzi*	

5.1 Individual Language Histories

(171)

hair	PCC	*(ma-) **s(a)b(a)ta** (-y, -kʷ)	
	PLH	*swda-y	PLH *b > w; *t > d
		Lamang	Hdi	
		sØda-y sØdØ-y	— swdØ-y	3a. deletion of C₂ *w > Ø 3b. deletion of final lexical /a/
		səd-y	səwəd-y	4. epenthesis
		səd-yʸ	səwəd-yʸ	7. Y-prosodification
		səd-iʸ	səwəd-iʸ	9. Y-syllabification
		səʸd-i	səwəʸd-i	14. Y-prosody on vowels
		sidi	*səwidi*	

(172)

hare	PCC	*(ma-, na-) **xʷ(a)d(a)y(a)va** (-k, -kʷ, -n; FV)	
	PLH	*Øvyla-kʷa	PLH *xʷ > Ø; *d > l; metathesis lyv > vyl
		Lamang	Hdi	
		—	vyla-kʷØ	3. deletion/apocope FV /a/
		vila-kʷa	vila-kʷ	9. Y-syllabification
		vilakʷa	*vilakʷ*	

(173)

horn₁	PCC	***d(a)r(a)ma** (-y, -kʷ)	
	PLH	*dlma-y-kʷ	PLH *r > l
		Lamang	Hdi	
		dlma-kʷ-y	dlma-kʷ-y	1. metathesis (augment)
		dlØa-kʷ-y dlØØ-kʷ-y	dlØa-kʷ-y dlØØ-kʷ-y	3a. deletion of C₃ *m > Ø 3b. deletion of lexical final /a/
		dkʷl-y	dkʷl-y	1. metathesis
		dwl-y	dwl-y	5. partial desegmentalisation kʷ > w
		dul-y	dul-y	8. W-syllabification
		dul-i	dul-i	9. Y-syllabification
		duli	*duli*	

Note the much simpler alternative scenario based on the assumption of a known yet only 'sporadic' sound change m : w in the languages of the LAMANG group:

(173a)

horn₁	PCC	*d(a)r(a)ma (-y, -kʷ)	
	PLH	*dlwa-y	PLH *r > l, *m > w
		Lamang / Hdi	
		dwla-y / dwla-y	1. metathesis
		dwlØ-y / dwlØ-y	3. deletion, apocope
		dul-y / dul-y	8. W-syllabification
		dul-i / dul-i	9. Y-syllabification
		duli / *duli*	

(174)

horse	Pseudo-PCC	*(a-) p(a)r(a)sa (-y, -k, -kʷ, -ŋ; FV) (< ultimately Arabic loan)	
	Pseudo-PLH	*plsa-y	Pseudo-PLH *r > l
		Lamang / Hdi	
		plsØ-y / plsØ-y	3. deletion of lexical final /a/
		pləs-y / pləs-y	4. epenthesis
		pləs-yʸ / pləs-Øʸ	7. Y-prosodification Lamang: partial Hdi: complete
		pləs-iʸ / —	9. Y-syllabification
		pləʸs-i / pləʸs	14. Y-prosody on vowel
		plisi / *plis*	

(175)

laugh, to	PCC	*(ma-) ɣʷ(a)b(a)sa (-a,-y, -k, -n; FV)	
	PLH	*m-ɣʷbasa *ɣᵐbasa *ɣʷɓasa	Lamang *ɣʷ > ɣ; *b > ᵐb Hdi *b > ɓ
		Lamang / Hdi	
		— / ɣʷəɓasa	4. epenthesis
		/ ɣəʷɓasa	12. W-prosody on vowel
		ghmbasa / *ghuɓasa*	

5.1 Individual Language Histories

(176)

lion	PCC	*(w-, RED-) **l(a)vara** (-y)	
	PLH	*rvara-y	PLH *l > r
		Lamang	Hdi	
		—	rvarØ-y	3. deletion of lexical final /a/
		rvara-Ø^y	rvar-y^y	7. Y-prosodification Lamang: complete Hdi: partial
		—	rvar-i^y	9. Y-syllabification
		rvara^y	rva^{y}r-i	14. Y-prosody on vowel
		rvare	*rveri*	

(177)

moon	PCC	*(n-, ŋ-) **t(a)ra** (-y, -k^w; FV)	
	PLH	*tra-y *tla-y *tra-y	Hdi *r > l
		Lamang	Hdi	
		—	t lØ-y	3. deletion of lexical final /a/
		—	təl-y	4. epenthesis
		tra-Ø^y	təl-y^y	7. Y-prosodification Lamang: complete Hdi: partial
		—	təl-i^y	9. Y-syllabification
		tra^y	tə^{y}l-i	14. Y-prosody on vowel
		tre	*tili*	

(178)

night	PCC	*(a-, x-, m-/n-, sa-, ta-) **r(a)v(a)ɗa** (-a, -y, -k, -k^w, -n, -ŋ; FV)	
	PLH	*rvɗa(-y-k) *rvɗa-y *rvɗa-y-k	Lamang: *-y Hdi: *-y-k
		Lamang	Hdi	
		rvɗØ-y	rvɗØ-y-k	3. deletion of lexical final /a/
		rvəɗ-y	rvəɗ-y-k	4. epenthesis

172 CC Languages and the Neogrammarian Hypothesis

	rvəɗ-yʸ	rvəɗ-yʸ-k	7. Y-prosodification
	rvəɗ-iʸ	rvəɗ-iʸ-k	9. Y-syllabification
	rvəʸɗ-i	rvəʸɗ-i-k	14. Y-prosody on vowel
	rvidi	*rvidik*	

(179)

quiver	PCC	*ɣʷ(a)dza (-y,-n, -l)		
	PLH	*ɣʷadza-y		
		Lamang	Hdi	
		—	ɣʷadzØ-y	3. deletion of lexical final /a/
		ɣʷadza-Øʸ	—	7. Y-prosodification
		—	ɣʷadz-i	9. Y-syllabification
		—	ɣaʷdz-i > ɣodzi	12. W-prosody on vowel (optional)
		ɣʷaʸdzaʸ	—	14. Y-prosody on vowel
		ghʷedze	*ɣʷadzi~ghodzi*	

(180)

root	PCC	*(RED-) ɫ(a)r(a)ka (-a, -y, -kʷ, -n; FV)		
	PLH	*ɫrka(-y-n) *ɫrka-y-n *ɫrka-n		Lamang: *-y-n Hdi: -n
		Lamang	Hdi	
		ɫrka-n-y	—	1a. metathesis (augment)
		ɫrkØ-n-y	ɫrkØ-n	3. deletion of lexical final /a/
		ɫrnk-y	ɫrnk	1b. metathesis
		ɫrŋ-y	ɫrŋ	fusion *nk > ŋ
		ɫərŋ-y	ɫərəŋ	4. epenthesis
		ɫərŋ-i	—	9. Y-syllabification
		ɫərŋi	*ɫərəŋ*	

5.1 Individual Language Histories

(181)

spit, to	PCC	*(m(a)-, n-, ŋ-) **t(a)fa** (-a, -y, -k^w, -n, -l; FV)		
	PLH	*tfa(-y) *tfa *tfa-a-y		Hdi: *-a-y
		Lamang	Hdi	
		tfØ	tfØ-a-y	3. deletion/apocope
		təf	təf-a-y	4. epenthesis
		təf	*təfay*	

(182)

sun	PCC	*(a-, xa-, d-, RED-) **p(a)ta** (-a, -y, -k, -k^w, -n; FV)		
	PLH	*fta(-y-k) *fta-y *fta-y-k		PLH *p > f Lamang: *-y Hdi: *-y-k
		Lamang	Hdi	
		ftØ-y	ftØ-y-k	3. deletion of lexical final /a/
		fət-y	fət-y-k	4. epenthesis
		fət-y^y	fət-y^y-k	7. Y-prosodification
		fət-i^y	fət-i^y-k	9. Y-syllabification
		fə^y t-i	fə^y t-i-k	14. Y-prosody on vowels
		fiti	*fitik*	

(183)

thorn	PCC	*(a-, xa-, ma-, va-) **d(a)yka** (-t, -y)		
	PLH	*t(a)yka *tyka *tayka		PLH *d > t Lamang √ C C Ca Hdi √ CaC Ca
		Lamang	Hdi	
		ty^y ka	taØ^y ka	7. Y-prosodification Lamang: partial Hdi: complete
		ti^y ka	—	9. Y-syllabification
		ti^y kə	ta^y kə	10. centralisation of /a/
		ti^y kə^y	ta^y kə^y	14. Y-prosody on vowel
		tiki	*teki*	

(184)

three	PCC	*(ma-) **x(a)k(a)na** (-y, -k^w, -ɗ; FV)		
	PLH	*xkna		
		Lamang	Hdi	
		—	xknØ	3. deletion/apocope
		xkəna	xəkən	4. epenthesis
		hkəna	*həkən*	

(185)

two	PCC	*(k-) **k(a)sa** (-y, -k^w, -ɗ; FV)			
	PLH	*x(a)sa-y *xasa-y *xsa-y			PLH *k > x Lamang √ CaCa Hdi √ C Ca
		Lamang	Hdi		
		—	xsØ-y	3. deletion of lexical final /a/	
		—	xəs-y	4. epenthesis	
		xasa-Ø^y	xəs-Ø^y	7. Y-prosodification	
		xa^y sa	xə^y s	14. Y-prosody on vowel	
		hesa	*xis*		

(186)

water	PCC	*(a(x^w)-) **ʔy(a)ma** (-a, -y, -k^w, -n; FV)		
	PLH	*yma		PLH *ʔy > y
		Lamang	Hdi	
		y^y ma	y^y ma	7. Y-prosodification
		i^y ma	i^y ma	9. Y-syllabification
		i^y mə	i^y mə	10. centralisation of /a/
		imə^y	imə^y	14. Y-prosody on vowel
		imi	*imi*	

5.1 Individual Language Histories

(187)

work	PCC	*(a-, ka-, ma-) ɬ(a)na (-t, -y, -k, -kʷ, -n, -l; FV)	
	PLH	*ɬna	
		Lamang	Hdi
		ɬəna	ɬəna	4. epenthesis
		sləna	hləna	

Summarising the sound changes occurring in the data above, we note that out of the pool of 15 diachronic rules (including sporadic metathesis, which does not qualify as 'rule' in a narrow sense), only 12 'rules' apply to the two languages of the LAMANG group. This could mirror accidental gaps in the data. Not found were the following three sound changes, which do occur elsewhere in Central Chadic:

- Rule 2. Split of labialised $C^w > C + w$;
- Rule 11. Centralisation of FV /a/ > [ə] (which actually could be seen as being a variant of Rule 3 deletion/apocope);
- Rule 15. Y-prosody affecting consonants.[4]

Prosodification of C^w/w (Rule 6) has only been found to operate in Lamang, not in Hdi; likewise W-prosody affecting consonants (Rule 13), yet only with the loan 'camel'.

Table 5.1 *Frequency of rule applications*

Rule	Lamang	Hdi	Total
3. Deletion	13	25	38
4. Epenthesis	14	17	31
9. Y-Syllabification	13	15	28
7. Y-Prosodification	14	13	27
14. Y-Prosody on vowel	14	13	27
1. Metathesis	4	5	9
12. W-Prosody on vowel	4	5	9
5. $C^w > w$	2	2	4
8. W-Syllabification	1	3	4
10. /a/ centralisation	2	2	4
6. W-Prosodification	2	—	2
13. W-Prosody on consonant	1	—	1

---

[4] Note that 'lectal' variants of both languages allow occasional or regular palatalisation of consonants triggered by the surface phonological environment, but not found in the above list of shared cognates.

Among the 34 shared reconstructed lexical items (out of a total of 64 used in the present study), the 12 diachronic rules found operating have differing frequencies of occurrence. See the count of rule applications for the two languages of the LAMANG group in Table 5.1. Note again that we are neither considering nor counting apparently unconditioned articulatory changes of consonants, like *r > l, *l > r, *k > x, *g > ɣ, *p > f, *m > b, *dz > z, *ts > t, *d > t, etc. The table clearly shows that segment deletion (mainly targeting final root vowels, i.e. apocope) and vowel epenthesis are highly frequent changes, and that palatalisation effects largely outnumber labialisation effects (Table 5.1).

5.2 Scrutinising the Notion of 'Regular Sound Correspondence' in the Vocalic Domain

As already sketched out further above, the classic comparative method approach by attempting to match surface vowels in pairs of languages in order to establish series of regular sound correspondences between these vowels fails almost across the board when applied to Central Chadic languages. The reason being that surface vowels in present-day languages are – in diachronic systemic perspective – not what they appear to be, namely 'vowels' of identical phonological status. This is easily illustrated with two examples from closely related Lamang and Hdi, which both belong to the LAMANG group.

(188) 'arm'   Lamang   *dzvo*   Hdi   *dzvu*
       'night' Lamang   *rvidî*   Hdi   *rvidîk*

Approaching these apparently straightforward examples from a naïve Neogrammarian position, we would come up with statements like the following: (a) In the examples for 'arm', Lamang /o/ corresponds to Hdi /u/, and this would be a 'regular' correspondence for which one could find many examples in the available data (cf. Wolff 2015, Vol. 1, Chapters 3 and 4). (b) In the examples for 'night', Lamang /i/ corresponds to Hdi /i/ in both medial and final positions, and again several similar examples could be found in the available data.

Based on our current insights into the linguistic history of Central Chadic, however, these statements would be false. The characteristically much more complex situation as we currently understand it rather has to be described as follows.

(a) For 'arm': there is no vowel phoneme ^{x}/o/ in Lamang in the first place, so any 1:1 correspondence between Lamang ^{x}/o/ and Hdi /u/ is excluded on the phonemic level. The surface phonetic realisation [o] in *dzvo* 'arm' does not represent ^{x}/o/, but rather represents the result of monophthongisation of a diphthong-like sequence /a+w/: *dzvo* < *dzva-w < *dzva-k^w, i.e. it is of

5.2 Notion of 'Regular Sound Correspondence'   177

morphophonological nature. Similarly, the vowel [u] in Hdi *dzvu* 'arm' does not represent an underlying phoneme ˣ/u/, but is the phonetic manifestation of syllabified /w/ which ends up in syllable-nucleus position: *dzvu* < *dzvØ-w < *dzva-k^w. This surface vowel, too, is of morphophonological nature. The historical source form for both languages is *dzva-k^w. Thus, the surface vowels [o] and [u] do not form a 1:1 sound correspondence necessarily involving segmental vowel phonemes of the languages compared, but both contain reflexes of a diachronic suffix *{-k^w} > *{-w}, which together with the lexical vowel /a/ likely forms an underlying intermediate diphthong [aw] in Lamang to be finally monophthongised to [o], and syllabifies directly to [u] in Hdi after deletion of the preceding final vowel /a/. Accordingly, despite apparent evidence from surface representations, for 'arm' there is no /o/ : /u/ sound correspondence in the language pair Lamang : Hdi. The existing but underlying and diachronic correspondence is twofold and trivial: */a/ : */a/, and *{-k^w} : *{-k^w}. The rest is language-specific morphophonology.

(b) For 'night': the two occurrences of a high front vowel [i] in the word for 'night' are by no means identical in terms of their phonological status and, therefore, must not be confused. In the first syllable, [i] represents the palatalised variant of epenthetic schwa, while in the second syllable [i] represents the syllabification of underlying */y/, which likely originates from morphological palatalisation stemming from a marker *{-y} in the proto-language. Thus, identical surface vowels do not necessarily represent identical phonological units even in the same language; only internal reconstruction can tell us what we are dealing with in a particular case. Therefore, in the current example, we are dealing with two different sets of surface-vowel correspondences, and the underlying and diachronic correspondence is again twofold and trivial: (i) between fronted+raised epenthetic schwa *[ə]^y : *[ə]^y in the first syllable, and (ii) between *{-y} : *{-y} involving instantiations of syllabification of underlying */y/ in syllable-nucleus position in the second syllable:

(189)   Lamang   *rvidi*   < *rvə^{y}ɗ-i   < *rvəɗ-i^y < *rvɗ-y
        Hdi   *rvidik*   < *rvə^{y}ɗ-i-k   < *rvəɗ-i^y-k   < *rvɗ-y-k

Let us now revisit – for historical reasons and in the light of what we now think we know – the small set of examples from the then so-called Wandala-Lamang group that had already been discussed in the pioneer efforts to tackle the problem (Wolff et al. 1981; Wolff 1981, 1983b) and that was taken up in sub-section 1.1 above. Starting out from the relevance of prosodies, we can easily recognise their presence with some, and absence with other, languages of the set, indicated in Table 5.2 by Ø (absence), +Y (palatalisation), +W (labialisation).

178   CC Languages and the Neogrammarian Hypothesis

Table 5.2 *'nose' and 'ear' in so-called Wandala-Lamang (3)*

	'nose'			'ear'		
	∅	+Y	+W	∅	+Y	+W
Dghweɗe		x t i r e			ɬ e m e	
Glavda	x t ə r a				x^y i m ia	
Gvoko			x t o r			ɬ u w o
Guduf		x t e r e			ɬ i m e	
Podoko	f t r a			ɬ a m a		
Wandala		ə k t a r e		ɬ ə m a		
Gwara		a k^w c i n			ɬ i m i	
Lamang		x ts i n i		ɬ ə m ə ŋ i		

Let's start with a more detailed diachronic reanalysis of surface vowels in the word for 'nose'.

(1) Surface vowels in word-initial position
Only two languages in our data set have vowels in word-initial position. Wandala has long been known to have a shallow synchronic rule of regularly inserting a prothetic vowel in front of a consonant cluster. About Gwara frightfully little is known; presumably in this example it shares the same shallow rule with Wandala. So, both word-initial vowels for 'nose' are likely to represent prothetic, i.e. non-phonemic, vowels. They would correspond to ∅ prothesis in all other languages of the set.

(2) Surface vowels in word-medial position
In terms of our PCC reconstructions, the languages under analysis reflect different root types to begin with. Subgroup (a) below would reflect medial */a/, subgroup (b) would reflect medial epenthetic schwa. Systemic vowel correspondences can only be identified within the same subgroups.

(a)   √ C CaCa   Gvoko *xtor*, Guduf *xtere*, Wandala *əktare*
(b)   √ C C Ca   Dghweɗe, Glavda, Podoko, Gwara, Lamang

In subgroup (a), medial */a/ is retained as [a] in Wandala *əktare*, but comes under prosody impact in Gvoko *xtor* (+W) and in Guduf *xtere* (+Y), yielding surface [o] and [e]. While the presence of Y-prosody in Guduf is corroborated from the behaviour of the word-final vowel (see below), the exceptional W-prosody in Gvoko needs explanation. W-prosody in Gvoko reflects the original presence of a labialised initial consonant *x^w in this PCC root, which Gravina (2014a) has reconstructed as *h^w itsin^y. Note that Gwara also shows this labialisation of the initial consonant in the shape of /k^w/. All other languages of the set have diachronically lost their labialisation feature: *x^w > x~f and *k^w > k. In subgroup (b), surface Ø (Podoko), ə (Glavda), and i (under Y-prosody in Dghweɗe, Gwara, Lamang) represent conditioned variants of non-phonemic (epenthetic) schwa.

(3) Surface vowels in word-final position
Under the assumption that all PCC reconstructed roots end in /a/ by default, Gvoko and Gwara can be assumed to have deleted lexical final */a/ (see Rule 3 for deletion/apocope further above). Final */a/ has been retained in Glavda and Podoko.

(190)	Gvoko	x t o r Ø	Glavda	x t ə r a
	Gwara	a k^w c i n Ø	Podoko	f t r a

Dghweɗe, Guduf, Wandala and Lamang each show a front vowel in final position, which is likely the petrified result of morphological palatalisation by *{-y}, which we would need to reconstruct for the diachronic source. This *{-y} is the source for the occurrence of Y-prosody in these four languages, in three of them affecting also medial */a/ (Guduf) and schwa (Dghweɗe, Lamang), the exception being Wandala where medial */a/ is retained despite Y-prosody.

(191)	Dghweɗe	x t i r e	(*{-y})
	Guduf	x t e r e	(*{-y})
	Wandala	ə k t a r e	(*{-y})
	Lamang	x ts i n i	(*{-y})

In Lamang, the *{-y} would have deleted the preceding lexical final */a/. In the other three languages, *{-y} would have fused with and diphthongised final */a/ > *ay, which would monophthongise to [e]. With the exception of Wandala, where Y-prosody remains localised with the final vowel, Y-prosody spreads onto the medial vowels in the other three languages, affecting medial /a/ > e in Guduf, and medial schwa > i in Dghweɗe and Lamang.

With the above observations and analyses in mind, we can now reconstruct the historically underlying forms for 'nose' in the eight languages (Table 5.3). We note that five of the eight languages opted for a Ø-vocalised simple root √ C C Ca, while three opted for an a-vocalised simple root √ C CaCa.

To complete the picture, the consonantal sound changes involved are given in Table 5.4.

Our deep internal and prosody-based reconstruction for this one lexical item also confirms the more recent reclassification into subgroups along classic

Table 5.3 *Reconstructing 'nose' in so-called Wandala-Lamang*

	'nose'			Internal reconstruction	Reconstructed for proto-language	
	Ø	+Y	+W			
Glavda	xtəra			*/x t ra/	*xt ra(-y)	*x^{w}ts na(-y)
Podoko	ftra			*/x t ra/		
Dghwede		xtire < xtə^{y}ra^y		*/x t ra-y^y/		
Gwara		[a]k^{w}cin < k^{w}ts^{y}ə^{y}nØ		*/k^w ts na-y^y/		
Lamang		xtsini < xtsə^{y}nØ-i		*/x ts na-y^y/		
Gvoko			xtor < xta^{w}rØ	*/x^w tara/	*x^{w}tsana(-y)	
Guduf		xtere < xta^{y}ra^y		*/x tara-y^y/		
Wandala		[ə]ktare < ktara^y		*/k tara-y^y/		

Table 5.4 *Consonantal sound changes in so-called Wandala-Lamang (1)*

*x^w	>	k^w	Gwara
	>	k	Wandala
	>	x +^{w}	Gvoko
	>	x	Glavda, Dghwede, Lamang, Guduf
	>	f	Podoko
*ts	>	t	Glavda, Podoko, Dghwede, Gvoko, Guduf, Wandala
*n	>	r	Glavda, Podoko, Dghwede, Gvoko, Guduf, Wandala

comparative method-based criteria. Languages of the MANDARA group proper all undergo C$_3$ *n > r, while Lamang of the more recently identified LAMANG group retains C$_3$ *n. Note that Gwara currently remains unclassified; it was discovered and described by Wolff (1975) as a 'substratum' of present-day Margi (MARGI group) around Izge near the Yadzeram River, whose characteristic deviations from surrounding Margi point not only towards Mandara (both share initial /k/) and Gvoko (both share the labial feature ^{w} with their initial consonant, i.e. Gwara k^w and Gvoko x^w, but note the

5.2 Notion of 'Regular Sound Correspondence'   181

absence of W-prosody in Gwara as opposed to its presence in Gvoko), but also Lamang (both share the retention of C_3 *n). Maintaining both the labialisation feature of their C_1 and the retention of C_3 *n makes Gvoko and Gwara rather 'conservative' among all these languages. Unfortunately, both languages rank among the least researched in the area.

Let's continue with a more detailed diachronic analysis of surface vowels in the word for 'ear'.

(1) Surface vowels in word-initial position
There are no word-initial vowels; the conditions for prothetic vowel insertion are not met.

(2) Surface vowels in word-medial position
Again and in terms of our PCC reconstructions, the languages under analysis reflect different root types to begin with. Subgroup (a) below would reflect medial */a/, subgroup (b) would reflect epenthetic schwa.

(a)   √ CaCa   Dghweɗe ɬeme, Podoko ɬama,
(b)   √ C Ca   Glavda, Gvoko, Guduf, Wandala, Gwara, Lamang

In subgroup (a), medial */a/ is retained in Podoko ɬama, but comes under Y-prosody impact in Dghweɗe ɬeme. The presence of Y-prosody in Dghweɗe is corroborated from the behaviour of the word-final vowel (see below). In subgroup (b), surface ə (Wandala, Lamang), i (under Y-prosody in Glavda, Guduf, Gwara), and u (under W-prosody in Gvoko) represent conditioned variants of non-phonemic (epenthetic) schwa.

(3) Surface vowels in word-final position
Under the assumption that all PCC reconstructed roots end in /a/ by default, all languages can be assumed to have retained the lexical final vowel. It has remained unaffected by prosodies in Podoko and Wandala: ɬama and ɬəma. It would appear to have been deleted in Gwara and Glavda to be replaced by *{-y} to yield intermediate Gwara *ɬəm-y and Glavda *x^{y}əm-ya. In Lamang it became centralised (cf. Rule 10 further above) *ɬəmə(-ŋ-y) and remained otherwise unaffected before the suffix chain *{-ŋ-y}. Gvoko is exceptional by again showing effects of W-prosody that merit explanation. W-prosody in Gvoko here is the result of phonological ('lexical') labialisation stemming from the second root consonant /w/ < */m/. (This prosodification by partial desegmentalisation is symbolised in Table 5.5 by w^w.)

Table 5.5 *Reconstructing 'ear' in so-called Wandala-Lamang*

	'ear'			Internal reconstruction	Reconstructed for proto-language
	Ø	+Y	+W		
Gvoko			łuwo < łə^wwa^w	*ɬ w^wa/	
Wandala	ləma			*ɬ ma/	
Guduf		łime < łə^yma^y		*ɬ ma-y^y/	*ɬ ma(-ŋ-y(a))
Gwara		łimi < łə^ymØ-i		*ɬ ma-y^y/	
Glavda		h^yimia < h^yə^ymØ-ia		*/h^y ma-ya/	
Lamang	ləmə-ŋ-i			*ɬ ma-ŋ-y/	
Podoko	łama			*/łama/	*łama(-y)
Dghwede		łeme < ła^yma^y		*/łama-y^y/	

Dghwede, Guduf and Gwara each show a front vowel (monophthong) in simple-root final position, Glavda retains a diphthong (in this particular case reflecting the presence of FV */a/). The final front vowel, however, reflects two different underlying phonological processes, namely (i) syllabification of *{-y} > i (Glavda, Gwara, Lamang), and (ii) monophthongisation of the sequence */a-y/ > *ay > e (Dghwede, Guduf). Both monophthongs and diphthongs here reflect the petrified result of morphological palatalisation by *{-y}, which we would need to reconstruct as the diachronic source. This *{-y} accounts for the occurrence of Y-prosody in these five languages, in four of them also affecting the medial vowel, the exception being Lamang. In Lamang, the simple root is followed by an augmental chain *{-ŋ-y}, in front of which simple-root final lexical /a/ became centralised to [ə].

(192) Dghwede   ł e m e   (*{-y})
       Glavda   h^y i m i-a   (*{-y})
       Guduf   ł i m e   (*{-y})
       Gwara   ł i m i   (*{-y})
       Lamang   ł ə m ə-ŋ-i   (*{-y})

In Glavda and Gwara, the *{-y} would have deleted the preceding lexical final */a/; in Glavda being followed by the FV /a/. In Lamang, *{-y} syllabifies in final position following a preceding root-augmental suffix *{-ŋ}. In the

5.2 Notion of 'Regular Sound Correspondence'

Table 5.6 *Consonantal sound changes in so-called Wandala-Lamang (2)*

*ɬ	> x^y	Glavda (possibly just a transcription variant)
*m	> w^w	Gvoko

other two languages, *{-y} would have fused with and diphthongised final */a/ > *ay, which would further monophthongise to [e]. Y-prosody spreads onto the medial vowels, affecting medial /a/ > e in Dghwede, and medial schwa > i in Guduf, Gwara and Glavda. There is no Y-prosody effect in Lamang.

With the above observations and analyses in mind, we can now reconstruct the historically underlying forms for 'ear' in the eight languages. We note that in this set of examples, six of the eight languages opted for a Ø-vocalised simple root √ C Ca, while two opted for an a-vocalised simple root √ CaCa.

The consonantal sound changes involved are given in Table 5.6.

In terms of low-level sub-classification, we note that – unlike in the case of 'nose' – we here see few if any diagnostic innovations, other than in Lamang (by the use of a rare root augment -ŋ). The odd man out here is Gvoko, given its sound change C_2 *m > w, which triggers W-prosody, as would appear to be quite characteristic for Gvoko anyway (*m > w sound changes sporadically also occur elsewhere among a number of CC languages).

Even after the detailed historical analysis of, for instance, the forms for 'nose' and 'ear' in the eight languages under review above, we still cannot proceed to establish 1:1 individual sound correspondences between any kind of surface vowels by naïvely following the received Neogrammarian principles and methods. First, we must consider the essential difference between phonemic and non-phonemic vowels and their respective allophones. Second, and since the regime of prosodies in Central Chadic languages supersedes what might be called the equipollent phonological autonomy of segments in the vocalic domain, it needs to be established in each individual case whether a segment is affected by a prosody or not. If a segment is affected by a prosody, then the generalised correspondence rules outlined below apply. At the current state of our knowledge, the likely 'affectedness' or 'non-affectedness' of segments and types of segments cannot be predicted in any general manner for each individual language. However, Gravina's (2014a) distinction and typological classification of 'Prosody-type languages' (see 2.6.1) suggests that there could be an areal clustering of typological pulls towards either consonants, or vowels, or both, or none at all. Much more and intensive research is needed to reconcile Gravina's 'prosody types' with the alternative lexical reconstructions proposed in this book.

'Vowel correspondence rules' affecting phonemic /a/

Since there is only one vowel phoneme */a/ to be scrutinised for regular sound correspondences in the individual languages, and since */a/ only contrasts with its absence on the level of diachronically underlying root-and-pattern structures, we end up with only one assimilation-type correspondence rule across languages. This rule would affect */a/ independent of position in the word (initial, medial, final), but subject to the prosodic phonological environment. Note that this rule (Rule 1) would only apply if /a/ did not undergo two rules to be previously applied, which, however, and according to current knowledge, would appear to be 'sporadic' (and therefore 'irregular') and language-specific, if not word-specific.

$$/a/ \quad > \quad \begin{bmatrix} [o] \\ [e] \\ [a] \end{bmatrix} \quad / \quad \begin{bmatrix} \text{W-prosody} \\ \text{Y-prosody} \\ \text{elsewhere} \end{bmatrix}$$

Unless:
/a/ > Ø   apocopation ('sporadic')
/a/ > [ə]   centralisation ('sporadic')

Rule 1. Prosody-sensitive phonetic realisations of /a/

'Vowel correspondence rule' affecting [ə]

Both epenthetic schwa and [ə] reflecting centralised /a/ undergo a comparable 'assimilation-type' rule as in Rule 1 above for /a/, see Rule 2.

$$[ə] \quad > \quad \begin{bmatrix} [ʉ] \\ [ɨ] \\ [ə] \end{bmatrix} \quad / \quad \begin{bmatrix} \text{W-prosody} \\ \text{Y-prosody} \\ \text{elsewhere} \end{bmatrix}$$

Rule 2. Prosody-sensitive phonetic realisations of schwa

In more general terms and for Central Chadic as a whole, i.e. beyond the lexical items for 'nose' and 'ear' in the formerly so-called Wandala-Lamang group of languages, we could state that 'regularities', somewhat at variance with the classic comparative method approach, can be powerfully

5.2 Notion of 'Regular Sound Correspondence'

generalised in a principled way. These regularities may or may not affect individual words in individual languages across Central Chadic, i.e. they do not apply to all languages and to all words at all times. The overarching principle is that *if and only if* the identified units of the vocalic domain in Central Chadic undergo any sound changes, they will do so under the following regularities.

1. Phonemic /a/ in any Central Chadic language may undergo the following sound changes and entertain correspondences in other Central Chadic languages:

None of the following	Y-prosody /a/^{y}	W-prosody /a/^{w}	W+Y-prosodies /a/^{yw}	centralisation
[a]	[ay ~ e ~ ɛ]	[aw ~ o ~ ɔ]	[œ]	[ə]

2. Phonemic /y/ in any Central Chadic language will undergo the following sound changes and entertain correspondences in other Central Chadic languages:

Syllable onset	Syllable coda	Syllable nucleus
[y]	[y]	[i]

3. Phonemic /w/ in any Central Chadic language will undergo the following sound changes and entertain correspondences in other Central Chadic languages:

Syllable onset	Syllable coda	Syllable nucleus
[w]	[w]	[u]

4. Schwa [ə] in any Central Chadic language may undergo the following sound changes and entertain correspondences in other Central Chadic languages:

Epenthesis Ø-prosody	Prothesis Ø-prosody	Y-prosody [ə]^y	W-prosody [ə]^w	W+/Y-prosodies [ə]^{yw}	
[ə]	[a ~ ə]	[i ~ ɨ ~ ɪ]	[u ~ ʉ ~ ʊ]	IPA [ʏ]	

Note 1: Such sound changes and correspondences would also apply to phonetic [ə] when it represents a centralised allophone of /a/.

Note 2: The choice of the graphic representation of pro- and epenthetic vowels may vary according to the conventions used by individual field linguists or in published and unpublished sources. In synchronic perspective, these vowels tend to be phonetically unstable and subject to assimilations by immediate phonological environment. Palatalised and labialised variants [i ~ ɨ ~ ɪ] and [u ~ ʉ ~ ʊ], therefore, need not automatically reflect the impact of prosodies, but may come about by very shallow and local assimilation processes.

6 Full Lexical Reconstructions

6.1 Alternative Option for Not Reconstructing ˣ/ə/

In his study, Gravina (2014a), at variance with assumptions discussed at length in previous studies by other authors like, for instance, Newman (1977a, 2006), Wolff (1983b), Barreteau (1987), proposes three vowel phonemes for PCC plus contrastive Y-prosody. However, he feels forced to take a rather vague position on the status of schwa.

The vowel ɨ [i.e. schwa, which is transcribed as ə according to traditional convention including our own and for the purpose of this book – HEW] is often considered to be epenthetic in individual languages, i.e. as not existing in the underlying form of the word. Here it will be treated as a vowel phoneme, largely for pragmatic reasons. It plays an important role in many phonological processes, and these can be described with greater clarity by considering ɨ as a phoneme. Establishing the status of this vowel is difficult with living languages, and with reconstructed languages it is not possible to reach a reliable conclusion. (Gravina 2014a: 333)

Besides observing that schwa 'is the most common of the three vowels' (2014a: 351), Gravina uses syllable-structure considerations for attributing schwa phonemic status in PCC (2014a: 352), namely by identifying an 'essentially CV nature of Proto-Central Chadic syllables' with 'slots' provided by such structures to be filled by phonemic vowels. In our own and alternative approach, this is taken care of by

(a) assuming a diachronic and underlying root-and-pattern structure, which rests in the Afroasiatic history of Chadic as a whole, and which exactly relies on the identification of sequences of slots filled by either consonants (providing the skeletal 'roots' in the narrow sense of Afroasiatic scholarship) or phonemic vowels, i.e. */a/, and thereby creating vocalisation 'patterns', which interact in a two-tier fashion with the consonantal skeleton of the root (in the term's narrowest sense);
(b) leaving other potential vowel slots to be filled, or not to be filled, by epenthetic schwa.

Gravina attempts to handle this characteristic typological and genetic Afroasiatic feature, to which he makes no reference in his study, by his typologically neutral notion of vowel slots:

> the essentially CV nature of Proto-Central Chadic syllables indicates that there is a vowel slot following each consonant in the underlying form. The structural requirement for these slots to be filled has resulted in a strong tendency for Central Chadic vowels to move between slots diachronically, or for these vowel slots to be filled from sources such as the labialisation of consonants. It is rare for a vowel slot to be left unfilled. (2014a: 352)

Based on our own reconstructions of PCC lexical items, this is considered an over-generalisation. Firstly, we found no evidence that 'vowels … move between slots diachronically'. Rather, the position of vowels, in particular */a/, being the only vowel phoneme, is governed by the choice of root type (see 3.1.1) and tends to remain very stable. Further, roots do not relate to a 'structural requirement for these [vowel] slots to be filled'. Our own reconstructions show that, with a fair number of roots, some slots are never filled, i.e. these underlying roots may be of the shape $\sqrt{}\ C_1aC_2C_3a$, for instance, with no evidence from known languages that the slot between C_2 and C_3 would have to have been filled. Gravina further maintains that 'these vowel slots (are) to be filled from sources such as the labialisation of consonants'. In our approach, labialisation or palatalisation as such do not fill vowel slots. This is done either by */a/ or by epenthetic schwa; as independent processes, both */a/ and schwa may then undergo 'colouring' under the effect of prosodies stemming from segments anywhere else in the word. This is something entirely different from saying that such slots can 'be filled from sources such as the labialisation of consonants'. Also, the statement that '[i]t is rare for a vowel slot to be left unfilled' needs precision: as our own reconstructions show, certain roots, whether in underlying structure or on the surface in phonetic transcription, do systematically allow such unfilled vowel slots and thus contradict the 'essential … CV nature of Proto-Chadic syllables'. While some underlying roots show consistent root type (in terms of number of consonants and vocalisation) across all languages in the database, others allow considerable variation as to which root type and which underlying vocalisation pattern they follow in a particular language. See sub-sections 3.1.1.3 and 3.1.2.2 above, where we illustrate, for instance, the choice of three possible root types for the PCC reconstruction of 'dream': $\sqrt{}\ C\ C\ Ca$, $\sqrt{}\ C\ CaCa$, and $\sqrt{}\ CaCaCa$. This observation is reflected in our convention to give conflated root type structures for our PCC reconstructions, such as $\sqrt{}\ C(a)C(a)Ca$.

6.1 Alternative Option for Not Reconstructing ^{x}/ə/

Table 6.1 *Neutralisation of structural contrasts*

Root type input	Phonological process		Neutralised phonetic output
/CaCa/	Centralisation of /a/ > [ə]		[CəCa]
/CaCa/	Deletion of /a/ and schwa epenthesis	> /CØCa/	[CəCa]
/C Ca/	Epenthetic insertion of schwa		[CəCa]

The central question of whether to reconstruct schwa as a phoneme or always treat it as an epenthetic vowel in diachronic analyses would appear to remain eternally open, so we could easily agree with the following statement by Gravina:

> This gives two viable analyses. The first is to reconstruct *ɨ [i.e. schwa ə – HEW] as a phoneme. The second is to reconstruct vowel slots following each consonant, some of which may be empty at an underlying level and are filled by [ɨ]. The two analyses are essentially equivalent. (Gravina 2014a: 352)

For the purpose of this study, schwa is not reconstructed as a PCC vowel phoneme. Surface phonetic representations of schwa [ə] and its context-induced 'coloured' variants (mainly [ɨ, ʉ]) are diachronically considered to be of epenthetic nature, unless schwa can be analysed as being a centralised allophone of */a/. Such phonemic diachronic origin of schwa deriving from */a/ is made evident from the internal reconstruction of the lexical item in question, i.e. the underlying root type in which */a/ would figure. Note, however, that we do not always have robust comparative evidence for schwa to unequivocally derive surface [ə ~ ɨ ~ ʉ] from */a/ rather than accepting it as simply an epenthetic vowel. Under our chosen approach, it is difficult if not impossible to tell whether we are dealing with differences of root type to start with, or with centralisation of medial */a/. In an even more problematic way, one might occasionally want to assume that underlying */a/ has been deleted and that the vocalic slot is re-filled in surface representation by epenthetic schwa. Table 6.1 illustrates the ensuing neutralisation of structural contrasts (using a biliteral root for exemplification). Currently and under the general methodological principles adhered to in this study (see 2.1), I would favour root type input differences over the other (theoretically and methodologically possible) solutions.

Note that both phonemic */a/ and epenthetic schwa are subject to prosodic impact, so that they can give rise to characteristic synchronic phonetic surface vowels:

- */a/ will usually become [e] under Y-prosody and [o] under W-prosody;
- schwa will become [i] (~ɨ~ɪ) under Y-prosody and [u] (~ʉ~ʊ) under W-prosody.

See the following examples that show the different behaviour of phonemic and epenthetic vowels under the impact of prosodies. In the first set of examples from Vame and Gidar, the underlying phonemic vowel */a/ is retained and undergoes the effect of prosodies:

(193) 'butterfly' PCC *(k^wa-, ma-, ma-ta-RED, RED ...) **p(a)ra** (-y, -k^w, -n; FV)
  HURZA Vame √ CaCa   *pal+pala-y   > pa^ylpa^yla^y-Ø^y
                                       > *pelpele*
  GIDAR Gidar √ CaCa   *ma-ta-pala   > ma^wta^wpa^wla^wpa^wla^w-Ø^w
                       +pala-k^w   > *motopolopolo*

The second set of examples for 'butterfly' from dialects of Giziga shows deletion or centralisation of the phonemic vowel */a/ in the prefix. If we assume */a/ to have been deleted, the slot is then filled again by epenthetic schwa, which undergoes assimilation by prosodies (as would do schwa if it were the centralised allophone of /a/), whose quality is linked to the reconstructed source segment in the suffixal augment.[1]

(194) MAROUA Giziga-   √ CaCa *ma-pala+pala   > *mapalapala*
             Muturwa
             Giziga-   √ C Ca *ma-pla+pla-y   > mə^yplapla-Ø^y   > *miplapla*
             Muturwa
             Giziga-   √ C Ca *ma-pla+pla-k^w > mə^wplapla-Ø^w   > *muplapla*
             Muturwa

This compares to a third set of examples for the word 'butterfly' where the prefix is either absent (Kilba, Bura) or is incorporated between the reduplicated parts of the word and there remains unaffected by prosody like the rest of the word (Nyimatli):

(195) MARGI Kilba   √ C Ca *pr+prØ   > pərpər   > *pərpər*
            Bura   √ C Ca *pr+prØ-y   > pə^yrpə^yr-Ø^y > *pirpir*
      TERA Nyimatli √ C Ca *pr+ma-prØ > pər-ma-pər   > *pərmapər*

Not to reconstruct schwa as a phoneme in PCC means to accept that the diachronic roots will not follow a neat *CV.(CV.)CV. structure as postulated by Gravina (2014a). Rather, PCC roots are here considered to allow for clustering of radical consonants, even operating with medially vowelless roots, such as represented by the root types √ C C Ca and √ C Ca, and even allowing the lexical final /a/ to be deleted, which results in completely vowelless synchronic underlying roots, like √ C C C and √ C C, which some researchers may find hard to accept. Syllables and syllable structures are here considered to be phonetic in nature rather than providing strict phonological constraints for the underlying level of representation. This means that reconstructed and

---

[1] See also notes on examples (37, 77) further above for a non-prosodic alternative analysis.

6.2 Alternative Option for Not Reconstructing ^{x}/i/

underlying roots will have to undergo syllabification processes before they can be considered real phonological and phonetically 'pronounceable' words. Such syllabification processes encompass the following observations in particular with regard to medially 'vowelless' roots of the shapes √ C C C(a) and √ C C(a):

1. *Syllabification* of [±syllabic] vocoids in syllable-nucleus positions creating surface vowels (*/y/ > [i], */w/ > [u]).
2. Insertion of *epenthetic* schwa dissolving clusters of radical consonants and root-augmental materials in order to create phonologically and phonetically acceptable syllables. In a language-specific manner, *prothetic* vowel insertion dissolves word-initial consonant clusters to end up in two different syllables.
3. Sonorants have a stronger tendency than non-sonorants to attract epenthetic vowels, or occasionally become syllabified themselves in the creation of syllables in surface representations.
4. Abutting (particularly voiced) consonants allow for 'open phonetic transition' between them; such open phonetic transitions are almost impossible to tell from epenthetic vowel insertion and may thus also play a role in the phonetic syllabification of underlying forms.

As it would appear, syllabification of [±syllabic] vocoids would chronologically precede *epenthetic* schwa insertion in the overall process of syllabification of underlying structures.

6.2 Alternative Option for Not Reconstructing ^{x}/i/

For the three vowels reconstructed by Gravina (2014a), he states that '[t]he phonemes *a and *ɨ [= schwa ə – HEW] are relatively stable', and that

[t]he phoneme *i is more varied in its reflexes. In some languages it has the reflex /ə/, in others it is /i/, and in many cases it has merged with either *ɨ or *a. (Gravina 2014a: 333)

Such observations raise considerable doubt as to the validity of the reconstruction of */i/ for PCC. Another suspicious observation is the relatively low frequency of occurrence of */i/ in reconstructions. As a matter of fact, out of 250 reconstructions in the database, only 29, i.e. less than 12 per cent, show */i/: 9 in final position, and 20 in medial position (see 6.3.1). If reconstructed vowels could be expected to be equally distributed over the available corpus, we would have expected more than 80 occurrences of */i/ in the reconstructions. These figures provide additional justification to look for potential alternative analyses.

At variance with Gravina's work, therefore, and based on my own previous research (see 1.1 further above), for the purpose of this study the vowel ^{x}/i/ is not reconstructed as a PCC vowel phoneme. Rather, phonetic surface representations of [i] are internally reconstructed as stemming from two diachronic sources:

- syllabification of the vocoid */y/ in syllable-nucleus positions;
- epenthetic schwa under the impact of Y-prosody.

Partly, at least, our own diachronic explanations for the occurrence of surface [i] in present-day Central Chadic languages rests on accepting

- internal reconstruction as a valid method of historical linguistic research, and
- the notion of 'weak radical' as a plausible and legitimate tool for comparative work in Afroasiatic languages.

Honouring Gravina's pioneer efforts, we will discuss his data concerning reconstructable ^{x}/i/ and at least final ^{x}/ə/ separately in sub-sections 6.3.1 and 6.3.4 below and primarily make use of these potentially controversial reconstructions as illustrations in the present book.

6.3 Alternative Reconstructions of the Proto-Central Chadic Lexicon

In this section, we confront the results from Gravina's groundbreaking comparative work with our own reconstructions as based on the particular approach chosen for this study. We focus on reconstructions that contain potentially controversial issues, like the treatment of schwa (as either phonemic or epenthetic in nature) and the need to reconstruct or not to reconstruct a high front vowel ^{x}/i/ as a phonemic unit in Proto-Central Chadic (PCC). We discuss prosodies as affecting Central Chadic languages in general and PCC reconstructions in particular, and we discuss Y-prosody and W-prosody on equal terms, i.e. we do not single out Y-prosody over W-prosody for whatever reasons. Gravina had made it a point to reconstruct Y-prosody as a phonemic unit for PCC, while not attributing the same status to W-prosody. In our approach, neither are considered phonemic 'units', but rather are phonological processes that both played a decisive role in the historical development of the Central Chadic languages.

In terms of reconstructed consonants, we largely follow Gravina's notations with his comments on sound correspondences implied (see the verbatim quotations from his database in 6.4 for each reconstructed lexical item). Note that quoting from and thereby linking to Gravina's work does not mean that all of Gravina's reconstructions and observations concerning consonants are accepted as valid, since our assumptions about the inventory of PCC consonants differ slightly (see 3.2.1). The present study simply does not focus on the reconstruction of consonants for PCC, but rather focuses on surface vowels

6.3 Alternative Reconstructions of the PCC Lexicon 193

and their underlying representations and historical reconstructions. It is our firm belief that final judgements on PCC consonants can only be made after the nature of and complexities concerning vowels and prosodies have been satisfactorily solved. And this is the major concern of the present study. Accordingly and for subsequent comparative Chadic linguistic research, Gravina's (2014a) observations regarding the reconstruction of both consonants and vowels will have to be modified and adjusted, should the results of the present study be taken as a valid alternative starting point for reconstructions of the PCC lexicon. See Wolff (forthcoming).

6.3.1 Reconstructions Licensing [i] in Phonetic Surface Representation

A major and controversial issue in comparative work on Central Chadic languages is the identification of the diachronic sources of high surface vowels, which appear as [i] and [u] in the transcriptions of individual language data. Further, it is received wisdom in Chadic linguistics that structural constraints govern the availability of vowel inventories for different positions in the word (cf. Newman 1977a, 2006). Generally speaking, experts would expect only /a/ and /i/ in word-initial position (plus or including a prothetic vowel preceding initial consonant clusters in some languages, which may take any 'colouring' depending on environment, including occasional phonetic transcription as [a]). In word-initial position, we would regularly derive phonetic [u] from syllabification of an initial labial(ised) consonant /C^w/ or /w/, or from a prothetic vowel preceding such a labial(ised) initial consonant in an initial cluster. Occasionally, initial [i] reflects the same story when a palatal consonant is part of an initial consonant cluster.

Medial [i] and [u] could be analysed, as is done in the current study, as either syllabifications of underlying */y/ and */w/ (cf. the notion of 'weak radical') or as epenthetic schwa under the effect of Y-prosody and W-prosody, respectively (often presumably a convenient simplification in the transcription of data instead of using the phonetically likely more appropriate special symbols [ɨ] ands [ʉ], which anyway would not be contrastive with [i] and [u]). This leaves only the word-final position to allow for the appearance of all phonemic vowels that any given language may synchronically possess (but see 3.4; cf. also Newman 1977a).

Presumably, it was the fairly frequent occurrence of final and non-final [i] (and [e], for that matter) in phonetic surface representations that motivated Gravina (2014a) to reconstruct ^{x}/i/ for PCC. His rich database (Gravina 2014b), however, provides only 29 examples for reconstructions containing ^{x}/i/. In this section and others, we will revisit these 29 lexical reconstructions and provide alternative forms, which could also and quite plausibly explain the surface occurrences of [i] in these examples without necessarily reconstructing ˣ/i/ for PCC. As a result of applying our alternative approach as outlined across this book, we maintain that even for these examples, there is no reason or necessity to reconstruct for PCC either ˣ/i/ or independent Y-prosody as phonemic units, as does Gravina (2014a).

Another major theoretical and methodological decision to take is whether to identify the segmental source of prosodies as phonological or morphological in nature (see 3.2.3). With regard to the surface vowel [i] being itself both the result of and a potential source of Y-prosody, the *phonology hypothesis* would reconstruct *i as part of the lexical root, either as phonemic vowel or as weak radical consonant */y/. Reconstructing */i/ in roots is basically the line followed by Gravina (2014a), while in our study underlying */y/ is reconstructed instead. For examples see 3.2.5. The *morphology hypothesis* is based on the observation that morphological palatalisation has been well established to exist in Chadic languages (see the discussions in Schuh 2002; Wolff 2019b). Hence and in the absence of radical /y/ in the simple root and disregarding the option of reconstructing ˣi in simple roots, the present reconstructions opt for the morphology hypothesis concerning the origin of Y-prosody. Given the rich evidence for the existence of petrified suffixal root-augment material throughout Central Chadic, and the high frequency of *{-y} among these elements, we feel safe to suggest a grammatical (suffixal) origin whenever necessary (i.e. when we can exclude a phonological source of the prosody from within the simple root). For examples see the discussion in 3.2.5.1 and 4.4.1. Note, however, that at the current state of our knowledge, we are not in a position to unequivocally identify any grammatical functions with reconstructed occurrences of *{-y}, but see the discussion in Wolff (2019b).

6.3.1.1 [i] in Final Position
In confrontation with the comparative research by Gravina (2014a, 2014b), it is of great interest to look at his only 9 (out of 250) reconstructions in which ˣ/i/ is assumed to occur in word-final position. Remember that it is this position in which we would expect all possible vowel contrasts to occur in a Chadic language (cf. Newman 1977a).

Our alternative prosody-based approach does not provide any justification to reconstruct a phonemic high-front vowel ˣ/i/ for the final position of a root or word even where and although final [i] is present in many surface representations of words. According to our own reconstruction hypotheses, such final [i] can be accounted for most frequently by the presence and syllabification of a reconstructed suffixal root-augment *{-y}, and only occasionally by palatalisation of a centralised allophone [ə] of underlying /a/. In the case of *{-y}, we

6.3 Alternative Reconstructions of the PCC Lexicon

would deal with one or several diachronic marker(s), which also give(s) rise to morphological palatalisation elsewhere and across both Central and West Chadic (Schuh 2002; Wolff 2019b). Nonetheless, it needs pointing out as a caveat that postulating underlying *{-y} any time it is needed to account for surface palatalisation remains a kind of *deus ex machina* strategy, even though *{-y} has frequent independent segmental reflexes in modern Central Chadic languages.

The segmental reflexes of this hypothetical suffixal *{-y} have different shapes in present-day languages. In some, there is straightforward vocalisation to yield a final vowel [i] that replaces the lexical final /a/ of the root (as in Kilba below), in other languages *{-y} is simply added to the final /a/ to yield a diphthong /ay/ (as in Matal below), in yet other languages it monophthongises such intermediate underlying diphthong to /ay/ > [e] (as in Gemzek below). E.g.

(196) 'cry, to' PCC *(ma-) **ts(a)wa** (-a, -y, -k, -k^w; a)
      MARGI   Kilba   *t wØ-y   > təw-i^y > tə^{y}wi   > *tiwi*
      MANDARA   Matal   *t wØ-a-y   > təway   > *təway*
      MOFU   Gemzek   *t wa-y   > tə^w^{w}a-Ø^y > tə^{w}wa^y > *tuwe*

This *{-y} is often, but not always (see 3.2.5), the source also for Y-prosody affecting other segments of the root or word (like in Kilba above), and therefore needs to be reconstructed on independent grounds, whether or not it syllabifies as final [i] in present-day languages.

Another source of synchronic final [i] is to be found with assumed centralisations of final /a/ (> [ə]) under phonological Y-prosody. E.g.

(197) 'bone' PCC *(...) **ɗ y(a)ɬa** (-a, -y, -k^w, -t, -n)
      MARGI   Kilba   *ɗ y xa   > ɗi^{y}xə   > ɗix^{y}ə^y > *ɗih^{y}i*

(198) 'earth' PCC *(a-, ya-, RED) **x^w(a)yɗa** (-y, -k; FV)
      HIGI   Kamwe-Futu   *x yɗa   > xi^{y}ɗə > x^{y}iɗə^y > *hyiɗi*
                    Bana   *x yɗa   > xi^{y}ɗə > x^{y}iɗə^y > *x^{y}iɗi*

(199) 'thorn' PCC *(a-, xa-, m-, va-) **d(a)y(a)ka** (-t, -y)
      LAMANG   Lamang   *t y ka   > ti^{y}kə > tikə^y > *tiki*

6.3.1.2 [i] in Medial Position

For medial [i] to emerge in phonetic surface representations of present-day languages, we see two diachronic sources and processes to be responsible:

- syllabifications of reconstructed medial */y/ in the simple root (phonological palatalisation);

196   Full Lexical Reconstructions

- epenthetic schwa under the effect of morphological or phonological Y-prosody, transcribed as both [ɨ] and [i] in the data.

Some PCC roots can be reconstructed with medial vocoids as so-called weak radicals, such as */y/ (see also examples 197–199 above). Syllabification of */y/ underlying the vowel [i] in such roots is not likely to be transparent from purely synchronic analysis, but presupposes the application of the methodology of internal reconstruction (see 2.3). The medial radical */y/ may or may not function as source for phonological palatalisation affecting other segments. (Note that with loss of the original initial root consonant, medial /*y/ may surface as initial segment of the root (see also 6.3.1.3 below) yielding vowel-initial forms in surface structures.) The following examples are all reconstructed with original medial (C_2) */y/. E.g.

(200)   'bone' PCC *(...) ɗ y(a)ɬa (-a, -y, -k^w, -t, -n)

BATA	Gude	*Ø y la			> ila
	Tsuvan	*Ø y ɮa	> i^{y}ɮa	> iɮa^y	> iɮe
MARGI	Kilba	*ɗ y xa	> ɗi^{y}xə	> ɗix^{y}ə^y	> ɗih^{y}i
KOTOKO-SOUTH	Mazera	*a-RED+ʔØ^{y}sa	Metathesis a-RED+ʔsØ^{y}a Metathesis a-RED+sʔØ^{y}a > asə^y+sʔa$^{y=}$		> asis'e

(201)   'earth' PCC *(a-, ya-, RED) x^w(a)yɗa (-y, -k; FV)

HURZA	Vame	*x yØØ-y-ka	Metathesis xy-ka-y		> higay
MARGI	Bura	*x yØØ			> hi
HIGI	Kamwe-Futu	*x yɗa	> xi^{y}ɗə	> x^{y}iɗə^y	> hyidi
	Bana	*x yɗa	> xi^{y}ɗə	> x^{y}iɗə^y	> x^{y}idi

(202)   'grasshopper' PCC *(a-) x^w(a)y(a)k^{w}a (...)

BATA	Gude	*a-Ø y wa	> a-y^{y}wa	> a-yə^{y}wa	> ayiwa
MANDARA	Podoko	*x yawa	> xy^{y}awa	> xə^{y}yawa	> hiyawa
	Mandara	*Ø y wa			> iwa
	Malgwa	*Ø y wa	> əy^{y}wa	> ə^{y}ywa^y	> iiwe

(203)   'hare' PCC *(ma-, na-) x^w(a)d(a)y(a)va (-k, -k^w, -n ; FV)

BATA	Gude	*Ø t y pa	> py^{y}ta	> pit^{y}a	
	Jimi	*Ø d y va-n	> vyda-n	> vidən	
	Tsuvan	*Ø t y va-k-n	> vy^{y}tə-kən > vitə^y-kən	> vitikən	
SUKUR	Sukur	*Ø l y va	> vly^{y}a > və^{y}lya	> vil^{y}a	

6.3 Alternative Reconstructions of the PCC Lexicon   197

	MARGI	Margi	*Ø t y pa	> pyta	> pitə
		Margi- South	*Ø t y pa-kʷ	> pyta-kʷ > pitØ-w	> pitu
		Kilba	*Ø t y pa	> pyta	> pita
	MANDARA	Podoko	*Ø r y va	> vyra	> vira
		Mandara	*na-Ø r y va	> navyʸra > naviraʸ	> navire
		Malgwa	*na-Ø r y va	> navəyʸra > navəʸira	> naviira
		Glavda	*Ø Ø y vØ *Ø d y va	> vyʸ > vəʸi > vyʸda > vəʸida	> vii > vi:da
	LAMANG	Lamang	*Ø l y va-kʷa	> vyla-kʷa	> vilakʷa
		Hdi	*Ø l y va-kʷ	> vyla-kʷ	> vilakʷ
	HIGI	Kamwe- Futu	*Ø r y va	> vyra	> vira
		Kirya	*Ø t y pa	> pyta	> pitə

(204)   'thorn' PCC *(a-, xa-, m-, va-) **d(a)y(a)ka** (-t, -y)
	SUKUR	Sukur	*dz y kØ	> dziʸk	> dzʸik	> dʒik
	LAMANG	Lamang	*t y ka	> tiʸkə	> tikəʸ	> tiki
	HIGI	Kamwe-Nkafa	*t y ka			> tikə

(205)   'whistle, to' PCC *(ma-, RED) **f(a)y(a)kʷa** (-a, -y, -n)
	BATA	Gude	*f y kʷa	> fikʷə	> fikəʷ	> fiku
		Jimi	*f y kʷa-n	> fikʷan		> fikʷən
	MANDARA	Mandara	*f y kʷa	> fikʷa		> fikʷa
		Malgwa	*f y kʷa	> fyʸkʷa	> fəʸykʷa	> fiikʷa
		Glavda	*fa-f y kʷa	> fafikʷa		> fafikʷa
	MOFU	Muyang	*f y kʷ-a-y	> fiʸkʷayʸ	> fikʷaʸy	> fikʷey
	HIGI	Kamwe- Futu	*f y gʷa	> fiʸgʷa	> figʷaʸ	> figʷe

For the very frequent and transparent instances of reconstructed morphological palatalisation of epenthetic schwa, see the following few examples from a plethora of comparable cases in the data (6.4):

(206)   'ashes' PCC *(a-) **p ts(a)ɗa** (-y, -kʷ,-n)
	TERA	Tera	*p dz tØ-y	> pədzət-Øʸ	> pədzʸəʸt	> pədʒit
		Nyimatli	*p z tØ-y	> pəzət-Øʸ	> pəzʸəʸt	> pəʒit
		Hwana	*f s Øa-y	> fəsa-Øʸ	> fəʸsʸaʸ	> fiʃe
	MOFU	Muyang	*v t ØØ-y	> vət-iʸ	> vəʸt-i	> viti
		Zulgo	*b t Øa-y	> bəta-Øʸ	> bəʸtaʸ	> bite

(207)   'blow, to' PCC *(ma-) **v ɮa** (-a, -y, -kʷ, -n)
	BATA	Bata	*f lØ-y	> fəl-Øʸ	> fəʸl	> fil
	MOFU	Zulgo	*v ɮØ-y	> vəɮ-Øʸ	> vəʸɮ	> viɮ

6.3.1.3 [i] in Initial Position

The examples for 'bone' discussed above can also serve to illustrate the emergence of [i] in initial position from originally medial position, for instance after loss of the original initial consonant. Note that in Tsuvan, the syllabified */y/ > i^y has a prosodising effect (on final /a/ > [e]), which is missing in the other three languages.

(208) 'bone' PCC *(...) ɗ y(a)ɬa (-a, -y, -k^w, -t, -n)

BATA	Gude	*Ø y la	> ila		> ila
	Tsuvan	*Ø y ʓa	> i^{y}ʓa	> iʓa^y	> iʓe
HIGI	Kirya	*Ø y ɬa	> iɬə		> iɬə
	Kamwe-Futu	*Ø y ɬa	> iɬa		> iɬa

A somewhat intermediate stage is represented by two other HIGI group languages, in which original */ɗ+y/ fuse to yield initial ['y]. This is accompanied by a prosodic effect on the immediately following medial epenthetic schwa:

(209) HIGI Kamwe-Nkafa *ɗ y ɬa > 'y^{y}əɬə > 'yə^{y}ɬə > 'yiɬə
            Bana   *ɗ y ɬa > 'y^{y}əɬə > 'yə^{y}ɬə > 'yiɬə

See also 'grasshopper' in the following examples:

(210) 'grasshopper' PCC (a-) x^w(a)y(a)k^{w}a (-ɗ,-ŋ?)
      MANDARA   Mandara *Ø y wa   > iwa
                Malgwa   *Ø y wa > əy^{y}wa > əy^{y}wa^y > iiwe

6.3.2 Reconstructions Licensing [u] in Phonetic Surface Representation

As outlined above, the identification of the diachronic sources of high surface vowels is a major and controversial issue in comparative work on Central Chadic languages. It is received wisdom in Chadic linguistics that structural constraints govern the availability of vowel inventories for different positions in the word (cf. Newman 1977a). Experts would expect only /a/ and /i/ in word-initial position and would, in word-initial position, regularly derive phonetic [u] from syllabification of an initial labial(ised) consonant /C^w/ or /w/, or from a prothetic vowel preceding such labial(ised) initial consonant in an initial cluster. Medial [i] and [u] could be analysed, as in the current study, as either syllabifications of underlying */y/ and */w/ (cf. the notion of weak radical) or as epenthetic schwa under the effect of Y- and W-prosody respectively. This leaves only the word-final position to allow for the appearance of all phonemic vowels that any given language may synchronically possess (but see 3.4; cf. also Newman 1977a).

6.3.2.1 [u] in Final Position

Final [u] ought to be looked at in terms of language-specific diachronic developments. For its diachronic origin, we assume vocalisation of the labial

6.3 Alternative Reconstructions of the PCC Lexicon   199

component of (often final) labial(ised) consonants, whether of simple or augmented roots (see also 3.2.4.1).

In some cases such as in the following examples, we are dealing with phonological labialisation prosody where syllabification of /w/ in final position yields word-final [u]. In the root for 'five' in MARGI languages, such final [u] would appear to derive from a double metathesis involving the labial root consonant /w/, which ends up in final position of the word where it is syllabified to [u].

(211) 'five' PCC *(m-, n-) **x^w t(a)fa** (-y, -k; FV)
                              Metathesis   Metathesis
       MARGI   Bura   *n-w^wtfØ   n-tw^wf   n-tfw^w   > n-tə^wfw   > *ntufu*

Note that, once again, the two occurrences of the same phonetic surface vowel [u] represent different underlying phonological units, namely epenthetic schwa under W-prosody in the first syllable, and syllabified /w/ in the final syllable, where we are dealing with a case of phonological labialisation originating from root-internal /w/ (< /x^w/) > [u].

(212) 'belly' PCC *(a-) **x^w(a)ɗa** (-y, -ɗ, -k^w)
       MAROUA Mbazla *(a-)w^wra   > (a-)w^wərə   > (a-)wə^wrə^w   > *(a)wuru*

Note that in the Mbazla example, on the other hand, the two occurrences of the same phonetic surface vowel [u] both represent schwa under W-prosody, albeit stemming from an epenthetic vowel in the first syllable, but from centralised lexical final /a/ in the ultimate syllable.

In another set of cases, we would appear to be dealing with weakening of *{-k^w} > w and subsequent syllabification of /w/ > [u] from suffixal root-augment material, i.e. these would be cases of morphological labialisation.

(213) 'ashes' PCC *(a-) **p ts(a)ɗa** (y, -k^w, -n)
       MAROUA Mbazla *f ts ØØ-y-k^w   > fəts-Ø^y-w^w   > fə^wts^y-w   > *futfu*
       MARGI   Kilba   *p ts dØ-k^w   > pətsəɗ-w   > *pətsədu*

(214) 'bone' PCC *(...) **ɗ y(a)ɬa** (-a, -y, -k^w, -t, -n)
       MARGI   Margi   *ɗ yaxØ-k^w   > ɗyax-w   > *ɗyahu*

(215) 'dream' PCC *(...) **s(a)w(a)na** (-a, -y, -k, -n; a)
       HIGI   Kirya   *s w Øa-y   > səw^wə-Ø^y   > s^yə^ywə^w   > *ʃiwu* (vb)

(216) 'root' PCC *(RED) **ɬ(a)r(a)ka** (-a, -y, -k^w, -n; a)
       HIGI   Psikye *ɬ Ø gØ-k^w   > ɬəg-w^w   > ɬə^wg-w   > *ɬugu*

However, final [u] may also come about by the effect of W-prosody on a centralised allophone [ə] of underlying /a/. E.g.

(217) 'whistle, to' PCC *(ma-, RED) **f(a)y(a)k^wa** (-a, -y, -n)
BATA   Gude   *f y k^wa   > fik^wə   > fikə^w   > *fiku*

6.3.2.2 [u] in Medial Position

Many cases of medial [u] in phonetic surface representation result from syllabification of a medial weak radical /w/. Occasionally, such weak radicals take part in metathesis of root consonants.

(218) 'dream' PCC *(...) **s(a)w(a)na** (...)
HURZA   Mbuko   *s w na-y   > suna-Ø^y   > suna^y   > *sune*
MARGI   Bura   *s w nØ-y   > sun-i   > *suni*

        Kilba   *s 'w nØ-y   > sə'wn-i^y   > s^yə^y'un-i > *ʃi'uni*

MOFU   Zulgo   *s w na   > *suna*
        Merey   *ma-s w na-y > masuna-Ø^y   > masuna^y   > *məsune*
LAMANG Hdi   *s w nØ-y   > sun-i   > *suni*

(219) 'suck, to' PCC *(ma-, n-, RED) **s(a)wɓa** (a-, -y, -n)
MAFA   Mafa   *RED+sawɓØ   > sa+sØw^wɓ
                                      > sa^w+swɓ   > *sosuɓ*
MANDARA   Dghweɗe   *ts wɓa   Metathesis
                                      tsɓwa
                                      Metathesis
                                      ɓtswa
                                      Metathesis
                                      ɓwtsa   > *p'utsa*
MOFU   Zulgo   *RED+sawɓa   > sa+sØwɓa   > *sasuɓa*
          Gemzek   *s wɓØ   > *suɓ*
          Merey   *RED+s wɓØ   > sw+swɓ   > *susuɓ*
MAROUA   Giziga-Marva *s wɓa   > *suɓa*
          Mbazla   *RED+s wɓØ-y   > sw+swɓ-i   > *susuɓi*
GIDAR   Gidar   *a-RED+s wɓa   > a-s+sw^wɓa
                                      > a-s+swɓa^w   > *əssuɓo*

6.3.2.3 [u] in Initial Position

It had long been noted (Newman 1977a) that Proto-Chadic allowed vowel-initial roots and words, but that only /a/ and /i/ needed to be reconstructed for this position, and not */u/. The reason is quite obvious from synchronic analyses of Central Chadic languages (see, for instance, Lamang in Wolff 2015, Vol.1: 81), which tend to show that initial [u] is underlyingly or historically the representation of a labial(ised) consonant /C^w/, which became weakened to the vocoid /w/ (or would have been /w/ from the beginning), and would emerge in syllable-nucleus positions as surface vowel [u]. Initial labialised consonants (*/C^w/) may become diachronically reduced ('weakened') to underlying synchronic /w/. By syllabification they yield phonetic [u] on the surface. E.g.

(220)   'ram' PCC *(a-, ma-) **gʷ(a)z(a)ma** (-y)
       KOTOKO- Lagwan   *w z mØ-y   > uzəm-iʸ   > uzəʸm-i   > *uzimi*
       CENTRAL
                     Mser   *w zamØ   > uzam   > *uzam*

If the initial consonant is a labialised one (/Cʷ/), then occasionally occurring prothetic schwa may receive a labialised 'colouring' from it and thereby create initial [u] in phonetic surface representation, cf.

(221)   'faeces' PCC *(ŋ-) **ɣʷ va** (-a, -y, -n)
       MANDARA   Mandara   *gʷva-y   > əgʷva-Øʸ   > əʷgvaʸ   > *ugve*

6.3.3 Reconstructions Licensing Mid Vowels [e] and [o] in Both Medial and Final Positions in Phonetic Surface Representation

Mid vowels [e] and [o] in Chadic typically represent the diachronic phonemic vowel */a/ under the effect of Y- and W-prosodies, both in medial and final positions.

       (a) Medial and final [e]:

(222)   'butterfly' PCC *(..., RED) **p(a)ra** (-y, -kw, -n; FV)
       HURZA   Vame   *pal+pala-y   > palpala-Øʸ   > paʸlpaʸlaʸ   > *pelpele*

       (b) Medial and final [o]:

(223)   'ashes' PCC *(a-) **p ts(a)ɗa** (y, -kʷ, -n)
       MAROUA   Giziga-   *a-f tsa-y-kʷ   > aftsa-Øʸ-Øʷ   > aftsʸaʷ   > *aftʃo*
                     Marva

(224)   'belly' PCC *(a-) **xʷ(a)ɗa** (-y, -ɗ, -kʷ)
       MAROUA   Mada   *xʷaɗØ   > xaʷɗ   > *hoɗ*

(225)   'butterfly' PCC *(..., ma-ta-, RED) **p(a)ra** (-y, -kʷ, -n; FV)
       HURZA   Mbuko   *ma-pra-kʷ   > mapəraʷk   > *mapərok*
       GIDAR   Gidar   *ma-ta-pala-pala-kʷ   > matapalapala-Øʷ
                                          > maʷtaʷpaʷlaʷpaʷlaʷ   > *motopolopolo*

6.3.4 Reconstructions Licensing Final Schwa in Phonetic Surface Representation

For the purpose of this study and for the sake of completeness, this sub-section looks at the occurrence of final schwa in phonetic surface representations. Currently and for lack of any other plausible hypothesis, final schwa is phonologically identified as a centralised allophone of underlying phonemic *\/a/. Final /a/ centralisation to allophone schwa would appear to be language-specific and not governed by a principle already valid at the level of PCC.

Final /a/ centralisation affects both lexical final /a/ and suffixal root-augmental final /a/ (FV) following other root-augmental material in the segmental chain. (Note that, given the fact that grammatical reconstruction of PCC has hardly begun, we currently have no evidence for the potential original systemic identity of the final vowel *\/a/ with both simple and augmented roots.) In order not to become guilty of premature under-analysis, we keep both distinct in our current analysis under the terms 'lexical final /a/' and 'FV'. We first present some examples of lexical /a/ centralisation.

(226)   'bone' PCC *(a-, a-n-, a-ta-, ma-, ma-ta-, RED, . . .) **ɗ y(a)ɬa** (-a, -y, -kʷ, -t, -n)

	BATA	Sharwa	*a-Ø y ɬa	> a-lla	> allə
	HIGI	Kamwe-Nkafa	*' y ɬa		> 'yithlə
		Kirya	*Ø y ɬa		> iɬə
		Bana	*' y ɬa		> 'yiɬə
	KOTOKO-SOUTH	Zina	*a-sa-Ø Ø sa		> asasə

(227)   'eight' PCC *(m-) **tɣ(a)sa** (-y, -kʷ)

	BATA	Gude	*t ɣ sa	> təɣəsa	> təɣəsə
	HIGI	Psikye	*d g sa	> dəgəsa	> dəgəsə
		Bana	*d ɣ sa	> d(ə)ɣəsa	> d(ə)ɣəsə

(228)   'five' PCC *(m-, n-) **xʷ t(a)fa** (-y, -k; FV)

	BATA	Gude	*w t fa	Metathesis twfa	> tufə
		Jimi	*w tafa-y	Metathesis tawfa-y	
				Metathesis tafwa-y	
				> tafwa-Øʸ	
				> taʸfwa	> tefᵛə
	HIGI	Kamwe-Nkafa	*n-w ts fa-y	Metathesis n-tswfa-y	
				> n-tswfa-Øʸ	
				> n-tsʸufa	> ntʃufə
		Kamwe-Futu	*m-w tsafa-y	Metathesis m-tsawfa-y	
				> m-tsawʷfa-Øʸ	
				> m-tsʸʷafa	> mtʃʷafə
		Kirya	*n-Ø ts fa-y	> n-tsəfa-Øʸ	
				> n-tsʸəʸfa	> ntʃifə
		Psikye	*m-Ø tsafa-y	> m-tsafa-Øʸ	
				> m-tsʸaʸfa	> mtʃefə
		Bana	*Ø ts fa-y	> tsəfa-Øʸ	
				> tsʸəʸfa	> tʃifə

6.3 Alternative Reconstructions of the PCC Lexicon   203

(229)   'hare' PCC *(ma-, na-) **x^w(a)d(a)y(a)va** (-k, -k^w, -n ; FV)
        MARGI   Margi   *Ø t y pa   > pyta   > pitə

(230)   'moon' PCC *(n-, ŋ-) **t(a)ra** (-y, -k^w; FV)
        HIGI   Kamwe-Nkafa   *t ra   > təra   > tərə°
                Psikye   *t ra   > trə

(231)   'navel' PCC *(ma-) **z(a)b(a)-x^w(a)ɗa** (-y, -n)
        BATA   Sharwa   *m-z b Ø^w ɗa-y   > zə^{m}b^{w}ə^{w}ɗa-Ø^y
                                               > zə^{ym}bə^{w}ɗa   > zɨ^{m}budə

The following examples show that the so-called final vowel (FV) /a/ following a petrified suffixal root augment may also undergo centralisation in final position.

(232)   'butterfly' PCC *(..., ma-ta-, RED) **p(a)ra** (-y, -kw, -n; FV)
        BATA   Gude   *pry+pr-y-na   > pəri+pəri-na   > pəripərinə

(233)   'dog' PCC ***k(a)ra** (-a, -y, -k^w; FV)
        KOTOKO-ISLAND   Buduma   *k lØ-ya   > kəli(a)   > kəli(ə)

(234)   'dream' PCC *(...) **s(a)w(a)na** (...)
        BATA   Sharwa   *s Ø na-y'a   > səna-Ø^y'a
                                         > s^{y}ə^{y}na'a   > ʃinə'ə

(235)   'root' PCC *(RED) **ɬ(a)r(a)ka** (-a, -y, -k^w, -; FV)
        BATA   Gude   *ɬ r g-y-na   > ɬərəgina   > lhərəginə
        HIGI   Bana[2] *x l g-y-na   Metathesis
                                        xlygna
                                        REDuplication:
                                        > xly^y-ly^y-gna
                                        Metathesis
                                        xly^y-ly^y-nga
                                        > x^{y}ə^{y}liliŋa   > x^{y}ililiŋə

6.3.5 Reconstructions Involving */a/ as Medial Vowel

The stunning complexity of Central Chadic reconstructions, in particular with a focus on surface vs. synchronically underlying vs. diachronic vowels and

---

[2] Quite exceptional in the data, Bana, besides undergoing metathesis of C_3 and *{-y} plus fusion of the metathesised sequence -gn- > -ŋg-, uses medial (2nd-syllable-based) reduplication for root augmentation rather than the much more frequent initial (1st-syllable-based) reduplication.

prosodies, becomes particularly obvious when we look at what should be easy and highly transparent reconstructions that involve only /a/. The database contains several such which Gravina (2014a, 2014b) has reconstructed as, for instance, √ CaCa roots.

As straightforward as such reconstructions should be, obvious differences pertain to the choice of root type in individual languages or language groups, which trigger, in combinations with suffixal root-augments, considerable surface variation across languages. The first choice is between a-vocalisation √ CaCa and Ø-vocalisation √ C Ca. Both morphological Y-prosody and morphological W-prosody occur, at times within the same augmented root. The options are illustrated below with the verb root 'to wash', which shows the various reflexes of what would appear to be the same underlying simple root. The 16 apparent surface root shapes can first be neatly grouped according to root types reflecting Ø-vocalisation vs. a-vocalisation, namely *bna~bana:

(236) | Root type | simple root | surface representations |
|---|---|---|
| √ C Ca | *b na | buna, bun, bin, pər, pi |
| √ CaCa | *bana | bara, bar, ban, baŋ, bere, ber, para, pana, pan, pal, pe |

Apart from unspectacular consonant changes (C_1 */b/ > p, C_2 */n/ > r ~ l ~ Ø), such variation of a single simple root, as characteristic as it would appear to be of Central Chadic languages at first sight, and looking at phonetic surface representations of vowels only (u ~ i ~ ə ~ a ~ e), is counter-intuitive and would in any case deserve detailed explication. Our explication comes from internal reconstruction of underlying and diachronic forms under a rigid prosody-based approach and representing both simple and augmented roots.

(237) 'wash, to' PCC *(ma-) **b(a)na** (-a,-y,-k^w,-n, (fa-)ŋ,-x, RED; FV)

(a) Root type √ C Ca

BATA	Jimi	*bna-y-n	> bəna-Ø^y-n	
			> bə^{y}nan	> binən
	Vame	*bna-y-k^{w}a	Metathesis bna-k^w-ya	
			> bənə-Ø^w-y^{y}a	
			> bə^{w}nə^{y}ya	> buniya
MOFU	Mofu North	*ma-prØ-a-y	> mapəray^y	
			> ma^{y}pəra^{y}y	> mepərey
	Mofu-Gudur	*prØ	> pər	> pər
MAROUA	Giziga-Muturwa, -Marva	*bnØ-k^w	> bən-Ø^w	
			> bə^{w}n	>bun
	Giziga-Marva	*bna-k^w	> bəna-Ø^w	
			> bə^{w}na	> buna
HIGI	Bana	*pØØ-y	> p-i	> pi

6.3 Alternative Reconstructions of the PCC Lexicon   205

(b) Root type √ CaCa
DABA	Buwal, Gavar	*banØ		> ban
	Mbudum	*banØ(-k^w ?)		> baŋ
	Daba	*panØ		> pan
MAFA	Mafa	*panØ		> pan
	Cuvok	*pana		> pana
SUKUR	Sukur	*banØ		> ban
HURZA	Mbuko	*banØ-a-y		> banay
MANDARA	Matal	*ma-palØ-a-y		> mapalay
	Podoko	*para		> para
	Glavda	*barØ-ka		> barga
MOFU	Ouldeme	*bara-y-ŋ	> bara-Ø^y-ŋ	
			> ba^yra^y-ŋ	> bereŋ
		*bara-ka		> baraka
		*barØ-ya	> bar-y^ya	
			> barə^ya	> bariya
		*bara-ya	> bara-y^ya	
			> ba^yra^y-ya	> bereya
		*bara-xa		> baraha
	Muyang	*bara-RED		> baraba
		*bara-fa-ŋ		> barafəŋ
		*barØ-a-y		> baray
	Mada	*ma-bala(-fa-ŋa)		> mabala(faŋa)
	Moloko	*balØ-a-y		> balay
	Zulgo	*bara		> bara
	Gemzek	*bara		> bara
		*ma-bara-y	> mabara-Ø^y	
			> ma^yba^yra^y	> mebere
	Merey	*bara		> bara
	Dugwor	*ma-bar-ay	> ma-bar-ay^y	
			> maba^yra^yy	> məberey
MAROUA	Mbazla	*banØ		> ban
HIGI	Psikye	*paØØ-y	> pa-Ø^y	
			> pa^y	> pe

It would appear to be received wisdom in Chadic linguistics that so-called mono-structures, i.e. those that only have a single root consonant (and often also emerge as monosyllabic words phonetically), may form subsystems of their own – and that this would be particularly true for verbs (known as 'monoverbs'). With regard to our PCC reconstructions, however, this appears not to be the case since we have not noted any peculiarities. *Ca structures tend to behave like any other reconstructed lexical items. See the following monoradical verb that we reconstruct with a lexical final /a/ by default (note that Gravina 2014b reconstructs no vowel for such roots).

(238) 'cook, to' PCC *(k-, ma-, RED) **da** (-a, -y, -k, -k^w; FV)

For this verb, and disregarding any obvious augmental material to the simple root, we find the following apparent surface forms of the simple root which vary with regard to their final vowel, features of the initial consonant, and the presence or absence of initial vowels preceding the root consonant:

1. There are voicing distinctions of the root consonant: *da~ta, di~ti*.
2. One language (Malgwa) has a (predictable) change of place of articulation of the palatalised initial consonant: *d^y > *g^y.
3. Final vowel qualities found are
    - a: *da, ta, əda~ida*
    - i: *di, ti, tii*
    - e: *de*
    - ə: *də* (only Sukur)
    - o: *udo* (only Mazera)
    - ay ~ ey: *day, dey, tey*
4. Two languages have an initial (prothetic) vowel:
    - Mazera   *udo*
    - Gidar   *əda~ida*
5. One language has a long final vowel:
    - Mbara   *tii*

The first two issues are taken care of by the more or less regular sound correspondences, according to Gravina (2014b):

The devoicing of *d to *t in the Margi and Higi groups is a regular change. The Malgwa root /g^ja/ is due to a regular general process where palatalised alveolar consonants become palatalised velar consonants.

Let us look now at the differences in surface vowels under the impact of prosody. In the first group under Ø-prosody, we have [a] and [ə], which we assume to represent underlying and diachronic /a/ (unless underlying /a/ is deleted).

(a) Prosody-neutral (Ø-prosody) forms

DABA	Buwal, Gavar		da	
	Mbudum	kə-d(-)u-	da	
		kə-	da	
	Daba		ta	
SUKUR	Sukur		də	
HURZA	Mbuko		da	
MARGI	Bura. Margi, Kilba		ta	
MANDARA	Matal	ma-	t	-ay
	Podoko		ta	
	Glavda		ta	
MOFU	Zulgo		da	
MOFU	Merey		da	
	Dugwor	ma-	d	-ay

6.3 Alternative Reconstructions of the PCC Lexicon   207

	Mofu-Gudur	t
LAMANG	Lamang	da
HIGI	Kamwe-Nkafa, Kirya	ta
	Bana	ta
KOTOKO-NORTH	Mpade	da
GIDAR	Gidar	Prothesis
		əda

Some vowel reflexes obviously represent the impact of Y-prosody stemming from suffixal root-augmentation material.

(b) Y-prosody effects

MARGI	Bura	*tØ-y	> t-i		ti
MANDARA	Malgwa	*da-y	> da-Ø^y		
			> d^{y}a	>	g^{y}a
MOFU	Ouldeme,				
	Muyang	*dØ-y	> d-i	>	di
	Mada	*ma-da-y	> ma-da-Ø^y		
			> ma^y-da^y	>	mede
	Moloko	*da-y	> da-Ø^y		
			> da^y	>	de
	Gemzek	*ma-da-y	> ma-da-Ø^y		
			> ma^y-da^y	>	mede
MOFU	Mofu North	*ma-t-a-y	> ma-t-ay^y		
			> ma^{y}ta^{y}y	>	metey
MAROUA	Giziga-Muturwa,				
	-Marva, Mbazla	*dØ-y	> d-i	>	di
MUSGUM	Mulwi	*dØ-y	> d-i	>	di
GIDAR	Gidar	*da-y	Prothesis		
			> əda-Ø^y		
			> ə^{y}da	>	ida

Note that the following form in Psikye shows the simple root unaffected by prosodies, but – somewhat unusually – the final vowel of the augmented root alone shows the impact of Y-prosody:

HIGI   Psikye   *ta-y-ka   > ta-Ø^y-ka^y > take

Vowel length in Mbara can be explained as result of vowel epenthesis (instead of syllabification of *{-y} as, for instance, in Mulwi of the same MUSGUM group):

MUSGUM   Mbara   *tØ-y   > t-y^y > tə^{y}y   > tii

A third group reflects the effect of W-prosody, which is also due to suffixal root-augmentation material.

(c) W-prosody effect

KOTOKO-SOUTH   Mazera   *da-k^w Prothesis
                                    > əda-Ø^w > ə^{w}da^w >   udo

Looking now at a mono-structure noun, we see that there is basically no difference in the phonological behaviour of the reconstructed forms. Obviously, we are dealing in our reconstructions with the most generalised features of Central Chadic diachronic phonology irrespective of root types and word class. With regard to diachronic morphology as reflected in the (partly) petrified root-augmental material, we note both shared markers, in particular *{-y} and much less often *{-k} and *{-k^w}, as well as presumably some word-class sensitive markers, i.e. different ones for verbs and nouns. A detailed study of these goes beyond the purpose of the present study and must await further research. The following Ca-structure noun is rather stable in maintaining its lexical vowel /a/, and takes less varied suffixal root-augmentation material. There are no traces of W-prosody in this example, but some cases of morphological Y-prosody. It is the most widely spread reconstructable root in Central Chadic: out of 54 languages from all 18 language groups of Central Chadic, only 8 show traces of morphological Y-prosody, which is remarkably few. In the following set of examples, only these cases are illustrated.

(239) 'cow' *(a-, k-, n-, wur-, wa-) ɬa (-a, -y, -n; FV)

MAFA	Mafa	*ɓa-y	> ɓa-Ø^y	> ɓa^y	> ɓe
TERA	Nyimatli	*ɓa-y	> ɓa-Ø^y	> ɓa^y	> ɓe³
MARGI	Bura	*ɬØ-y	> ɬ-i		> ɬi
MANDARA	Mandara	*a-ɬa-y	> a-ɬa-Ø^y	> a^y-ɬa	> eɬa
KOTOKO-NORTH	Mpade	*sa-y	> sa-Ø^y	> s^ya	> ʃa
KOTOKO-SOUTH	Mazera	*k-sa-y	> kə-sa-Ø^y	> kə^y-sa	> kisa
MUSGUM	Mulwi	*ɬa-y	> ɬa-Ø^y	> ɬa^y	> ɬe
GIDAR	Gidar	*wa-ɬØ-ya	> waɬə-y^ya	> waɬə^yya	> waɬiya

The following example is interesting to look at, since Gravina (2014b) reconstructs */y/ as a final radical consonant and this would be a potential source for phonological Y-prosody, whereas our own reconstruction takes this root to be monoradical, so that instances of Y-prosody would have to be analysed as being morphological in nature (which, however, is an academic distinction only). Gravina's motivation to opt for radical */y/ is obviously based on the observation that among a fairly restricted distribution of this root in only five groups anyway, most reconstructed roots show traces of palatalisation, to the exception of Gavar *ŋ-tsa, Matal and Ouldeme *ma-ts-ay, Gemzek dz-ay, Dghweɗe ⁿdza-xa, and Mofu-Gudur *z-. Note that final [i] and endings [ay~ey] have been found all over the place in Central Chadic and are attributed in this study to suffixal root-augmental material.

---

³ According to P. Newman (p.c. 2020), the final vowel is /a/ in all Tera dialects, i.e. ɓa. Y-prosody appears when the word is inflected, e.g. ɓe-ku 'cows'. Gravina's database, however, gives ɓe for 'Nyimatli' without any further comments.

6.3 Alternative Reconstructions of the PCC Lexicon   209

(240)   'bite, to' PCC *(ŋ-, ⁿga-, ma-, n-) **dza** (-a, -y, -n, -w, -x ; FV)
Note: Gravina (2014b) gives the root as **dzay**.

DABA	Buwal	*ŋ-tsa-y	> ŋ-tsa-Ø^y		> ŋtʃa
	Gavar	*ŋ-tsa			> ŋtsa
	Daba	*ⁿga-tsØ-y	> ⁿgats-Ø^y	> ⁿgats^y	> ⁿgatʃ
MAFA	Mafa	*ndza-y	> ndza-Ø^y	> ndz^{y}a^y	> ndʒe
		*dzØ-y	> dz-Ø^y	> dz^y	> dʒ-
MANDARA	Matal	*ma-ts-a-y	> ma-ts-ay		> matsay
	Podoko	*n-dza-y-wa	> ndzawa-Ø^y	> ndz^{y}a^{y}wa^y	> ⁿdʒewe
	Malgwa	*dza-y	> dza-Ø^y	> dz^{y}a	> dʒa
	Dghwede	*n-dza-xa			> ⁿdzaxa
MOFU	Ouldeme	*ma-ts-a-y	> ma-ts-ay		> matsay
	Zulgo	*dza-y(-n)	> dza-Ø^y(-r)	> dza^y(-r)	> dze(-r)
	Gemzek	*dz-a-y	> dz-ay		> dzay
		*ma-dza-y	> madza-Ø^y	> ma^{y}dza^y	> medze
	Mofu North	*ma-z-a-y	> maz-ay^y	> ma^{y}za^{y}y	> mezey
	Mofu-Gudur	*zØ-			> z-
MAROUA	Mbazla	*tsØ-y	> ts-i^y	> ts^y-i	> tʃi

Further in this context, one particular – and, at least as surface form in many individual languages, apparently monoradical – root deserves to be looked at which contains, possibly or likely, both */y/ and /*w/ as radical consonants (unless /y/ is again attributed to augmental material of the root). The reconstructions show a remarkable loss (see 3.1.2.2) of any of the three radical consonants, so that in many languages the root becomes synchronically monoradical. There are surprisingly few effects of phonological labialisation prosody originating from the postulated first radical /w/. Y-prosody is noticed much more often, with the entailing problem of deciding whether this is always attributable to the third radical /y/, or whether there is not also evidence for morphological palatalisation stemming from suffixal *{-y}. There are no formal criteria to say which would be which. Also, there are some cases of potential reduplicative (RED) root augmentation. Note that this root is again very widespread in Central Chadic (found in 43 languages from 16 of the 18 groups).

(241)   'give birth, to' PCC *(ma-, RED) **w(a)x(a)ya** (-k, -k^w, -n, -l; FV)

MAFA	Mafa	*Ø Ø ya		ya
	Cuvok	*Ø xaya		haya
TERA	Tera	*Ø x Øa		xa
SUKUR	Sukur	*w x ya	Metathesis	
			wyxa	
			> yy^{y}xa	
			> yə^{y}ixa	yiiha
		*w x ya	Metathesis	
			wyxa	
			> yy^{y}xa	
			> yyØØ	
			> y-i	yi

210   Full Lexical Reconstructions

HURZA	Mbuko	*waxayØ		*wahay*
	Vame	*waxaØØ		*wah(a)*
MARGI	Bura	*w x ya	Metathesis	
			wyxa	
			> yyØa	
			> yia	*iya*
		*w x ya	Metathesis	
			wyxa	
			> yyØa	
			> yia	*yia*
	Margi, Margi-South, Kilba	*Ø Ø ya		*ya*
MANDARA	Podoko	*Ø x Øa		*ha*
	Malgwa	*Ø Ø ya		*ya*
	Glavda	*w x ya-ka	Metathesis	
			wyxa-ka	
			> yyØØ-ga	
			> yiga	*yiga*
		*RED+Ø Ø ya-na	> ya+ya-na	*yayana*
	Dghweɗe	*w x ya-ka	Metathesis	
			wyxa-ka	
			> yyØØ-ga	
			> yi^y-ga	
			> yiga^y	*yige*
MOFU	Ouldeme	*w Ø ØØ-y	> w-i	*wì*
	Moloko	*w Ø Øa-y	> wa-Ø^y	
			> wa^y	*we*
	Zulgo	*w Ø Øa		*wa*
	Gemzek	*ma-w Ø Øa-y	> mawa-Ø^y	
			> ma^{y}wa^y	*mewe*
		*ma-w Ø Øa	> ma-wa	*mawa*
	Merey	*w Ø Øa		*wa*
	Mofu North	*ma-Ø Ø y-a-y	> may-ay^y	
			> ma^{y}ya^{y}y	*meyey*
	Mofu-Gudur	*Ø Ø yØ	> y-	*y-*
MAROUA	Giziga-Marva	*w x yØ	Metathesis	
			wyx	
			> yyØ	
			> yi	*yi*
		*Ø Ø ya	> y^{y}a	
			> ya^y	*ye*
	Mbazla	*w x yØ	Metathesis	
			wyx	
			> yyØ	
			> yi	*yi*
		*RED+wax yØ	Metathesis	
			RED+wayx	
			> RED+yayx	

6.3 Alternative Reconstructions of the PCC Lexicon   211

			> ya+yʸa-y'	
			> yaʸ-yØy'	
			> yaʸyi'	yéyi'
LAMANG	Lamang	*Ø Ø ya		ya
	Hdi	*RED+Ø Ø yØ	> ya+y	yay
HIGI	Kamwe-Nkafa	*Ø Ø ya		yə
	Kamwe-Futu	*Ø Ø ya-ka	> yʸa-ka	
			> yaʸkə	yekə
		*Ø Ø ya-k-kʷa	> yʸakəgʷa	
			> yaʸkəgʷaʷ	yekəgʷo
	Kirya, Bana	*Ø Ø ya		ya
KOTOKO-ISLAND	Buduma	*w Ø yØ	> wʷy	
			> wəʷy	wuy
		*w Ø yØ	> wʷy	
			> wəʷəy	wuəy
KOTOKO-NORTH	Afade, Mpade	*w Ø ya	> wØʸa	
			> waʸ	we
		*w Ø Øa-n	> wa-n	wan
	Malgbe	*RED+waØ ØØ-n	> wa+wʷə-n	
			> wa+wəʷn	wawun
KOTOKO-CENTRAL	Lagwan	*w Ø ya-l	> wØʸa-l	
			> waʸ-l	wel
		*RED+w Ø Øa-n	> wa+wəʷ-n	wawun
	Mser	*w Ø ya	> wa-Øʸ	
			> waʸ	we
KOTOKO-SOUTH	Zina	*w Ø ya	> wəyʸa	
			> wəʸya	wiya
MUSGUM	Mulwi	*w Ø yØ	> wi	wi
	Mbara	*w Ø yØ	> wəyʸ	
			> wəʸi	wii
GIDAR	Gidar	*RED+w Ø Øa	> w+wʷa	
			> əw-wʷa	
			> əʷuwa	uuwa
		*RED+w Ø Øa	> w+wa	uwa
		*w Ø yØ-na	> wyʸ-na	
			> wəʸyna	wiina

6.3.6 Regarding Glottal Stop and Glottalisation

Throughout the data and in an apparently non-systematic manner, transcriptions of modern Central Chadic language data contain unexpected indications of a glottal stop or indication towards glottalised articulation (mainly but not exclusively in the KOTOKO groups). The data remain partly inconclusive in this regard, but deserve to be taken note of in this book for the sake of completeness, see Wolff (forthcoming). Note that neither Newman (1977a) for Proto-Chadic nor Gravina (2014a) for PCC suggested reconstructing the glottal stop as a phoneme of the proto-language; Jungraithmayr and Shimizu (1981: 20) list '(ʔ)' as doubtful. Stolbova (2016: 43) regards the 'problem of Ch[adic] *ʔ' as unsolved.

6.3.6.1 Emergence of Glottal Stops in Surface Representations

On both synchronic and diachronic levels of description of Central Chadic languages, /ɗ/ and /ɗ+y/ have allophonic variation ['] and ['y] (simplifying to ['] before [i]). Occasionally, also /ɓ/ (< PCC */ɓ/) is reflected by a glottal stop, as for instance in the word for 'to laugh' (after metathesising with the initial root consonant). In our reconstructions, this is borne out by comparative evidence regarding languages of the MARGI, MAROUA and HIGI groups, e.g.

(242)	Gloss	PCC simple root	GROUP	language	underlying	surface
	bone	*ɗ y(a)ɬa	MAROUA	Mbazla	ɗa-ɗ ØaɬØ	'a-'aɬ
			HIGI	Kamwe-Nkafa, Bana	ɗʸ y ɬa	'yithlə
	night	*r(a)v(a)ɗa	MARGI	Margi	Ø v ɗʸØ-y	vi'i
				Margi-South	Ø v ɗʸØ-y-kʷ	vʷi'i
				Kilba	Ø v ɗʸØ-y-kʷ	vu'i
	laugh, to	*ɣʷ(a)b(a)sa	HIGI	Psikye	'w sʸØ-y	
					< 'w sʸØ-y	'wuʃi
				Kamwe-Nkafa		'uʃi
				cf. Kirya	Øʷ ɓ sʸØ-y	ɓʷiʃi

Slightly more complicated are the issues with regard to the word for 'brain' (see 6.4), for which Gravina (2014a) discusses two different potential PCC forms: *raⁿgaɬ ʸ and *ɗaraɬ ʸ. For the latter option, he states that '[t]he *ɗ is lost in Matal, Zulgo, Gemzek and Giziga-Marva, and has combined with *ɬ in Afade, Maltam and Mser. These are common sporadic processes.' In order to explain the otherwise erratic occurrence of the glottal stop in the KOTOKO group languages, a reconstructed */ɗ/ would indeed be a plausible source that could be assumed to have metathesised into C₃ position.

(243)	Gloss	PCC simple root	GROUP	language	underlying	surface
	brain	*ɗ(a)r(a)ɬa	KOTOKO-NORTH	Afade	ʔar ɬØ-yʸ	
					> aʸrɬʔ-i	erɬ'i
				Maltam	ʔar ɬØ-yʸ	
					> aʸrəʸɬʔ-i	eriɬ'i
			KOTOKO-CENTRAL	Mser	m-ʔaraɬa-yʸ	
					> maʸraʸsʔəʸ	meres'i

Occasionally, there appear to be allophonic reflexes of */k/, */kʷ/, */gʷ/ and */x/ as glottal stop in all positions (initial, medial, final), as we might assume for the following examples.

6.3 Alternative Reconstructions of the PCC Lexicon   213

(244) | Gloss | PCC simple root | GROUP | language | underlying | surface |
|---|---|---|---|---|---|
| fly | *dz(a)k^w(a)ɗa | BATA | Jimi | *dz k^w yØ-n | dʒi'in |
| | | | Sharwa | *dz k^w yØ | dʒi'i |
| give birth, to | *w(a)x(a)ya | MAROUA | Mbazla | *RED+wax yØ Metathesis RED+wayx > RED+yayx > ya+yØyx | yɛyi' |
| grasshopper | *xw(a)y(a)k^{w}a | MARGI | Kilba | *xayk^{w}a Metathesis xak^{w}yə | ha'yi |
| | | LAMANG | Hdi | *x y k^{w}a Metathesis xk^{w}ya > xə'y^y > xə^y'i | hi'i |
| ram | *g^w(a)z(a)ma | MAROUA | Mbazla | *ʔazamØ-y > 'azam-Ø^y > 'a^{y}z^{y}a^{y}m | 'eʒem |
| | | KOTOKO-NORTH | Afade | *ʔ s mØ-y Metathesis sʔm-y > sʔm-Ø^y > sʔə^{y}m | s'im |
| white | *k^w(a)ɗ(a)ka | MAFA | Mafa | *RED+k^{w}ɗɗaka-y > k^{w}əɗ+k^{w}əɗɗaka-Ø^y > k^{w}ə^{y}ɗk^{w}ə^{y}ɗɗa^{y,y}a^y | k^{w}iɗk^{w}iɗɗe'e |

6.3.6.2 ['w] (and [p']?) Reflecting PCC */C^w/

In two of our restricted set of selected examples, surface ['w] is a reflex of a reconstructed PCC labial(ised) consonant, namely */ɣ^w/ in the root for 'laugh' and */w/ in the root for 'dream'. This begs the question whether or not 'dream' should not be reconstructed also with */x^w/ rather than with plainly */w/ (note that Gravina (2014a, 2014b) indeed reconstructs C_2 as */h^w/).

(245) | Gloss | PCC simple root | GROUP | language | underlying | surface |
|---|---|---|---|---|---|
| laugh | *ɣ^w(a)b(a)sa | HIGI | Kamwe-Nkafa | *'w Ø sØ-y | 'uʃi |
| | | | Psikye | *'w Ø sØ-y | 'wuʃi |
| | | | Bana | *'w Ø sØ-y | 'wəʃi |
| dream | *s(a)w(a)na ~ *s(a)x^w(a)na | MARGI | Kilba | *s 'w nØ-y | ʃi'uni |

In a third example, surface /p'/ could be a reflex of underlying /k^w/, as in the following example.

(246) | Gloss | PCC simple root | GROUP | language | underlying | surface |
|---|---|---|---|---|---|
| grasshopper | *x^w(a)y(a)k^{w}a | DABA | Daba | *wayk^{w}Ø | wayəp' |

6.3.6.3 */ʔ/ as an Unidentified Root Augment?

In quite a number of examples, a glottal stop ['] is indicated at the end of a word in the transcriptions of data. The frequency of its unexpected occurrence in this particular position could be an indication as to its potential origin, namely as another suffixal root augment. Personally, I do not see enough evidence for it, but the following list of examples offers the respective data in a slightly manipulated representation in order to allow interpretation in terms of a hypothetical root-augmental nature of *{-ʔ}. (Note that in the reconstructions under 6.4, this aspect has been left unconsidered and the final glottal stop is in some cases simply not accounted for in the PCC reconstructions.)

(247)	Gloss	PCC simple root	GROUP	language	underlying?	surface
	dog	*k(a)ra	MAROUA	Mbazla	*k ra-y-ʔ	krɛ'
	dream	*sw(a)na	BATA	Sharwa	*s Ø na-ʔa	ʃinə'ə
	extinguish	*m(a)ta	DABA	Daba	*m tsØ-y-ʔ-n	mitʃi'n
	grasshopper	*xʷ(a)y(a)kʷa	DABA	Daba	*way pØ-ʔ	wayəp'
			MARGI	Kilba	*xay ØØ-y-ʔ Metathesis xay-ʔ-y Metathesis xaʔy-i	ha'yi
			LAMANG	Hdi	*x y ØØ-y-ʔ Metathesis xy-ʔ-y	hi'i

6.3.6.4 Another Look at the Root for 'Water'

In the context of glottalisation, it may be in order to take another look at the root for 'water', which P. Newman (1977a: 10) explicitly reconstructs as vowel-initial for PC (*am), but which by Gravina (2014a, 2014b) and in this study is reconstructed as consonant-initial in PCC. For Central Chadic, Gravina sees 'evidence for a glottal element, in most cases [ʔ]', but he reconstructs */d/ (*dəyəm), quite likely in order to avoid a contradiction to the a priori postulation that no glottal stop should be reconstructed for PCC. Indeed, there is a remarkable presence of a glottal element in some languages, while it is lacking in many others. The presence of this glottal element would remain unaccounted for if it wasn't reconstructed for in the PCC root. Languages that show reflexes of an initial glottal element, which in some cases undergoes metathesis, strongly suggest reconstructing a triradical PCC root *ʔ y(a)ma, which also happens to largely match Gravina's reconstruction *dəyəm. Our own PCC reconstruction, however, also conflicts with the widely held assumption (see 3.2.1) that *ʔ cannot or should not be reconstructed for PCC. Some Central Chadic languages, however, and as it would appear, do consider this root to be triradical in underlying structure (√ C C(a)Ca *ʔy(a)ma) and to show reflexes of both the glottal element *ʔ and *y, occurring either individually in a word, or combined. Therefore, a tentative triradical structure will be reflected in our reconstructions of individual language roots under 6.4. Note that in quite a number of CC languages, either *ʔ or *y or both are missing in the synchronic forms of present-day languages (see 6.4). For languages displaying the assumed triradical diachronic structure, see the following list.

(248)	Gloss	PCC simple root	GROUP	language	underlying √ C C(a)Ca	surface
	water	*ʔy(a)ma	BATA	Gude	*ʔy ma-na Metathesis ʔmay-na Metathesis maʔy-na	maʼinə
				Jimi, Sharwa	*ʔy ma Metathesis ʔmay Metathesis maʔy	maʼi
			TERA	Tera	*ɗy mØ	ɗyim ~ yim
			HURZA	Mbuko	*a-ʔØamØ	aʼam
			MARGI	Margi	*ʔy ma > ʔyʸmə > ʔiməʸ	ʼimi
			MANDARA	Matal	*ʔyawØ > yyaw	y:aw
			KOTOKO-SOUTH	Mazera	*a-ʔy mØ > aʔØʸəm > aʔəʸm	aʔim
			MUSGUM	Mbara	*ʔØamØ	ʼam

6.3.6.5 Are There Traces of 'Glottalisation Prosody'?

Languages belonging to the KOTOKO groups, in particular, but in one case also in Sukur of the one-member SUKUR group, show a remarkable behaviour regarding the feature glottalisation, which in Central Chadic is usually and reconstructably associated with the so-called 'implosives' ɓ and ɗ plus likely a third member of the series with yet uncertain place of articulation (see 3.2.1). As was already noted further above, P. Newman (1977a: 9–10) reconstructed three glottalised consonants for PC, namely ɓ and ɗ, plus *'J ('probably a glottalized palatal stop'); he explicitly excluded the glottal stop as a phoneme in PC. Likewise, Gravina (2014a) excludes the glottal stop from his list of PCC consonants, and only recognises */ɓ/ and */ɗ/ for PCC.

More remarkable is that some Central Chadic languages show glottalisation apparently independent of the generally assumed inventory of glottalised (so-called 'implosive') consonants, namely they associate a glottalisation feature with consonants of other places and manners of articulation, namely s', ɫ' and k'. Interestingly, in four out of the seven instances in our alternative reconstructions, the PCC reconstructions do contain a glottalised consonant, but elsewhere in the word. In a more traditional way, the situation could be explained by assuming sequencing of metathesis, i.e. we could relate the

216   Full Lexical Reconstructions

position of the glottalisation feature to instances of (multiple) metathesis, which would have shifted it from the original position to another. Even though the quantitative basis is small, this still raises the question whether we are witnessing the operation of 'glottalisation prosody', according to which possibly any one of the consonants of the particular root must carry the feature [+glottal], not necessarily identical to the one from which it originally stems. See the following list of examples and the accompanying notes.

(249) bone *ɗ y(a)ła   KOTOKO-   Afade   *a-n-ɗ y łØ
                         NORTH   Metathesis
                                               a-n-ɗły
                                               Metathesis
                                               a-n-łɗy
                                               > anłɗi
                                               > aʸnłɗi   enł'i

                         KOTOKO-   Mazera *a-RED+ɗ y sa
                         SOUTH   Metathesis
                                               a-RED+yɗsa
                                               Metathesis
                                               a-RED+ysɗa
                                               > a-RED+Øʸsɗa
                                               > a-səʸ-s'aʸ   asis'e

Note: In Afade and in Mazera, the original glottalised alveolar */ɗ/ could be assumed to have been 'weakened' to glottal stop; by double metathesis the glottal stop now follows /ł/ (in Afade), respectively /s/ (in Mazera), with possible fusion to become a glottalised lateral fricative /ł'/ in Afade and a glottalised /s'/ in Mazera.

(250) fly   *dz(a)kʷ(a)ɗa KOTOKO-   Maltam *s w ɗØ-y
                            NORTH   Metathesis
                                              sɗw-y
                                              > sɗw-iʸ
                                              > s'əʸwi   s'ɨwi

                            KOTOKO-   Mser   *m-s w ɗØ-y
                            CENTRAL   Metathesis
                                              m-sɗw-y
                                              > m-s'əw-iʸ
                                              > m-s'əʸw-i   ms'ɨwi

Note: In Maltam and Mser, the original glottalised alveolar */ɗ/ has been 'weakened' to glottal stop; by metathesis the glottal stop now follows /s/ with possible fusion to yield glottalised /s'/.

(251) suck, to *s(a)wɓa KOTOKO-   Afade   *s wɓØ
                           NORTH   Metathesis
                                              sɓw
                                              > sʔfwʷ
                                              > s'əʷfw   s'ufu

6.3 Alternative Reconstructions of the PCC Lexicon

	Mpade	*sawɓØ	
		Metathesis	
		saɓw	
		> saʔfw	
		> sʔafw	
		> s'afw	s'afu
	Malgbe	*sawɓa-y	
		> saØʔfə-Ø^y	
		> saʔfə^y	
		Metathesis	
		sʔafə^y	s'afi
KOTOKO- CENTRAL	Lagwan	*s wɓØ-y-n	
		Metathesis	
		sɓw-y-n	
		> sʔfw^w-Ø^y-n	
		> s'ə^{y}fə^{w}wə^{w}n	s'ifuwun
	Mser	*n-sawɓa-y	
		> n-saØʔfa-Ø^y	
		Metathesis	
		n-sʔafə^y	ns'afi

Note: In all KOTOKO languages, the glottal feature may at one point in history have been associated with PCC */ɓ/, which in the modern languages has re-segmentalised > ʔ+f in the synchronic underlying structure. The glottalisation feature apparently 'floats' around, finally associating with initial /s/ and fusing to yield glottalised /s'/. (Note that in Mpade, Malgbe and Mser we observe – unique in our selected data – metathesis involving a consonant */ʔ/ and the vowel /a/. The implication of this observation for a more comprehensive analysis of the historical phonology of Central Chadic remains at present unexplored.) This is the closest we can get to 'glottalisation prosody' in any of the Central Chadic languages in the reconstructed data. (Afade and Lagwan show phonological W-prosody effects originating from root-internal /w/, while Malgbe, Lagwan and Mser show morphological Y-prosody stemming from *{-y}.)

(252) razor₁ ***p(a)ɗ(a)k^{w}a** SUKUR Sukur *p dak^{w}Ø-y
> pədak^w-Ø^y
> pə^{y}da^{yw}k *pidæk'*

*p ɗ k^{w}Ø-y
> pəɗək^w-Ø^y
> pə^{y}ɗə^{y}kw *piɗik'u*

Note: In Sukur, the evidence is inconclusive, since one of the forms displays /ɗ/, the other plain /d/ (if this is not due to faulty transcription). Either the glottal feature in *pidæk'* has indeed been transferred from originally /d/ > /k'/, or the form *pidîk'u* does indeed allow glottal feature 'spreading' and manifestation on two different consonants (/d/ and /k'/). If any of these explanations holds, this again comes close to 'glottalisation prosody'.

The above ought to be compared to the following example, in which the KOTOKO language Mser carries one of the 'exceptional' glottalised consonants, but where our PCC reconstruction does not contain a glottalised consonant that we could assume to have been the diachronic source of the glottalisation feature. The emergence of glottalised /s'/ must here remain unaccounted for by comparative evidence and be considered a likely Mser innovation.

(253)   foot   *tsa   KOTOKO-CENTRAL   Mser   *m-sa-y-ka
                                              > m-sə-$Ø^y$-kə
                                              > msə^{y}kə^y *ms'ikɨ*

Note, however, that quite likely in languages of the KOTOKO groups as well, a synchronic glottal stop may originate from the weakening of a diachronic velar, whether labialised or not, as described for other CC languages under 6.3.6.1, so that we are not necessarily dealing with a KOTOKO group innovation in all cases where there appears to be no underlying glottalised consonant from where the glottalisation feature could have originated. See Afade *g^w > *ʔ in the following example.

(254)   ram   *g^w(a)z(a)ma   KOTOKO-NORTH   Afade   *ʔ s mØ-y
                                                       Metathesis
                                                       sʔm-y
                                                       > sʔəm-$Ø^y$
                                                       > sʔə^{y}m   *s'im*

6.4 PCC Lexical Reconstructions: Data and Details

In this final section, we will confront Gravina's most welcome and groundbreaking comparative work with our own detailed reconstructions based on the particular approach chosen for this study. We address in great detail a selection out of the total of 250 items of the available database (Gravina 2014b), which Gravina had built from 60 Central Chadic languages, along with a number of variants and different sources totalling to 66, out of a total of 78 Central Chadic languages listed in the Ethnologue (Lewis 2009). Our selection of 64 lexical reconstructions covers about 25 per cent of the lexical items in the database. This was considered to be sufficient to meet the goals of this study, namely:

(a) to show the general principles and recurring diachronic processes related to PCC lexical reconstruction based on the particular approach chosen;
(b) to provide an illustrative corpus of reconstructed items, including in particular those that could be a priori considered problematic or controversial;
(c) not to overload this book with another 300 pages of meticulous data presentation if we were to address all 250 lemmata (Wolff forthcoming).

6.4 PCC Lexical Reconstructions

We have focused on reconstructions that contain potentially controversial issues, like:

- the treatment of schwa (as either phonemic */ə/ or as pro-/epenthetic in nature);
- the need to reconstruct or not to reconstruct a high front vowel */i/ as phonemic in Proto-Central Chadic (PCC) in addition to */a/;
- the reconstruction of both Y-prosody and W-prosody as diachronic phonological processes in a unified fashion rather than reconstructing just Y-prosody (and treating it as a phonemic unit almost on a par with three reconstructed vowels).

This study is based on individually looking at and historically analysing some 1,500 words representing up to 64 languages or language varieties, which gives an average of about 25 language representations for each lexical item that has been reconstructed. (In reality, lexical items are represented in between 3 and more than 50 languages, depending on their regional spread among Central Chadic languages, which may differ considerably. In this sense, not all reconstructions presented here are truly Proto-Central Chadic roots; some have only areal significance, and a few are so-called pseudo-PCC roots when they reflect fully integrated loans from neighbouring non-Chadic languages, in particular Nilo-Saharan Kanuri.) All items that were analysed and used for reconstruction are listed below in considerable detail.

As said, and in order to illustrate both methodology and detailed results of our alternative reconstructions, it was not considered necessary to subject all 250 lexical items in the database to such detailed alternative reconstruction. The selection and number of those reconstructions presented are considered sufficient to allow critical evaluation and stimulus for further comparative (Central) Chadic research by fellow Chadicists, Afroasiaticists and linguists of other specialisations who are interested in historical-comparative research on human languages.

The data and PCC reconstructions will be presented in a standardised manner. For the sake of convenience and where available, possible or likely related reconstructions for Proto-Chadic (PC) will be added for reference from three sources: PN (Newman, Paul. 1977a. *Chadic Classification and Reconstructions*), JS (Jungraithmayr, Herrmann & Kiyoshi Shimizu. 1981. *Chadic Lexical Roots.* Vol II.), and OS (Stolbova, Olga. 2016. *Chadic Etymological Dictionary*). Diacritics for pitch and tone will not be indicated either in the reconstructions or in the quotations of the original data from the database. In a few cases, missing items from LAMANG group languages (Lamang, Hdi) are added from my own data (Wolff 2015) and a recent dictionary of Hdi (Frajzyngier et al. 2015); both published sources were not accessible to Richard Gravina at the time of his study and were not available for inclusion in his database (Gravina 2014b).

The representation of consonants within the root will largely follow Gravina (2014a, 2014b) and thus implies reference to his observations and remarks on sound changes, which will be cited verbatim for each reconstructed item. (For slight differences of opinion about the PCC consonant inventory, see 3.2.1.) The format is described by Gravina in the introduction to his database (no page numbers in the electronic version consulted) as follows:

The first part of the entry gives the headword in bold, the part of speech, and the gloss in English and French (in italic). Following this, figures are given in parentheses for the number of present-day languages where reflexes of the reconstructed form have been attested, and the number of groups within Central Chadic represented by these languages. There are eighteen groups in total.

After the language statistics, there is an indication of the reliability of the reconstruction. This takes the form of a letter from A to E, with A being the most reliable. The level is determined according to the consistency of the data, the difficulty of the reconstruction, and the quantity of data available.

There then follows a commentary on the reconstruction, indicating where sound changes have taken place, how the reconstruction has been determined, and whether the word has come from Proto-Central Chadic, a later neologism, or is borrowed. Sound changes are categorised as 'regular' if they follow an established rule, 'irregular' if they go against an established rule, 'sporadic' if the change is common but not predictable (e.g. loss of *h), and 'unestablished' if the change has not been researched and it is not yet known if it is regular or not.

All this information will be quoted verbatim for each lexical item that has been reconstructed in the present study. Note that quoting from and thereby linking to Gravina's work does not mean that all of Gravina's reconstructions and observations concerning consonants are accepted as valid. The present study just is not concerned with the reconstruction of consonants for PCC, but rather focuses on surface vowels and their underlying representations and reconstructions. It is our firm belief that final judgements on PCC consonants can only be made after the nature of and complexities concerning vowels and prosodies have been satisfactorily solved. And this is the sole concern of the present study. Accordingly, Gravina's observations regarding the reconstruction of both consonants and vowels may have to be modified and adjusted, should the results of the present study be taken as a valid starting point for alternative reconstructions of the PCC lexicon.

After quoting Gravina's PCC reconstructions and observations, we proceed to the internal reconstruction of selected diachronic forms underlying the synchronic phonetic surface representations in the individual languages, according to our own prosody-based approach, which allows for only one single true vowel phoneme: */a/. The resulting synchronic segmental surface realisations are then given in *italics*. The reader is encouraged to cross-check

6.4 PCC Lexical Reconstructions

these forms with the quotations in Gravina's (2014b) database, which is freely available electronically.

Note that the telegram-style short explanations of diachronic processes following the examples are not meant to serve as complete descriptions of word histories, but just to highlight the most significant processes. For more details, the reader is referred to the topical sections in the body of the book.

The standardised format for the presentation of the data is the following:

gloss	Alternative reconstruction (**PCC**)					
	Optional left augment	Root C(a)C(a)Ca	Optional right augment	FV	+Y, +W	PC: * ... (PN) * ... (JS) * ... (OS)
	Quote from: Richard Gravina (2014b). *Proto-Central Chadic Reconstructions.*					
LANGUAGE GROUP 1.-18.	language glossonym	Left augment	Simple root type root type *root underlying form incl. vowel epenthesis and prosodies *surface form* Comments: highlighted diachronic processes	Right augment	FV	+Y, +W

Note that, in this section and for reasons of saving space, diachronic processes are indicated simultaneously in the same lines of the illustrations. This refers to metathesis, deletion of segments, vowel pro-/epenthesis, marking both the segmental sources and targets of prosodification by raised ^{y} and ^{w}, syllabification of weak radicals, centralisation of /a/, etc., which are highlighted in the comments. For instance, for the internal reconstruction of the lexical item 'ashes' in Bachama (BATA), i.e. *f taɗa-y-k^{w}a in Proto-Bachama, the transcription conventions fə^{y}ta^{yw}ɗə^y-Ø^w-y^{y}a^y here include reference to metathesis *-y-k^w > -k^w-y; complete prosodification k^w > Ø^w; partial prosodification of /y/ > y^y; vowel epenthesis; Y-prosody affecting all vowels; W- and Y-prosodies combined affecting medial /a/.

arm

	Alternative reconstruction (**PCC**)					
	dz va	-y, -k^w, -n	a	+Y, +W	PC: *db (-r) (JS), *dVb- (OS)	

dzivi ^{y} n. arm *bras* (4 groups, 14 languages) C syn: paɮa, hira.
This root is found in the south-west of the Central Chadic area. Evidence for the palatalisation prosody comes only from the BATA group. The *dz is realised as /ts/ or /t/ in the BATA group, and as /d/ or /r/ in the MANDARA group. There is a regular change *d to /r/ within the Mandara group, but only in intervocalic position. The other changes are unestablished.

222   Full Lexical Reconstructions

BATA	Bata	√ C Ca	+Y

Bata
√ C Ca   +Y
*t fa   -y
təʸfaʸ   -Øʸ
tife
Vowel epenthesis; prosody affecting all vowels

Gude
√ C Ca   +Y
*ts ØØ   -y-n   a
tsʸəʸ   -yʸn   a
tʃiinə
Vowel epenthesis; prosody affecting epenthetic vowel and initial consonant; syllabification of /y/; centralisation of FV; Cəʸ+y > Cii

Jimi
√ C Ca   +Y
*ts ØØ   -y-n
tsʸəʸ   -yʸən
tʃiyən
Vowel epenthesis; prosody affecting first syllable epenthetic vowel and initial consonant

Sharwa
√ C Ca   +Y
*t vØ   -y
təʸv   -iʸ
tivi
Vowel epenthesis; prosody affecting epenthetic vowel; syllabification of /y/

Tsuvan
√ C Ca   +Y
*ts va   -y
tsʸəvaʸ   -Øʸ
tʃəve
Vowel epenthesis; prosody affecting initial consonant and final /a/

MANDARA   **Mandara**
√ C Ca   +Y
*r va   -y
aʸrva   -Øʸ
erva
Vowel prothesis; prosody affecting prothetic vowel

Malgwa
√ C Ca
*r va

6.4 PCC Lexical Reconstructions

		ǝrva Vowel prothesis	
	Glavda	√ C Ca *dØa dǝ Centralisation of final /a/	
		√ C Ca *d va -y dǝʸva -Øʸ dɨva Vowel epenthesis; prosody affecting epenthetic vowel	+Y
	Dghweɗe	√ C Ca *d va dǝva Vowel epenthesis	
LAMANG	Lamang	√ C Ca *dz va -kʷ dzǝvaʷ -Øʷ dzǝvo Vowel epenthesis; prosody affecting final /a/	+W
	Hdi	√ C Ca *dz vØ -kʷ dzǝv -w dzǝvu Vowel epenthesis; desegmentalisation of *{-kʷ} > /w/; syllabification /w/ > u	+W
HIGI	Kamwe- Futu	√ C Ca *dz ɓa -y dzǝʸɓǝ -Øʸ dzɨɓǝ Vowel epenthesis; prosody affecting epenthetic vowel; centralisation of final /a/	+Y
	Psikye	√ C Ca *dz va dzǝvǝ Vowel epenthesis; centralisation of final /a/	

	Bana	√ C Ca		
		*d va		
		dəvə		
		Vowel epenthesis; centralisation of final /a/		

ashes

Alternative reconstruction (**PCC**)
p ts(a)ɗa   -y, -k^w, -n   a   +Y, +W   PC *bətuə (PN),
                                                         *bt(u) (h-, m-, -r)
                                                         (JS)

pitsiɗ n. ash *cendres* (7 groups, 17 languages) B

The *p has the reflex *f in several groups, even though *p is expected. In Proto-Mofu this has become *v, which is an irregular change. The subsequent change *v > b in Zulgo and Dugwor is regular. *ts has the reflex *t in Proto-Bata and Proto-Mofu, which is a regular process, and the *t has developed into /d/ in Buduma, which is an unestablished process. The Mofu North form may be a borrowing. There is no clear explanation for the presence of *u in Proto-Margi and Proto-Mandara. The *ɗ has been lost in several groups, which is a common sporadic process.

BATA	Bata	√ C C Ca		+Y
		*f tØa	-y	
		fə^{y}ta^y	-Ø^y	
		fite		
		Vowel epenthesis; prosody affecting epenthetic vowel and final /a/		
	Bachama	√ C CaCa		+Y, +W
		*f taɗa	-y -k^w	a
		fə^{y}ta^{yw}ɗə^y	-Ø^w-y^y	a^y
		fitœdiye		
		Metathesis *-y-k^w > -k^w-y; prosodification k^w > ^{w}; vowel epenthesis; Y-prosody affecting all vowels; W- and Y-prosodies combined affecting medial /a/		
TERA	Tera	√ C C Ca		+Y
		*p dz tØ	-y	
		pədz^{y}ə^{y}t	-Ø^y	
		pədʒit		
		Vowel epenthesis; prosody affecting final syllable onset consonant and (epenthetic) vowel		
	Nyimatli	√ C C Ca		+Y
		*p z tØ	-y	

6.4 PCC Lexical Reconstructions

		pəz^{y}ə^{y}t -Ø^y	
		pəʒit	

Vowel epenthesis; prosody affecting final syllable onset consonant and (epenthetic) vowel

	Hwana	√ C C Ca	
		*f s Øa -y	+Y
		fə^{y}s^{y}a^y -Ø^y	
		fiʃe	

Vowel epenthesis; prosody affecting final syllable consonant and all vowels

MARGI	Kilba	√ C C Ca	
		*p ts ɗØ -k^w	
		pətsəɗ -w	
		pətsəɗu	

Vowel epenthesis; weakening *k^w > /w/; syllabification of /w/

MANDARA	Glavda	√ C C Ca	
		*f t ØØ	
		aft	
		aft	

Vowel prothesis

		√ C C Ca
		*f ts Øa
		aftsa
		aftsa

Vowel prothesis

	Dghweɗe	√ C C Ca	+Y, +W
		*f ts ɗa -y -k^w	
		ftsə^{w}ɗa^y -Ø^y-Ø^w	
		ftsut'e	

Vowel epenthesis; W-prosody affecting epenthetic vowel, Y-prosody affecting final /a/

MOFU	Muyang	√ C C Ca	+Y
		*v t ØØ -y	
		və^{y}t -i^y	
		viti	

Vowel epenthesis; prosody affecting epenthetic vowel; syllabification of /y/

	Moloko	√ C C Ca	+Y
		*v t Øa -y	
		vəta^y -Ø^y	
		vəte	
		Vowel epenthesis; prosody affecting final /a/	
	Zulgo	√ C C Ca	+Y
		*b t Øa -y	
		bə^{y}ta^y -Ø^y	
		bite	
		Vowel epenthesis; prosody affecting all vowels	
	Dugwor	√ C C Ca	
		*b t Øa	
		bəta	
		bəta	
		Vowel epenthesis	
	Mofu North	√ C C Ca	
		*p ts Øa -k^w	
		pətsa -w	
		pətsaw	
		Vowel epenthesis; weakening *k^w > /w/; syllabification of /w/	
MAROUA	Giziga-Muturwa, Mbazla	√ C C Ca	+Y, +W
		*f ts ØØ -y -k^w	
		fə^{w}ts^y -Ø^y-w^w	
		futʃu	
		Vowel epenthesis; weakening *{-k^w} > /w/; syllabification of /w/; W-prosody affecting epenthetic vowel; Y-prosody affecting final consonant	
	Mbazla	√ C C Ca	+Y, +W
		*p ts ØØ -y -k^w	
		pə^{w}ts^y -Ø^y-w^w	
		putʃu	
		Vowel epenthesis; weakening *{-k^w} > /w/; syllabification of /w/; W-prosody affecting epenthetic vowel; Y-prosody affecting final consonant	
	Giziga-Marva	√ C C Ca	+Y, +W
		*f ts Øa -y -k^w	
		afts^{y}a^w -Ø^y-Ø^w	

6.4 PCC Lexical Reconstructions   227

			aftʃo
			Vowel prothesis; Y-prosody affecting final
			consonant; W-prosody affecting /a/

KOTOKO- ISLAND	Buduma		√ C C Ca	
			*f d ØØ	-n
			fəd	-ən
			fədən	
			Vowel epenthesis	

beard

Alternative reconstruction (**PCC**)
a-, m(a)-, RED   **gʷ ma**[4]   -a, -y   +Y, +W   PC *grm (JS),
                                                    *ɣVm- (OS)

ɣʷimiɗ ʸ n. beard *barbe* (9 groups, 14 languages) B
The final *ɗ under palatalisation is realised as *j in almost all cases, which is a regular change. This has then been vocalised in Proto-Margi and Proto-Mandara. The palatalisation prosody is retained only in Gidar. *ɣʷ has a wide range of reflexes, as expected.

SUKUR	Sukur		√ C Ca	
			*ɣ mØ	-a-y
			ɣəm	-ay
			ɣəmay	
			Vowel epenthesis	

HURZA	Mbuko		√ C Ca	
			*x mØ	-a-y
			xəm	-ay
			həmay	
			Vowel epenthesis	

MARGI	Bura		√ C Ca		+W
			*kʷ mØ	-y	
			kʷəʷm	-i	
			kumi		
			Vowel epenthesis; prosody affecting		
			epenthetic vowel; syllabification of /y/		

MANDARA	Matal		√ C Ca	
		a-	*gʷ ØØ	-a-y
		a-	gʷ	-ay
			agʷay	

---

[4] Gravina reconstructs the PCC initial consonant as */ɣʷ/, which is here considered a later development from PCC */gʷ/.

228   Full Lexical Reconstructions

                        √ C Ca   +W
a-   *g^w ØØ   -a-y
a- g^w -a^wy
ag^woy
Prosody affecting /a/ in final syllable

    Podoko   √ C Ca   +Y
          m-   *w ma   -y
          m-   wma^y -Ø^y
mume
Syllabification of initial /w/ < *$ɣ^w$; prosody affecting final /a/

    Mandara   √ C Ca
                 *w ma
uma
Syllabification of initial /w/ < *$ɣ^w$

    Malgwa   √ C Ca   +W
                 > C C Ca
                 *k^w ma
                 > k wma
                 k^wə^{w}wma
kuuma
Re-segmentalisation *k^w > /k+w/; vowel epenthesis; prosody affecting epenthetic vowel; syllabification of medial /w/; Cə^w+w > Cuu

                        √ C Ca   +W
                        *w ma
                        ə^{w}wma
uuma
Vowel prothesis; prosody affecting prothetic vowel; syllabification of medial /w/; ə^w+w > uu

MOFU   Ouldeme   √ C Ca
          ma-   *Ø mØ   -a-y
          ma-   m   -ay
mamay

      Gemzek   √ C Ca
                      *x ma
                      xəma
həma
Vowel epenthesis

6.4 PCC Lexical Reconstructions

MAROUA	Giziga-Muturwa		√ C Ca		+W
			*x^w mØ	-ŋ	
		RED	x^{w}mØ	-ŋ	
	x^{w}ə^w-		mmə^w	-ŋ	
			hummuŋ		
			Vowel epenthesis; prosody affecting epenthetic vowels; note assimilation x^{w}m > mm		
LAMANG	Lamang		√ C Ca		
			*ɣma		
			ɣma		
	Hdi		√ C Ca		+W
			*ɣ^w mØ	-a-y	
			ɣ^{w}ə^{w}m	-ay	
			ɣumay		
			Vowel epenthesis; prosody affecting epenthetic vowel		
HIGI	Kamwe-Futu		√ C Ca		+Y, +W
			*ɣ^w ɓa	-y	
			ɣ^{w}ə^{w}ɓa^y	-Ø^y	
			ɣuɓe		
			Vowel epenthesis; W-prosody affecting epenthetic vowel; Y-prosody affecting final /a/		
	Kirya		√ C Ca		+W
			*ɣ^w mØ	-y	
			ɣ^{w}ə^{w}m	-i	
			ɣumi		
			Vowel epenthesis; W-prosody affecting epenthetic vowel; syllabification of /y/		
GIDAR	Gidar		√ CaCa		+Y
		a-m-	*gama	-y	
		a^y-n-	ga^{y}ma^y	-Ø^y	
			eⁿgeme		
			Prosody affecting all /a/		
			√ CaCa		+Y
		a-m-	*gama	-y	
		a-n-	ga^{y}ma^y	-Øy	
			aⁿgeme		
			Prosody affecting /a/ in ultima and penultima		

230   Full Lexical Reconstructions

beer

Alternative reconstruction (**PCC**)
ma-, n-, ŋg-   **v(a)xʷa**   -y, -n   +Y, +W   PC : —

vihʷ n. beer *bière* (4 groups, 12 languages) D syn: ɣʷizim, ᵐbaʣa.
   This is one of several roots for beer. ... The labialisation has transferred from *hʷ to *vʷ in Proto-Bata. *hʷ has the reflex *h in Proto-Mandara and *w in Proto-Daba. All these are common sporadic processes.

BATA	Bata		√ C Ca	+Y, +W
			*v xʷa -y	
			v Øʷa -y	
			vʷaʸ -Øʸ	
			vʷe	
			Prosodification *xʷ > ʷ; W-prosody affecting initial consonant; Y-prosody affecting final /a/	
	Gude		√ C Ca	+W
		n-	*v xʷa	
		n-	v Øʷa	
			ənvʷa	
			Prosodification *xʷ > ʷ; vowel prothesis; prosody affecting initial root consonant	
	Jimi		√ C Ca	+W
		ŋg-	*v xʷØ -n	
		ŋg-	v Øʷ -n	
		ŋgə-	vʷ -əʷn	
			ŋgəvun	
			Prosodification *xʷ > ʷ; vowel epenthesis; prosody affecting epenthetic vowel in final syllable	
	Sharwa		√ C Ca	+W
			> C C Ca	
			*v x wØ	
			> v w x	
			vʷəx	
			vʷəh	
			Re-segmentalisation *xʷ > x+w; metathesis *x w > w x; prosodification w > ʷ; vowel epenthesis; prosody affecting initial consonant	
	Tsuvan		√ C Ca	+Y, +W
			*v xʷa -y	
			əvØʷaʸ -Øʸ	
			əvʷe	

6.4 PCC Lexical Reconstructions   231

			Vowel prothesis; prosodification $*x^w > ^w$;
			W-prosody affecting initial consonant;
			Y-prosody affecting final /a/

DABA   Buwal   √ CaCa
                   ma- $*vax^w\emptyset$
                   ma-   vaw
                           mavaw
                           Weakening $*x^w > $ /w/ ; syllabification of /w/

          Gavar   √ C Ca
                   ma- $*v\,\emptyset a$
                   ma-   və
                           mavə
                           Centralisation of final /a/

          Mbudum   √ C Ca   +W
                   ma- $*v\,x^w\emptyset$
                   ma-   vw
                   ma-   vu
                           mavu
                           Weakening $*x^w > $ /w/; syllabification of /w/

          Daba   √ C Ca   +W
                   ma- $*v\,x^w\emptyset$
                   ma- vw^w
                   ma^w- vu
                           movu
                           Weakening $*x^w > $ /w/; syllabification of /w/;
                           prosody affecting prefixal /a/

MANDARA   Podoko   √ C Ca   +Y
                           *p xa   -y
                           $pə^y xa^y$ $-\emptyset^y$
                           pihe
                           Vowel epenthesis; prosody affecting all vowels

belly

Alternative reconstruction (**PCC**)
a- $x^w(a)ɗa$ -y, -ɗ, $-k^w$ +Y, +W   PC $*k^w t$ (JS),
                                                       $*ḥVw/y$- (OS)

$h^w iɗ$ n. stomach *ventre* (9 groups, 29 languages) B
   The basic sense of this root is the interior of the belly, i.e. the lower
part of the abdomen, and in particular the stomach. In some
languages the word is used in prepositional constructions to mean

'inside something'. The *hʷ is retained in most groups, but has the reflex *w in Proto-Maroua, Proto-Musgum and Dugwor, which is a common sporadic change. The *ɗ has the reflex *r in Ga'anda, Mbazla and Proto-Musgum, which is an unestablished change. This is also a regular change word-finally for several Higi group languages, as is the loss of final consonants. The *i is reconstructed from the evidence from Proto-Tera, Proto-Lamang and Proto-Higi.

MAFA	Mafa, Cuvok	√ CaCa *xʷaɗØ *hʷaɗ*	
TERA	Ga'anda	√ C Ca *xʷ ra -y xʷəʸra -Øʸ *hʷira* Vowel epenthesis; prosody affecting epenthetic vowel	+Y
SUKUR	Sukur	√ C Ca *xʷ ɗØ xʷəʷɗ *huɗ* Vowel epenthesis; prosody affecting epenthetic vowel	+W
MANDARA	Matal	√ C Ca *xʷ ɗØ xʷəɗ *hʷəɗ* Vowel epenthesis	
	Podoko	√ C Ca *xʷ ɗa xʷəʷɗa *huɗa* Vowel epenthesis; prosody affecting epenthetic vowel	+W
	Mandara, Malgwa	√ C Ca *xʷ ɗa -y xʷəʷɗaʸ -Øʸ *huɗe* Vowel epenthesis; W-prosody affecting epenthetic vowel; Y-prosody affecting final /a/	+Y, +W

6.4 PCC Lexical Reconstructions

	Glavda	√ C Ca	+W
		*xʷ ɗa	
		xʷəʷɗa	
		xuɗa	
		Vowel epenthesis; prosody affecting epenthetic vowel	

		√ C Ca	
		*xʷ ɗØ	
		xʷəɗ	
		Vowel epenthesis	

	Dghweɗe	√ C Ca	+Y
		*xʷ ɗa -y	
		xʷɗaʸ -Øʸ	
		xʷt'e	
		Prosody affecting final /a/	

MOFU	Ouldeme	√ C Ca	+W
		*xʷ ra -ɗ	
		xʷəʷra -ɗ	
		xuraɗ	
		Vowel epenthesis; prosody affecting epenthetic vowel	

	Muyang, Zulgo, Gemzek, Merey	√ C Ca	+W
		*xʷ ɗØ	
		xʷəʷɗ	
		huɗ	
		Vowel epenthesis; prosody affecting epenthetic vowel	

	Mada, Moloko, Gemzek	√ CaCa	+W
		*xʷaɗØ	
		xʷaʷɗ	
		hoɗ	
		Prosody affecting medial /a/	

	Dugwor	√ CaCa	
		*waɗØ	
		waɗ	

	Mofu North, Mofu-Gudur	√ CaCa	
		*xʷaɗØ	
		hʷaɗ	

MAROUA	Mbazla	√ C Ca	+W
		*w ra	
		wʷəʷrəʷ	

wuru
Vowel epenthesis; centralisation of final /a/; prosody affecting all vowels

		√ C Ca		+W
a-		*w ra		
a-		wʷəʷrəʷ		

awuru
Vowel epenthesis; centralisation of final /a/; prosody affecting epenthetic and final vowel

LAMANG Lamang
√ C Ca   +W
xʷ ɗØ   -y
xʷəʷɗ   -i
xudî
Vowel epenthesis; syllabification of /y/; prosody affecting epenthetic vowel

Hdi
√ C Ca   +W
*xʷ ɗØ   -y
xʷəʷɗ   -i
xudî
Vowel epenthesis; syllabification of /y/; prosody affecting epenthetic vowel

HIGI Kamwe-Nkafa, Kamwe-Futu
√ C Ca
*xʷ ØØ   -y
xʷ   -i
hʷi
Syllabification of /y/

Kirya
√ C Ca   +W
*xʷ rØ
xʷəʷr
hʷur
Vowel epenthesis; prosody affecting epenthetic vowel

Bana
√ C Ca
*xʷ rØ
xʷər
Vowel epenthesis

MUSGUM Vulum, Mbara
√ CaCa
*warØ
war

6.4 PCC Lexical Reconstructions

bite, to

Alternative reconstruction (**PCC**)
ŋ-, ⁿga-,   **dza**   -a, -y, -n, -w⁵, -x   a   +Y   PC:
ma-, n-   different
                                                                      root

dzaj v. to bite *mordre* (5 groups, 14 languages) syn: hʷipid̂.

This root is largely stable, with the only change being the unestablished change *dz to /ts/ in the Daba and Maroua groups. The final *j is realised as the palatalisation prosody in the Mafa, Mandara and Maroua groups, which is a common sporadic process. The Proto-Daba root is prenasalised, which is also a common sporadic process.

DABA	Buwal		√ Ca		+Y
		ŋ-	*tsa	-y	
		ŋ-	tsʸa	-Øʸ	
			ŋtʃa		
			Prosody affecting root-initial consonant		
	Gavar		√ Ca		
		ŋ-	*tsa		
			ŋtsa		
	Daba		√ Ca		+Y
		ⁿga-	*tsØ	-y	
		ⁿga-	tsʸ	-Øʸ	
			ⁿgatʃ		
			Prosody affecting root-initial consonant		
MAFA	Mafa		√ Ca		+Y
		n-	*dza	-y	
		n-	dzʸaʸ	-Øʸ	
			ndʒe		
			Prosody affecting initial consonant and final /a/		
			√ Ca		+Y
			*dzØ	-y	
			dzʸ	-Øʸ	
			dʒ-		
			Prosody affecting initial consonant		
MANDARA	Matal		√ Ca		
		ma-	*tsØ	-a-y	

---

⁵ It still remains an open question whether a separate suffixal root augment *{-w} existed besides the more frequently found *{-kʷ}, or whether occurrences of /w/ in such positions are all a reflex of the latter.

236   Full Lexical Reconstructions

			ma-	ts	-ay		
				matsay			
		Podoko		√ Ca			+Y
			n-	*dza	-y-k^w(?)	a	
			n-	dz^{y}a^y	-Ø^y-w	a^y	
				^{n}dʒewe			
				Prosody affecting initial consonant and all vowels			
		Malgwa		√ Ca			+Y
				*dza	-y		
				dz^{y}a	-Ø^y		
				dʒa			
				Prosody affecting initial consonant			
		Dghweɗe		√ Ca			
			n-	*dza	-x	a	
			n-	dza	-x	a	
				^{n}dzaxa			
MOFU	Ouldeme			√ Ca			
			ma-	*tsØ	-a-y		
			ma-	ts	-ay		
				matsay			
		Zulgo		√ Ca			+Y
				*dza	-y (-n)		
				dza^y	-Ø^y (-r)		
				dze(-r)			
				Prosody affecting final /a/			
		Gemzek		√ Ca			
				*dzØ	-a-y		
				dz	-ay		
				dzay			
				√ Ca			+Y
			ma-	*dza	-y		
			ma^y-	dza^y	-Ø^y		
				medze			
				Prosody affecting all vowels			
		Mofu North		√ Ca			+Y
			ma-	*zØ	-a-y		
			ma^y-	z	-a^{y}y^y		
				mezey			
				Prosody affecting all vowels			

6.4 PCC Lexical Reconstructions

	Mofu- Gudur	√ Ca *zØ z		
MAROUA	Mbazla	√ Ca *tsØ ts^y t∫i Prosody affecting initial consonant; syllabification of *{-y}	-y -i^y	

blow, to

Alternative reconstruction (**PCC**)
ma-   v ɮa   -a, -y, -k^w, -n   +Y, +W   PC: *fVč-
                                                   (OS)

viɮ v. to blow *souffler* (6 groups, 11 languages) B cf: vats, v₂, pik^w/pik$^{w\ y}$.

This root is found in a diverse collection of languages. The change *v→f in Proto-Kotoko-North is regular, as is the change *ɮ→l in Bata. The other changes affecting *ɮ are not known to be regular, but data is limited.

BATA	Bata	√ C Ca *f lØ fə^{y}l *fil* Vowel epenthesis; prosody affecting epenthetic vowel	-y -Ø^y	+Y
HURZA	Mbuko	√ C Ca *v ɮa vəɮa^y *vəɮe* Vowel epenthesis; prosody affecting final /a/	-y -Ø^y	+Y
MOFU	Zulgo	√ C Ca *v ɮØ və^{y}ɮ *viɮ* Vowel epenthesis; prosody affecting epenthetic vowel	-y -Ø^y	+Y
	Gemzek ma-	√ C Ca *v ɮa	-y	+Y

238   Full Lexical Reconstructions

		ma^y-	vəɮa^y		-Ø^y
			mevəɮe		
			Vowel epenthesis; prosody affecting all /a/		
	Merey		√ C Ca		
			*v ɮØ		
			vəɮ		
			Vowel epenthesis		
	Dugwor		√ C Ca		+Y
		ma-	*v ɮa	-y	
		ma-	vəɮa^y	-y^y	
			məvəɮey		
			Vowel epenthesis; prefix /a/ centralised; prosody affecting final /a/		
LAMANG	Hdi		√ C CØ		+W
			*v ɬØ	-a-y-k^w	
			və^{w}ɬ	-ay-Ø^w	
			vułay		
			Vowel epenthesis; prosody affecting epenthetic vowel		
KOTOKO-NORTH	Mpade		√ C Ca		+Y
			*f lØ	-y	
			fə^{y}l	-Ø^y	
			fil		
			Vowel epenthesis; prosody affecting epenthetic vowel		
	Malgbe		√ C Ca		+Y
			*f la	-y	
			fə^{y}la^y	-Ø^y	
			file		
			Vowel epenthesis; prosody affecting all vowels		
KOTOKO-CENTRAL	Lagwan		√ C Ca		+Y
			*v lØ	-y-k^w-n	+W
			və^{y}l	-Ø^y-wə^w-n	
			vilwun		
			Vowel epenthesis; Y-prosody affecting first syllable epenthetic vowel; weakening		

6.4 PCC Lexical Reconstructions   239

	Mser	*kʷ > /w/, W-prosody affecting second syllable epenthetic vowel		
		√ C Ca		+Y
		*v lØ	-y	
		vəʸl	-Øʸ	
		vil		
		Vowel epenthesis; prosody affecting epenthetic vowel		

boil, to

Alternative reconstruction (**PCC**)
ma-   **kʷ(a)ɗ(a)xa**   -a,-y,-ŋ   +Y, +W   PC: *[k]Vd-
                                                     > *kVɗ- (OS)

kʷaɗax v. boil *bouillir* (9 groups, 20 languages) A

The basic sense of this word is to cook by boiling. In most cases it is a transitive verb with a person being the agent and the liquid being the patient. *kʷ is retained in all groups, though the labialisation has been lost in a few languages (a sporadic process). The *ɗ→r in Tera is an unestablished process. *h is widely retained, which is unusual, and has the irregular reflex /s/ in Bachama. Two groups have palatalisation in the forms given, but this may be a property of the citation form that is used rather than of the root itself.

BATA	Bachama	√ CaCaCa		+Y
		*kʷaɗasa	-y	
		kʷaɗʸasa	-Øʸ	
		kʷaɗʸasa		
		Prosody affecting medial consonant		
DABA	Mbudum	√ C CaCa		+Y
		*k ɗaxØ	-y	
		kʸɗaʸx	-Øʸ	
		kydeh		
		Prosody affecting initial consonant and medial /a/		
	Daba	√ C C Ca		+W
		*kʷ ɗ ØØ	-a-y	
		kʷəʷɗ	-ay	
		kuɗay		
		Vowel epenthesis; prosody affecting epenthetic vowel		

240   Full Lexical Reconstructions

MAFA	Cuvok	√ C CaCa	+W
		*kʷ ɗaxa	
		kʷəʷɗaxa	
		kuɗaha	
		Vowel epenthesis; prosody affecting epenthetic vowel	
TERA	Tera	√ C CaCa	+W
		*kʷ raxØ -y	
		kʷəʷrax -i	
		kuraxi	
		Vowel epenthesis; prosody affecting epenthetic vowel; syllabification of /y/	
	Nyimatli	√ C CaCa	+W
		*kʷ ɮaxØ	
		kʷəʷɮax	
		kuɮakh	
		Vowel epenthesis; prosody affecting epenthetic vowel	
HURZA	Mbuko	√ CaCaCa	
		*kʷaɗaxØ	
		kʷaɗah	
	Vame	√ CaCaCa	
		*kʷaɗaxa	
		kʷaɗaha	
MARGI	Bura	√ C C Ca	+W
		*kʷ ɗ Øa	
		kʷəʷɗəʷ	
		kudu	
		Vowel epenthesis; centralisation of final /a/; prosody affecting all vowels	
MANDARA	Podoko	√ CaCaCa	
		*kʷaɗaxa	
		kʷaɗaha	
	Malgwa	√CaCa(Ca)	
		*kʷaɗØØa	
		kʷaɗa	
MOFU	Ouldeme	√ CaCaCa	+Y
		*kʷaɗaxa -y-ŋ	

6.4 PCC Lexical Reconstructions

		kʷaɗaʸxaʸ -Øʸ-ŋ	
		kʷaɗeheŋ	
		Prosody affecting /a/ in penultimate and ultimate syllables	
Muyang		√ CaCaCa	+W
		*kʷaɗaxØ -a-y	
		kʷaʷɗax -ay	
		koɗahay	
		Prosody affecting first syllable /a/	
Mada		√ CaCaCa	
	ma-	*kʷaɗaxØ	
		makʷaɗah	
Zulgo		√ CaC Ca	
		*kʷaɗØa	
		kʷaɗa	
Gemzek		√ CaCaCa	+Y
	ma-	*kʷaɗaxa -y	
	maʸ-	kʷaʸɗaʸxaʸ -Øʸ	
		mekʷeɗehe	
		Prosody affecting all /a/	
Dugwor		√ CaCaCa	+Y
	ma-	*kʷaɗaxØ -a-y	+W
	ma-	kʷaʷɗaʸx -aʸyʸ	
		məkʷoɗehey	
		Centralisation of /a/ in prefix; W-prosody affecting /a/ in antepenultima; Y-prosody affecting /a/ in penultima and ultima	
Mofu North		√ CaCaCa	+Y
	ma-	*kʷaɗaxØ -a-y	
	maʸ-	kʷaʸɗaʸx -aʸyʸ	
		mekʷeɗehey	
		Prosody affecting all vowels	
LAMANG Lamang		√ CaCaCa	
		*kʷaɗaxa	
		kʷaɗaha	
Hdi		√ C CaCa	
		*k ɗaxØ -a-y	
		kəɗahay	
		Vowel epenthesis	

bone

Alternative reconstruction (**PCC**)
(')a-, a-n-,   **ɗ y(a)ɬa**   -a, -y, -kʷ,   +Y, +W   PC: *'Jaṣu (PN),
a-ta-, ma-,   -t, -n, -ŋ   *s₃ (-n, -k) ~
ma-ta-,   *ɬ (<*ɬs₃) ~ *tɬ
RED-a-   (JS)

dɨɬ nm. bone *os* (14 groups, 43 languages) B syn: kɨrakaɬ ʸ.

This widely attested root is close to the root *ɗɨɬij 'egg', but the presence of *i in the root rather than a final *j makes a big difference to the reflexes in individual languages. The initial *ɗ is realised as *t in Proto-Mafa, Proto-Sukur, Proto-Mofu and Proto-Maroua, an unestablished change. It has been lost in many groups, triggering compensatory reduplication in the Mandara and Kotoko-South groups, and in some Mofu group languages. It has fused with the *i in the Tera and Higi groups to create a palatalised glottal or a velar implosive. In the Kotoko-North and South groups it has fused with the *ɬ to create an ejective. These fusion processes are common sporadic changes. The *ɬ is expected to have the reflex *ɮ in the groups of the South sub-branch, but for this root this is only the case in the Bata group. Within the Bata group there is a subsequent change *ɮ to *l. In the Margi group and in Mandara and Malgwa in the Mandara group, *ɬ has become palatalised by processes originating with *i, and *ɬʲ has then been velarised to /hʲ/ as part of a regular process. Regular processes give *ɬ the reflexes *s in the Proto-Kotoko-South and Mser, /ʃ/ in Mpade and /h/ in Buduma. In Mser the /ʃ/ is due to the effect of the front vowel on *s.

BATA	Bachama	√ C C Ca		+Y
		*Ø y la	-kʷ	+W
		> Ø y kʷ la		
		əʷØʸwʷlaʸ		
		əʷulaʸ		
		uule		
		Metathesis *l kʷ > kʷ l; weakening */kʷ/ > /wʷ/; syllabification of medial /w/ > u; vowel prothesis; W-prosody affecting prothetic vowel; prosodification of medial /y/ > ʸ; Y-prosody affecting final /a/; əʷ+w > uu		
	Gude	√ C C Ca		
		*Ø y la		
		ila		
		Syllabification of /y/		
	Jimi	√ C C Ca		
		*Ø y lØ	-n	
		yl	-ən	

6.4 PCC Lexical Reconstructions

			ilən Syllabification of /y/; vowel epenthesis	
	Sharwa		√ C C Ca *Ø y la *allə* Vowel prothesis; assimilation yl > ll; centralisation of final /a/	
	Tsuvan		√ C C Ca *Ø y ɮa *iɮe* Syllabification of /y/ ; prosody affecting /a/	+Y
MAFA	Mafa	ta- ta-	√ C C Ca *Ø Ø ɬØ ɬ *taɬ*	
	Cuvok	RED ɬa	√ C C Ca ØØɬa *ɬaɬar*	-n -n
TERA	Tera		√ C C Ca *ɗ y ɬØ ɗyʸəɬ *ɠəɬ* Vowel epenthesis; prosodification of medial /y/ > ʸ; prosody affecting initial consonant: fusion *ɗ+yʸ > ɠ	+Y
	Nyimatli		√ C C Ca *ɗ y ɬa ɗʸəɬəʸ *qəɬi* Vowel epenthesis; prosodification of medial /y/ > ʸ; Y-prosody affecting initial consonant and centralised final /a/	+Y
	Ga'anda		√ C C Ca *Ø y la aʸla *ela* Vowel prothesis; prosodification of medial /y/ > ʸ; Y-prosody affecting prothetic vowel	+Y
SUKUR	Sukur	ta-	√ C C Ca *Ø Ø ɬØ	

244   Full Lexical Reconstructions

			ta-	ɬ	
				taɬ	
MARGI	Margi			√ C CaCa	
				*ɗ yaxØ	-kʷ
				ɗyax	-w
				ɗyahu	
				Weakening *{-kʷ} > /w/; syllabification of /w/	
	Kilba			√ C C Ca	+Y
				*ɗ y xa	
				ɗiʸxəʸ	
				ɗihʸi	
				Syllabification of medial /y/; prosody affecting final consonant and centralised final /a/	
MANDARA	Matal			√ C C Ca	
		a-RED		*Ø Ø ɬØ	
		a-ɬa-		ɬ	
				aɬaɬ	
	Podoko			√ C C Ca	
		RED		*Ø Ø ɬa	
		ɬa-		ɬa	
				ɬaɬa	
	Mandara			√ C C Ca	+Y
		RED		*Ø y xʸa	
		RED		ØØʸxʸa	
		xʸa-		xʸaʸ	
				hʸahʸe	
				Prosodification of /y/ > ʸ; prosody affecting final /a/	
	Malgwa			√ C C Ca	+Y
		RED		*Ø y xʸa	
		xʸaʸ-		ØØʸxʸaʸ	
				hʸehʸe	
				Prosodification of medial /y/ > ʸ; prosody affecting all /a/	
	Glavda			√ C C Ca	
				*Ø Ø ɬa	
				ɬa	
				√ C C Ca	
		RED		*Ø Ø ɬa	

6.4 PCC Lexical Reconstructions

			ɬa-	ɬa	
				ɬaɬa	
	Dghweɗe			√ C C Ca	+Y
		RED		*Ø y ɬa	
		ɬa-		ØØʸɬaʸ	
				ɬaɬe	
				Prosodification of medial /y/ > ʸ; prosody affecting final /a/	
MOFU	Ouldeme			√ C C Ca	
		a-RED		*Ø Ø ɬØ	
		a-ɬa-		ɬ	
				aɬaɬ	
	Muyang			√ C C Ca	
		a-		*Ø Ø ɬa	-t
		a-		ɬa	-t
				aɬat	
	Mada			√ C C Ca	
		a-RED		*Ø Ø ɬØ	
		a-ɬa		ɬ	
				aɬaɬ	
	Zulgo, Gemzek			√ C C Ca	
		a-ta-		*Ø Ø ɬØ	
		a-ta-		ɬ	
				ataɬ	
	Merey, Dugwor			√ C C Ca	
		ma-ta-		*Ø Ø ɬØ	
		ma-ta-		ɬ	
				mətaɬ	
				Centralisation of prefix /a/ in first syllable	
	Mofu North			√ C C Ca	
		ma-ta-		*Ø Ø ɬØ	
		mØ-ta-		ɬ	
				ⁿdaɬ	
				Reduction of prefix *ma- > prenasalisation ⁿd	
MAROUA	Giziga-Muturwa			√ C C Ca	+Y
		ta-		*Ø y ɬ(a)	
		taʸ-		Ø Øʸ ɬ(aʸ)	
				teɬ(e)	
				Prosodification of medial /y/ > ʸ; prosody affecting all /a/	

	Muturwa, Marva		√ C C Ca	+Y
		a-ta-	*Ø y ɬØ	
		a-ta-	Ø Ø^y ɬØ	
		a-ta^y-	ɬ	
			ateɬ	
			Prosodification of medial /y/ > ^y; prosody affecting prefix-final /a/	

	Muturwa		√ C C Ca	+Y
		a-ta-	*Ø y ɬa	
		a-ta-	Ø ^yɬ	
		a^y-ta^y-	ɬ	
			eteɬ	
			Prosodification of medial /y/ > ^y; prosody affecting all /a/	

	Mbazla		√ C CaCa	
		RED	*' ØaɬØ	
		'a-	'aɬ	
			'a'aɬ	

HIGI	Kamwe-Nkafa		√ C C Ca	+Y
			*' y ɬa	
			'yɔ^yɬa	
			'yithlə	
			Vowel epenthesis; prosody affecting epenthetic vowel; centralisation of final /a/	

	Kamwe-Futu		√ C C Ca	
			*Ø y ɬa	
			iɬa	
			Syllabification of /y/	

	Kirya		√ C C Ca	
			*Ø y ɬa	
			iɬə	
			Syllabification of /y/; centralisation of final /a/	

	Bana		√ C C Ca	+Y
			*Ø y ɬa -n	
			a^yɬa^y -r	
			eɬer	
			Vowel prothesis; prosodification of medial /y/ > ^y; prosody affecting all /a/	

6.4 PCC Lexical Reconstructions

			√ C C Ca	+Y
			*' y ɬa	
			'yəʸɬa	
			'yiɬə	
			Vowel epenthesis; prosody affecting epenthetic vowel; centralisation of final /a/	

KOTOKO-ISLAND   Buduma

√ C C Ca
a-   *Ø Ø xØ   -a-y
a-   x   ay
ahay

KOTOKO-NORTH   Afade

√ C C Ca   +Y
a-n-   *' y ɬa
a-n-   yɬ'a
aʸ-n-   ʸɬ'əʸ
enɬ'i
Double metathesis: *' y ɬ > y ' ɬ > y ɬ '; Prosodification of medial /y/ > ʸ; prosody affecting prefixal /a/ and centralised final vowel

           Mpade

√ C C Ca   +Y
a-n-   *Ø y sa
aʸ-n-   Ø Øʸ sʸəʸ
enʃi
Prosodification of medial /y/ > ʸ; prosody affecting prefixal /a/ and remaining root consonant plus centralised final vowel

           Malgbe

√ C C Ca   +Y
a-n-   *Ø y ɬa
aʸ-n-   Ø Øʸ ɬəʸ
enɬi
Prosodification of medial /y/ > ʸ; prosody affecting prefixal /a/ and centralised final vowel

KOTOKO-CENTRAL   Lagwan

√ C C Ca
a-   *Ø y ɬa
a-   Ø Øʸ ɬəʸ
aɬi
Prosodification of medial /y/ > ʸ; prosody affecting centralised final vowel

           Mser

√ C C Ca   +Y
a-n-   *Ø y sa
aʸ-n-   Ø Øʸsʸəʸ
enʃi

248   Full Lexical Reconstructions

			Prosodification of medial /y/ > ʸ; prosody affecting prefixal /a/ and remaining root consonant plus centralised final vowel	
KOTOKO-SOUTH	Zina	a-RED a-sa	√ C C Ca *Ø Ø sa sa *asasə* Centralisation of final /a/	
	Mazera	a-RED a-s- a-sə ʸ-	√ C C Ca *' y sa s'Ø ʸa s'a ʸ *asis'e* Metathesis ' y s > ' s y > s ' y; prosodification of /y/ > ʸ; vowel epenthesis; prosody affecting epenthetic vowel and final /a/	+Y
GIDAR	Gidar	RED ła ʸŋ-	√ C C Ca *Ø y ła -ŋ Ø Ø ʸ ła ʸ -ŋ *łeŋłeŋ* Prosodification of medial /y/ > ʸ; prosody affecting all /a/	+Y

bow

	Alternative reconstruction (**PCC**)			
	a-, xa-, ma-ⁿga-, ⁿg-, g-nd-, RED	**r(a)ga**	-a, -y, -ɗ, -n, -ŋ	+Y PC: *rəga (PN), *rg (i) (-a, -n) (JS), *dVgVn- > *dVŋg- (OS)

rigiɗ ʸ nm. bow *arc* (12 groups, 36 languages) A

This word denotes the bow used for hunting or warfare. There was a regular change *r→l in the groups of the North sub-branch and Cuvok. Here we also find /l/ in Mafa where /r/ is expected. The *g has the reflex *k in Proto-Mafa, Proto-Mandara and Proto-Maroua. It has the reflex *ɣ in Proto-Lamang, and has been lost in Proto-Tera and Proto-Sukur, possibly following an earlier *g→ɣ. These are unestablished changes. *ɗ has been lost in most groups. This may be due to interaction with the palatalisation prosody, i.e. *ɗ ʸ→j, with *j being lost or reanalysed in some groups. This is a common sporadic process.

BATA	Bata		√ CaCa *raga -y	+Y

6.4 PCC Lexical Reconstructions   249

			raga^y	-Ø^y	
			rage		
			Prosody affecting final /a/		
	Gude		√ CaCa		
			*raga		
			raga		
	Jimi		√ CaCa		
			*ragØ	-n	
			rag	-ən	
			ragən		
			Vowel epenthesis		
MAFA	Mafa		√ CaCa		+Y
			*laka	-y-ɗ	
			la^{y}ka^y	-Ø^y-ɗ	
			lekeɗ		
			Prosody affecting all /a/		
	Cuvok		√ C Ca		
		RED-	*l Øa	-ŋ	
		la-	la	-ŋ	
			lalaŋ		
TERA	Tera, Nyimatli		√ C Ca		
			*r ØØ	-y	
			r	-i	
			ri		
			Syllabification of /y/		
SUKUR	Sukur		√ C Ca		
			*r ØØ	-a-y	
			r	-ay	
			ray		
HURZA	Mbuko		√ C Ca		+Y
		ŋg-	*l Øa	-y	
			l ŋga	-y	
			lə^{ŋ}ga^y	-Ø^y	
			liŋge		
			Metathesis *ŋg l > l ŋg; vowel epenthesis; prosody affecting all vowels		
	Vame		√ C Ca		
			*l ka		

250 Full Lexical Reconstructions

			ləka Vowel epenthesis		
MARGI	Bura		√ C Ca		
		RED-	*l ØØ	-y	
		la-	l	-i	
			lali Syllabification of /y/		
	Margi, Kilba		√ CaCa *laga *laga*		
	Margi-South		√ CaCa *laga *lagga* Consonant length remains obscure		
MANDARA	Matal		√ CaCa		
		a-	*lakØ		
		a-	lak *alak*		
	Podoko		√ C Ca		+Y
			*l ka	-y	
			lə^yka	-Ø^y	
			lika Vowel epenthesis; prosody affecting epenthetic vowel		
	Mandara		√ C Ca		+Y
			*l ka	-y	
			a^ylka^y	-Ø^y	
			elke Vowel prothesis; prosody affecting all vowels		
	Malgwa		√ C Ca	-y	+Y
			əlka^y	-Ø^y	
			əlke Vowel prothesis; prosody affecting final /a/		
	Glavda		√ CaCa *laɣa *laːʁa* Vowel length remains obscure		

6.4 PCC Lexical Reconstructions

MOFU					
	Ouldeme		√ CaCa		
		a-	*lakØ		
		a-	lak		
			alak		
	Mada		√ CaCa		+Y
		a-	*laka	-y-ɗ	
		aʸ-	laykay	-Øʸ-ɗ	
			eleked̂		
			Prosody affecting all vowels		
	Moloko		√ CaCa		+Y
		ma-ᵑga-	*lakØ	-y	
		maʸ-ᵑgaʸ-	laʸk	-Øʸ	
			meᵑgelek		
			Prosody affecting all vowels		
	Zulgo		√ C Ca		+Y
			*l ka	-y-ɗ	
			ləʸkəʸ	-Øʸ-ɗ	
			likiɗ		
			Vowel epenthesis; prosody affecting all vowels		
	Gemzek		√ C Ca		
		xa-	*l Øa	-ŋ	
		xa-	la	-ŋ	
			halaŋ		
	Merey		√ C Ca		
		RED-	*l Øa	-ŋ	
		la-	la	-ŋ	
			lalaŋ		
	Dugwor		√ CaCa		+Y
		xa-	*lakØ	-y	
		xa-	laʸk	-Øʸ	
			həlek		
			Prosody affecting second syllable /a/; centralisation of prefixal /a/		
	Mofu North		√ C Ca	-ŋ	
		RED-	*l Øa	-ŋ	
		la-	la		
			lalaŋ		

252   Full Lexical Reconstructions

	Mofu-Gudur		√ C Ca	+Y
		RED-	*l Øa	-y-ŋ
		laʸ-	laʸ	-Øʸ-ŋ
			leleŋ	
			Prosody affecting all vowels	
MAROUA	Giziga-Marva,		√ CaCa	+Y
	Mbazla	xa-	*lakØ	-y
		xaʸ-	laʸk	-Øʸ
			helek	
			Prosody affecting all vowels	
LAMANG	Lamang		√ CaCa	+Y
			*laɣa	-y
			laʸɣaʸ	-Øʸ
			leɣe	
			Prosody affecting all vowels	
	Hdi		√ C Ca	+Y
			*l ɣa	-y-ɗ
			ləɣaʸ	-Øʸ-ɗ
			ləyeɗ	
			Vowel epenthesis; prosody affecting final /a/	
HIGI	Kamwe-Nkafa		√ C Ca	+Y
			*l gØ	-y
			ləʸgʸ	-iʸ
			ligʸi	
			Vowel epenthesis; prosody affecting epenthetic vowel and final consonant; syllabification of /y/	
	Kamwe-Futu		√ CaCa	+Y
			*ragØ	-y
			raʸg	-iʸ
			regi	
			Prosody affecting medial /a/; syllabification of /y/	
	Bana		√ C Ca	
			*r gØ	-y
			rəg	-i
			rəgi	
			Vowel epenthesis; syllabification of /y/	

MUSGUM	Mbara		√ C Ca		+Y
		g-nd-	*1 ØØ	-y-ŋ	
		gə^y-ndə^y-	lə^y-	-Ø^y-ŋ	
			gi^{n}diliŋ		
			Vowel epenthesis; prosody affecting epenthetic vowels		

brain

Alternative reconstruction (**PCC**)
a-, an-, (a-)^{ŋ}ga-, ma-ka-(^{ŋ}ga-)   **r(a)ɬa**   -y   +Y   PC: —

Note: For a different reconstruction having relevance for the languages of the KOTOKO groups, see quotation from Gravina (2014b) below and under 6.3.6.1.

ra^{ŋ}gaɬ ^{y} nm. brain *cerveau* (6 groups, 12 languages) D
The forms given here can be divided between those that include a prenasalised consonant and those that don't. Those that don't could be reflexes of a form such as *ɗaraɬ ^{y}. The *ɗ is lost in Matal, Zulgo, Gemzek and Giziga-Marva, and has combined with *ɬ in Afade, Maltam and Mser. These are common sporadic processes. The change *ɬ→s in Mser is regular. It is harder to show relatedness for the forms with a prenasalised consonant. It is also not possible to say that all these forms are cognate.

HURZA	Mbuko		√ CaCa		+Y
		ma-ka-^{ŋ}ga-	*laɬØ	-y	
		ma-ka -	l^{ŋ}gaɬ	-y	
		ma-ka-	lə^{yŋ}ga^{y}ɬ	-Ø^y	
			məkəli^{ŋ}geɬ		
			Metathesis *^{ŋ}g l > l ^{ŋ}g; vowel epenthesis; prosody affecting epenthetic vowel and medial /a/ in penultimate and ultimate syllables; centralisation of /a/ in first and second syllables		
MANDARA	Matal		√ C Ca		+Y
		a-	*r ɬØ	-y	
		a-	rə^{y}ɬ	-Ø^y	
			ariɬ		
			Vowel epenthesis; prosody affecting epenthetic vowel		
MOFU	Ouldeme		√ CaCa		+Y
		an-	*daɬØ	-y	

254 Full Lexical Reconstructions

		an-	da^{y}ɨ	-Ø^y	
			a^{n}deɬ		
			Prosody affecting medial /a/		
	Muyang		√ C Ca		+Y
		an-	*ɗ ɨØ	-y	
		a^{y}n-	də^{y}ɨ	-Ø^y	
			e^{n}diɬ		
			Vowel epenthesis; prosody affecting all vowels		
	Zulgo, Gemzek		√ CaCa		+Y
		a-	*raɮØ	-y	
		a-	ra^{y}ɮ	-Ø^y	
			areɮ		
			Prosody affecting medial /a/		
	Merey		√ CaCa		+Y
		^{ŋ}ga-	*ɗaɬØ	-y	
			ɗa^{ŋ}gaɬ	-y	
			ɗa^{yŋ}ga^{y}ɨ	-Ø^y	
			de^{ŋ}geɬ		
			Metathesis *^{ŋ}g ɗ > ɗ ^{ŋ}g; prosody affecting all vowels		
	Dugwor		√ CaCa		+Y
		a-^{ŋ}ga-	*laɬØ	-y	
		a-	la^{yŋ}ga^{y}ɨ	-Ø^y	
			ale^{ŋ}geɬ		
			Metathesis *^{ŋ}g l > l ^{ŋ}g; prosody affecting all medial /a/		
MAROUA	Giziga-Marva		√ CaCa		+Y
		a-	*laɬØ	-y	
		a-	la^{y}ɨ	-Ø^y	
			aleɬ		
			Prosody affecting medial /a/		
KOTOKO-NORTH	Afade		√ C Ca		+Y
		a-	*r ɨØ	y	
		a^y-	rɨ	-i^y	
			erɬ'i		
			Prosody affecting /a/; syllabification of /y/; origin of glottalisation feature remains obscure – but see note above		
	Maltam		√ C Ca		+Y
		a-	*r ɨØ	-y	

6.4 PCC Lexical Reconstructions   255

			aʸ-	rəʸɬ	-iʸ	
				eriɬ'i		
				Vowel epenthesis; prosody affecting all vowels; syllabification of /y/; origin of glottalisation feature remains obscure – but see note above		
KOTOKO- CENTRAL	Mser			√ CaCa		+Y
			ma-	*rasa	-y	
			maʸ-	raʸsəʸ	-Øʸ	
				meres'i		
				Centralisation of final /a/; prosody affecting all vowels; origin of glottalisation feature remains obscure – but see note above		

butterfly

Alternative reconstruction (**PCC**)
kʷa-, ma-(ta-), (n)a-)RED RED-ma- **p(a)ra** -y, -kʷ, -n a +Y, +W PC: —

piri n. butterfly *papillon* (11 groups, 17 languages)
   In many cases, this root is reduplicated, and in some cases there is a prefix, which implies that there may have been more material at the start of this root, or else that the word was a nominalisation of a root with a different meaning. *r has the reflex *l in the groups of the North sub-branch and in Proto-Daba as part of a regular change. The final *i is reconstructed from its presence in the three Consonant Prosody groups, Proto-Bata, Proto-Margi and Proto-Higi.

BATA	Gude		√ C Ca			
		RED-	*p rØ	-y-n	a	
		pəry-	pər	-yn	a	
			pəripərinə			
			Vowel epenthesis; syllabification of /y/; FV /a/ centralisation			
DABA	Mbudum		√ C Ca			+W
		ma-RED-	*p la	-kʷ		
		mə-pəʷl-	pəʷla	-Øʷ		
			məpulpula			
			Prosodification of *kʷ > ʷ; vowel epenthesis; prosody affecting epenthetic vowels in reduplicated root; /a/ centralisation in prefix			

256   Full Lexical Reconstructions

TERA	Nyimatli		√ C Ca	
		RED-ma-	*p rØ	
		pər-ma-	pər	
			pərmapər	
			Vowel epenthesis	

SUKUR	Sukur		√ C Ca	
		RED-	*p rØ	
		pər-	pər	
			məɮə-pərpər	
			Vowel epenthesis; composite with preposed *məɮə-*	

HURZA	Mbuko		√ C Ca	+W
		ma-	*p ra -k^w	
		ma-	pəra^w -k^w	
			mapərok	
			Vowel epenthesis; prosody affecting lexical final /a/	

	Vame		√ CaCa	+Y
		RED-	*pala -y	
		pa^{y}l-	pa^{y}la^y -Ø^y	
			pelpele	
			Prosody affecting all vowels	

MARGI	Bura		√ C Ca	+Y
		RED-	*p rØ -y	
		pə^{y}r-	pə^{y}r -Ø^y	
			pirpir	
			Vowel epenthesis; prosody affecting all vowels	

	Kilba		√ C Ca	
		RED-	*p rØ	
		pər-	pər	
			pərpər	
			Vowel epenthesis	

MANDARA	Malgwa		√ CaCa	
		na-RED-	*pala	
		na-pala-	pala	
			napalapala	

	Glavda		√ CaCa	
		a-RED-	*pala	

6.4 PCC Lexical Reconstructions

		a-pala-	paØØ	
			apalapa	
			Loss of final syllable	
MOFU	Mofu-Gudur		√ C Ca	
		ma-RED-	*p la	
		ma-pəla-	pəla	
			mapəlapəla	
			Vowel epenthesis	
MAROUA	Giziga-Muturwa		√ CaCa	
		ma-RED-	*pala	
		ma-pala-	pala	
			mapalapala	
			√ C Ca	+Y
		ma-RED-	*p la -y	
		mə^y-pla-	pla -Ø^y	
			miplapla	
			Prosodification of *y > ^{y}; centralisation of prefix /a/; prosody affecting centralised /a/	
			√ C Ca	+W
		ma-RED-	*p la -k^w	
		ma-pla	pla -k^w	
		mə^w-pla	pla -Ø^w	
			muplapla	
			Prosodification of *k^w > ^{w}; centralisation of prefix /a/; prosody affecting centralised /a/	
HIGI	Kamwe-Nkafa		√ CaCa	
		k^{w}a-RED-	*pala	
		k^{w}a-pal-	paØØ	
			k^{w}apalpa	
			Loss of final syllable	
	Kamwe-Futu		√ CaCa	
		RED-	*pala	
		palə-	paØØ	
			paləpa	
			Vowel epenthesis; loss of final syllable	
	Bana		√ C Ca	
		RED-	*p lØ -y	
		pəl-	pəl -i	

258   Full Lexical Reconstructions

                      pəlpəli
                      Vowel epenthesis; syllabification of /y/

GIDAR   Gidar   √ CaCa   +W
                  ma-ta-RED-   *pala   -k^w
                  ma^w-ta^w-   pa^{w}la^w -Ø^w
                  pa^{w}la^w

                              motopolopolo
                              Prosodification of *k^w > ^{w}; prosody
                              affecting all vowels

camel[6]

                Alternative reconstruction (**PCC**/loan)
                n- **k(a)l(a)g(a)m(a)wa** -y, -n, -t a +Y, +W   Kanuri:
                                                                       kaligimo,
                                                                     Fulfulde:
                                                                   ^{n}*geelooba*

                kaligimo n. camel *chameau* (3 groups, 6 languages) A
                syn: ɓig^{w}amɨ ^{y}, ^{n}g^{j}aluba.
                This root is a borrowing from the old Kanuri /kaligimo/, and is
                found in three of the Kotoko groups. There were no back vowels in
                these groups at an earlier point in their history, and this has led to
                the displacement of the back vowel next to velar consonants in
                Lagwan, Mser and Mazera. The back vowel was reanalysed as
                labialisation of the velar consonants, which then condition a
                following *ɨ to be realised as [u].

---

[6] This is an obvious loan and thus qualifies as a 'pseudo'-PCC root insofar as it has been streamlined into Central Chadic phonology systems to the extent of being apparently 'reconstructable'.
    Note, however, that this root may have entered CC languages at different times via different donors, like Fulfulde (^{n}*geelooba*) and Old Kanuri (*kaligimo*). Ultimately, the original source may be Berber *alγəm. Gravina (2014b) keeps three – as we see it, cognate – proto-language forms distinct; all three will be cited here. At variance with Gravina, however, in this study we propose a common 'pseudo'-PCC root from which all modern forms could be diachronically derived. This does not exclude repeated borrowing from different donor languages in individual CC languages, for which we would appear to have evidence.
    Note further, that the Central Chadic languages treat this 'pseudo'-PCC root as if it was a (rare!) 5-radical simple root in order to dissolve, for instance, the final [o] of *kaligimo* to underlying /aw/. Characteristically for Central Chadic languages, they allow manipulation in terms of different root types in underlying structure, namely √ C C C C Ca, √ C C C CaCa, √ C CaCaC Ca, √ C C CaC Ca, √ CaCaCaC Ca, √ CaC C CaCa, √ CaC C C Ca, √ C C CaCaCa, √ C CaCaCaCa, √ C C CaCaCa, √ CaC CaC Ca.

6.4 PCC Lexical Reconstructions

ɓigʷamɨ ʸ nf. camel *chameau* (14 groups, 32 languages) A syn: kaligimo, ⁿgʲaluba.

This root has come into Central Chadic from the Berber *alɣʷəm. The change from Berber *l to *ɮ is consistent with a considerable degree of time-depth, since it implies that the word was adopted before the creation of *l in Proto-Central Chadic North. This conflicts with evidence from archaeology, which leads to a more recent date for the arrival of the camel in the Central Chadic region. The *ɮ is realised as *l in Proto-Kotoko-Island, Proto-Kotoko-North and Proto-Musgum, and is devoiced in Proto-Higi and Proto-Gidar. The change in Proto-Gidar is a regular change, but the change is unestablished in the other groups. The evidence for the palatalisation prosody is inconsistent. The prosody is present in Jimi in the Bata group, and in the Hurza and Mofu groups, but is absent in other groups where it would be expected. There is support from the *i in Proto-Tera and Proto-Higi, the *e in Proto-Kotoko-Island and Proto-Kotoko-North and from some languages in the Mandara group.

ⁿgʲaluba n. camel *chameau* (4 groups, 5 languages) D syn: kaligimo, ɓigʷamɨ ʸ.

This is one of several Central Chadic roots for camel. This root is a recent borrowing from the Fulfulde ⁿgeelooba.

BATA	Bata		√ C C CaC Ca		+W
			*Ø l kap Øʷ Ø	-t	a
			ləʷkʷap	-t	aʷ
			lukʷapto		
			Vowel epenthesis; prosody affecting epenthetic vowels and FV		
	Jimi		√ C C CaC Ca		+Y, +W
			*Ø l gam wʷ Ø	-y-n	
			ləʸgʷamØʷ	-Øʸən	
			ligʷamən		
			Vowel epenthesis; W-prosody on /g/ > gʷ; Y-prosody affecting epenthetic vowel in first syllable		
	Sharwa		√ CaC C C Ca		+Y
		n-	*galØbwa	-y	
		n-	gʸalwba	-Øʸ	
			ngyaluba		
			Metathesis b w > w b; syllabification of /w/; prosody affecting initial consonant		

	Tsuvan		√ C C C C Ca		+Y
		n-	*Ø ɮ g m wa	-y	
		n-	ɮəgwmay	-Ø^y	
			ɮə-n-guma^y		
			ɮəŋgume		

Metathesis m w > w m; metathesis n- ɮ > ɮ -n-; vowel epenthesis; syllabification of /w/; prosody affecting final /a/

DABA	Daba	√ C CaCaC Ca	+W
		*Ø ɮakamaØ^{w}Ø	
		ɮa^{w}ka^{w}ma^w	
		ɮokomo	

Prosodification of /w/; prosody affecting all vowels

TERA	Nyimatli	√ C C CaC Ca	+Y, +W
		*Ø ɮ xamØ^{w}Ø	-y
		ɮə^{y}ma^{w}x	-Ø^y
		ɮimokh	

Metathesis x m > m x; vowel epenthesis, Y-prosody affecting epenthetic vowel; W-prosody affecting medial /a/

	Ga'anda		√ CaC C C Ca		+Y
		n-	*gal Ø p wa	-y	
		n-	ga^{y}lwpa	-Ø^y	
			ŋelupa		

Metathesis p w > w p; syllabification of /w/; prosody affecting first syllable /a/

SUKUR	Sukur	√ C C CaC Ca	+W
		*Ø ɮ gamØ^{w}Ø	
		ɮəg^{w}am	
		ɮəg^{w}am	

Prosodification of /w/; prosody affecting 2nd consonant; vowel epenthesis

HURZA	Mbuko	√ C C CaC Ca	+Y, +W
		*Ø ɮ gamØ^{w}a	-y
		ɮə^{w}g^{w}a^{y}ma^y	-Ø^y
		ɮug^{w}eme	

Prosodification of /w/; vowel epenthesis; W-prosody affecting epenthetic vowel and

6.4 PCC Lexical Reconstructions   261

		2nd consonant; Y-prosody affecting medial and final /a/	
	Vame	√ CaC CaC Ca	+Y, +W

                                              *Øaʒ gamØʷa   -y
                                              aʒəgʷaʸmaʸ   -Øʸ
                                              aʒəgʷeme
                                              Prosodification of /w/; W-prosody affecting 2nd consonant; vowel epenthesis; Y-prosody affecting /a/ in penultima and ultima

| MARGI | Bura | √ C C CaC Ca | +Y, +W |

                                              *Ø l kamaØʷØ   -y
                                              ləʸkamaʷ   -Øʸ
                                              likamo
                                              Prosodification of /w/; vowel epenthesis; W-prosody affecting final /a/; Y-prosody affecting epenthetic vowel

| | Margi-South | √ C C CaC Ca | +W |

                                              *Ø ʒ gamØʷØ
                                              ʒəʷgʷam
                                              ʒugʷam
                                              Prosodification of /w/; vowel epenthesis; prosody affecting epenthetic vowel and 2nd consonant

| MANDARA | Matal | √ C C C C Ca | +W |

                                            *Ø ʒ g mØʷə   -y
                                              ʒəgʷmə   -y
                                              ʒəgʷməy
                                            Prosodification of /w/; vowel epenthesis; prosody affecting 2nd consonant; centralisation of final /a/

                                            √ C C C C Ca   +W
                                            *Ø ʒ g mØʷØ   -y
                                              ʒəgʷm   -i
                                              ʒəgʷmi
                                            Prosodification of /w/; vowel epenthesis; prosody affecting 2nd consonant; syllabification of /y/

                                            √ C C C C Ca   +W
                                            *Ø ʒ g mØʷØ   -y

262   Full Lexical Reconstructions

		ɮəʷgm	-i
		ɮugmi	
		Prosodification of /w/; vowel epenthesis; prosody affecting epenthetic vowel; syllabification of /y/	

	Podoko	√ C C CaC Ca	+W
		*Ø ɮ gamØʷa	
		ɮəgʷama	
		ɮəgʷama	
		Prosodification of /w/; vowel epenthesis; prosody affecting 2nd consonant	

	Mandara	√ CaCaCaC Ca	+Y, +W
		*Øaɮagamɸʷa	-y
		aʸɮaʸgʷamaʸ	-Øʸ
		eɮegʷame	
		Prosodification of /w/; W-prosody affecting 2nd consonant; Y-prosody affecting 1st and 2nd and final syllable /a/	

	Malgwa	√ C C CaC Ca	+Y, +W
		*Ø ɮ gamØʷa	-y
		əɮəʷgʷamaʸ	-Øʸ
		ədhlugʷame	
		Vowel prothesis and epenthesis; prosodification of /w/; W-prosody affecting epenthetic vowel and 2nd consonant; Y-prosody affecting final vowel	

	Glavda	√ CaCaCaC Ca	+W
		*Øaɮagamɸʷa	
		aɮagʷama	
		aɮagʷama	
		Prosodification of /w/; prosody affecting 2nd consonant	

	Dghweɗe	√ C C CaC Ca	+W
		*Ø ɮ gamØʷa	
		ɮəʷgʷama	
		ɮugʷama	
		Prosodification of /w/; vowel epenthesis; prosody affecting epenthetic vowel and 2nd consonant	

| MOFU | Ouldeme | √ CaC CaC Ca | +Y, +W |
| | | *Øaɮ gamØʷa | -y |

6.4 PCC Lexical Reconstructions

	aɮəgʷaʸmaʸ	-Øʸ
	aɮəgʷeme	
	Prosodification of /w/; vowel epenthesis; W-prosody affecting 2nd consonant; Y-prosody affecting /a/ in penultimate and ultimate syllables	
Muyang	√ CaC CaC Ca	+Y, +W
	*Øaɮ gamØʷØ	-y
	aʸɮəʸgʷaʸm	-iʸ
	eɮigʷemi	
	Prosodification of /w/; vowel epenthesis; W-prosody affecting 2nd consonant; Y-prosody affecting all vowels; syllabification of /y/	
Moloko	√ CaCaCaC Ca	+Y, +W
	*ØaɮagamØʷa	-y
	aʸɮaʸgʷaʸmaʸ	-Øʸ
	eɮegʷeme	
	Prosodification of /w/; W-prosody affecting 2nd consonant; Y-prosody affecting all vowels	
Zulgo	√ C C C C Ca	+Y, +W
	*Ø ɮ g mØʷa	-y
	ɮəʸgʷəʸmaʸ	-Øʸ
	ɮigʷime	
	Prosodification of /w/; W-prosody affecting 2nd consonant; Y-prosody affecting all vowels	
Gemzek	√ CaC C C Ca	+Y, +W
	*Ø ɮag mØʷa	-y
	ɮaʸgəʷmaʸ	-Øʸ
	ɮegume	
	Prosodification of /w/; vowel epenthesis; W-prosody affecting epenthetic vowel; Y-prosody affecting /a/ in first and final syllable	
	Alternative option: Metathesis m w > w m: *Øɮagwma-y Syllabification of /w/: ɮaguma-y Y-prosody on /a/: ɮaʸgumaʸ	

264   Full Lexical Reconstructions

		√ C C C C Ca		+Y, +W
		*Ø ɮ g mØʷa	-y	
		ɮəʷgmaʸ	-Øʸ	
		ɮugme		
		Prosodification of /w/; vowel epenthesis; W-prosody affecting epenthetic vowel; Y-prosody affecting final /a/		
		Alternative option: Double metathesis m w > w m, g w > w g: *Øɮwgma-y Syllabification of /w/: ɮugma-y Y-prosody on final /a/: ɮugmaʸ		
	Merey	√ C C CaC Ca		+Y, +W
		*Ø ɮ gamØʷa	-y	
		ɮəgʷaʸmaʸ	-Øʸ	
		ɮəgʷeme		
		Prosodification of /w/; vowel epenthesis; W-prosody affecting 2nd consonant; Y-prosody affecting all /a/		
	Dugwor	√ C C CaC Ca		+Y, +W
		*Ø ɮagamØʷa	-y	
		ɮaʸgʷaʸmaʸ	-Øʸ	
		ɮegʷeme		
		Prosodification of /w/; W-prosody affecting 2nd consonant; Y-prosody affecting all vowels		
	Mofu North			
		ɮeg[iveme⁷	-y	+Y
	Mofu-Gudur	√ C CaCaC Ca		+W
		*Ø łagamØʷa		
		łagʷama		
		łagʷama		
		Prosodification of /w/; W-prosody affecting 2nd consonant		
MAROUA	Giziga-Muturwa	√ CaCaCaC Ca		+W
		*Øaɮagamaʷa	(-ŋ)	
		(a)ɮaʷgaʷmaʷ	(-ŋ)	
		(a)ɮogomo(ŋ)		

---

[7] Unclear transcription, therefore no analysis attempted.

6.4 PCC Lexical Reconstructions

			Prosodification of /w/; W-prosody affecting all medial and final vowels	
	Mbazla		√ CaC CaC Ca	+W
			*ʔaɮgamØʷa	
			ʔaɮgaʷmaʷ	
			'aɮgomo	
			Prosodification of /w/; W-prosody affecting /a/ in penultimate and ultimate syllable	
LAMANG[8]	Lamang		√ C C CaCaCa	+W
			*Ø ɮ gamaØʷØ	
			ɮ gʷama	
			ɮgʷama	
			Prosodification of /w/; prosody affecting *g > gʷ	
	Hdi		√ CaC C C Ca	+Y
		n-	*galØbwa	-y
		n-	galəʸbwa	-Øʸ
			ngalibwa	
			Vowel epenthesis; prosody affecting epenthetic vowel	
			√ CaC C C Ca	+Y, +W
		n-	*galØbwa	-y
		n-	galəʸbəʷwʷa	-Øy
			ŋalibuwa	
			Vowel epenthesis; Y-prosody affecting epenthetic vowel in 2nd syllable; W-prosody affecting epenthetic vowel in 3rd syllable	
HIGI	Kamwe-Futu		√ C C CaC Ca	+W
			*Ø ɬ gamØʷØ	-y
			ɬəgʷam	-i
			thəgʷami	
			Prosodification of /w/; prosody affecting 2nd consonant; vowel epenthesis; syllabification of /y/	
	Kirya		√ CaCaC C Ca	+Y, +W
		n-	*galaʷØ p Øʷa	-y

---

[8] Lamang ɮgʷama and Hdi ngalibwa are not in Gravina's database.

		n-	gʸalaʷba	-Øʸ
		n-	Øʸalaʷba	
			nyaloba	

Prosodification of /w/; W-prosody affecting 2nd syllable /a/; Y-prosody affecting (later deleted) initial root consonant

	Bana		√ CaC C C Ca
		n-	*gal Ø b wa
		n-	galwba
			ŋgaluba

Metathesis b w > w b; syllabification of /w/

KOTOKO-ISLAND	Buduma		√ C CaCaCaCa +Y, +W
			*Ø lag maØʷa -y
			laʷgʷəmaʸ -Øy
			loguəme

Prosodification of /w/; W-prosody affecting /a/ in 1st syllable and 2nd consonant
*g > gu ~ gʷ; Y-prosody affecting final /a/

KOTOKO-NORTH	Afade		√ C C C CaCa +Y
			*g rg m wØ -y
			gəʸrgəʸmw -Øʸ
			gɨrgimu

Vowel epenthesis; prosody affecting epenthetic vowels; syllabification of /w/

	Mpade		√ CaC C CaCa +Y, +W
			*galgmawØ -y
			galgʸəʸmaʷ Ø-ʸ
			galdʒimo

Prosodification of /w/ > ʷ; vowel epenthesis; Y-prosody affecting epenthetic vowel and 3rd root consonant; W-prosody affecting final /a/

	Malgbe		√ C CaCaCaCa +Y, +W
			*Ø lag maØʷa -y
			laʷgaʷmaʸ -Øʸ
			logome

Prosodification of /w/; W-prosody affecting /a/ in 1st and 2nd syllables; Y-prosody affecting final /a/

6.4 PCC Lexical Reconstructions   267

	Maltam	√ C C C C Ca	+Y
		*g rg m wØ -y	
		gə^{y}rg^{y}ə^{y}mw Ø-^{y}	
		girdʒimu	
		Vowel epenthesis; Y-prosody affecting epenthetic vowel and 3rd root consonant; syllabification of /w/	
KOTOKO- CENTRAL	Lagwan	√ C C C CaCa	+W
		*k rg mawØ	
		> kə^{w}rgə^{w}maØ^w	
		kurguma	
		Prosodification of /w/ > ^{w}; vowel epenthesis; prosody affecting epenthetic vowels	
	Mser	√ C C C CaCa	+W
		*g rg mawØ	
		gə^{w}rgə^{w}maØ^w	
		gurguma	
		Prosodification of /w/ > ^{w}; vowel epenthesis; prosody affecting epenthetic vowels	
KOTOKO- SOUTH	Mazera	√ C C C CaCa	+W
		*k rg mawØ	
		kə^{w}rgə^{w}maØ^w	
		kurguma	
		Prosodification of /w/ > ^{w}; vowel epenthesis; prosody affecting epenthetic vowels	
MUSGUM	Mbara	√ C C C C Ca	
		*Ø l k m wa	
		> l k w ma	
		> l w k ma	
		lukma	
		lukma	
		Double metathesis m w > w m; k w > w k; syllabification of /w/	
GIDAR	Gidar	√ C CaCaC Ca +W	
		*Ø lagam Ø^{w}a	
		la^{w}ga^{w}ma^w	
		logomo	
		Prosodification of /w/; prosody affecting all vowels	

cook, to

Alternative reconstruction (**PCC**)
k-, ma-, RED   **da**   -a, -y, -k, -k^w a   +Y, +W   PC *da
                                                           (PN)

d v. to cook *préparer* (13 groups, 37 languages) A cf: tɨsaw, sɨwra$_2$.

This is the generic root for 'to cook'. The devoicing of *d to *t in the Margi and Higi groups is a regular change. The Malgwa root /g^{j}a/ is due to a regular general process where palatalised alveolar consonants become palatalised velar consonants.

DABA	Buwal, Gavar		√ Ca *da da		
	Mbudum[9]	k-RED kə-də^w-	√ Ca *da da kəduda Prosodification of /w/ > ^{w}; vowel epenthesis; prosody affecting epenthetic vowel in penultimate	-k^w -Ø^w	+W
		k- kə-	√ Ca *da da kəda Vowel epenthesis		
	Daba		√ Ca *ta ta		
SUKUR	Sukur		√ Ca *da də Centralisation of /a/		
HURZA	Mbuko		√ Ca *da da		
MARGI	Bura, Margi, Kilba		√ Ca *ta ta		

---

[9] The origin and nature of 'prefixal' d-(u)- remains obscure. Its consonantal part could be a not yet verified REDuplication from √ da, but still the vowel [u] would require explanation, possibly from the 'suffixal' augment *{-k^w}?

6.4 PCC Lexical Reconstructions

	Bura		√ Ca	-y	
			*tØ	-i	
			ti		
			Syllabification of /y/		
MANDARA	Matal		√ Ca		
		ma-	*tØ	-a-y	
		ma-	t	-ay	
			matay		
	Podoko		√ Ca		
			*ta		
			ta		
	Malgwa		√ Ca		+Y
			*da	-y	
			dʸa	-Øʸ	
			gya		
			Prosody affecting initial consonant		
	Glavda		√ Ca		
			*ta		
			ta		
MOFU	Ouldeme,		√ Ca		
	Muyang		*dØ	-y	
			d	-i	
			di		
			Syllabification of /y/		
	Mada		√ Ca		+Y
		ma-	*da	-y	
		maʸ-	daʸ	-Øʸ	
			mede		
			Prosody affecting all /a/		
	Moloko		√ Ca		+Y
			*da	-y	
			daʸ	-Øʸ	
			de		
			Prosody affecting /a/		
	Zulgo		√ Ca		
			*da		
			da		

	Gemzek		√ Ca			+Y
		ma-	*da		-y	
		ma^y-	da^y		-Ø^y	
			mede			
			Prosody affecting all /a/			

	Merey		√ Ca	
			*da	
			da	

	Dugwor		√ Ca	
		ma-	*dØ	-a-y
		ma-	d	-ay
			maday	

	Mofu North		√ Ca		+Y
		ma-	*tØ	-a-y	
		ma^y-	t	-a^{y}y^y	
			metey		
			Prosody affecting all /a/		

	Mofu-Gudur		√ Ca
			*tØ
			t

MAROUA	Giziga-Muturwa, -Marva, Mbazla		√ Ca *dØ *di* Syllabification of /y/	-y -i	+Y

LAMANG	Lamang		√ Ca
			*da
			da

HIGI	Kamwe-Nkafa, Kirya		√ Ca
			*ta
			ta

	Psikye		√ Ca			+Y
			*ta	-y-k	a	
			ta	-Ø^y-k	a^y	
			take			
			Prosody affecting FV; note the somewhat exceptional 'spread' rather than the much more frequent 'anticipation' of Y-prosody			

6.4 PCC Lexical Reconstructions

	Bana	√ Ca		
		*ta		
		ta		
KOTOKO-NORTH	Mpade	√ Ca		
		*da		
		da		
KOTOKO-SOUTH	Mazera	√ Ca		+W
		*da	-k^w	
		ə^{w}da^w	-Ø^w	
		udo		
		Vowel prothesis; prosodification of		
		*k^w > ^{w}; prosody affecting all vowels		
MUSGUM	Mulwi	√ Ca		+Y
		*dØ	-y	
		d	-i	
		di		
		Syllabification of /y/		
	Mbara	√ Ca		+Y
		*tØ	-y	
		tə^y	-i^y	
		tii		
		Vowel epenthesis; prosody affecting		
		epenthetic vowel; syllabification of /y/;		
		Cə^y+y > Cii		
GIDAR	Gidar	√ Ca		+Y
		*da	-y	
		ə^{y}da	-Ø^y	
		ɨda		
		Vowel prothesis; prosody affecting		
		prothetic vowel		

cow

Alternative reconstruction (**PCC**)

a-, k-, n-, wr-, wa-   **ɬa**   -a, -y, -n   a   +Y, +W   PC *hla (PN),
                                                          *ɬ$_2$- (a) (JS),
                                                          *n-ɬV > *ɬa (OS)

ɬa nf. cow *bœuf* (18 groups, 54 languages)

This is the best attested root in Central Chadic, occurring in all eighteen groups. *ɬ has the regular reflex *ɮ in the South sub-branch, with the further regular reflex *l within part of the Bata group. *ɬ also has the regular reflexes *h in Buduma, *s in Proto-Kotoko-South and some of the other Kotoko languages, and *ʃ in Mpade.

BATA	Gude	√ Ca *la *la*		
	Jimi	√ Ca *la -n *lan*		
	Sharwa	√ Ca *la *la*		
	Tsuvan	√ Ca *ɮa *ɮa*		
DABA	Mazagway Hidi, Daba	√ Ca *ɮa *ɮa*		
MAFA	Mafa	√ Ca *ɮa -y ɮaʸ -Øʸ *ɮe* Prosody affecting final /a/		+Y
	Cuvok	√ Ca *ɮa *ɮa*		
TERA	Tera, Nyimatli	√ Ca *ɮa *ɮa*		
	Nyimatli	√ Ca *ɮa -y ɮaʸ -Øʸ *ɮe* Prosody affecting final /a/		+Y
SUKUR	Sukur	√ Ca *ɮa *ɮə* Centralisation of final /a/		
HURZA	Mbuko	√ Ca *ɬa *ɬa*		

6.4 PCC Lexical Reconstructions   273

	Vame		√ Ca		
		a-	*ɬa		
			aɬa		

MARGI	Margi, Margi-		√ Ca		
	South, Kilba		*ɬa		
			ɬa		

	Bura		√ Ca		
			*ɬØ	-y	
			ɬ	-i	
			ɬi		
			Syllabification of /y/		

MANDARA	Matal, Podoko		√ Ca		
			*ɬa		
			ɬa		

	Mandara		√ Ca		+Y
		a-	*ɬa	-y	
		aʸ-	ɬa	-Øʸ	
			eɬa		
			Prosody affecting first syllable /a/		

	Malgwa		√ Ca		
		a-	*ɬa		
			əthla		
			Centralisation of prefixal /a/		

	Glavda		√ Ca		
			*ɬa		
			ɬa		

MOFU	Ouldeme,		√ Ca		
	Moloko, Zulgo,		*ɬa		
	Gemzek, Merey,		ɬa		
	Dugwor, Mofu North,				
	-Gudur				

MAROUA	Giziga-Muturwa,		√ Ca		
	-Marva, Mbazla		*ɬa		
			ɬa		

LAMANG	Lamang, Hdi		√ Ca		
			*ɬa		
			ɬa		

274   Full Lexical Reconstructions

HIGI	Kamwe-Nkafa, Kirya, Psikye, Bana		√ Ca *ɬa ɬa	
KOTOKO-ISLAND	Buduma		√ Ca *xa ha	
KOTOKO-NORTH	Afade, Malgbe		√ Ca *ɬa ɬa	
	Mpade		√ Ca *sa sʸa ʃa Prosody affecting initial consonant	+Y -y -Øʸ
KOTOKO-CENTRAL	Lagwan	n-	√ Ca *ɬa nɬa	
	Mser		√ Ca *sa sa	
KOTOKO-SOUTH	Zina	a-	√ Ca *sa asa	
	Mazera	k- kəʸ-	√ Ca sa sa kɨsa Vowel epenthesis; prosody affecting epenthetic vowel	+Y -y -Øʸ
MUSGUM	Vulum		√ Ca *ɬØ ɬ ɬay	-a-y -ay
	Mulwi		√ Ca *ɬa ɬaʸ ɬe Prosody affecting final /a/	+Y -y -Øʸ

6.4 PCC Lexical Reconstructions   275

	Mbara		√ Ca		+W
		wr-	*ɮØ	-a-y	
		wəʷr-	ɮ	-ay	
			wurɮay		
			Vowel epenthesis; prosody		
			affecting epenthetic vowel		

GIDAR	Gidar		√ Ca		+Y
		wa-	*ɬØ	-y	a
		wa-	ɬəʸ	-yʸ	a
			waɬiya		
			Vowel epenthesis; prosody		
			affecting epenthetic vowel		

crocodile

Alternative reconstruction (**PCC**)
m-   **r ga**   -y, -kʷ   +Y, +W

rigɨ n. crocodile *crocodile* (4 groups, 7 languages) B syn: kɨdɨm.
This root is only found within the Kotoko languages. *kɨdɨm is the
Proto-Chadic root.

KOTOKO-	Buduma		√ C Ca		+Y
ISLAND			*l ga	-y	
			ləʸgə	-Øʸ	
			ligə		
			Vowel epenthesis; prosody affecting epenthetic		
			vowel; centralisation of final /a/		

KOTOKO-	Afade		√ C Ca		+Y, +W
NORTH			*l ga	-y -kʷ	
			ləʸgaʷ	-Øʸ-Øʷ	
			ligo		
			Prosodification of *kʷ > ʷ; vowel epenthesis;		
			Y-prosody affecting epenthetic vowel; W-prosody		
			affecting final /a/		

	Mpade,		√ C Ca		+Y
	Malgbe		*l ga	-y	
			ləʸgəʸ	-Øʸ	
			ligɨ		
			Vowel epenthesis; centralisation of final /a/; prosody		
			affecting all vowels		

KOTOKO-	Lagwan		√ C Ca		+Y
CENTRAL		m-	*d ga	-y	
		məʸ-	dəʸgaʸ	-Øʸ	
			midige		
			Vowel epenthesis; prosody affecting all vowels		

276   Full Lexical Reconstructions

	Mser		√ C Ca		+Y
	m-	*r ga	-y		
	mə^y-	rga^y	-Ø^y		
		mirge			
		Vowel epenthesis; prosody affecting all vowels			
KOTOKO- SOUTH	Mazera		√ C Ca		+Y
		*l ɣa	-y		
		lə^yɣa^y	-Ø^y		
		liye			
		Vowel epenthesis; prosody affecting all vowels			

cry, to

Alternative reconstruction (**PCC**)
ma-   **ts(a)wa**   -a, -y, -k   a   +Y, +W   PC: *tVʔ/w-
                                                                      ~ *cVw/ʔ- (OS)

tsiwi v. to cry *pleurer* (11 groups, 34 languages) B
The initial *ts has the reflex *t in several groups. In Proto-Bata, Proto-Lamang, Proto-Mofu and Proto-Musgum this is part of a regular process, but in other groups it is a sporadic change. The change *ts→s in Proto-Kotoko Centre is regular. In Mandara and Malgwa, the palatalisation prosody has developed, which has caused the palatalisation of *t. There is a regular process whereby palatalised alveolars are realised as palatalised velars, which here gives *t^j→k^j.

BATA	Bata, Gude		√ C Ca		+W
			*t wØ		
			tə^wwØ		
			tuu		
			Syllabification of /w/; vowel epenthesis; prosody affecting epenthetic vowel; Cə^w+w > Cuu		
	Sharwa		√ C Ca		+W
			*t wa		
			tə^wwə		
			tuwə		
			Prosodification of /w/ > w^w; vowel epenthesis; prosody affecting epenthetic vowel; final /a/ centralisation		
MARGI	Bura		√ C Ca		+W
			*t wa		
			tə^wwa		
			tuwa ~ tua		
			Vowel epenthesis; prosody affecting epenthetic vowel		

6.4 PCC Lexical Reconstructions

	Margi	√ C Ca		
		*t ØØ	-y	
		t	-i	
		ti		
		Syllabification of /y/		
	Margi-South, Kilba	√ C Ca		+Y
		*t wØ	-y	
		tə^{y}w	-i^y	
		tiwi		
		Vowel epenthesis; prosody affecting epenthetic vowel; syllabification of /y/		
MANDARA	Matal	√ C Ca		
	ma-	*t wØ	-a-y	
	ma-	təw	-ay	
		matəway		
		Vowel epenthesis		
	Podoko	√ CaCa		
		*tawa		
		tawa		
	Mandara	√ C Ca		+Y
		*t wa	-y	
		t^{y}ua	-Ø^y	
		k^{y}ua		
		Syllabification of /w/; prosody affecting initial consonant		
	Malgwa	√ C Ca	-y	+Y, +W
		*t wa	-Ø^y	
		t^{y}ə^{w}w^{w}a		
		k^{y}uwa		
		Prosodification of /w/ > w^w; Y-prosody affecting initial consonant, W-prosody affecting epenthetic vowel		
	Glavda	√ C Ca		+W
		*t wØ	-k	a
		tə^{w}u	-k	a
		tu:ga		
		Syllabification of /w/; vowel epenthesis; prosody affecting epenthetic vowel: tə^{w}w > tu:		
MOFU	Ouldeme	√ C Ca		+W
		*t wa		
		tə^{w}wa^w		

		tuwo	
		Prosodification of /w/ > w^w; vowel epenthesis; prosody affecting all vowels	
Muyang		√ C Ca	+W
		*t wØ	-y
		tə^{w}w^w	-i
		tuwi	
		Prosodification of /w/ > w^w; vowel epenthesis; prosody affecting epenthetic vowel; syllabification of /y/	
Moloko		√ C Ca	+Y
		*t wa	-y
		təwa^y	-Ø^y
		təwe	
		Vowel epenthesis; prosody affecting final /a/	
Zulgo		√ C Ca	+W
		*t wa	
		tə^{w}w^{w}a	
		tuwa	
		Prosodification of /w/ > w^w; vowel epenthesis; prosody affecting epenthetic vowel	
Gemzek		√ C Ca	+Y, +W
	ma-	*t wa	-y
	ma^y-	tə^{w}w^{w}a^y	-Ø^y
		metuwe	
		Prosodification of /w/ > w^w; vowel epenthesis; W-prosody affecting epenthetic vowel; Y-prosody affecting all /a/	
Merey		√ C Ca	+W
		*t wa	
		tə^{w}w^{w}a	
		tuwa	
		Prosodification of /w/ > w^w; vowel epenthesis; prosody affecting epenthetic vowel	
Dugwor		√ C Ca	+W
	ma-	*t wØ	-a-y
	mə-	tə^{w}w^w	-ay
		mətuway	

6.4 PCC Lexical Reconstructions 279

		Prosodification of /w/ > w^w; vowel epenthesis; prosody affecting epenthetic vowel; /a/ centralisation in prefix	
	Mofu-Gudur	√ C Ca *t wØ təw Vowel epenthesis	
MAROUA	Giziga-Muturwa	√ C Ca *t wØ -y tə^{w}w^{w}ə^w -y tuwuy Prosodification of /w/ > w^w; vowel epenthesis; prosody affecting epenthetic vowels	+W
	Giziga-Marva	√ C Ca *t wØ -a-y tə^{w}w^w -ay tuway Prosodification of /w/ > w^w; vowel epenthesis; prosody affecting epenthetic vowel	+W
	Giziga-Marva	√ C Ca *t wa tə^{w}w^{w}a tuwa Prosodification of /w/ > w^w; vowel epenthesis; prosody affecting epenthetic vowel	+W
	Mbazla	√ C Ca *t wØ -a-y tə^{w}w^w -ay tuway Prosodification of /w/ > w^w; vowel epenthesis; prosody affecting epenthetic vowel	+W
LAMANG	Lamang	√ CaCa *tawa tawa	

	Hdi	√ CaCa	-a-y
		*tawØ	-ay
		taw	
		taway	
KOTOKO-ISLAND	Buduma	√ C Ca	+Y
		*ts wØ	-y
		ts^{y}w	-y
		tʃuy	
		Syllabification of /w/; prosody affecting initial consonant; syllabification of /y/	
KOTOKO-NORTH	Afade	√ C Ca	+Y
		*ts wa	-y
		tsə^{y}wa^y	-Ø^y
		tsɨwe	
		Vowel epenthesis; prosody affecting all vowels	
	Mbade	√ C Ca	+Y
		*s wa	-y
		swa^y	-Ø^y
		swe	
		Prosody affecting final vowel /a/	
	Malgbe	√ C Ca	+Y, +W
		*s wa	-y
		sə^{w}w^{w}a^y	-Ø^y
		suwe	
		Prosodification of /w/ > w^w; vowel epenthesis; W-prosody affecting epenthetic vowel; Y-prosody affecting /a/	
KOTOKO-CENTRAL	Lagwan	√ C Ca	+Y
		*s wa	-y
		sə^{y}wa^y	-Ø^y
		sɨwe	
		Vowel epenthesis; prosody affecting all vowels	
	Mser	√ C Ca	+Y
		*s wa	-y
		swa^y	-Ø^y
		swe	
		Prosody affecting final vowel /a/	

6.4 PCC Lexical Reconstructions

KOTOKO-SOUTH	Zina	√ C Ca *ts wØ -y a ts^{y}ə^{w}w^w -y^y a *t∫uwya* Prosodification of /w/ > w^w; vowel epenthesis; W-prosody affecting epenthetic vowel; Y-prosody affecting initial consonant	+Y, +W
MUSGUM	Mulwi	√ C Ca *t wØ -y tə^{w}w^w -i *tuwi* Prosodification of /w/ > w^w; vowel epenthesis; prosody affecting epenthetic vowel; syllabification of /y/	+W
	Mbara	√ C Ca *t wa tə^{w}w^{w}a *tuwa* Prosodification of /w/ > w^w; vowel epenthesis; prosody affecting epenthetic vowel	+W

die, to

Alternative reconstruction (**PCC**)
k-, ma-   **m(a)ta**[10]   -a, -y,   a   +Y, +W   PC: *mətə (PN),
                           -k, -k^w,   *mwt (JS),
                           -n, -ŋ   *mV(wV)t- (OS)

mits v. to die *mourir* (18 groups, 47 languages) A rel. to: mits.
    This is one of the most widely-attested Central Chadic roots, and reflexes are found in all eighteen groups. There is a regular change *ts→t which took place independently in several different groups. The resulting *t has the unestablished reflexes *d in Proto-Kotoko North, *ɗ in Proto-Musgum and *r in Proto-Kotoko South. If the Sukur word is cognate, then we have the regular change *ts→s, and the initial *m has the irregular reflex /ŋ^w/.

BATA	Jimi	√ C Ca *m ta -n

---

[10] Gravina reconstructs the PCC second consonant as */ts/, which is here considered a later development from PCC */t/.

			mətə -n
			mətən
			Vowel epenthesis; centralisation of final /a/

        Sharwa   √ C Ca   +Y
                        *m ta   -y
                        mə^{y}tə   -Ø^y
                        mitə
                        Vowel epenthesis; prosody affecting
                        epenthetic vowel; centralisation of final /a/

DABA   Buwal   √ CaCa   +Y
                        *matsØ   -y
                        mats^y -Ø^y
                        matʃ
                        Prosody affecting final consonant

        Gavar   √ C Ca   +Y
                        *m tsa   -y
                        mts^{y}a   -Ø^y
                        mtʃa
                        Prosody affecting final consonant

        Mbudum   √ C Ca   +Y
                     k- *m tsØ   -y
                     kə- məts^y -Ø^y
                        kəmatʃ
                        Vowel epenthesis; prosody affecting final
                        consonant

        Daba   √ C Ca   +Y
                        *m tsØ   -y
                        məts^y -Ø^y
                        mətʃ
                        Vowel epenthesis; prosody affecting final
                        consonant

MAFA   Mafa,   √ C Ca
            Cuvok   *m tsa
                        mətsa
                        Vowel epenthesis

TERA   Tera   √ C Ca
                        *m ɗØ   -y
                        məɗ   -i
                        məɗi
                        Vowel epenthesis; syllabification of /y/

6.4 PCC Lexical Reconstructions

	Nyimatli		√ C Ca		
			*m tØ		
			m t		
			mt		
			mət		
			Vowel epenthesis		
SUKUR	Sukur		√ C Ca		
			*m sØ	-kʷ	
			mkʷs		
			> ŋkʷs		
			ŋws		
			ŋus		
			Metathesis *s kʷ > kʷ s; assimilation *m > ŋ/_kʷ; weakening /kʷ/ > /w/; syllabification of /w/		
HURZA	Mbuko		√ CaCa		
			*matsØ		
			mats		
	Vame		√ C Ca		
			*m tsa		
			mətsa		
			Vowel epenthesis		
MARGI	Bura		√ C Ca		
			*m ta		
			mta		
MANDARA	Matal		√ C Ca		
		ma-	*m tsØ	-a-y	
		ma-	mts	-ay	
			mamtsay		
	Podoko		√ C Ca		+Y
			*m tsa	-y	
			məʸtsʸaʸ	-Øʸ	
			mitʃe		
			Vowel epenthesis; prosody affecting all vowels and final consonant		
	Malgwa		√ C Ca		
			*m tsa		
			mtsa		
	Glavda		√ C Ca		+Y
			*m tsØ	-y-k	a

284   Full Lexical Reconstructions

			əʸmts -Øʸ-g a

imtsᵊga
Vowel prothesis; prosody affecting
prothetic vowel; vowel epenthesis/open
phonetic transition

	Dghweɗe		√ C Ca *m tsa *mtsa*
MOFU	Ouldeme		√ C Ca *m tØ *mət* Vowel epenthesis
	Mada	ma-	√ C Ca *m ta *mamta*
	Moloko		√ CaCa *matØ *mat*
	Zulgo		√ C Ca *m tØ *mət* Vowel epenthesis
	Gemzek	ma- maʸ-	√ C Ca +Y *m ta -y mətaʸ -Øʸ *memәte* Vowel epenthesis; prosody affecting all /a/
	Merey		√ C Ca *m tØ *mət* Vowel epenthesis
	Dugwor	ma- ma-	√ C Ca *m tØ -a-y mt -ay *məmtay* Centralisation of prefixal /a/
	Mofu- Gudur		√ C Ca *m tsØ

6.4 PCC Lexical Reconstructions   285

| | | məts |
| | | Vowel epenthesis |

		√ C Ca	+Y
	ma-	*m tsØ -a-y	
	ma^y-	məts -a^yy^y	
		memətsey	
		Vowel epenthesis; prosody affecting	
		all /a/	

MAROUA   Giziga-   √ C Ca   +Y, +W
          Muturwa,   *m tsØ   -y-k^w
          Giziga-   mə^wts^y   -Ø^y-Ø^w
          Marva,   mutʃ
          Mbazla   Prosodification of /k^w/ > ^w; vowel
                       epenthesis; W-prosody affecting
                       epenthetic vowel; Y-prosody affecting
                       final consonant

          Mbazla   √ C Ca   +Y, +W
                       *m tsØ   -y-k^w
                       > m y ts   -Ø^w
                       mə^wyts^y
                       muitʃ
                       Metathesis *ts y > y ts; vowel
                       epenthesis; W-prosody affecting
                       epenthetic vowel; Y-prosody affecting
                       final consonant; syllabification of
                       medial /y/

LAMANG   Lamang   √ C Ca
                       *m ta
                       mta

          Hdi   √ C Ca
                       *m tØ   -a-y
                       mət   -ay
                       mətay
                       Vowel epenthesis

HIGI   Kamwe-   √ C Ca
          Nkafa   *m ta
                       mtə
                       mtə
                       Centralisation of final /a/

	Kamwe- Futu	√ C Ca +W *m ta -k^w mta^w -Ø^w *mto* Prosodification of /k^w/ > ^{w}; prosody affecting final /a/
	Psikye	√ C Ca *m ta mtə *mtə* Centralisation of final /a/
	Bana	√ C Ca *m tØ -y mət -i *m(ə)ti* Vowel epenthesis; syllabification of /y/
KOTOKO- ISLAND	Buduma	√ CaCa *mata matə *matə* Centralisation of final /a/
KOTOKO- NORTH	Afade, Mpade	√ CaCa +Y *mada y madə^y -Ø^y *madɨ* Centralisation of final /a/; prosody affecting centralised /a/
	Malgbe	√ CaCa *madØ -y mad -i *madi* Syllabification of /y/
KOTOKO- CENTRAL	Lagwan	√ C Ca +Y *m tØ -y mə^{y}t -i^y *mɨti* Vowel epenthesis; prosody affecting epenthetic vowel; syllabification of /y/

6.4 PCC Lexical Reconstructions

	Mser	√ CaCa	+W
		*mata -kʷ	
		mataʷ -Øʷ	
		mato	
		Prosodification of /kʷ/ > ʷ; prosody affecting final /a/	
KOTOKO-SOUTH	Zina	√ CaCa	
		*mara	
		mara	
MUSGUM	Vulum, Mulwi	√ C Ca	+Y
		*m rØ -y	
		məʸr -iʸ	
		miri	
		Vowel epenthesis; prosody affecting epenthetic vowel; syllabification of /y/	
	Mbara	√ C Ca	+Y
		*m ɗØ -y-ŋ	
		məʸɗ -iʸ-ŋ	
		mi'diŋ	
		Vowel epenthesis; prosody affecting epenthetic vowel; syllabification of /y/	
GIDAR	Gidar	√ C Ca	
		*m ta	
		əmta	
		əmta	
		Vowel prothesis	
		√ C Ca	+W
		*m ta -kʷ	
		əʷmta -Øʷ	
		umta	
		Prosodification of /kʷ/ > ʷ; vowel prothesis; prosody affecting prothetic vowel	

dog

Alternative reconstruction (**PCC**/loan?)
        k(a)ra   -a, -y, -kʷ   a   +Y   PC: *kər- (PN), *kɗ(u) (JS), *kVr- (OS)

kɨri nm. dog *chien* (13 groups, 35 languages) C
    This root may have come into Central Chadic from Kanuri or from Nilo-Saharan. The root presents some unusual difficulties. *r

has the reflex *d in some languages, and *l in others. If this root were a Proto-Central Chadic root, then we would expect *r→l in the North sub-branch, but this is the case only in a few groups, some of which have a separate, later *r→l change. A Proto-Central Chadic root with *d in medial position should give *r in the North sub-branch. There is a reasonable degree of consistency in this, but there are many exceptions. The best explanation for the forms is that the word entered Central Chadic at the time of the group proto-languages. The final vowel is reconstructed as *i, as in Kanuri, and this is reflected in Proto-Margi, Proto-Lamang and Proto-Higi. In the Higi group the *i has been reanalysed as palatalisation of *l.

MAFA	Mafa	√ C Ca *k da kəda Vowel epenthesis	
	Cuvok	√ C Ca *g da gəda Vowel epenthesis	
SUKUR	Sukur	√ C Ca *k ra kəra Vowel epenthesis	
HURZA	Mbuko, Vame	√ C Ca *k la kəla Vowel epenthesis	
MARGI	Bura	√ C Ca +Y *k la -y kə^{y}la -Ø^y kila Vowel epenthesis; prosody affecting epenthetic vowel	
MANDARA	Matal, Podoko	√ C Ca *k da kəda Vowel epenthesis	
	Mandara	√ CaCa +Y *kara -y ka^{y}ra^y -Ø^y kere Prosody affecting all vowels	

6.4 PCC Lexical Reconstructions

	Malgwa	√ C Ca *k ra kəra^y *kəre* Vowel epenthesis; prosody affecting final /a/	+Y -y -Ø^y
	Dghweɗe	√ C Ca *g da gda^y *gde* Prosody affecting /a/	+Y -y -Ø^y
MOFU	Ouldeme, Muyang, Moloko, Zulgo, Gemzek, Dugwor	√ C Ca *k ra *kəra* Vowel epenthesis	
	Mofu North, Mofu- Gudur	√ C Ca *g dØ gəd *gədey* Vowel epenthesis; prosody affecting /a/	+Y -a-y -a^{y}y^y
MAROUA	Giziga- Muturwa	√ C Ca *k rØ kə^{y}r *kiri* Vowel epenthesis; prosody affecting epenthetic vowel; syllabification of /y/	+Y -y -i^y
	Giziga- Marva	√ C Ca *k ra kra^y *kre* Prosody affecting /a/	+Y -y -Ø^y
	Mbazla	√ C Ca *k ra kə^{y}ra^y *kire* Vowel epenthesis; prosody affecting all vowels	+Y -y -Ø^y
		√ C Ca *k ra kra^y *krɛ'* Prosody affecting /a/; unclear origin of final '	+Y -y -Ø^y

290   Full Lexical Reconstructions

LAMANG	Lamang	√ C Ca		+Y
		*k ra	-y	
		kəra^y	-Ø^y	
		kəre		
		Vowel epenthesis; prosody affecting /a/		
	Hdi	√ C Ca		
		*k rØ	-y	
		kər	-i	
		kəri		
		Vowel epenthesis; syllabification of /y/		
HIGI	Kamwe-Nkafa	√ C Ca		+Y
		*k la	-y	
		kəl^{y}ə	-Ø^y	
		kəlyə°		
		Vowel epenthesis; prosody affecting final consonant; centralisation of final /a/		
	Kamwe-Futu	√ C Ca		+Y
		*k la	-y	
		kəl^{y}a^y	-Ø^y	
		kəlye		
		Vowel epenthesis; prosody affecting final consonant and final /a/		
	Kirya	√ C Ca		+Y
		*k rØ	-y	
		kəɾ	-i^y	
		kəɾi		
		Vowel epenthesis; prosody affecting final consonant; syllabification of /y/		
KOTOKO-ISLAND	Buduma	√ C Ca		
		*k lØ	-y	a
		kəl	-i	ə
		kəli(ə)		
		Vowel epenthesis; syllabification of /y/; centralisation of FV /a/		
KOTOKO-NORTH	Afade, Malgbe	√ C Ca		+Y
		*g la	-y-k^w	
		gə^{y}la^y	-Ø^y-w	
		gilew		
		Weakening of /k^w/ > /w/; vowel epenthesis; prosody affecting vowels; syllabification of /w/		
	Mpade	√ C Ca		+Y
		*k la	-y-k^w	

6.4 PCC Lexical Reconstructions

		kəʸlaʸ -Øʸ-w	
		k*i*lew	
		Weakening of /kʷ/ > /w/; vowel epenthesis; prosody affecting vowels; syllabification of /w/	
KOTOKO-CENTRAL	Lagwan, Mser	√ C Ca	+Y
		*k la -y	
		klaʸ -Øʸ	
		kle	
		Prosody affecting /a/	
	Lagwan	√ C Ca	+Y
		*k la -y	
		kəʸlaʸ -Øʸ	
		k*i*le	
		Vowel epenthesis; prosody affecting all vowels	
GIDAR	Gidar	√ C Ca	
		*k ra	
		kəra	
		Vowel epenthesis	
		√ C Ca	
		*kra	
		kra	

donkey₁

Alternative reconstruction (**PCC**)
a-, xa-   **z(a)ᵑgʷa**   -y, -kʷ   +Y, +W   PC : —

ziᵑgʷa n. donkey *âne* (8 groups, 22 languages) B syn: koro, ᵐburi.
This is one of three common roots for 'donkey'. It is found in the languages of the Mandara Mountains. It is one of the few roots reconstructed with *ᵑgʷ.

DABA	Mbudum	√ CaCa	+W
		*zaᵑgʷa	
		zaʷᵑgʷaʷ	
		zoᵑgo	
		Prosody affecting all /a/	
MAFA	Cuvok	√ CaCa	
		*zaᵑgʷa	
		zaᵑgwa	
SUKUR	Sukur	√ C Ca	+W
		*z ᵑgʷa	
		zəʷᵑgʷa	
		zuᵑgʷa	
		Vowel epenthesis; prosody affecting epenthetic vowel	

292   Full Lexical Reconstructions

$\sqrt{}$ C Ca
*z $^{\emptyset}$g^{w}a
zəg^{w}a
zəg^{w}a
Vowel epenthesis

HURZA	Mbuko	$\sqrt{}$ C Ca	+W

*z ^{ŋ}g^{w}a
zə^{wŋ}g^{w}a^{w}
zu^{ŋ}go
Vowel epenthesis; prosody affecting all vowels

	Vame	$\sqrt{}$ C Ca		+Y
		a-	*z ŋ^{w}a	-y
		a-	zə^{y}ŋ^{w}a	-Ø^{y}

aziŋ^{w}a
Vowel epenthesis; prosody affecting epenthetic vowel

MANDARA	Matal	$\sqrt{}$ CaCa	+Y

*zaŋ^{w}a   -y -k^{w}
z^{y}aŋ^{w}ə   -Ø^{y}-w
ʒaŋ^{w}əw
Prosody affecting initial consonant; partial desegmentalisation of k^{w} > w; syllabification of /w/; centralisation of lexical final /a/

$\sqrt{}$ CaCa   +Y
*zaŋ^{w}Ø   -y -k^{w}
z^{y}aŋ^{w} -Ø^{y}-w
ʒaɲu
Partial desegmentalisation of k^{w} > w; syllabification of /w/; prosody affecting initial consonant

$\sqrt{}$ CaCa   +Y
*zaŋ^{w}Ø   -y -k^{w}
za^{y}ŋ^{w} -Ø^{y}-w
zeɲu
Partial desegmentalisation of k^{w} > w; syllabification of /w/; prosody affecting /a/

$\sqrt{}$ CaCa   +Y
*zaŋ^{w}Ø   -y -k^{w}

6.4 PCC Lexical Reconstructions 293

	za^{y}ŋə	-Ø^y-w	
	zeŋəw		
	Partial desegmentalisation of k^w > w; prosody affecting medial /a/; syllabification of /w/; centralisation of lexical final /a/		

Podoko   √ C Ca   +Y
          *zŋ^{w}a   -y
          z^{y}əŋ^{w}a   -Ø^y
          ʒəŋ^{w}a
          Vowel epenthesis; prosody affecting initial consonant

Mandara   √ CaCa   +Y
     a-   *zaŋ^{w}a   y
     a^y- za^{y}ŋ^{w}a -Ø^y
          ezeŋ^{w}a
          Prosody affecting initial and medial /a/

Malgwa   √ C Ca   +W
     a-   *z ŋ^{w}a
     ə-   zə^{w}ŋ^{w}a
          əzuŋ^{w}a
          Vowel epenthesis; prosody affecting epenthetic vowel; centralisation of prefixal /a/

Glavda   √ C Ca   +Y
     a-   *z ŋØ   -y
     a-   z^{y}ə^{y}ŋ   -Ø^y
          ayiŋ
          Vowel epenthesis; prosody affecting initial consonant and epenthetic vowel

          √ C Ca   +W
     a-   *z ŋ^{w}a   -y
     a-   z^{y}ə^{w}ŋ^{w}a -Ø^y
          ayuŋ^{w}a
          Vowel epenthesis; prosody affecting initial consonant and epenthetic vowel

Dghweɗe   √ C Ca   +Y, +W
          *z ^{ŋ}g^{w}a   -y
          zə^{wŋ}g^{w}a^y -Ø^y
          zu^{ŋ}g^{w}e

294   Full Lexical Reconstructions

			Vowel epenthesis; W-prosody affecting epenthetic vowel; Y-prosody affecting final /a/	
MOFU	Ouldeme		√ C Ca	+Y
		a-	*z ŋʷa -y	
		a-	zəʸŋʷa -Øʸ	
			aziŋʷa	
			Vowel epenthesis; prosody affecting epenthetic vowel	
	Muyang		√ CaCa	+W
		a-	*zaᵑgʷØ -kʷ	
		a-	zaʷᵑgʷ -w	
			azoᵑgu	
			Weakening of /kʷ/ > /w/; prosody affecting medial /a/; syllabification of /w/	
	Moloko		√ CaCa	+W
		a-	*zaᵑgʷa	
		aʷ-	zaʷᵑgʷaʷ	
			ozoŋgo	
			Prosody affecting all /a/	
	Zulgo		√ CaCa	+W, +Y
		xa-	*zaŋʷa -y	
		xaʸ-	zʷaʸŋØaʸ -Øʸ	
			hezʷeŋe	
			W-prosody shifting from C₂ to C₁ of the simple root, i.e. affecting initial root consonant; Y-prosody affecting all /a/	
	Gemzek, Dugwor		√ C Ca	+W
			*z ᵑgʷa	
			zəʷᵑgʷaʷ	
			zuᵑgo	
			Vowel epenthesis; prosody affecting all vowels	
	Merey		√ C Ca	
			*z ᵑga -kʷ	
			zəᵑga -w	
			zəᵑgaw	
			Vowel epenthesis; weakening of /kʷ/ > /w/; syllabification of /w/	
	Mofu North		√ CaCa	
			*zaᵑga -kʷ	
			zaᵑga -w	

6.4 PCC Lexical Reconstructions   295

		zaᵑgaw
		Weakening of /kʷ/ > /w/; syllabification
		of /w/
	Mofu-	√ C Ca
	Gudur	*z ᵑgʷa -kʷ
		zəᵑgʷa -w
		zəᵑgʷaw
		Vowel epenthesis; weakening of /kʷ/ >
		/w/; syllabification of /w/
MAROUA	Giziga-	√ C Ca +W
	Muturwa	*z ᵑgʷØ -kʷ
		zəʷᵑgʷ -w
		zuᵑgʷu
		Vowel epenthesis; prosody affecting
		epenthetic vowel; weakening of /kʷ/ > /w/;
		syllabification of /w/
	Giziga-	√ C Ca +W
	Marva	*z ᵑgʷa
		zəʷᵑgʷaʷ
		zuᵑgo
		Vowel epenthesis; prosody affecting all
		vowels
LAMANG	Lamang	√ C Ca +W
		*z ŋʷa
		zəʷŋØa
		zuŋa
		Vowel epenthesis; prosody shifting from
		C₂ to epenthetic vowel

donkey₂[11]

Alternative reconstruction (**PCC**/loan)
ᵐb(a)rdza   -y, -kʷ, -ŋ   +Y, +W

ᵐburi nm. donkey *âne* (5 groups, 6 languages) C syn: koro, ziᵑgʷa.
This is one of three roots for 'donkey' within Central Chadic. The forms cited come from three distinct areas, and may or may not be cognate. The root found in the Kotoko groups is almost certainly a fairly recent borrowing.

| BATA | Bata | √ C C Ca | +Y |
| | | *ᵐb rsa   -y | |

---

[11] If this word was a loan into some CC languages, as Gravina (2014b) assumes, its donor language has not (yet) been identified.

		ᵐbə ʸrsaʸ	-Øʸ
		ᵐ*birse*	
		Vowel epenthesis; prosody affecting epenthetic vowel and final /a/	
DABA	Buwal	√ CaC Ca	+Y
		*bardza -y –ŋ	
		baʸrdzʸaʸ -Øʸ-ŋ	
		berdʒeŋ	
		Prosody affecting final root consonant and all vowels	
KOTOKO-NORTH	Afade	√ CaC Ca	
		*ɓarØa -kʷ	
		ɓaʷraʷ -Øʷ	
		ɓoro	
		Prosodification of *kʷ > ʷ; prosody affecting all vowels	
KOTOKO-CENTRAL	Lagwan	√ C C Ca	+W
		*ᵐb r ØØ -y -kʷ	
		ᵐbəʷr -i-Øʷ	
		ᵐ*buri*	
		Prosodification of *kʷ > ʷ; vowel epenthesis; W-prosody affecting epenthetic vowel; syllabification of /y/	
KOTOKO-SOUTH	Mazera	√ C C Ca	+Y, +W
		*ᵐb r ØØ -y -kʷ	
		ᵐbəʷr -i-Øʷ	
		ᵐ*buri*	
		Prosodification of *kʷ > ʷ; vowel epenthesis; W-prosody affecting epenthetic vowel; syllabification of /y/	

donkey$_3$[12]

Alternative reconstruction (**PCC**/loan)

k(a)w(a)ra   -y, -t   a   +Y, +W   Kanuri: *koro*

koro n. donkey *âne* (9 groups, 20 languages) B syn: ziⁿgʷa, ᵐburi.

This is a widespread African root that may have come into Central Chadic from Kanuri. Many Central Chadic languages do not have back

---

[12] This is an obvious loan from or via Kanuri and thus qualifies as a 'pseudo'-PCC root insofar as it has been streamlined into Central Chadic phonology systems to the extent of being apparently 'reconstructable'.

6.4 PCC Lexical Reconstructions

vowels, and the *o has been reinterpreted as labialisation of *k, the labialisation prosody or as the sequence /aw/. The *r has not changed in any languages, which indicates a very short time-depth for the introduction of this root into Central Chadic.

BATA	Bata	√ C CaCa			+Y, +W
		*k wara	-y-t	a	
		k^{w}ara^y	-Ø^y-t	a^w	
		k^{w}aareeto			
		Prosodification of /w/ > ^{w}; W-prosody affecting initial consonant and FV; Y-prosody affecting root-final /a/; origin of vowel length remains unaccounted for			
	Gude, Jimi, Sharwa	√ C CaCa			+W
		*k wara			
		k^{w}ara			
		Prosodification of /w/ > ^{w}; prosody affecting initial consonant			
TERA	Tera	√ CaC Ca			+W
		*kawra			
		ka^{w}Ø^{w}ra^w			
		koro			
		Prosodification of /w/ > ^{w}; prosody affecting all vowels			
	Nyimatli	√ CaC Ca			+W
		*kawra			
		ka^{w}w^{w}ra^w			
		kooro			
		Prosodification of /w/ > ^{w}; prosody affecting all vowels; Ca^{w}w > Coo			
MARGI	Bura, Margi-South, Kilba	√ C CaCa			
		*k wara			
		k^{w}ara			
MAROUA	Giziga-Muturwa	√ CaC Ca			
		*kawra			
		kawra			
		√ CaC Ca			
		*kawra			
		Øawra			
		awra			

298   Full Lexical Reconstructions

HIGI	Kamwe-Nkafa	√ C CaCa	
	Kamwe-Futu,	*k wara	
	Kirya, Psikye	*k^w ara*	
KOTOKO-NORTH	Mpade	√ CaC Ca	+W
		kaʷØʷraʷ	
		koro	
		Prosodification of /w/ > ʷ; prosody affecting all /a/	
	Malgbe	√ C C Ca	+W
		*g wra	
		> g Øʷraʷ	
		gro	
		Prosodification of /w/ > ʷ; prosody affecting final /a/	
MUSGUM	Vulum	√ C C Ca	+Y, +W
		*k wra -y	
		kəʷØʷraʸ -Øʸ	
		kure	
		Prosodification of /w/ > ʷ; vowel epenthesis; W-prosody affecting epenthetic vowel; Y-prosody affecting final /a/	
	Mbara	√ C C Ca	+W
		*k wra	
		kəʷØʷraʷ	
		kuro	
		Prosodification of /w/ > ʷ; vowel epenthesis; W-prosody affecting all vowels	
	Muskum	√ C C Ca	+Y, +W
		*k wra -y-t	
		kəʷØʷraʸ -Øʸ-t	
		kuret	
		Prosodification of /w/ > ʷ; vowel epenthesis; W-prosody affecting epenthetic vowel; Y-prosody affecting root-final /a/	
GIDAR	Gidar	√ CaC Ca	+W
		*kawra	
		kaʷØʷraʷ	
		koro	
		Prosodification of /w/ > ʷ; prosody affecting all /a/	

6.4 PCC Lexical Reconstructions 299

Note: Central Chadic languages integrate this loan from Kanuri by reanalysing it as a triradical root *kawra, and allowing two root types √ C C Ca and √ CaC Ca: *kwra and *kawra.

dream

Alternative reconstruction (**PCC**)
ma-, ma-RED-, **s(a)w(a)na** -a, -y, -k, -n a +Y, +W   PC: *səwnə (PN),
RED-, n-   *swn (m-) (JS),
                                                        *sVn-
                                                        /*sVw/yVn- (OS)

sɨhʷani ʸ n. dream *rêve* (15 groups, 37 languages) B

The *s has the reflex *z in West Tera as part of a regular change. The change *n→r in Proto-Kotoko North and Mser is a common sporadic change. *hʷ is realised as /hʷ/ only in Podoko. The reflex is *w in several groups, and the consonant has been completely lost in other groups. This is a common sporadic process. In Proto-Margi it has the irregular reflex *ʔʷ. The palatalisation prosody is easily reconstructed, with evidence from all groups. *i can also be reconstructed based on the evidence from the Bata, Margi, Mandara and Lamang groups.

BATA	Bata	√ C C Ca		+Y
		*s ∅ r∅	-y	
		sʸəʸr	-iʸ	
		ʃiri		
		Vowel epenthesis; prosody affecting initial consonant and epenthetic vowel; syllabification of /y/		
	Gude	√ C C Ca		+Y
		*s ∅ na	-y	
		sənəʸ	-iʸ	
		sənii		
		Vowel epenthesis; prosody affecting centralised /a/ in final syllable; syllabification of /y/; Cə-iʸ > Cəʸiʸ > Cii creating long vowel [ii]		
	Jimi	√ C C Ca		+Y
		*s ∅ n∅	-y-n	
		səʸn	-iʸ-n	
		sinin		
		Vowel epenthesis; prosody affecting epenthetic vowel; syllabification of /y/		
	Sharwa	√ C C Ca		+Y
		*s ∅ na	-y ʼa	

300   Full Lexical Reconstructions

			sʸəʸnə	-Øʸ	'ə
			ʃinə'ə		

Vowel epenthesis; prosody affecting initial consonant and epenthetic vowel in 1st syllable; centralisation of final /a/ and FV; unclear origin of ' preceding FV

DABA	Buwal		√ C CaCa		+Y
		RED	s ØaŋØ	-y	
		saʸŋ-	saʸŋ	-Øʸ	
			seŋseŋ		

Prosody affecting all vowels

	Gavar		√ C C Ca		+Y
		RED	*s Ø ŋØ	-y	
		sʸəʸŋ-	sʸəʸŋ	-Øʸ	
			ʃiŋʃiŋ		

Vowel epenthesis; prosody affecting initial root consonant and vowels

	Mbudum		√ C C Ca		+Y
		RED	*s Ø nØ	-y	
		sə-	səʸn	-Øʸ	
			səsin		

Vowel epenthesis; prosody affecting vowel in final syllable

	Daba		√ C C Ca		+Y
			*s Ø nØ	-y	
			səʸn	-iʸ	
			sini		

Vowel epenthesis; prosody affecting epenthetic vowel; syllabification of /y/

MAFA	Mafa		√ C C Ca		+Y, +W
		n-	*s w na	-y	
		n-	sʸəʷwʷəʸnaʸ	-Øʸ	
			nʃuwine		

Prosodification of /w/ > wʷ; vowel epenthesis; W-prosody affecting first syllable epenthetic vowel; Y-prosody affecting initial consonant and all vowels in penultimate and ultimate syllable

	Cuvok		√ C CaCa		+W
			*s wana		
			səʷwʷana		

6.4 PCC Lexical Reconstructions 301

		suwana Prosodification of /w/ > w^w; vowel epenthesis; prosody affecting epenthetic vowel	
TERA	Tera, Nyimatli	√ C C Ca *z Ø na -y $z^y ə^y na^y$ -$Ø^y$ *ʒine* Vowel epenthesis; prosody affecting initial consonant and all vowels	+Y
HURZA	Mbuko	√ C C Ca *s w na -y $swna^y$ -$Ø^y$ *sune* Syllabification of /w/; prosody affecting /a/	+Y
MARGI	Bura	√ C C Ca *s w nØ -y swn -i *suni* Syllabification of /w/ and /y/	
	Kilba	√ C C Ca *s w nØ -y $s^y ə^y wn$ -i^y *ʃi'uni* Vowel epenthesis; prosody affecting epenthetic vowel and initial consonant; syllabification of medial /w/ and final /y/; unclear origin of medial '	+Y
MANDARA	Matal	√ C C Ca ma-RED *s Ø ŋ Ø -a-y ma-sa- $sə^y ŋ$ -ay^y *masasiŋay* Vowel epenthesis; prosody affecting epenthetic vowel	+Y
		√ C C Ca ma-RED *s Ø ŋ Ø a-y ma-s^ya- $s^y ə^y ŋ$ -ay^y *maʃaʃiŋay* Vowel epenthesis; prosody affecting epenthetic vowel and initial consonant (2×)	+Y

302   Full Lexical Reconstructions

	Podoko[13]	√ C CaCa		
		*s xʷana		
		səhʷana		
		Vowel epenthesis		

	Mandara	√ C CaCa		+Y
		*s Øana	-y	
		sʸaʸnaʸ	-Øʸ	
		ſene		
		Prosody affecting initial consonant and all vowels		

	Malgwa	√ C C Ca		+Y
		*s Ø na	-y	
		sʸəʸnaʸ	-Øʸ	
		ſine		
		Prosody affecting initial consonant and all vowels		

	Glavda	√ C C Ca		+Y
		*s Ø nØ	-y –k a	
		səʸn	-Øʸ-g a	
		siŋga		
		Vowel epenthesis; prosody affecting epenthetic vowel		

MOFU	Zulgo	√ C C Ca		
		*s w na		
		suna		
		Syllabification of /w/		

	Gemzek	√ C C Ca		+Y, W
		*s w na	-y	
		səʷØʷnaʸ	-Øʸ	
		sʉne		
		Prosodification of /w/ to ʷ; W-prosody affecting epenthetic vowel; Y-prosody affecting /a/		

	Merey	√ C C Ca		+Y
		ma- *s w na	-y	

---

[13] Medial /xʷ/ in Podoko raises the pertinent question whether, possibly, the simple root in PCC should not be reconstructed as **s xʷ(a)na** instead, assuming that reconstructed */w/ derived from */xʷ/ rather than the other way round.

6.4 PCC Lexical Reconstructions

		mə-	swna^y	-Ø^y
			məsune	
		Syllabification of /w/; prosody affecting /a/; centralisation of prefix /a/		
	Dugwor	√ C C Ca		+Y
		ma-	*s Ø na	-y
		mə-	sna^y	-Ø^y
		məsne		
		Prosody affecting final /a/; centralisation of prefix /a/		
	Mofu North	√ C C Ca		+Y
		ma-	*s Ø nØ	-a-y
		ma^y-	sən	-a^y y^y
		mesəney		
		Vowel epenthesis; prosody affecting all /a/		
MAROUA	Giziga-Marva	√ C C Ca		+Y
		ma-	*s Ø nØ	-y
		mə-	sə^y n	-Ø^y
		məsin		
		Vowel epenthesis; prosody affecting epenthetic vowel; centralisation of prefix /a/		
LAMANG	Lamang	√ C CaCa		+W
		*s waŋa		
		sə^w w^w aŋa		
		suwaŋa		
		Prosodification of /w/ to w^w; vowel epenthesis; prosody affecting epenthetic vowel		
	Hdi	√ C C Ca		
		*s w nØ	-y	
		swn	-i	
		suni		
		Syllabification of /w/ and /y/		
HIGI	Kamwe-Futu	√ C C Ca		+W
		*s w Øa		
		sə w^w a^w		
		səwo		
		Prosodification of /w/ to w^w; vowel epenthesis; prosody affecting /a/		

304   Full Lexical Reconstructions

	Kirya (noun)	√ C C Ca *s Ø nØ -y s^{y}ə^{y}n -Ø^y *ʃin* Vowel epenthesis; prosody affecting epenthetic vowel and initial consonant		+Y
	Kirya (verb)	√ C C Ca *s w Øa -y s^{y}ə^{y}w^{w}ə^w -Ø^y *ʃiwu* Prosodification of /w/ to w^w; vowel epenthesis; prosody affecting initial consonant and epenthetic vowel in 1st syllable; centralisation of final /a/; W-prosody affecting centralised /a/		+Y, +W
	Bana	√ C C Ca *s w ØØ -y s^{y}ə^{y}w -Ø^y *ʃiw* Vowel epenthesis; prosody affecting epenthetic vowel and initial consonant		+Y
KOTOKO- NORTH	Mpade	√ C CaCa *s wara -y swara^y -Ø^y *sware* Prosody affecting final /a/		+Y
	Malgbe	√ CaCaCa *yawara -y yawara^y -Ø^y *yaware* Prosody affecting final /a/		+Y
KOTOKO- CENTRAL	Lagwan	√ C CaCa *s wana -y swana^y -Ø^y *swane* Prosody affecting final /a/		+Y
	Mser	√ C CaCa *s wara -y swara^y -Ø^y *sware* Prosody affecting final /a/		+Y

6.4 PCC Lexical Reconstructions 305

MUSGUM	Mulwi[14]	√ C C Ca		+Y
		*x w nØ	-y	
		> x y n	-y	
		xə^{y}yn	-i^y	
		hiini		

Vowel epenthesis; prosody affecting epenthetic vowel; syllabification of /y/ (2×); Cə^{y}y > Cii creating vowel length

GIDAR	Gidar[15]	√ C C Ca		+Y
		*s w na	-y	
		> s y na	-y	
		ə^{y}ssə^{y}na^y	-Ø^y	
		issine		

Vowel prothesis and epenthesis; assimilation sy > ss; prosody affecting all vowels

earth

Alternative reconstruction (**PCC**)
a-, ya-, RED   **x^w(a)yɗa**   -y, -k   a   +Y, +W   PC: *hy (n, -t, -k)
                                                   ~ *hn ~ *gy (JS)

h^{w}aɗik n. earth *terre* (12 groups, 24 languages) C

The basic meaning of this root is the soil or earth that the ground is made from. The evidence for *h^w rather than *h comes from Cuvok, Mbuko and Lamang. In Cuvok the *h component has been lost, resulting in /w/. In Mbuko the labialisation is reanalysed as the labialisation prosody, and in Lamang it has resulted in /o/. These are common sporadic processes. In several languages the *ɗ and *i have fused, resulting in *j. In the Kilba the result is /ʔʲ/. In Kamwe-Futu and Bana the *i has caused the palatalisation of the *h. *k has been lost in all groups except for the Daba, Mafa and Hurza, which is not a regular process. The final /k/ in Hdi is a frozen suffix, and not a reflex of *k. The *i has direct support from the Margi, Lamang and Higi groups.

DABA	Buwal,	√ CaC Ca	
	Gavar,	*xay Øa	-k
	Mbudum	xaya	-k
		hayak	

---

[14] For Mulwi, we presently offer two reconstruction options subject to revision after clarity on two still open questions: (1) Is it plausible to assume a sound shift medial /w/ > /y/ to account for the internal long vowel? How else to explain the internal long vowel? (2) Is this a cognate in the first place, or rather a reflex of the noun meaning 'sleep'?

[15] The internal reconstruction for Gidar rests on the ad hoc assumption that, like possibly in Mulwi, there is a sound shift medial /w/ > /y/, which feeds into an assimilation of s-y- > -ss-. This remains a guess and cannot be considered established.

306   Full Lexical Reconstructions

MAFA	Cuvok	√ C C Ca		
		*x^w yØa	-k	
		wya	-k	
		uyak		
		Partial desegmentalisation and syllabification of initial *x^w > w > u		
TERA	Tera, Nyimatli	√ CaC Ca		
		*ɣayØØ		
		ɣay		
SUKUR	Sukur	√ CaC Ca		
		*xaØdØ		
		hadˊ		
HURZA	Mbuko	√ C C Ca		+W
		*x^w yØØ	-k	a
		> y x^w	-g	a
		yw^w	-g	a^w
		yugo		
		Metathesis *x^w y > *y x^w; syllabification of /w/ < *x^w; prosody affecting FV /a/		
	Vame	√ C C Ca		+Y
		*x yØØ	-y-k	a
		xy	-ka-y	
		higay		
		Syllabification of medial /y/; metathesis -y-ka > -ka-y		
MARGI	Bura	√ C C Ca		
		*xyØØ		
		hi		
		Syllabification of medial /y/		
	Kilba	√ C C Ca		+Y
		*xy'Ø		
		xə'y		
		hə'i		
		Metathesis y' > 'y; vowel epenthesis; syllabification of /y/		
MANDARA	Mandara, Malgwa	RED xa-	√ C C Ca *x ØØa xa *haha*	

6.4 PCC Lexical Reconstructions   307

| | Dghwede | √ CaC Ca
| | | *xayØa
| | | xaya

MOFU | Zulgo | √ C C Ca
| | a- | *xØdØ
| | a- | xəd
| | | ahəd
| | | Vowel epenthesis

MAROUA | Mbazla | √ CaC Ca
| | | *xayØØ
| | | hay

LAMANG | Lamang | √ CaC Ca   +W
| | | *xʷaØda
| | | xʷaʷdaʷ
| | | hodo
| | | Partial prosodification of xʷ: prosody affecting all /a/

| | Hdi | √ CaC Ca
| | | *xaydØ   -k
| | | > xady   -k
| | | hadik
| | | Metathesis *y d > d y; syllabification of /y/

HIGI | Kamwe-Futu | √ C C Ca   +Y
| | | *xyda
| | | > xʸiʸdəʸ
| | | hʸidi
| | | Prosodification and syllabification of medial /y/; prosody affecting initial consonant and centralised final vowel

| | Kirya | √ CaC Ca
| | RED | *xayØØ
| | xa- | xay
| | | hahay

| | Psikye | √ C C Ca
| | | *x y dØ
| | | xdy
| | | hədi
| | | Metathesis y d > d y; vowel epenthesis; syllabification of /y/

308   Full Lexical Reconstructions

	Bana		√ C C Ca *x ɣdØ xʸyʸɗəʸ *xʸidi Prosodification and syllabification of medial /y/; prosody affecting initial consonant and centralised final vowel		+Y
MUSGUM	Mbara	ya- ya-	√ CaC Ca *xayØØ xay *yahay*		

eight[16]

Alternative reconstruction (**PCC**)

m-	**tɣ(a)sa**	-y, -kʷ	+Y, +W	PC: —

tiɣis num. eight *huit* (4 groups, 11 languages) B

It is unlikely that Proto-Central Chadic had a root for 'eight'. This is the most widely attested root, and it is only present in four groups. These groups are not genetically related at a close level, so the root may be a comparatively recent coinage that has spread.

BATA	Gude		√ C C Ca *t ɣ sa *təɣəsə* Vowel epenthesis; centralisation of final /a/		
	Jimi		√ C C Ca *t ɣ sØ təɣəʸs *təɣis* Vowel epenthesis; prosody affecting epenthetic vowel in final syllable	-y -Øʸ	+Y
SUKUR	Sukur		√ C C Ca *t k zØ *təkəz* Vowel epenthesis		
MANDARA	Matal	m-	√ C C Ca t g sØ	-y	+Y

---

[16] As already noted by Gravina (see quote below), the word for 'eight' is unlikely to be reconstructable for PCC, but may be a later areal development; it would thus, like loans, qualify as being a 'pseudo'-PCC root.

6.4 PCC Lexical Reconstructions   309

| | | m- | təgᵊˀs | -Øʸ | |
| | | | *mtəgis* | | |

Vowel epenthesis; prosody affecting
epenthetic vowel in final syllable

√ C C Ca   +Y
m-   *t g sØ   -y
m-   təgᵊʸsʸ   -Øʸ
mtəgiʃ

Vowel epenthesis; prosody affecting final
consonant and epenthetic vowel in final
syllable

        Mandara   √ C C Ca   +Y
                              *t Ø sa   -y
                              təʸsaʸ   -Øʸ
                              tise

Vowel epenthesis; prosody affecting
epenthetic vowel and final /a/

        Glavda   √ C C Ca
                              *t x sa
                              txsa

LAMANG Lamang   √ C CaCa
                              *t ɣasa
                              tɣasa

        Hdi   √ C CaCa
                              *t ɣasØ
                              tɣas

HIGI   Kamwe-   √ C C Ca   +Y
           Nkafa   *t k sa   -y
                            təkəsaʸ   -Øʸ
                            təkəse

Vowel epenthesis; prosody affecting
final /a/

        Kamwe-Futu   √ C CaCa   +W
                              *d ɣasa   -kʷ
                              dəɣaʷsaʷ -Øʷ
                              dəɣoso

Vowel epenthesis; prosodification of
/kʷ/ > ʷ; prosody affecting all /a/

310   Full Lexical Reconstructions

	Kirya	√ C C Ca
		*t ɣ sØ
		təɣəs
		Vowel epenthesis
	Psikye	√ C C Ca
		*d g sa
		dəgəsə
		Vowel epenthesis; centralisation of final /a/
	Bana	√ C C Ca
		*d ɣ sa
		dəɣəsə
		d(ə)ɣəsə
		Vowel epenthesis; centralisation of final /a/

elephant

Alternative reconstruction (**PCC**)
    n va   -y, -k^w +Y

nivi n. elephant *éléphant* (2 groups, 5 languages) B syn: ^{m}bilala ^{y}, dziwin ^{y}, giwin.

This is one of four roots for 'elephant' which have been reconstructed, and is only found in some of the Kotoko languages. The change from *v to *f in Proto-Kotoko North is a regular change. The *n is only found in Lagwan. There is a common sporadic sound change in these groups *n to *r, but there is no evidence of a regular change in the other direction, and so *n is preferred in the reconstruction.

KOTOKO-NORTH	Afade	√ C Ca	
		*r fØ	-y
		arf	-i
		arfi	
		Vowel prothesis; syllabification of /y/	
	Mpade	√ C Ca	
		*r fØ	-k^w
		arf	-w
		arfu	
		Vowel prothesis: weakening of k^w > w; syllabification of /w/ > u	
	Malgbe	√ C Ca	+Y
		*r fa	-y
		arfə^y	-Ø^y
		arfɨ	

6.4 PCC Lexical Reconstructions 311

		Vowel prothesis; centralisation of final /a/; prosody affecting centralised /a/	
KOTOKO-CENTRAL	Lagwan	√ C Ca	+Y
		*n vØ -y	
		nə^{y}v -i^y	
		nivi	
		Vowel epenthesis; prosody affecting epenthetic vowel; syllabification of /y/	
	Mser	√ C Ca	
		*r vØ -y	
		arv -i	
		arvi	
		Vowel prothesis; syllabification of /y/	

extinguish, to

Alternative reconstruction (**PCC**)
k-, m(a)-   **m(a)ta**[17]   -a, -y, -k^w,   a   +Y,+W   PC: *(m)bətə
                              -n, -ŋ   (PN)

mits v. to extinguish *éteindre* (8 groups, 14 languages) B rel. to: mits.
  The basic meaning of this verb is 'to put out a fire'. This root is very similar to the root for 'to die', the only difference is that *i is reconstructed. It could possibly be a causative form, i.e. 'to cause (a fire) to die'. There is a regular word-final change *ts→t in several groups.

BATA	Jimi		√ C Ca	+Y
			*m ta -y –n	
			> m y ta -n	
			mə^{y}y^{y}tə -n	
			miitən	
			Metathesis *t y > y t; vowel epenthesis; prosodification of /y/; prosody affecting epenthetic vowel; centralisation of final /a/; Cə^{y}y > Cii;	
DABA	Mbudum		√ C Ca	+Y, +W
		k-	*m tsØ -y -k^w	
		kə-	mə^{w}ts^y -Ø^y-Ø^w	
			kəmutʃ	

---

[17] Gravina reconstructs the PCC second consonant as */ts/, which is here considered a later development from PCC */t/.

312   Full Lexical Reconstructions

			Prosodification of $k^w > {}^w$; vowel epenthesis; W-prosody affecting root-internal epenthetic vowel; Y-prosody affecting final consonant		
	Daba		√ C Ca		+Y
			*m tsØ	-y-k^w-n	
			mə^{y}ts^y	-i^y-'-n	
			mitʃi'n		
			Vowel epenthesis; prosody affecting epenthetic vowel and final root consonant; syllabification of /y/; glottal stop preceding *-n possibly deriving from *-k^w		
MAFA	Cuvok		√ C Ca		
			*m tsa		
			mətsa		
			Vowel epenthesis		
HURZA	Vame		√ C Ca		+Y, +W
		m-	*m dza	-y-k^w	a
		mə^w-	mdz^{y}ə^y	-y^y-Ø^w	a
			mu^{n}dʒiya		
			Prosodification $k^w > {}^w$; vowel epenthesis; centralisation of final /a/; W-prosody affecting epenthetic vowel in prefix; Y-prosody affecting final root consonant and centralised final /a/; homorganic nasal assimilation md > ^{n}d		
MANDARA	Matal		√ CaCa		+Y
		ma-	*matsa	-y –ŋ	
		ma-	matsəy	-Ø^y-ŋ	
			mamatsiŋ		
			Centralisation of final /a/; prosody affecting centralised final /a/		
	Podoko		√ CaCa		+Y
			*matsa	-y	
			ma^{y}ts^{y}a^y	-Ø^y	
			metʃe		
			Prosody affecting C$_2$ and all /a/		
	Glavda		√ C Ca		+Y
			*m tsa	-y	

6.4 PCC Lexical Reconstructions

			əymtsa	-Ø^y	

                                                imtsa
                                                Vowel prothesis; prosody affecting prothetic vowel

MOFU   Ouldeme $\sqrt{}$ CaCa   +Y
                                      *mata   -y -ŋ
                                      ma^yta^y   -Ø^y-ŋ
                                      meteŋ
                                      Prosody affecting all /a/

                Muyang $\sqrt{}$ CaCa   +Y
                                    *matØ   -y
                                    ma^yt   -Ø^y
                                    met
                                    Prosody affecting medial /a/

                                   $\sqrt{}$ CaCa   +Y
                                   *matØ   -y -ŋ
                                    ma^yt   -i^y-ŋ
                                    metiŋ
                                    Syllabification of /y/; prosody affecting medial /a/

                Mofu $\sqrt{}$ CaCa   +Y
                North   ma-   *matsØ   -a-y
                               ma^y-   mØts   -a^yy^y
                                    memtsey
                                    Prosody affecting all non-deleted /a/

MAROUA   Giziga- $\sqrt{}$ C Ca   +Y, +W
                Muturwa   *m tsØ   -y -k^w
                                      mə^wtsy   -Ø^y-Ø^w
                                      mutʃ
                                      Prosodification k^w > ^w; vowel epenthesis; W-prosody affecting epenthetic vowel; Y-prosody affecting final consonant

                Giziga- $\sqrt{}$ C Ca   +Y, +W
                Marva   *m tsa   -y -k^w
                                      mə^wtsya   -Ø^y-Ø^w
                                      mutʃa
                                      Prosodification k^w > ^w; vowel epenthesis; W-prosody affecting epenthetic vowel; Y-prosody affecting final consonant

314   Full Lexical Reconstructions

LAMANG	Hdi	√ C Ca	
		*m tØ	-a-y
		mətay	
		Vowel epenthesis	

faeces

Alternative reconstruction (**PCC**)

ŋ-   ɣʷ va   -a, -y, -n   +Y, +W   PC: *gb (JS),
                                               *ɦu[ɓ]- (OS)

ɣʷívi n. faeces *selles* (7 groups, 15 languages) A syn: zaj, ⁿgʷi̧.
The initial *ɣʷ is retained only in the Lamang group, and its loss is irregular in almost all cases. In Proto-Daba it has been lost, and in Proto-Bata, Proto-Sukur and Proto-Higi the labialisation component has transferred to the *v, which is a common sporadic process. There is support for *i in all groups where this vowel has been retained.

BATA	Jimi	√ C Ca		+W
		*w vØ	-y-n	
		> v w	-in	
		vʷin		
		Metathesis *w v > v w; prosodification of /w/ > labialisation vʷ; syllabification of /y/		
	Sharwa	√ C Ca		+W
		*w vØ	-a-y	
		> v w	-ay	
		vʷay		
		Metathesis *w v > v w; prosodification of /w/ > labialisation vʷ		
DABA	Buwal, Gavar, Mbudum	ŋ-	√ C Ca	
			*Ø va	
			ŋva	
SUKUR	Sukur	√ C Ca		
		*w vØ		
		> v w		
		vu		
		Metathesis *w v > v w; syllabification of /w/		
MARGI	Bura	√ C Ca		+Y
		*k vØ	-y	
		kəʸv	-iʸ	

6.4 PCC Lexical Reconstructions

		kivi		
		Vowel epenthesis; prosody affecting epenthetic vowel; syllabification of /y/		
		√ C Ca		+Y
		*k vØ	-y	
		kʸəʸv	-iʸ	
		tʃivi		
		Vowel epenthesis; prosody affecting initial consonant and epenthetic vowel; syllabification of /y/		
	Kilba[18]	√ C Ca		+Y
		*Ø bØ	-y	
		əʸØb	-iʸ	
		ibi		
		Vowel prothesis; prosody affecting prothetic vowel; syllabification of /y		
MANDARA	Mandara, Malgwa	√ C Ca		+Y, +W
		*gʷ va	-y	
		əʷgʷvaʸ	-Øʸ	
		ugve		
		Vowel prothesis; W-prosody affecting prothetic vowel; Y-prosody affecting /a/		
	Glavda	√ C Ca		+W
		*gʷ va		
		gʷəʷva		
		guva		
		Vowel epenthesis; prosody affecting epenthetic vowel		
	Dghwed̶e	√ C Ca		+Y
		*g va	-y	
		gəvaʸ	-Øʸ	
		gəve		
		Vowel epenthesis; prosody affecting /a/		
LAMANG	Lamang, Hdi	√ C Ca		+W
		*ɣʷ vØ	-y	
		ɣʷəʷv	-i	
		ɣuvi		

---

[18] Kilba would appear to 'remember' the initial consonant cluster (of which C_1 became eventually deleted) and, consequently, inserted a prothetic vowel.

316   Full Lexical Reconstructions

		Vowel epenthesis; prosody affecting epenthetic vowel; syllabification of /y/
HIGI	Kirya	√ C Ca
		*w vØ -y
		> v w -i
		$v^w i$
		Metathesis *w v > v w; prosodification of /w/ > labialisation v^w; syllabification of /y/

five

Alternative reconstruction (**PCC**)
m-, n- x^w **t(a)fa**   -y, -k   a   +Y, +W   PC: *tp (-u)(-n)
                                                                      (JS)

h^w**itif** num. five *cinq* (4 groups, 14 languages) B syn: ƙidim, łensi.

This is one of three widely attested roots for 'five'. It is found in the groups of the Nigerian Plains. Proto-Central Chadic had no *f, but *p was realised as [f] in word-final position. If this root comes from Proto-Central Chadic, then the final consonant would be *p. However it is more likely that this root originated later, at a time when the *p/*f distinction had been phonemicised, and for this reason the final consonant is given as *f. The initial *h^w is retained only in the Lamang group. In Proto-Higi it has the reflex *w. In the Bata and Margi groups, the labialisation component has transferred to the *f, from where it has become vocalised. These are common sporadic changes. The *t has become *ts in Proto-Higi, which is an irregular change, and this has been palatalised by the following *i. There is metathesis of *w and *ts in the two Kamwe dialects, a sporadic process.

BATA	Bata	√ C C Ca	+W
		*wt fØ	
		> twf	
		tuf	
		Metathesis *w t > t w; syllabification of /w/	
	Gude	√ C C Ca	+W
		*wtfa	
		> twfə	
		tufə	
		Metathesis *w t > t w; syllabification of /w/; centralisation of final /a/	
	Jimi	√ C CaCa	+Y, +W
		*wtafa -y	
		> tawfa -y	

6.4 PCC Lexical Reconstructions

			> tafwa	-y
			ta^{y}f^{w}ə	-Ø^y
			tef^{w}ə	

Double metathesis: *w t > t w and subsequently w f > f w; prosodification of w > ^{w}; W-prosody affecting and fusing with final consonant *f > f^w; Y-prosody affecting medial /a/; centralisation of final /a/

	Sharwa		√ C C Ca		
			*Øt fØ	-k	a
			təf	-k	ə
			təf(kə)		

Vowel epenthesis; centralisation of FV /a/

MARGI	Bura		√ C C Ca	+W
		n-	*wt fØ	
		n-	> twf	
		n-	> tfw^w	
		n-	tə^{w}fu	
			ntufu	

Double metathesis: *w t > t w and subsequently w f > f w; vowel epenthesis; prosodification of w > w^w; W-prosody affecting epenthetic vowel; syllabification of /w/ > u

	Margi-South		√ C C Ca
			*wt fØ
			> twf
			> tfw
			təfu
			təffu

Double metathesis *w t > t w and w f > f w; vowel epenthesis; syllabification of /w/ > u; consonant length remains unaccounted for

	Kilba		√ C C Ca
			*wtf Ø
			> twf
			> tfw
			təfu
			təfu

318   Full Lexical Reconstructions

			Double metathesis *w t > t w and w f > f w; vowel epenthesis; syllabification of /w/ > u	
LAMANG	Lamang		√ C CaCa *xʷtafa *hʷtafa*	
	Hdi		√ C CaCa *xʷtafØ xʷəʷtaf *hutaf* Vowel epenthesis; prosodification of xʷ affecting epenthetic vowel	+W
HIGI	Kamwe-Nkafa	n- n-	√ C C Ca *wts fa -y tsʸwfə -Øʸ *ntʃufə* Metathesis *w ts > ts w; prosody affecting initial consonant; syllabification of /w/; centralisation of final /a/	+Y
	Kamwe-Futu	m- m-	√ C CaCa *wtsafa -y tsʸwafə -Øʸ *mtʃwafə* Metathesis *w ts > ts w; prosody affecting initial consonant; centralisation of final /a/	+Y
	Kirya	n- n-	√ C C Ca *Øts fa -y tsʸəʸfə -Øʸ *ntʃifə* Vowel epenthesis; prosody affecting root-initial consonant and epenthetic vowel; centralisation of final /a/	+Y
	Psikye	m- m-	√ C CaCa *Øtsafa -y tsʸaʸfə -Øʸ *mtʃefə* Prosody affecting initial consonant and medial /a/; centralisation of final /a/	+Y

6.4 PCC Lexical Reconstructions   319

           Bana   √ C C Ca   +Y
                                   *Øts fa   -y
                                   tsʸəʸfə   -Øʸ
                                   t∫if ə
                                   Vowel epenthesis; prosody affecting
                                   initial consonant and epenthetic
                                   vowel; centralisation of final /a/

fly

           Alternative reconstruction (**PCC**)
           a-, xa-, m-,   **dz(a)kʷ(a)ɗa**   -y, -n, -ŋ   +Y, +W   PC: *diwa (PN),
           n-, RED   *db (-n) (JS),
                                                                      *zi/*zVw/y- ~
                                                                      čVw/y- (OS)

           Note a particular problem of reconstruction here. There is independent
           evidence for both C3 */ɗ/ and *{-y}, because both may co-occur in a
           fair number of languages. Also, there would appear to be a massively
           occurring sound change */ɗ/ > y in languages of the following groups:
           Likely in BATA, certainly in MAFA, SUKUR, HURZA,
           MANDARA, MOFU, HIGI, KOTOKO-ISLAND, KOTOKO-
           NORTH (Afade), and KOTOKO-SOUTH (Zina). There are no
           examples of languages where both would co-occur, since prosodies
           cannot accumulate. Presently, it is impossible to tell whether the */ɗ/
           > y change was triggered by morphological addition of *{-y} (as
           implied by Gravina, see quote immediately below) and *{-y} was
           afterwards lost or deleted, or whether all occurrences of final /y/ in the
           absence of underlying */ɗ/ were indeed reflexes of *{-y} with */ɗ/
           having become deleted. In keeping with our methodological principles
           established for this study, we prioritise phonological prosodies over
           morphological prosodies, i.e. we will reconstruct */ɗ/ > y. This,
           however, could be cases of under-differentiation if historically the
           sound change was indeed triggered by the presence of *{-y}, i.e. if we
           were dealing with morphological rather than phonological prosody.

           dziwɗ ʸ nf/m fly *mouche* (17 groups, 44 languages) A
           This well-attested root is found in all groups except for the Tera
           group. There is support for the palatalisation prosody across the
           reconstructions of the forms of the group proto-languages. In many
           cases there is the common change *ɗ to /j/ under palatalisation. In Proto-
           Bata *ɗ has been reduced to *ʔ, and in Proto-Kotoko North it has fused
           with *dz to form the ejective *ts'. Both of these are common sporadic
           changes. The *dz is variously realised as /d/, /z/, /ts/. The changes in
           Proto-Margi, Proto-Musgum and Proto-Kotoko Centre are regular, but
           the rest are unestablished. The *w has been lost in Proto-Bata, Proto-
           Margi and Proto-Gidar, which is a common sporadic change.

Full Lexical Reconstructions

BATA	Bata	√ C C Ca		+Y, +W
		*dz kʷ ta	-y	
		dzʸəʸkʷtaʷ	-Øʸ	
		dʒitto		

Vowel epenthesis; Y-prosody affecting initial consonant and epenthetic vowel; W-prosody affecting final /a/; assimilation kʷt > ttʷ

Alternative option (tentative):
√ C C Ca
*dz kʷ Øʸ Ø   -t   a
dzʸəʸkʷ   -t   aʷ
dʒitto

Vowel epenthesis; Y-prosody affecting initial consonant and epenthetic vowel; W-prosody affecting FV /a/; assimilation kʷt > ttʷ

	Gude	√ C C Ca	+Y
		*dz Ø yØ	
		dzʸiʸ	
		dʒi	

Prosody affecting initial consonant; syllabification of /y/

	Jimi	√ C C Ca	+Y
		*dz ' yØ	-n
		dzʸəʸ'iʸ	-n
		dʒi'in	

Vowel epenthesis; prosody affecting initial consonant and epenthetic vowel; syllabification of /y/

	Sharwa	√ C C Ca	+Y
		*dz ' yØ	
		dzʸəʸ'iʸ	
		dʒi'i	

Vowel epenthesis; prosody affecting initial consonant and epenthetic vowel; syllabification of /y/

DABA	Buwal		√ CaCaCa		+Y
		RED	*dzØwadØ	-y	
	dzʸaʸ-		dzʸəwaʸɗ	-Øʸ	
			dʒedʒəwed		

Vowel epenthesis after deletion of medial /a/ in first syllable; prosody affecting initial consonant and all non-deleted /a/

6.4 PCC Lexical Reconstructions

	Gavar		√ C C Ca	+Y
			*dz w ɗØ -y	
			dzʸəʸwəʸɗ -Øʸ	
			dʒiwiɗ	
			Vowel epenthesis; prosody affecting epenthetic vowels	
	Mbudum		√ C C Ca	+Y
		RED	*dz w ɗØ -y	
		dzʸəʸ-	dzʸəʸwəɗ -Øʸ	
			dʒidʒiwəɗ	
			Vowel epenthesis; prosody affecting first and second syllable epenthetic vowel	
	Daba		√ CaC Ca	+Y
			*tsaØ dØ -y	
			tsʸaʸd -iʸ	
			tʃedi	
			Prosody affecting initial consonant and medial /a/; syllabification of /y/	
MAFA	Mafa		√ C CaCa	+W
			*dz wayØ	
			dzəʷway	
			dzuway	
			Vowel epenthesis; prosody affecting epenthetic vowel	
SUKUR	Sukur		√ C C Ca	+Y, +W
			*dz w yØ	
			dzʸəʷwyʸ	
			dʒuwi	
			Vowel epenthesis; Y-prosody affecting initial consonant; W-prosody affecting epenthetic vowel; syllabification of /y/	
			√ C C Ca	+Y
			*dz w yØ	
			dzʸwyʸ	
			dʒui	
			Y-prosody affecting initial consonant; syllabification of /w/ and /y/	
HURZA	Mbuko, Vame		√ C CaCa	+W
			*dz wayØ	
			dzəʷway	
			dzuway	

322   Full Lexical Reconstructions

		Vowel epenthesis; prosody affecting epenthetic vowel	
MARGI	Margi	√ C C Ca	+Y
		*ts Ø dØ -y	
		ts^{y}ə^{y}ɗ -i^y	
		t∫idi	
		Vowel epenthesis; prosody affecting initial consonant and epenthetic vowel; syllabification of /y/	
	Kilba	√ C C Ca	+Y
		*ts Ø dØ -y	
		ts^{y}ə ɗ -i^y	
		t∫ədi	
		Vowel epenthesis; prosody affecting initial consonant; syllabification of /y/	
	Bura	√ C C Ca	+Y
		*ts Ø rØ -y	
		ts^{y}ə^{y}r -i^y	
		t∫iri	
		Vowel epenthesis; prosody affecting initial consonant and epenthetic vowel; syllabification of /y/	
MANDARA	Matal	√ C CaCa	
		*z wayØ	
		zway	
		√ C CaCa	
		*z wayØ	
		zəway	
		zəway	
		Vowel epenthesis	
		√ C CaCa	+W
		*z wayØ	
		zə^{w}way	
		zuway	
		Vowel epenthesis; prosody affecting epenthetic vowel	
	Podoko	√ C CaCa	+Y
		n- *dz waØ^{y}Ø	
		n- dz^{y}əwa^y	
		^{n}dʒəwe	

6.4 PCC Lexical Reconstructions   323

                                  Prosodification of root-final /y/ > ^{y}; prosody
                                  affecting initial consonant and final /a/

	Mandara		√ CaC Ca	+Y
		n-	*dzawØ^{y}a -ŋ	
		n-	> dz^{y}aŋwa	
			^{n}dʒaŋ^{w}a	

                                    Metathesis *w ŋ > ŋ w; prosody affecting initial
                                    root consonant

	Malgwa		√ C C Ca	+Y
		n-	*dz w Ø^{y}a -ŋ	
		n-	> dz^{y}əŋwa	
			^{n}dʒəŋ^{w}a	

                                    Metathesis *w ŋ > ŋ w; vowel epenthesis;
                                    prosody affecting initial root consonant

	Glavda		√ C C Ca	+Y
		n-	*dz w Ø^{y}Ø	
		n-	dz^{y}w	
			^{n}ǧu	

                                    Syllabification of /w/ ; prosody affecting initial root
                                    consonant

			√ C C Ca	
		n-	*dz w ya	
		n-	dzwya	
			^{n}dzuya	

                                    Syllabification of /w/

MOFU	Ouldeme		√ C CaCa	+W
			*z wayØ	
			zə^{w}way	
			zuway	

                                    Vowel epenthesis; prosody affecting epenthetic
                                    vowel

	Muyang		√ C C Ca	+Y, +W
		a-	*z w yØ	
		a^y-	zə^{w}wy^y	
			ezʉwi	

                                    Vowel epenthesis; W-prosody affecting
                                    epenthetic vowel; Y-prosody affecting prefix /a/;
                                    syllabification of /y/

	Moloko		√ C CaCa	+Y
			*dz wayØ	

324   Full Lexical Reconstructions

	dz^{y}əway	
	dʒəway	
	Vowel epenthesis; prosody affecting epenthetic vowel and initial consonant	
Zulgo	√ C CaCa	+Y
	*dz waØ^{y}Ø	
	dzə^{y}wa^y	
	dziwe	
	Vowel epenthesis; prosodification of /y/ > ^{y}; prosody affecting all vowels	
Gemzek	√ C CaCa	+Y, +W
	*dz waØ^{y}Ø	
	dzə^{w}w^{w}a^y	
	dzuwe	
	Vowel epenthesis; prosodification of /w/ > w^w; W-prosody affecting epenthetic vowel; prosodification of /y/ > ^{y}; Y-prosody affecting final /a/	
Merey	√ C CaCa	+W
	*dz wayØ	
	dzə^{w}w^{w}ay	
	dzuway	
	Vowel epenthesis; prosodification of /w/ > w^w; prosody affecting epenthetic vowel	
Dugwor	√ C CaCa	+Y, +W
	*dz wayØ	
	dz^{y}ə^{w}w^{w}ay^y	
	dʒuway	
	Vowel epenthesis; prosodification of /w/ > w^w and /y/ > y^y; W-prosody affecting epenthetic vowel; Y-prosody affecting initial consonant	
Mofu North	√ C CaCa	+W
	*dz wayØ	
	dzə^{w}w^{w}ay	
	dzuway	
	Vowel epenthesis; prosodification of /w/ > w^w; prosody affecting epenthetic vowel	
Mofu-Gudur	√ CaCaCa	+Y
	RED *dzawayØ	
	dza- dzØway^y	
	dz^{y}a- dz^{y}əway^y	

6.4 PCC Lexical Reconstructions   325

			dʒadʒəway Vowel epenthesis; prosodification of /y/ > y^y; prosody affecting initial consonant; deletion of and epenthetic schwa substitution for 1st syllable medial /a/ of the simple root		
MAROUA	Giziga- Muturwa	RED $dz^yə^y$-	√ C C Ca *dz w ɗØ $dz^yə^ywə^y$ɗ *dʒidʒiwiɗ(i)* Vowel epenthesis; prosody affecting initial consonant and all vowels; syllabification of /y/	-y -i^y	+Y
	Giziga- Marva	RED $dz^yə^y$-	√ C CaCa *dz waɗØ $dz^yə^ywa^y$ɗ *dʒidʒiweɗ* Vowel epenthesis; prosody affecting initial consonant and all vowels	-y -Ø^y	+Y
LAMANG	Lamang		√ C C Ca *z Ø ɗØ $zə^y$ɗØ *ziɗi* Vowel epenthesis; prosody affecting epenthetic vowel; syllabification of /y/	-y -i^y	+Y
	Hdi		√ C C Ca *z k^w ɗØ > $zə^y$ɗə$^yk^w$ *ziɗik^w* Metathesis *k^w ɗ > ɗ k^w; vowel epenthesis; prosody affecting epenthetic vowels	-y -Ø^y	+Y
HIGI	Kamwe- Futu		√ C C Ca *z w yØ $z^yə^ywy^y$ *ʒiwi* Vowel epenthesis; prosody affecting initial consonant and epenthetic vowel; syllabification of /y/		+Y
	Kirya		√ CaC Ca *zaw Ø^{y}Ø $z^ya^yw^y$ *ʒew* Prosody affecting initial consonant and medial /a/		+Y

	Bana		√ C C Ca	+Y

                    Bana   √ C C Ca   +Y
                                    *z ɓ y Ø
                                    zʸəʸɓyʸ
                                    ʒiɓ(i)
                                    Vowel epenthesis; prosody affecting epenthetic
                                    vowel and initial consonant; syllabification
                                    of /y/

KOTOKO-   Buduma   √ C C Ca   +Y
ISLAND   xa-   *dz w yʸØ
                    xa-   dzʸwØʸ
                           hadʒu
                           Prosody affecting root-initial consonant;
                           syllabification of /w/

KOTOKO-   Afade   √ C C Ca   +Y
NORTH   *ts w yØ
                           tsəʸwyʸ
                           tsɨwi
                           Vowel epenthesis; prosody affecting epenthetic
                           vowel; syllabification of /y/

            Maltam   √ C C Ca   +Y
                           *s w ɗØ   -y
                           > sɗw   -y
                           sɗəʸw   -iʸ
                           s'ɨwi
                           Metathesis *w ɗ > ɗ w; vowel epenthesis;
                           prosody affecting epenthetic vowel;
                           syllabification of /y/

KOTOKO-   Lagwan   √ C C Ca
CENTRAL   *z w ØØ
                           zu
                           Syllabification of /w/

            Mser   √ C C Ca   +Y
                    m-   *s w ɗØ   -y
                    m-   > sɗw   -y
                    m-   sɗəʸw   -iʸ
                           ms'ɨwi
                           Metathesis *w ɗ > ɗ w; vowel epenthesis;
                           prosody affecting epenthetic vowel;
                           syllabification of /y/

KOTOKO-   Zina   √ CaC Ca   +Y
SOUTH   RED   *dzaØw yØ

6.4 PCC Lexical Reconstructions

		dza- dzØwy	
		dz^{y}a dz^{y}wy^y	
		dʒadʒwi	
		Prosody affecting initial consonant; syllabification of /y/	

MUSGUM	Vulum	√ C CaCa	+W
		a- *d wayØ	
		a- də^{w}w^{w}ay	
		aduway	
		Vowel epenthesis; prosodification of /w/ > w^w; prosody affecting epenthetic vowel	

	Mbara	√ C CaCa	+W
		*t wayØ	
		tə^{w}w^{w}ay	
		tuway	
		Vowel epenthesis; prosodification of /w/ > w^w; prosody affecting epenthetic vowel	

GIDAR	Gidar	√ C C Ca	+Y
		*z k ɗa	-y
		zə^{y}kɗa^y	-Ø^y
		zikɗe	
		Vowel epenthesis; prosody affecting epenthetic vowel and final /a/	

foot[19]

Alternative reconstruction (**PCC**)
a(-n)-, m-   **sa**   -y, -k, -k^w a   +Y, +W   Kanuri: ʃi
                                                    PC:
                                                    *(ʔa)cVm- (OS)

ʃi n. foot *pied* (4 groups, 8 languages) [e] syn: sɨk ^{y}, sɨraj.

There are two far more widely attested roots for 'leg' or 'foot'. The forms presented here may come from different sources, with the Kotoko forms being more likely to come from *tsɨ. It is possible that these are borrowed from the Kanuri 'ʃi'.

---

[19] This item could be a potential loan (see Gravina's quoted remarks), at least in the KOTOKO group languages, in which case it would there qualify as a 'pseudo'-PCC root insofar as it has been streamlined into Central Chadic phonology systems to the extent of being apparently 'reconstructable'. Accordingly, the common etymology suggested here for both KOTOKO and MARGI group languages must remain open to further research.

328 Full Lexical Reconstructions

MARGI	Margi		√ Ca		+Y
			*xØ	-y	
			x^y	-i^y	
			h^{y}i		
			Syllabification of /y/; prosody affecting initial consonant		
	Margi-South		√ Ca		+Y
			*xØ	-y	
			x	-i^y	
			hi		
			Syllabification of /y/		
	Kilba		√ Ca		+Y
			*xØ	-y	
			x^y	-i^y	
			h^{y}i		
			Syllabification of /y/; prosody affecting initial consonant		
KOTOKO-ISLAND	Buduma		√ Ca		+Y, +W
			*tsØ	-y-k^w	
			ts	-Ø^y-w	
			ts^{y}w		
			tʃu		
			Weakening of k^w > w; syllabification of w; Y-prosody affecting initial consonant		
KOTOKO-NORTH	Afade	an-	√ Ca		+Y
		a^{y}n-	*tsØ	-y	
			ts	-i^y	
			entsi		
			Syllabification of /y/; prosody affecting prefixal /a/		
	Mpade	an-	√ Ca		+Y
		a^{y}n-	*sa	-y	
			səy	-Ø^y	
			ensɨ		
			Centralisation of final /a/; prosody affecting all vowels		
KOTOKO-CENTRAL	Lagwan	a-	√ Ca		+Y
		a-	*sa	-y	
			sə^y	-Ø^y	
			asɨ		
			Centralisation of final /a/; prosody affecting centralised /a/		

6.4 PCC Lexical Reconstructions   329

    Mser   √ Ca   +Y
              m- *sa   -y-k   a
              m- s'ə^y -Ø^y-k ə^y
                   ms'ɨkɨ
                   Centralisation of lexical final /a/ and FV /a/;
                   prosody affecting all centralised /a/; glottalisation
                   feature remains unaccounted for

Note: While the obvious Kanuri loan *beli* 'razor$_2$' has been fully integrated into CC phonology with just one suffixal root augment, namely *{-y} to account for internal [i, e] palatalisation and endings in [e], if *fi* 'foot' was a likely Kanuri loan, this has a more complex derivational ('root-augmental') history in those rather few Central Chadic languages in which cognates are found. Either we are dealing with a much older loan or simply with an accidental similarity of form and meaning.

give birth, to

        Alternative reconstruction (**PCC**)
        ma-, RED- **w(a)x(a)ya** -a, -y, -k,   a   +Y, +W PC: *wa (PN),
                                -k^w, -n, -l   *y/w- ~ *yw
                                                                                          (JS),
                                                                                          *ɣVy/w/ʔ-
                                                                                           (> C C *ɣV-)
                                                                                           (OS)

wahaj v. to give birth *naître* (16 groups, 43 languages) C syn: ^{m}bɨw. This is the most widely attested root for 'to give birth'. All three consonants in the root are prone to sporadic deletion or reanalysis, and only in a few cases are all three consonants preserved in the reflexes of individual languages.

MAFA	Mafa	√ C C Ca *Ø Ø ya *ya*	
	Cuvok	√ C CaCa *Ø xaya *haya*	
TERA	Tera, Nyimatli	√ C C Ca *Ø x Øa *xa*	
	Nyimatli	√ C C Ca *Ø x Øa *kha*	

330   Full Lexical Reconstructions

SUKUR	Sukur	√ C C Ca	+Y
		*w x ya	
		> w y xa	
		yy^{y}xa	
		yə^{y}yxa	
		yiiha	
		Metathesis *w x y > w y x with assimilation to yyx; vowel epenthesis; syllabification of /y/; prosody affecting epenthetic vowel; Cə^{y}y > Cii	
		√ C C Ca	
		*w x ya	
		> w y xa	
		yyxa	
		yyØØ	
		yi	
		Metathesis *w x y > w y x with assimilation to yyx; syllabification of /y/	
HURZA	Mbuko	√ CaCaCa	
		*waxayØ	
		wahay	
	Vame	√ CaC Ca	
		*wax Øa	
		wah(a)	
MARGI	Bura	√ C C Ca	
		*w x ya	
		> w y xa	
		yyØa	
		iya	
		iya	
		Metathesis *w x y > w y x with assimilation to yyx; syllabification of /y/	
		√ C C Ca	
		*w x ya	
		w Ø ya	
		yya	
		yia	
		Assimilation *wy > yy; syllabification of /y/	
	Margi, Margi-South, Kilba	√ C C Ca	
		*Ø Ø ya	
		ya	

6.4 PCC Lexical Reconstructions

MANDARA	Podoko		√ C C Ca *Ø x Øa *ha*		
	Malgwa		√ C C Ca *Ø Ø ya *ya*		
	Glavda		√ C C Ca *w x ya w Ø ya yyØ *yiga* Assimilation *wy > yy; syllabification of /y/	-k -k -g	a a a
		RED ya-	√ C C Ca *Ø Ø ya ya *yayana*	-n -n	a a
	Dghweɗe		√ C C Ca *w x ya w Ø ya yyØ *yige* Assimilation *wy > yy; syllabification of /y/; prosody affecting FV /a/	-k -k -g	+Y a a a^y
MOFU	Ouldeme		√ C C Ca *w Ø yØ *wi* Syllabification of /y/		
	Moloko		√ C C Ca *w Ø Ø^{y}a wa^y *we* Prosodification of /y/ > ^{y}; prosody affecting final /a/		+Y
	Zulgo		√ C C Ca *w Ø Øa *wa*		
	Gemzek	ma-	√ C C Ca *w Ø Ø^{y}a		+Y

332   Full Lexical Reconstructions

                              ma^y- wa^y
                              mewe
                              Prosody affecting all /a/

                              √ C C Ca
                         ma- *w Ø Øa
                         ma- wa
                              mawa

              Merey   √ C C Ca
                              *w Ø Øa
                              wa

              Dugwor   √ CaC Ca
                         ma- *waØyØ
                         ma- way
                              maway

              Mofu   √ C C Ca   +Y
              North   ma- *Ø Ø yØ   -a-y
                         ma^y- y^y -a^{y}y^y
                              meyey
                              Prosody affecting all /a/

              Mofu-   √ C C Ca
              Gudur   *Ø Ø yØ
                              y-

MAROUA   Giziga-   √ C C Ca
              Marva   *w x ya
                              > wyxa
                              yy
                              yi
                              Metathesis *w x y > w y x with assimilation to
                              yyx; syllabification of /y/

                              √ C C Ca   +Y
                              *Ø Ø ya
                              y^{y}a^y
                              ye
                              Prosody affecting /a/

              Mbazla   √ C C Ca
                              *w x ya
                              w y xa

6.4 PCC Lexical Reconstructions   333

```
                      w Ø yØ
                      yy
                      yi
                      Assimilation *wy > yy; syllabification of /y/

                      √ CaC Ca                              +Y
              RED    *wax yØ
              RED    way x
              ya-    yay'
              ya-    yØy'
              yaʸ-   yi'
                      yɛyi'
                      Metathesis *w x y > w y x with assimilation
                      to yyx and */x/ > '; prosody affecting
                      reduplicated first syllable; syllabification
                      of /y/
```

LAMANG   Lamang
```
                      √ C C Ca
                      *Ø Ø ya
                      ya
```

        Hdi
```
                      √ C C Ca
              RED    *Ø Ø ya
              ya-    yØ
                      yay
```

HIGI   Kamwe-
      Nkafa
```
                      √ C C Ca
                      *Ø Ø ya
                      yə
                      yə
                      Centralisation of final /a/
```

      Kamwe-
      Futu
```
                      √ C C Ca                              +Y
                      *Ø Ø ya        -k          a
                      yʸaʸ           -k          ə
                      yekə
                      Prosody affecting lexical final /a/; centralisation
                      of FV /a/

                      √ C C Ca                              +Y, +W
                      *Ø Ø ya        -k -kʷ      a
                      yʸaʸ           -kəkʷ       aʷ
                      yekəgʷo
                      Vowel epenthesis; Y-prosody affecting lexical
                      final /a/; W-prosody affecting FV /a/
```

	Kirya, Bana	√ C C Ca *Ø Ø ya *ya*	
KOTOKO-ISLAND	Buduma	√ C C Ca *w Ø yØ wʷəʷy *wuy* Vowel epenthesis; prosodification of /w/ > wʷ; prosody affecting epenthetic vowel	+W
		√ C C Ca *w Ø yØ wʷəy wəʷəy *wuəy* Vowel epenthesis; prosodification of /w/ > wʷ; prosody affecting first syllable epenthetic vowel	+W
KOTOKO-NORTH	Afade, Mpade	√ C C Ca *w Ø ya wØʸa waʸ *we* Prosody affecting /a/	+Y
		√ C C Ca *w Ø Øa -n wa -n *wan*	
	Malgbe	√ Ca C Ca RED- *wa Ø ØØ -n wa- wʷØ -n wa- wəʷ -n *wawun* Prosodification /w/ > wʷ; vowel epenthesis; prosody affecting epenthetic vowel	+W
KOTOKO-CENTRAL	Lagwan	√ C C Ca *w Ø ya -l wØʸa -l *wel* Prosody affecting final /a/	+Y

6.4 PCC Lexical Reconstructions 335

		√ C C Ca	+W
	RED	*w Ø Øa	-n
	wa-	w^w	-n
	wa-	wə^w	-n
		wawun	

Centralisation of final /a/; prosodification of /w/ > w^w; prosody affecting centralised final /a/

	Mser	√ C C Ca	+Y
		*w Ø Ø^{y}a	
		wa^y	
		we	

Prosody affecting final /a/

KOTOKO-	Zina	√ C C Ca	+Y
SOUTH		*w Ø ya	
		wə^{y}y^{y}a	
		wiya	

Vowel epenthesis; prosody affecting epenthetic vowel

MUSGUM	Mulwi	√ C C Ca	
		*w Ø yØ	
		wi	

Syllabification of /y/

	Mbara	√ C C Ca	+Y
		*w Ø yØ	
		wə^{y}y^y	
		wii	

Vowel epenthesis; prosody affecting epenthetic vowel; syllabification of /y/; Cə^{y}y > Cii

GIDAR	Gidar		√ C C Ca	+W
		RED	*w Ø Øa	
		w-	wa	
		ə^{w}w-	w^{w}a	
			uuwa	

Vowel prothesis; prosodification of /w/ > w^w; syllabification of /w/ > u; prosody affecting prothetic vowel; Cə^w+w > Cuu

			√ C C Ca	
		RED	*w Ø Øa	
		w-	wa	
			uwa	

Syllabification of /w/

√ C C Ca   +Y
*w Ø yØ   -na
wə^{y}y^y -na
wiina
Vowel epenthesis; prosody affecting epenthetic
vowel; syllabification of /y/, Cə^{y}y > Cii

grandfather

Alternative reconstruction (**PCC**)
a-, b-, a-d-   **dz(a)dza**   -a, -y, -k^w, -n   a   +Y   PC: —

dzɨdzɨ ^{y} nm. grandfather *grand-père* (8 groups, 17 languages) A

The initial *dz has the reflex *ts in Proto-Hurza and Proto-Margi, which is an unestablished change in both cases. In Proto-Mandara both *dz have become *d, also an unestablished change. The palatalisation prosody is supported by the data from all the groups. In the Mandara group, the palatalisation prosody has affected the *d. This was followed by a regular change where palatalised alveolars become palatalised velars, resulting in *d^j→g^j. In Mbuko and Sukur, the reflex of the root is not reduplicated, but other material has been added.

BATA	Gude	√ C Ca	
		*dz dza	
		dzədzə	
		dzədzə	
		Vowel epenthesis; centralisation of final /a/	
	Jimi	√ C Ca	
		*dz dzØ	-n
		dzədz	-ən
		dzədzən	
		Vowel epenthesis	
	Sharwa	√ C Ca	+Y
		*dz dza	-y
		dz^{y}ə^{y}dz^{y}ə	-Ø^y
		dʒidʒə	
		Vowel epenthesis; prosody affecting consonants and first syllable epenthetic vowel; centralisation of final /a/	
	Tsuvan	√ C Ca	+Y
		*dz dza	-y
		dzədza^y	-Ø^y

6.4 PCC Lexical Reconstructions   337

			dzədze	
			Vowel epenthesis; prosody affecting final /a/	
DABA	Buwal		√ CaCa	+Y
			*dzadza	-y
			dz^{y}a^{y}dz^{y}a^y	-Ø^y
			dʒedʒe	
			Prosody affecting consonants and all /a/	
	Gavar		√ CaCa	+Y
			*dzadzØ	-y
			dz^{y}a^{y}dz^y	-i^y
			dʒedʒi	
			Prosody affecting consonants and medial /a/; syllabification of /y/	
SUKUR	Sukur		√ C Ca	+Y
			*Ø dzØ	-y-k^w
			dz^y	-i^y-k+w
			dz^{y}ikw	
			dʒiku	
			Prosody affecting consonant; syllabification of /y/; re-segmentalisation of *{-k^w} > /k+w/; syllabification w > u	
HURZA	Mbuko		√ C Ca	+Y
		b-	*Ø dza	-y
		bə^y-	dz^{y}a^y	-Ø^y
			bidʒe	
			Vowel epenthesis; prosody affecting root-initial consonant and all vowels	
	Vame		√ CaCa	+Y
			*tsadza	-y
			ts^{y}a^{y}dz^{y}a^y	-Ø^y
			tʃedʒe	
			Prosody affecting all consonants and vowels	
MARGI	Margi		√ C Ca	+Y
			*ts dzØ	-y
			ts^{y}ə^{y}dz^y	-i^y
			tʃidʒi	
			Vowel epenthesis; prosody affecting epenthetic vowel and all consonants; syllabification of /y/	
	Margi-South		√ C Ca	+Y
			*ts dzØ	-y

338   Full Lexical Reconstructions

			ts^{y}ə^{y}dz^y	-i^y	
			tʃidʒi		
			Vowel epenthesis; prosody affecting epenthetic vowel and all consonants; syllabification of /y/		

	Kilba		√ C Ca		+Y
		a-	*Ø dzØ	-y	
		a-	dz^y	-i^y	
			adʒi		
			Prosody affecting consonant; syllabification of /y/		

MANDARA	Mandara		√ C Ca		+Y
			*d da	-y	
			d^y d^{y}a^y	-Ø^y	
			a^{y}dd^{y}a^y		
			eggye		
			Vowel prothesis; prosody affecting consonants and all /a/		

		√ C Ca			+Y
		*d dØ	-a-y	a	
		d^y d^y	-ay	a	
		a^{y}dd^y	-ay	a^y	
		egg^{y}aaye			
		Vowel prothesis; prosody affecting prothetic vowel and initial consonants and FV /a/; vowel length remains unaccounted for			

	Malgwa		√ C Ca		+Y
			*d da	y	
			d^y d^{y}a^y	-Ø^y	
			ədd^{y}a^y		
			əgg^{y}e		
			Vowel prothesis; prosody affecting consonants and final /a/		

LAMANG	Lamang, Hdi		√ C Ca		+Y
			*dz dzØ	y	
			dzə^{y}dz	-i^y	
			dzidzi		
			Vowel epenthesis; prosody affecting epenthetic vowel; syllabification of /y/		

| HIGI | Bana | | √ C Ca | -y | +Y |

6.4 PCC Lexical Reconstructions   339

                        *dz dzØ   -i^y
                        dz^yə^ydz^y
                        dʒidʒi
                        Vowel epenthesis; prosody affecting epenthetic
                        vowel and consonants; syllabification of /y/

grasshopper
           Alternative reconstruction (**PCC**)
           a-   **x^w(a)y(a)k^wa**   (-ɗ,-ŋ?)   +Y, +W   PC: *hVy/w-
                                                                     (OS)

           haɗik^w nm. grasshopper *sauterelle* (11 groups, 32 languages) B cf:
           dzaraj.
              This root is difficult to reconstruct. The initial *h is retained in
           most groups, but was lost in Proto-Mafa and many individual
           languages, which is a common sporadic process. The *ɗ is retained
           only in Gidar. In many groups it has fused with the *i to become *j,
           and this *j triggered the creation of the palatalisation prosody in
           several languages in the Mofu group. These are both sporadic
           processes. However, in Hdi *ɗ has the reflex /ʔ/ and in Kilba /ʔʲ/.
           These are unestablished changes. The final *k^w has been lost in
           several groups. In Proto-Bata, Proto-Margi and Proto-Mandara it has
           become *w, and this change also led to the creation of *o in Mpade.
           In Proto-Daba the labialisation component became *w and replaced
           the lost *h. In the Maroua group the labialisation component was
           reanalysed as the labialisation prosody. In the Higi group, *i and *k
           fused to create /gʲ/. In Bata, the *k fused with *ɗ to create /q/. All
           these processes are known sporadic processes.

BATA	Bata[20]	√ C CaCa	+Y, +W
		*x^w yawa	
		x^w ^yawa^y	
		qaawe	
		Desegmentalisation of /y/ > ^y; Y-prosody	
		affecting final /a/; possibly: /x^wa+^y/ > /qaa/	
	Gude	√ C C Ca	+Y
		a- *Ø y wa	
		a- y^yə^ywa	
		ayiwa	

---

[20] I have no plausible explanation for the emergence of initial *x^wya > q+aa in Bata. Gravina (2014b) assumes that 'the *k fused with *ɗ to create /q/', i.e. C_2 (*/ɗ/) with C_3 (*/k^w/) which, in my understanding, cannot explain the character of /q/ in C_1 position, nor the long vowel. I rather assume the combined effect of both prosodies to play a role here.

340   Full Lexical Reconstructions

		Partial desegmentalisation of /y/ to /y^y/; vowel epenthesis; prosody affecting epenthetic vowel	
DABA	Buwal, Gavar, Mbudum	√ CaCaCa *wayakØ *wayak*	
	Daba	√ CaC Ca *way k^{w}Ø wayəp' *wayəp'* Vowel epenthesis; /p'/ < */k^w/ (?)	
MAFA	Cuvok	√ C CaCa *Ø yak^{w}Ø yak^w *yak^w*	
MARGI	Bura	√ CaC Ca *xaØwa xa^{w}w^{w}a *hauwa* Partial desegmentalisation of */k^w/ > /w^w /; prosody affecting medial /a/ > au	+W
	Kilba	√ CaC Ca *xay'a > xa'ya xa'y^{y}ə^y *ha'yi* Metathesis y' >' y; partial desegmentalisation /y/ > y^y; prosody affecting centralised final vowel; for somewhat speculative accounting for the glottal stop, see 6.3.6.3	+Y
MANDARA	Matal	√ CaCaCa *xayawØ *hayaw*	
	Podoko	√ C CaCa *x yawa xə^{y}y^{y}awa *hiyawa*	+Y

6.4 PCC Lexical Reconstructions   341

			Vowel epenthesis; prosody affecting epenthetic vowel	

	Mandara		√ C C Ca
			*Ø y wa
			ywa
			iwa
			Syllabification of /y/

	Malgwa		√ C C Ca	+Y
			*Ø y wa
			əʸyʸwaʸ
			iiwe
			Vowel prothesis; prosody affecting final and prothetic vowel; *əʸy > iy > ii

MOFU   Ouldeme | | √ CaCaCa |
| | a- | *wayakØ |
| | | *awayak* |

	Muyang		√ C CaCa	+Y
		a-	*Ø yawØ
		aʸ-	yʸaʸw
			eyew
			Partial desegmentalisation of /y/ > /yʸ/; prosody affecting all /a/

	Mada		√ C CaCa
		a-	*Ø yawØ
		a-	yaw
			ayaw

	Moloko,		√ CaCaCa	+Y
	Gemzek,		*xayawØ
	Merey		xaʸyʸaʸw
			heyew
			Partial desegmentalisation of /y/ > /yʸ/; prosody affecting all /a/

	Zulgo		√ CaCaCa
			*xayawØ
			hayaw

	Dugwor		√ CaCaCa	+Y
			*xʷayakØ
			xʷaʸyʸaʸk
			hʷeyek
			Partial desegmentalisation of /y/ > /yʸ/; prosody affecting all /a/

	Mofu North		√ CaCaCa *xʷayakʷØ *hʷayakʷ*
	Mofu- Gudur	a- a-	√ C CaCa *Ø yakʷØ yakʷ *ayakʷ*
MAROUA	Giziga- Muturwa		√ C C Ca +W *Ø y kʷa yəʷkʷəʷ *yuku* Centralisation of final /a/, vowel epenthesis; prosody affecting epenthetic vowel and centralised /a/. Alternative: Deletion of final /a/; re-segmentalisation /kʷ/ > /k+w/, syllabification of /w/ > [u] in final syllable
	Giziga- Marva		√ CaCaCa +W *xʷayakʷØ xʷaʷyaʷkʷØ *hoyok* Prosody affecting all /a/
LAMANG	Hdi		√ C C Ca +Y *x y 'a > x ' yØ xəʸ'yʸ *hi'i* Metathesis y' > 'y; vowel epenthesis; syllabification of /y/ and partial prosodification y > yʸ; prosody affecting epenthetic vowel
HIGI	Kamwe- Nkafa		√ CaC Ca +Y *xay gØ > xagy xagyʸ *hagʸi* Metathesis *y g > g y; partial desegmentalisation of /y/ > /yʸ/; prosody affecting final consonant; syllabification of /y/
	Kamwe- Futu		√ CaC Ca +Y *xay ga

6.4 PCC Lexical Reconstructions   343

		xagyØ	
		hagi	
		Metathesis *y g > g y; syllabification of /y/	

	Kirya	√ CaC Ca	
		*xay ØØ	
		hay	

	Bana	√ CaC Ca	
		*xay ØØ	
		xay	

KOTOKO-NORTH	Mpade	√ CaCaCa	+W
		*xayawØ	
		xayaØʷ	
		hayo	
		Prosodification of /w/ > ʷ; prosody affecting /a/ in final syllable	

		√ CaCaCa	+W
		*gayawØ	
		gayaØʷ	
		gayo	
		Prosodification of /w/ > ʷ; prosody affecting /a/ in final syllable	

Note on Lamang (LAMANG) and Gidar (GIDAR):
Lamang *hdeŋe* 'locust' (not contained in Gravina's database), and Gidar *heeydeŋ* 'locuste (migrateur), sauterelle, criquet', *heydeŋ ~ heydeŋ* 'criquet, sauterelle' would appear to be cognates, but may not belong to the same root as all the other examples in this set. If they did, this would point to hitherto unidentified suffixal augment material of the shape *-ɗaŋ(a) plus phonological Y-prosody, i.e. Lamang √ C C Ca *x Øʸ ØØ-Øʸ-ɗaʸŋaʸ > *hdeŋe*; Gidar √ C C Ca *xaʸyʸØØ-Øʸ-ɗaʸŋ > *heydeŋ* with still no explanation for the occurrence of the long vowel in Gidar *heeydeŋ*.

hair

Alternative reconstruction (**PCC**)
    (ma-) **s(a)b(a)ta** -y, -kʷ   +Y, +W   PC: *gasi (PN),
                                                                                 *ⁿgz , *sʷk- (-a,-l) (JS),
                                                                                 *sV(ʔV)m- (OS)

siᵐbiti ʸ nf. hair *cheveux* (5 groups, 8 languages) D syn: ⁿgʷits ʸ.
    This root is found in the south-west of the Central Chadic area. The *ᵐb has reflexes including /ɓʷ/, /w/ and zero, none of which are known to be regular. The root is difficult to reconstruct with confidence.

BATA	Bata	√ CaC Ca	+Y, +W
		*saw ta -y	
		sʸaʸwʷtaʷ -Øʸ	
		ʃewto	

Partial prosodification of w > wʷ; Y-prosody affecting initial consonant and medial /a/; W-prosody affecting final /a/

	Sharwa	√ C C Ca	+Y
		*s ɓʷ tØ -y	
		sʸəɓʷət -iʸ	
		ʃəɓʷəti	

Vowel epenthesis; prosody affecting initial consonant; syllabification of /y/

	Tsuvan	√ C C Ca	+Y, +W
		*s ɓʷ ta -y	
		səʷɓʷtaʸ -Øʸ	
		suɓte	

Vowel epenthesis; W-prosody affecting epenthetic vowel; Y-prosody affecting /a/

SUKUR	Sukur	√ C C Ca	+Y, +W
		mØ- *s b tØ -y -kʷ	
		sØ- ʸəʷmbəʷt -Øʸ-Øʷ	
		ʃuᵐbut	

Prosodification kʷ > ʷ; vowel epenthesis; W-prosody affecting epenthetic vowels; Y-prosody affecting initial consonant; prenasalisation of C_2

MOFU	Moloko	√ C CaCa	+Y, +W
		mØ- *s bata -y-kʷ	
		Ø- səᵐbaʸtaʸʷ -Øʸ-kʷ	
		səᵐbetewk	

Vowel epenthesis; Y-prosody affecting /a/ in penultima and ultima; W-prosody also affecting /a/ in ultima: combined prosodies yielding diphthong [ew][21]

---

[21] The process by which the labial feature of underlying *kʷ should be realised on the preceding vowel to form a diphthong has no parallel in the data that have so far been reanalysed. Note, however, that there are instances in the data where labialised consonants are indeed separated from their labial feature in terms of creating a sequence C+w (which we refer to as 're-segmentalisation' in this study). In order to account for this unique Moloko case, we would need to assume such re-segmentalisation and subsequent metathesis.

6.4 PCC Lexical Reconstructions

LAMANG	Lamang	√ C C Ca		+Y
		*s Ø dØ	-y	
		sə^{y}d	-i^y	
		sidi		
		Vowel epenthesis; prosody affecting epenthetic vowel; syllabification of /y/		
	Hdi	√ C C Ca		+Y
		*s w dØ	-y	
		səwə^{y}d	-i^y	
		səwidi		
		Vowel epenthesis; prosody affecting epenthetic vowel in penultimate syllable; syllabification of /y/		
HIGI	Kamwe-Nkafa	√ C C Ca		+Y
		*s m tØ	-y	
		s^{y}ə^{y}nt^y	-i^y	
		ʃint^{y}i		
		Vowel epenthesis; prosody affecting epenthetic vowel plus initial and final consonants; syllabification of /y/		
	Bana	√ C C Ca		
		*s Ø tØ	-y	
		sət	-i	
		səti		
		Vowel epenthesis; syllabification of /y/		
		√ C C Ca		+Y
		*s Ø tØ	-y	
		s^{y}t	-i^y	
		ʃti		
		Syllabification of /y/		

hare

                     Alternative reconstruction (**PCC**)

ma, na-   **x^w(a)d(a)y(a)va** -k, -k^w, -n a +Y,   PC: *bnd
                                                        +W   (t-,k-; -t,-k)
                                                                     ~ *bd (JS),
                                                                     *ʔarnVb-
                                                                     (> nbVr- >
                                                                     bVr-) (OS)

               vida nf. hare lièvre (6 groups, 16 languages) C syn: h^{w}a^{n}dav.

               This is one of two possibly related roots for 'hare', the other being *h^{w}a^{n}dav. There was a regular intervocalic change *d→r in the North sub-branch, and there were subsequent regular changes *r→l in various languages. However, these changes do not account for all the surface forms. In particular, the Margi form appears cognate but does not conform with established rules. There is no known rule that would predict the presence of *p as the initial consonant. There is good evidence for *i from all groups, though in Sukur /i/ would be expected rather than the palatalisation prosody.

BATA	Gude	√ C C C Ca *Ø t y pa > py^y ta *pit^y a* Multiple metathesis typ > pyt; partial desegmentalisation of medial /y/ > /y^y/ and syllabification > [i]; prosody affecting final consonant		+Y
	Jimi	√ C C C Ca *Ø d y va vydə *vidən* Multiple metathesis dyv > vyd; syllabification of medial /y/; centralisation of final /a/	-n -n	
	Tsuvan	√ C C C Ca *Ø t y va > vy^y tə^y *vitikən* Vowel epenthesis; multiple metathesis tyv > vyt; syllabification of medial /y/; centralisation of final /a/; prosody affecting centralised final /a/	-k -n -kə-n	
SUKUR	Sukur	√ C C C Ca *Ø l y va > vlya vəl^y a *vəl^y a* Multiple metathesis *lyv > vly; prosodification of medial /y/ > ^y; prosody affecting final root consonant		+Y
		√ C C C Ca *Ø l y va > vy^y la *vil^y a* Multiple etathesis *lyv > vyl; partial desegmentalisation of medial /y/ > /y^y/; prosody affecting final root consonant; syllabification of /y/		+Y

6.4 PCC Lexical Reconstructions

MARGI	Bura		√ C C C Ca	
			*Ø t y pØ	
			> pty	
			pti	
			Multiple metathesis *typ > pty; syllabification of /y/	

                Margi
                            √ C C C Ca
                            *Ø t y pa
                            > pytə
                            pitə
                            Multiple metathesis *typ > pty; syllabification of medial /y/; centralisation of /a/

                Margi-South
                            √ C C C Ca
                            *Ø t y pØ   -k^w
                            > pyt   -w
                            pitu
                            Multiple metathesis *typ > pty; syllabification of medial /y/; weakening of /k^w/ > /w/ > u

                Kilba
                            √ C C C Ca
                            *Ø t y pa
                            > pyta
                            pita
                            Multiple metathesis *typ > pty; syllabification of medial /y/

MANDARA   Podoko
                            √ C C C Ca
                            *Ø r y va
                            > vyra
                            vira
                            Multiple metathesis *ryv > vyr; syllabification of medial /y/

                Mandara   √ C C C Ca   +Y
                          na-   *Ø r y va
                          na-   > vy^{y}ra^y
                                    navire
                                    Multiple metathesis *ryv > vyr; syllabification of medial /y/ and partial desegmentalisation > i^y; prosody affecting final /a/

                Malgwa   √ C C C Ca   +Y
                          na-   *Ø r y va
                          na-   > vy^{y}ra
                                    və^{y}yra
                                    naviira
                                  Multiple metathesis *ryv > vyr; vowel epenthesis; prosody affecting epenthetic vowel; syllabification of /y/; Cə^{y}y > Ciy > Cii

348   Full Lexical Reconstructions

	Glavda	√ C C C Ca *Ø Ø y vØ > vy > və^{y}y *vii* Metathesis *yv > vy; vowel epenthesis; prosody affecting epenthetic vowel; syllabification of /y/; Cə^{y}y > Ciy > Cii	+Y
		√ C C C Ca *Ø d y va > vy^{y}da və^{y}yda *vi:da* Multiple metathesis *dyv > vyd; vowel epenthesis; prosody affecting epenthetic vowel; syllabification of /y/; Cə^{y}y > Ciy > Ci:	+Y
LAMANG	Lamang	√ C C C Ca -k^w a *Ø l y va > vyla -k^w a *vilak^{w}a* Multiple metathesis *lyv > vyl; syllabification of medial /y/	
	Hdi	√ C C C Ca -k^w *Ø l y va > vyla -k^w *vilak^w* Multiple metathesis *lyv > vyl; syllabification of medial /y/	
HIGI	Kamwe- Futu	√ C C C Ca *Ø r y va > vyra *vira* Multiple metathesis *ryv > vyr; syllabification of medial /y/	
	Kirya	√ C C C Ca *Ø t y pa > pytə *pitə* Multiple metathesis *typ > pty; syllabification of medial /y/; centralisation of /a/; (likely loan from Margi)	
	Bana	√ C C C Ca *Ø l y va > vØ^{y}la vəla^y *v(ə)le* Multiple metathesis *lyv > vyl; vowel epenthesis; prosody affecting final /a/	+Y

hedgehog

Alternative reconstruction **PCC**
a-, ɗa-, m-,   **xʷ(a)s(a)sa**   -ɓ, -y   +Y, +W   PCC: *-ss (u)
(a-)RED   (JS)

hʷisis nf. hedgehog *hérisson* (6 groups, 15 languages) C

The initial *hʷ has become *w in Proto-Hurza and Margi, *u in Proto-Mandara, and has developed into the labialisation prosody in Mbuko and Gemzek, with or without the *h component. It has become *h in Proto-Higi and has been lost in several languages of the Mofu group. These are all common sporadic changes. The /f/ in Kirya could be a development of *h, or the root could be unrelated. In Buwal, Merey and Mofu North there is evidence for a glottal consonant in the word. The form that we have reconstructed could be a reflex of a reduplicated form such as *hʷisa-hʷisa. If there was a glottal consonant, the original root may have been *hʷisaɗ, with the other forms coming from simplified versions of the reduplicated root. More data is needed to clarify this.

DABA	Buwal		√CaCaCa -ɓ	
			*xʷasasa	
			hʷasasaɓ	
HURZA	Mbuko		√C CaCa	+W
			*w sasØ	
			wʷsaʷs	
			usos	
			Partial desegmentalisation of /w/ > /wʷ/ and syllabification of /w/; prosody affecting medial /a/	
	Vame		√C C Ca	+Y, +W
		a-RED	*w Ø sa y	
		a-wəʷsʸa-	wʷəʷsʸa -Øʸ	
			awuʃawuʃa	
			Partial desegmentalisation of /w/ > /wʷ/ and syllabification of /w/; vowel epenthesis; W-prosody affecting epenthetic vowels; Y-prosody affecting final root consonant	
MARGI	Bura		√C C Ca	+Y
			*xʷ Ø sa -y	
			xʷəʸsa -Øʸ	
			hʷisa	
			Vowel epenthesis; prosody affecting epenthetic vowel	
	Margi		√C C Ca	+Y
			*w Ø sa -y	
			wəʸsə -Øʸ	

350   Full Lexical Reconstructions

			wisə	
			Vowel epenthesis; prosody affecting epenthetic vowel; centralisation of final /a/	
MANDARA	Mandara, Malgwa		√C C Ca	+W
			*w s sa	
			wsə^{w}sa	
			ususa	
			Syllabification of initial /w/; vowel epenthesis; prosody affecting epenthetic vowel	
MOFU	Ouldeme		√C CaCa	
		a-	*Ø sasØ	
		a-	sas	
			asas	
	Muyang, Zulgo		√C C Ca	
		a-	*w s sØ	
			> sws	
		a-	sus	
			asus	
			Metathesis *w s > s w; syllabification of medial /w/	
	Gemzek		√CaCaCa	+W
			*x^{w}asasØ	
			x^{w}a^{w}sa^{w}s	
			hosos	
			Prosody affecting all /a/	
	Merey		√C C Ca	
		ɗa-	*w s sØ	
			> sws	
		ɗa-	sus	
			ɗasus	
			Metathesis *w s > s w; syllabification of medial /w/	
	Mofu North		√CaC Ca	+W
		RED	*ʔ^{w}as ØØ	
		ʔa^w-	ʔ^{w}a^{w}s	
			ʔoʔos	
LAMANG	Hdi[22]		√C C Ca	+W
		m-	x^w t sØ	

---

[22] Not in Gravina's database.

6.4 PCC Lexical Reconstructions 351

		mə^w- x^{w}tə^{w}s		
		muxtus		
		Vowel epenthesis; prosody affecting epenthetic vowels; *s > t unexpected change, if at all cognate (dissimilation from ^{x}*muxsus*?)		
HIGI	Kirya	√C C Ca		+Y
		*f s Øa	-y	
		fə^{y}sa	-Ø^y	
		fisa		
		Vowel epenthesis; prosody affecting epenthetic vowel		
	Bana	√CaC Ca		
		*xas sa		
		xasəsə		
		xasəsə		
		Vowel epenthesis; centralisation of final /a/		

hide, to

Alternative reconstruction (**PCC**)
k-   ɓ(a)ɣ^{w}a   -n   +W   PC: *ɓgw (JS), *[ɦ]Vɓʔ- (OS)

ɓaɣ^w v. to hide *cacher* (5 groups, 11 languages) B

Although this root is only attested in 11 languages, these are from a wide area and diverse groups, and so this root is likely to have come from Proto-Central Chadic. In Proto-Daba there is an unestablished change *ɣ^w→h^w. The labialisation component was lost in all languages, except for Daba where it was reanalysed as the labialisation prosody. The same unestablished change took place in Podoko in the Mandara group. In the Mofu group there was a regular change *ɣ^w→h^w in the Tokombere subgroup, and in Muyang the *h was lost in a sporadic change, leaving behind the labialisation component. In the Mofu subgroup there was a regular change *ɣ^w→w. In Mofu-Gudur the *w was lost as a sporadic change. In Bata the labialisation has transferred to the *ɓ. In Bana there has been metathesis of the two consonants.

BATA	Bata	√ CaCa		+W
		*ɓaØ^{w}a		
		ɓa^{w}a^w		
		ɓoo		
		Prosody retained from lost final consonant and affecting all /a/		

352 Full Lexical Reconstructions

	Jimi		√ C Ca	+W
			*ɓ ɣʷa -n
			ɓʷəɣə -n
			ɓʷəyən
			Vowel epenthesis; centralisation of final /a/; W-prosody: transfer of ʷ from velar C_2 to labial C_1
	Sharwa		√ CaCa	+W
			*ɓaxʷØ
			ɓʷax
			ɓʷah
			W-prosody: transfer of ʷ from velar C_2 to labial C_1
DABA	Buwal, Gavar		√ CaCa
			*ɓaxØ
			ɓah
	Mbudum		√ CaCa
		k-	*ɓaxØ
		kə-	ɓax
			kəɓah
			Vowel epenthesis
	Daba		√ CaCa	+W
			*ɓaxʷØ
			ɓaʷxʷ
			ɓoh
			Prosody affecting medial /a/
MANDARA	Podoko		√ C Ca
			*ɓ xʷa
			ɓəhʷa
			Vowel epenthesis
MOFU	Muyang		√ C Ca	+W
			*ɓ wØ
			ɓu
			Weakening of */Cʷ/ > w; syllabification of /w/
HIGI	Bana		√ C Ca	+W
			*ɓ ɣʷa
			> ɣʷ ɓa
			ɣʷəʷɓə
			ɣuɓə

6.4 PCC Lexical Reconstructions

Metathesis *ɓ ɣʷ > ɣʷ ɓ; vowel epenthesis; prosody affecting epenthetic vowel; centralisation of final /a/

horn₁

Alternative reconstruction (areal root)
    d(a)r(a)ma   -y, -kʷ   +Y, +W   PC: Different root (JS)
                                                                  Central Chadic: *drm (JS)

dirim nf. animal horn *corne d'un animal* (8 groups, 26 languages) C syn: lagan, ᵐbikʷim, mahʷa.

This root poses some interesting problems in reconstruction. The change *d to t in the Margi and Higi groups is regular. We also expect to find *r becoming *l in all groups except for Mafa and Sukur. However, there are exceptions in the Mandara, Mofu and Maroua groups. The Mafa and Mofu data indicate that there are two cognate roots interfering, with *dirim being the horn of an animal, and *tilim being an animal horn used as a musical instrument. Another difficulty is the presence of labialisation in many of the groups. The change *m to /w/ in the Mandara group is regular, and in the Lamang group is a common sporadic change. However we also have labialisation in the Mafa, Sukur, Maroua and Higi groups that has not come from *m. In the Maroua group this is a common sporadic change, but the present reconstruction does not account for the introduction of labialisation in the other groups.

MAFA	Mafa	√ CaCaCa		+W
		*talamØ	-kʷ	
		taʷlaʷm	-Øʷ	
		tolom		
		Prosodification of /kʷ/ > ʷ; prosody affecting all /a/		
		√ C CaCa		+W
		*d ramØ	-kʷ	
		dəʷraʷm	-Øʷ	
		durom		
		Prosodification of /kʷ/ > ʷ; vowel epenthesis; prosody affecting all vowels		
	Cuvok	√ C CaCa		+Y
		*d ramØ	-y	
		dəraʸm	-Øʸ	
		dərem		
		Vowel epenthesis; prosody affecting medial /a/		
	Mefele	√ C C Ca		+W
		*d r mØ	-kʷ	

354   Full Lexical Reconstructions

		dərə^{w}m	-Ø^w	
		dərum		
		Prosodification of /k^w/ > ^{w}; vowel epenthesis; prosody affecting second-syllable epenthetic vowel		
SUKUR	Sukur	√ C CaCa		+W
		*t ØamØ	-k^w	
		t^{w}am	-Ø^w	
		t^{w}am		
		Prosodification of /k^w/ > ^{w}; prosody affecting initial consonant		
MARGI	Bura	√ C C Ca		+Y, +W
		*t l mØ	-y, -k^w	
		> t^{m}bl	-y, -k^w	
		tə^{y}mbə^{w}l	-Ø^y-Ø^w	
		ti^{m}bul		
		Metathesis *l m > ^{m}b l; prosodification of /k^w/ > ^{w} and /y/ > ^{y}; Y-prosody affecting first syllable epenthetic vowel; W-prosody affecting second syllable epenthetic vowel		
	Kilba	√ C C Ca		
		*t l mØ		
		tələm		
		tələm		
		Vowel epenthesis		
MANDARA	Matal	√ C CaCa		
		*d rawØ		
		draw		
		√ C CaCa		
		*d rawØ		
		dəraw		
		Vowel epenthesis		
	Podoko	√ C CaCa		
		*d rawa		
		dərawa		
		Vowel epenthesis		
	Mandara	√ CaC Ca		+Y
		*dar ma	-y	
		da^{y}rma	-Ø^y	
		derma		
		Prosody affecting /a/ in first syllable		

6.4 PCC Lexical Reconstructions

	Malgwa	√ C C Ca	+Y
		*d r ma -y	
		dərma^y -Ø^y	
		dərme	
		Vowel epenthesis; prosody affecting final /a/	

	Glavda	√ C CaCa
		*d r aØØ
		dəra
		Vowel epenthesis

		√ C CaCa
		*d rawa
		drawa

	Dghweɗe	√ C CaCa
		*d rawa
		dərawa
		Vowel epenthesis

MOFU	Muyang	√ C CaCa	+Y
	a-	*d ramØ -y	
	a^y-	dra^{y}m -Ø^y	
		edrem	
		Prosody affecting all /a/	

	Mada	√ C CaCa
		*d ramØ
		dram

	Merey	√ C CaCa
		*d ramØ
		dəram
		Vowel epenthesis

	Dugwor	√ C CaCa	+W
		*d ramØ -k^w	
		dəra^{w}m -Ø^w	
		dərom	
		Prosodification of /k^w/ > ^{w}; vowel epenthesis; prosody affecting medial /a/	

	Mofu North	√ C CaCa
		*t lamØ
		təlam
		təlam
		Vowel epenthesis

356   Full Lexical Reconstructions

		√ CaCaCa	
		*talamØ	
		talam	
	Mofu-Gudur	√ C CaCa	
		*t lamØ	
		təlam	
		Vowel epenthesis	
MAROUA	Giziga-Muturwa	√ C C Ca	+W
		*d r mØ -k^w	
		də^{w}rə^{w}m -Ø^w	
		durum	
		Prosodification of /k^w/ > ^{w}; vowel epenthesis; prosody affecting epenthetic vowels	
		√ C C Ca	+W
		*d r mØ -k^w	
		drə^{w}m -Ø^w	
		drum	
		Prosodification of /k^w/ > ^{w}; vowel epenthesis; prosody affecting epenthetic vowel	
	Giziga-Marva	√ C CaCa	+W
		*d ramØ -k^w	
		də^{w}ra^{w}m -Ø^w	
		durom	
		Prosodification of /k^w/ > ^{w}; vowel epenthesis; prosody affecting all vowels	
	Mbazla	√ C C Ca	+W
		*d r mØ -k^w	
		də^{w}rə^{w}m -Ø^w	
		durum	
		Prosodification of /k^w/ > ^{w}; vowel epenthesis; prosody affecting epenthetic vowels	
LAMANG	Lamang, Hdi	√ C C Ca	
		*d l ØØ -y-k^w	
		> d l -k^w-y	
		> d w l -y	
		dwl -i	
		duli	

6.4 PCC Lexical Reconstructions

Double metathesis: *y k^w > k^w y; l k^w > k^w l; weakening of k^w > w; syllabification of /w/; syllabification of /y/

HIGI	Kamwe-Nkafa	√ C C Ca		+W
		*t r mØ	-y-k^w	
		tərm^w	-w^w-y	
		tərm^w	-i	
		tərm^{w}i		

Metathesis: *y k^w > k^w y; partial desegmentalisation and prosodification of /k^w/ > /w^w/; vowel epenthesis; prosody affecting final consonant; syllabification of /y/

	Kamwe-Futu	√ C C Ca		+W
		*t r ma	-y-k^w	
		> təryma^w	-Ø^w	
		tərimo		

Metathesis *m y > y m; vowel epenthesis; syllabification of /y/; prosody affecting final /a/

	Bana	√ C C Ca	
		*t l ma	-y
		> təlymə	
		təlima	

Metathesis *m y > y m; vowel epenthesis; syllabification of /y/; centralisation final /a/

horn$_2$

Alternative reconstruction (areal root)
a-, m(a)-   **x^w(a)la**   -y   +Y, +W   PC: —

mah^{w}a n. horn *corne* (3 groups, 4 languages) C syn: lagan, dirim, ^{m}bik^{w}im.

This is one of the rarer roots for 'horn', and is found only in three groups in the Eastern Plains area. The labialisation component of the *h has been reanalysed as the labialisation prosody in Proto-Musgum and Proto-Gidar, which is a common sporadic process.

KOTOKO-SOUTH	Zina		√ CaCa
		a-	*x^{w}alØ
		a-	x^{w}al
			ah^{w}al

358   Full Lexical Reconstructions

	Mazera		$\sqrt{}$ C Ca		+Y
		m-	*x^w Øa	-y	
		mə^y-	xwa^y	-Ø^y	
			mihue		
			Re-segmentalisation /x^w/ > /x+w/; syllabification of /w/ > [u]; Y-prosody affecting epenthetic vowel in prefix and final /a/		
MUSGUM	Mbara		$\sqrt{}$ CaCa		+W
		ma-	*x^{w}aØØ		
		ma^w-	x^{w}a^w		
			moho		
			Prosody affecting all /a/		
GIDAR	Gidar		$\sqrt{}$ CaCa		+W
		ma-	*x^{w}aØØ		
		ma^w-	x^{w}a^w		
			moho		
			Prosody affecting all /a/		

horse[23]

Alternative reconstruction (PCC/loan)
a-   **p(a)r(a)sa**   -y, -k,   a   +Y, +W   PC: *pərsi (JS)
                       -k^w, -ŋ

piris ^{y} n. horse *cheval* (10 groups, 32 languages) A syn: tak^w, bisk^{w}an.

This root is a borrowing from the Arabic 'FRS', denoting a mare. The Arabic /f/ appears as a Proto-Central Chadic *p, since there was no *p/*f contrast in the early stages of Central Chadic, and [p] was the word-initial allophone. Likewise, the *r has the regular reflex *l in the languages of the North sub-branch and Proto-Daba. However, it is also realised as *l in Proto-Mafa and Proto-Hurza, where *r is expected. The palatalisation prosody is present in all groups where it is expected, except for Gidar.

DABA	Daba		$\sqrt{}$ C C Ca		+Y
			*p l sØ	-y	
			pə^{y}lə^{y}s	-Ø^y	
			pilis		
			Vowel epenthesis; prosody affecting epenthetic vowels		

---

[23] This is an obvious loan and thus qualifies as a 'pseudo'-PCC root insofar as it has been streamlined into Central Chadic phonology systems to the extent of being apparently 'reconstructable'.

6.4 PCC Lexical Reconstructions

MAFA	Mafa	√ C CaCa	+Y
		*p lasØ -y	
		pəʸlaʸsʸ -Øʸ	
		pileʃ	
		Vowel epenthesis; prosody affecting all vowels and final consonant	
	Cuvok	√ C CaCa	+Y
		*p lazØ -y	
		pəlaʸz -Øʸ	
		pəlez	
		Vowel epenthesis; prosody affecting medial /a/	
TERA	Tera	√ C C Ca	
		*p r sØ -y	
		pərs -i	
		pərsi	
		Vowel epenthesis; syllabification of /y/	
	Nyimatli	√ C C Ca	
		*p r sØ -y	
		pərs -i	
		pərsi	
		Vowel epenthesis; syllabification of /y/	
		√ C C Ca	
		*p r sa -ŋ-k	
		pərsa -ŋg	
		pərsaŋg	
		Vowel epenthesis; fusion of root-augmental -ŋ-k > ŋg	
	Ga'anda	√ C C Ca	+Y
		*p r sa -y	
		pəʸrsʸa -Øʸ	
		pirʃa	
		Vowel epenthesis; prosody affecting epenthetic vowel and final consonant	
HURZA	Mbuko	√ C CaCa	+Y
		*p lasØ -y	
		pəlaʸs -Øʸ	
		pəles	
		Vowel epenthesis; prosody affecting medial /a/	

360   Full Lexical Reconstructions

	Vame	√ C CaCa	+Y
		*p lasØ -y	
		pəla^{y}s^y -Ø^y	
		pəleʃ	
		Vowel epenthesis; prosody affecting medial /a/	
		and final consonant	

MANDARA   Matal   √ C C Ca   +Y
                   *p l sØ   -y
                   pələ^{y}s   -Ø^y
                   pəlis
                   Vowel epenthesis; prosody affecting second
                   syllable epenthetic vowel

                   √ C C Ca   +Y
                   *p l sØ   -y
                   pələ^{y}s^y -Ø^y
                   pəliʃ
                   Vowel epenthesis; prosody affecting second
                   syllable epenthetic vowel and final consonant

          Podoko   √ C C Ca   +Y
                   *p r sa   -y
                   pə^{y}rəs^{y}a^y -Ø^y
                   pirəʃe
                   Vowel epenthesis; prosody affecting first
                   syllable epenthetic vowel and final consonant
                   and final /a/

          Mandara √ CaC Ca   +Y
                   *bal sa   -y
                   ba^{y}lsa   -Ø^y
                   belsa
                   Prosody affecting medial /a/

          Malgwa   √ C C Ca
                   *b l sa
                   bəlsa
                   Vowel epenthesis

          Glavda   √ C C Ca
                   *p l sØ
                   pəls
                   Vowel epenthesis

                   √ C C Ca   +Y
                   *p l sa   -y
                   pə^{y}ls^{y}a   -Ø^y

6.4 PCC Lexical Reconstructions

		pilːʃa Vowel epenthesis; prosody affecting epenthetic vowel and final consonant; consonant length (?) remains unaccounted for	
MOFU	Ouldeme	√ C C Ca *p l sØ -y pələʸs -Øʸ *pəlis* Vowel epenthesis; prosody affecting second syllable epenthetic vowel	+Y
	Moloko	√ C CaCa *p lasØ -y pəlaʸs -Øʸ *pəles* Vowel epenthesis; prosody affecting medial /a/	+Y
	Zulgo	√ C C Ca *p r sØ -y pəʸrəʸs -Øʸ *piris* Vowel epenthesis; prosody affecting epenthetic vowels	+Y
	Gemzek, Merey, Dugwor, Mofu- Gudur	√ C CaCa *p lasØ -y pəlaʸs -Øʸ *pəles* Vowel epenthesis; prosody affecting medial /a/	+Y
	Mofu North	√ CaCaCa *palasØ -y paʸlaʸs -Øʸ *peles* Vowel epenthesis; prosody affecting medial /a/	+Y
MAROUA	Giziga- Muturwa	√ C C Ca *p l sØ -y pəʸləʸs -iʸ *pilis(i)* Vowel epenthesis; prosody affecting epenthetic vowels; syllabification of /y/	+Y
		√ C C Ca *p l sØ -y	+Y

362   Full Lexical Reconstructions

          pləʸs   -Øʸ
          plis
          Vowel epenthesis; prosody affecting epenthetic vowel

          √ C C Ca   +Y +W
          *p Ø tsa -y-kʷ
          pəʷtsʸəʷ -Øʸ-Øʷ
          putʃu
          Vowel epenthesis; prosodification of /kʷ/ > ʷ; Y-prosody affecting medial consonant; W-prosody affecting epenthetic vowel and centralised final /a/

    Giziga-   √ C CaCa   +Y
    Marva   *p lasØ -y
          pəʸlaʸs -Øʸ
          piles
          Vowel epenthesis; prosody affecting all vowels

    Mbazla   √ C C Ca   +Y
          *p l sØ -y
          pəʸləʸsʸ -Øʸ
          piliʃ
          Vowel epenthesis; prosody affecting epenthetic vowels and final consonant

LAMANG Lamang   √ C C Ca   +Y
          *p l sØ y
          pələʸs -iʸ
          pəlis(i)
          Vowel epenthesis; prosody affecting second syllable epenthetic vowel; syllabification of /y/

    Hdi   √ C C Ca   +Y
          *p l sØ -y
          pələʸs -Øʸ
          pəlis
          Vowel epenthesis; prosody affecting second syllable epenthetic vowel

MUSGUM Mulwi,   √ C C Ca   +Y
    Vulum a- *p l sØ -y
        a- pləʸs -Øʸ
          aplis

6.4 PCC Lexical Reconstructions   363

	Mbara	√ C C Ca	+Y
		*p l sØ -y	
		pə^{y}lə^{y}s -Ø^y	
		pilis	

Vowel epenthesis; prosody affecting epenthetic vowel

	Mbara	√ C C Ca	+Y
		*p l sØ -y	
		pə^{y}lə^{y}s -Ø^y	
		pilis	

Vowel epenthesis; prosody affecting epenthetic vowels

	Muskum	√ C CaCa	+Y
		*p lasa -y-k a	
		pla^{y}sa^y -Ø^y-k a^y	
		pleseke	

Prosody affecting all /a/

GIDAR | Gidar | √ C C Ca |
| | | *p l sa |
| | | *pəlsa* |

Vowel epenthesis

		√ C C Ca	+Y
		*p l sa -y	
		pə^{y}lsa -Ø^y	
		pɨɨlsa	

Vowel epenthesis; prosody affecting epenthetic vowel; long [ɨ] remains unaccounted

laugh, to

Alternative reconstruction (**PCC**)
a-, m- ɣ^w(a)b(a)sa -a,-y, -k, -n   a   +Y, +W   PC: *gamsə (PN), *gms$_2$ (JS), *[ɦ]Vm(V)c- (OS)

ɣ^{w}iɓis v. laugh *rire* (12 groups, 29 languages) C
   This is a difficult root to reconstruct. The three consonants of the reconstructed form are found only in the Mandara and Lamang groups. In all other groups the *ɣ^w and *ɓ have interacted or been lost. *ɣ^w has been lost in Proto-Daba and Proto-Sukur, which is an unestablished change. In Podoko the labialisation component was retained and vocalised, and in Proto-Higi the labialisation component transferred onto *ɓ. Within the Higi group, *ɓ^w→ʔ^w in several languages, which

is an unestablished change. There has been an unestablished change *ɓ→ᵐb, giving the forms in Mbuko, Moloko and Lamang. The sporadic change *ᵐb→m took place subsequently, giving the forms in Daba, Proto-Tera, Ouldeme, Vame and Gidar. The labialisation component of *ɣʷ combined with this in Proto-Bata, Vame and Proto-Margi. In another path, the *m combined with *ɣʷ to create *ŋgʷ, giving the forms in Mafa, Merey and Dugwor. These examples of fusion are common sporadic processes. There is evidence for reconstructing *i from the Sukur, Margi and Higi groups.

BATA	Gude		√ C C Ca			
			*w m sa			
			> mwsa			
			mwʷəʷsa			
			nwʷəʷsənʷ			
			nwusə			
			Metathesis *w m > m w; vowel epenthesis; prosody affecting epenthetic vowel; dissimilation mw > nwʷ; centralisation of final /a/			
	Sharwa		√ C C Ca			+Y
		a-	*w m sØ	-y -k	a	
		a-	> mwəʸs	-Øʸ-k	ə	
			amʷiskə			
			Metathesis *w m > m w; vowel epenthesis; prosody affecting epenthetic vowel; centralisation of FV /a/			
	Tsuvan		√ C CaCa			+Y, +W
		a-	*w masØ	-y -k -n		
		a-	> mwəʸs	-Øʸ-kən		
			amʷeskən			
			Metathesis *w m > m w; prosodification of w > ʷ + labialisation of preceding /m/; vowel epenthesis; Y-prosody affecting medial /a/			
DABA	Buwal, Gavar, Mbudum		√ C CaCa			
			*Ø ɓasØ			
			ɓas			
	Daba		√ C C Ca			+Y
			*Ø m sØ	-y		
			məʸs	-Øʸ		
			mis			

6.4 PCC Lexical Reconstructions   365

		Vowel epenthesis; prosody affecting epenthetic vowel		
MAFA	Mafa	√ C CaCa *g^w masa > mg^wasØ *ng^was* Metathesis *g^w m > m g^w; assimilation mg^w > ng^w		
TERA	Tera	√ C C Ca *Ø m sØ məs *məsi* Vowel epenthesis, syllabification of /y/	-y -i	
	Nyimatli	√ C C Ca *Ø m sØ məs		
SUKUR	Sukur	√ C C Ca *Ø ɓ sØ ɓə^{y}s *ɓis* Vowel epenthesis; prosody affecting epenthetic vowel	-y -Ø^y	+Y
HURZA	Mbuko m- Ø-	√ C CaCa *Ø basØ ^{m}bas *^{m}basay* Prenasalisation of C_2 *b > mb	-a-y -ay	
	Vame	√ C C Ca *w m sØ > mws^y *muʃ* Metathesis *w m > m w; syllabification of /w/; prosody affecting final consonant	-y -Ø^y	+Y
		√ C C Ca *w m sa > mws^{y}ə^y *muʃiya* Metathesis *w m > m w; syllabification of /w/; centralisation of root-final /a/; prosody affecting final consonant and centralised /a/	-y -y^y	+Y a a

366   Full Lexical Reconstructions

MARGI	Bura		√ C C Ca		+Y, +W
			*k^w m sØ	-y	
			k^{w}ə^{w}ms^y	-i^y	
			kumʃi		
			Vowel epenthesis; W-prosody affecting epenthetic vowel; Y-prosody affecting final consonant; syllabification of /y/		
			√ C C Ca		+Y
			*w m sa	-y	
			> mws^{y}a	-Ø^y	
			muʃa		
			Metathesis *w m > m w; syllabification of medial /w/; prosody affecting final consonant		
			√ C C Ca		+Y
			*Ø m sa	-y	
			mə^{y}s^{y}a	-Ø^y	
			miʃa		
			Vowel epenthesis; prosody affecting epenthetic vowel and final consonant		
MANDARA	Podoko		√ C CaCa		
			*w ɓasa		
			uɓasa		
			Syllabification of initial /w/		
	Glavda		√ C CaCa		+W
			*ɣ^w ɓasØ	-k	a
			ɣ^{w}ə^{w}ɓas	-g	a
			ʁuɓas^{ə}ga		
			Vowel epenthesis; prosody affecting first syllable epenthetic vowel		
	Dghwede		√ C CaCa		
			*g ɓasa		
			gəp'asa		
			Vowel epenthesis		
MOFU	Ouldeme		√ C CaCa		
			*ØmasØ	-a -y	
			mas	-ay	
			masay		
	Moloko		√ C CaCa		
		m-	*Ø basØ		
		Ø-	^{m}bas		
			^{m}bas		
			Prenasalisation of C$_2$ *b > ^{m}b		

6.4 PCC Lexical Reconstructions   367

	Merey		√ C CaCa	
			*g^w masa	
			> mg^wasa	
			ŋg^wasa	
			Metathesis *g^w m > m g^w; (homorganic) assimilation mg^w > ŋg^w	
	Dugwor		√ C CaCa	+Y
		m-	*g^w masØ	-a-y
		mə-	> mg^wa^{y}s	-a^{y}y^y
			məŋg^wesey	
			Metathesis *g^w m > m g^w; vowel epenthesis; prosody affecting all /a/; assimilation mg > ng	
LAMANG	Lamang		√ C CaCa	
		m-	*ɣ basa	
		Ø-	ɣə^{m}basa	
			Prenasalisation of C_2 *b > ^{m}b; vowel epenthesis	
	Hdi		√ C CaCa	+W
			*ɣ^w ɓasØ	-a-y
			ɣ^{w}ə^{w}ɓas	-ay
			ɣuɓasay	
			Vowel epenthesis; prosody affecting epenthetic vowel	
HIGI	Kamwe-Nkafa		√ C C Ca	+Y
			*w ' sØ	-y
			> 'ws	-y
			'us^y	-i^y
			'uʃi	
			Metathesis w ' > ' w; syllabification of /w/; prosody affecting final consonant; syllabification of /y/	
	Kamwe-Futu		√ C C Ca	+Y
			*w Ø sØ	-y
			us^y	-i^y
			uʃi	
			Syllabification of initial /w/; prosody affecting final consonant; syllabification of /y/	
	Kirya		√ C C Ca	+Y, +W
			*w ɓ sØ	-y
			> ɓws	-y
			ɓ^{w}ə^{y}s^y	-i^y

368   Full Lexical Reconstructions

                        ɓʷiʃi
                        Metathesis *w ɓ > ɓ w; prosodification of /w/ > ʷ; W-prosody affecting initial consonant; vowel epenthesis; Y-prosody affecting epenthetic vowel and final consonant; syllabification of /y/

        Psikye   √ C C Ca   +Y, +W
                        *w ' sØ   -y
                        > 's Ø   -iʸ
                        'wəʷsʸ
                        'wuʃi
                        Metathesis w ' > ' w; vowel epenthesis; W-prosody affecting epenthetic vowel; Y-prosody affecting final consonant; syllabification of /y/

                        √ C C Ca   +Y, +W
                 m-   *w ' sa   -y
                 m-   m'wəʷsʸ   -iʸ
                        ŋ'wuʃi
                        Metathesis *' w > ' w; vowel epenthesis; W-prosody affecting epenthetic vowel; Y-prosody affecting final consonant; syllabification of /y/

        Bana   √ C C Ca   +Y
                        *w ' sØ   -y
                        'wəsʸ   -iʸ
                        'wəʃi
                        Metathesis w ' > ' w; vowel epenthesis; prosody affecting final consonant; syllabification of /y/

GIDAR   Gidar   √ C CaCa
                 a-   *Ø masa
                 ə-   masa
                        əmasa
                        Centralisation of prefixal /a/

lion

        Alternative reconstruction (**PCC**)
        w-, RED   **l(a)vara**   -y   +Y, +W   PC: *rbn (JS), *lVb-(r)- (OS)

6.4 PCC Lexical Reconstructions

lɨvarɨ n. lion *lion* (8 groups, 14 languages) D syn: mabor, zɨjɨl.

There are a variety of apparently cognate forms collected here. The root is unlikely to have existed in Proto-Central Chadic, but was a later innovation or borrowing. The initial consonant was probably *l, which is not a native Central Chadic phoneme. In languages of the South sub-branch, where *l had not yet developed, the reflex was *ɮ. In other languages it had the reflex *r. The Mbara form is possibly cognate, though the balance of likelihood is that it is not.

BATA	Gude		√ C CaCa		+Y
			*l vara	-y	
			ləʸvʸara	-Øʸ	
			livʸara		
			Vowel epenthesis; prosody affecting epenthetic vowel and medial consonant		
	Tsuvan		√ CaCaCa		+Y
		RED	*ɮawara	-y	
		ɮʸa	ɮʸawaraʸ	-Øʸ	
			ɮʸaɮʸaware		
			Prosody affecting initial consonant and final /a/		
DABA	Buwal		√ CaCaCa		+Y
			*lavara	-y	
			laʸvaʸraʸ	-Øʸ	
			levere		
			Prosody affecting all /a/		
	Daba		√ C CaCa		
			*ɮ varØ	-y	
			ɮʸəvar	-iʸ	
			ɮʸəvari		
			Vowel epenthesis; prosody affecting initial consonant; syllabification of /y/		
SUKUR	Sukur		√ C CaCa		+Y
			*l varØ	-y	
			ləʸvar	-iʸ	
			livari		
			Vowel epenthesis; prosody affecting epenthetic vowel; syllabification of /y/		
			√ C CaCa		+Y
			*r varØ	-y	
			rəʸvar	-iʸ	
			rivari		
			Vowel epenthesis; prosody affecting epenthetic vowel; syllabification of /y/		

HURZA	Vame	√ C CaCa	+Y
		*l vara -y	
		alvara^y -Ø^y	
		alvare	
		Vowel prothesis; prosody affecting final /a/	

MARGI	Margi- South	√ C CaCa
		*l varØ -y
		ləvar -i
		ləvari
		Vowel epenthesis; syllabification of /y/

MANDARA	Podoko	√ C CaCa	
		*r vara	
		rəvara	
		Vowel epenthesis	
	Mandara[24]	√ C CaCa	+Y
		*Ø vara -y	
		a^y vara^y -Ø^y	
		evare	
		Vowel prothesis (see fn.); prosody affecting prefixal and root-final /a/	
	Malgwa	√ C CaCa	+Y
		*r vara -y	
		ərvara^y -Ø^y	
		ərvare	
		Vowel prothesis; prosody affecting final /a/	
	Glavda	√ C CaCa	
		*r vara	
		arvara	
		arvara	
		Vowel prothesis	
		√ C CaCa	
		*r vaØØ	
		arva	
		arva	
		Vowel prothesis	

---

[24] Mandara is a language that as a rule inserts a prothetic vowel before an initial consonant cluster, which historically is also the case here with 'lion' (see closely related Malgwa and Glavda). Therefore, it would appear that Mandara lost the initial root consonant after prothetic vowel insertion, which may give us a welcome idea about relative chronology of diachronic processes.

6.4 PCC Lexical Reconstructions   371

LAMANG	Lamang		√ C CaCa		+Y
			*r vara	-y	
			ərvara^y	-Ø^y	
			ərvare		
			Vowel prothesis; prosody affecting final /a/		
	Hdi		√ C CaCa		+Y
			*r varØ	-y	
			rva^y r	-i^y	
			rveri		
			Prosody affecting medial /a/; syllabification of /y/		
HIGI	Kamwe-Futu		√ C CaCa		
			*l varØ	-y	
			ləvar	-i^y	
			ləvari		
			Vowel epenthesis; syllabification of /y/		
	Kirya		√ CaCaCa		+W
		w-	*ravana		
		w^w ə^w -	ravanə		
			wuravanə		
			Vowel epenthesis; prosody affecting epenthetic vowel; centralisation of final /a/		
MUSGUM	Mbara		√ C CaCa	-y	+Y
			*d vaŋØ	-Ø^y	
			də^y vaŋ		
			divaŋ		
			Vowel epenthesis; prosody affecting epenthetic vowel		

market[25]

Alternative reconstruction (**PCC**)
RED   **k(a)s(a)wka**   -b, -y   +Y, +W   Kanuri : *kasugu*

k^w asik^w a nm. market (n) *marché* (12 groups, 24 languages) B

This root derives ultimately from the Arabic 'suq', through Shoa Arabic 'sug' and Kanuri 'kasugu'. The back vowels are reinterpreted as labialisation of *k or *g. The Fulfulde word 'luumo' is replacing this root in many areas. There are no real indicators in the data of the age of this borrowing.

---

[25] This is an obvious loan and thus qualifies as a 'pseudo'-PCC root insofar as it has been streamlined into Central Chadic phonology systems to the extent of being apparently 'reconstructable'.

TERA	Hwana	√ CaC C Ca
		*kas wØØ
		kasw
		kasu
		Syllabification of /w/

SUKUR	Sukur	√ C C C Ca	+W
		*Ø s wkØ	
		> skw	
		sə^{w}kw^w	
		suku	
		Metathesis *w k > k w; partial desegmentalisation of /w/ > /w^w/; vowel epenthesis; prosody affecting epenthetic vowel; syllabification of /w/	
		√ C C C Ca	
		*Ø s wkØ	
		> skw	
		səkw	
		səku	
		Metathesis *w k > k w: vowel epenthesis; syllabification of /w/	

HURZA	Mbuko	√ CaC C Ca	+W
		*kaswka	
		k^{w}asw^{w}ka^w	
		k^{w}asuko	
		Partial desegmentalisation of /w/ > /w^w/; prosody affecting initial consonant and final /a/; syllabification of /w/	
	Vame	√ CaC C Ca	
		*kaswka	
		kasuka	
		Syllabification of /w/	

MARGI	Kilba	√ C C C Ca
		*Ø s wkØ
		> skw
		səkw
		səku
		Metathesis *w k > k w; vowel epenthesis; syllabification of /w/

6.4 PCC Lexical Reconstructions   373

MANDARA   Matal   √ CaC C Ca   +W
                         *kas wka
                         > kaskwa
                         kʷaskʷa
                         kʷasəkʷa
                         kʷasəkʷa
                         Metathesis *w k > k w; prosodification of
                         /w/ > ʷ; vowel epenthesis; prosody affecting
                         velar consonants

                         √ CaC C Ca   +W
                         *kaswka
                         kaʷswʷka
                         kosuka
                         Partial desegmentalisation of /w/ > /wʷ/;
                         syllabification of /w/; prosody affecting 1st
                         syllable /a/

          Podoko   √ CaCaC Ca   +W
                         *kasawka
                         > kasakwʷa
                         kʷasakʷa
                         kʷasakʷa
                         Metathesis *w k > k w; prosodification of
                         /w/ > ʷ; prosody affecting velar consonants

          Malgwa   √ CaC C Ca   +Y, +W
                         *kas wka   -y
                         > kaskwʷa   -y
                         kʷaskʷaʸ   -Øʸ
                         kʷaskʷe
                         Metathesis *w k > k w; desegmentalisation
                         of /w/ > ʷ; W-prosody affecting velar
                         consonants; Y-prosody affecting final /a/

          Glavda   √ CaC C Ca
                         *kas wØØ
                         kasw
                         kasu
                         Syllabification of /w/

                         √ CaC C Ca
                         *kaswkØ
                         kaswk
                         kasuk
                         Syllabification of /w/

374   Full Lexical Reconstructions

		√ CaC C Ca	+W
		*kas wka	
		kasw^wka	
		kasuk^wa	
		kasuk^wa	

Partial desegmentalisation of /w/ > /w^w/; prosody affecting final consonant; syllabification of /w/

MOFU   Ouldeme   √ CaC C Ca   +W
                        *kas wka
                        > kaskw^wa
                        kask^wa
                        k^wask^wa
                        k^wask^wa
                        Metathesis *w k > k w; prosodification of
                        /w/ > ^w; prosody affecting velar consonants

          Muyang   √ CaC C Ca   +W
                        *gas wkØ
                        > gaskw^w
                        ga^wskw
                        gosku
                        Metathesis *w k > k w; partial
                        desegmentalisation of /w/ > /w^w/; prosody
                        affecting medial /a/; syllabification of /w/

          Mada   √ CaC C Ca   +W
                        *gas wka
                        > gaskwa
                        gask^wa
                        ga^wska^w
                        gosko
                        Metathesis *w k > k w; Prosodification
                        of /w/ > ^w; prosody affecting all /a/

          Moloko   √ CaCaC Ca   +W
                        *kasawka
                        kasa^wka
                        ka^wsa^wka^w
                        kosoko
                        Prosodification of /w/ > ^w; prosody affecting
                        all /a/

          Zulgo   √ CaC C Ca   +W
                        *kas wka

6.4 PCC Lexical Reconstructions

> kaskwa
kaskʷa
kʷaskʷa
kʷaskʷa
Metathesis *w k > k w; prosodification of /w/ > ʷ; prosody affecting velar consonants

MAROUA	Giziga-Marva	√ CaC C Ca	+W

*kas wka
> kasØʷka
kaskʷa
kaʷskaʷ
kosko
Prosodification of /w/ > ʷ; prosody affecting all /a/

HIGI	Kamwe-Futu	√ C C C Ca	+Y, W

*Ø s wkØ   -y
> skwʷ   -y
sʸəʸkʷ   -iʸ
ʃikʷi
Metathesis *w k > k w; vowel epenthesis; Y-prosody affecting epenthetic vowel and initial consonant; prosodification of /w/ > ʷ; W-prosody affecting final consonant; syllabification of /y/

	Psikye	√ C C C Ca	+Y, +W

*Ø s wkØ   -y
> skwʷ   -y
sʸkʷw   -Øʸ
ʃkʷu
Metathesis *w k > k w; syllabification of /w/ plus partial prosodification of /w/ > ʷ; W-prosody affecting final consonant; Y-prosody affecting initial consonant

√ C CaC Ca   +Y, +W
*Ø sawkØ   -y
> sakwʷ   -y
sʸaʸkʷw   -Øʸ
ʃekʷu
Metathesis *w k > k w; syllabification of /w/ plus partial prosodification of /w/ > ʷ; W-prosody affecting final consonant; Y-prosody affecting initial consonant and medial /a/

376   Full Lexical Reconstructions

KOTOKO- ISLAND	Buduma	√ CaCaC Ca *kaxawga > kaxagwa kaxaguə *kaxaguə* Metathesis *w g > g w; syllabification of /w/; centralisation of final /a/		
KOTOKO- NORTH	Afade	√ CaC C Ca *gas ØØØ gasə^y *gasɨbi* Vowel epenthesis; prosody affecting epenthetic vowel; syllabification of /y/	-b-y -b-i^y	+Y
	Mpade	√ CaC C Ca *kas wgØ > kasgw^w kasə^{w}gw *kasugu* Metathesis *w g > g w; partial desegmentalisation of /w/ > /w^w/; vowel epenthesis; prosody affecting epenthetic vowel; syllabification of /w/		+W
	Malgbe RED ga-	√ CaC C Ca *gaØ ØØØ ga ga^{y}gØ *gegbɨ* Vowel epenthesis; prosody affecting epenthetic vowel and medial /a/	-b-y -b-y -bə-^{y}	+Y
KOTOKO- CENTRAL	Lagwan, Mser	√ CaC C Ca *kas wkØ > kaskw *kasku* Metathesis *w k > k w; syllabification of /w/		
MUSGUM	Mbara	√ CaC C Ca *kas wka > kasØ^{w}kwa kask^{w}a kask^{w}a^w *kasko* Prosodification of /w/ > ^{w}; prosody affecting final /a/		+W

moon

Alternative reconstruction (**PCC**)
n-, ŋ-   **t(a)ra** -y, -k^w a   +Y, +W   PC : *təra (PN),
                                                 *tr (a) (k-; -n) ~
                                                 *k^{y}r (JS),
                                                 *tV-ʔVr- (OS)

tira nm. moon *lune* (10 groups, 31 languages) A syn: kija.
This root is the original Proto-Central Chadic root, and goes back at least as far as Proto-Chadic. There is a regular change *r→l in the North sub-branch, though here Proto-Higi has *r, and Proto-Kotoko North and Proto-Kotoko Centre have *ɗ. It is expected that Sukur has /r/, but this is not the case. Evidence for *i comes from the three groups where *i exists as a phoneme, i.e. the Mandara, Lamang and Higi groups. In Glavda, *i has been reanalysed as the palatalisation of *t. There is a regular process in Glavda where palatalised alveolar consonants become palatalised velar consonants, and this explains the presence of /k^j/. The change *t→k in Muskum is regular.

DABA	Buwal		√ C Ca
		ŋ-	*t ra
		ŋ-	təra
			ŋtəra
			Vowel epenthesis
	Gavar		√ C Ca
		ŋ-	*t ra
			ŋtra
	Mbudum		√ C Ca
		n-	*t ra
		n-	təra
			ntəra
			Vowel epenthesis
			√ C Ca
		n-	*t ra
			ntra
	Daba, Mazagway Hidi		√ C Ca
			*t ra
			təra
			təra
			Vowel epenthesis

378   Full Lexical Reconstructions

TERA	Tera		√ CaCa	+Y
			*tara -y	
			ta^{y}ra -Ø^y	
			tera	
			Prosody affecting medial /a/	
	Nyimatli		√ CaCa	+Y
			*tsara -y	
			ts^{y}a^{y}ra^y -Ø^y	
			tʃere	
			Prosody affecting initial consonant and all /a/	
			√ CaCa	+Y
			*tsara -y	
			ts^{y}a^{y}ra -Ø^y	
			tʃera	
			Prosody affecting initial consonant and medial /a/	
	Hwana		√ C Ca	+Y
		n-	*d ra -y	
		n-	dra^y -Ø^y	
			^{n}d*r*e	
			Prefixal nasal > prenasalisation; prosody affecting final /a/	
SUKUR	Sukur		√ C Ca	+Y
			*t Øa -y a	
			ta^y -y^y a	
			teya	
			Prosody affecting medial /a/	
			√ C Ca	+Y
			*t ØØ -y a	
			t -y a	
			tya	
MANDARA	Matal		√ C Ca	
			*t la	
			təla	
			Vowel epenthesis	
	Podoko		√ C Ca	
			*t ra	
			təra	
			Vowel epenthesis	

6.4 PCC Lexical Reconstructions

	Mandara, Malgwa	√ C Ca		+Y
		*t ra	-y	
		təra^y	-Ø^y	
		təre		
		Vowel epenthesis; prosody affecting final /a/		

	Glavda	√ C Ca		+Y
		*t ØØ	-y	
		t^y	-i^y	
		k^yi		
		Prosody affecting initial consonant; syllabification of /y/		

		√ C Ca		+Y
		*t la	-y	
		t^yla	-Ø^y	
		k^yla		
		Prosody affecting initial consonant		

	Dghwede	√ C Ca		+Y
		*t la	-y	
		tə^yla^y	-Ø^y	
		tile		
		Vowel epenthesis; prosody affecting all vowels		

LAMANG	Lamang	√ C Ca		+Y
		*t ra	-y	
		təra^y	-Ø^y	
		tər(e)		
		Vowel epenthesis; prosody affecting final /a/		

	Hdi	√ C Ca		+Y
		*t lØ	-y	
		tə^yl	-i^y	
		tili		
		Vowel epenthesis; prosody affecting epenthetic vowel; syllabification of /y/		

HIGI	Kamwe-Nkafa	√ C Ca		
		*t ra		
		tərə°		
		tərə°		
		Centralisation of final /a/		

	Kamwe-Futu	√ C Ca		+W
		*t ra	-k^w	
		təra^w	-Ø^w	

380   Full Lexical Reconstructions

		tǝro	
		Prosodification of /kʷ/ > ʷ; vowel epenthesis; prosody affecting final /a/	
	Kirya	√ C Ca	+Y
		*t rØ -y	
		tǝr -iʸ	
		tǝɾi	
		Vowel epenthesis; prosody affecting final consonant; syllabification of /y/	
	Psikye	√ C Ca	
		*t ra	
		trǝ	
		trǝ	
		Centralisation of final /a/	
	Bana	√ C Ca	+Y
		*t rØ -y	
		tǝʸr -Øʸ	
		tir	
		Vowel epenthesis; prosody affecting epenthetic vowel	
KOTOKO- NORTH	Afade	√ CaCa	+Y
		*daɗ Ø -y	
		daʸɗ -iʸ	
		deɗi	
		Prosody affecting medial /a/; syllabification of /y/	
	Mpade	√ CaCa	+Y
		*taɗa -y	
		taʸɗǝʸ -Øʸ	
		teɗi	
		Centralisation of final /a/; prosody affecting all vowels	
KOTOKO- CENTRAL	Lagwan, Mser	√ CaCa	+Y
		*taɗa -y	
		taʸɗǝʸ -Øʸ	
		teɗi	
		Centralisation of final /a/; prosody affecting all vowels	
MUSGUM	Vulum	√ C Ca	+Y
		*t la -y	

6.4 PCC Lexical Reconstructions

		tla^y	-Ø^y	
		tle		
		Vowel epenthesis; prosody affecting final /a/		

	Mbara	√ C Ca		+Y
		*t la	-y	
		tə^yla^y	Ø^y	
		tile		
		Vowel epenthesis; prosody affecting all vowels		

	Muskum	√ C Ca		+Y
		*t la	-y	
		t^yə^yla^y	-Ø^y	
		kile		
		Vowel epenthesis; prosody affecting all vowels and intial consonant *t^y > k^y		

GIDAR	Gidar	√ C Ca		+Y
		*t la	-y	
		tə^yla	-Ø^y	
		tɨla		
		Vowel epenthesis; prosody affecting epenthetic vowel		

√ C Ca
*t la
təla
Vowel epenthesis

navel

Alternative reconstruction (**PCC**)
z(a)b(a)-x^w(a)ɗa   -y, -n   +Y, +W   PC: *'tb (m-, -k)
                                          ~ *tb ~ *ɗb (-n) (JS)

Note: The widespread occurrence of medial *^mb^w in this root is an invitation to reconstruct */^mb^w/, i.e. ^xz(a)^mb^w(a)ɗa, but PCC did not have any labialised labials, only labialised velars. Since there is no labialised velar in the simple root, the labialisation feature could have originated from morphological labialisation, which we symbolise in our reconstructions by *{-k^w}. However, Gravina's hypothesis (see immediately below) is quite plausible that we are dealing with a compound containing the root for 'belly', whose initial consonant would account for the labial feature to be prosodised: *mØ-**z(a)ba** + ***x^w(a)ɗa** > ***z(a)^mb-x^w(a)ɗa**. We, therefore, tentatively reconstruct such a compound, irrespective of the fact that the first part of it (***z(a)ba**) remains obscure. Note, however, that the MANDARA group languages would appear not to use such a compound, i.e. there is no labialisation reflex of *x^w(a)ɗa 'belly'.

zi^{m}b^{w}iɗ nm. navel *nombril* (8 groups, 23 languages) B

This root is attested in a wide distribution of languages. In most respects, this root behaves in a regular fashion. The changes *z→s in Proto-Margi and Proto-Kotoko North are regular. *ɗ is lost in many cases (a common sporadic process), and has the regular reflex *r in part of the Higi group. A similar change, followed by an irregular change *r→l would account for the forms in Mafa, Ouldeme and Muyang. The difficulty lies in accounting for the presence of back vowels and labialisation in the Bata, Margi, Higi and Kotoko North groups, since there were no labialised labial phonemes in Proto-Central Chadic. The phoneme *^{m}b^w was created in the Bata, Margi and Higi groups by the reanalysis of *w as labialisation, or the transfer of the labialisation component from a labialised velar. It is possible that this root is a compound such as *zɨ^{m}bɨ-h^{w}iɗ, with *h^{w}iɗ being the Proto-Central Chadic root for 'belly' and *zɨ^{m}bɨ being a root of unknown meaning. This would also account for the variation between the presence of the palatalisation prosody and *i in the group-level reconstructions.

BATA	Bata		√ C C-C Ca		+W, +Y
		mØ-	*s b x^w ɗa	-y	
		Ø-	sə^{wm}b w^{w}ə^{w}ɗa^y	-Ø^y	
			su^{m}buɗe		
			Vowel epenthesis; nasal prefix > prenasalisation of C$_2$; W-prosody affecting epenthetic vowel; syllabification of /w/; Y-prosody affecting /a/		
	Jimi		√ C C-C Ca		+W, +Y
		ma-	*z b x^w ɗØ	-y -n	
		Ø-	z^{y}ə^{m}bw^w əɗ	-y-n	
			z^{y}ə^{m}bØ^w əɗ	-Ø^y-ən	
			ʒə^{m}b^{w}əɗən		
			Vowel epenthesis; nasal prefix > prenasalisation of C$_2$; W-prosody affecting second consonant; Y-prosody affecting initial consonant		
	Sharwa		√ C C-C Ca		+W, +Y
		ma-	*z b x^w ɗa	-y	
		Ø-	zə^{ym}bwɗə	-Ø^y	
			zɨ^{m}buɗə		
			Vowel epenthesis; nasal prefix > prenasalisation of C$_2$; Y-prosody affecting epenthetic vowel in first syllable; syllabification of /w/; centralisaton of final /a/		

6.4 PCC Lexical Reconstructions 383

| MAFA | Mafa | | √ C C-CaCa | | +Y |

*z m ØalØ   -y
zə^{y}ma^{y}l   -Ø^y
zimel
Vowel epenthesis; prosody affecting all vowels

| MARGI | Margi-South | ma-
Ø- | √ C C-C Ca | | +Y, +W |

*s b x^w ɗa   -y
s^{y}ə^{ym}b w^{w}ɗə^w -Ø^y
ʃə^{m}budu
Vowel epenthesis; nasal prefix > prenasalisation of C$_2$; centralisation of final /a/; W-prosody affecting vowels in ultimate and penultimate syllables; Y-prosody affecting initial consonant

| | Kilba | ma-
Ø- | √ C C-C Ca | | +Y, +W |

*s b x^w ɗa   -y
s^{y}ə^{ym}b w^{w}ɗə^w -Ø^y
ʃi^{m}budu
Vowel epenthesis; nasal prefix > prenasalisation of C$_2$; centralisation of final /a/; W-prosody affecting vowels in ultimate and penultimate syllables; Y-prosody affecting first syllable consonant and vowel

| MANDARA | Podoko | ma-
Ø- | √ C Ca | | +Y |

*z ba   -y
z^{y}ə^{ym}ba   -Ø^y
ʒi^{m}ba
Vowel epenthesis; nasal prefix > prenasalisation of C$_2$; prosody affecting first syllable consonant and vowel

| | Mandara,
Malgwa,
Glavda | ma-
Ø- | √ CaCa | | +Y |

*zaba   -y
z^{y}a^{m}ba   -Ø^y
ʒa^{m}ba
Prosody affecting initial consonant; nasal prefix > prenasalisation of C$_2$

| | Dghweɗe | ma-
Ø- | √ C Ca | | +Y |

*z ba   -y
z^{y}ə^{ym}ba^y -Ø^y
ʒi^{m}be
Vowel epenthesis; nasal prefix > prenasalisation of C$_2$; prosody affecting first syllable consonant and all vowels

384   Full Lexical Reconstructions

MOFU	Ouldeme, Muyang	ma- Ø-	√ C C-CaCa *z bØalØ zəʸmbaʸl zi^mbel Vowel epenthesis; nasal prefix > prenasalisation of C_2; prosody affecting all vowels	-y -Øʸ	+Y
LAMANG	Lamang	ma- Ø-	√ C C-C Ca *z b xʷ Øa zəʸmb Øʷaʷ zi^mbo Vowel epenthesis; nasal prefix > prenasalisation of C_2; Y-prosody affecting epenthetic vowel; W-prosody affecting final /a/	-y -Øʸ	+Y, +W
HIGI	Kamwe-Nkafa	ma- Ø-	√ C C-C Ca *z b xʷ ØØ zʸəʸmbw $ʒi^mb^wi$ Vowel epenthesis; nasal prefix > prenasalisation of C_2; W-prosody affecting second consonant; Y-prosody affecting first syllable consonant and vowel; syllabification of /y/	-y -iʸ	+Y, +W
	Kamwe-Futu	ma- Ø-	√ CaC-C Ca *zab xʷ ØØ zʸaʸmbʷØʷ $ʒe^mb^wi$ W-prosody affecting second consonant; nasal prefix > prenasalisation of C_2; Y-prosody affecting first syllable consonant and vowel; syllabification of /y/	-y -iʸ	+Y, +W
	Kirya	ma- Ø-	√ C C-C Ca *z b xʷ rØ zʸəʸmb w r $ʒi^mbur$ Vowel epenthesis; nasal prefix > prenasalisation of C_2; Y-prosody affecting first syllable consonant and vowel; syllabification of /w/	-y -Øʸ	+Y, +W
	Bana	ma- Ø-	√ C C-CaCa *z b ØarØ zʸəʸmbaʸr $ʒi^mber$	-y -Øʸ	+Y

6.4 PCC Lexical Reconstructions

			Vowel epenthesis; nasal prefix > prenasalisation of C_2; Y-prosody affecting first syllable consonant and all vowels	
KOTOKO-NORTH[26]	Mpade	ma- Ø-	√ CaC-C Ca *sab x^w Øa sa^{m}b w *sa^{m}bu* Syllabification of /w/; nasal prefix > prenasalisation of C_2	+W

night

Alternative reconstruction (**PCC**)
a-, x-, **r(a)v(a)ɗa**   -a, -y, -k,   a   +Y, +W   PC: *bəɗi (PN),
m-/n-,   -k^w, -n, -ŋ   *-bɗ- (t-, m-, k-;
sa-, ta-   -m, -k) ~*vɗ (JS)

viɗ nf. night *nuit* (17 groups, 45 languages) B
   This root is attested in all groups except for Kotoko Island. *v is realised as *f in Proto-Kotoko North as a regular reflex, and in Proto-Gidar where *b is expected. *f is also expected in Proto-Musgum, but *v is present. *ɗ is unusually stable. In Mbuko and Zina we find /n/ where we would expect a reflex of *ɗ. Many languages have an initial consonant on the root, which can be /l/, /h/, /s/, /t/, /r/ or /d/. Often an initial consonant is appended when an original consonant was lost. This may have been *h^w, with the labialisation accounting for the forms in Proto-Daba, Proto-Hurza, Proto-Margi and Proto-Maroua. However, each language has a particular consonant that is used to compensate for lost material, and the consonants found here don't match the compensatory consonants. Until a good explanation is available, we will assume that the original root had no initial consonant.

BATA	Gude	√ C C Ca *Ø v ɗa vəɗa *vəɗa* Vowel epenthesis	
	Jimi	√ C C Ca *Ø v ɗa vəɗə *vəɗən* Vowel epenthesis; centralisation of final /a/	-n -n

---

[26] For the time being, I am hesitant to consider Afade *tsimtsim*, Mpade *simsim*, Maltam *simsim* to be cognate to this root. Further study may, however, reveal that they are. In that case, they would stem from a non-compound form ***z(a)ba-y** (see MANDARA group languages) with reduplication likely to compensate for the lost second element of the compound structure.

	Sharwa	√ C C Ca		+Y
		*Ø v ɗa	-y	
		vəʸɗə	-Øʸ	
		viɗə		
		Vowel epenthesis; prosody affecting epenthetic vowel; centralisation of final /a/		
MAFA	Mafa, Cuvok	√ C CaCa		
		*Ø vadØ		
		vad		
	Cuvok	√ C CaCa		
		*l vaØØ	-ŋ	
		ləva	-ŋ	
		ləvaŋ		
		Vowel epenthesis		
TERA	Tera	√ C C Ca		+Y
		*Ø v ɗØ	-y-k	
		vəʸɗ	-k-iʸ	
		viɗki		
		Metathesis *y k > k y; vowel epenthesis; prosody affecting epenthetic vowel; syllabification of /y/		
	Nyimatli[27]	√ C C Ca		+Y
		*Ø v rØ	-y-k-n	
		> vər	-k-r-iʸ	
		vəʸr	-kəʸ-r-iʸ	
		virkiri		
		Multiple metathesis *y k n > k n y; vowel epenthesis; prosody affecting epenthetic vowels; syllabification of /y/		
	Hwana	√ C C Ca		+Y
		*Ø f ɗØ	-y-k-n	a
		fəʸɗ	-iʸ-g-r	a
		fiɗigɹa		
		Vowel epenthesis; prosody affecting epenthetic vowel; syllabification of /y/		

---

[27] According to P. Newman (p.c. 2020), the generally somewhat doubtful variant forms identified as 'Nyimatli' in Gravina's database in this example represent 'an indefinite form' (Tera: *viɗki-r-i*).

6.4 PCC Lexical Reconstructions   387

SUKUR   Sukur   √ C C Ca
                     *Ø v dØ
                     vəɗ
                     vəɗ
                     Vowel epenthesis

                     √ C C Ca
                     *Ø v ØØ   -a-y
                     v   -ay
                     vay

HURZA   Mbuko   √ C C Ca   +W
                     *l v Øa   -k^w -n
                     lə^{w}va^w -Ø^w-n
                     luvon
                     Vowel epenthesis; prosodification of
                     /k^w/ > ^{w}; prosody affecting all vowels

        Vame   √ C CaCa   +W
                     *l vaɗØ   -k^w
                     lə^{w}vaɗ   -Ø^w
                     luvaɗ
                     Vowel epenthesis; prosodification of /k^w/ > ^{w};
                     prosody affecting epenthetic vowel

MARGI   Margi   √ C C Ca   +Y
                     *Ø v dØ   -y
                     və^{y}ɗ   -i^y
                     vi'i
                     Vowel epenthesis; prosody affecting epenthetic
                     vowel; syllabification of /y/

        Margi-   √ C C Ca   +Y, +W
        South   *Ø v dØ   -y -k^w
                     v^{w}ə^{y}ɗ   -i^y-Ø^w
                     v^{w}i'i
                     Vowel epenthesis; Y-prosody affecting
                     epenthetic vowel; prosodification of /k^w/ > ^{w};
                     W-prosody affecting initial consonant;
                     syllabification of /y/

        Kilba   √ C C Ca   +W
                     *Ø v dØ   -y -k^w
                     və^{w}ɗ   -i-Ø^w
                     vu'i
                     Vowel epenthesis; prosodification of /k^w/ > ^{w};
                     W-prosody affecting epenthetic vowel;
                     syllabification of /y/

388   Full Lexical Reconstructions

	Bura	√ C C Ca			+Y
		*Ø v rØ	-y		
		və^yr	-i^y		
		vir(i)			
		Vowel epenthesis; prosody affecting epenthetic vowel; syllabification of /y/			
MANDARA	Matal	√ C C Ca			
		*Ø v ɗØ			
		vəɗ			
		Vowel epenthesis			
	Podoko	√ C C Ca			
		*Ø v ɗa			
		vəɗa			
		Vowel epenthesis			
	Mandara	√ C CaCa			+Y
		*Ø vaɗØ	-y	a	
		vaɗ^y	-i^y	a	
		vayia			
		Prosody affecting final consonant: assumption *ɗ^y > y; syllabification of /y/			
	Glavda	√ C C Ca			
		*Ø v ɗa			
		avɗa			
		av^əɗ(a)			
		Vowel prothesis			
	Dghweɗe	√ C C Ca			+Y
		*Ø v ɗa	-y		
		və^yɗa^y	-Ø^y		
		vit'e ~ vit'e			
		Vowel epenthesis; prosody affecting all vowels			
MOFU	Ouldeme	√ CaCaCa			
		*lavaɗØ			
		lavaɗ			
	Muyang	√ C CaCa			
		*Ø vaɗØ			
		vaɗ			
	Zulgo	√ C C Ca			
		x- *Øv ɗØ			
		xə- vəɗ			
		həvəɗ			
		Vowel epenthesis			

6.4 PCC Lexical Reconstructions

	Gemzek		√ C CaCa		
		x-	*Ø vadØ		
		xə-	vaɗ		
			həvaɗ		
			Vowel epenthesis		

	Mofu		√ C CaCa		+Y
	North	sa-	*Ø vadØ	-y	
		saʸ-	vad	-Øʸ	
			sevad		
			Prosody affecting /a/ in prefixal augment		

	Mofu-		√ C CaCa		
	Gudur	ta-	*Ø vadØ		
		ta-	vaɗ		
			tavaɗ		

MAROUA   Mbazla   √ C C Ca   +W
                              *Ø v ɗØ   -kʷ
                              avɗ   -kʷ
                              avəʷɗ   -Øʷ
                              avuɗ ~ avut
                              Vowel prothesis and epenthesis;
                              prosodification of /kʷ/ > ʷ; prosody affecting
                              epenthetic vowel

LAMANG   Lamang   √ C C Ca   +Y
                              *r v ɗØ   -y
                              rvəʸɗ   -iʸ
                              rvidi
                              Vowel epenthesis; prosody affecting epenthetic
                              vowel; syllabification of /y/

          Hdi   √ C C Ca   +Y
                              *r v ɗØ   -y -k
                              rəvəʸɗØ   -iʸ -k
                              rəvidik
                              Vowel epenthesis; prosody affecting second
                              syllable epenthetic vowel; syllabification of /y/

HIGI   Kamwe-   √ C C Ca
          Nkafa   *Ø v ra
                              vərə
                              vərə
                              Vowel epenthesis; centralisation of final /a/

                              √ C C Ca
                              Ø v ɹa
                              vəɹə

                                                    vəɟə
Vowel epenthesis; centralisation of /a/

            Kamwe-   √ C C Ca   +Y
            Futu   *Ø v ɗØ   -y
                                  vəʸɗ   -iʸ
                                  vidî
Vowel epenthesis; prosody affecting epenthetic vowel; syllabification of /y/

            Kirya   √ C C Ca   +Y
                                *Ø v la   -y
                                vəlaʸ   -Øʸ
                                vəle
Vowel epenthesis; prosody affecting /a/

            Psikye   √ C C Ca   +Y
                                *Ø v ɗØ   -y
                                vəʸɗ   -iʸ
                                vidî
Vowel epenthesis; prosody affecting epenthetic vowel; syllabification of /y/

KOTOKO-   Afade,   √ C CaCa   +Y
NORTH   Mpade,   *Ø faɗa   -y
            Malgbe   faɗaʸ   -Øʸ
                                faɗe
Prosody affecting final /a/

KOTOKO-   Lagwan   √ C CaCa   +Y
CENTRAL   m-   *Ø vaɗa   -y
                             m-   vaɗaʸ   -Øʸ
                                    mvaɗe
Prosody affecting final /a/

                                    √ C CaCa   +Y
                          n-   *Ø vaɗa   -y
                          n-   vaɗaʸ   -Øʸ
                                  nvaɗe
Prosody affecting final /a/

            Mser   √ C CaCa   +Y
                         n-   *Ø vaɗa   -y
                         n-   vaɗaʸ   -Øʸ
                               nvaɗe
Prosody affecting final /a/

6.4 PCC Lexical Reconstructions

KOTOKO-SOUTH	Zina	√ C C Ca		+Y
		*l v ØØ	-y-n	
		ləv	-in	
		ləvin		
		Vowel epenthesis; syllabification of /y/		

MUSGUM	Mulwi	√ C C Ca		+Y
		*d v ØØ	-y-k	
		dəʸv	-iʸ-k	
		divik		
		Vowel epenthesis; prosody affecting epenthetic vowel; syllabification of /y/		

	Vulum	√ C C Ca		+Y
		*d v Øa	-y -k	
		dəʸvəʸ	-Øʸ-k	
		divɨk		
		Vowel epenthesis; centralisation of /a/; prosody affecting all vowels		

	Mbara	√ C C Ca		+Y
		*d v ɗØ	-a-y	
		dəʸvəʸɗ	-ay	
		divi'day		
		Vowel epenthesis; prosody affecting epenthetic vowels		

	Muskum	√ C C Ca		+Y
		*r v lØ	-y	
		arvəʸl	-Øʸ	
		arvɨl		
		Vowel pro- and epenthesis; prosody affecting epenthetic vowel		

GIDAR	Gidar	√ C C Ca		
		*d f ɗa		
		dəfɗa		
		Vowel epenthesis		

quiver

Alternative reconstruction (**PCC**)
ɣʷ(a)dza   -y,-n, -l   +Y, +W   PC: *kd- (JS)

ɣʷadzi nm. quiver *carquois* (5 groups, 11 languages) B

This root is found in languages around the Nigerian Plains area, and reflects a technological innovation rather than an ancient Proto-Central Chadic root. The sound changes indicate that the root was introduced during the time of the group proto-languages. The *ɣʷ has become *gʷ in the Higi group, and has developed into *kʷ in the Bata and Margi groups, all of which are unestablished changes. In Sukur the fricative component was lost, leaving /w/, also an unestablished change. The *dz has been devoiced to *ts in the Higi group, which is also an unestablished change. The final *i is reanalysed as the palatalisation prosody in the Margi group.

BATA	Gude	√ CaCa	
		*kʷadza	
		kʷadza	
	Jimi	√ CaCa	
		*kʷadza	-n
		kʷadzan	
	Sharwa	√ CaCa	
		*kʷadza	
		kʷadza	
SUKUR	Sukur	√ CaCa	
		*wadzØ	-y
		wadz	-i
		wadzi	
		Syllabification of /y/	
		√ CaCa	
		*wadza	-y
		wadzə	-i
		wadzəi	
		Centralisation of final /a/; syllabification of /y/	
MARGI	Bura	√ CaCa	+Y
		*kʷadza	-y
		kʷadzʸa	-Øʸ
		kʷadʒa	
		Prosody affecting final consonant	
	Margi-South	√ CaCa	
		*kʷadza	
		kʷadza	
	Kilba	√ CaCa	+Y
		*gʷadza	-y
		gʷadzʸa	-Øʸ
		gʷadʒa	
		Prosody affecting final consonant	

6.4 PCC Lexical Reconstructions

LAMANG	Lamang	√ CaCa	+Y
		*ɣʷadza -y	
		ɣʷaʸdzaʸ -Øʸ	
		ɣʷedze	
		Prosody affecting all /a/	
	Hdi	√ CaCa	
		*ɣʷadzØ -y	
		ɣʷadz -i	
		ɣʷadzi	
		Syllabification of /y/	
HIGI	Kamwe-Nkafa	√ C Ca	+Y, +W
		*gʷ tsa -y	
		gʷəʷtsʸə -Øʸ	
		gutʃə	
		Vowel epenthesis; W-prosody affecting epenthetic vowel; Y-prosody affecting final consonant; centralisation of final /a/	
	Kirya	√ C Ca	+Y, +W
		*gʷ tsØ -y-l	
		gʷəʷtsʸ -iʸ-l	
		gutʃil	
		Vowel epenthesis; W-prosody affecting epenthetic vowel; Y-prosody affecting final consonant; syllabification of /y/	
	Bana	√ C Ca	+Y, +W
		*gʷ tsØ -y	
		gʷəʷtsʸ -iʸ	
		gutʃi	
		Vowel epenthesis; W-prosody affecting epenthetic vowel; Y-prosody affecting final consonant; syllabification of /y/	

ram

        Alternative reconstruction (**PCC**)
        ma-   **gʷ(a)z(a)ma**   -y   +Y   PC: *gam (PN),
                                                                *gm (a) (N-;
                                                                -k, -l) (JS)

wìzim nm. ram *bélier* (6 groups, 12 languages) C

This root for 'ram' is far less widespread than the root for 'sheep'. There is a regular word-final change *m→w in Proto-Mandara, which may be behind the Matal form, if it is truly cognate. There was a regular change *z→s in Proto-Kotoko North, and a regular subsequent change *s→j in Malgbe.

MAFA	Cuvok		√ C CaCa	+Y
			*Ø zamØ -y	
			za^{y}m -Ø^y	
			zem	
			Prosody affecting medial /a/	
MANDARA	Matal		√ CaCaCa	
		ma-	*gadzawØ	
		ma-	gadzaw	
			magadzaw	
MOFU[28]	Dugwor		√ C CaCa	+Y
			*Ø zamØ -y	
			aza^{y}m -Ø^y	
			azem	
			Vowel prothesis; prosody affecting medial /a/	
	Mofu North		√ C CaCa	+Y
			*Ø zamØ -y	
			za^{y}m -Ø^y	
			zem	
			Prosody affecting /a/	
	Mofu-Gudur		√ C CaCa	+Y
			*Ø zamØ -y	
			a^{y}za^{y}m -Ø^y	
			ezem	
			Vowel prothesis; prosody affecting all /a/	
MAROUA	Giziga-Marva[29]		√ C C Ca	+Y
			*Ø z mØ -y	
			ə^{y}zə^{y}m -Ø^y	
			izim	
			Vowel pro- and epenthesis; prosody affecting all vowels	

---

[28] For Dugwor and Mofu-Gudur, we assume vowel prothesis based on the original situation of initial consonant cluster. The same holds for Giziga-Marva of the MAROUA group.

[29] See preceding footnote.

6.4 PCC Lexical Reconstructions 395

	Mbazla	√ CaCaCa	+Y
		*ʔazamØ -y	
		'aʸzʸaʸm -Øʸ	
		'eʒem	
		Prosody affecting second root consonant and all /a/	

√ CaCaCa   +Y
*ʔazamØ   -y
'azʸaʸm   -Øʸ
'aʒem
Vowel prothesis; prosody affecting second root consonant and 2nd syllable /a/

KOTOKO-   Afade   √ C C Ca   +Y
NORTH   *ʔ s mØ   -y
                           > s ʔ m   -y
                           s'əʸm   -Øʸ
                           s'ɨm
                           Metathesis ʔ s > s ʔ; vowel epenthesis; prosody affecting epenthetic vowel

             Mpade   √ C CaCa
                           *Ø samØ
                           sam

             Malgbe   √ C CaCa   +Y
                           *w yamØ   -y
                           wəʸyam   -Øʸ
                           wiyam
                           Vowel epenthesis; prosody affecting epenthetic vowel

KOTOKO-   Lagwan   √ C C Ca   +Y
CENTRAL   *w z mØ   -y
                           wzəʸm   -iʸ
                           uzimi
                           Vowel epenthesis; prosody affecting epenthetic vowel; syllabification of /w/; syllabification of /y/

             Mser   √ C CaCa
                           *w zamØ
                           uzam
                           Syllabification of /w/

razor₁

    Alternative reconstruction (**PCC**)
    p(a)ɗ(a)kʷa   -y, -ɗ   +Y, +W   PC: —

piɗakʷ ʸ nm. razor *rasoir* (9 groups, 13 languages) A cf: beli.

It is not possible to determine whether this root was present in Proto-Central Chadic, or whether it was an early technological innovation that spread through the languages at a later point. The regularity of the root is consistent with an early origin. *ɗ has the regular reflex /r/ in Bura, Kirya and Bana.

BATA	Gude	√ C C Ca		+Y
		*p ɗ kʷa	-y	
		pəʸɗəkʷa	-Øʸ	
		piɗakʷa		
		Vowel epenthesis; prosody affecting first syllable epenthetic vowel		
DABA	Buwal	√ C CaCa		+Y
		*p ɗakʷØ	-y	
		pəɗaʸkʷ	-Øʸ	
		pədekʷ		
		Vowel epenthesis; prosody affecting medial /a/		
	Mbudum	√ C C Ca		+Y
		*p ɗ Øa	-y-ɗ	
		pʸɗaʸ	-Øʸ-ɗ	
		pʸɗeɗ		
		Prosody affecting initial consonant and medial /a/		
	Daba	√ C CaCa	-y	+Y
		pəʸɗaʸkØ	-Øʸ	
		pidek		
		Vowel epenthesis; prosody affecting epenthetic vowel and medial /a/		
MAFA	Cuvok	√ C CaCa		+Y
		*p ɗakØ	-y	
		pəɗaʸkʷ	-Øʸ	
		pəɗekʷ		
		Vowel epenthesis; prosody affecting medial /a/		
SUKUR	Sukur	√ C CaCa		+Y, +W
		*p ɗakʷØ	-y	
		pəʸɗaʸʷk	-Øʸ	
		pidoek'		
		Vowel epenthesis; Y-prosody affecting epenthetic vowel and medial /a/; W-prosody also affecting		

6.4 PCC Lexical Reconstructions 397

    medial /a/; final ' (glottalisation transfer?) possibly originating from underlying medial */ɗ/

    √ C C Ca   +Y, +W
    *p ɗ k^w Ø   -y
    pə^{y}ɗə^{y}kw   -Ø^y
    pidik'u
    Vowel epenthesis; Y-prosody affecting epenthetic vowels in first and second syllable; re-segmentalisation *k^w > k+w; syllabification of w; final k' (glottalisation spread?) possibly originating from underlying medial */ɗ/

HURZA	Mbuko	√ C CaCa	+Y, +W

    *p ɗak^{w}Ø   -y
    pəɗa^{yw}k^w -Ø^y
    pəɗæk
    Vowel epenthesis; Y-prosody affecting medial /a/; W-prosody also affecting medial /a/

MARGI	Bura	√ CaC Ca	+Y, +W

    *par k^wa   -y
    p^{y}a^{y}rkw   -Ø^y
    p^{y}erku
    Y-prosody affecting initial consonant and medial /a/; re-segmentalisation *k^w > k+w; syllabification of w

    √ CaC Ca   +Y, +W
    *par k^wa   -y
    pa^{y}rkw   -Ø^y
    perku
    Y-prosody affecting medial /a/; re-segmentalisation *k^w > k+w; syllabification of w

MANDARA	Matal	√ C CaCa	+Y

    *p ɗak^{w}Ø   -y
    pəɗ^{y}a^{y}k^w -Ø^y
    p^{ə}ɗ^{y}ɛk^w
    Vowel epenthesis; prosody affecting medial consonant and /a/

MOFU	Mofu-Gudur	√ C CaCa	+Y

    *p ɗak^{w}Ø   -y
    pəɗa^{y}k^w -Ø^y
    pəɗek^w
    Vowel epenthesis; prosody affecting medial /a/

LAMANG	Lamang	√ C CaCa	

    *p Øaka
    paka

398   Full Lexical Reconstructions

HIGI	Kamwe-Futu	√ C C Ca	
		*p ɗ ØØ	-y
		pəɗ	-i
		pədi	
		Syllabification of /y/	

                Kirya   √ C C Ca   +Y, +W
                                  *p r k^{w}Ø   -y
                                  pə^{y}rə^{w}kw^w -Ø^y
                                  piruku

Re-segmentalisation and prosodification of /k^w/ > /k+w^w/; vowel epenthesis; Y-prosody affecting 1st syllable vowel; W-prosody affecting 2nd syllable vowel; syllabification of /w/ > [u]

                Bana   √ C C Ca   +Y
                                  *p r Øa   -y
                                  pə^{y}rə   -Ø^y
                                  pirə

Vowel epenthesis; prosody affecting epenthetic vowel; centralisation of final /a/

razor₂

                Alternative reconstruction (**PCC**)
                         b(a)la   -y   +Y   Kanuri: *beli*

Note: This obvious loan *beli* from Kanuri (partly via Fulfulde *beliihi*) has been adapted to Central Chadic phonology and is treated as if it was a retention from PCC (i.e. 'pseudo'-PCC root).

beli nm. razor *rasoir* (6 groups, 12 languages) Loan cf: *piɗak$^{w\ y}$*.
   This root is borrowed from Kanuri, in some cases via Fulfulde, and is found in languages covering a wide spread of the north and east of the Central Chadic area. The *l is not a native Central Chadic phoneme. It was introduced in the North sub-branch of Central Chadic by a general change from *r to *l. All the languages using this root are from this sub-branch, so no adaptation of the *l was necessary. The vowel *e is also absent from Proto-Central Chadic and many of the languages cited. In the case of Mbara, this has been re-analysed as the palatalisation prosody.

MARGI	Bura	√ CaCa	+Y
		*balØ	-y
		ba^{y}l	-Ø^y
		bel	
		Prosody affecting medial /a/	

6.4 PCC Lexical Reconstructions

MANDARA	Mandara	√ C Ca		+Y
		*b la	-y	
		bə^{y}la	-Ø^y	
		bila		
		Vowel epenthesis; prosody affecting epenthetic vowel		
MOFU	Ouldeme	√ C Ca		+Y
		*b la	-y	
		bə^{y}la	-Ø^y	
		bila		
		Vowel epenthesis; prosody affecting epenthetic vowel		
	Zulgo[30]	√ C C Ca		+Y
		*b y la	-y	
		bə^{y}yə^{y}la	-Ø^y	
		biyila		
		Vowel epenthesis; prosody affecting epenthetic vowels		
	Mofu North	√ C Ca		+Y
		*b la	-y	
		bə^{y}la	-Ø^y	
		bila		
		Vowel epenthesis; prosody affecting epenthetic vowel		
	Mofu-Gudur	√ C Ca		+Y
		*b la	-y	
		bə^{y}la	-Ø^y	
		bila		
		Vowel epenthesis; prosody affecting epenthetic vowel		
KOTOKO-NORTH	Afade	√ C Ca		+Y
		*b lØ	-y	
		bə^{y}l	-Ø^y	
		bil		
		Vowel epenthesis; prosody affecting epenthetic vowel		

---

[30] Zulgo is unique insofar as it reanalyses the root to be triradical of the root type √ C C Ca, namely *b y la.

	Mpade	√ C Ca		+Y

√ C Ca +Y
*b lØ   -y
bəʸl   -Øʸ
bil
Vowel epenthesis; prosody affecting epenthetic vowels

Malgbe

√ C Ca +Y
*b la   -y
bəʸla   -Øʸ
bila
Vowel epenthesis; prosody affecting epenthetic vowels

KOTOKO-CENTRAL   Lagwan, Mser

√ CaCa +Y
*balØ   -y
baʸl   -Øʸ
bel
Prosody affecting medial /a/

MUSGUM   Mbara

√ CaCa +Y
*bala   -y
baʸlaʸ -Øʸ
bele
Prosody affecting all /a/

root

Alternative reconstruction (**PCC**)
RED   **ɬ(a)r(a)ka**   -a, -y,   a   +Y, +W   PC: *ʂar- (PN),
                        -kʷ, -n   *ɬ₂rw (a) (JS),
                                               *ɬVrVw-/
                                               *ɬVwVr- (OS)

ɬirigi nf. root *racine* (11 groups, 31 languages) C

This root presents some difficulties in its reconstruction. The *ɬ is expected to have the reflex *ɮ in the South sub-branch, but this is not the case in any of the South groups (Bata, Daba, Mafa, Sukur). In the Bata group, there should also have been a subsequent change *ɮ→l in most languages, and this has not taken place. However, the regular change *r→l in the North sub-branch has taken place with a good degree of consistency. The *g has the unestablished reflexes /k/, /h/, /ᵑg/, /ŋ/ and /j/. In the Daba, Mafa and Maroua groups, and in some Mofu group languages, there is reduplication of the *ɬ. This is normally a sign that an initial consonant such as *h has been lost, but there is no direct evidence for such an initial consonant.

6.4 PCC Lexical Reconstructions   401

BATA	Gude		√ C C Ca		
			*ɬ r gØ	-y-n	a
			ɬərəg	-i-n	ə
			lhərəginə		
			Vowel epenthesis; syllabification of /y/; centralisation of FV /a/		
	Jimi		√ C C Ca		
			*ɬ r gØ	-y -n	
			ɬərəg	-i-n	
			ɬərəgin		
			Vowel epenthesis; syllabification of /y/		
	Sharwa		√ C C Ca		+Y
			*ɬ r gØ	-y	
			ɬʸərʸəg	-iʸ	
			ɬʸərʸəgi		
			Vowel epenthesis; syllabification of /y/; prosody affecting first and second root consonant		
	Tsuvan		√ CaC Ca		+Y
			*ɬar Øa	-y	
			ɬaʸraʸ	-Øʸ	
			ɬere		
			Prosody affecting all /a/		
DABA	Buwal		√ CaC Ca		
		RED	*ɬal ØØ	-a-y	
		ɬa	ɬal	-ay	
			ɬaɬalay		
MAFA	Cuvok		√ CaC Ca		
		RED	*ɬal ØØ	-a-y	
		ɬa	ɬal	-ay	
			ɬaɬalay		
SUKUR	Sukur		√ C C Ca		
			*ɬ Ø ØØ	-y	
			ɬ	-i	
			ɬi		
			Syllabification of /y/		
			√ C C Ca		
			*ɬ Ø Øa	-y	
			ɬə	-i	
			ɬəi		
			Syllabification of /y/; centralisation of lexical final /a/		

402   Full Lexical Reconstructions

HURZA	Mbuko	√ C C Ca	
		*ɬ l ØØ	-a-y
		ɬəl	-ay
		ɬəlay	
		Vowel epenthesis	
	Vame	√ C C Ca	
		*ɬ l ka	-y
		ɬəlkaʸ	-Øʸ
		ɬəlke	
		Vowel epenthesis; prosody affecting lexical final /a/	

MANDARA	Matal	√ C C Ca		+Y
		*ɬ l xØ	-y	
		ɬəʸləʸx	-Øʸ	
		ɬiɬɪx		
		Vowel epenthesis; prosody affecting epenthetic vowels		
	Mandara	√ CaC Ca		+Y
		*ɬal wa	-y	
		ɬalwaʸ	-Øʸ	
		ɬalwe		
		Prosody affecting final /a/		
	Malgwa	√ CaCaCa		+Y
		*ɬalawa	-y	
		ɬalawaʸ	-Øʸ	
		thlalawe		
		Prosody affecting final /a/		
	Glavda	√ CaC Ca		+Y
		*ɬal Øa	-y	a
		ɬaləʸ	-yʸ	a
		thlaliya		
		Prosody affecting centralised root-final /a/		
	Dghwede	√ C C Ca		
		*ɬ l Øa		
		ɬəla		
		ɬəla		
		Vowel epenthesis		

MOFU	Ouldeme	√ C C Ca		+Y
		*ɬ l kØ	-y	
		> ɬ k l	-y	
		ɬəʸkəʸl	-iʸ	
		ɬikili		

6.4 PCC Lexical Reconstructions

Metathesis ɬ-l-k- > ɬ-k-l-; vowel epenthesis; prosody affecting epenthetic vowels; syllabification of /y/

Moloko
√ C C Ca
*ɬ l ØØ   -a-y
ɬəl   -ay
ɬəlay
Vowel epenthesis

Zulgo
√ C C Ca   +Y
*ɮ l Øa   -y
ɮəʸlaʸ   -Øʸ
ɮile
Vowel epenthesis; prosody affecting all vowels

Gemzek
√ C C Ca   +Y
*ɮ l Øa   -y
ɮəlaʸ   -Øʸ
ɮəle
Vowel epenthesis; prosody affecting /a/

Merey
√ C C Ca
*ɮ l ØØ   -a-y
ɮəl   -ay
ɮəlay
Vowel epenthesis

Dugwor
√ C C Ca
RED   *ɮ l ØØ   -a-y
ɮə-   ɮəl   -ay
ɮəɮəlay
Vowel epenthesis

Mofu North
√ C C Ca
*ɬ Ø fØ   -a-y
ɬəf   -ay
ɬəfay
Vowel epenthesis

Mofu-Gudur
√ CaC Ca
RED   *ɬal ØØ   -a-y
ɬa-   ɬal   -ay
ɬaɬalay

MAROUA	Giziga-Muturwa, Giziga-Marva	RED ɬa	√ CaCaCa *ɬalaka ɬalak(a) ɬaɬalak(a)	
	Mbazla		√ C C Ca *s l kØ sʸəʸlk ʃilki Vowel epenthesis; syllabification of /y/; prosody affecting initial consonant and epenthetic vowel	+Y -y -iʸ
			√ CaC Ca *tsal kØ tsʸaʸlk tʃelki Prosody affecting initial consonant and /a/; syllabification of /y/	+Y -y -iʸ
			√ C C Ca *x l kØ x⁽ʸ⁾əʸləʸk hiliki Vowel epenthesis; prosody affecting initial consonant(?) and epenthetic vowels; syllabification of /y/	+Y -y -iʸ
LAMANG	Lamang		√ C C Ca *ɬ r k Ø > ɬ r k > ɬ r nk ɬərŋ ɬərŋi Metathesis *-y-n > -n-y and k n > n k; fusion nk > ng > ŋ; vowel epenthesis; syllabification of /y/	-y-n -n-y -y -i
	Hdi		√ C C Ca *ɬ r kØ > ɬ r nk ɬərəng ɬərəŋ Metathesis *k n > n k; fusion nk > ng > ŋ; vowel epenthesis	-n

6.4 PCC Lexical Reconstructions   405

HIGI	Kamwe-Nkafa		√ C C Ca		
			*ɬ r ØØ	-n	a
			ɬərə	-n	a
			thlərəna		
			Vowel epenthesis		
			√ C C Ca		
			*ɬ r ØØ	-n	a
			ɬər	-n	a
			thərna		
			Vowel epenthesis		
	Kirya		√ C C Ca		+Y
			*ɬ r gØ	-y-n	a
			> ɬryg	-n	a
			> ɬryng		a
			ɬəʸrØʸng		a
			ɬirᵑga		
			Double metathesis: *g y n > y g n > y n g; prosodification of /y/ > ʸ; vowel epenthesis; prosody affecting epenthetic vowel		
	Psikye		√ C C Ca		+W
			*ɬ Ø gØ	-kʷ	
			ɬəʷg	-wʷ	
			ɬugu		
			Partial desegmentalisation of /kʷ/ > /wʷ/; vowel epenthesis; prosody affecting epenthetic vowel; syllabification of /w/		
	Bana		√ C C Ca		+Y
		-RED-	*x l gØ	-y-n	a
			> xlyg	-n	a
		-ly-	> xlyng		a
		-li-	xʸəʸling		ə
			xʸililiŋə		
			Double metathesis: *g y > y g, g n > n g; vowel epenthesis; prosody affecting first consonant and epenthetic vowel; syllabification of /y/; centralisation of FV /a/		
GIDAR	Gidar		√ CaC Ca		
			*ɬal wa	-y	a
			ɬalwa	-y	a
			ɬalwaya		

six

  Alternative reconstruction (areal root)
    ɬ(a)ra -y   +Y PC : —

  ɬira num. six *six* (2 groups, 3 languages) C syn: kɨwah, vɨnahkɨr, markɨdˀ ʸ.

  This is one of several roots for 'six', and is found only in the Musgum and Gidar groups. The vowel *i is tentatively reconstructed, but without great confidence.

MUSGUM	Vulum	√ CaCa		
		*ɬara		
		ɬaara		
		Vowel length remains unaccounted for		
	Mbara	√ C Ca		+Y
		*ɬ ra	-y	
		ɬəʸra	-Øʸ	
		ɬira		
		Vowel epenthesis; prosody affecting epenthetic vowel		
GIDAR	Gidar	√ C Ca		+Y
		*ɬ ra	-y	
		ɬəraʸ	-Øʸ	
		ɬəre		
		Vowel epenthesis; prosody affecting final /a/		
		√ C Ca		+Y
		*ɬ ra	-y	
		ɬraʸ	-Øʸ	
		ɬre		
		Prosody affecting lexical final /a/		

spit, to

  Alternative reconstruction (**PCC**)
  m(a)-, **t(a)fa**[31] -a, -y, -kʷ, a +Y, +W PC: *təfə~təfu
  n-, ŋ-   -n, -l   (PN),
                      *tp (JS),
                      *tVf(f)- (OS)

---

[31] Our PCC reconstruction purposefully contains *f (while Gravina maintains */p/). By this we wish to indicate that the question remains open whether or not */f/ could be reconstructed for PCC parallel to */p/ (as suggested by P. Newman, p.c. 2020, and at variance with Gravina 2014a), or whether we are dealing with an onomatopoeic origin of this root/word, which would 'explain' the violation of the reconstructed set of PCC consonants.

6.4 PCC Lexical Reconstructions

tip v. to spit *cracher* (14 groups, 31 languages) A

This common root is almost certainly onomatopoeic in origin. A similar word is found in both Hausa and Kanuri. It is significant though that *i is present in almost all the groups where this vowel is part of the phonemic inventory. This implies that the word may have been adopted as a word rather than as a sound at an early period in the history of Central Chadic. *p was realised as [f] word-finally in Proto-Central Chadic, so the presence of the final *f in all groups does not contradict the early origin of the word.

BATA	Bata	√ C Ca *t fØ *təf* Vowel epenthesis		
	Gude	√ C Ca *t fØ təʸf *tifi* Vowel epenthesis; prosody affecting epenthetic vowels; syllabification of /y/	-y -iʸ	+Y
	Jimi	√ CaCa *tafa taʸfʷə *tefʷən* Y-prosody affecting medial /a/; prosodification of /kʷ/ > ʷ; W-prosody affecting final root consonant; centralisation of final /a/	-y-kʷ-n -Øʸ-Øʷ-n	+Y, +W
DABA	Buwal	√ CaCa ŋ- *tafØ ŋ- taʸf *ŋtef* Prosody affecting medial /a/	-y -Øʸ	+Y
	Gavar	√ C Ca ŋ- *t fØ ŋ- təʸf *ŋtif* Vowel epenthesis; prosody affecting epenthetic vowel	-y -Øʸ	+Y
	Daba	√ C Ca *t fØ təʸf *tif*	-y -Øʸ	+Y

			Vowel epenthesis; prosody affecting epenthetic vowel	

MAFA	Mafa	√ C Ca		+Y
	n-	*dz fØ	-y	
	n-	dz^{y}ə^{y}f	-Ø^y	
		^{n}dʒif		

Vowel epenthesis; prosody affecting epenthetic vowel and initial root consonant; prenasalisation of initial root consonant by prefix

SUKUR	Sukur	√ C Ca		+Y
		*t fa	-y	
		tə^{y}fa	-Ø^y	
		tifa		

Vowel epenthesis; prosody affecting epenthetic vowel

HURZA	Mbuko	√ C Ca		+Y
		*t fa	-y	
		təfa^y	-Ø^y	
		təfe		

Vowel epenthesis; prosody affecting /a/

	Vame	√ C Ca		+Y
		*t fa	-y	
		tə^{y}fa	-Ø^y	
		tifa		

Vowel epenthesis; prosody affecting epenthetic vowel

MARGI	Bura	√ C Ca		+Y	
		*t fØ	-y-k^w		+W
		tə^{y}f	-Ø^y-w		
		tifu			

Vowel epenthesis; Y-prosody affecting epenthetic vowel; weakening of /k^w/ > /w/; syllabification of /w/

		√ C Ca		+Y
		*t fa	-y	
		tə^{y}fa	-Ø^y	
		tifa		

Vowel epenthesis; Y-prosody affecting epenthetic vowel

6.4 PCC Lexical Reconstructions

	Kilba	√ C Ca			
		*t fa			
		təfa			
		Vowel epenthesis			
MANDARA	Matal	√ C Ca			+Y
		ma- *t fØ	-y -l	a	
		ma^y- t^{y}f	-Ø^y-l	a	
		mæt^{y}fla			
		Prosody affecting initial root consonant and /a/ of prefix			
	Podoko	√ C Ca			
		*t fa			
		təfa			
		Vowel epenthesis			
MOFU	Moloko	√ CaCa			
		*tafØ			
		taf			
	Gemzek	√ CaCa			+Y
		ma- *tafa	-y		
		ma^y- ta^{y}fa^y	-Ø^y		
		metefe			
		Prosody affecting all /a/			
	Merey	√ C Ca			
		*t fØ			
		təf			
		Vowel epenthesis			
	Dugwor	√ C Ca			+Y
		m- *t fØ	-a-y		
		mə- təf	-a^{y}y^y		
		mətəfey			
		Vowel epenthesis; prosody affecting /a/ in suffix			
	Mofu North	√ C Ca			+Y
		ma- *t fØ	-a-y		
		ma^y- təf	-a^{y}y^y		
		metəfey			
		Vowel epenthesis; prosody affecting all /a/			
	Mofu-Gudur	√ C Ca			
		təfØ			
		təf			
		Vowel epenthesis			

410   Full Lexical Reconstructions

MAROUA	Mbazla		√ C Ca	+W
			*t fØ	-k^w
			tə^{w}f	-w^w
			tufu	
			Vowel epenthesis; partial desegmentalisation of /k^w/ > /w^w/; prosody affecting epenthetic vowel; syllabification of /w/	
LAMANG	Lamang		√ C Ca	
			*t fØ	
			təf	
			Vowel epenthesis	
	Hdi		√ C Ca	
			*t fØ	-a-y
			təf	-ay
			təfay	
			Vowel epenthesis	
HIGI	Kamwe-Nkafa, Kamwe-Futu	n- n-	√ C Ca *t vØ tə^{y}v ntivi	+Y -y -i^y
			Vowel epenthesis; prosody affecting epenthetic vowel; syllabification of /y/	
	Kirya	n- n-	√ C Ca *t fa təfə ntəfə	
			Vowel epenthesis; centralisation of final /a/	
	Bana		√ C Ca *t fa tfə tfə	
			Centralisation of final /a/	
KOTOKO-NORTH	Mpade		√ CaCa *tafa tafə^y tafɨ	+Y -y -Ø^y
			Centralisation of final /a/; prosody affecting final vowel	
KOTOKO-CENTRAL	Lagwan		√ C Ca *t fa tə^{y}fə^y	+Y, +W -y-k^w-n -Ø^y-w^{w}ə^w-n

6.4 PCC Lexical Reconstructions 411

		tifiwun		
		Vowel epenthesis; centralisation of final /a/; Y-prosody affecting vowels in first and second syllable; weakening and prosodification of /k^w/ > w^w; W-prosody affecting epenthetic vowel in suffix		

		√ C Ca		+Y
		*t fØ	-y-k^w	
		tə^{y}f	-Ø^y-w	
		tifu		
		Vowel epenthesis; Y-prosody affecting epenthetic vowel; weakening of /k^w/ > /w/; syllabification of /w/		

		√ C Ca		+Y
		*t fa	-y -l	
		tə^{y}fa^y	-Ø^y-l	
		tifel		
		Vowel epenthesis; prosody affecting all vowels		

	Mser	√ CaCa		+Y
		*tafa	-y	
		tafə^y	-Ø^y	
		tafi		
		Centralisation of final /a/; prosody affecting final vowel		

MUSGUM	Mbara	√ C Ca		+W
		*t fØ	-k^w	
		tə^{w}f	-Ø^w	
		tuf		
		Vowel epenthesis; prosodification of *k^w > ^{w}; prosody affecting epenthetic vowel		

suck, to

Alternative reconstruction (**PCC**)

ma-, n-, RED	s(a)wɓa	-a, -y, -n	+Y, +W	PC: *səɓə (PN), *s^{m}b (-ɗ) ~ *sɓ (JS), *sVH(V)b- > suɓ- (OS)

Note: In a number of languages from the KOTOKO groups, there is a remarkable re-segmentalisation process that splits */ɓ/ > /ʔ+f/, with /ʔ/ undergoing metathesis and ending up as glottalisation feature of initial /s/ > [s'].

412   Full Lexical Reconstructions

siwiɓ ʸ v. to suck *sucer* (15 groups, 35 languages) A

This well-attested root has a complex history. *w has been lost in many cases. Where it is present, it has been reanalysed as a vowel, or else as the labialisation prosody, which is a common sporadic process. This process has led to the loss of a syllable, and in several languages the first syllable of the root has been reduplicated to compensate for the lost material, which is also a common sporadic process. In the Kotoko groups, the *ɓ has transferred its glottal component to the *s, resulting in *ts or *s'. There is good evidence in support of the palatalisation prosody, and *i is found in those groups where it is expected.

BATA	Gude		√ C C Ca		+Y
			*s Øɓa	-y	
			sʸəʸɓə	-Øʸ	
			ʃiɓə		
			Vowel epenthesis; prosody affecting initial consonant and epenthetic vowel; centralisation of final /a/		
	Sharwa		√ C C Ca		+Y
			*s ØɓØ	-y	
			sʸəɓ	-Øʸ	
			ʃəɓ		
			Vowel epenthesis; prosody affecting initial consonant		
DABA	Buwal		√ CaC Ca		+Y
		RED	*saØɓØ	-y	
		sa-	saɓ	-y	
		saʸ-	saʸɓ	-Øʸ	
			seseɓ		
			Prosody affecting all /a/		
	Gavar		√ CaC Ca		+Y
			*saØɓØ	-y	
			sʸaʸɓ	-Øʸ	
			ʃeɓ		
			Prosody affecting initial consonant and medial /a/		
	Mbudum		√ CaC Ca		+Y
		RED	*saØɓØ	-y	
		sa-	saɓ	-y	
		sə-	saʸɓ	-Øʸ	
			səseɓ		
			Centralisation of prefixal /a/; prosody affecting medial /a/		

6.4 PCC Lexical Reconstructions

	Daba		√ CaC Ca		+Y
			*saØɓØ	-y	
			saʸɓ	-Øʸ	
			seɓ		
			Prosody affecting medial /a/		

MAFA³²	Mafa		√ CaC Ca		+W
		RED	*sawɓØ		
		sa-	sØwɓ		
		saʷ-	swɓ		
			sosuɓ		
			Prosody affecting prefixal /a/; syllabification of /w/		

	Cuvok		√ CaC Ca		
		RED	*saØɓa		
		sa-	sØØɓa		
		sa-	sɓa		
			sasɓa		

HURZA	Mbuko		√ CaC Ca		+W, +Y
		RED	*sawɓØ	-y	
		sa-	saØʷɓ	-y	
		səʷ-	saʷʸɓ	-Øʸ	
			susœɓ		
			Centralisation of prefixal /a/; prosodification of /w/ to W-prosody affecting all vowels; Y-prosody affecting root-medial /a/ combining with W-prosody to yield [œ]		

MARGI	Kilba		√ C C Ca		+Y
			*s Øɓa	-y	
			sʸəʸɓa	-Øʸ	
			ʃiɓa		
			Vowel epenthesis; prosody affecting initial consonant and epenthetic vowel		

MANDARA	Podoko		√ C C Ca		+Y
			*s Øɓa	-y	
			> ɓsa	-Øʸ	

---

³² Note that in MAFA but also MOFU group languages, the shape of the reduplicative prefix containing /a/ indicates an originally underlying root-pattern shape *CaC Ca. While the /a/ in the prefix may be retained, the medial /a/ in the root may be deleted and replaced by epenthetic schwa.

414   Full Lexical Reconstructions

			ɓəʸsʸaʸ
			ɓiʃe
			Metathesis *s ɓ > ɓ s; vowel epenthesis; prosody affecting all vowels and second root consonant
	Dghweɗe		√ C C Ca
			*ts wɓa
			> tsɓwa
			> ɓtswa
			> ɓwtsa
			p'utsa
			Triple metathesis *ts-w-ɓa > ts-ɓ-wa > ɓ-ts-wa > ɓ-w-tsa; syllabification of /w/
MOFU	Ouldeme		√ C C Ca
			*s ØɓØ -a-y
			səɓ -ay
			səɓay
			Vowel epenthesis
	Moloko		√ CaC Ca +W
			*sawɓØ
			saØʷɓ
			saʷɓ
			soɓ
			Prosodification of medial /w/ > ʷ; prosody affecting /a/
	Zulgo		√ CaC Ca
		RED	*sawɓa
		sa-	sawɓa
		sa-	sØwɓa
			sasuɓa
			Syllabification of medial /w/
	Gemzek		√ C C Ca
			*swɓØ
			suɓ
			Syllabification of medial /w/
	Merey		√ C C Ca
		RED	*swɓØ
		sw-	swɓ
			susuɓ
			Syllabification of medial /w/

6.4 PCC Lexical Reconstructions

	Dugwor		√ CaC Ca		+W, +Y
		m-	*sawɓØ	-a-y	
		mə-	saØʷɓ	-aʸyʸ	
			məsoɓey		

Vowel epenthesis; prosodification of /w/ > ʷ; W-prosody affecting medial /a/; Y-prosody affecting final syllable /a/

	Mofu North		√ CaC Ca		+Y
		ma-RED	*saØɓØ	-a-y	
		ma-sa-	sØɓ	-ay	
		maʸ-saʸ-	səɓ	-aʸyʸ	
			mesesəɓey		

Vowel epenthesis; prosody affecting all prefix augment and final syllable /a/

	Mofu-Gudur		√ CaC Ca	
		RED	*saØɓØ	
		sa-	saɓ	
		sa-	sØɓ	
			sasəɓ	

Vowel epenthesis

MAROUA	Giziga-Marva		√ C C Ca
			*swɓa
			suɓa

Syllabification of /w/

	Mbazla		√ C C Ca	
		RED	*swɓØ	-y
		sw-	swɓ	-i
			susuɓi	

Syllabification of /w/; syllabification of /y/

LAMANG	Hdi	√ C C Ca		+Y
		*s ØɓØ	-a-y	
		> ɓs	-a-y	
		ɓəʸØs	-ay	
		ɓisay		

Metathesis *s ɓ > ɓ s; vowel epenthesis; prosody affecting epenthetic vowel

HIGI	Kamwe-Nkafa, Kamwe-Futu	√ C C Ca		+Y
		*s ØɓØ	-y	
		> ɓs	-iʸ	

| | | | ɓəʸs | -iʸ |
| | | | ɓisi | |

Metathesis *s ɓ > ɓ s; vowel epenthesis; prosody affecting epenthetic vowel; syllabification of /y/

	Psikye		√ C C Ca		+Y
		m-	*s Øɓa	-y	
		m-	> ɓsa	-Øʸ	
			ɓəʸsə		
			mɓisə		

Metathesis *s ɓ > ɓ s; centralisation of final /a/; vowel epenthesis; prosody affecting epenthetic vowel

	Bana		√ C C Ca	
			*s Øɓa	
			> ɓsa	
			ɓəsə	
			ɓ(ə)sə	

Metathesis *s ɓ > ɓ s; centralisation of final /a/; vowel epenthesis

			√ C C Ca		+Y
			*s Øɓa	-y	
			sʸəʸɓə	-Øʸ	
			ʃiɓə		

Vowel epenthesis; prosody affecting initial consonant and epenthetic vowel; centralisation of final /a/

			√ C C Ca		+Y
		RED	*s Øɓa	-y	
		sʸəʸ-	sʸəɓə	-Øʸ	
			ʃiʃəɓə		

Vowel epenthesis; prosody affecting root initial consonant and prefixal epenthetic vowel; centralisation of final /a/

KOTOKO-	Buduma		√ CaC Ca		+Y
ISLAND		RED	*tsawɓØ	-y	
			> tsaɓw		
		tsa-	tsaɓw	-y	
		tsʸaʸ-	tsʸaɓu	-Øʸ	
			tʃetʃaɓu		

6.4 PCC Lexical Reconstructions

		Metathesis *w ɓ > ɓ w; prosody affecting root initial consonant and prefixal epenthetic vowel; syllabification of /w/	
KOTOKO-NORTH	Afade	√ C C Ca *s wɓØ > s ɓw sʔfw s'ə^{w}fw^w *s'ufu*	+W
		Metathesis *w ɓ > ɓ w; re-segmentalisation *ɓ > ʔ+f; vowel epenthesis; partial desegmentalisation of /w/ > /w^w/; W-prosody affecting epenthetic vowel; syllabification of /w/	
	Mpade	√ CaC Ca *sawɓØ > saʔfw *s'afu*	
		Metathesis *w ɓ > ɓ w; re-segmentalisation *ɓ > ʔ+f; syllabification of /w/	
	Mpade, Malgbe	√ CaC Ca *saØɓa -y saʔfə^y -Ø^y *s'afi*	+Y
		Re-segmentalisation *ɓ > ʔ+f; centralisation of final /a/; prosody affecting centralised /a/	
KOTOKO-CENTRAL	Lagwan	√ C C Ca *s wɓØ -y-n > s ɓw -y-n s ʔfw -y-n s'ə^{y}fə^{w}w^w -Ø^y-ə^{w}n *s'ifuwun*	+Y, +W
		Metathesis *w ɓ > ɓ w; re-segmentalisation *ɓ > ʔ+f; vowel epenthesis; partial desegmentalisation and prosodification of /w/ > /w^w/; W-prosody affecting epenthetic vowels in ultima and penultima; Y-prosody affecting first syllable epenthetic vowel	

418   Full Lexical Reconstructions

	Mser		√ CaC Ca		+Y
			*saØɓa	-y	
			saʔfə^y	-Ø^y	
			s'afi		

Re-segmentalisation *ɓ > ʔ+f; (metathesis saʔ f > sʔaf); centralisation of final /a/; prosody affecting centralised /a/

			√ CaC Ca		+Y
		n-	*saØɓa	-y	
		n-	saʔfə^y	-Ø^y	
			ns'afi		

Re-segmentalisation *ɓ > ʔ+f; saʔ f > sʔaf; centralisation of final /a/; prosody affecting centralised /a/

MUSGUM	Vulum		√ C C Ca		+W
		RED	*sØ^wɓØ	-y	
		s-	swɓ	-y	
		sə^w-	sə^wɓ	-i	
			susuɓi		

Vowel epenthesis; desegmentalisation of /w/ > ^w; prosody affecting epenthetic vowels; syllabification of /y/

GIDAR	Gidar		√ C C Ca		+W
		a-RED	*swɓa		
		a-s-	swɓa		
		əs-	su^wɓa^w		
			əssuɓo		

Centralisation of prefixal /a/; partial desegmentalisation and prosodification of /w/ > /w^w/; syllabification of /w/; prosody affecting final /a/

sun

Alternative reconstruction (**PCC**)

a-, x-, d-,	**p(a)ta**[33]	-a, -y, -k,	a	+Y, +W	PC: *fati (PN),
RED		-k^w, -n			*pt (JS)

---

[33] Gravina reconstructs the PCC second consonant as */ts/, which is here considered a later development from PCC */t/.

6.4 PCC Lexical Reconstructions   419

pitsɨ nf. sun *soleil* (14 groups, 45 languages) A

In Proto-Central Chadic [p] and [f] were allophones of *p, but they split into separate phonemes by the time of the group proto-languages. [p] was the word-initial allophone of *p, and so *p is found in many groups. *f is the reflex in Proto-Bata, Proto-Tera, Proto-Mandara, Proto-Lamang, Proto-Kotoko South and Proto-Musgum, with Proto-Higi *v being a development from *f. There is no known rule to account for this change. *ts has the reflex *s in Proto-Sukur (regular) and in Proto-Maroua (irregular). It has the regular reflex *t in Proto-Lamang and Proto-Musgum, with Proto-Tera *ɗ being an unestablished development from *t.

BATA	Jimi	√ C Ca		+Y
		*f tØ	-y -n	
		fəʸt	-Øʸ-ən	
		fitən		
		Vowel epenthesis; prosody affecting first syllable epenthetic vowel		
	Sharwa	√ C Ca		
		*f ta		
		fətə		
		fətə		
		Vowel epenthesis; centralisation of final /a/		
	Tsuvan	√ CaCa		+Y
		*fata	-y	
		faʸtaʸ	-Øʸ	
		fete		
		Prosody affecting all /a/		
DABA	Buwal	√ CaCa		+Y
		*pasØ	-y	
		paʸs	-Øʸ	
		pes		
		Prosody affecting /a/		
	Gavar	√ C Ca		+Y
		*p sØ	-y	
		pəʸsʸ	-Øʸ	
		piʃ		
		Vowel epenthesis; prosody affecting epenthetic vowel and second consonant		
	Mbudum	√ C Ca		+Y
		*p sØ	-y	

420   Full Lexical Reconstructions

		pə^{y}s -Ø^y	
		pis	
		Vowel epenthesis; prosody affecting epenthetic vowel	
	Daba	√ C Ca	+Y
		*p tsØ -y	
		pə^{y}ts^y -Ø^y	
		pitʃ	
		Vowel epenthesis; prosody affecting epenthetic vowel and second consonant	
MAFA	Mafa	√ CaCa	
		*patsØ	
		pats	
	Cuvok	√ CaCa	
		*pasØ	
		pas	
TERA	Tera	√ C Ca	
		*f ɗa	
		fəɗa	
		Vowel epenthesis	
	Nyimatli	√ C Ca	
		*f ɗa -n	
		fəɗa -r	
		fəɗar	
		Vowel epenthesis	
SUKUR	Sukur	√ C Ca	+Y
		*p sØ -y	
		pə^{y}s -Ø^y	
		pis	
		Vowel epenthesis; prosody affecting epenthetic vowel	
HURZA	Mbuko	√ CaCa	
		*patsØ	
		pats	
	Vame	√ CaCa	
		a- *pasØ	
		apas	
MARGI	Bura	√ C Ca	+Y
		*p tsØ -y	

6.4 PCC Lexical Reconstructions 421

			pts^y	-i^y		
			ptʃi			
			Prosody affecting final root consonant; syllabification of /y/			

	Margi- South, Kilba		√ C Ca *p tsØ pəts^y *pətʃi* Vowel epenthesis; prosody affecting final root consonant; syllabification of /y/	-y -i^y		+Y

MANDARA	Matal	a-	√ CaCa *fatsØ *afats*			

	Podoko		√ CaCa *patsa *patsa*			

	Malgwa		√ CaCa *vatsØ vəts^y *vatʃiya* Vowel epenthesis; prosody affecting final root consonant and epenthetic vowel	-y -ə^{y}y^y	a a	+Y

	Glavda		√ CaCa *fatsØ fats^y *fac* Prosody affecting final root consonant	-y -Ø^y		+Y

			√ CaCa *fatsØ fats^y *fatʃiya* Vowel epenthesis; prosody affecting final root consonant and epenthetic vowel	-y -ə^{y}y^y	a a	+Y

		d- d-	√ CaCa *vatsØ vəts^y *dvatʃiya* Vowel epenthesis; prosody affecting final root consonant and epenthetic vowel	-y -ə^{y}y^y	a a	+Y

Full Lexical Reconstructions

	Dghweɗe	√ C Ca		+Y
		*f tsa	-y	
		fəʸtsaʸ	-Øʸ	
		fitʃe		
		Vowel epenthesis; prosody affecting final root consonant and all vowels		

MOFU   Ouldeme, Muyang, Moloko, Zulgo, Gemzek

        √ CaCa
        *fatØ
        fat

           Merey   √ CaCa
                   x-   *patØ
                   xə-   pat
                         həpat
                         Vowel epenthesis

           Dugwor   √ CaCa
                         *patØ
                         pat

           Mofu North, Mofu-Gudur

                         √ CaCa
                         *pasØ
                         pas

           Mofu-Gudur   √ CaCa
                   RED   *pasØ
                   pa-   pas
                            papas

MAROUA   Giziga-Marva, Mbazla
                         √ CaCa
                         *pasØ
                         pas

LAMANG   Lamang   √ C Ca   +Y
                         *f tØ   -y
                         fəʸt   -iʸ
                         fiti
                         Vowel epenthesis; prosody affecting epenthetic vowel; syllabification of /y/

           Hdi   √ C Ca   +Y
                         *f tØ   -y-k
                         fəʸt   -iʸ-k

6.4 PCC Lexical Reconstructions

			fitik		
			Vowel epenthesis; prosody affecting epenthetic vowel; syllabification of /y/		
HIGI	Kamwe-Nkafa		√ CaCa		+Y
			*vatsØ	-y	
			va^{y}ts^y	-i^y	
			vetʃi		
			Prosody affecting medial /a/ and second consonant; syllabification of /y/		
	Kamwe-Futu		√ C Ca		+Y
			*v tsØ	-y	
			və^{y}ts^y	-i^y	
			vitʃi		
			Vowel epenthesis; prosody affecting epenthetic vowel and second consonant; syllabification of /y/		
	Kirya, Psikye		√ C Ca		+Y
			*v tsØ	-y	
			vəts^y	-i^y	
			vətʃi		
			Vowel epenthesis; prosody affecting second consonant; syllabification of /y/		
	Bana		√ C Ca		+Y
			*v tsØ	-y	
			vts^y	-i^y	
			vtʃi		
			Prosody affecting second consonant; syllabification of /y/		
			√ C Ca		+Y
			*f tsa	-y	
			fts^{y}a	-Ø^y	
			ftʃa		
			Prosody affecting second consonant		
KOTOKO-SOUTH	Zina		√ CaCa		+Y
		a-	*vatsa	-y	
		a-	vats^{y}a	-Ø^y	
			avatʃa		
			Prosody affecting second consonant		
	Mazera		√ CaCa		+Y
			*fatsa	-y	
			fats^{y}a	-Ø^y	

		fatʃa Prosody affecting second consonant		

MUSGUM	Vulum, Mulwi	√ C Ca *f ta fəʷtəʸ *futii* Vowel epenthesis; centralisation of final /a/; prosodification of /kʷ/ > ʷ; W-prosody affecting first syllable; Y-prosody affecting centralised /a/; syllabification of /y/; Cəʸy > Cii	-y -kʷ -iʸ-Øʷ	+Y, +W
	Mbara	√ C Ca *f tØ fəʷt *futay* Vowel epenthesis; desegmentalisation and prosodification of /kʷ/ > ʷ; prosody affecting epenthetic vowel	-a-y-kʷ -ay-Øʷ	+W
	Muskum	√ CaCa *fasa *fasa*		

thorn

Alternative reconstruction (**PCC**)
a-, xa-, m-, va-   **d(a)yka**   -t, -y   +Y   PC: —

hadik nm. thorn *épine* (10 groups, 31 languages) A
    The initial *h in this root is retained in Proto-Mafa, Proto-Mofu and Proto-Musgum, and the initial vowels in Proto-Hurza and Proto-Mandara support the reconstruction of an initial consonant, since Proto-Central Chadic did not permit initial vowels. In the Mafa group, the loss of *h has been compensated for by the addition of a prefix /v/ in Mafa and /m/ in Cuvok. This is a common process in these languages. *d has become *t in Proto-Mafa and Proto-Lamang, and in Proto-Higi, where this is a regular change. The reflex /dz/ in Sukur is unestablished. The *k is realised as *h in Proto-Bata, an unestablished change, and as /t/ in Muskum, a regular change. *i is reconstructed, rather than the palatalisation prosody, primarily on the evidence from the Bata and Higi groups, with support from the Tera, Sukur, Lamang and Musgum groups. In the Bata group, *i has the reflex /ə/ in both Gude and Sharwa. In Sharwa, *i has the contrasting reflex /i/. The Bata group data therefore supports the reconstruction of *i.

6.4 PCC Lexical Reconstructions   425

BATA   Gude   √ C C Ca
                        *d Øxa
                        dəxa
                        dəha
                        Vowel epenthesis

        Sharwa   √ C C Ca
                        *d Øxa
                        dəxə
                        dəhə
                        Vowel epenthesis; centralisation of
                        final /a/

MAFA   Mafa   √ CaC Ca
                va-   *taØkØ
                va-   tak
                        vatak

        Cuvok   √ CaC Ca
                m-   *taØkØ
                mə-   tak
                        mətak
                        Vowel epenthesis

TERA   Tera   √ CaC Ca   +Y
                m-   *dayka
                n-   daØʸkəʸ
                        ⁿ*deki*
                        Prosodification of medial /y/ to ʸ;
                        prosody affecting root-medial /a/ and
                        centralised final vowel

        Nyimatli   √ CaC Ca   +Y
                m-   *dzayxØ   -t-y
                m-   dzaʸx   -t-y
                n-   dzʸax   -t-iʸ
                        ⁿ*dʒakhti*
                        Prosodification of medial /y/ > ʸ;
                        prosody affecting root-initial consonant;
                        syllabification of suffixal /y/

        Hwana   √ CaC Ca
                m-   *daØxa
                n-   daxa
                        ⁿ*daxa*

SUKUR   Sukur   √ C C Ca   +Y
                        *dz y kØ

426   Full Lexical Reconstructions

			dz^{y}yk	
			dʒik	
			Partial desegmentalisation and prosodification of medial /y/ to /y^y/; prosody affecting root-initial consonant; syllabification of medial /y/	
HURZA	Mbuko		√ CaC Ca	
		a-	*daØkØ	
		a-	dak	
			adak	
	Vame		√ C C Ca	
		a-	*d Øga	
		a-	dəga	
			adəga	
			Vowel epenthesis	
MANDARA	Matal		√ CaC Ca	
		a-	*taØkØ	
		a-	tak	
			atak	
	Podoko		√ CaC Ca	
			*taØka	
			taka	
	Mandara, Malgwa		√ CaC Ca	+Y
			*dayka	
			daØ^{y}ka^y	
			dake	
			Prosodification of /y/ > ^{y}; prosody affecting final /a/	
	Glavda		√ CaC Ca	
			*taØka	
			taka	
MOFU	Ouldeme, Muyang, Zulgo, Gemzek, Merey, Dugwor	a- a-	√ CaC Ca *daØkØ dak *adak*	
	Moloko		√ CaC Ca	
		xa-	*daØkØ	

6.4 PCC Lexical Reconstructions   427

		xa-	dak	
			hadak	
	Mofu North		√ CaC Ca	
		m-	*daØkØ	
		n-	dak	
			ⁿdak	
	Mofu-Gudur		√ CaC Ca	
		xa-	*taØkØ	
		xa-	tak	
			hatak	
LAMANG	Lamang		√ C C Ca	+Y
			*t y ka	
			tikə^y	
			tiki	
			Syllabification of /y/; prosody affecting centralised final vowel	
	Hdi		√ CaC Ca	+Y
			*tayka	
			taØ^{y}kə^y	
			teki	
			Desegmentalisation and prosodification of medial /y/ > ^{y}; prosody affecting medial /a/ and centralised final vowel	
HIGI	Kamwe-Nkafa		√ C C Ca	
			*t y ka	
			tykə	
			tikə	
			Syllabification of medial /y/; centralisation of final /a/	
	Bana		√ C C Ca	+Y
			*t y ka	
			təØ^{y}kə^y	
			t(ə)ki	
			Prosodification /y/ > ^{y}; vowel epenthesis; prosody affecting centralised final vowel	
MUSGUM	Vulum		√ CaC Ca	+Y
		xa-	*daykØ	
		xa^y-	daØ^{y}k	
			hedek	

			Desegmentalisation of medial /y/ > ʸ; prosody affecting all /a/	
Mbara			√ CaC Ca *taØxa *taha*	
Muskum		xa- xaʸ-	√ CaC Ca *dayØØ -t daØʸ -t *hedet* Desegmentalisation and prosodification of medial /y/ > ʸ; prosody affecting all /a/	+Y

three

Alternative reconstruction (**PCC**)
ma-   **x(a)k(a)na**   -y, -kʷ, -ɗ   a   +Y, +W   PC: *k(w)ən (PN),
                                              *knɗ (u,a) (mʷ-, b-, y-, k-) (JS)

Note: Quite a few (but not all) of the languages show a long vowel [aa] in the first syllable at the juncture of the petrified prefix *ma- and the simple root, when the initial consonant of the root (*/x/) is lost. Here we follow Gravina (see immediately below): 'In several groups, the *h has been lost, triggering compensatory lengthening of the *a from the prefix.'

hikin num. three *trois* (12 groups, 42 languages) A
   This root is attested across all groups except for Gidar, Musgum and the Kotoko groups. The final *n has become *r in the Margi, Mandara and Mofu groups as part of a regular change. However *r is also found in the Mafa group and in the Giziga languages, and the /ɗ/ in the Daba group is also a reflex of *r. These forms are the result of borrowing. The unestablished *r→ɗ change also took place in Mandara, Malgwa and Glavda. In Mandara the *i and *ɗ fused to create /j/. In Malgwa, there was an intermediate /ɗʲ/, which moved to a velar position as part of a regular process of velarisation of palatalised alveolars. All groups except for the Mandara and Lamang groups have *ma- prefixed to the root. In several groups, the *h has been lost, triggering compensatory lengthening of the *a from the prefix. The *i vowel is reconstructed on the basis of evidence from the Margi, Mandara and Maroua groups. The evidence is not conclusive as there is no support for *i from the Bata or Higi groups.

6.4 PCC Lexical Reconstructions

BATA	Bata[34]		√ CaC Ca		+Y, +W
		ma-	*xaknØ	-y-k^w	
		m^{w}a-	Økə^{y}n	-Ø^y-Ø^w	
			m^{w}aakin		

Vowel epenthesis; prosodification of k^w > ^{w}; W-prosody affecting prefix consonant; Y-prosody affecting epenthetic vowel; fusion/ compensatory lengthening of 1st syllable vowel

	Gude		√ C C Ca
		ma-	*ØkØa
		ma-	kə
			makə

Centralisation of final /a/

	Jimi		√ C C Ca
		ma-	*x k nØ
		ma-	xəkən
			mahəkən

Vowel epenthesis

DABA[35]	Buwal, Gavar		√ C CaCa
		ma-	*x kadØ
		ma-	xkaɗ
			mahkaɗ

	Mbudum, Daba		√ C CaCa
		ma-	*ØkadØ
		ma-	kaɗ
			makaɗ

---

[34] The unique occurrence of labialised /m^w/ in Bata is somewhat enigmatic. It is here explained as resulting from the desegmentalisation of suffixal {-k^w} to prosodising /^{w}/ with subsequent leftward transfer of the labialisation to yield m^w. There is segmental loss of */x/ in root-initial position, which is compensated by lengthening the vowel /a/ of the prefix, which synchronically is interpreted as having the shape m^{w}a-.

[35] The reflex /ɗ/ of PCC */n/ in the DABA group is questionable in view of the appearance of clearly root-augmental *-ɗ in Glavda (MANDARA), which definitely is not a reflex of PCC */n/; see also other MANDARA group languages below.

430   Full Lexical Reconstructions

			Alternative option for analysis (DABA): Augmented root *ma-xkaØØ-ɗ ~ *ma-ØkaØØ-ɗ	
MAFA	Mafa	ma- ma	√ C CaCa *ØkarØ kar *makar*	
	Cuvok	ma- ma-	√ C CaCa *x karØ xkar *mahkar*	
TERA	Ga'anda	ma- ma-	√ C CaCa *x kanØ xkan *mahkan*	
SUKUR	Sukur	ma- ma-	√ CaC Ca *Øak nØ akən *maakən* Vowel epenthesis; fusion/ compensatory lengthening of 1st syllable vowel	
HURZA	Mbuko	ma- ma-	√ CaCaCa *ØakanØ akan *maakan* Fusion/compensatory lengthening of 1st syllable vowel	
	Vame[36]	ma- ma-	√ C CaCa *Ø kanØ gan *maŋgan*	
MARGI	Bura	ma- ma-	√ C C Ca *Ø k rØ kə^{y}r *makir*	+Y -y -Ø^y

[36] The origin of the prenasalisation element in ŋg remains obscure, unless we assume assimilation by the two surrounding nasals of the augmented underlying root: *magan > maŋgan.

6.4 PCC Lexical Reconstructions

				Vowel epenthesis; prosody affecting epenthetic vowel
	Margi-South			√ CaC Ca
		ma-		*Øak rØ
		ma-		akər
				maakər
				Fusion/compensatory lengthening of 1st syllable vowel
	Kilba			√ CaC Ca
		ma-		*Øak rØ -kʷ
		ma-		akər -w
				maakəru
				Vowel epenthesis; weakening of /kʷ/ > /w/; syllabification of /w/; fusion/compensatory lengthening of 1st syllable vowel
MANDARA	Matal			√ C C Ca
		ma-		*Ø k rØ
		ma-		kər
				makᵊr
				Vowel epenthesis
	Podoko			√ C C Ca
		ma-		*Ø k ra
		ma-		kəra
				makəra
				Vowel epenthesis
	Mandara[37]			√ C CaCa +Y
				*Ø kØa -y a
				kaʸ -yʸ aʸ
				keye
				Prosody affecting all /a/
	Malgwa			√ C CaCa +Y
				*Ø ɗkØa -ɗ-y a
				kaʸɗʸaʸ -Øʸ a
				keɠʸe

---

[37] The surface /y/ in Mandara cannot be related to root-final *n > ɗ+ʸ > ɗʸ > y, because, like in Malgwa below and in other examples in the data, in the MANDARA group languages palatalised /ɗʸ/ > /gʸ~ɟ/.

432   Full Lexical Reconstructions

			Prosody affecting all /a/ and final root consonant *ɗ + ^{y} > ɠ^y		
	Glavda		√ C C Ca		
			*x k rØ	-ɗ	a
			xkrɗa		
	Dghweɗe		√ C C Ca		+Y
			*x k ra	-y	
			xkra^y	-Ø^y	
			xkre		
			Prosody affecting final /a/		
MOFU	Ouldeme		√ C CaCa		
		ma-	*Ø karØ		
		ma-	kar		
			makar		
	Muyang		√ C C Ca		
		ma-	*x k rØ		
		ma-	xkər		
			mahkər		
	Moloko,		√ C CaCa		
	Gemzek,	ma-	*ØkarØ		
	Dugwor,	ma-	kar		
	Mofu North		makar		
	Gemzek		√ C C Ca		
		ma-	*Ø k rØ		
		ma-	kər		
			makər		
	Merey		√ C CaCa		
		ma-	*x karØ		
		ma-	xkar		
			mahkar		
	Mofu-Gudur		√ CaCaCa		
		ma-	*ØakarØ		
		ma-	akar		
			maakar		
			Fusion/compensatory lengthening of 1st syllable vowel		

6.4 PCC Lexical Reconstructions   433

MAROUA	Giziga-Muturwa, Giziga-Marva	ma- ma-	√ C C Ca *Ø k rØ kə^{y}r *makir*	+Y -y -Ø^y
	Mbazla	ma- ma-	√ C CaCa *Ø kaŋØ kaŋ *makaŋ*	
		ma- ma-	√ CaCaCa *ØakanØ akaŋ *maakaŋ* Fusion/compensatory lengthening of 1st syllable vowel	
LAMANG	Lamang		√ C C Ca *x k na xkəna *hkəna* Vowel epenthesis	
	Hdi		√ C C Ca *x k nØ *həkən* Vowel epenthesis	
HIGI	Kamwe-Nkafa	ma- ma-	√ C C Ca *Ø k na kənə *makənə* Vowel epenthesis; centralisation of final /a/	
	Kamwe-Futu	ma- ma-	√ C C Ca *Ø k Øa kə *makəo* Vowel epenthesis; centralisation of lexical final /a/; prosodification of /k^w/ > ^{w}; prosody affecting FV /a/	+W -k^w a -Ø^w a^w
	Kirya	ma- ma-	√ C C Ca *Ø k nØ kən	

| | | | *makən* | |
| | | | Vowel epenthesis | |

Psikye		√ C C Ca
	ma-	*x k na
	ma-	xkənə
		maxkən(ə)
		Vowel epenthesis; centralisation of final /a/

Bana		√ C CaCa
	ma-	*x kanØ
	ma-	xkan
		mahkan

two

Alternative reconstruction (**PCC**)
k- **k(a)sa** -y, -k^w, -ɗ   a   +Y, +W   PC: different roots

kasi num. two *deux* (3 groups, 5 languages) B syn: ɓiwak, tsɨjiw, sɨwra₁.

This root is found in the Kotoko Island, North and Centre groups, but not Kotoko South. The change *s→x in Buduma is regular. The *k has reflexes *k, *g and *x, which are unestablished changes.

LAMANG[38]	Lamang	√ CaCa		+Y
		*xasa	-y	
		xa^ysa	-Ø^y	
		hesa		
		Prosody affecting medial /a/		

		*xasa -y +Y
		xas^ya -Ø^y
		hasha
		Prosody affecting 2nd root consonant

	Hdi	√ C Ca		+Y
		*x sØ	-y	
		xə^ys	-Ø^y	
		his		
		Vowel epenthesis; prosody affecting epenthetic vowel		

---

[38] Not contained in the database (Gravina 2014a).

6.4 PCC Lexical Reconstructions 435

KOTOKO-ISLAND	Buduma	√ C Ca k- *x ØØ -y kə^y- x -i^y *kixi* Vowel epenthesis; prosody affecting epenthetic vowel; syllabification of /y/		+Y
KOTOKO-NORTH	Afade, Mpade	√ CaCa *gasØ -y gas -i^y *gasi* Syllabification of /y/		+Y
KOTOKO-CENTRAL	Lagwan	√ C Ca *x sØ -y-ɗ a xsə^y -Ø^y-ɗ a *xsɨda* Vowel epenthesis; prosody affecting epenthetic vowel		+Y
	Mser	√ C Ca *k tsa -y-k^w kə^{y}ts^{y}a^w -Ø^y-Ø^w *kitʃo* Vowel epenthesis; Y-prosody affecting epenthetic vowel; prosodification of /k^w/ > ^{w}; W-prosody affecting final /a/		+Y, +W

wash, to

Alternative reconstruction (**PCC**)
ma- **b(a)na** -a, -y, -k^w, (fa-)ŋ, a +Y, +WPC: *bəna (PN), *bn (JS)
           -x, RED

bana v. to wash *laver* (13 groups, 34 languages) A

This root is unusual in that it contains *b. There was a general change from Proto-Chadic *b to *v in Proto-Central Chadic, but this root appears as an exception to this change. The change of the medial *n to /r/ in the Mandara and Mofu groups is a regular change in the Mandara group, but in the Mofu group the data from other roots is less consistent and the change is unestablished.

BATA	Jimi	√C Ca *b na -y bə^{y}nə -Ø^y *binə*	+Y

436   Full Lexical Reconstructions

		Vowel epenthesis; prosody affecting epenthetic vowel; centralisation of final /a/		
DABA	Buwal, Gavar	√ CaCa *banØ *ban*		
	Mbudum	√ CaCa *banØ (-k^w?) *baŋ* Velarisation of final /n/ remains unaccounted for (reflex of lost root-augmental *{-k^w}?) Alternative option for analysis: Augmented root *baØØ-ŋ > *baŋ*		
	Daba	√ CaCa *panØ *pan*		
MAFA	Mafa	√ CaCa *panØ *pan*		
	Cuvok	√ CaCa *pana *pana*		
SUKUR	Sukur	√ CaCa banØ *ban*		
HURZA	Mbuko	√ CaCa *banØ -a-y ban -ay *banay*		
	Vame	√C Ca +Y, +W *b na -y-k^w a bə^{w}nə^y -y^y-Ø^w a *buniya* Vowel epenthesis; centralisation of final /a/; prosodification of /k^w/ > ^{w}; W-prosody affecting first syllable epenthetic vowel; Y-prosody affecting centralised /a/		

6.4 PCC Lexical Reconstructions

MANDARA	Matal		√ CaCa			
		ma-	*palØ	-a-y		
		ma-	pal	-ay		
			mapalay			
	Podoko		√ CaCa			
			*para			
			para			
	Glavda		√ CaCa			
			*barØ	-k	a	
			bar	-g	a	
			barga			
MOFU	Ouldeme		√ CaCa			+Y
			*bara	-y-ŋ		
			baʸraʸ	-Øʸ-ŋ		
			bereŋ			
			Prosody affecting all /a/			
			√ CaCa			
			*bara	-k	a	
			baraka			
			√ CaCa			+Y
			*bara	-y	a	
			barəʸ	-yʸ	a	
			bariya			
			Centralisation of final /a/; prosody affecting centralised /a/			
			√ CaCa			+Y
			*bara	-y	a	
			baʸraʸ	-yʸ	a	
			bereya			
			Prosody affecting all /a/			
			√ CaCa			
			*bara	-x	a	
			baraha			
	Muyang		√ CaCa			
			*bara	RED		
			bara	-ba		
			baraba			
			√ CaCa			
			*bara	-f-ŋ		
			bara	-fəŋ		

438 Full Lexical Reconstructions

          barafəŋ
          Vowel epenthesis

          √ CaCa
          *barØ   -a-y
          bar   -ay
          baray

Mada
          √ CaCa
    ma- *bala   (-fa-ŋ- a)
          mabala(faŋa)

Moloko
          √ CaCa
          *balØ   -a-y
          bal   -ay
          balay

Zulgo,
Gemzek
          √ CaCa
          *bara
          bara

Gemzek
          √ CaCa   +Y
    ma- *bara   -y
    ma^y- ba^{y}ra^y -Ø^y
          mebere
          Prosody affecting all /a/

Merey
          √ CaCa
          *bara
          bara

Dugwor
          √ CaCa   +Y
    ma- *barØ   -a-y
    mə- ba^{y}r   -a^{y}y^y
          məberey
          Prosody affecting /a/ in ultima and
          penultima; centralisation of prefixal /a/

Mofu North
          √ C Ca
    ma- *p rØ   -a-y
    ma^y- pər   -a^{y}y^y
          mepərey
          Vowel epenthesis; prosody affecting
          first and final syllable

Mofu-Gudur
          √ C Ca
          *p rØ
          pər
          Vowel epenthesis

6.4 PCC Lexical Reconstructions

MAROUA	Giziga-Muturwa, Giziga-Marva	√ C Ca *b nØ bəʷn *bun*	-kʷ -Øʷ	+W
		Vowel epenthesis; prosodification of /kʷ/ > ʷ; prosody affecting epenthetic vowel		
	Giziga-Marva	√ C Ca *b na bəʷna *buna*	-kʷ -Øʷ	+W
		Vowel epenthesis; prosodification of /kʷ/ > ʷ; prosody affecting epenthetic vowel		
	Mbazla	√ CaCa *banØ *ban*		
HIGI	Psikye	√ C Ca *p Øa paʸ *pe*	-y -Øʸ	+Y
		Prosody affecting /a/		
	Bana	√ C Ca *p ØØ p *pi*	-y -i	+Y
		Syllabification of /y/		

water

	Alternative reconstruction (**PCC**)				
a(xʷ)-	ʔy(a)ma[39]	-a, -y, -kʷ, -n	a	+Y, +W	PC: *am (PN), *maa/*maʔ- (OS)

---

[39] The initial segment(s) of the reconstructed form remain(s) enigmatic. P. Newman (1977a: 10) had reconstructed a somewhat rare but phonologically acceptable vowel-initial root for PC. For Central Chadic, Gravina sees 'evidence for a glottal element, in most cases [ʔ]', but reconstructs */d/. I have chosen the representation */ʔy/ to highlight this enigmatic case, without any idea as to whether we are dealing with a glottalised palatal */ʔy/ or a sequence of */ʔ + y/. Some Central Chadic languages, as it would appear, do consider this root to be triradical in underlying structure: √ C C(a)Ca ***ʔ y(a)ma**. This triradical structure will be reflected in our (tentative) reconstructions of individual language roots.

ɗijim nm. water *eau* (17 groups, 53 languages) A

The *ɗ is reconstructed on the evidence from the Bata, Tera, Hurza, Kotoko South and Musgum groups. In all of these groups there is evidence for a glottal element, in most cases [ʔ]. In the Tera group the *ɗ and *j have fused to form /ɗʲ/.

BATA	Gude	√ C CaCa
		*ʔyama -n a
		> ma'yØ -n ə
		ma'inə
		Metathesis *ʔy m > m ʔy; syllabification of */ʔy/ > 'i
	Jimi, Sharwa	√ C CaCa
		*ʔyama
		> ma'yØ
		ma'i
		Metathesis *ʔy m > m ʔy; syllabification of */ʔy/ > 'i
DABA	Buwal	√ C CaCa
		*ʔyamØ
		Øyam
		yam
	Gavar	√ C C Ca
		*ʔy mØ
		Øyəm
		yəm
		Vowel epenthesis
	Mbudum	√ C C Ca +Y
		*ʔy mØ
		Øyʸəʸm
		yim
		Partial desegmentalisation of /y/ > /yʸ/; vowel epenthesis; prosody affecting epenthetic vowel
	Daba	√ C C Ca
		*ʔy mØ
		Øyəm
		yəm
		Vowel epenthesis
MAFA	Mafa, Cuvok	√ C CaCa
		*ʔyamØ
		Øyam
		yam

6.4 PCC Lexical Reconstructions

TERA	Tera, Nyimatli		√ C C Ca *ɗy mØ ɗyə^{y}m *ýim (ɗyim)* Partial desegmentalisation and prosodification of /ɗy/ > /ɗy^y/; vowel epenthesis; prosody affecting epenthetic vowel	+Y
	Hwana	a- a-	√ C CaCa *ʔyama ØØama *aama* Prefix or prothetic vowel; fusion/ compensatory lengthening of 1st-syllable vowel	
SUKUR	Sukur[40]		√ C CaCa *ʔyamØ ə^{y}Øy^{y}am *iyam* Partial desegmentalisation and prosodification of /y/ > /y^y/; vowel prothesis; prosody affecting prothetic vowel	+Y
			√ C CaCa *ʔyamØ Øyam *yam*	
HURZA	Mbuko	a- a-	√ C(C)aCa *ʔyamØ 'Øam *a'am*	
	Vame	a-x^w- a-x^w-	√ C CaCa *ʔyamØ ØØam *ah^{w}am*	

---

[40] Vowel prothesis is a fairly frequent process in some Central Chadic languages in cases of initial consonant clusters; vowel prothesis in Sukur could be an indication of an underlying reanalysis of the root as triradical √C CaCa, i.e. ***ʔyama**.

MARGI	Margi	√ C C Ca *ʔy ma 'yməʸ 'imi Syllabification of initial /y/; prosody affecting centralised final vowel	+Y
	Margi-South	√ C C Ca *ʔy ma Øyməʸ imi Syllabification of initial /y/; prosody affecting centralised final vowel	+Y
	Bura	√ C C Ca *ʔy ma Øyəʸməʸ yimi Syllabification of /y/; vowel epenthesis; prosody affecting epenthetic medial vowel and centralised final vowel	+Y
MANDARA	Matal	√ C CaCa *ʔyawØ yyaw y:aw Consonant length < assimilation *ʔy > yy	
	Podoko	√ C C Ca *ʔy wa Øyəwa yəwa Vowel epenthesis	
	Mandara, Malgwa	√ C CaCa *ʔyawa Øyʸawaʸ yawe Partial desegmentalisation and prosodification of /y/ > /yʸ/; prosody affecting final /a/	+Y
	Glavda	√ C C Ca *ʔy wa Øyəʷwʷa	+W

6.4 PCC Lexical Reconstructions 443

yuwa
Vowel epenthesis; partial desegmentalisation and prosodification of /w/ > wʷ; prosody affecting epenthetic vowel

√ C C Ca   +Y
*ʔy Øa
Øyʸəʸ
ii
Partial desegmentalisation and prosodification of /y/ > /yʸ/; vowel epenthesis; prosody affecting epenthetic vowel and centralised final /a/; yəʸ > yi > ii

√ C C Ca
*y wØ
Øy w
yu
Syllabification of /w/

	Dghwede	√ C C Ca *ʔy wa Øyʸəʸwaʸ *yiwe* Partial desegmentalisation and prosodification of /y/ > /yʸ/; vowel epenthesis; prosody affecting epenthetic vowel and final /a/	+Y
MOFU	Ouldeme, Muyang, Moloko, Zulgo Gemzek, Merey, Dugwor, Mofu North, Mofu-Gudur	√ C C Ca *ʔyamØ Øyam *yam*	
MAROUA	Giziga-Marva. Mbazla	√ C C Ca *ʔyamØ Øyam *yam*	
LAMANG	Lamang, Hdi	√ C C Ca *ʔy ma Øyʸməʸ	+Y

		imi Syllabification of initial /y/ and partial desegmentalisation and prosodification > yʸ; prosody affecting final centralised vowel	
HIGI	Kamwe-Nkafa	√ C CaCa *ʔyama Øyʸamaʸ *yame* Partial desegmentalisation and prosodification of /y/ > /yʸ/; prosody affecting final /a/	+Y
	Kamwe-Futu	√ C CaCa *ʔyama Øyʸaʸmʸəʸ *yemʸi* Partial desegmentalisation and prosodification of /y/ > /yʸ/; prosody affecting final consonant and both medial /a/ and centralised final /a/	+Y
	Kirya	√ C CaCa *ʔyama Øyamə *yamə* Centralisation of final /a/	
	Psikye	√ C CaCa -kʷ *ʔyamØ -w Øyʸaʸm *yemu* Partial desegmentalisation and prosodification of /y/ > /yʸ/; prosody affecting medial /a/ ; weakening of /kʷ/ > /w/; syllabification of /w/	+Y
	Bana	√ C CaCa *ʔyamØ Øyam *yam*	
KOTOKO-ISLAND	Buduma	√ C CaCa *ʔyamØ -a-y	

6.4 PCC Lexical Reconstructions 445

		ØØam -ay *amay*	
KOTOKO- NORTH	Afade, Mpade	√ C CaCa *?yama ØØ^{y}ama^y *ame* Prosodification of /y/ > ^{y}; prosody affecting final /a/	+Y
	Malgbe	√ C CaCa *?yamØ ØØam *am*	
KOTOKO- CENTRAL	Lagwan, Mser	√ C CaCa *?yamØ ØØam *am*	
KOTOKO- SOUTH	Zina	√ C CaCa *?yama ØØ^{y}amə^y *ami* Prosodification of /y/ > ^{y}; prosody affecting centralised final vowels	+Y
	Mazera	√ C C Ca *?y mØ	+Y

a-   ?Ø^{y}m
a-   ?ə^{y}m
a-   *a?im*
Prosodification of /y/ > ^{y}; vowel
epenthesis; prosody affecting
epenthetic vowel

| MUSGUM | Vulum | √ C CaCa
*?yamØ
Øy^{y}a^{y}m
yem
Partial desegmentalisation and
prosodification of /y/ > /y^y/; prosody
affecting medial /a/ | +Y |
| | Mbara | √ C CaCa
*?yamØ | |

446   Full Lexical Reconstructions

		ʔØam	
		'am	
Muskum		√ C CaCa	
		*ØyamØ -kʷ	
		yam -w	
		yamu	
		Prosodification of /kʷ/ > ʷ;	
		syllabification of /w/	

whistle, to

Alternative reconstruction (**PCC**)
m-, RED   f(a)y(a)kʷa[41]   -a, -y, -n   +Y   PC: —

pikʷ/pikʷ ʸ v. whistle *siffler* (6 groups, 18 languages) B cf: vats, vikɮ, v₂.

Two alternative roots are proposed due to the contradictory evidence. The data from the Daba, Mafa and Mofu groups supports reconstructing the palatalisation prosody, whilst the data from the other groups indicates that the vowel *i should be reconstructed. *p has the reflex *f in all groups, which is not expected in word-initial position. The word may therefore have an onomatopoeic origin.

BATA	Gude		√ C C Ca	+W
			*f y kʷa	
			fikw	
			fiku	
			Re-segmentalisation *kʷ > k+w;	
			syllabification of medial /y/;	
			syllabification of final /w/	
	Jimi		√ C C Ca	
			*f y kʷa -n	
			fikʷə -n	
			fikʷən	
			Centralisation of final /a/;	
			syllabification of medial /y/	
DABA	Buwal		√ CaC Ca	+Y
		RED	*fay kʷØ	

---

[41] Our PCC reconstruction purposefully contains *f (while Gravina maintains */p/). By this we wish to indicate that the question remains open whether or not */f/ could be reconstructed for PCC parallel to */p/ (as suggested by P. Newman, p.c. 2020, and at variance with Gravina 2014a), or whether we are dealing with an onomatopoeic origin of this root/word, as also assumed by Gravina, which would 'explain' the violation of the reconstructed set of PCC consonants.

6.4 PCC Lexical Reconstructions

		fa-	faØʸkʷ	
		faʸ-	faʸkʷ	
			fefekʷ	
			Prosodification of medial /y/ > ʸ; prosody affecting all /a/	
	Mbudum		√ CaC Ca	+Y
		RED	*faykØ	
		fa-	faØʸk	
		fə	faʸk	
			fəfek	
			Prosodification of medial /y/ > ʸ; prosody affecting root-medial /a/; centralisation of prefixal /a/	
		RED	√ C C Ca	
		f-	fØkØ	
		fə-	fək	
			fəfək	
			Vowel epenthesis	
MAFA	Mafa		√ C C Ca	+W
			*f Ø kʷ Ø	
			fəʷkʷ	
			fukʷ	
			Partial desegmentalisation and prosodification of /kʷ/ > /k + ʷ/; vowel epenthesis; prosody affecting epenthetic vowel	
	Cuvok		√ C C Ca	
		RED	*f Ø kʷa	
		f-	fkʷa	
		fə-	fkʷa	
			fəfkʷa	
			Vowel epenthesis	
			√ CaC Ca	
		RED	*faØkʷa	
		fa-	fakʷa	
		fa-	fØkʷa	
		fa-	fkʷa	
			fafkʷa	
			Note deletion of medial /a/ in root under reduplication	

448   Full Lexical Reconstructions

MANDARA	Podoko, Mandara		√ C C Ca	
			*f y kʷa	
			fikʷa	
			fikʷa	
			Syllabification of /y/	

	Malgwa		√ C C Ca	+Y
			*f y kʷa	
			fəʸykʷa	
			fiikʷa	
			Partial desegmentalisation and prosodification of /y/ > /yʸ/; vowel epenthesis; prosody affecting epenthetic vowel; syllabification of medial /y/; Cəʸ+y > Cii	

	Glavda		√ CaC Ca	
		RED	*faykʷa	
		fa-	faykʷa	
		fa-	fØykʷa	
		fa-	fikʷa	
			fafikʷa	
			Syllabification of medial /y/; note deletion of medial /a/ in root under reduplication	

	Dghweɗe		√ C C Ca	+Y
			*f y ga	
			f Øʸ ga	
			fgaʸ	
			fəge	
			Prosodification of /y/ > ʸ; vowel epenthesis; prosody affecting final /a/	

MOFU	Muyang		√ C C Ca	+Y
			*f y kʷØ -a-y	
			fyʸkʷ -aʸyʸ	
			fikʷey	
			Prosody affecting final /a/; syllabification of medial /y/	

	Moloko		√ CaC Ca	+W
			*faØkʷØ -a-y	
			faʷk -ay	
			fokay	

6.4 PCC Lexical Reconstructions   449

                                    Partial desegmentalisation and
                                    prosodification of /kʷ/ > /k + ʷ/;
                                    prosody affecting medial /a/

Zulgo   √ CaC Ca   +Y
                    RED   *fayka
                    fa-   faØʸkʷa
                    faʸ-   faʸkʷaʸ
                                fefekʷe
                                Prosodification of medial /y/ > ʸ;
                                prosody affecting all /a/

Gemzek   √ C C Ca   +Y,
                                                                 +W
                    ma-   *f y kʷa
                    ma-   f Øʸ kʷa
                    mə-   fəʷkʷaʸ
                                məfukʷe
                                Prosodification of medial /y/ > ʸ;
                                partial desegmentalisation of /kʷ/
                                > /k + ʷ/; centralisation of prefixal
                                /a/; vowel epenthesis; W-prosody
                                affecting epenthetic vowel in
                                penultimate; Y-prosody affecting
                                final /a/

                                √ C C Ca   +W
                                *f Ø kʷØ
                                fəʷkʷ
                                fuk
                                Partial desegmentalisation and
                                prosodification of /kʷ/ > /k + ʷ/;
                                vowel epenthesis; prosody
                                affecting epenthetic vowel

Merey   √ C C Ca
                    RED   *f Ø kʷØ
                    f-   fkʷ
                    fə-   fəkʷ
                                fəfəkʷ
                                Vowel epenthesis

Mofu-Gudur   √ CaC Ca
                    RED   *faØkʷØ
                    fa-   fakʷ
                                fafakʷ

450   Full Lexical Reconstructions

HIGI   Kamwe-Futu   √ C C Ca   +Y
                                    *f y gʷa
                                    fyʸgʷaʸ
                                    *fig*ʷe*
                                    Partial desegmentalisation and
                                    prosodification of /y/ > /yʸ/;
                                    syllabification of medial /y/;
                                    prosody affecting final /a/

white

            Alternative reconstruction (**PCC**)
            m(a)-,   **kʷ(a)ɗ(a)ka** -y, -l   a   +Y, +W   PC: *ḳVr- (OS)
            RED

            ɗakʷa ʸ adj. white *blanc* (7 groups, 17 languages) B
            This root has two primary reflexes, *ɗakʷ and *kʷaɗ. The first is
            found in the Mandara and Musgum groups, and the second in the groups
            around the Mandara Mountains. It is not possible to be certain which of
            these constituted the Proto-Central Chadic root, or if it took the form
            *kʷaɗak. Palatalisation is attested in many of the groups.

DABA   Mbudum   √ C CaCa   +Y
                        RED   *k ɗakØ   -y
                        k-   kɗak   -y
                        kʸ-   kʸɗ:aʸk   -Øʸ
                                    kʸkʸɗ:ek
                                    Prosody affecting initial consonant and
                                    medial /a/; source of consonant length [ɗ:]
                                    remains obscure

MAFA   Mafa   √ C CaCa   +Y
                        RED   *kʷ ɗaka   -y
                        kʷəʸɗ-   kʷəʸɗaʸ'aʸ   -Øʸ
                                    kʷidkʷidɗe'e
                                    Vowel epenthesis; prosody affecting
                                    epenthetic vowel; source of consonant length
                                    [ɗɗ] obscure

            Cuvok   √ CaC Ca   +Y
                                    *kʷaɗ ØØ   -y
                                    kʷaʸɗ   -Øʸ
                                    kʷeɗ
                                    Prosody affecting /a/

HURZA   Mbuko   √ CaCaCa   +Y
                                    *kʷaɗakØ   -y
                                    kʷaʸɗaʸk   -Øʸ
                                    kʷeɗek
                                    Prosody affecting all /a/

6.4 PCC Lexical Reconstructions

		√ CaCaCa		+Y
	RED	*kʷaɗakØ	-y	
	kʷaʸ-	kʷaʸɗaʸk	-Øʸ	
		kʷekʷeɗek		
		Prosody affecting all /a/		

Vame

	√ CaC Ca		+Y
ma-	*kʷaɗØa	-y	
ma-	> ɗakʷa	-y	
maʸ-	ɗaʸkʷaʸ	-Øʸ	
	meɗekʷe		
	Metathesis *kʷ ɗ > ɗ kʷ; prosody affecting all /a/		

MANDARA   Matal

	√ C C Ca		+Y, +W
ma-	*kʷ ɗ ga	-y	
ma-	> ɗ kʷ ga	-y	
maʸ-	ɗəʸkʷəʷga	-Øʸ	
	mæɗikʷᵘga		
	Metathesis *kʷ ɗ > ɗ kʷ; vowel epenthesis; Y-prosody affecting antepenultima epenthetic vowel; W-prosody affecting penultima epenthetic vowel		

Podoko

	√ CaC Ca		+Y
ma-	*kʷaɗ Øa	-y	
	> ɗakʷa		
maʸ-	ɗaʸkʷaʸ	-Øʸ	
	meɗekʷe		
	Metathesis *kʷ ɗ > ɗ kʷ; prosody affecting all /a/		

	√ CaC Ca			+Y, +W
ma-	*kʷaɗ ØØ	-y-l	a	
ma	> ɗakʷ	-y-l	a	
maʸ-	ɗaʸkʷə ʷ	-Øʸ-l	a	
	meɗekula			
	Metathesis *kʷ ɗ > ɗ kʷ; vowel epenthesis; W-prosody affecting epenthetic vowel; Y-prosody affecting medial /a/			

Glavda

	√ C C Ca
ma-	*kʷ ɗ Øa
ma-	> ɗkʷa
ma-	ɗəkʷa

			madᵊkʷa	
			Metathesis *kʷ ɗ > ɗ kʷ; vowel epenthesis	
	Dghweɗe		√ CaC Ca	
		ma-	*kʷaɗØa	
		ma-	> ɗakʷa	
			mat'akʷa	
			Metathesis *kʷ ɗ > ɗ kʷ	
MOFU	Ouldeme		√ CaC Ca	+Y
		ma-	*kʷaɗØa -y	
		ma-	> ɗakʷa -y	
		maʸ-	ɗaʸkʷaʸ -Øʸ	
			medekʷe	
			Metathesis *kʷ ɗ > ɗ kʷ; prosody affecting all /a/	
	Gemzek		√ CaCaCa	+Y
			*kʷaɗakØ -y	
			kʷaʸɗaʸk -Øʸ	
			kʷedek	
			Prosody affecting all /a/	
	Merey		√ C CaCa	+Y, +W
		RED	*kʷɗakØ -y	
		kʷəʷɗaʸ-	kʷəʷɗaʸk -Øʸ	
			kuɗekuɗek	
			Vowel epenthesis; W-prosody affecting epenthetic vowel; Y-prosody affecting /a/	
			√ CaCaCa	+Y
			*kʷaɗakØ -y	
			kʷaʸɗaʸk -Øʸ	
			kʷedek	
			Prosody affecting all /a/	
	Mofu North, Mofu-Gudur		√ CaCaCa	+Y
			*kʷaɗakØ -y	
			kʷaʸɗaʸk -Øʸ	
			kʷedek	
			Prosody affecting all /a/	
MAROUA	Giziga-Muturwa		√ CaCaCa	+Y
			*kʷaɗakØ -y	
			kʷaʸɗaʸk -Øʸ	
			kʷedek	
			Prosody affecting all /a/	

6.4 PCC Lexical Reconstructions 453

MUSGUM	Mulwi, Vulum	√ C C Ca		+Y, +W
		m- *kʷ ɗ Øa	-y	
		m- > ɗkʷa	-y	
		mə^w- ɗə^wkʷə^y	-y^y	
		muɗukʷii		

Metathesis *kʷ ɗ > ɗ kʷ; vowel epenthesis; W-prosody affecting first and second syllable epenthetic vowels; Y-prosody affecting third syllable epenthetic vowel; syllabification of /y/; Cə^yy > Cii

work

Alternative reconstruction (**PCC**)

a-, ka-,	ɬ(a)na	-t, -y,	a	+Y, +W	PC
ma-		-k, -kʷ,			*ṣəna (PN)
		-n, -l			

ɬini nf., v. work *travail* (11 groups, 34 languages) A
    *ɬ has the regular reflex *ɮ in the South sub-branch, and here that is the case in Proto-Daba and Proto-Sukur. However, in the Tera group we expect /ɮ/ but find /l/, and in the Bata group we expect /ɮ/ in Tsuvan and /l/ in the other languages cited, but find /l/ in all languages except Bata. The *n has the regular reflex *r in the Margi-Mandara-Mofu major group, and here also in the Giziga languages, borrowed from Mofu-Gudur. *i is reconstructed based on its presence in Proto-Bata, Proto-Margi, Proto-Mandara and Proto-Higi. In most other groups *i is no longer contrastive.

BATA	Bata	√ CaCa		+W +Y
		*ɬanØ	-t -y -kʷ a	
		la^yn	-t-Ø^y-Ø^w a^w	
		lento		

Y-prosody affecting medial /a/; W-prosody affecting FV /a/

	Gude	√ C Ca
		*ɬ na
		ɬənə
		ɬənə

Vowel epenthesis; centralisation of final /a/

√ C Ca
*ɬ na
ɬəna
Vowel epenthesis

454   Full Lexical Reconstructions

	Jimi	√ C Ca		+Y
		*ɬ na	-y-n	
		ɬəʸnə	-Øʸ-n	
		linən		
		Vowel epenthesis; prosody affecting epenthetic vowel; centralisation of final /a/		
	Sharwa	√ C Ca		
		*ɬ nØ		
		ɬən		
		Vowel epenthesis		
	Tsuvan	√ C Ca		+Y
		*ɬ nØ	-y-k-n	
		ɬəʸn	-iʸ-kən	
		linikən		
		Vowel epenthesis; prosody affecting epenthetic vowel in first syllable; syllabification of /y/		
DABA	Buwal	√ CaCa		
		*ɮanØ		
		ɮan		
	Gavar	√ C Ca		
		*ɮ nØ		
		ɮən		
		Vowel epenthesis		
TERA	Tera, Nyimatli	√ C Ca		
		*ɬ na		
		ɬəna		
		Vowel epenthesis		
SUKUR	Sukur	√ C Ca		
		*ɮ nØ		
		ɮən		
		Vowel epenthesis		
HURZA	Mbuko	√ CaCa		
		a- *ɬanØ		
		a- ɬan		
		aɬan		
	Vame	√ C Ca		
		*ɬ ra		
		ɬəra		
		Vowel epenthesis		

6.4 PCC Lexical Reconstructions

MARGI	Bura		√ C Ca		+Y
		k-	*ɬ rØ	-y	
		kə^y-	ɬə^{y}r	-Ø^y	
			kiɬir		
			Vowel epenthesis; prosody affecting epenthetic vowels		
	Margi		√ C Ca		
			*ɬ rØ		
			ɬər		
			Vowel epenthesis		
	Kilba		√ C Ca		
			*ɬ ra		
			ɬəra		
			Vowel epenthesis		
MANDARA	Matal		√ C Ca		
			*ɬ rØ	-a-y	
			ɬər	-ay	
			ɬ^{w}ray		
			Vowel epenthesis		
	Podoko		√ C Ca		
			*ɬ ra		
			ɬəra		
			Vowel epenthesis		
	Malgwa		√ C Ca		
			*ɬ ra		
			thləra		
			Vowel epenthesis		
	Glavda		√ C Ca		
			*ɬ ra		
			ɬra		
			√ C Ca		
			*ɬ Øa		
			ɬə		
			ɬə		
			Centralisation of /a/		
	Dghweɗe		√ C Ca		
			*ɬ ra		
			ɬəra		
			Vowel epenthesis		

Full Lexical Reconstructions

MOFU	Ouldeme		√ C Ca	
		a-	*ɬ rØ	
		a-	ɬər	
			alər	
			Vowel epenthesis	
	Moloko		√ C Ca	+Y
			*ɬ ra -y -l a	
			ɬəra^y -Ø^y-l a^y	
			ɬərele	
			Vowel epenthesis; prosody affecting /a/ in ultimate and penultimate syllables	
	Gemzek, Dugwor, Merey	ma- mə-	√ C Ca *ɬ rØ ɬər *mələr* Centralisation of prefixal /a/; vowel epenthesis	
	Mofu-Gudur		√ C Ca *ɬ ra *ɬəra* Vowel epenthesis	
MAROUA	Giziga-Muturwa		√ C Ca *ɬ ra *ɬra*	
	Giziga-Marva		√ C Ca *ɬ ra -y ɬə^yra -Ø^y *ɬira* Vowel epenthesis; prosody affecting epenthetic vowel	+Y
LAMANG	Lamang, Hdi		√ C Ca *ɬ na *ɬəna* Vowel epenthesis	
HIGI	Kamwe-Nkafa		√ C Ca *ɬ na ɬənə *ɬənə* Vowel epenthesis; centralisation of final /a/	

6.4 PCC Lexical Reconstructions

Kamwe- √ C Ca   +Y
Futu   *ɬ na   -y
       ɬəʸnə   -Øʸ
       linə
       Vowel epenthesis; prosody affecting epenthetic vowel; centralisation of final /a/

Kirya, √ C Ca
Psikye *ɬ na
        ɬənə
        lənə
        Vowel epenthesis; centralisation of final /a/

Bana   √ C Ca
        *ɬ nØ   -y
        ɬən   -i
        ləni
        Vowel epenthesis; syllabification of /y/

APPENDIX Alphabetical List of Glosses with Alternative Reconstructions and Prosodies

In this appendix and for quick and easy reference, we list all our alternative reconstructed PCC roots and pseudo-roots in alphabetical order of their glosses. Details and individual language data are found in section 6.4.

The following list also allows for quick comparison of both prefixal and suffixal root-augmental inventories, the presence or absence of FV, and the occurrence of Y- and/or W-prosody with any of the listed items.

Gloss	Prefixal root augment	Simple root	Suffixal root augment	FV	Prosodies
arm		**dz va**	-y, -kʷ, -n	a	+Y, +W
ashes		**p ts(a)ɗa**	-y, -kʷ, -n	a	+Y, +W
beard	a-, m(a)-, RED-	**gʷ ma**	-a, -y		+Y, +W
beer	ma-, n-, ᵑg-	**v(a)xʷa**	-y, -n		+Y, +W
belly	a-	**xʷ(a)ɗa**	-y, -ɗ, -kʷ		+Y, +W
bite, to	ma-, n-, ŋ-, ᵑga-	**dza**	-a, -y, -n, -w, -x	a	+Y
blow, to	ma-	**v ɮa**	-a, -y, -kʷ, -n		+Y, +W
boil, to	ma-	**kʷ(a)ɗ(a)xa**	-a, -y, -ŋ		+Y, +W
bone	(')a-, a-n-, a-ta-, ma-, ma-ta-, RED-a-	**ɗ y(a)ɬa**	-a, -y, -kʷ, -t, -n, -ŋ		+Y, +W
bow	a-, xa-, ma-ᵑga-, ᵑg-, g-nd-, RED-	**r(a)ga**	-a, -y, -ɗ, -n, -ŋ		+Y
brain	a-, a-n-, a-ᵑga-, ᵑga-, ma-ka-, ma-ka-ᵑga-	**r(a)ɬa**	-y		+Y
butterfly	kʷa-, ma-(ta-), (n)a-) RED, RED-ma-	**p(a)ra**	-y, -kʷ, -n	a	+Y, +W
camel	n-	**k(a)l(a)g(a)m(a)wa**	-y, -n, -t	a	+Y, +W
cook, to	k-, ma-, RED	**da**	-a, -y, -k, -kʷ	a	+Y, +W
cow	a-, k-, n-, wa-, wr-	**ɬa**	-a, -y, -n	a	+Y, +W

Appendix

crocodile	m-	**r ga**	-y, -kʷ		+Y, +W
cry, to	ma-	**ts(a)wa**	-a, -y, -k	a	+Y, +W
die, to	k-, ma-	**m(a)ta**	-a, -y, -k, -kʷ, -n, -ŋ	a	+Y, +W
dog		**k(a)ra**	-a, -y, -kʷ	a	+Y
donkey₁	a-, xa-	**z(a)ⁿgʷa**	-y, -kʷ		+Y, +W
donkey₂		**ᵐb(a)rdza**	-y, -kʷ, -ŋ		+Y, +W
donkey₃		**k(a)w(a)ra**	-y, -t	a	+Y, +W
dream	ma-, ma-RED, RED, n-	**s(a)w(a)na**	-a, -y, -k, -n		+Y, +W
earth	a-, ya-, RED	**xʷ(a)yɗa**	-y, -k	a	+Y, +W
eight	m-	**tɣ(a)sa**	-y, -kʷ		+Y, +W
elephant		**n va**	-y, -kʷ		+Y
extinguish, to	k-, m(a)-	**m(a)ta**	-a, -y, -kʷ, -n, -ŋ	a	+Y, +W
faeces	ŋ-	**ɣʷ va**	-a, -y, -n		+Y, +W
five	m-, n-	**xʷ t(a)fa**	-y, -k	a	+Y, +W
fly	a-, xa-, m-, n-, RED	**dz(a)kʷ(a)ɗa**	-y, -n, -ŋ		+Y, +W
foot	a(-n)-, m-	**sa**	-y, -k, -kʷ	a	+Y, +W
give birth, to	ma-, RED	**w(a)x(a)ya**	-a, -y, -k, -kʷ, -n, -l	a	+Y, +W
grandfather	a-, b-, a-d-	**dz(a)dza**	-a, -y, -kʷ, -n		+Y
grasshopper	a-	**xʷ(a)y(a)kʷa**	(-ɗ,-ŋ?)		+Y, +W
hair	ma-	**s(ab(a)ta**	-y, -kʷ		+Y
hare	ma-, na-	**xʷ(a)d(a)y(a)va**	-k, -kʷ, -n	a	+Y, +W
hedgehog	a-, ɗa-, m-, (a-)RED	**xʷ(a)s(a)sa**	-ɓ, -y		+Y, +W
hide, to	k-	**ɓ(a)ɣʷa**	-n		+W
horn₁		**d(a)r(a)ma**	-y, -kʷ		+Y, +W
horn₂	a-, ma-	**xʷ(a)la**	-y		+Y, +W
horse	a-	**p(a)r(a)sa**	-y, -k, -kʷ, -ŋ	a	+Y, +W
laugh, to	a-, m-	**ɣʷ(a)b(a)sa**	-a, -y, -k, -n	a	+Y, +W
lion	w-, RED	**l(a)vara**	-y		+Y, +W
market	RED	**k(a)s(a)wka**	-b, -y		+Y, +W
moon	n-, ŋ-	**t(a)ra**	-y, -kʷ	a	+Y, +W
navel	ma-	**z(a)b(a)-xʷ(a)ɗa**	-y, -n		+Y, +W
night	a-, x-, m-/n-, sa-, ta-	**r(a)v(a)ɗa**	-a, -y, -k, -kʷ, -n, -ŋ	a	+Y, +W
quiver		**ɣʷ(a)dza**	-y, -n, -l		+Y, +W

Appendix

ram	ma-	**gʷ(a)z(a)ma**	-y		+Y
razor₁		**p(a)ɗ(a)kʷa**	-y, -ɗ		+Y,+W
razor₂		**b(a)la**	-y		+Y
root	RED	**ɬ(a)r(a)ka**	-a, -y, -kʷ, -n	a	+Y, +W
six		**ɬ(a)ra**	-y		+Y
spit, to	m(a)-, n-, ŋ-	**t(a)fa**	-a, -y, -kʷ, -n, -l	a	+Y, +W
suck, to	ma-, n-, RED	**s(a)wɓa**	-a, -y, -n		+Y, +W
sun	a-, xa-, d-, RED	**p(a)ta**	-a, -y, -k, -kʷ, -n	a	+Y, +W
thorn	a-, xa-, ma-, va-	**d(a)yka**	-t, -y		+Y
three	ma-	**x(a)k(a)na**	-y, -kʷ, -ɗ	a	+Y, +W
two	k-	**k(a)sa**	-y, -kʷ, -ɗ	a	+Y, +W
wash, to	ma-	**b(a)na**	-a,-y,-kʷ, -x, (fa-)ŋ, RED	a	+Y, +W
water	a(xʷ)-	**ʔy(a)ma**	-a, -y, -kʷ, -n	a	+Y, +W
whistle, to	m-, RED	**f(a)y(a)kʷa**	-a, -y, -n		+Y
white	m(a)-, RED	**kʷ(a)ɗ(a)ka**	-y, -l	a	+Y, +W
work	a-, ka-, ma-	**ɬ(a)na**	-t, -y, -k, -kʷ, -n, -l	a	+Y, +W

References

Amha, Azeb. 2012. Omotic. In *Frajzyngier and Shay* (eds.), 423–504.
Barreteau, Daniel. 1983. Phonémique et prosodie en Higi. In *Wolff and Meyer-Bahlburg* (eds.), 249–276.
   1987. Du vocalisme en Tchadique. In *Langues et Cultures Dans Le Bassin du Lac Tchad*, ed. by Daniel Barreteau, 161–191. Paris: ORSTOM.
   1988. *Description du mofu-gudur: langue de la famille tchadique parlée au Cameroun*. Paris: Éditions de L'ORSTOM.
Bow, Catherine. 1999. *The Vowel System of Moloko*. MA, University of Melbourne.
Diakonoff, Igor M. 1965. *Semito-Hamitic Languages: An Essay in Classification*. Moscow: Akademia Nauk.
Eberhard, David M., Gary F. Simons and Charles D. Fennig (eds.). 2021. *Ethnologue: Languages of the World*, 24th edition. Dallas, TX: SIL International. Online version: www.ethnologue.com.
Eguchi, Paul Kazuhisa. 1971. Matériaux pour servir à l'étude de la langue hide: Vocabulaire. *Kyoto University African Studies* 6: 195–283.
Frajzyngier, Zygmunt with Erin Shay. 2002. *A Grammar of Hdi* (Mouton Grammar Library 21). Berlin: Mouton de Gruyter.
Frajzyngier, Zygmunt and Erin Shay (eds.). 2012. *The Afroasiatic Languages*. Cambridge: Cambridge University Press.
Frajzyngier, Zygmunt, Paul Eguchi, Roger Prafé, Megan Schwabauer (with assistance from Erin Shay and Henry Tourneux). 2015. *Dictionary of Hdi: A Central Chadic Language of Cameroon*. Cologne: Rüdiger Köppe.
Gerhardt, Ludwig and Justus Roux (eds). 1998. *Otto Dempwolff: Induktiver Aufbau des Urbantu* (Archiv afrikanistischer Manuskripte 5). Cologne: Rüdiger Köppe.
Gragg, Gene and Robert Hoberman. 2012. Ancient Egyptian and Coptic. In *Frajzyngier and Shay* (eds.), 145–235.
Gravina, Richard. 2007. Classification and reconstruction in Chadic Biu-Mandara A. In *Topics in Chadic Linguistics III: Historical Studies*, ed. by Henry Tourneux, 37–91 (Chadic Linguistics 4). Cologne: Rüdiger Köppe.
   2011. The internal classification of Chadic Biu-Mandara. In *Topics in Chadic Linguistics VI: Comparative and Descriptive Studies*, ed. by Doris Löhr and Ari Awagana, 67–84 (Chadic Linguistics 7). Cologne: Rüdiger Köppe.
   2013. The history of vowels and prosodies in Central Chadic. In *Topics of Chadic Linguistics VII*, ed. by Henry Tourneux, 87–99 (Chadic Linguistics 8). Cologne: Rüdiger Köppe.

2014a. *The Phonology of Proto-Central Chadic. The Reconstruction of the Phonology and Lexicon of Proto-Central Chadic, and the Linguistic History of the Central Chadic Languages*. Utrecht: LOT.

2014b. *Proto-Central Chadic Reconstructions*. http://centralchadic.webonary.org.

Greenberg, Joseph H. 1963. *The Languages of Africa*. Bloomington, IN: Indiana University Press.

Hoffmann, Carl. 1963. *A Grammar of the Margi Language*. London: Oxford University Press.

1965. *A Tentative Analysis of the Phonology of Higi*. Unpubl. conference paper, University of Legon, Accra, Ghana.

1987. Were there labial alveolars and labial palatals in Proto-Bura-Margi? In *Proceedings of the Fourth International Hamito-Semitic Congress*, ed. by Herrmann Jungraithmayr and Walter W. Müller, 451–474. Amsterdam: John Benjamins.

Hoskison, James T. 1974. Prosodies and verb stems in Gude. *Linguistics* 141: 17–26.

1983. *A Grammar and Dictionary of the Gude Language*. MA, Ohio State University.

Jungraithmayr, Herrmann. 1978 (1974). A tentative four stage model for the development of the Chadic languages. In *Atti del Secondo Congresso Internazionale di Linguistica Camito-Semitica*, ed. by Pelio Fronzaroli, 381–388. Florence: Istituto de Linguistica [e] di Lingue Orientali, Universita di Firenze.

Jungraithmayr, Herrmann and Dymitr Ibriszimow. 1994. *Chadic Lexical Roots. Vol. 1: Tentative Reconstruction, Grading, Distribution and Comments. Volume 2: Documentation* (Sprache und Oralität in Afrika, 20). Berlin: Dietrich Reimer.

Jungraithmayr, Herrmann and Kiyoshi Shimizu. 1981. *Chadic Lexical Roots. Vol. 2: Tentative Reconstruction, Grading and Distribution* (Marburger Studien zur Afrika- und Asienkunde, Serie A, Afrika, 26). Berlin: Dietrich Reimer.

Kossmann, Maarten. 2012. Berber. In *Frajzyngier and Shay* (eds.), 18–101.

Lewis, M. P. 2009. *Ethnologue: Languages of the World*. Dallas: SIL International.

Lienhard, Ruth and Marti Giger. 1975. *Daba (parler de Pologozom): Description phonologique*. Yaoundé: Office National de la Recherche Scientifique et Technique.

Loprieno, Antonio and Matthias Müller. 2012. Ancient Egyptian and Coptic. In *Frajzyngier and Shay* (eds.), 102–144.

Lukas, Johannes. 1936. The linguistic situation in the Lake Chad Area in Central Africa. *Africa: Journal of the International African Institute* 9(3): 332–349.

Meyer, Ronny and H. Ekkehard Wolff. 2019. Afroasiatic linguistic features and typologies. In *The Cambridge Handbook of African Linguistics*, ed. by H. Ekkehard Wolff, 246–325. Cambridge: Cambridge University Press.

Mirt, Heide. 1969. Einige Bemerkungen zum Vokalsystem des Mandara. In *ZDMG Supplementa I. Vorträge, Teil 3*, ed. by W. Voigt, 1096–1103.

Mohrlang, Roger. 1971. Vectors, prosodies, and Higi vowels. *Journal of African Languages* 10(1): 75–86.

1972. *Higi Phonology* (Studies in Nigerian Languages, 2). Zaria and Kano: SIL and CSNL.

Mous, Maarten. 2012. Cushitic. In *Frajzyngier and Shay* (eds.), 342–422.

Newman, Paul. 1970. *A Grammar of Tera: Transformational Syntax and Texts*. Berkeley, CA: University of California Press.

1977a. Chadic classification and reconstructions. *Afroasiatic Linguistics* 5: 1–42.
1977b. The formation of the imperfective verb stem in Chadic. *Afrika und Übersee* 60: 178–192.
1980. *The Classification of Chadic within Afroasiatic*. Leiden: Universitaire Pers.
1990. *Nominal and Verbal Plurality in Chadic* (Publications in African Languages and Linguistics, 12). Dordrecht: Foris Publications.
1991. Historical decay and growth in the Hausa lexicon. In *Semitic Studies in Honor of Wolf Leslau*, vol. 2, ed. by Alan S. Kaye, 1131–1139. Wiesbaden: Harrassowitz. http://hdl.handle.net/2022/21470.
2004. *Klingenheben's Law in Hausa* (Chadic Linguistics – Linguistique Tchadique – Tschadistik 2). Cologne: Rüdiger Köppe.
2006. Comparative Chadic revisited. In *West African Linguistics: Papers in Honor of Russell G. Schuh*, ed. by Paul Newman and Larry M. Hyman, 188–202. (Studies in African Linguistics, Supplement 11). Columbus: Ohio State University. http://hdl.handle.net/2022/21185.
2013. *The Chadic Language Family: Classification and Name Index*. Indiana: Mega-Chad Miscellaneous Publications, 1–11. http://hdl.handle.net/2022/20964.
2014. The range and beauty of internal reconstruction: Probing Hausa linguistic history. *Studies of the Department of African Languages and Cultures* [Warsaw] 48: 13–32. http://hdl.handle.net/2022/20959.
2018. *Comprehensive Bibliography of Chadic and Hausa Linguistics*, 4th edn. Bloomington, IN: IUScholarWorks. http://hdl.handle.net/2022/22181.
2019. Russell G. Schuh: An overview of his Chadic scholarship. In *Topics in Chadic Linguistics X*, ed. by Henry Tourneux and Yvonne Treis, 13–22. Cologne: Rüdiger Köppe.
Newman, Paul and Roxana Ma. 1966. Comparative Chadic: Phonology and lexicon. *Journal of African Languages* 5: 218–251.
Newman, Paul and Roxana Ma Newman (eds.). 1977. *Papers in Chadic Linguistics*. Leiden: Afrika-Studiecentrum.
Newman, Roxana Ma. 1971. *A Case Grammar of Ga'anda*. PhD dissertation, UCLA.
1977. Y-prosody as a morphological process in Ga'anda. In *Newman and Newman* (eds.), 212–230.
Peust, Carsten. 2019. *A Dictionary of Margi (Nigeria). Margi–English with English–Margi Index. Based on Carl Hoffmann's Material.* (Westafrikanische Studien 40). Cologne: Rüdiger Köppe.
Schuh, Russell G. 1983. The evolution of determiners in Chadic. In *Wolff and Meyer-Bahlburg* (eds.), 157–210.
2002. Palatalisation in West Chadic. *Studies in African Linguistics* 31: 97–128.
2017. *A Chadic Cornucopia*, ed. by Paul Newman. Oakland: eScholarship, California Digital Library. http://escholarship.org/uc/uclaling_chadic.
Seetzen, Ulrich J. 1810. Ueber das große afrikanische Reich Burnu und dessen Nebenländer, und über die Sprache von Áffadéh. *Monatliche Correspondenz zur Beförderung der Erd- und Himmelskunde*, 22: 269–341.
Sölken, Heinz. 1957. Seetzens Áffadéh – Eine Einführung in die Bearbeitung eines älteren Kotokovokabulars. *Anthropos* 53: 877–900.
Stolbova, Olga. 2016. *Chadic Etymological Dictionary*. Moscow: Institute of Oriental Studies Russian Academy of Sciences.

Thomason, Sarah and Terrence Kaufman. 1988. *Language Contact, Creolisation, and Genetic Linguistics.* Berkeley, CA: University of California Press.

Westermann, D. and M. A. Bryan (eds.). 1952. *The Languages of West Africa. Handbook of African Languages Part II.* London: Oxford University Press.

Wolff, [H.] Ekkehard. 1975. Sprachwandel und Sprachwechsel in Nordostnigeria. *Afrika und Übersee* 58: 7–27.

— 1977. Patterns in Chadic (and Afroasiatic?) verb base formations. In *Newman and Newman*, 199–233.

— 1979. Grammatical categories of verb stems and the marking of mood, aktionsart, and aspect in Chadic. *Afroasiatic Linguistics* 6(5): 1–48.

— 1981. Vocalisation patterns, prosodies, and Chadic reconstructions. In *Précis from the Twelfth Conference on African Linguistics* (Studies in African Linguistics, Supplement 8), ed. by William R. Leben, 144–148. Los Angeles: Department of Linguistics, UCLA.

— 1982. 'Aspect' and aspect-related categories in Chadic. In *The Chad Languages in the Hamitosemitic-Nigritic Border Area*, ed. by Herrmann Jungraithmayr, 183–191. Berlin: Dietrich Reimer.

— 1983a. *A Grammar of the Lamang Language (Gwàd Làmàŋ)* (Afrikanistische Forschungen, 10). Glückstadt: J. J. Augustin.

— 1983b. Reconstructing vowels in Central Chadic. In *Wolff and Meyer-Bahlburg* (eds.), 211–232.

— 1984a. New proposals concerning the nature and development of the Proto-Chadic tense/aspect system. In *Current Progress in Afro-Asiatic Linguistics: Papers of the Third International Hamito-Semitic Congress*, ed. by James Bynon, 225–239. Amsterdam: John Benjamins.

— 1984b. Adverb and verbal noun formation in the Musgu language of Mogroum (Vulum/Mulwi): Studies on consonant-tone interference in Chadic languages II. *Afrika und Übersee* 67: 175–197.

— 1993. *Referenzgrammatik des Hausa. Zur Begleitung des Fremdsprachenunterrichts und Einführung in das Selbststudium.* Münster-Hamburg: LIT.

— 1994. *Our People's Own (Ina Lamaŋ): Traditions and Specimens of Oral Literature from a Dying Culture in the Southern Lake Chad Basin in Central Africa* (Afrikanistische Forschungen Vol. 11). Cologne: Rüdiger Köppe (in cooperation with Abdullahi Ndaghra [postum] and E. Adwiraah).

— 1995. Proto-Chadic determiners and nominal plurals in Hausa. In *Studia Chadica et Hamitosemitica*, ed. by D. Ibriszimow and R. Leger, 118–128. Cologne: Rüdiger Köppe.

— 2001. Verbal plurality in Chadic: Grammaticalization chains and early Chadic history. In *Berkeley Linguistics Society: Special Session on Afroasiatic Languages* (March 22–25, 2001), ed. by Andrew Simpson, 123–167. Berkeley: Berkeley Linguistics Society.

— 2004. Segments and prosodies in Chadic: On descriptive and explanatory adequacy, historical reconstructions, and the status of Lamang-Hdi. In *Proceedings of the 4th World Congress of African Linguistics at Rutgers University, New Brunswick N.J. 2003*, ed. by Akinbiyi Akinlabi, 43–65. Cologne: Rüdiger Köppe.

— 2006a. Suffix petrification and prosodies in Central Chadic (Lamang-Hdi). In *Topics in Chadic Linguistics II*, ed. by Dymitr Ibriszimow, 141–154 (Chadic Linguistics – Linguistique tchadique – Tschadistik 3). Cologne: Rüdiger Köppe.

2006b. Genealogical continuity and discontinuity in Hidkala oral traditions. In *Africa in the Long Run. Festschrift in the Honour of Professor Arvi Hurskainen*, ed. by L. Harjula and M. Ylänkö, 111–129 (Studia Orientalia 103). Helsinki: Finnish Oriental Society.

2009. Another look at 'internal a' in Chadic. In *Topics in Chadic Linguistics V: Comparative and Descriptive Studies. Papers from the 4th Biennial International Colloquium on the Chadic Languages*, ed. by Eva Rothmaler, 161–172. Cologne: Rüdiger Köppe.

2011. Language variation, theoretical preoccupations and the Lamang–Hdi language continuum in Central Chadic. Review of Zygmunt Frajzyngier with Erin Shay: *A Grammar of Hdi* (Mouton Grammar Library 21). Berlin: Mouton de Gruyter. 2002. *Afrika und Übersee* 90 (2008/09): 213–258.

2015. *The Lamang Language and Dictionary. Vol. 1: The Lamang Language; Vol. 2: A Dictionary of Lamang*. Cologne: Rüdiger Köppe.

2017. Vocalogenesis in (Central) Chadic languages. In *African Linguistics in the 21st Century: Essays in Honor of Paul Newman*, ed. by Samuel G. Obeng and Christopher R. Green, 13–32. Cologne: Rüdiger Köppe.

2019a. *A History of African Linguistics*. Cambridge: Cambridge University Press.

2019b. On morphological palatalisation in Chadic. In *Schuhschrift: Papers in Honor of Russell Schuh*, ed. by Margit Bowler, Travis Major and Harold Torrence, 178–191. https://escholarship.org/uc/item/7c42d7th.

(in press). Chadic linguistics in the 21st century: Attempting a state-of-the-art account. In *Proceedings of the 47th Annual Meeting of the North Atlantic Conference on Afroasiatic Linguistics*, ed. by Lameen Souag and Mena Lafkioui. Villejuif: Les Publication du LACITO.

(forthcoming). Lexical Reconstruction in Central Chadic (Afroasiatic). A Comparative Study of Vowels, Consonants and Prosodies Based on Internal Reconstructions for 66 Languages.

Wolff, [H.] Ekkehard, Andrea Hauenschildt and Thomas Labahn. 1981. Biu-Mandara vowel systems. In *Berliner Afrikanistische Vorträge, XXI. Deutscher Orientalistentag*, ed. by Herrmann Jungraithmayr and Gudrun Miehe, 259–276. Berlin: Dietrich Reimer.

Wolff, [H.] Ekkehard and Hilke Meyer-Bahlburg (eds.). 1983. *Studies in Chadic and Afroasiatic Linguistics*. Hamburg: Helmut Buske.

Wolff, H. Ekkehard and Christfried Naumann. 2004. Frühe lexikalische Quellen zum Wandala (Mandara) und das Rätsel des Stammauslauts. In *Egyptian and Semito-Hamitic (Afro-Asiatic) Studies in Memoriam W. Vycichl*, ed. by G. Takács, 372–413. Leiden: Brill.

Index: Languages and Lexical Items

Afade 1, 63, 92, 103, 119, 121, 131, 211–213, 216–218, 247, 253–254, 266, 274–275, 280, 286, 290, 296, 310, 319, 326, 328, 334, 376, 380, 384, 390, 394, 399, 417, 435, 445
Afroasiatic 3–6, 9, 12–16, 18, 27–28, 33, 48, 52–54, 65, 67–68, 72, 76, 79, 87, 126, 129, 145, 152, 160, 187–188, 192
Arabic 29, 130, 170, 358, 371
arm 148, 163, 176–177, 221, 458
ashes 2, 24–25, 37, 50, 118, 125, 197, 199, 201, 221, 224, 458

Bachama 2, 50, 108, 112, 125, 150, 221, 224, 239, 242
Bana 45–46, 81, 89, 92, 100, 109, 117, 120, 122, 137, 156–157, 195–196, 198, 202–204, 207, 211–213, 224, 234, 246, 252, 257, 266, 271, 274, 286, 304–305, 308, 310, 319, 326, 334, 338, 343, 345, 348, 351–352, 357, 368, 380, 384, 393, 395, 398, 405, 410, 416, 423, 427, 434, 439, 444, 457
Bantu 94, 160
Bata 50, 58, 83, 88, 90, 93, 102, 109, 112, 118, 120, 124, 131–132, 136, 149, 197, 221–222, 224, 230, 237, 248, 259, 276, 295, 297, 299, 316, 320, 339, 344, 351, 382, 407, 428–429, 453
BATA 20–23, 26, 50, 58, 63, 79, 81, 83–84, 88–89, 90, 93–94, 99–100, 102, 108–109, 112–114, 118, 120–121, 124–125, 131, 136–137, 140, 148–150, 152, 156, 196–198, 200, 202–204, 213–215, 221–222, 224, 230, 237, 239, 242, 248, 255, 259, 271–272, 276, 281, 295, 297, 299, 308, 311, 314, 316, 319–320, 336, 339, 344, 346, 351, 364, 369, 382, 385, 391, 395, 400, 407, 412, 419, 424–425, 428–429, 435, 440, 446, 453
beard 2, 63, 81, 110, 138–139, 150, 155–156, 227, 458

beer 22, 26, 63, 113, 230, 458
belly 123, 139, 163, 199, 201, 231, 381–382, 458
Berber 4–5, 74, 131–132, 258–259
bite, to 63, 209, 235, 458
blow, to 51, 118, 122, 197, 237, 458
boil, to 111, 152, 239, 458
bone 2, 23–24, 63, 90, 108, 110, 114, 140, 150, 195–196, 198–199, 202, 212, 216, 242, 458
bow 152, 163, 248, 458
brain 63, 212, 253, 458
Buduma 2, 92, 123, 131–132, 136, 203, 211, 224, 227, 242, 247, 266, 271, 274–275, 280, 286, 290, 326, 328, 334, 376, 416, 434–435, 444
Bura 24, 40–41, 53, 60, 63, 79, 82–83, 90–91, 94, 100, 112, 116, 120, 122–123, 125, 135–136, 139, 142, 152, 155, 190, 196, 199–200, 206–208, 210, 227, 240, 250, 256, 261, 268–269, 273, 276, 283, 288, 297, 301, 306, 314, 317, 322, 330, 340, 347, 349, 354, 366, 387, 392, 395, 397–398, 408, 420, 430, 442, 455
Bura-Margi 7
butterfly 25–26, 58–59, 81, 94, 114, 137, 190, 201, 203, 255, 458
Buwal 81, 93, 95, 109, 113, 152, 205–206, 209, 231, 235, 268, 282, 296, 300, 305, 314, 320, 337, 340, 349, 352, 364, 369, 377, 396, 401, 407, 412, 419, 429, 436, 440, 446, 454

camel 63, 131, 164, 175, 258–259, 458
Cineni 8
cook, to 53, 148, 152, 164, 205, 268, 458
Coptic 4
cow 5, 152, 165, 208, 271, 458
crocodile 275, 458
cry, to 36, 39–40, 58, 93, 108, 118–119, 123–124, 136–137, 149, 152, 165, 195, 276, 459

Cushitic 4
Cuvok 20–21, 23, 38, 81, 84, 89, 91, 95, 111–112, 115, 152, 205, 209, 232, 240, 243, 248–249, 272, 282, 288, 291, 300, 305–306, 312, 329, 340, 353, 359, 385, 393, 396, 401, 413, 420, 424–425, 430, 436, 440, 447, 450

Daba 6, 84, 90, 109, 111–113, 120, 205–206, 209, 213–214, 231, 235, 239, 260, 268, 272, 282, 300, 312, 321, 340, 351–352, 358, 364, 369, 377, 396, 407, 413, 420, 429, 436, 440
DABA 59, 63, 81, 84, 90, 93, 95, 109, 111–113, 120, 152, 205–206, 209, 213–214, 230–231, 235, 239, 255, 260, 268, 272, 282, 291, 296, 300, 305, 311, 314, 320, 337, 339–340, 349, 351–352, 358, 363–364, 369, 377, 385, 396, 400–401, 407, 412, 419, 428–430, 436, 440, 446, 450, 453–454
Dghwede 8–9, 40–41, 50, 63, 91–92, 94, 99–100, 115, 141–142, 178–183, 200, 208–210, 223, 225, 233, 236, 245, 262, 284, 289, 293, 307, 315, 331, 355, 366, 379, 383, 388, 402, 414, 422, 432, 443, 448, 452, 455
die, to 84–85, 152, 165, 281, 311, 459
dog 58, 119–120, 123, 137, 152, 165, 203, 214, 287, 459
donkey$_1$ 152, 157, 291, 459
donkey$_2$ 295, 459
donkey$_3$ 151, 296, 459
dream 20–21, 23–26, 38, 53, 58, 73, 79, 89, 95, 114, 120, 123–124, 135, 148, 166, 188, 199–200, 203, 213–214, 299, 459
Dugwor 2, 90–92, 109, 112, 116, 122, 152, 205–206, 224, 226, 232–233, 238, 241, 245, 251, 254, 264, 270, 273, 278, 284, 289, 294, 303, 324, 332, 341, 355, 361, 364, 367, 393, 403, 409, 415, 422, 426, 432, 438, 443, 456

ear 8–9, 41, 178, 181–184
earth 69, 166, 195–196, 305, 459
Egyptian 4–5, 74
eight 152, 167, 202, 308, 459
elephant 310, 459
English 29, 151, 220
extinguish, to 84–85, 148, 214, 311, 459

faeces 22, 40–41, 93–94, 99, 113, 120, 123–124, 140, 157, 167, 201, 314, 459
five 63, 100, 152, 167, 199, 202, 316, 459

fly 35, 37, 45–46, 63, 95, 99, 107–108, 168, 213, 216, 319, 459
foot 63, 131, 218, 327, 329, 459
Fulfulde 29, 129, 131–132, 258–259, 371, 398

Ga'anda 1, 6, 23, 108, 117, 131–132, 232, 243, 260, 430
Gava 8
Gavar 93, 109, 112–113, 205–206, 208–209, 231, 235, 268, 282, 300, 305, 314, 321, 337, 340, 352, 364, 377, 407, 412, 419, 429, 436, 440, 454
Gemzek 91–92, 109, 112, 119, 123–124, 139, 195, 200, 205, 207–210, 212, 228, 233, 236–237, 241, 245, 251, 253–254, 263, 270, 273, 278, 284, 289, 294, 302, 324, 331, 341, 349–350, 361, 388, 403, 409, 414, 422, 426, 432, 438, 443, 449, 452, 456
Gidar 2, 25, 58, 63, 81–82, 93, 111, 114, 138–139, 149–150, 152, 190, 200–201, 206–208, 211, 227, 229, 248, 258–259, 267, 271, 275, 287, 291, 298, 305, 327, 335, 339, 343, 358, 363–364, 368, 381, 391, 405, 418
GIDAR 25, 58, 63, 81, 93, 111, 114, 139, 149–150, 152, 190, 200–201, 207–208, 211, 229, 248, 258–259, 267, 271, 275, 287, 291, 298, 305, 319, 327, 335, 343, 357–358, 363, 368, 381, 385, 391, 405, 418, 428
give birth, to 59–60, 91, 95, 107, 148, 150, 168, 209, 213, 329, 459
Giziga 82, 108, 190, 428, 453
Giziga-Marva 2, 25, 37, 90–92, 116, 118, 151–152, 200–201, 204, 207, 210, 212, 226, 252–254, 270, 273, 279, 285, 289, 295, 303, 313, 325, 332, 342, 356, 362, 375, 393–394, 404, 415, 422, 433, 439, 443, 456
Giziga-Muturwa 50, 59, 81–82, 84, 91, 108, 114, 116, 118, 120, 130, 139, 190, 204, 207, 226, 229, 245, 257, 264, 270, 273, 279, 285, 289, 295, 297, 313, 325, 342, 356, 361, 404, 433, 439, 452, 456
Glavda 2, 8–9, 36, 39–41, 63, 79, 83–84, 90–92, 108, 115, 136, 141–142, 149, 178–183, 197, 205–206, 210, 223, 225, 233, 244, 250, 256, 262, 269, 273, 277, 283, 293, 302, 309, 312, 315, 323, 331, 348, 355, 360, 366, 370, 373, 377, 379, 383, 388, 402, 421, 426, 428–429, 432, 437, 442, 448, 451, 455
grandfather 108, 168, 336, 459

468   Index

grasshopper 64, 69, 81, 149, 196, 198, 213–214, 339, 459
Gude 1–2, 6, 22, 26, 63, 81, 90, 93–94, 113, 121, 136–137, 148–149, 152, 156, 196–198, 200, 202–203, 215, 222, 230, 242, 249, 255, 272, 276, 297, 299, 308, 316, 320, 336, 339, 346, 364, 369, 385, 391, 395, 400, 407, 412, 424–425, 429, 440, 446, 453
Guduf 8–9, 178–183
Gvoko 8–9, 178–183
Gwara 8–9, 178–183

hair 88, 114, 120, 124, 169, 343, 459
hare 79, 136, 141, 149, 152, 169, 196, 203, 345, 459
Hausa 1, 29, 38, 41, 72, 83, 85, 106, 129, 158, 407
Hdi 1, 8, 15, 21, 42–44, 47, 49, 63, 79, 81, 84, 89–90, 92, 101, 111–112, 117, 120–123, 135–137, 139, 161–177, 197, 200, 211, 213–214, 219, 223, 229, 234, 238, 241, 252, 265, 273, 280, 285, 290, 303, 305, 307, 309, 314–315, 318, 325, 333, 338–339, 342, 345, 348, 350, 356, 362, 367, 371, 379, 389, 392, 404, 410, 415, 422, 427, 433–434, 443, 456
hedgehog 349, 459
hide, to 102, 109, 351, 459
Higi 6–7
HIGI 37, 45–46, 53, 61, 63, 81, 89–90, 92, 99–100, 108–110, 113–115, 117, 119–123, 125, 127, 136–137, 139–140, 156–157, 195–199, 202–207, 211–213, 223, 229, 232, 234, 242, 246, 252, 255, 257, 259, 265, 268, 270, 274, 285, 288, 290, 298, 303, 305, 307, 309, 314, 316, 318–319, 325, 333, 338–339, 342, 345, 348–349, 351–353, 357, 363–364, 367, 371, 375, 377, 379, 382, 384, 389, 391–392, 397, 405, 410, 415, 419, 423–424, 427–428, 433, 439, 444, 450, 453, 456
horn₁ 82, 100, 114–115, 150, 169–170, 353, 459
horn₂ 111, 357, 459
horse 170, 358, 459
HURZA 26, 58, 79, 81, 84, 90–91, 112, 123, 126, 139, 152, 190, 196, 200–201, 205–206, 210, 215, 227, 237, 240, 249, 253, 256, 259–260, 268, 272, 283, 288, 292, 301, 305–306, 312, 319, 321, 330, 336–337, 349, 358–359, 365, 370, 372, 385–386, 397, 401, 408, 413, 420, 424, 426, 430, 436, 440–441, 450, 454

Hwana 50, 63, 118, 197, 225, 372, 378, 386, 425, 441

Indo-European 11, 30, 75, 143, 151, 158

Jimi 79, 84, 90, 93, 99–100, 102, 109, 113, 131–132, 136, 140, 148, 196–197, 202, 204, 213, 215, 222, 230, 242, 249, 259, 272, 281, 297, 299, 308, 311, 314, 316, 320, 336, 346, 352, 382, 385, 391, 401, 407, 419, 429, 435, 440, 446, 454

Kamwe-Futu 2, 37, 45–46, 92, 101, 117, 120–123, 136, 139, 195–198, 202, 211, 223, 229, 234, 246, 252, 257, 265, 286, 290, 298, 303, 305, 307, 309, 318, 325, 333, 342, 348, 357, 367, 371, 375, 379, 384, 389, 397, 410, 415, 423, 433, 444, 450, 457
Kamwe-Nkafa 63, 89, 92, 108, 117, 120–123, 197–198, 202–203, 207, 211–213, 234, 246, 252, 257, 270, 274, 285, 290, 298, 309, 318, 333, 342, 345, 357, 367, 379, 384, 389, 392, 405, 410, 415, 423, 427, 433, 444, 456
Kanuri 29, 129–132, 151, 162, 164, 219, 258, 287, 296, 299, 327, 329, 371, 398, 407
Kilba 24, 26, 40–41, 79, 92, 100, 115, 119, 122, 136–137, 142, 190, 195–197, 199–200, 206, 210, 212–214, 225, 244, 250, 256, 268, 273, 277, 297, 301, 305–306, 315, 317, 322, 328, 330, 338–340, 347, 354, 372, 383, 387, 392, 409, 413, 421, 431, 455
Kirya 45–46, 53, 63, 90, 92, 99–100, 110, 113–114, 120–123, 125, 136–137, 139, 157, 197–199, 202, 207, 211–212, 229, 234, 246, 265, 270, 274, 290, 298, 304, 307, 310, 316, 318, 325, 334, 343, 348–349, 351, 367, 371, 380, 384, 389, 393, 395, 398, 405, 410, 423, 433, 444, 457
KOTOKO 51, 70, 97, 102, 211–212, 215, 217–218, 253, 258, 271, 275, 295, 310, 327, 411–412, 428
KOTOKO-CENTRAL 25, 51–52, 63, 89, 97–98, 103, 131–132, 201, 211–212, 216–218, 238, 247, 255, 267, 274–276, 280, 286, 291, 296, 304, 311, 319, 326, 328, 334, 376–377, 380, 390, 395, 400, 410, 417, 434–435, 445
KOTOKO-ISLAND 92, 123, 131, 203, 211, 227, 247, 259, 266, 274–275, 280, 286, 290, 319, 326, 328, 334, 376, 385, 416, 434–435, 444

Index

KOTOKO-NORTH 20, 22, 51–52, 64, 89, 92, 95, 103, 119, 121, 131, 207–208, 211–213, 216, 218, 237–238, 242, 247, 254, 259, 266, 271, 274–275, 280–281, 286, 290, 296, 298–299, 304, 310, 319, 326, 328, 334, 343, 376–377, 380, 382, 384–385, 390, 393–394, 399, 410, 417, 434–435, 445

KOTOKO-SOUTH 58, 93, 97–98, 108, 111, 124, 131–132, 196, 202, 207–208, 211, 215–216, 242, 248, 267, 271, 274, 276, 281, 287, 296, 319, 326, 335, 357, 390, 419, 423, 434, 440, 445

Lagwan 25, 51–53, 63, 89, 97, 103, 131, 201, 211, 217, 238, 247, 258, 267, 274–275, 280, 286, 291, 296, 304, 310–311, 326, 328, 334, 376, 380, 390, 395, 400, 410, 417, 435, 445

Lamang 1, 8–9, 15, 20, 24, 28, 42–44, 47, 49, 53, 79, 89, 92, 101, 111–112, 116, 120–123, 136, 139, 143, 150, 152, 161–183, 195, 197, 200, 207, 211, 219, 223, 229, 234, 241, 252, 265, 270, 273, 279, 285, 290, 295, 303, 305, 307, 309, 315, 318, 325, 333, 338, 343, 345, 348, 356, 362–364, 367, 371, 379, 384, 389, 392, 397, 404, 410, 422, 427, 433–434, 443, 456

LAMANG 8, 15, 20–21, 24, 42–44, 47, 49, 53, 63, 79, 81, 83–84, 89–90, 92, 100–101, 112, 115–116, 120–123, 135–137, 139, 150, 152, 161–162, 169, 174–176, 180, 195, 197, 200, 207, 211, 213–214, 219, 223, 229, 232, 234, 238, 241, 248, 252, 265, 270, 273, 276, 279, 285, 288, 290, 295, 299, 303, 305, 307, 309, 314–316, 318, 325, 333, 338, 342–343, 345, 348, 350, 353, 356, 362–363, 367, 371, 377, 379, 384, 389, 392, 397, 404, 410, 415, 419, 422, 424, 427–428, 433–434, 443, 456

Lamang-Hdi *See* LAMANG
Latin 52
laugh, to 170, 212–213, 363, 459
lion 121, 171, 368, 370, 459

Mabas 8
Mada 91, 112, 115, 201, 205, 207, 233, 241, 245, 251, 269, 284, 286, 341, 355, 374, 438
Mafa 25, 38, 63, 89, 91, 95, 115–116, 124, 200, 205, 208–209, 213, 232, 235, 243, 248–249, 272, 282, 288, 300, 305, 321, 329, 353, 359, 364–365, 382, 385,

408, 413, 420, 424–425, 430, 436, 440, 447, 450

MAFA 25, 38, 63, 81, 89, 91, 95, 111–112, 115–116, 124, 152, 155, 200, 205, 208–209, 213, 232, 235, 240, 242–243, 248, 272, 282, 288, 291, 300, 306, 312, 319, 321, 329, 339–340, 353, 358–359, 365, 382, 385, 393, 396, 400–401, 408, 413, 420, 424–425, 428, 430, 436, 440, 446–447, 450

Malgbe 20, 22, 63, 89, 93, 95, 103, 131–132, 211, 217, 238, 247, 266, 274–275, 280, 286, 290, 298, 304, 310, 334, 376, 390, 393, 395, 400, 417, 445

Malgwa 8, 22, 40–41, 81, 90, 92, 99–100, 108, 112, 116, 124, 136, 139, 141, 149–150, 155–156, 196–198, 206–207, 209–210, 222, 228, 232, 236, 240, 242, 244, 250, 256, 262, 268–269, 273, 276–277, 283, 289, 293, 302, 306, 315, 323, 331, 338, 341, 347, 350, 355, 360, 370, 373, 379, 383, 402, 421, 426, 428, 431, 442, 448, 455

Maltam 131, 212, 216, 253–254, 267, 326, 384
Mandara 1, 5, 8, 22, 40–41, 63, 81, 90–91, 99, 108–109, 116, 124, 136–137, 139, 141, 143, 148, 155–156, 178–182, 196–198, 201, 208, 222, 228, 232, 240, 244, 250, 262, 273, 276–277, 288, 293, 302, 306, 309, 315, 323, 338, 341, 347, 350, 354, 360, 370, 379, 383, 388, 398, 402, 426, 428, 431, 442, 448

MANDARA 8, 22, 35–36, 39, 40–41, 50, 53, 63–64, 79, 81, 83–84, 89–90, 92, 94, 99, 108–109, 112–113, 115–117, 119, 124, 136, 138–139, 141, 149–150, 152, 155, 180, 195–198, 200–201, 205–210, 215, 221–222, 224–225, 227, 230–232, 235, 240, 242, 244, 248, 250, 253, 256, 259, 261, 269, 273, 277, 283, 288, 292, 299, 301, 306, 308, 312, 315, 319, 322, 331, 336, 338–340, 347, 349–354, 360, 363, 366, 370, 373, 377–378, 381, 383–384, 387, 393, 397–398, 402, 409, 413, 419, 421, 424, 426, 428–429, 431, 435, 437, 442, 448, 450–451, 453, 455

Margi 1–2, 8, 24, 26, 92, 110, 114, 121, 123, 136–137, 140, 142, 180, 197, 199, 203, 206, 210, 212, 215, 244, 250, 268, 273, 276, 322, 328, 330, 337, 346–349, 387, 442, 455

MARGI 8, 24, 26, 40–41, 53, 60, 63, 79, 82–83, 90–91, 94, 100, 110, 112, 114–116, 119–123, 125, 135–140, 142, 152, 155, 180, 190, 195–197, 199–200,

203, 206–208, 210, 212–215, 224–225, 227, 240, 242, 244, 250, 255–256, 261, 268, 273, 276, 283, 288, 297, 299, 301, 305–306, 314, 316–317, 319, 322, 327–328, 330, 336–337, 339–340, 347, 349, 353–354, 364, 366, 370, 372, 382–383, 385, 387, 391–392, 397–398, 408, 413, 420, 428, 430, 442, 453, 455
Margi-Mandara-Mofu major group 453
Margi-South 92, 119, 121–122, 136–137, 142, 197, 210, 212, 250, 261, 273, 277, 297, 317, 328, 330, 337, 347, 370, 383, 387, 392, 421, 431, 442
market 130, 371, 459
MAROUA 24–25, 37, 50, 58–59, 81–82, 84, 91–92, 95, 108, 114–116, 118–121, 130, 139–140, 151–152, 190, 199–201, 204–205, 207, 209–210, 212–214, 226, 229, 232–233, 235, 237, 242, 245, 248, 252, 254, 257, 264, 270, 273, 279, 285, 289, 295, 297, 303, 307, 313, 325, 332, 339, 342, 353, 356, 361, 375, 385, 389, 393–394, 400, 404, 410, 415, 419, 422, 428, 433, 439, 443, 452, 456
Matal 2, 8, 35–36, 39–40, 64, 81, 84, 90, 108, 115, 119, 139, 141, 195, 205–206, 208–209, 212, 215, 227, 232, 235, 244, 250, 253, 261, 269, 273, 277, 283, 288, 292, 301, 308, 312, 322, 340, 354, 360, 373, 378, 387, 393, 397, 402, 409, 421, 426, 431, 437, 442, 451, 455
Mazagway Hidi 272, 377
Mazera 2, 108, 111, 131, 196, 206–208, 215–216, 248, 258, 267, 271, 274, 276, 296, 358, 423, 445
Mbara 53, 93, 111, 148, 206–207, 211, 215, 234, 253, 267, 271, 275, 281, 287, 298, 308, 327, 335, 358, 363, 369, 371, 376, 381, 391, 398, 400, 406, 411, 424, 428, 445
Mbazla 2, 24, 50, 58, 92, 95, 116, 121, 140, 199–200, 205, 207, 209–210, 212–214, 226, 232–233, 237, 246, 252, 265, 270, 273, 279, 285, 289, 307, 332, 356, 362, 389, 394, 404, 410, 415, 422, 433, 439, 443
Mbudum 59, 63, 84, 93, 109, 111–113, 205–206, 231, 239, 255, 268, 282, 291, 300, 305, 311, 314, 321, 340, 352, 364, 377, 396, 412, 419, 429, 436, 440, 447, 450
Mbuko 26, 79, 90–91, 112, 123, 126, 139, 152, 200–201, 205–206, 210, 215, 227, 237, 240, 249, 253, 256, 260, 268, 272, 283, 288, 292, 301, 305–306, 321, 330, 336–337, 349, 359, 364–365, 372, 385–386, 397, 401, 408, 413, 420, 426, 430, 436, 441, 450, 454
Mefele 116, 353
Merey 78–79, 82, 90–92, 108, 115, 200, 205–206, 210, 233, 238, 245, 251, 254, 264, 270, 273, 278, 284, 294, 302, 324, 332, 341, 349–350, 355, 361, 364, 367, 403, 409, 414, 422, 426, 432, 438, 443, 449, 452, 456
MOFU 20, 22, 63, 79, 82–84, 89–92, 94–97, 102, 107–109, 112, 114–116, 118–119, 121–124, 130, 137, 139, 143, 152, 157, 195, 197, 200, 204–207, 209–210, 224–225, 228, 233, 236–237, 240, 242, 245, 251, 253, 257, 259, 262, 269, 273, 276–277, 284, 289, 294, 302, 307, 313, 319, 323, 331, 339, 341, 344, 349–353, 355, 361, 366, 374, 383, 388, 393, 397, 399–400, 402, 409, 413–414, 422, 424, 426, 428, 432, 435, 437, 443, 446, 448, 452, 456
Mofu North 90–92, 95, 107, 112, 115, 119, 204, 207, 209–210, 224, 226, 233, 236, 241, 245, 251, 264, 270, 273, 289, 294, 303, 313, 324, 332, 342, 349–350, 355, 361, 388, 394, 399, 403, 409, 415, 422, 427, 432, 438, 443, 452
Mofu-Gudur 92, 95, 115, 119, 143, 204, 207–210, 233, 237, 252, 257, 264, 270, 273, 279, 284, 289, 295, 324, 332, 342, 351, 356, 361, 388, 393–394, 397, 399, 403, 409, 415, 422, 427, 432, 438, 443, 449, 452–453, 456
Moloko 5, 65, 83, 89, 92, 96, 109, 114, 118, 143, 205, 207, 210, 226, 233, 251, 263, 269, 273, 278, 284, 289, 294, 323, 331, 341, 344, 361, 364, 366, 374, 403, 409, 414, 423, 426, 432, 438, 443, 448, 456
moon 63, 108, 121, 171, 203, 377, 459
Mpade 2, 51–52, 63–64, 89, 92, 95, 103, 131, 207–208, 211, 217, 238, 242, 247, 266, 271, 274–275, 286, 290, 298, 304, 310, 328, 334, 339, 343, 376, 380, 384, 390, 395, 399, 410, 417, 435, 445
Mser 51–52, 63, 89, 97, 103, 131, 201, 211–212, 216–218, 239, 242, 247, 253, 255, 258, 267, 274, 276, 280, 287, 291, 299, 304, 311, 326, 329, 335, 376, 380, 390, 395, 400, 411, 418, 435, 445
Mulwi 53, 93, 123, 137, 148–149, 207–208, 211, 271, 274, 281, 287, 305, 335, 362, 390, 424, 453
MUSGUM 48, 53, 93, 111, 123, 137, 148–149, 152, 207–208, 211, 215, 232, 234, 253,

259, 267, 271, 274, 276, 281, 287,
298, 305, 308, 319, 327, 335, 357–358,
362, 371, 376, 380, 385, 390, 400, 406,
411, 418–419, 424, 427–428, 440, 445,
450, 453
Muskum 298, 363, 377, 381, 391, 424, 428,
446
Muyang 63, 91, 96–97, 102, 109, 112, 116,
118, 123, 137, 197, 205, 207, 225, 233,
241, 245, 254, 263, 269, 278, 289, 294,
313, 323, 341, 350–352, 355, 374,
382–383, 388, 422, 426, 432, 437,
443, 448

navel 121, 203, 381–382, 459
Niger-Congo 5
night 63, 69, 97, 121, 142, 171, 176–177, 212,
385, 459
Nilo-Saharan 5, 129, 151, 219, 287
nose 8–9, 41, 73, 178–180, 183–184
Nyimatli 34, 50, 112, 131–132, 190, 197, 208,
224, 240, 243, 249, 256, 260, 272, 283,
297, 301, 306, 329, 359, 365, 378, 386,
420, 425, 441, 454

Omotic 4
Ouldeme 63, 84, 91–92, 96, 108, 121, 139,
155, 205, 207–210, 228, 233, 236, 240,
245, 251, 253, 262, 269, 273, 277, 284,
289, 294, 302, 313, 323, 331, 341, 350,
361, 364, 366, 374, 382–383, 388, 399,
402, 414, 422, 426, 432, 437, 443,
452, 456

Podoko 2, 8–9, 39–40, 53, 63, 79, 81, 84,
89–90, 92, 109, 112–113, 115, 117, 136,
139, 152, 178–182, 196–197, 205–206,
209–210, 228, 231–232, 236, 240, 244,
250, 262, 269, 273, 277, 283, 288, 293,
299, 302, 312, 322, 331, 340, 347,
351–352, 354, 360, 363, 366, 370, 373,
378, 383, 387, 409, 413, 421, 426, 431,
437, 442, 448, 451, 455
Psikye 121–122, 140, 199, 202, 205, 207, 213,
223, 270, 274, 286, 298, 307, 310, 318,
368, 375, 380, 390, 405, 416, 423, 434,
439, 444, 457

quiver 172, 391, 459

ram 201, 213, 218, 393, 460
razor₁ 125, 155, 217, 395, 460
razor₂ 329, 398, 460
root 100, 121, 123, 140–141, 155–156, 172,
199, 203, 400, 460

Semitic 4–6, 12, 14, 33, 52, 72, 74, 76
Sharwa 89–90, 93–94, 99, 102, 109, 113–114,
120–121, 131–132, 140, 202–203,
213–215, 222, 230, 243, 259, 272, 276,
282, 297, 299, 314, 317, 320, 336, 344,
352, 364, 382, 385, 391, 401, 412, 419,
424–425, 440, 454
Shoa Arabic *See* Arabic
six 152, 406, 460
spit, to 63, 121, 173, 406–407, 460
suck, to 63, 95, 99–100, 102, 122, 152, 200,
216, 411–412, 460
Sukur 60, 79, 89, 91, 93, 99, 114, 116, 121,
123, 125–126, 136, 139, 141, 148,
196–197, 205–206, 209, 215, 217, 227,
232, 243, 249, 256, 260, 268, 272, 281,
283, 288, 291, 306, 308, 314, 321, 330,
336–337, 344, 346, 354, 365, 369, 372,
377–378, 386, 391–392, 396, 401, 408,
420, 424–425, 430, 436, 441, 454
SUKUR 60, 79, 89, 91, 93, 99, 114–116, 121,
123, 125, 136, 139, 141, 148, 196–197,
205–206, 209, 215, 217, 227, 232,
242–243, 248–249, 256, 260, 268, 272,
283, 288, 291, 306, 308, 314, 319, 321,
330, 337, 344, 346, 353–354, 363–365,
369, 372, 378, 386, 392, 396, 400–401,
408, 419–420, 424–425, 430, 436, 441,
453–454
sun 21, 122, 149, 152, 173, 418, 460

Tera 1–2, 34, 50, 91, 108, 111–112, 118,
197, 208–209, 215, 224, 239–240, 243,
249, 272, 282, 297, 299, 301, 306,
329, 359, 365, 378, 386, 420, 425,
441, 454
TERA 23, 34, 50, 63, 91, 108, 111–112,
117–118, 131, 190, 197, 208–209, 215,
224, 232, 240, 242–243, 248–249, 256,
259–260, 272, 282, 297, 301, 306, 319,
329, 359, 364–365, 372, 378, 386,
419–420, 424–425, 430, 440–441,
453–454
thorn 69, 173, 195, 197, 424, 460
three 174, 428, 460
Tsuvan 23, 79, 83, 89, 108, 113–114, 125,
131–132, 136, 196, 198, 222, 230, 243,
260, 272, 336, 344, 346, 364, 369, 401,
419, 453–454
Tumak 65
two 174, 434, 460

Vame 58, 81–82, 84, 91, 112, 152, 190, 196,
201, 204, 210, 240, 249, 256, 261, 273,
283, 288, 292, 306, 312, 321, 330, 337,

349, 360, 364–365, 370, 372, 387, 402, 408, 420, 426, 430, 436, 441, 451, 454
Vulum 48, 149, 152, 234, 274, 287, 298, 327, 362, 380, 390, 406, 418, 424, 427, 445, 453

Wandala *See* Mandara
Wandala-Lamang 8–9, 48, 79, 177–178, 180, 182–184
wash, to 96–97, 204, 435, 460
water 14, 149, 174, 214–215, 439–440, 460
whistle, to 149, 197, 200, 446, 460
white 149, 213, 450, 460

work 83, 175, 453, 460
wound 42

Zina 58, 93, 97, 111, 124, 202, 211, 248, 274, 281, 287, 319, 326, 335, 357, 385, 390, 423, 445
Zulgo 2, 20–22, 79, 90–92, 94–96, 109, 112, 118, 130, 157, 197, 200, 205–206, 209–210, 212, 224, 226, 233, 236–237, 241, 245, 251, 253–254, 263, 269, 273, 278, 284, 289, 294, 302, 307, 324, 331, 341, 350, 361, 374, 388, 399, 403, 414, 422, 426, 438, 443, 449

For EU product safety concerns, contact us at Calle de José Abascal, 56–1°,
28003 Madrid, Spain or eugpsr@cambridge.org.

www.ingramcontent.com/pod-product-compliance
Lightning Source LLC
LaVergne TN
LVHW011753060526
838200LV00053B/3587